In memory of
William F. Lewis

Contents

PART ONE
Anthropology and Culture   1

CHAPTER 6

Learning Culture   131

PART TWO

Sociocultural Adaptations   153

CHAPTER 7

Making a Living   155

Preface

Cultural Anthropology is intended for a one-semester course in introductory cultural anthropology. It has been designed with the idea that, even though the majority of students in the course will not major in anthropology, they will find it a fascinating and useful subject. The core concept of the text is *culture,* and the ethnographic data from our own and other cultures are organized around three major themes: (1) the impact of culture on human behavior, (2) the interrelationships between the different parts of a culture, and (3) the view of cultures as adaptive systems. The ethnographic data have also been chosen to highlight contrasts with our own culture so that the student is led into asking questions about behavior, values, and cultural patterns in the United States that normally would be taken for granted.

Students' understanding of these three themes will lead to an increasing awareness of themselves and the world they live in, of the human past and present, and of the unity and diversity that characterize the human species. With this anthropological perspective, students can begin to "make sense" of the behavior and cultures of peoples unlike themselves as well as to gain insight into their own behavior and society. This awareness is becoming increasingly necessary in order to deal with the plurality of cultures and life-styles that characterizes the contemporary United States as well as the world. For both liberal arts and preprofessional students, particularly those who enter human services careers, anthropology is an essential intellectual, scientific, humanistic, and practical foundation.

The importance of the anthropological perspective in today's world is paralleled by the growing use of anthropologists as professionals in a wide variety of settings and fields. A glance at the topics on the agenda of the recent annual meetings of the American Anthropological Association indicates that more anthropologists are making a living practicing anthropology than ever before, and the number is increasing every year. The recognition of the importance of applied anthropology is reflected in Chapter 16, "The Uses of Anthropology," and also by increased references throughout the text to the ways in which anthropologists apply their knowledge to the service of humankind.

New in This Edition

The fifth edition features some major organizational changes and much new ethnographic material, as well as updated bibliography and suggested readings sections that include the best of the current work in the field. Most of the information from the fourth edition is retained, with a few deletions made to keep the text length from getting unwieldy.

I have made three major changes in organization from the fourth edition. The first change is the combining of two chapters from the previous edition—Chapter 2, "Theory in Cultural Anthropology," and Chapter 3, "Human Adaptation and Culture," into a new Chapter 3, "The Culture Concept and Anthropological Theory." This chapter integrates the study of the characteristics of culture with the development of theories of culture; all of the theoretical material from the fourth edition is retained, but it is now presented in a way that demonstrates the relationship between knowledge in cultural anthropology and the way that knowledge develops over time. An important addition to this chapter is the introduction of the world systems approach. Marxist and feminist approaches in cultural anthropology, which are important contemporary perspectives in the field, now have expanded treatment. For those who wish to treat the rise of anthropological theory as part of the intellectual current of their times, I have added an appendix with a briefly annotated chronological listing of some of the most important theoretical works in the field. Though the new Chapter 3 omits a few details on the biological aspects of human adaptation that were included in the earlier edition, the idea of culture as the major means of human adaptation remains an important theme of the chapter, and of the book.

A second organizational change is the addition of a new chapter, "Doing Cultural Anthropology," which is Chapter 2 of this edition. The addition is warranted not only by the traditional importance of ethnography in cultural anthropology, but also by the new directions ethnography has taken in the postmodern era. The chapter combines all the material on ethnography that appeared in the introductory chapter of the fourth edition with new material on current interpretive perspectives on ethnography, a detailed account of a fieldwork experience that highlights the steps in doing an ethnography, ethical and practical considerations in doing ethnography, and the influence of feminist theory on ethnography.

The third major organizational change involves dropping the fourth edition's Chapter 11, "Nonkin-Based Forms of Association," and distributing the material among other chapters. Associations based on age and sex are now discussed in Chapter 10, "Kinship and Nonkin Bases of Association"; ethnicity has been added to the new Chapter 11, "Social Ranking and Stratification"; and the material on association in urban settings has been added to Chapter 15, "Change in the Contemporary World."

In this edition, I have substantially expanded the ethnographic focus on culture in the United States by adding new ethnographies on gender communication, downward social mobility among the middle class, and a comparison between kinship terminology systems in North America and North India, as well as chapter opening excerpts and material on coming of age. The ethnographic descriptions of cultural contrasts between the United States and other societies, which has been a consistent theme throughout earlier editions, are thus continued and strengthened in this edition.

Chapter Overview

Many students in our cultural anthropology courses will not major in anthropology. Indeed, many of our colleges (including my own) do not offer an anthropology major. We would all agree, however, that even one course in cultural anthropology has a great deal to offer every student. This text is meant both for students who may not take any other anthropology course and for those who will major in anthropology. It introduces the fundamental concepts, theories, methods, data, and references that enable the student to gain a grasp of the discipline and to move successfully into more specialized and advanced anthropology courses. The topics included in the text cover the traditional scope of cultural anthropology, while drawing on the most recent anthropological research. I have also made an effort to present a number of different theoretical viewpoints and arguments in approaching the data.

In **Chapter 1**, "Anthropology and Human Diversity," the focus is on anthropology as a discipline centered on the subject of human diversity. The chapter introduces the major perspectives of anthropology and the subfields of the discipline. The ethnography "Body Ritual among the Nacirema" has been retained from the fourth edition as an excellent model of how our culture may be looked at from the outside, and a way for students to examine their own ethnocentrism early in the semester.

Chapter 2, "Doing Cultural Anthropology," is new. It examines the recent issues concerning ethnography, includes a detailed description of a field study in India, and explores the topics of doing ethnography in one's own culture and in dangerous situations.

Chapter 3, "The Culture Concept and Anthropological Theory," is also a new chapter. It contains almost all of the material on the culture concept and theory from the fourth edition, but in an integrated, less repetitive way. Each aspect of the culture concept is introduced and then followed by a discussion of the theoretical approaches in cultural anthropology that are most significant in that context. Thus, for example, the discussion of culture as a system of meaning is followed by a presentation of the theories of Clifford Geertz and the French structuralists, among others. As noted above, in order to retain the chronological approach to anthropological theory, an appendix keyed to this chapter has been added.

Chapter 4, "The Cultural Context of Human Behavior," is retained from the fourth edition. It emphasizes the many aspects of human behavior that are patterned by culture, such as perceptions of reality, space and time, body movement and gestures, sex and gender, cognition and emotions. The ethnography on the hijras raises questions about cultural categories such as sex and gender that are frequently taken for granted. An added ethnographical description of maternal reactions to child death in Brazil also presents provocative material about behavior many students assume is universal, that of the "maternal instinct."

Chapter 5, "Language," retains all the material from the fourth edition. A highlight here is the focus on linguistic culture in the United States through ethnographic material on Black English, the Apache "Whiteman" stories, and, new in this edition, genderlect, the differences in the conversational styles of men and women.

Chapter 6, "Learning Culture," examines the ways in which children are brought up to become functioning adults in a culture. The material from the fourth edition has been retained in its entirety, including ethnographic cases of personality in adaptation, transitions from adolescence to adulthood, and a socioeconomic perspective on educational achievement among different ethnic groups in the United States from the work of a Nigerian anthropologist, John Ogbu. Two important additions to this chapter are material on the culture-and-personality school (from the theory chapter in the fourth edition) and new material on coming of age in the United States.

These six chapters form Part One of the text, "Anthropology and Culture."

Part Two, "Sociocultural Adaptations," examines variations in the major universal dimensions of human sociocultural systems and comprises Chapters 7–16. **Chapter 7**, "Making a Living," brings cultural adaptation into focus, describing the major human food-getting strategies through extended ethnographies on hunting and gathering, pastoral, horticultural, and agricultural societies. The emphasis in this chapter is on the relationship between cultural diversity and adaptation to different environments with different kinds of technologies.

Chapter 8, "Economics," discusses systems of production and exchange, including an ecological perspective on such classic anthropological topics as the kula ring and the potlatch. The ethnography in this chapter is on the Kapauku, a culture whose economic system has many features of capitalism but differs from it in important respects. The chapter also returns to the world systems approach to understanding culture change, and retains the ethnographic description of the Gypsies of Spain as an example of resistance to the spread of capitalism.

Chapter 9, "Marriage, Family, and Domestic Groups," is retained essentially complete from the fourth edition, with some added material on the changing structure and demographics of families in the United States. The chapter opening material describing the positive aspects of arranged marriages in India, which challenges the North American view of romantic love as the primary basis for marriage, sets the tone of the chapter's comparative approach in which students are encouraged to look at their own family structures as just one alternative in a wide range of possibilities. Throughout the chapter the ethnographic material on polygyny, polyandry, collectivism, and other forms of family and domestic life emphasizes the adaptive nature of culture and motivates students to examine their own ethnocentrism.

Chapter 10, "Kinship and Nonkin Bases of Association," introduces the major kinship ideologies and the kinds of social groups formed by kinship and other bases for association such as sex and age. A new ethnography comparing the kinship terminology systems of North America and North India demonstrates how kinship classification systems are related to larger cultural interests and values; in addition, its comparative and personalized perspective draws the student into what is probably the most difficult topic in the introductory cultural anthropology course. Moving from kinship to sex and age as important bases for association in all societies, this chapter also discusses age grading in Africa, with an ethnographic example from the Maasai, and sex-based associations among indigenous populations in both North and South America.

Chapter 11, "Social Ranking and Stratification," examines basic differences between egalitarian and stratified societies. Compared to the fourth edition, this revised chapter goes more deeply into the nature of social stratification, examining gender, race, ethnicity, and caste as aspects of stratification, or "invidious distinctions." The new ethnography added to this chapter, "Downward Mobility among the Middle Class in the United States," adds a rarely considered perspective on our own stratification system. This chapter includes an expanded treatment of race as a socially constructed category, as well as the material on ethnicity from Chapter 11 in the fourth edition.

The focus of Chapter 12, "Political Systems and Social Control," is the variation in political institutions and control of behavior in band, tribal, chiefdom, and state societies. The section on tribal warfare has been updated to include the application of a world systems perspective to our understanding of Yanomamo warfare. The chapter opening description of how traditional Mexican villages dealt with the potential for corruption in political office is both amusing and a serious commentary on some universal human concerns. The ethnographies on the Kpelle Moot and deviance in the People's Republic of China raise important questions about alternative views of human nature that underlie different systems of law and punishment. The material from "Tribes on the Hill," about kinship links in the U.S. Congress, provides another means for students to think more objectively, and less ethnocentrically, about their own political system.

"Religion," in Chapter 13, is viewed in light of its symbolism and functions in human society. The chapter focuses on the relation of religious beliefs, practices, and organization to other aspects of the sociocultural system. A new chapter opener on religion in a small town in the United States reminds the student that an analysis of the functions of religion also includes our own society. Material on myth and its functions is now included in this chapter (moved from the previous edition's Chapter 15).

New material on Santeria presents students with an example of religious syncretism, which is becoming increasingly widespread in the United States.

Chapter 14, formerly named "The Arts," is renamed "Expressive Culture" to more accurately reflect the wide range of activities described, which include plastic and graphic arts, music, dance, folklore, play, and sports. The ethnography on the Balinese cockfight gives a vivid example of the contribution a symbolic perspective makes to our understanding of a culture.

Chapter 15, "Change in the Contemporary World," begins with a critical examination of the modern/traditional dichotomy and the emergence of the world systems perspective on culture change. The poem by Pablo Neruda that opens the chapter, the new ethnography on the impact of industrialized agriculture on the Bakairi of the Amazon forest, and ethnographic material on the effect of market economies and heavy agricultural machinery on women's work roles all serve to carry through one theme of this chapter, which may be articulated in the form of a question: Is change progress? The different ways in which changes in the global economy have affected various peoples are described through the ethnographic material on tourism including a new ethnography on the effects of tourism on the Toraja of Indonesia. This chapter also now includes the material on urban voluntary associations and social networks that appeared in Chapter 11 in the fourth edition.

Chapter 16, "The Uses of Anthropology," emphasizes the different kinds of contributions anthropologists are making to solving problems in the contemporary world: The material here includes new ethnographic approaches to combatting AIDS, an expanded section on the work of cultural survival, anthropologists as expert witnesses, the role of anthropologists in development projects, and how data on cultural differences in values and practices can be applied to international business and conflict resolution.

Features and Study Aids

Each chapter is pedagogically constructed to help students identify, learn, and remember key concepts.

- **Study questions** at the beginnings of chapters are keyed to major topics and/or concerns.
- **Ethnographic examples** are featured at the beginning of each chapter to engage the student's interest and to provide a context for thinking about more abstract concepts.
- A **summary of main points** at the end of each chapter helps study and review.
- A **glossary** at the end of the book defines major terms and concepts, which are printed in bold type in the text so students can quickly identify them.

Maps, charts, drawings, and photographs have been chosen and placed to illustrate the main points of each chapter. A map showing the location of many of the societies mentioned in this text is found at the beginning of the book.

To aid students' further study, the end of each chapter contains a list of suggested readings that are both interesting and accessible to the introductory student. In addition, a list of sources, in the notation system of the *American Anthropologist*, is included at the end of the book.

Although each chapter stands on its own and the sequence of study can be rearranged to fit individual teachers' preferences, the material is also integrated for greater comprehensibility. The substance of each chapter is organized so that the main ideas, secondary ideas, and ethnographic material stand out clearly. Ethnographic examples and extended ethnographic cases are presented at the beginning of and within each chapter, with the aim of providing interesting and appropriate illumination of basic concepts, rather than in an attempt to cover the field of anthropological research exhaustively.

An Instructor's Manual includes new multiple-choice, short-answer, and essay questions; updated film suggestions keyed to each chapter; and student-oriented exercises for both class participation and assignments outside of class.

Acknowledgments

It gives me great pleasure to thank the many people who have been associated with this book. I am most appreciative of the helpful comments made by the reviewers of the fifth edition: John Fritz, University of Notre Dame; Nancy Hickerson, Texas Tech University; John McDaniel, Washington and Lee University; N.J.C. Vasantkumar, Susquehanna University; Michael Whiteford, Iowa State University; and Michael Winkelman, Arizona State University.

For the use of their photographs, I would like to thank Kathleen Adams, Ann Brody, Charles Brooks, Deena Burton, Soo Choi, Kathy Clark, Chander Dembla, Richard Feinberg, Joan Gregg, Sarah Grossman, William S. Grossman, James Hamilton, Jane Hoffer, Raymond Kennedy, David Klein, Bernhard Krauss, John Lenoir, Joan Morriss, Marilyn Omifunke Torres, and Jean Zorn, as well as the American Museum of Natural History, the United Nations Photography Library, and the Museum of the American Indian (Heye Foundation). For help with other materials, I would like to thank Wendy Demegret, and particularly Mrs. Raksha Chopra, who was my invaluable informant on the intricacies of kinship terminology in North India. Ruth and Stanley Freed and Owen Lynch have always been a great source of friendship and intellectual stimulation and most generous about sharing their wide and deep knowledge with me. My colleagues at John Jay College, whose concerns for teaching cultural anthropology animate our discussions, are also an important source of support for my work.

I had the good fortune to participate in the 1991 National Endowment for the Humanities (NEH) Summer Seminar, "The Politics of Culture and Identity: Pacific Perspectives," led by Geoffrey White and Lamont Lindstrom. That seminar was particularly helpful in expanding my interest in contested images, cultural politics, and the Pacific. Much of that summer's work has found its way into these pages, and I want to thank the NEH, the seminar leaders, and the seminar members for providing such an exciting and collegial atmosphere in which to delve into some of the most important new directions in contemporary anthropology.

The Wadsworth staff, as always, has been helpful throughout. I particularly enjoyed working with my editor and friend, Peggy Adams. I also appreciate the enthusiasm and advice from Sheryl Fullerton, who always has good ideas, and from Serina Beauparlant, who will be taking up where Peggy Adams left off.

My family continues to form an important cheering section for my work. For their support and enthusiasm I thank my wonderful parents, Harry and Sylvia Young; the younger generation, Raj, Jai, and Paisley; my sister and colleague, Joan Gregg; and especially my husband, Robin, who is particularly helpful in not letting me take anything for granted about my own or other cultures and the discipline of anthropology.

Anthropology and Human Diversity

What are the aims of cultural anthropology?

In what ways is anthropology unique in its study of humankind?

How does anthropology help us understand our own and other cultures?

How is Kominsky, described on the next page, like a person from one culture observing people from another culture?

How have changes in the world affected the practice of anthropology?

This Kominsky [recently deposed president of the Senior Citizen Center] is like a man who is deaf. He comes across a bunch of people with fiddles and drums, jumping around every which way and he thinks they are crazy. He can't hear the music, so he doesn't see they are dancing.

Basha, from Barbara Myerhoff, Number Our Days, *New York: Simon and Schuster, 1978.*

Anthropology is the comparative study of human societies and cultures. The aim of anthropology is to describe, analyze, and explain the different ways of life, or cultures, through which human groups, or societies, have adapted to their environments. Anthropology is comparative in that it attempts to understand both similarities and differences among human societies, in both the past and the present. Only by the study of humanity in its total variety can we understand the origins and development of our species.

Anthropologists study our species from its beginnings several million years ago right up to the present. We study human beings as they live in every corner of the earth, in all kinds of physical environments. Some anthropologists are now trying to project how human beings will live in outer space. It is this interest in humankind throughout time and in all parts of the world that distinguishes anthropology as a scientific and humanistic discipline. In other academic disciplines, human behavior is studied primarily from the point of view of Western

society. "Human nature" is thought to be the same as the behavior of people as they exist in the modern industrial nations of Europe and the United States.

Human beings everywhere consider their own behavior not only right, but natural. For example, both "common sense" and Western economic theory see human beings as "naturally" individualistic and competitive. But in some societies, human beings are not competitive, and the group is more important than the individual. Anthropologists see the Western idea of "economic man"—the individual motivated by profit and rational self-interest—as the result of the particular socioeconomic and political system we live in. It is not an explanation of the behavior of the Arapesh hunter in New Guinea, who makes sure he is not always the first to sight and claim the game, so that others will not leave him to hunt alone (Mead 1963:38). In anthropology, more than any other discipline, concepts of human nature and theories of human behavior are based on studies of human groups whose goals, values, views

Included in cultural behavior are simple acts, like eating with a fork, with chopsticks, or with one's fingers. The daily rice meal of this Burmese family is one of thousands of patterns of behavior that must be learned by each new generation. (United Nations)

beings as whole organisms who adapt to their environments through a complex interaction of biology and culture.

Because anthropologists have this "holistic" approach to the study of the human experience, they are interested in the total range of human activity. They study the small dramas of daily living as well as dramatic events. They study the ways in which mothers hold their babies, or sons address their fathers. They want to know not only how a group gets its food but also the rules for eating it. Anthropologists are interested in how human societies think about time and space and in how they see colors and name them. They are interested in health and illness and in the human body and the cultural significance of physical variation. Anthropologists are interested in sex and marriage and in giving birth and dying. They are interested in folklore and fairy tales, political speeches, and everyday conversation. For the anthropologist, great ceremonies and the ordinary rituals of greeting a friend are all worth investigating. When presented out of context, some of the behaviors anthropologists are interested in and write about seem strange or silly, but every aspect of human behavior is significant as part of the attempt to understand human life and society.

of reality, and environmental adaptations are very different from those of industrial Western societies.

In their attempts to explain human variation, anthropologists combine the study of both human biology and the learned and shared patterns of human behavior we call culture. Other academic disciplines focus on one factor — biology, psychology, physiology, or society — as the explanation of human behavior. Anthropology seeks to understand human

Specialization in Anthropology

The broad range of anthropological interest has led to specialization of research and teaching. The major divisions of anthropology are cultural anthropology, anthropological linguistics, archeology, and biological or physical anthropology.

Cultural Anthropology

Culture is human behavior that is learned, rather than genetically transmitted, and that is typical of a particular human group, or society. A **society** is a group of people who are dependent on one another for survival and/or well-being and who share a particular way of life, or **culture**. **Cultural anthropology** is the study of human culture and society.

Culture is the major way in which human beings adapt to their environments. Cultural anthropologists attempt to understand culture in this general sense: They study its origins, its development, and its diversity as it changes through time and among peoples. They also examine its transmission through teaching and learning and its relation to our species, *Homo sapiens*. Cultural anthropologists are also interested in particular cultures; they want to know how different societies adapt to their environments. In its comparative perspective, cultural anthropology attempts to discover what is specific and variable in human behavior and what is general and uniform. Cultural anthropologists ask questions like these: "Is religion universal?" "What kinds of family structures are found in different societies?" They are also interested in the relationships among the different subsystems of a culture — in particular, in their cause-and-effect relationship to cultural change. One goal of cultural anthropology is to understand how culture change works so that we can predict and perhaps direct or control change in productive ways.

Linguistics

Language is the means by which human beings communicate with each other and as such it is an essential part of what it means to be human and an essential part of culture. The field of

Dr. Anne-Marie Cantwell carefully uncovers an artifact from a historical site in the heart of a North American city. From bits and pieces of material culture, archeologists add to our knowledge about prehistoric, historic, and contemporary populations. (John P. McCabe)

cultural anthropology that is concerned with language is called **linguistics**. Anthropological linguists study linguistic variation, the ways in which human languages have developed, the ways in which they are related to one another, how language is learned, and the relationship between language and other aspects of culture. One aim of anthropological linguistics is ultimately to understand the process of thought and the organization of the human mind as they are expressed in language.

Archeology

Anthropological **archeology** specializes in studying culture through material remains. Most archeologists study past societies for which there are either no written records or no writing systems that have been deciphered. Archeology thus adds a vital time dimension to our understanding of culture and how cultures change.

A biological anthropologist, David Klein, observes vervet monkeys in East Africa. Field observations of nonhuman primates have greatly added to our knowledge of the variety of primate behavior patterns, which until about thirty years ago was obtained only from animals in captivity. (David Klein)

The archeologist does not observe human behavior and culture directly but reconstructs them from material remains — pottery, tools, garbage, ruins of houses and public buildings, burials, and whatever else a society has left behind. Until about 1960, archeologists were mainly concerned with describing the artifacts, or material remains, of prehistoric sites. They would describe the procedures they had followed and the relative frequency and locations of the artifacts, and they would compare those artifacts with similar ones in the same region. Contemporary archeology redirects the interests of archeologists to new questions and research. It is interested not simply in describing prehistoric sites and artifacts but in interpreting and explaining these data in terms of what they say about the culturally patterned behavior that produced them.

Biological Anthropology

The human ability to survive under a broad and varied range of conditions is based in the enormous flexibility of cultural behavior. The capacity for culture, however, is grounded in our unique biological history and physical makeup. The human adaptation — the way people contend with environmental conditions — is *biocultural* in nature in that it involves both biological and cultural dimensions. Therefore, to understand fully what it is to be human, we need a sense of how the biological aspects of this adaptation came about and how they influence human cultural behavior.

Biological, or **physical**, **anthropology** is the study of humankind from a biological perspective. A major task of biological anthropology is to study the evolution of the human species over time and the biological processes involved in human adaptation.

Paleontology is the study of tracing human evolution in the fossil record. Paleontologists study the remains of the earliest human forms, as well as those nonhuman forms that can suggest something about our own origin and development. Paleontology is a particularly fascinating subject because it tries to answer the question "Where did we come from?"

Biological anthropologists are also interested in the evolution of culture. In the evolution of the human species, biological and cultural evolution interacted in a complex feedback system; neither is independent of the other. The process of biological evolution is responsible for the cultural aspects of human adaptation. Our unique evolutionary history resulted in the development of a biological structure, the human brain, capable of inventing, learning, and using cultural adaptations. Cultural adaptation has, in turn, "freed" humans from the relatively slow process of biological adaptation: Populations can invent, or adopt from other societies, new ways of dealing with problems on an almost immediate basis. The study of the complex interrelationship between biological and cultural evolution is the link among biological anthropology, cultural anthropology, and archeology.

Because early human populations were hunters and gatherers, biological anthropologists study contemporary foraging societies in order to fill in the fragmentary physical evidence left by early humans. In addition to studying living human groups, biological anthropologists also study living nonhuman **primates**, which is the *order* within the mammalian *class* that includes monkeys, apes, and humans. Primates are studied for the clues that their chemistry, physiology, morphology (physical structure), and behavior can give us in understanding our own species. Although at one time primates were mainly studied in the artificial settings of laboratories and zoos, now much of the work of biological anthropologists involves studying these animals in the wild.

One of the important outcomes of human evolution is the wide diversity in human form. Some people are short, others are tall; skin color covers a spectrum from very light to very dark; there are people with slight builds, others are husky. The degree to which humans vary is even more startling when less obvious differences, such as in blood type and other biochemical traits, are taken into account. Additionally, there are geographic patterns to this biological diversity, with people from the same region tending to share more traits than do people from distant lands.

What is the nature of these differences, and how should scientists describe and classify populational diversity? What accounts for this biological variation, and is it of any evolutionary significance? These intriguing questions form still another major interest of biological anthropologists: the study of differences among human groups that are transmitted genetically. In addition to the practical benefits of genetic analysis — for example, in the treatment and prevention of some harmful hereditary abnormalities — population genetics contributes to our understanding of human evolution and adaptation.

Applying Anthropology

Although anthropology as an academic discipline is mainly concerned with basic research — that is, asking the "big" questions about the origins of our species, the development of culture and civilization, and the functions of human social institutions such as the family or religion — anthropologists are also putting their knowledge to work to solve human problems. Biological anthropologists, for example, can shed light on some of the major diseases of the modern, industrial world by comparing our diet and life-style with those of prehistoric and contemporary hunter-gatherer societies who do not suffer from heart disease, high blood pressure, and diabetes (Eaton and Konner 1989). Forensic anthropologists, specialists in analyzing bones, identify remains from airplane crashes and in criminal investigations. Archeologists' research about what people in our contemporary society throw into the garbage is being used to help solve our nation's "garbage crisis" — a problem partly caused by our consumerism — and also to address more theoretical problems, such as how eating habits differ in different social classes (Rathje 1993).

Interdisciplinary work by anthropologists and others in the natural sciences is put to use in helping people with such projects as reforestation, development of agriculture (Rhoades 1984), population control, and water management. Other anthropologists study our legal and criminal justice systems to help address such problems as drug abuse or racial/ethnic conflict. Some new forms of conflict resolution, such as mediation, are being tried in our court systems as litigation proves an unproductive way to resolve all conflicts. These new methods grew out of anthropological studies of non-Western societies where such methods have been more effective than courts of law in dealing with problems in human relationships.

Psychological anthropologists study areas in which anthropology overlaps with psychology, such as cognition (mental processes), which has implications for educational policy, and mental health, where anthropologists can draw upon their knowledge of healing practices in non-Western societies. Medical anthropology has been a particularly useful specialty, studying how cultural patterns of different people encourage or inhibit attitudes toward health, disease and illness, medical practitioners, population control, and such important customs as dietary habits.

Anthropology, with its comparative, holistic, and cultural perspective, emphasizing the interrelatedness of human culture with the environment and the links among different elements of a culture, is particularly well suited for helping to solve human problems in a wide variety of fields. Throughout this text, we will see in more detail the great variety of ways in which anthropologists have been involved in applying their knowledge to contemporary issues and human problems.

What We Learn from Anthropology

Understanding Human Differences

Anthropology contributes to our understanding of genetically transmitted differences among human groups, as well as those that result from learning. By increasing our understanding of the importance of culture in human adaptation, anthropology enables us to look more critically at popular ideas about "human nature." Anthropology helps remove the blinders of **ethnocentrism**, the tendency to view the world through the narrow lens of one's own culture or social position. The American tourist who, when presented with a handful of Italian *lira*, asks "How much is this in *real* money?" is ethnocentric. In my own anthropological fieldwork among women in India, I found myself pitied because my informants heard that "in America sons leave their parents' home when they marry." It was difficult to convince anyone that I would be pleased when my own two sons set up homes of their own.

All over the world, people are ethnocentric. They tend to see things from their own culturally patterned point of view, to value what they have been taught to value, and to see the meaning of life in their own culturally defined purposes. But ethnocentrism is more than just the biases of perception and knowledge; it is also the practice of judging other cultures by the standards of one's own. Most peoples in the world regard their own culture as superior, and many consider peoples from other cultures to be less than human. But although all peoples are ethnocentric, the ethnocentricity of Western societies has had greater consequences than that of smaller, less technologically advanced,

Ethnocentrism is universal but because Western military technology is so powerful, our own ethnocentrism has had a great, and often destructive, impact on other cultures. (Serena Nanda)

and geographically isolated peoples. The historical circumstances that led to the spread of Western civilization have given us a strong belief in its rightness and superiority. We have been in a position to impose our beliefs and practices on other peoples because of our superior military technology and because our industrial technology provides an abundance of consumer goods that other people quickly learn to want. Their acceptance of refrigerators and washing machines has led us to believe that our values and other social institutions are also superior.

The paradox is that, although ethnocentrism gets in the way of understanding, some ethnocentrism seems necessary as a kind of glue to hold a society together. When a people's culture loses value for them, they may experience great emotional stress and even lose interest in living. To the extent that ethnocentrism prevents building bridges between cultures, however, it becomes maladaptive. Where one culture is motivated by ethnocentrism to trespass on another, the harm done can be enormous. It is but a short step from this kind of ethnocentrism to **racism**, the belief that some human populations are superior, or inferior, to others because of inherited, genetically transmitted characteristics, and one that has been made in both popular and scientific thought in the West.

Human Biological Diversity: Race and Racism

The most familiar aspect of the study of human diversity is the concept of "race," the idea that there are clearly bounded categories of people sharing the same biological traits into which any individual can be placed. Early racial studies attempted to construct racial categories, and many such groupings have been constructed over the years. The schemes were based on easily visible biological characteristics, such as

Physical characteristics, language, and culture vary independently of one another. (United Nations)

hair texture, skin color, and nose form, and were ascribed to populations inhabiting particular geographical regions (e.g., African Negroid). As it became apparent that there was no exact correlation between continents and so-called racial traits, classifications became more elaborate and studies talked about composite races, micro-races, or local races — that is, groups limited to a small, localized area (Garn 1969).

Many criticisms have been made of the racial typology approach. It is clear, for example, that there are no discrete boundaries between racial groups; rather, there is a merging between them at their peripheries. Also, the racial categories are based on a very small number of readily visible traits, such as skin color and head shape, when in fact there are thousands of genetically inherited characteristics that might be used for classification, many of which are "invisible," such as blood type. In addition, we know little about the inheritance of most of these characteristics.

Another important point is that racial classifications, even when not so intended by their authors, are frequently used for political purposes, including to distinguish so-called superior and inferior peoples. These schemes became the basis for discriminatory policies, such as restrictive immigration.

The idea that cultural variation, and specifically cultural superiority, resulted from physical or "racial" variation seemed to make sense: Peoples who looked different from each other also behaved differently. The theory that the peoples of Asia and Africa and those native to North and South America were biologically inferior was comforting to Europeans who exploited their natural resources, took over their lands, and used them as slaves and servants. Up until the late nineteenth century, even some scientists believed in these ideas. This "scientific racism" was used as a justification for building social, political, and economic structures that favored the interests of the "superior" race. Even today, in spite of a century of scientific evidence to the contrary, racism and racial discrimination are still powerful factors in contemporary societies. One of the most important things we can learn by studying anthropology is that the big differences among human groups are the result of culture, not biological inheritance or "race." Because the biological similarities among human groups far outweigh the differences, and because racial classifications tell us little or nothing about other kinds of variation, some anthropologists want to drop the word *race* altogether.

While biological anthropologists are interested in physical variation among human populations, the division of societies into groups of people called races is a matter of social and cultural construction. Cultural labels of different "races" are not based on scientifically valid or relevant categories, but on the political, social, and economic positions groups have in a society, a topic we will discuss further in Chapter 11. The focus on so-called racial differences

The anthropologist has become so familiar with the diversity of ways in which different peoples behave in similar situations that he [or she] is not apt to be surprised by even the most exotic customs. In fact, if all of the logically possible combinations of behavior have not been found somewhere in the world, he is apt to suspect that they must be present in some yet undescribed tribe. . . . In this light, the magical beliefs and practices of the Nacirema present such unusual aspects that it seems desirable to describe them as an example of the extremes to which human behavior can go.

Professor [Ralph] Linton first brought the ritual of the Nacirema to the attention of anthropologists twenty years ago, but the culture of this people is still very poorly understood. They are a North American group living in the territory between the Canadian Cree, the Yaqui and Tarahumare of Mexico, and the Carib and Arawak of the Antilles. Little is known of their origin, although tradition states that they came from the east. . . .

Nacirema culture is characterized by a highly developed market economy which has evolved in a rich natural habitat. While much of the people's time is devoted to economic pursuits, a large part of the fruits of these labors and a considerable portion of the day are spent in ritual activity. The focus of this activity is the human body, the appearance and health of which loom as a dominant concern in the ethos of the people. While such a concern is certainly not unusual, its ceremonial aspects and associated philosophy are unique.

The fundamental belief underlying the whole system appears to be that the human body is ugly and that its natural tendency is to debility and disease. Incarcerated in such a body, man's only hope is to avert these characteristics through the use of the powerful influences of ritual and ceremony. Every household has one or more shrines devoted to this purpose. The more powerful individuals in the society have several shrines in their houses and, in fact, the opulence of a house is often referred to in terms of the number of such ritual centers it possesses. Most houses are of wattle and daub construction, but the shrine rooms of the more wealthy are lined with stone. Poorer families imitate the rich by applying pottery plaques to their shrine walls.

While each family has at least one such shrine, the rituals associated with it are not family ceremonies but are private and secret. The rites are normally only discussed with children, and then only during the period when they are being initiated into these mysteries. I was able, however, to establish sufficient rapport with the natives to examine these shrines and to have the rituals described to me.

The focal point of the shrine is a box or chest which is built into the wall.

In this chest are kept the many charms and magical potions without which no native believes he could live. These preparations are secured from a variety of specialized practitioners. The most powerful of these are the medicine men, whose assistance must be rewarded with substantial gifts. However, the medicine men do not provide the curative potions for their clients, but decide what the ingredients should be and then write them down in an ancient and secret language. This writing is understood only by the medicine men and by the herbalists who, for another gift, provide the required charm.

The charm is not disposed of after it has served its purpose, but is placed in the charm-box of the household shrine. As these magical materials are specific for certain ills, and the real or imagined maladies of the people are many, the charm-box is usually full to overflowing. The magical packets are so numerous that people forget what their purposes were and fear to use them again. While the natives are very vague on this point, we can only assume that the idea in retaining all the old magical materials is that their presence in the charm-box, before which the body rituals are conducted, will in some way protect the worshipper.

Beneath the charm-box is a small font. Each day every member of the family, in succession, enters the shrine room, bows his head before the charm-box, mingles different sorts of holy water in the font, and proceeds with a brief rite of ablution. The holy waters are secured from the Water Temple of the community, where the priests conduct elaborate ceremonies to make the liquid ritually pure.

In the hierarchy of magical practitioners, and below the medicine men in prestige, are specialists whose designation is best translated "holy-mouth-men." The Nacirema have an almost pathological horror of and fascination with the mouth, the condition of which is believed to have a supernatural influence on all social relationships. Were it not for the rituals of the mouth, they believe that their teeth would fall out, their gums bleed, their jaws shrink, their friends desert them, and their lovers reject them. They also believe that a strong relationship exists between oral and moral characteristics. For example, there is a ritual ablution of the mouth for children which is supposed to improve their moral fiber.

The daily body ritual performed by everyone includes a mouth-rite. Despite the fact that these people are so punctilious about care of the mouth, this rite involves a practice which strikes the uninitiated stranger as revolting. It was reported to me that the ritual consists of inserting a small bundle of hog

(*continued*)

hairs into the mouth, along with certain magical powders, and then moving the bundle in a highly formalized series of gestures.

In addition to the private mouth-rite, the people seek out a holy-mouth-man once or twice a year. These practitioners have an impressive set of paraphernalia, consisting of a variety of augers, awls, probes, and prods. The use of these objects in the exorcism of the evils of the mouth involves almost unbelievable ritual torture of the client. The holy-mouth-man opens the client's mouth and, using the above mentioned tools, enlarges any holes which decay may have created in the teeth. Magical materials are put into those holes. If there are no naturally occurring holes in the teeth, large sections of one or more teeth are gouged out so that the supernatural substance can be applied. In the client's view, the purpose of these ministrations is to arrest decay and to draw friends. The extremely sacred and traditional character of the rite is evident in the fact that the natives return to the holy-mouth-men year after year, despite the fact that their teeth continue to decay.

It is to be hoped that, when a thorough study of the Nacirema is made, there will be careful inquiry into the personality structure of these people. One has but to watch the gleam in the eye of a holy-mouth-man, as he jabs an awl into an exposed nerve, to suspect that a certain amount of sadism is involved. If this can be established, a very interesting pattern emerges, for most of the population shows definite masochistic tendencies. It was to these that Professor Linton referred in discussing a distinctive part of the daily body ritual which is performed only by men. This part of the rite involves scraping and lacerating the surface of the face with a sharp instrument. Special women's rites are performed only four times during each lunar month, but what they lack in frequency is made up in barbarity. As part of this ceremony, women bake their heads in small ovens for about an hour. The theoretically interesting point is that what seems to be a preponderantly masochistic people have developed sadistic specialists.

The medicine men have an imposing temple, or *latipso*, in every community of any size. The more elaborate ceremonies required to treat very sick patients can only be performed at this temple. These ceremonies involve not only the *thaumaturge* [a person who supposedly works miracles] but a permanent group of vestal maidens who move sedately about the temple chambers in distinctive costume and headdress.

The *latipso* ceremonies are so harsh that it is phenomenal that a fair proportion of the really sick natives who enter the temple ever recover. Small children whose indoctrination is still incomplete have been known to resist attempts to take them to the temple because "that is where you go to die." Despite this fact, sick adults are not only willing but eager to undergo the protracted ritual purification, if they can afford to do so. No matter how ill the supplicant or how grave the emergency, the guardians of many temples will not admit a client if he cannot give a rich gift to the custodian. Even after one has gained admission and survived the ceremonies, the guardians will not permit the neophyte to leave until he makes still another gift.

The supplicant entering the temple is first stripped of all his or her clothes. In everyday life the Nacirema avoids exposure of his body and its natural functions. Bathing and excretory acts are performed only in the secrecy of the household shrine, where they are ritualized as part of the body-rites. Psychological shock results from the fact that body secrecy is suddenly lost upon entry into the *latipso*. A man, whose own wife has never seen him in an excretory act suddenly finds himself naked and assisted by a vestal maiden while he performs his natural functions into a sacred vessel. This sort of ceremonial treatment is necessitated by the fact that the excreta are used by a diviner to ascertain the course and nature of the client's sickness. Female clients, on the other hand, find their naked bodies are subjected to the scrutiny, manipulation, and prodding of the medicine men.

Few supplicants in the temple are well enough to do anything but lie on their hard beds. The daily ceremonies, like the rites of the holy-mouth-men, involve discomfort and torture. With ritual precision, the vestals awaken their miserable charges each dawn and roll them about on their beds of pain while performing ablutions, in the formal movements of which the maidens are highly trained. At other times they insert magic wands in the supplicant's mouth or force him to eat substances which are supposed to be healing. From time to time the medicine men come to their clients and jab magically treated needles into their flesh. The fact that these temple ceremonies may not cure, and may even kill the neophyte, in no way decreases the people's faith in the medicine men.

There remains one other kind of practitioner, known as a "listener." This witchdoctor has the power to exorcise the devils that lodge in the heads of people who have been bewitched. The Nacirema believe that parents bewitch their own children. Mothers are particularly suspected of putting a curse on children while teaching them the secret body rituals. The counter-magic of the witchdoctor is unusual in its lack of ritual. The patient simply tells the "listener" all his troubles and fears, beginning with the earliest difficulties he can

(continued)

remember. The memory displayed by the Nacirema in these exorcism sessions is truly remarkable. It is not uncommon for the patient to bemoan the rejection he felt upon being weaned as a babe, and a few individuals even see their troubles going back to the traumatic effects of their own birth.

In conclusion, mention must be made of certain practices which have their base in native esthetics but which depend upon the pervasive aversion to the natural body and its functions. There are ritual fasts to make fat people thin and ceremonial feasts to make thin people fat. Still other rites are used to make women's breasts larger if they are small, and smaller if they are large. General dissatisfaction with breast shape is symbolized in the fact that the ideal form is virtually outside the range of human variation. A few women afflicted with almost inhuman hypermammary development are so idolized that they make a handsome living by simply going from village to village and permitting the natives to stare at them for a fee.

Reference has already been made to the fact that excretory functions are ritualized, routinized, and relegated to secrecy. Natural reproductive functions are similarly distorted. Intercourse is taboo as a topic and scheduled as an act. Efforts are made to avoid pregnancy by the use of magical materials or by limiting intercourse to certain phases of the moon. Conception is actually very infrequent. When pregnant, women dress so as to hide their condition. Parturition takes place in secret, without friends or relatives to assist, and the majority of women do not nurse their infants.

Our review of the ritual life of the Nacirema has certainly shown them to be a magic-ridden people. It is hard to understand how they have managed to exist so long under the burdens which they have imposed upon themselves. But even such exotic customs as these take on real meaning when they are viewed with the insight provided by [Bronislaw] Malinowski when he wrote:

"Looking from far and above, from our high places of safety in the developed civilization, it is easy to see all the crudity and irrelevance of magic. But without its power and guidance early man could not have mastered his practical difficulties as he has done, nor could man have advanced to the higher stages of civilization."

From Horace Miner, "Body Ritual among the Nacirema." Reproduced by permission of the American Anthropological Association from The American Anthropologist, *1956, 58:503–507. Not for further reproduction.*

far too often overlooks the facts that all human beings belong to the same species and that the biological features essential to human life are common to us all. A human being from any part of the world, falling anywhere in the range of human physical variation, can learn the cultural and behavioral patterns of any group she or he is born into. Adaptation through culture and the potential for cultural richness and creativity are part of a universal human heritage and override any physical variation existing among human groups.

Cultural Relativity

Anthropology helps us understand peoples whose ways of life are different from our own but with whom we share a common human destiny. The idea that each culture must be approached on its own terms is called **cultural relativity**. Cultural relativity is a tool for understanding other cultures. With this attitude, we understand cultural patterns in terms of the total culture of which they are a part. Cultural relativity does not mean that all patterns must be judged as equally "good"; every culture has a set of values that serve as criteria in judging human behavior. It does mean that other patterns make sense, even if we would not want them for ourselves.

The concept of cultural relativity emphasizes an insider's view of a culture, what is sometimes called the native's point of view or an **emic** perspective. With the emic perspective, anthropologists use concepts and distinctions that are meaningful to members of the culture, attempting to acquire a knowledge of how that culture looks from the inside and what one must know in order to think and act as a native of that culture. But anthropology, as a science, also incorporates an **etic**, or outsider's, perspective. This perspective allows anthropologists to analyze data in a way that may not be part of the native's cultural awareness or may even be in conflict with it. The aim of emic research is to generate understanding that a native would find meaningful; the aim of etic research is to generate useful scientific theories. It is by this latter criterion, which may lie outside the native's ability to judge, that etic research is tested. The discussion over whether the emic or etic perspective is more appropriate for the goals of anthropological research continues to be part of professional debate, as we will see in Chapter 2.

Older arguments about the value of the emic and etic perspectives in anthropology distract from understanding the potentially complementary relationship between them. The ability to look at another culture from the inside, the emic perspective, helps develop our ability to look at our own culture from the outside, an etic perspective. This objective anthropological perspective gives us better insight into our own behavior. By introducing the idea that human behavior is learned, not biologically inherited, anthropology helps us understand ourselves as individuals influenced by our own cultural patterns and by society as a whole. The comparative, cross-cultural perspective of anthropology allows us to see that our own culture is only one design for living among the many in the history of humankind, a much needed corrective for ethnocentrism. Our culture is an adaptation to one kind of environment with a particular level of technology, and it came into being under a particular set of historical circumstances. An outsider's view of our culture and its historical context is an important contribution anthropology can make to understanding and constructively addressing our problems as a society. From its beginnings, anthropology held out a dual promise: that of contributing to the understanding of human diversity and that of serving as a cultural critique of our own society (Marcus and Fischer 1986). By becoming conscious of cultural alternatives, we would become better able to "see ourselves as others see us" and to use that knowledge to make constructive changes in our own society. It was by looking at the "other" that we could come to understand ourselves.

Anthropology in a Changing World

One source that allows us to see ourselves as others see us could be accounts about our own society by outsiders. But because anthropology is a Western science, growing out of our own particular intellectual traditions, as well as out of the Western colonial past, we have many more accounts of other societies by Europeans and Americans than we have accounts of our own society by non-Western observers. Indeed, one of the most insightful accounts of the culture and society of the United States, written more than one hundred years ago, is that by a Frenchman, Alexis de Tocqueville (1956).

With the formal dismantling of colonialism since World War II, this anthropological focus on "the other" has been challenged, and the role of anthropology as cultural critique is again gaining attention. Until the end of World War II, the major audience for anthropology was the educated public in the United States and Western Europe. The peoples among whom anthropologists worked, for the most part, could not read European languages and did not have access to the published materials in which anthropological descriptions and theories appeared. Thus, there was little political pressure to consider their responses to anthropological descriptions of them, or to take a hard look at the sources of political and economic power implicit in the relationships between anthropologists and the peoples whose cultures they described.

This attitude has changed in the postcolonial world, and many of the ideas, products, and practices of cultural anthropology that were perhaps taken too much for granted are now being contested and reexamined. Serious questions are being asked about whether or not non-Western cultures can be accurately represented and written about by Western anthropologists, and about the impact such representations have on the people whose culture is being described. This challenge is not merely to bias and factual inaccuracy but goes to the very core of the discipline.

As contemporary social groups, whether nations or smaller units within nations, embark on a search for identity and autonomy, cultural representations become important resources, and traditions once taken for granted become a subject of heightened political consciousness. Indigenous peoples, as well as minority groups within nations, including our own, wish their cultures to be represented to the outside world in ways acceptable to them, and are holding anthropologists responsible for the political impact of their work. The political consciousness raised by decolonization and the civil and human rights movements since the 1960s, in addition to a postmodernist perspective that calls all so-called truths into question, have both had a significant impact on contemporary anthropology.

Like all cultures, the culture of anthropology must adapt to changes in the world it inhabits, if it is to survive. Those of us engaged in the anthropological enterprise are optimistic that, as our studies become more reflective on issues of politics, history, and context (Lee 1992a), we will continue to make a valuable contribution to illuminating cultural diversity and, in doing so, leave the world a better place than we found it.

Summary

1. Anthropology is a comparative study of humankind. It studies human beings in the past and the present and in every corner of the world.

2. Anthropology is holistic. It studies the whole range of human behavior and the interrelationships among the different aspects of human behavior.

3. Anthropology focuses on what is typical within a human group, rather than on individual differences.

4. The aim of anthropology is to discover and explain the similarities and differences among human groups.

5. Biological anthropology focuses on human characteristics that are transmitted genetically.

6. Cultural anthropology focuses on culture, the learned and shared ways of behaving typical of a particular human group. Anthropologists also study culture in general and attempt to discover laws of cultural development that apply to the whole of humankind.

7. Two specialties in cultural anthropology are archeology and linguistics. Archeologists study societies that existed in the past and did not leave written records. Linguists study human speech and linguistic variation.

8. Anthropologists not only do basic research but also apply their knowledge to solving human problems.

9. By showing the importance of culture in human adaptation, anthropology makes us examine biological explanations of differences among human populations more critically.

10. Anthropology reduces ethnocentrism, that is, looking at and judging other people through the narrow perspective of one's own culture.

11. Anthropology demonstrates that race is not a valid scientific category but rather a cultural construct.

12. Anthropology introduces the concept of cultural relativity, which means understanding a culture from the point of view of its participants. Anthropology can thus present the emic, or insider's, view of a particular culture.

13. Anthropology can also present an etic, or outsider's, view of a culture; it can point out causes and consequences of particular patterns of which people in that culture may not be conscious.

14. By taking the outsider's view of our own society and culture, we can understand it more objectively and perhaps use this understanding to make more rational changes in our own lives.

15. With the end of colonialism, the theories and practices of anthropology are being challenged by peoples whose cultures have traditionally been studied by anthropology.

Suggested Readings

Cole, Johnnetta B.
1988 *Anthropology for the Nineties: Introductory Readings.* New York: Free Press. An interesting anthology that largely succeeds in its explicit aim of "teaching respect for diversity in the human condition" by placing American culture squarely within a cross-cultural perspective.

DeVita, Philip R., and Armstrong, James D.
1993 *Distant Mirrors: America as a Foreign Culture.* Belmont, Calif.: Wadsworth. An entertaining series of articles with a serious message: how the U.S. culture looks to foreign anthropologists. This book gives the United States a chance to "see ourselves as others see us."

Gould, Stephen Jay
1982 *The Mismeasure of Man.* New York: Norton. A brilliant and important book that attacks the theories of biological determinism in a well-argued and carefully documented manner.

Hymes, Dell, ed.
1972 *Reinventing Anthropology.* New York: Vintage. Provocative essays on the role of anthropology in the contemporary world.

Peacock, James L.
1986 *The Anthropological Lens: Harsh Light, Soft Focus.* New York: Cambridge University Press. A readable introduction to the substance, method, and significance of anthropology as both a scientific and humanistic discipline.

Doing Cultural Anthropology

What are the aims of fieldwork and ethnography?

How has ethnography changed from the beginning of the twentieth century to the present?

In what ways may the personalities, social status, and culture of anthropologists affect their ethnographies?

How does an anthropologist go about doing an ethnographic field study?

Anthropology inevitably involves an encounter with the Other. . . . In many cases this [ethnographic] distancing leads to an exclusive focus on the other as primitive, bizarre, and exotic. The gap between a familiar "we" and an exotic "they" is a major obstacle to a meaningful understanding of the Other, an obstacle that can only be overcome through some form of participation in the world of the Other. . . . If it is possible to reduce the distance between the anthropologist and the Other, to bridge the gap between "us" and "them," then the goal of a truly humanistic anthropology can be achieved.

From L. Danforth, The Death Rituals of Rural Greece *(Princeton, N.J.: Princeton University Press, 1982), pp. 5–7.*

The field-working anthropologist undergoes a unique experience; no one else knows quite so personally what it is like to live in an entirely alien culture. Missionaries do not know; government officials do not know; traders and explorers do not know. Only the anthropologist wants nothing from the people with whom he lives — nothing, that is, but . . . an understanding of and an appreciation for the texture of their lives.

From K. E. Read, The High Valley *(New York: Charles Scribner and Sons, 1965), p. ix.*

Doing Cultural Anthropology

Anthropologists, like professionals in every other academic discipline, have developed a particular way of looking at the world, especially that part of the world that is the subject of their study — the world of humankind. This anthropological perspective has grown out of the method of anthropology called fieldwork. **Fieldwork** is the firsthand, systematic exploration of the variety of human cultures by anthropologists. Anthropology uses the naturally existing diversity of human cultures as a substitute for the controlled experimental situation of the laboratory, which for both technical and ethical reasons is of little use in gathering anthropological data and testing anthropological theories. Anthropologists can hardly go out and start a war somewhere to see the effect of warfare on family life. Nor can they control in a laboratory all the factors involved in examining the impact of multinational corporations on a horticultural village in the Amazon rain forest.

In order to get information and test hypotheses, anthropologists go out into the field to observe their subjects in a natural setting and to participate in their lives on an ongoing, daily basis. From the results of this method, anthropologists write up an account of the lives of people in a particular society. This written account is called an **ethnography**. Ethnographic data from many societies are the evidence around which anthropological theories are built and tested. **Ethnology** refers to the comparative statements about cultural and social processes that are based on cross-cultural ethnographic data.

In order to include the widest possible range of cultural variation, the earliest ethnographers concentrated their studies on the small-scale, technologically simpler societies that had developed for thousands of years outside the orbit of European culture. Only by looking at these culturally different societies could we learn about the very diverse ways of being human. Also, because these societies were structurally less complex than those of the industrialized world, it was easier to understand in them the interrelationships of the different aspects of culture and the dynamics of cultural change.

Twentieth-century anthropologists hoped that detailed ethnographies would illuminate the richness and human satisfactions in a wide range of cultures and increase respect among Europeans and North Americans for peoples whose lives were very different from their own. After World War I, and even more so after World War II, anthropologists turned their attention to peasant and urban societies, which were enmeshed in more complex regional and national systems. This required some changes in the way fieldwork and ethnography were practiced.

The earliest observers of the societies later studied by anthropologists were typically "amateurs" — travelers, explorers, missionaries, and colonial officers who had recorded their experiences in remote corners of the world. In the nineteenth and early twentieth centuries, much of anthropological theory was developed by "armchair anthropologists," who had not done fieldwork and who based their theories on the often ethnocentric and unsystematic writings of the amateurs. Only after devastation, demoralization, and disenchantment with European "civilization" resulted from World War I did academically trained ethnographers begin doing intensive fieldwork in distant places and among peoples whose cultures were not only different from, but often in striking contrast to, Western culture (Tedlock 1991). This new emphasis on ethnography is linked particularly with the names of Bronislaw Malinowski in Europe and Franz Boas in the United States.

If Edward Tylor (see Chapter 3) has sometimes been referred to as the "father of anthropology," then Bronislaw Malinowski might be called the "father of ethnography." Malinowski, whose fieldwork was carried out in the Trobriand Islands, saw the goal of the ethnographer as "grasp[ing] the native's point of view, his relation to life, to realize *his* vision of *his* world" ([1922]1961:25). Only an anthropologist who could learn to think, feel, and behave as a member of another culture could enter into another cultural experience. And this could only be done through fieldwork, living among the people, observing their behavior first-hand, and participating in their lives. With the publication of Malinowski's unmatched ethnographies of the Trobriand Islands, fieldwork became the dominant way of "doing anthropology."

Franz Boas, the primary influence in anthropology in the United States in the first half of the twentieth century, also turned away from armchair anthropology and urged anthropologists to do more fieldwork before these small non-Western cultures disappeared. Boas himself produced an enormous amount of ethnographic data on native American cultures, particularly those of the Pacific Northwest. For Boas, the status of anthropology as a science would depend on the most complete and objective gathering of ethnographic data on specific cultural systems. He insisted that grasping the whole of a culture could be achieved only through fieldwork. Boas and Malinowski together set the high standards for fieldwork, the unique methodology of cultural anthropology.

The major criterion of good ethnography that grew out of the work of Malinowski and Boas was that it grasp the native point of view,

objectively and without bias. This, of course, was related to the goals of positivist, empirical science, which was based on the confidence that trained investigators could, through observation of behavior, comprehend the reality of a phenomenon — in the case of anthropology, of culture. An important contribution of the new approaches of interpretivist and feminist anthropology has been to raise questions about whether it is possible to have a totally unbiased view of another cultural reality.

For example, an important question now raised about earlier ethnography is the degree to which gender bias has shaped our view of different cultures and of the culture concept itself. Much fieldwork was — and continues to be — done by men who have limited, or even no, personal access to women's lives. This is particularly true in cultures where men and women lead very separate lives, fraught with hostility, as in New Guinea (Hammar 1989), or in Muslim cultures where notions of honor and shame severely restrict the interactions of men and women who are not related (Abu-Lughod 1987). This restricted interaction had not been seen as problematical; descriptions of cultures based on male activities were accepted as accurate, on the assumption that the most important cultural activities were dominated by men. A good example is the work of Malinowski himself. His descriptions of exchange among the Trobriand Islanders almost completely excluded women's gift exchanges, an omission rectified more than fifty years later by a woman anthropologist whose restudy of the Trobriand Islands focuses on exchanges among women (Weiner 1976).

Gender bias had its effect not only on the accuracy of ethnographies, but also on the development of theories about culture. When the culture of a small society is based on information from just one segment of the community — i.e., men — the culture appears to be much more homogeneous than it really is. When such inaccurate descriptions accumulate, anthropologists can draw the conclusion that cultural homogeneity and integration are characteristic of such societies. This conclusion may not only be theoretically misleading, but it also helps

Margaret Mead, shown here on one of her early field trips to the South Pacific, was a leading ethnographer and one of the first to focus her studies on women's lives in different cultures. (Institute for Intercultural Studies)

perpetuate oppression of women in those communities by ignoring their perspective on their own culture (Keesing 1987), which may be quite different from that of the men.

The recognition of the gender bias of male-centered ethnographies has led to a new concern with the lives, thoughts, and activities of women. Anthropologists are now investigating the ways in which female personality is shaped, the meanings that a culture has for its female as well as its male participants, and the possibilities of autonomy and power, control and abuse, in the domestic and public spheres of life. By incorporating data on women's lives, feminist anthropology has led to new concerns in ethnography with how cultural beliefs and practices result in unequal allocation of resources and unequal opportunities for different groups in a society. In addition, by demonstrating, in detail, how an anthropologist's gender becomes a lens through which another culture is filtered — that who we are shapes what we know, or think we know — feminist anthropology has contributed in very significant ways to the current reexamination of both ethnography and anthropological theory.

Anthropological Fieldwork: Participant Observation

Fieldwork involves participating in and observing the lives of people in the group the anthropologist wishes to study. The writing up of the field data is aimed at presenting as authentic and coherent a picture of the cultural system as possible. The holistic perspective of anthropology developed through doing fieldwork. It is only by living with people and engaging in their activities over a long period of time that we can see culture as a system of interrelated patterns. Good ethnography is based both on the fieldworker's ability to see things from the other person's point of view and on the ability to see

In the letter below, Lisa, a graduate student doing fieldwork for her doctoral dissertation, writes to her dissertation advisor about some of her experiences. The letter expresses many of the personal and professional issues that arise in the field. Some of Lisa's experiences reflect changes in the discipline: As anthropologists move from the study of homogeneous, small societies as a whole, to the study of particular theoretical problems in heterogeneous large, complex societies, their techniques of research and perspectives change. Other aspects of Lisa's field experience are more personal; bringing the researcher's children into the field, for example, offers special opportunities but also poses some problems.

Dear Professor Ryan,

I'm not sure what I'm doing here but here I am. Sorry for the delay in writing but my typewriter just arrived — it took several weeks to get through customs. We left Chicago on July 18th and stopped in Mexico City for a few days. While going through customs — a fieldwork experience in itself — the children wandered off. Despite the indifference of the airport authorities during my frantic one-hour search for them, I found them safe and sound. After this hectic beginning, I only stayed long enough in Mexico to take a brief anthropological excursion to Tepoztlán, unrecognizable from Redfield's account.

After another brief halt in L___ (the capital) we flew to S___, the site of my fieldwork and a very small city in a valley about 8,000 feet above sea level surrounded by an arid countryside. The view in all directions of the surrounding mountains is quite lovely. The city is totally colonial with none of the usual pockets of modernity that pervade other Latin American cities. There is no daily newspaper, no television of course, and no telephone communication outside of the city. Vehicles are either pickup trucks or jeeps. Roads outside of the city are unpaved, rocky, narrow passages along the mountains — quite a hair-raising adventure, but I am getting used to it.

My work has not been progressing well. S___ has all the disadvantages of doing urban research combined with many of the inconveniences of rural living, i.e., no refrigerator or hot water, no bottled milk for the children. Upon arriving, we went directly to the agricultural organization that will be a main institutional unit of my study. The children and I were warmly received and served tea. While the staff was very helpful with some of the practical problems of settling in, they viewed me as someone checking up on them and feel they must present themselves in a positive light allowing me an exposure only to their official side. In addition, they perceive me as a student of the "natives" and do not consider themselves subjects of my investigation. It will take a while before I can participate in their meetings and can gain a sense of their problems and decision-making processes. Hanging around their headquarters, however, is beginning to yield data about the internal division of labor in the organization and their relations with the campesinos. But

I still feel a little like a sore thumb as they are very busy working and I don't appear to be working at all.

Eventually I will be visiting all of the rural cooperative affiliates and selecting a few for in-depth case study. I hadn't realistically anticipated how very rustic living conditions are in the countryside and have been introducing the children to it in small doses. I also hadn't fully appreciated how helpful it would be to speak Quechua in addition to Spanish. I am gradually beginning to remedy this with a more systematic language-learning campaign. However, I am concerned about neglecting my other work if I start to devote large chunks of my time to language study. I guess it is unavoidable and you will tell me it is all in the tradition of anthropology.

I was able to attend a conference, where the kids and I were asked to sit on the podium. After the formalities some of the campesinos performed on native instruments, sang and recited poetry, and asked me to dance with them. Everyone was enthralled with my dancing which, since I had never seen this kind of dancing, involved an on-the-spot adaptation of Latin American steps and some faking. I believe that along with graduate training, courses in dancing and holding liquor should be required for anthropologists. They are, at least in this cultural context, the best forms of gaining acceptance.

I haven't been able to read in the evenings because, lacking toys and television, the kids are very demanding of my attention. The easiest thing to concentrate on is Hortense Powdermaker's *Stranger and Friend*. I had never read it before and think it should be given to graduate students to read in the field. It is encouraging to read that she felt discouraged in the beginning, as I do, but also inspiring to read how systematic and compulsive she was in her first field experience.

I envy the simplicity of the small, intimate face-to-face community in which she first worked and realize a critical difference between her objectives and those of our generation. She was doing a holistic study of a culture and everything was data. With my problem orientation, I must screen out a good deal. My interviews so far have been informal, and I have given up the idea of using the tape recorder. I accidentally exposed my first roll of pictures. Even after six weeks I feel I have not yet started to do anthropology. In the context of real life, my original research design will have to be modified. The few studies I have read of this area seem to be wrong or don't apply to my problem.

Again, please forgive the delay in writing. We have been well except for the occasional flea invasions, which leave me with miserable welts. There was also a four-week delay getting my grant money transferred from my New York bank, causing me great concern about our subsistence — but it really helped me appreciate the cloud of insecurity under which campesinos live!

Well, my best regards to everyone at home.

Fondly,
Lisa

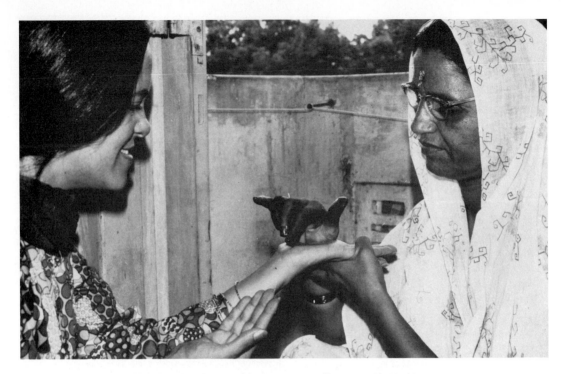

The author has her hands painted with vegetable dye as part of her participation in Karva Chowth, a ritual occasion in North India on which women observe a fast for their husbands' welfare. (Ravinder Nanda)

patterns, relationships, and meanings that may not be consciously understood by a person in that culture.

Because an anthropologist is a human being studying other human beings, it is difficult — some say impossible — to make a completely objective study of another culture. An anthropologist's own culture, personality, sex, age, and theoretical approach can all be sources of ethnographic bias.

Both participation and observation are necessary in good fieldwork. The anthropologist observes, listens, asks questions, and attempts to find a way through which she or he can participate in the life of the society over an extended period of time.

Anthropology, like every other scientific discipline, must be concerned with the accuracy of its data. Anthropology is unique among the sciences in that a human being is the major research instrument, and other human beings are supplying most of the data. At least in the initial stages of research — and, most frequently, throughout the fieldwork — anthropologists have to rely to a great extent on informants as well as observation for their data. Informants are people who have a deep knowledge of their own culture and are willing and able to pass this knowledge on to the anthropologist. All anthropologists have a few key informants with whom they work in the field. These informants are not only essential for explaining cultural patterns but are also helpful in introducing the anthropologist to the community and helping them establish a wide network of social relationships. It is the establishment of trust and cooperation in these relationships that is the basis for sound fieldwork.

The difficulty of establishing such relationships is humorously described by Napoleon Chagnon, who worked among the Yanomamo, the "fierce" people who live in the Amazon

Basin region in northern Brazil and southern Venezuela. Because of the importance of kinship in tribal societies, Chagnon (1983) made attempts early in his fieldwork to collect genealogies. What he did not know at that point was that the Yanomamo had very strong taboos against mentioning the names of people who had died and that they did not like to mention the personal names of living people out of courtesy, respect, and fear. So the Yanomamo made up false names for the living and dead members of their communities and passed these on to Chagnon as accurate data. The names, which were collected in public, were often graphically vulgar and caused great hilarity among the audience during the genealogy collection. It was only after months of painstaking, humiliating effort that Chagnon accidentally found out that he had been "taken for a ride" and had to start again from scratch. As his fieldwork progressed, however, he was very successful in finding some trustworthy informants and was eventually able to build up one of the most detailed ethnographies available in anthropology.

In the early stages of fieldwork, the anthropologist tends just to observe or to perform some seemingly neutral task such as collecting genealogies or taking a census. Within a short time, however, he or she will begin to participate in cultural activities as well. Participation is partly necessary because it is the best way to understand the difference between what people say they do, feel, or think and what kinds of action they take. It is not that people always deliberately lie; but often, when they are asked about some aspect of their culture, they give the cultural ideal, not what actually happens. This is especially true when the outsider has higher social status than the informant. For psychological or pragmatic reasons, the informant wishes to look good in the anthropologist's eyes.

Participation also forces the researcher to think about how to behave in a culturally approved manner and thus sharpens insight into right ways of behavior. Richard Lee (1974), for example, had this experience while working among the !Kung of Africa. The !Kung are an egalitarian society. Their ecological adaptation requires a high degree of sharing and a minimum of individualism and competition. In order to thank them for the cooperation they had given him in the field, Lee presented the group with a large ox at Christmas. In telling the !Kung about the gift, Lee stressed the large size of the animal and the great amount of meat it would provide. But the !Kung did not thank him for it; they even insulted him by calling the ox skinny and unfit to eat. Only through continued fieldwork and growing friendship was he able to find out what he had done wrong. His gift had been very welcome, but his manner of presentation — boasting and expecting gratitude — had not. !Kung values, in contrast to ours, stress generosity that does not call attention to itself.

The anthropologist's role as a stranger who comes to live in another society to learn its ways of life is not always well understood. One anthropologist from the United States, Roy Wagner, caused great confusion among members of the Diribi society in New Guinea. The Diribi could not figure out what kind of "work" he was doing. He was "not government, not mission, and not doctor." Finally, they classified him as a *storimasta*, someone interested in other people's ways of life, or "stories." It was hard for them to believe, however, that anyone would pay him for such an activity, as it did not fit any concept of work as they knew it (Wagner 1975).

Fieldwork and Ethnography: Changing Directions

Beginning in the 1970s, what had been a trickle of interest in raising explicit questions about the methodology of participant observation and the writing of ethnography turned into a stream and, by the 1990s, into a flood. From an earlier emphasis on participant observation, the new emphasis is on the process of fieldwork itself, what Barbara Tedlock (1991:69) calls the "observation of participation." Contemporary anthropologists are, in a more focused and

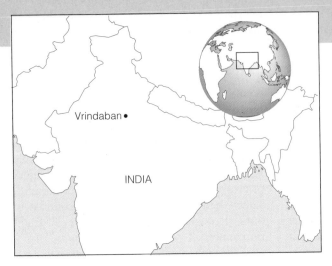

Charles Brooks is an American anthropologist who has carried out field research on the impact of Western Hare Krishnas in India. The Western Hare Krishna followers, with their orange robes and shaved heads, their public processions and festivals featuring drums and cymbals, and their vegetarian food, are by now well known in the United States. Brooks's fieldwork, like that of many other anthropologists today, took place not in a relatively isolated, small-scale society, but rather in a town in the very complex society of India. The following description of his fieldwork shows what anthropologists actually do as they go about understanding cultures. Although each fieldwork project is different, there are certain common steps: choosing the problem, choosing the site, locating informants, gathering and recording the data, and analyzing and writing up the results.

Choosing the Problem

Like much contemporary fieldwork, Brooks's approach to the culture he was studying was holistic, yet focused on a number of specific questions. Through his graduate study, Brooks had become interested in religion and change in India. This interest formed the background of his research. Brooks was also aware of the most visible representation of Indian religion in the United States, ISKCON, or the International Society for Krishna Consciousness. The Hare Krishna movement began in India as a way of spreading the worship of the Hindu god Krishna. In this religion, devoted worship to Krishna is the main path to religious or spiritual enlightenment. Krishna worship was brought to the United States in the 1960s by an Indian monk, Swami Bhaktivedanta, who aimed to save Westerners from what he saw as their materialism and atheism. His movement was very successful here and in Europe, attracting many converts from the counterculture of the 1960s. As part of their commitment to their new religion, many of these people went to India to help spread Krishna consciousness in the land where it originated.

Brooks was fascinated by this process and his research was guided by an overarching question: "How did a Western cultural version of Hare Krishna fit itself into the religious culture of India?" In order to answer this larger question, Brooks broke it down into smaller questions, which would actually guide his research. These questions included "What were the specific types of situations where foreign and Indian Krishna followers interacted?" "What were the similarities and differences in the ways in which foreigners and Indian devotees understood the symbols, rituals, meanings, and goals of Krishna worship?" "How did Indians react to foreigners who claimed they were Hindus — and Hindu priests at that?" "What opinions did Indians have about Westerners who were in India to spread the word about a religion that was originally Indian?" "Since Hindus believe that foreigners cannot become Hindus, as ISKCON members claim they have become, how was this paradox resolved?" "How did ISKCON's presence in India affect both Hindu religious culture and the Indian and Western Krishna followers who encountered each other?" In sum, Brooks was interested in the subjective experience of individuals from two different cultures who had come together through participation in the same religion.

Picking the Research Site

Sometimes anthropologists have a particular site in mind when they begin their fieldwork, but in many cases they have only a general idea about a location that might suit their research interests. While the ultimate choice involves some practical matters, such as the availability of housing, health care, or transportation, the major consideration is whether the site will allow the researchers to answer the questions they are interested in. Since Brooks wanted to study social interaction between foreign and Indian devotees to Krishna, his main criterion was to find a location where such interaction took place.

Anthropologists generally use the first month or so of their fieldwork to look over fieldsite possibilities. Brooks's initial choice for his research was the sacred pilgrimage town of Vrindaban, where Krishna is said to have been born and lived for part of his life. This town has many temples and religious sites dedicated to Krishna worship, and Brooks knew that ISKCON had also set up a temple there. He made an initial visit to discover whether significant social interaction took place among the Indian and foreign pilgrims and residents in Vrindaban and whether any Indians worshipped at ISKCON's temple. When he saw that such interactions did occur, and that the ISKCON temple attracted many Indian pilgrims, Brooks decided this would be an appropriate site for his fieldwork.

He chose as his residence a place where many foreign and Indian people stay while they are on pilgrimage at Vrindaban. As a "neutral" site, it would not associate Brooks with any particular religious faction, which would allow

(continued)

Children of the foreign members of the ISKCON march in a procession in Vrindaban, the site of Charles Brooks's field study. (Courtesy of Charles Brooks)

him greater access to a variety of social situations than if he had stayed at a place identified with a particular religious sect or temple. In addition, this residence was centrally located in the town and situated near a principal pilgrimage destination where Brooks could observe from his rooftop rooms the constant movement of pilgrims and the many cultural performances that were held in the adjacent public courtyard. Having found a suitable place to stay, Brooks turned his attention to beginning the research project.

Collecting and Recording Data

In anthropology, as in every science, method is connected to theory. The way we collect our data is related to the questions we hope our research will answer. Participant observation is the major method of anthropology, though this is usually augmented by one or more other methods such as census taking, structured interviews, archival research, surveys, mapmaking, taking genealogies, and photography.

Charles Brooks with his "identity kit," which is made up of clothing similar to that worn by most Indian pilgrims and residents of Vrindaban, though distinguished by the Western sunglasses. (Courtesy of Charles Brooks)

Because Charles Brooks's main interest was in the way people create meanings for their behavior through social interaction, participation observation was his major method of collecting data. Only in this way did Brooks feel he could develop the "intimate familiarity and sensitivity to the social world" he wished to understand (Brooks 1989:235). In order to do this, he also had to take account of his own role as anthropologist in these interactions.

As the initial step of participation is to find a role through which one interacts with others, Brooks defined his role as someone "looking for personal development," and also as a "research scholar" who had been certified by the Indian government to study Vrindaban's culture and history. Both these roles were familiar and valid to both pilgrims and town residents. In order to more effectively participate in the religious culture of the town, Brooks developed what he calls an "identity kit," Indian clothing and accessories that conveyed the impression of a religious devotee but were not specifically identified with any particular religious sect.

(continued)

Charles Brooks's key informant, Sripad Baba. Baba, as a religious figure, was both a source of information and a connection to other sources of information in Brooks's study. Key informants for anthropologists are usually people who are particularly knowledgeable about their own culture, articulate, and willing to spend extra amounts of time with the anthropologist. The anthropologist and informants develop a particular rapport. Sometimes, when Brooks would pose his Western rational "way of knowing" against Sripad Baba's intuitive sources of knowledge, Baba would admonish Brooks by saying, "Krishna works in mysterious ways. Baba works for Krishna, so his ways are also mysterious. Write that in your notebook!" (Courtesy of Charles Brooks)

Because of the public nature of many of the religious interactions Brooks wished to understand, gaining entry to these situations and observing behavior was not difficult. And because he had learned Hindi, the main language used for social interaction in this part of India, he rarely needed the assistance of an interpreter. But recording his observations presented more of a problem. Research situations differ: Many anthropologists use tape recorders or take notes at the time of observation, but in other cases this hinders interaction. On one occasion early in his research, when Brooks was recording an interview in a small notebook, one of his key informants, a guru, or religious leader, told him, "When you are ready to learn, come back without your notebook." From that point he stopped taking notes on the spot and waited until an encounter was over before writing it up. To help him remember and keep track of the many details of an interaction and record them in a consistent way, he developed a schematic flowchart into which he could fit his daily observations. A different flowchart was kept for each separate interaction, and each chart incorporated information on the actors, the content of their interaction, the symbols used, the goal of the interaction, and its conclusion. In addition, he also recorded his experiences in a more impressionistic way in a journal.

Second to participation observation in its importance for collecting data, Brooks also used unstructured, open-ended interviews, many of them with a group of informants rather than an individual. The goal of these interviews was to explore a particular topic in depth, for example, the meaning of a particular symbolic object used in religious practice. While a group interview is helpful in comparing the ways different individuals interpret a symbolic object or act, Brooks also conducted individual interviews, where people could speak about more private matters. This was the format he used for collecting life histories. These interviews were taped and more structured, that is, organized around preset questions, but Brooks also allowed the conversations to develop on their own if an informant showed a particular interest in or knowledge of a subject. Twenty-two of these life histories were collected, and they were particularly valuable in giving information about the background from which informants developed their interpretations of religious phenomena.

Brooks also used random verbal surveys to discover the castes and backgrounds of the pilgrims and town residents, and to learn their opinions and attitudes toward the foreign devotees in Vrindaban. He initially tried to use a written questionnaire to gather this kind of information but dropped that as counterproductive. Not only were written questionnaires foreign to Vrindaban culture, and thus not very effective, but, although Brooks assured informants of their confidentiality, many people were nervous at the idea of writing down private information. In addition, the use of such formal documents might be interpreted to confirm the belief of many Indians that all Americans in India are working for the CIA.

Hardly any anthropologist could be found today who does not take a camera to the field. Brooks used photographs in several specific ways related to his research project: documenting the physical aspects of Vrindaban's religious complex — the temples and pilgrimage sites; documenting the different people who visited and lived in Vrindaban and their "identity kits" as a way of preserving a record of cultural diversity; and photographing the sites and participants of social interactions as an aid to remembering and interpreting them.

Analyzing and Interpreting the Data

The conclusion Brooks drew from his study was that there is significant interaction between Indians and foreigners in Vrindaban. The ISKCON temple is accepted as a legitimate place of worship for Indian devotees of Krishna. The

(*continued*)

interaction of individuals from different cultures as they encounter one another in the religious complex of Krishna worship has led to changes in the meanings of the symbols involved in this worship. As the study uncovered some ways that outsiders — the foreigners — could be accepted in a Hindu religious and social universe, it opened up new perceptions of social organization in India, indicating that in religious settings, caste identity, which is normally essential in social interaction, could be subordinated to evaluations of the sincerity of a person's devotion.

A broader, cross-cultural application of Brooks's study is that it reveals the processes by which social reality is transformed into a meaningful universe. As people from different parts of the world come into contact with each other and participate in common social systems, they are forced to incorporate each other into their previous cultural concepts. This process applies to cultural diversity in our own society, as well as in the Indian town of Vrindaban. In his study of one small cultural space, Brooks illuminates larger dimensions of human behavior, which is the aim of all good ethnography.

From Charles Brooks, The Hare Krishnas in India *(Princeton, N.J.: Princeton University Press, 1989).*

explicit way, raising questions about subjectivity and objectivity in fieldwork, bias in the interpretation of field data, the accuracy of traditional ethnography as a representation of culture, the relationship of ethnography to anthropological theory, and the usefulness of definitions of culture itself. These concerns, sometimes grouped under the label of "interpretive anthropology," have been differently viewed, as a challenge, a threat, a crisis, or a fad. While many anthropologists would agree that the new focus on the observation of participation can be carried to an extreme so that we learn too little of a culture, and too much about the anthropologist, most anthropologists would also agree that raising explicit questions about field-

work as a methodology, and incorporating information about the fieldwork process into ethnographies, is a challenge anthropology can meet and grow from.

This emerging focus on fieldwork leads to a more intense consideration of the somewhat contradictory stances of objectivity and subjectivity inherent in participant observation. The anthropological fieldworker must "think like a native" to understand the culture from the inside, yet also think like a scientist in order to be objective. These two ways of viewing the world would seem to be incompatible or, at the very least, a source of stress. Traditionally, in anthropology the dominant requirement, at least in writing ethnography if not in the fieldwork itself, was to write like a scientist. This often led to omitting the lifeblood in a culture, describing norms and structures and patterns but leaving out any mention of specific events and individuals, including the ethnographer. Until the 1970s, few explicit accounts of the fieldwork process were included in ethnographies, and few ethnographies considered, in any central way, how interactions between ethnographer and informants affected the gathering, interpretation, and writing up of data.

This began to change in the 1960s with the publication of some first-person, experiential accounts of fieldwork (Berreman 1962), and by the 1970s, more ethnographies began to appear in which the observation of participation had as central a place as more standard cultural descriptions; indeed, such concerns have moved from the margins of anthropology to the center (though a center that continues to be shared by other interests and issues). These observations about participation are called **reflexivity**, as they lead anthropologists to reflect more consciously on how their own personalities or cultures shape their view of a culture, and how they personally interact with "the other" to produce cultural data. Thus, there is a new focus on the *interaction* between the self and the other — the ethnographer and her or his informants — and the kinds of communication they engage in, as part of, even central to, both the fieldwork experience and the written ethnography. Fieldwork and ethnography, from this perspective, become a dialogue, a coproduction between the self and the other, the ethnographer and the native informant.

Reflective anthropology means that anthropologists cannot ignore their own feelings as they participate in fieldwork, but rather must analyze them. Reflexivity ultimately incorporates the idea that the observer is not only the instrument of observation but also the subject of observation. Reflexive anthropology means finding ways to combine observations of others with observations of the self. The shape these reflections will take are difficult to know beforehand: They emerge as part of the interac-

Ethnography involves interaction, collaboration, and dialogue between the anthropologist and informants. (Raymond Kennedy)

tion with others that is central to fieldwork, and can be the source of those special insights that make fieldwork such an exciting, though risky, enterprise.

Studying One's Own Society

When anthropologists are studying a culture different from their own, their main task is to perceive things from the other people's point of view. Although training in the anthropological perspective is designed to help overcome cultural bias, even well-trained anthropologists slip into projecting their own culturally determined feelings and perceptions on other peoples. In studying their own culture, anthropologists must try to maintain the social distance of the outsider, because it is all too easy to take for granted what one knows. Remaining objective may be easier when studying cannibalism, kinship structure, or warfare in other cultures than when being confronted with child neglect, corporate structure, or armed conflict in one's own society.

Both the problems and the rewards of working as an anthropologist in one's own culture are beautifully illustrated in the work of Barbara Myerhoff, an American anthropologist who worked among elderly Jewish people in an urban ghetto in California (1978). Myerhoff had previously done research on the religion of the Huichol, who live in the mountains of northern Mexico. Because of her interest in aging and her previous work in Mexico, she decided to do a study of older Mexican people in southern California. But as she approached these elderly Chicanos, they kept asking her why she wanted to work with them, and they suggested that she "study her own people." This is something Myerhoff had not thought of doing, and she began to realize that such a project would have both difficulties and benefits. As she points out, working in "other cultures" — whether it involves a male trying to understand females, an American trying to understand Europeans, or a black trying to understand whites — is "an act of imagination, a means for discovering what one is not and will never be." For, as Myerhoff says about her own experiences among the Huichol, however much she learned from them, it was limited by the fact that she would never be a Huichol. But she knew that she would be a "little old Jewish lady someday" and that it would be essential for her, in a very personal way, to understand what that condition is like.

In North American culture, the young are increasingly cut off from the elderly. Partly because of the North American emphasis on youth and partly because we don't want to recognize the inevitability of decline and dependence that we associate with old age in North America, we shut out the elderly. So the elderly become "invisible" to us, and because we don't know what they are like, we fear old age even more. Our fear then leads us to shun the elderly, and the cycle becomes intensified. In working

with these elderly Jewish people, who had struggled to overcome and had triumphed in many small ways over the disabilities of being old and poor in North America, Myerhoff considers herself to have had a valuable and rare experience — that of being able to rehearse and contemplate her own future.

In addition to the problems of identification posed by her choice of a research topic, the personal involvement that came from being of the same community as the "natives" also presented both special difficulties and special rewards. The question of guilt frequently raised its head over a number of issues. One of them was the feeling Myerhoff expresses about whether she should just be studying old people or should be helping them. Many of these old people, who began to depend on her as a friend and perhaps to see in her their own children, sometimes tried to make her feel guilty if she missed some time with them at the senior citizens center. They were not intending to hurt her but were expressing one of their few powers — their ability to make others feel guilty. Also, her very lack of knowledge about *yiddishkeit*, the traditional Jewish culture of the *shtetl*, or village, in Europe from which her informants came, was a painful reminder to them that they had not passed this culture on to younger American Jews. The ethnography that Myerhoff produced of older Jewish people is not only a valuable look at a part of American life that has been shut out of the public eye but also a revealing account of the personal and professional pains and pleasures of doing ethnography among one's own people.

Because of the disappearance of "exotic" cultures and because of political sensitivities, it will be more and more difficult for Western anthropologists to limit themselves to studying "others." The process Barbara Myerhoff went through, first studying the Huichol and then her own people, is justifiable not only out of practical necessity, however. In some sense, it is perhaps the ideal anthropological journey, or what M. N. Srinivas, a distinguished anthropologist from India, calls being "thrice-born."

Soo Choi (center) is an anthropologist from Korea who studied in the United States and went back to do fieldwork in a Korean peasant village. He lived in the house of these two tenant farmers, who raised pigs. Choi, as an anthropologist working in his own culture, had the advantage of knowing the basic cultural patterns and the language. But his urban upbringing posed some difficulties in adapting to rural life; for example, the lack of water for washing was a source of particular discomfort in the sticky, sultry Korean summers. (Courtesy of Soo Choi)

First, we are born into our original, particular culture. Then, our second "birth" is to move away from this familiar place to a far place to do our fieldwork. In this experience, we are eventually able to understand the rules and meanings of other cultures, and the "exotic" becomes familiar. In our third "birth," we again turn toward our native land and find that the familiar has become exotic. We see it with new eyes. In spite of our deep emotional attachment to its ways, we are able to see it also with scientific objectivity. Anthropology originated with this ideal — that of eventually examining our own culture in the same objective way that we can come to understand others, and increasing numbers of anthropologists are studying their own societies. In Myerhoff's book, *Number Our Days* (1978), we have an example of what studying one's own people involves as both a personal and a professional quest for meaning.

In other cultures, both similar and different problems come up for the indigenous anthropologist. Recent accounts of fieldwork by Arab women in their own cultures (Altorki and Fawzi El-Solh 1988) suggest that the insider/outsider position of the ethnographer poses special difficulties in these cultures because of the limitations in such societies on women's activities, and a cultural emphasis on respectability and honor. Lila Abu-Lughod started out her fieldwork among the Bedouin accompanied by her father, an event that first irritated and embarrassed her. But she later concluded that her father's insistence was culturally correct, as a "young, unmarried woman traveling alone on uncertain business" would be suspect and "have a hard time persuading people of her respectability." This was all the more true because Abu-Lughod had lived in the West and was subject to the negative stereotypes the Arabs have of the morals of Western women.

While Abu-Lughod had confidence she could overcome this suspicion by her own culturally sensitive behavior, she did not realize until she reflected on her fieldwork that a young woman alone would be seen to have been abandoned or alienated from her family. This would cast doubts on her respectability (1987:9–24), hinder her fieldwork, or even make it impossible among the conservative Egyptian Bedouin whom she was studying.

Some Dilemmas in Fieldwork

As I suggested in Chapter 1, the changing political consciousness of many peoples has posed some new challenges for anthropology. While many of the ethical, practical, and emotional dilemmas that confront contemporary ethnographers also existed earlier (see, for example, Malinowski's personal diary [1967] of his fieldwork in the Trobriand Islands, published after his death), today there is much more awareness on the part of anthropologists and others about the importance of confronting these dilemmas and, indeed, discussing them as part of the fieldwork experience.

One role increasingly questioned since the 1960s is that of the legitimacy of the anthropologist as observer who cannot get involved in a partisan way with the activities of the people being studied. The political activism of the 1960s challenged anthropologists to play new roles. An early example of this was the work of Charles and Betty Lou Valentine (1970), anthropologists doing fieldwork in an African-American urban community. Along with the usual anthropological interest in accurately describing a human community, the Valentines more specifically wanted to correct the prevalent stereotyped impression of cultural uniformity about poor, black communities in the United States. In addition, they had a commitment to advancing the interests of the minority poor in our country and hoped that what they learned and wrote about could be used as the basis for more humane public policies. In order to achieve these goals, they participated with the community in some of their organized protests aimed at making government bureaucracies more responsive to community needs. The Valentines correctly anticipated that, in the 1960s context of demands for radical change, more than verbal expressions of sympathy with community activists would be needed to establish rapport and trust. Although the Valentines did not take leadership roles in community actions, they did go to mass demonstrations and participate in other ways with the community, even when this exposed them to police sanctions and harassment by bureaucrats. They were also confronted with the problem of taking sides *within* the community, because the community itself was not always united about which actions to engage in.

One aim of the Valentines in undertaking their fieldwork was to present an ethnography that would be free from the distortions that have marred descriptions of such communities written by outsiders. As part of this aim, the Valentines also wrote about community events from an insider's perspective that they compared point for point with the way such events were covered in the media. The role of advocate in a relatively powerless community vis-à-vis the larger culture not only posed practical problems but also raised challenging questions about the value-free stance of social science in general and anthropology in particular. The Valentines' conclusion was that, when anthropologists do fieldwork in communities whose members feel that they are being treated unjustly by the larger society, the anthropologists must participate to some extent in redressing these injustices.

Getting involved as the Valentines did may solve some dilemmas of the fieldworker, but it can create others, particularly in situations of political conflict and potential danger. Jeffrey Sluka is an anthropologist who studied the popular support for the Irish Republican Army (IRA) and the Irish National Liberation Army (INLA) in a Catholic-nationalist ghetto in Belfast, the scene of a violent and longstanding conflict between Irish nationalists and the British government (1990). In such ongoing, tense conflict situations, in which emotions run high, "no neutrals are allowed," and in any case, as Sluka points out, people will define the side they think the anthropologist is on and act accordingly. At the same time, it is not necessary, he found, to become an active partisan. One can indicate one's feelings through sympathizing with grievances and problems; "walking softly" around issues that involve illegal activities, such as the location of guns and explosives and the identification of guerillas; being honest about research interests; maintaining a heightened awareness about dangerous situations; and being flexible enough to redirect the research in the face of imminent danger. These are useful techniques for both building rapport and avoiding danger in the field.

Sluka's suggestions for minimizing danger by using "foresight, planning, skillful maneuver, and a conscious effort at impression management"; by becoming well acquainted with people in the community; by cultivating well-respected persons who will vouch for the researcher; and by avoiding contacts with the police, are also relevant for anthropologists working in the substance abuse field in the inner cities of the United States (Williams et al. 1992). Ethnographers studying the use and sale of crack cocaine, for example, are exposed to the irrational and often violent behavior of crack users, the routine violence used by drug dealers, the proliferation of guns and "random" shootings, and the possibility of being robbed or mugged. In spite of this, there has been relatively little violence in these ethnographic settings against anthropologists who follow the rules Sluka suggests.

Because ethnographic situations of these kinds involve persons acting against the law, who have every reason to hide their identities, locales, and activities, ethnographers in these special situations need to be particularly meticulous about following the rules of professional conduct and ethics, which guide all field research and ethnography.

Ethical Considerations in Fieldwork

Ethical considerations come up in every fieldwork experience. Three main ethical principles that must guide the fieldworker are: acquiring the consent of the people to be studied, protecting them from risk (an issue of particular importance in the dangerous situations described above), and respecting their privacy and dignity. The current concern with ethics in participant observation is an important, often agonizing matter, much more so than in the past, and surrounded by both professional codes and federal regulations (Murphy and Johannsen 1990). Some serious transgressions of ethical conduct, such as the participation of anthropologists in counterinsurgency work, have caused concern within the profession. Fieldwork is based above all upon trust, and as anthropologists involve themselves in a continually expanding range of research situations, including those with policy implications, ethical dilemmas will increase. In trying to address these issues, the American Anthropological Association adopted a statement of ethics in 1971, which holds that the anthropologist's paramount responsibility is to those being studied; the anthropologist must "do everything within his power to protect their physical, social and psychological welfare and to honor their dignity and privacy." This statement includes the obligation to allow informants to remain anonymous when they wish to do so and not to exploit them for personal gain. It also includes the responsibility to communicate the results of the research to the individuals and groups likely to be affected, as well as to the general public. Related to this obligation is the further one to reflect on the possible effects of one's research on the population being studied.

Thus, anthropologists are committed to taking responsibility for the policies that may be formulated by governments on the basis of heir research and for how these policies may affect various groups in the society. Their obligations to the public include a positive responsibility to speak out, both individually and collectively, in order to contribute to an "adequate definition of reality" that may become the basis of public opinion, public policy, or a resource in the politics of culture. These concerns bring us back to the challenge stated in Chapter 1, that of not only doing fieldwork in a way that appropriately involves the anthropologist working in collaboration with his or her informants, but also doing ethnography in a way that most accurately represents both the culture and the collaborative dialogues through which cultural description emerges.

Anthropology and the Uses of Ethnographic Data

The gathering of good ethnographic data through participant observation is the hallmark of cultural anthropology and the foundation on which anthropological theories are built. Although under the influence of anthropologists like Bronislaw Malinowski and Franz Boas the aim of anthropological fieldwork was the description of a *total* cultural pattern, today many anthropologists go into the field, or use the field data of others, to test a *specific* theoretical problem, rather than describe a culture in its totality. They may be interested in the relationship between the way people make a living and personality, or the relationship of urbanization to kinship organization, or the association between family type and sexual practices.

An important example of an early field study that had a particular theoretical problem in mind was that of Margaret Mead in Samoa. In the 1920s in the United States, psychologists saw the stress experienced by adolescents as a universal and "natural" condition of growing up. Mead believed that the rebellion and emotional distress experienced by American adolescents were related to the difficulties of making the transition from childhood to adulthood in our society. She chose to study life in Samoa,

where the transition from childhood to adulthood was known to be much easier. Mead found that the adolescent turmoil we know in the United States did not exist among this group of people. Her book *Coming of Age in Samoa* (1971; originally published 1928) is a classic example of the use of ethnographic study for testing a particular anthropological theory— in this case, one involving the relation of specific emotional disturbances to specific cultural patterns.

Fifty-five years after this work was first published and four years after her death, Mead's ethnography was challenged by sociobiologist Derek Freeman in a book entitled *Margaret Mead: The Making and Unmaking of an Anthropological Myth* (1983). Freeman's attack on Mead takes two forms. He first claims that she misinterpreted Samoan society because of her strong commitment to the theory that culture, not biology, is responsible for the ways in which human beings behave. Based on his own fieldwork over the last forty years, Freeman holds that Samoa was not the idyllic society Mead describes but rather one full of tension, aggression, and competition. Contrary to her assertion that Samoan society is one in which there is an absence of guilt and conflict over sex, Freeman, who used evidence from court cases, claims that adolescents and children are under considerable stress, that the culture has a preoccupation with virginity, and that the Samoans are prone to rape, violence, and jealousy. Freeman uses his criticisms of Mead's ethnographic work to put forth his own sociobiological view in which a large component of human behavior, particularly aggression, is seen as biologically determined. Many of Mead's former colleagues and students have defended her work, pointing out that her ethnography was done in 1925, when anthropology was still in its infancy as a science, and that she worked well within the tradition of ethnographic methodology as it was known at that time. They point out that although she may have been wrong about some of her facts and emphases, reinterpretation of ethnography is a standard practice in anthropology and is part of the growth and development of the field. Freeman's critics aptly point out that the attention given to his book in the media represents a current sympathy with politically conservative implications of his sociobiological stance (Lessinger 1983). Both Mead's and Freeman's work must be seen in the context of the "nature/nurture" controversy. It was due in great part to Mead's work that the theory that we are products of our environment and that we can reshape that environment if we are willing took hold in American scientific and popular thinking in the decades between 1930 and 1960. Beginning with the publication of Edward Wilson's *Sociobiology: The New Synthesis* (1975), the stage was set for criticism of the kind of cultural emphases that Mead's work embodies.

Another way of using ethnographic data is the **controlled cross-cultural comparison**, which requires using data from many societies to explore certain cultural relationships. An important source used by many anthropologists who wish to test explanations on a cross-cultural sample is the Human Relations Area File (HRAF). This is a collection of ethnographic books and articles on over 300 societies around the world cross-indexed for hundreds of cultural features. An example of the ways such files can be used is illustrated in the work of Peggy Sanday (1981), who wished to explore the question of whether male dominance is a universal cultural fact and, if it is not, under what conditions it arises. Sanday, using the HRAF, was able to show that male dominance is not universal. By correlating its existence with factors of ecological stress and warfare, she persuasively demonstrated that where the survival of the group rests more on male actions, such as in warfare, women accept male dominance for the sake of social and cultural survival. It should be emphasized here that because the HRAF (and other similar cross-cultural files) are only as good as the data they are based on, these statistical approaches to anthropological research highlight the need for meticulous ethnography.

Two young Samoan women, taken from a period a few decades before Margaret Mead worked there. Samoa, which was encountered by the Europeans in the eighteenth century, had already been influenced in important ways by the Europeans, especially the missionaries, by the early twentieth century. (Courtesy of Department Library Services, American Museum of Natural History)

As anthropologists increasingly work in cities or in villages, and even with tribal groups that are enmeshed in larger social structures and cultural patterns, however, it becomes more difficult and misleading to treat these units as encompassing a "total way of life." In conducting research in the contemporary world, anthropologists must place the group being studied in its larger political-economic-sociocultural context. Doing so often requires research outside the particular unit the anthropologist has chosen to study. This means anthropologists today are turning to a wider range of research techniques to supplement the still basic methodology of participant observation, including, for example, the use of questionnaires, social surveys, archival material, government documents, court records, and the like. It may mean following informants from villages to their workplaces in cities or collecting genealogies that spread over countries or even continents. Research in complex societies raises questions about how typical one's unit of study is within a larger cultural pattern, or even whether it is a culturally legitimate unit at all. Like other human groups, anthropologists themselves are adapting to a changing environment while retaining the core of their culture: that of understanding human society through an intense, day-to-day involvement with people over an extended period of time.

Summary

1. Anthropology uses the methods of the natural sciences rather than the controlled laboratory experiment. Participant observation, or fieldwork, is the main method of cultural anthropology. Ethnography is the written account of a culture based on fieldwork.

2. Anthropologists are becoming more reflexive, that is, concerned about how their own cultural, and particularly gender, biases may influence their perceptions of other cultures.

3. The most important ability in fieldwork is to see another culture from the point of view of members of that culture. Bronislaw Malinowski and Franz Boas were two twentieth-century anthropologists whose meticulous fieldwork set a standard for the profession.

4. A letter from the field shows how much fieldwork depends on being flexible and adaptable, both in one's research design and one's personality.

5. The study of a field experience in India shows the steps in doing ethnography: choosing a research problem, picking a research site, finding key informants, collecting and recording data, and analyzing and interpreting the data.

6. Doing fieldwork in the anthropologist's own culture presents different problems from doing fieldwork in another culture. But in either case the anthropologist must have both the insider's and the outsider's perspectives. An important example of an anthropologist working in her own culture is Barbara Myerhoff's study of Jewish senior citizens in California, called *Number Our Days*.

7. Some specific dilemmas facing anthropological fieldworkers involve questions of how actively one should become a partisan or advocate in the fieldwork situation, and how to do fieldwork in situations of ongoing conflict and violence.

8. Anthropological ethics require protecting the dignity, privacy, and anonymity of the people among whom one does fieldwork and not putting them at risk in any way.

9. Though the typical anthropological "product" is an ethnographic monograph, which is an in-depth description of a total culture, anthropologists also increasingly go into the field to look at a particular theoretical problem. An early example of this is Margaret Mead's study of adolescence in Samoa.

10. Some anthropologists examine theoretical problems by comparing ethnographic data from a large number of societies, using controlled cross-cultural comparison and such data sources as the Human Relations Area File.

Suggested Readings

Allen, Catherine
1989   *The Hold Life Has: Coco and Cultural Identity in an Andean Community*. Washington, D.C.: Smithsonian Institution. A sensitive and beautifully written account of anthropological fieldwork in a Latin American agricultural community.

Altorki, Soraya, and Fawzi El-Solh, Camillia, eds.

1988   *Arab Women in the Field: Studying Your Own Society.* Syracuse, N.Y.: Syracuse University Press. Six articles written by women anthropologists, each of whom is socially part Westerner and part Arab, about the personal, ethical, practical, and intellectual problems of doing fieldwork as an Arab woman in a range of Middle Eastern societies.

DeVita, Philip R., ed.

1991   *The Naked Anthropologist: Tales from Around the World.* Belmont, Calif.: Wadsworth. An anthology of original and often amusing articles written by anthropologists who have been taught some important lessons by their informants in the process of doing fieldwork.

Gwaltney, John L.

1980   *Drylongso.* New York: Random House. A black anthropologist studying black culture in the United States provides us with one of the few examples of native anthropology. This interesting and readable book utilizes the technique of folk seminars, in which the anthropologist serves as a facilitator while members of the community discuss and analyze their lives.

Narayan, Kirin

1989   *Storytellers, Saints, and Scoundrels: Folk Narrative in Hindu Religious Teaching.* Philadelphia: University of Pennsylvania Press. A delightful book whose rich portraits of the anthropologist and the swami who is her key informant become the vehicles for learning about one important kind of religious experience in India.

Powdermaker, Hortense

1966   *Stranger and Friend: The Way of an Anthropologist.* New York: Norton. An interesting, personal account of fieldwork in four different cultures, including the United States.

Stoller, Paul, and Olkes, Cheryl

1987   *In Sorcery's Shadow: A Memoir of Apprenticeship among the Songhay of Niger.* Chicago: University of Chicago Press. This extraordinary account of an ethnographic experience raises some important questions about the extent to which an anthropologist can or should become involved in the culture being studied.

The Culture Concept and Anthropological Theory

How does culture serve the needs of individuals and society?

What are the major characteristics of culture?

Can you outline the major theories of culture?

Do all people in a society share equally in its culture?

How and why do cultures change?

Humans are the learning animals par excellence. We have more to learn, take longer to do it, learn it in a more complex and yet more efficient way, and have a unique type of communication system to promote our learning. . . . The term "culture," a special one for the anthropologist, describes the specifically human type of learned behavior in which arbitrary rules and norms are so important. Thus, whether we have one or two spouses, wear black or white to a funeral, live in societies that have kings or lack chiefs entirely, is a function not of our genes but of learning. . . . Some behaviors make us feel comfortable, others do not; some behaviors may be correct in one situation and not in another . . . for example, singing rather than whistling in church; talking to domestic animals but not to wild ones. The appropriate or correct behavior varies from culture to culture.

From David Pilbeam, "The Naked Ape: An Idea We Could Live Without," Discovery *7(1972): 63–70.*

In 1873, Edward Tylor, sometimes called the "father of anthropology," introduced the concept of culture as an explanation of the differences among human societies. Tylor defined culture as "that complex whole which includes knowledge, belief, art, law, morals, custom, and any other capabilities acquired (learned) by man as a member of society" (1920:1), and he defined anthropology as the scientific study of human culture.

This chapter examines the concept of culture and the different anthropological theories that explain its nature,* its relationship to human adaptation, the similarities and differences among cultures, and the way culture changes. A **theory** is a systematic explanation of observed data that guides the scientific study of a subject. From the beginning of anthropology as a discipline, anthropologists have developed different theories about culture, each theory emphasizing a different aspect of culture in order to understand the whole. In this way anthropologists are similar to the seven blind men describing an elephant. The one who felt the tail described the elephant as a rope, the one who felt the leg described the elephant as a tree, and so on. As each anthropological theory emerges and fades, and sometimes reemerges, our understanding of culture and its relation to human behavior enlarges.

As the ethnography excerpt that opens this chapter suggests, human beings, more than any other animal, depend for their survival on learned behavior, or culture. This human capacity for culture is based on our biological

Human cultural adaptation — illustrated here in blowgun hunting — depends on our biological characteristics of bipedal posture, the ability to grasp objects with our hands, and stereoscopic vision. (Museum of the American Indian, Heye Foundation)

---

*See Appendix for a chronological ordering of anthropological theories.

heritage as primates, particularly the following characteristics: limbs adapted for grasping and exploration, with mobile digits, including an opposable thumb; an emphasis on vision over smell; development of areas of the brain associated with the mental functions of intelligence and learning; a complex social organization; a small number of young born from each pregnancy, a longer pregnancy, and a greater length of time during which an offspring is dependent on its mother; and a longer life span, which permits more time for development and learning.

The most important primate characteristic involved in human adaptation through culture is plasticity — the ability to change behavior in response to a wide range of environmental demands. This plasticity, based on the complexity of the human brain, makes learned behavior singularly important for primates. In the case of humans, since cultural adaptation can occur much more rapidly than biological adaptation, the capacity for culture gives our species an adaptational advantage in responding to changes in the environment and accounts for the wide distribution of humans over the face of the globe.

The Functions of Culture

It is obvious that culture functions to meet the needs of human beings in society. But it was Bronislaw Malinowski who developed the theory of culture called **functionalism**, which analyzed the functions of culture in great detail. Malinowski's theory holds that culture is the instrument which satisfies three types of human needs: basic needs, derived needs, and integrative needs. Basic needs for food, shelter, and physical protection are met by the technology and knowledge involved in making a living in a particular environment. Derived needs are the problems of social coordination — the organization of work, the distribution of food, defense, regulation of reproduction, and social control — which grow out of meeting basic

needs and are met by cultural institutions such as marriage and family, politics, the division of labor, and rules of exchange. Integrative needs, which include the needs for psychological security, social harmony, and purpose in life, are met by such cultural institutions as systems of knowledge, law, religion, magic, myth, and art, as we will see in later chapters. While Malinowski's insistence that every cultural element functions to meet a human need overlooked the dysfunctional, or destructive, elements in culture, the idea that culture functions to meet human needs is widely accepted as a basic premise in cultural anthropology.

In addition to meeting individual needs, cultural elements also function by contributing to social solidarity, and thus to the stability of a society over time. **Structural functionalism**, a theory associated with a generation of British social anthropologists led by A. R. Radcliffe-Brown, emphasized the ways in which social structures, the patterned role behaviors in a society, contributed to social stability. For example, "joking relations," which combine friendliness with underlying hostility, are a widespread cultural pattern among potentially hostile kin, such as in-laws. This obligatory "joking" inhibits overt conflict and thus contributes to social solidarity. The **social function** of a cultural trait is the contribution it makes to social solidarity.

Culture Is Adaptive

Adaptation is the ongoing process by which a living population survives and reproduces in its environment. The most directly adaptive aspect of a culture is the ways in which it uses tools and knowledge to transform the energy potential of an environment into food. Several anthropological theories, discussed below, focus on this relationship between a culture and its environment as the most dynamic factor in human adaptation and the most important explanation of cultural similarities and differences.

Anthropological Theory and Cultural Adaptation

Classic Evolutionary Theory

In attempting to understand the origin and development of culture, and to explain the differences and similarities among cultures, the earliest anthropological theories focused on the ways human societies adapted to their environments. Each culture was thought to have moved through different stages of **cultural evolution**, the process by which new cultural forms emerge out of prior ones. Each cultural stage was identified by a level of technology and a particular method of getting food, and this material aspect of a society was the basis upon which other cultural elements were built.

In 1877, for example, Lewis Henry Morgan, in *Ancient Society*, proposed an evolutionary scheme that included three stages of cultural development, each marked by a major technological breakthrough and accompanied by related cultural changes. The first stage, called "savagery," was marked by the acquisition of fire and the invention of the bow. Property was collectively owned and brothers and sisters were allowed to mate. "Barbarism," the second stage, began with the domestication of animals, the use of iron tools, the invention of pottery, and the development of agriculture. This new technology permitted the accumulation of wealth, and control of property fell into the hands of males. The patriarchal family (controlled by the father) emerged, and private ownership of property replaced collective ownership. The third stage, "civilization," was marked by the emergence of a phonetically written alphabet, the monogamous family, and the rise of the state, a society based on a politically organized territory, which replaced the tribe, a society based on kinship.

The material bases of culture were also emphasized in the evolutionary theories of Karl Marx and Friedrich Engels, who saw all aspects of culture — law, government, family, religion — as growing out of the ways society organized to satisfy its material needs. This organization, in turn, depended on a society's level of technology. These nineteenth-century theories of cultural evolution were later criticized by anthropologists as being too ethnocentric in putting Europeans at the top of the evolutionary scale, as being overly general, or as being too speculative, but they were important in directing attention to the primacy of the material bases of culture, and reemerged in different form in the mid-twentieth century.

Cultural Ecology

Even anthropologists who do not embrace materialist theories of culture would tend to agree that different food-getting strategies make different demands on human beings and have a tendency to be correlated with different cultural institutions such as the family, political structures, and religious organization (Cohen 1971). Thus, for example, the availability of food depends on the technology and knowledge of a society as it exploits its environment; the size of the group is dependent on the availability of food; and the organization of social groups correlates with population densities.

This view of culture as an integrated adaptive system, driven by a society's response to the problems of survival and reproduction, reemerged in the theories of **cultural ecology**, associated with Leslie White (1949) and Julian Steward (1972; originally published 1955). While the work of White, particularly, has clear links with classic evolutionary theory in its development of a universal scheme of cultural evolution based on increasing efficiency of energy transformation, contemporary cultural ecologists are more interested in demonstrating the specific, empirically identifiable ways in which cultural patterns and social organization help human societies adapt to their environments than in building grand universal theories of cultural development.

The emphasis on culture as adaptive is more easily seen in some areas of culture than in others. The ways in which humans satisfy their basic needs for food, shelter, and safety, for example, while part of a culturally constructed reality, are more directly adaptive to the requirements of the physical environment than, say, art. The material culture of societies with simple technologies is based on adaptive strategies that have developed slowly over long periods of trial and error and are finely suited to their physical environments, even when the people in the society cannot say why things are done in a certain way.

Anthropologist James Hamilton found this out the hard way, when he tried to build a house for himself while doing fieldwork among the Pwo Karen of northwestern Thailand (Hamilton 1987). To learn about house construction, Hamilton observed carefully the details of the building of a house. Karen houses are essentially wooden-post structures, raised about six feet off the ground, with bamboo walls, peaked roofs, and a verandah. There are no windows: The space between the thatch of the roof and the height of the walls serves for light and ventilation. The kitchen is in the house, with a water-storage area on one side of the verandah. This is an important feature of a house because Karen customs of sociability require that visitors and guests be offered water.

There were some features of the Karen house with which Hamilton, as an American, did not feel comfortable and which he tried to alter in building his own house. First of all, he insisted that, because the climate was very hot, his house be in a shaded area under some tall trees. The Karen villagers suggested that this was a bad location, but this didn't dissuade him. Like most Americans, Hamilton also liked the "lawn" — the wide grassy area in front of

his house — and protested when the villagers started pulling up the grass. He wasn't, he said, concerned about the snakes and scorpions that might be in the grass; besides, he had a flashlight and boots in case he had to go out at night.

In a traditional Karen house, a person cannot stand up straight as the side walls are less than five feet high. In order to allow for the American view that people ought to be able to stand up in their houses, Hamilton lowered the floor on his house to about two feet off the ground, to give the house more height. Furthermore, because the Karen house is dark and, to Americans, rather small, Hamilton decided to have his kitchen outside the house, in spite of the grumbling of the Karen that this was not the proper way to build a house. He built an extension on one side of the house with a lean-to roof covering made of leaves — this became his kitchen. Finally, when the Karen started to cut off the long overhanging thatch from the roof, Hamilton asked that they let it remain, as it gave him some privacy from eyes peering over the wall, which did not meet the top of the house.

After the house was finished and Hamilton had lived in it a while, he found out why the Karen had not liked the alterations he had made in his house. This part of Thailand has a heavy rainy season, and because the house was under the trees, the roof could not dry out properly and it rotted. In addition, so many twigs and branches fell through the roof that it was like a sieve. The slope of the lean-to over the kitchen was not steep enough; instead of running off, the water came through the roof. So the whole side of the house roof had to be torn off and replaced with a steeper roof, made of sturdier (and more expensive) thatch.

The nice "lawn" combined with the reachable thatch of the roof was too great a

The house of James Hamilton, with its characteristic features of Karen (Thailand) architecture. (Courtesy James Hamilton)

temptation for the local cows, who tried to make their meal out of it. One morning Hamilton woke up to find his lawn covered with piles of cow dung, with hundreds of dung beetles rolling little balls of dung all around the "yard." He cut off the thatch overhang that was left under the trees and pulled up all the grass.

Because the house had been built low to the ground (by Karen standards) in a shady, cool, wet area, there was insufficient ventilation and drying in and around the house to prevent mildew. This meant that Hamilton had to sweep the walls and wipe all leather objects once a week and tightly seal all his anthropological tools — field notes, camera, film, tape recorder, and typewriter.

The Karen house, like houses everywhere, has symbolic meanings and reflects the social organization and world view of a people. But there is no getting around the fact that it must also be built within the constraints posed by the physical environment. While some alterations have been made in the Karen house over the last eighty years, reflecting some changes in social organization, the materials and house construction are not so easily tinkered with.

Adapted from James W. Hamilton, "This Old House: A Karen Ideal." In Mirror and Metaphor: Material and Social Construction of Reality. *Daniel W. Ingersoll, Jr., and Gordon Bronitsky, eds. Lanham, Md.: University Press of America.*

Cultural materialists help explain how some apparently irrational customs, such as the prohibition on eating beef in India, a country in which some people starve, makes sense as an adaptation to long-run variation in the environment. (Serena Nanda)

Cultural Materialism

Cultural materialism, exemplified in the work of Marvin Harris, is another theoretical approach which emphasizes that the most basic aspect of culture is the material constraints of human existence that derive from the human need to satisfy basic needs and to reproduce within environmental and biological limits. Cultural materialists view all aspects of culture—ideology, social organization, values, religion, family, politics, law, child rearing—as varying in accordance with these material constraints. They thus analyze cultural elements in terms of how they help or limit societies in their adaptation to their environments.

A cultural materialist analysis can illuminate how some cultural patterns that seem irrational on the surface (and may not be consciously perceived even by the members of a society) result in rational utilization of the environment. For example, according to Harris (1966), while the Hindu taboo on eating beef despite widespread poverty and periodic famine in India seems ridiculous to outsiders, it makes adaptive sense. Cows are important in India not as a food source, but because they provide dung for fertilizer and give birth to bullocks, the draft animals that pull plows and carts, which are essential in agriculture. If a family ate its cows during a famine, it would deprive itself of the source of bullocks and could not continue farming. Thus, the Hindu religious taboo on eating beef strengthens the ability of Indian peasants to adapt to long-term changes in the environment.

Many anthropologists today do not accept the insistence of cultural materialists that *every* aspect of culture is best analyzed in terms of its adaptive value. Critics of this theory point out that human societies often cling to cultural patterns that have no demonstrative adaptive utility or even, as with the building of nuclear weapons, are potentially lethal to human health and survival (Edgerton 1992). Other critics also note that, in giving primacy to the adaptive results of cultural practices, cultural materialists have not sufficiently paid attention to the meanings that cultural elements have for members of a society. These meanings are important because the symbolic aspects of culture, such as the Hindu view of the cow as a holy animal, motivate and activate people in the absence of a conscious understanding of the adaptive (or maladaptive) effects of their behavior. In spite of this ongoing debate in contemporary anthropology, cultural materialism makes a valuable contribution in calling attention to the ways in which cultural patterns contribute to a society's ability to survive and reproduce in a particular physical and social environment.

Culture Is a System of Meaning

The view of culture as a system of meaning emphasizes the mental and symbolic aspects of culture as these are understood by the members of a society. This approach focuses on how human beings perceive, classify, and attribute cultural meaning to both the physical environment and social behavior. Its several theoretical perspectives all contribute to our understanding of culture as "something in the mind."

French structuralism, closely associated with the work of Claude Lévi-Strauss, draws on linguistic theory in its goal of understanding the mental structures that underlie human culture, particularly cultural systems of perception and classification of the world. According to Lévi-Strauss, human cultures everywhere are built upon the underlying mental structure of **binary oppositions**, that is, dualistic contrasts between one category of phenomena and another, such as male/female; hot/cold; good/

evil; right/left. While admitting that different environments or different histories may modify this universal mental structure, Lévi-Strauss's work does not sufficiently explain cultural differences. His theory has also been criticized as being too abstract and not empirically testable, though it has been useful in calling attention to the cognitive, or mental, aspects of culture, and is particularly interesting when applied to such cultural institutions as religious ritual, mythology, and totemism. (See Chapter 13.)

Cognitive anthropology identifies culture with rules, meanings, and classifications in language that give clues to the ways in which people perceive and understand their experiences. Cognitive anthropologists define culture as a "blueprint for action" (not action itself); a "grammar," or system of rules, for behavior; and a "code" for anthropologists to break. What people learn when they learn "culture" is not just customary ways of doing things but also, and primarily, ways of perceiving or conceptualizing experience. A description of a culture is thus not merely a description of what people do but also a description of the rules or collective ideas behind what people do.

Sometimes, members of a society know and can tell the anthropologist the rules behind their behavior, just as we can explain some of the grammatical rules that underlie our speech. But, in other cases, people cannot explain the rules underlying their behavior; they may not even be aware that such rules exist. It is then necessary for anthropologists to formulate the rules themselves, based on what they observe and on other, more formal techniques of inquiry.

Cognitive theories, like French structuralism, focus on culture as a device for classifying and categorizing the world; unlike French structuralists, however, cognitive anthropologists emphasize that different cultures do this differently. Thus, for example, as I will point out in Chapter 4, while many cultures in the world classify humans into the binary opposite categories of man and woman, there are some cultures that have three, or even several more, gender categories. In Chapter 5, we will also explore the issue of how language categories, which are part of culture, shape our perceptions of the world.

Interpretive Anthropology

Interpretive anthropology, along with cultural materialism, is a major contemporary approach to understanding culture, and has affected both theory and practice. Its most eloquent spokesman is Clifford Geertz (1973), whose main concern is with culture as a system of meaning.

Geertz and other interpretive anthropologists emphasize that human behavior is symbolic: It has meaning — it signifies something — to those who engage in it. A human being, Geertz says, is "an animal suspended in webs of significance which he himself has spun." These "webs of significance" are the systems of meaning that orient human beings to each other and to the world. It is these systems of meaning that Geertz calls culture, and the aim of the anthropologist is to understand the meanings of cultural acts or patterns.

What culture consists of, according to Geertz, is neither mere behavior that can be observed, nor mental constructs that are not necessarily observed in action. Rather, culture consists of "socially established [that is, universally understood within a culture, and publicly enacted in behavior] structures of meaning in terms of which people engage in social action" (Geertz 1973). Behavior is important to observe because it is through the flow of behavior, as social action, that culture is articulated.

For interpretive anthropologists, culture is not a power that causes behavior; rather culture is a *context* within which behavior can be understood. For native participants in a culture, doing something is saying something, and the anthropologist's goal is to understand what participants are saying, to search for the meanings of behavior — the hidden connections and deep significances in a culture — as these are constructed by the members of that culture. Culture, then, becomes a text to be interpreted, in that it can be "read" with different meanings, rather than behavior to be merely observed, or a social structure to be described.

Interpretive anthropologists interested in culture as symbolic behavior look for common themes that may underlie behavior in diverse areas of culture — ritual, law, the arts, ideology — or look for how one cultural event — for example, a religious ritual or a game — may embody several cultural meanings. Because interpretivists approach culture as a text to be interpreted, rather than as a way of adapting to an environment that has objectively verifiable results (as in materialist theories), they focus on each culture as a unique system and are more interested in an in-depth understanding of a particular culture than in searching for laws explaining similarities and differences across cultures.

Interpretivist anthropology attempts to grasp the whole of the native point of view. It opens up the "messier" side of culture, in its attempts not merely to describe cultures as abstract systems, but rather to understand a culture as the *experience* of being a member of that culture (Marcus and Fischer 1986) particularly through fieldwork. Interpretive anthropology is also reflective: It asks questions about how the ethnographer's cultural system of meaning affects the interpretation (and representation) of other cultures.

Culture Is a System of Norms and Values

Norms are the ideas a society has about the ways things *ought* to be done, for example, the expectation in the United States that two adult males will shake hands when introduced to each other for the first time. Cultural norms cluster around certain roles, or positions in society: Each culture has ideas about how a parent, or a politician, or a priest, ought to behave. Norms define the rights and obligations of persons in social interaction, and, as Radcliffe-

Brown suggested, form the building blocks of social structure and contribute to social solidarity and social stability.

Values are culturally defined ideals of what is true, right, and beautiful that underlie cultural patterns and guide society in its response to the physical and social environment. For example, the United States is significantly oriented toward the world by the value of science—the ideal that human beings can, and should, transform nature to meet human ends. Many specific kinds of North American behavior grow out of, and reflect, this underlying value orientation. As in the view of culture as an adaptive system, or as a system of meaning, culture can also be described as an interlocking *system* of norms and values.

The Relationship between Norms, Values, and Behavior

Human behavior is not always consistent with cultural norms or values. In all societies, there is some **deviance** from the norms. In describing the sexual behavior of the Trobriand Islanders, Malinowski (1929:503) noted that his informants stressed the importance of the taboo on incest within the clan. Clan incest was said to be punished by supernatural force, taking the form of a disease and eventual death. But further questioning brought out the fact that some people do engage in clan incest and that there is a patterned way of evading the supernatural punishment: a particular magical ritual performed over a wild ginger root wrapped up in leaves.

"Everyone knows" about the magic ritual to evade the supernatural sanctions for incest in the Trobriand Islands. Every society is apparently willing to pretend ignorance of certain kinds of deviance. But norms do exert pressure on behavior, even when they are not formally and legally expressed. Culture, as a system of norms, meanings, and expectations, does limit human behavior both by channeling it in culturally approved directions and by punishing known violations. Both norms and culturally

Rules of Conduct

For the safety and comfort of all customers, everyone must obey the rules. They're the law. Failure to pay the fare or violation of any other rule can result in arrest, fine and/or ejection.

— No destroying subway property
— No littering or creating unsanitary conditions
— No smoking
— No drinking alcoholic beverages
— No panhandling or begging
— No amplification devices on platforms
— No more than one seat per person
— No blocking free movement
— No lying down
— No unauthorized commercial activities
— No entering tracks, tunnels and non-public areas
— No bulky items likely to inconvenience others
— No radio playing audible to others

Ⓜ New York City Transit Authority

In a large, complex, anonymous society, such as that of major cities in the United States, cultural norms must increasingly be made explicit and sanctioned by formal means. (Serena Nanda)

patterned behavior change. Sometimes norms change before behavior does. Among the upper-middle-class Hindus living in large cities in India, for example, the norm of social equality among all classes of society is widely accepted. This norm is considerably in advance of actual behavior, which only rarely involves social interaction between individuals of the highest and lowest castes on a basis of equality. In other cases, a change in norms follows a change in behavior. The contemporary American cultural norm of small families followed the actual limiting of the number of children by parents who wanted to move up the social ladder.

Norms themselves may be contradictory in a particular society, so that people can justify their behavior in terms of more than one norm. In describing the political system among the

Cultural values do not exist in a vacuum. The high value placed on privacy and individual autonomy, which underlies the North American norm of children having their own rooms, is related to economic affluence, which permits some people to occupy large spaces just for themselves. (United Nations)

Soga of Uganda, Lloyd Fallers (1955) shows the conflict of two opposing norms. In traditional Soga society, political institutions emphasized personal rights and obligations. People owed loyalty to their own relatives, patrons, and local rulers. The administrative staff of the state was recruited through kinship and maintained through personal loyalty. With the coming of the British and the rise of a civil service bureaucracy, an opposing value system came into being. A bureaucracy should ideally treat everyone alike without regard to status or personal relationships. Recruitment to a bureaucracy is based on merit. Fallers emphasizes that both these norms are now institutionalized and have legitimacy in Soga society. This results in many conflicts, particularly for chiefs, who are sometimes pulled in the direction of one of the norms and sometimes in the direction of the other.

Norms may also be unclear. This allows for a wide range of legitimate behaviors. In the United States, for example, a norm is that a woman should be "a good mother" to her child. But this takes in a wide range of behavior, so patterns of mothering run from almost complete permissiveness to harsh discipline, and all are justified as being "for the good of the child."

Because culture is largely viewed as a limit on action, an individual's manipulation of the culture for personal ends has, until recently, been a neglected topic in cultural anthropology. All the ways in which behavior does not mesh with norms give a culture flexibility. They allow people to adjust behavior to changing circumstances. An example of manipulation of cultural norms for personal ends can be seen among upper-middle-class women in India. One important Indian ideal is that women should be in the home and not "moving about" with their friends. Another cultural ideal is that women should spend a lot of time in religious activities. Modern Indian women use the second ideal to get around the first. By forming clubs whose activities are religious, they have an excuse to get out of the house that their elders cannot object to too strongly.

Although too much contradiction, ambiguity, or discrepancy between cultural norms and actual behavior can lead to cultural disintegration, some leeway in the fit between norms and behavior actually adds an adaptive flexibility to culture, enabling it to change with changing circumstances.

Cultural Integration

A culture is not simply a list of norms, values, activities, and objects. Cultural elements are interrelated to form a system. Although anthropologists may analyze separate parts of a culture, the idea of culture as a complex whole, or integrated system, is basic to anthropology. One way of looking at **cultural integration** is in terms of the consistency of cultural themes or values.

Ruth Benedict is the anthropologist most closely associated with the idea that each culture is a unique configuration of integrated values, or themes, dominated by a particular theme, or **ethos**, which shapes all major institutions, such as family, religion, art, politics, and so forth. In her book, *Patterns of Culture* (1961; originally published 1934), Benedict accounted for cultural diversity by applying this

Fourth of July parades in the United States provide occasions for symbolically enacting important cultural norms and values. (Ravinder Nanda)

theory, called cultural **configurationalism**, to the study of the Kwakiutl, Zuni, and Plains Indians of North America and the Dobu of Melanesia. She suggested that the culture of the Plains tribes was dominated by extravagant sensation seeking and individualism, an ethos she called "Dionysian." This ethos appeared in many aspects of their culture, such as the fasting and self-torture involved in seeking supernatural visions, through which a warrior acquired the power needed in warfare. Zuni culture, on the other hand, which she called "Apollonian," was based on an ethos of moderation, and any seeking of extraordinary experiences or attempts to distinguish oneself from others were severely discouraged.

Although most anthropologists agree that there is a tendency for a culture to be dominated by a particular value, or ethos, most would also agree that no culture achieves complete integration. Cultures may have more than one dominant theme, and sometimes these themes may even be in conflict. For example, in addition to the Dionysian theme Benedict described for Plains culture, there was an opposing theme, that of the "considerate peace chief" (Hoebel 1960). This theme emphasized gentleness, generosity, reasonableness, and wisdom and called for self-restraint and consideration of others. These themes operated in different spheres of Plains life and provided a balance in the culture. It is clear that cultures can and do function with some disharmony and lack of integration, but this may be adaptive. A culture needs flexibility to respond to changes in the physical and social environment. On the other hand, too weak integration in a culture may impose intolerable stress on the individual.

The concept of cultural integration raises some interesting questions about American culture. Do we in fact have one theme that characterizes our culture? Or do different activities have different, even contradictory, themes? Is there a contradiction between our economic life, with its theme of individual competitiveness, and our family life, with its theme of altruism? Or is our family life, too, shaped by the themes of deception, individual competition, and the desire to control others in our own self-interest, which underlie our economic behavior (Henry 1963)? The history of the United States can also be seen as a continuing swing between the opposing themes of equality and inequality; democracy and hierarchy; and individualism and community.

Culture Is Shared

To be considered part of culture, a way of thinking or interacting must be shared among a group of people. Some cultural patterns, norms, values, meanings, and behaviors are shared by all people in a society. Societies in which important beliefs, values, and customs are shared by almost everyone are said to be homogeneous. Although anthropologists are now discovering that even small, traditional societies are less homogeneous than was previ-

ously believed, it is in the large, heterogeneous societies that discovering the degree of shared beliefs, values, and practices becomes a problem. In heterogeneous societies, written law may be a useful guide to the most widely shared cultural traits.

One universally shared cultural pattern in the United States is driving a car on the right side of the road. This custom is not simply the result of law but is built into our response system. Another cultural universal in the United States is our system of weights and measures. Here again, although this pattern is supported by formal teaching and law, it is a way of giving shape to the physical universe that is basic to the way we perceive the world.

Cultural Specialization

Some cultural patterns are shared only by people in certain social positions, or **statuses.** In most societies, for example, there is some cultural specialization between men and women. This specialization derives not only from the sexual division of labor, in which men customarily do different things than women, but also from cultural prohibitions on the kinds of activities women are allowed to engage in. Among the Arapesh of New Guinea, for example, women are not allowed to join the tamberan cult, because the tamberan is the supernatural patron of adult men. Not only are women not permitted to see the tamberan, but they are not even allowed to think about what he might look like or the meaning of the activities that accompany his entry into the village. Margaret Mead, who studied the Arapesh, notes that the intellectual passivity women must accept regarding the tamberan soon becomes a habit. All that is "strange, uncharted and unnamed" becomes unfamiliar to them. This not only cuts women off from speculative thinking on many subjects but also "from art, because among the Arapesh art and the supernatural are part and parcel of each other" (Mead 1963:81). Thus, intellectual and creative activity becomes a male cultural specialization.

Age is also a universal criterion of cultural specialization, though in most societies age specialization is not nearly as important as it is in the United States. In our own society, the degree to which cultural specialties — in language, music, and behavior — are associated with people between the ages of twelve and twenty has led to the label "youth culture" (Schwartz 1972).

Some occupational specialties exist in most societies. These cultural specialties are most often of a ritual kind. In some societies, they may be learned by anyone who wishes to engage in ritual activity and who seems to be successful at it. In others, ritual specialization may be limited to a few men or women who must first serve a long apprenticeship or join a secret association to learn ritual techniques and handle sacred materials. In India, most occupations are specialties of certain groups called castes, and only people born into a particular caste may practice its traditional occupational specialty.

Until recently, with few exceptions, the assumption made in cultural anthropology was that people in small, non-Western societies not only act in the same way in the same situation, but that they also attach the same meanings and values to cultural patterns and behaviors. Little or no emphasis was given to the different subjective meanings cultural patterns might have for persons in different social statuses, such as men in contrast to women, or the old in contrast to the young.

Anthropologists are now explicitly raising these kinds of questions (Keesing 1987), and it appears that cultural events, explanations, and norms do indeed have several interpretations within these societies, and that these differing, and sometimes conflicting, interpretations are linked to social position. These kinds of differences have always been expected in large, complex societies, but were incorrectly assumed to be unimportant in the small-scale, socially simpler societies typically studied by anthropologists. For example, a closer look at societies with significant sex segregation and hostility between the sexes, such as in New Guinea (Hammar 1989) and the Amazon (Murphy and

Murphy 1974), which was stimulated by feminist anthropology, makes it apparent that men and women do not attach the same meanings to the many myths and rituals that maintain the system of male dominance and do indeed experience their culture differently.

The anthropological emphasis on culture as shared has also given the inaccurate perception that in tribal and peasant societies there are few personality differences among individuals that would cause them to experience their cultures differently, or that individuals have any meaningful choices in acting in nonconventional ways. Although it is true that behavior, to be culture, must be shared, it is also true that in every culture there is some scope for individual variation, creativity, manipulation, choice, and resistance to cultural patterns. There are more options available for choice and behavioral variation in technologically and occupationally complex cultures, but even in small-scale societies, culture is not uniformly experienced and enacted.

Explicit questions into how widely a culture is shared, what are the boundaries of cultural sharing, how individuals in the same culture experience that culture differently, the relationship of culture to individual "deviance," and the connection between social position and interpretation of cultural events, are being raised in different forms: the life history, the person-centered ethnography, and the revived emphasis on political economy and social stratification, particularly by Marxist and feminist anthropologists. Both materialist and interpretive theories of culture make their contributions to our understanding of these varying interpretations of culture, as they exist among individuals and social groups.

The question of limits on cultural sharing within large, complex societies has, in contrast to this question in small, structurally simpler societies, long been an interest in anthropology. Sometimes the term **subculture** has been used to designate a cultural pattern — a system of perceptions, values, beliefs, and practices — that is shared by a group of people and is significantly different from the dominant culture,

In a socially stratified society, those at the very bottom of the social ladder do not share in many of the cultural patterns of society. In the United States, the homeless are sometimes said to have their own cultural specialization, or form a subculture. (Serena Nanda)

though it also shares some aspects of that culture. The terms *dominant culture* and *subculture* do not refer here to better and worse, superior and inferior, but rather to the idea that the dominant culture is the more *powerful* in a society, partly because it controls information through which images of the subcultures are filtered, or controls institutions like the law, which criminalizes some subcultural practices that conflict with the dominant culture and threaten to undermine its power (Norgren and Nanda 1988).

Modern nations contain many subcultures—based on region, religion, occupation, social class, ethnicity, age, gender, and lifestyle. The accompanying ethnography of the Rastafari illustrates the dynamic processes of cultural adaptation that may result in the creation and maintenance of a subculture.

Culture Changes

Every culture changes as it adapts to an ever-changing physical and social environment. Many changes in human societies are initially small and incremental, and have only a minor impact on a culture. But taken together, small changes can add up to major changes, until we perceive a culture to be qualitatively different from what it was before. This can happen slowly, as when a culture evolves; if this qualitative change comes about very rapidly and is far-reaching, it is cultural revolution. Because culture is a system, and each of the parts interacts with the others, as well as with the culture as a whole, change in one part of the system, even a small change, will lead to other changes over time.

There are three major processes by which all cultures change: innovation, invention, and diffusion. Understanding how these processes work, and the roles they play in culture change, has been a major interest in anthropological theory.

Innovation

An **innovation** is a variation of an existing cultural pattern that is then accepted or learned by the other members of the society. Most innovations are slight modifications of already existing habits of thought and action. Although

An innovation is a variation on an established cultural practice. Pictured are storage jars from Morocco, made in the traditional, centuries-old shape but using worn-out rubber tires instead of clay. (Joan Gregg)

material aspects of culture. New art forms and new ideas may all be considered inventions. All inventions involve human ingenuity and creativity, but even geniuses are limited in what they can invent by the nature and complexity of the existing cultural pattern. Had Einstein been born into a society that had not developed the complex scientific understandings of Western civilization, he could never have "invented" the theory of relativity. Each genius in a culture builds on what has gone before and moves in the direction of expanding an existing tradition.

Because inventions depend on the recombination of previously existing cultural elements, the more elements that are already present in a culture, the more likely it is to produce even more inventions. This partly explains why change occurs much faster in technologically complex societies than in technologically simple ones. This cumulative effect of change also applies to human culture as a whole. It took several million years for humans to change from hunters and gatherers to agricultural producers. After the first domestication of plants and animals about 10,000 or 12,000 years ago, it took about 5,000 or 6,000 years for writing and cities to be invented. All the other technological knowledge, and the social complexity that came with that knowledge, has been learned in the past few thousand years and involves a rate of change unlike anything known earlier.

each individual innovation may be slight, the accumulated effects may be great over the long run. An innovation can be the result of deliberate experimentation, or it can come about unintentionally.

An innovation means a slight modification of an existing cultural pattern; an **invention** is the combination of existing cultural elements into something altogether new. Although we are likely to think of inventions as primarily technological, invention is not limited to the

Diffusion

Diffusion is the spread of cultural elements through borrowing from one culture by another. Although both small and large changes can come from within a society, or through contact with other societies, it is usually direct cultural contact that results in the most far-reaching changes. That is why cultures located on the major paths of culture contact tend to change more rapidly than those in more isolated places. Diffusion does not automatically result from culture contact; it takes place only

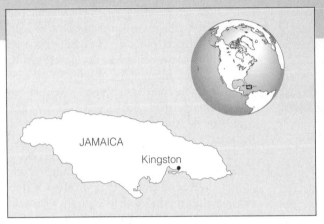

The Rastafari community emerged on the Caribbean island of Jamaica in the 1930s. Since that time, the Rastafari have spread throughout the islands of the Caribbean, into parts of the African states of Kenya and Ethiopia and the urban centers of the United States, England, and Canada. As part of a larger society, the Rastafari can be called a subculture (a term they would probably reject) and present an interesting example of a group specifically in resistance to the culture that surrounds it.

The Rastafari as a group has a value system that emphasizes economic communalism, solidarity within the group, and a rejection of the economic values of the culture that surrounds it. Also, Rastafari adherents value the beliefs and visible markers of identity, such as clothing, hair style, and special linguistic usages, that set it apart from the larger society. In addition, the Rastafari are often in trouble with the law, particularly because of their use and distribution of marijuana, and this negatively affects the way in which they are viewed by the outside world.

The Rastas emerged from the Jamaican peasantry at a time when much of the peasantry had been incorporated as wage labor into a modernizing, capitalist economy. Subsequent to the dissolution of slavery in Jamaica, in 1834, a peasant economy had developed, organized around a system of localized and small-scale exchanges involving interpersonal networks of extended kin. By the 1920s, capitalism had considerably undermined the peasant economy, which was considered backward and unproductive by the government and elite business class. In spite of the dominance of the capitalist market, there remained a conservative peasantry at the periphery who refused to participate in the modern economy and retained their own self-reliant economic systems. Although the limited trade and small opportunities for capital gain meant there was no large generation of profits, these peasants, in fact, were more immune to the difficulties of economic depression that occurred in the 1930s than were those peasants who participated in wage labor on the plantations.

It was out of this milieu that the Rastafari arose. Unlike the Marcus Garvey movement, occurring somewhat earlier, which tried to connect black identity to successful participation in the capitalist economy, the Rastas emphasized the positive identity of the black peasant as a nonparticipant in the modern economy and growing Jamaican nationalism. The emerging Rasta culture coalesced

The most visible sign of Rasta identity is their "dreads," or long, uncombed locks, which embodies their rejection of the world of wage labor. (William F. Lewis)

around the symbol of Ras (Prince) Tafari, who was crowned king of Ethiopia in 1930 and took the name Haile Selassie I. Through a belief in the divinity of Haile Selassie, the rejection of competitive markets and capitalism, their desire to repatriate to Africa, their use of marijuana, and the creation of a special language, the Rastas resolutely clung to the black cultural experience of the Jamaican peasantry.

Rejecting the aspirations of social mobility and participation in wage labor, the Rastas fashion a livelihood by forming networks of cooperation. In Jamaica they engage in fishing, handicrafts, and hustling in the cities, and, in the rural areas, in a family-based subsistence agriculture with minimal involvement in the market economy. The small group of Rastas living in Shashemane, Ethio-

(continued)

pia, rely on their agricultural produce and financial donations from abroad. In urban England, Canada, and the United States, Rasta economic activities tend to be small-scale cooperative businesses such as eateries, craft shops, small clothing stores, and the illegal sale of marijuana. All of these enterprises are based on the productivity and input of extended familylike networks. No Rasta enterprise is a lone venture.

In addition to their support of each other's businesses, they circulate their wealth through the community in the form of gifts, loans, and especially parties. The economic exchange among Rastas is ideally a highly personal event between community members. Even money from their ganja (marijuana) trade is distributed equitably within the community.

The central symbol of the Rastas that affirmed blackness and African roots, and disproved the stereotypical Jamaican image of the black peasant as poor and backward, was Haile Selassie, the king of Ethiopia from 1930 to 1974. Haile Selassie was the symbol from which the Rastas derived their name and their affirmation in blackness over and above any connection of black identity to social mobility. Haile Selassie embodied blackness, cooperative efforts, and conservatism. The Rastas ground their belief in their interpretations of biblical prophecies born out by the coronation of Haile Selassie I, when he was proclaimed "King of Kings and Lion of Judah." This orientation to Ethiopia was to some extent a continuity of the Jamaican peasant's continuing connection to African cultural patterns, modified by European culture and Christianity, which had been part of the slave culture.

In addition to "Ethiopianism" (the importance of Haile Selassie and the orientation to African cultural patterns), repatriation to Africa is another central theme in Rasta philosophy. While some Rastas actually did repatriate to Africa, repatriation (like all symbols) has several meanings: For the Rastas it vacillates between a literal passage to the African homeland and a retribalization of the Rastas in whichever country they find themselves. Ethiopianism and repatriation are the two key symbols of the Rastas' alienation from modern notions of progress, social mobility, and the status of propertyless wage labor.

Two other important symbols of their culture are the use of marijuana and their creation of special linguistic usages. Through their use of marijuana, and through their creation of a philosophy around that use, Rastas weaken their psychological disposition for participation in the dominant economy. The Rasta use of marijuana does not serve as a narcotic tool to create a future utopia for the Rastas. Rather, ganja sustains them in their own independent enterprises as craftspeople, fishermen, and hustlers, and it helps them assert their communal bonds against the world around them, giving them "an entire nontraditional and alternative system of power and control, influence, and prestige."

In addition, the illegal sale of marijuana is part of the underground economy of many Rasta groups. The networks for growing it, preparing it for sale, and its distribution are all based on friendship, alliances, and reciprocity. Although the Rastas have encountered difficulties with law enforcement in connection with their use and sale of marijuana, the drug has provided the Rastas with a livelihood that allows them independence and freedom from the capitalist system, a position they value highly. Ultimately, many Rastas hope that their world will become more and more based on reciprocity and redistribution where each member's work supports every other member's and money as a medium of exchange will disappear from their community.

Rastafari linguistic usages include the invention of "I"-centered words, phrases, and suffixes, such as "ital" for vital, and the substitution of such diminutives as "under" and "sub" with their opposites, such as coining the word *overstand* for understand. (This suggests that the use of the term *subculture* to characterize Rasta relations to the larger society would not be acceptable to them and represents the anthropologist's etic view over the native emic one.) In disavowing diminutives, the Rastas appear to be disavowing the hierarchical nature of relations in the marketplace. Rasta language contradicts the submissiveness that an employer expects of an employee through language that includes subtle forms of subordination. The Rastas have devised their language as an assertion of their black self-worth, and this, too, keeps them separate from the world of the boss and the worker.

The Rastas draw boundaries around themselves to exclude the outside world from participation in their economic and social relationships. They do this at the same time they participate in economic opportunities that extend beyond the group. Although there is jealousy, tension, and conflict within the group, occasionally resulting in violence, there is also strong solidarity against outsiders, particularly those in positions of authority. Rastas have rejected much of the social and psychological orientation of modern society, or Babylon, as the Rastas call it. They are a small group movement that deviates from the modern state and persists in a peasantlike identity. While much of their culture is a continuation of the milieu out of which they emerged, they have also created a new culture and adaptive strategies that allow them to survive in a manner consistent with their own view of the world.

Adapted with permission from William F. Lewis, Soul Rebels: The Rastafari. (Prospect Heights, Ill.: Waveland, 1993).

Useful innovations are accepted by peoples in ways consistent with their culture. Here Minmara, a member of the Ngatatjara aboriginal group of Australia, trims a spear using an old Landrover spring. (R. A. Gould, Courtesy Department of Library Services, American Museum of Natural History)

if the borrowed element proves rewarding in some way. Furthermore, once accepted, a borrowed element may undergo many changes, in both form and meaning, as it is worked into an existing cultural pattern. The article by Ralph Linton in the accompanying box reminds us of the adaptive value of diffusion and its importance in our own culture.

Culture Change and Anthropological Theory

Attention to culture change has waxed and waned in anthropology. The encounters between European and non-European peoples beginning in the fifteenth century led to cultural evolutionary theories that speculated on the origins and development of human culture. The tenet of these theories that cultural evolution proceeded by the same steps everywhere was based on the idea of the **psychic unity** of hu-

mankind: All human groups have the same mental capacities and the same ability to think logically; when faced with similar problems, they will invent similar solutions. Thus, **independent invention** explained similarities in culture among societies isolated from each other, and developmental stages explained cultural differences.

These classic evolutionary theorists were not interested in history, which is the study of the past through particular events, but rather in discovering the general laws by which cultural development occurred. Thus, while they acknowledged that diffusion did occur, and even affected a society's developmental stages, they did not give it much attention, believing that independent invention accounted for most cultural similarities.

In reaction to the evolutionary theorists' overemphasis on human inventiveness, anthropologists in both Europe and the United States turned their attention to studying cultural dif-

Cultures change, but some cultures, because they are less isolated, change faster than others. Twenty-five hundred years of culture change are shown in this view of Athens. (Ravinder Nanda)

fusion. These cultural diffusionists were, like the cultural evolutionists, interested in the origins and laws governing the development of human culture, which they hoped to discover by mapping cultural traits in nonliterate societies. Since they assumed the most widely distributed traits to be the oldest, they concluded that their trait mapping could tell them something about the original cultural traits of humankind and help determine which were the original human cultures.

The extreme diffusionists attempted to prove that all human culture originated in one place and then spread through diffusion. They concluded, for example, that the similarities in form among Egyptian pyramids, Mayan temples, and native American burial mounds demonstrated that Egypt was the sole source of human culture and civilization. What the extreme diffusionists failed to recognize was that, although there were similarities in form among these structures, they served entirely different

functions in society and the meanings attached to them were not the same.

The diffusion theorists in the United States, like their European counterparts, also sought to discover the laws of cultural process, but limited themselves to tracing culture trait distributions among the indigenous peoples of North America. These anthropologists of the **American historical tradition,** such as Robert Lowie, Clark Wissler, Alfred Kroeber, and Franz Boas, believed that the laws of cultural process could be discovered by reconstructing the particular cultural history of each society, rather than attempting to reconstruct the cultural history of humankind.

At the same time that historical particularism dominated American anthropology in the 1920s and 1930s, the functionalist theories of Malinowski and Radcliffe-Brown dominated in England, and indeed, influenced anthropology in the United States, as Boas and others in the American historical tradition turned their

There can be no question about the average American's Americanism or his desire to preserve this precious heritage at all costs. Nevertheless, some insidious foreign ideas have already wormed their way into his civilization without his realizing what was going on. Thus dawn finds the unsuspecting patriot garbed in pajamas, a garment of East Indian origin; and lying in a bed built on a pattern which originated in either Persia or Asia Minor. He is muffled to the ears in un-American materials: cotton, first domesticated in India; linen, domesticated in the Near East; wool from an animal native to Asia Minor; or silk whose uses were first discovered by the Chinese. All these substances have been transformed into cloth by methods invented in Southwestern Asia. If the weather is cold enough he may even be sleeping under an eiderdown quilt invented in Scandinavia.

On awakening he glances at the clock, a medieval European invention, uses one potent Latin word in abbreviated form, rises in haste, and goes to the bathroom. Here, if he stops to think about it, he must feel himself in the presence of a great American institution; he will have heard stories of both the quality and frequency of foreign plumbing and will know that in no other country does the average man perform his ablutions in the midst of such splendor. But the insidious foreign influence pursues him even here. Glass was invented by the ancient Egyptians, the use of glazed tiles for floors and walls in the Near East, porcelain in China, and the art of enameling on metal by Mediterranean artisans of the Bronze Age. Even his bathtub and toilet are but slightly modified copies of Roman originals. The only purely American contribution to the ensemble is the steam radiator, against which our patriot very briefly and unintentionally places his posterior.

In this bathroom the American washes with soap invented by the ancient Gauls. Next he cleans his teeth, a subversive European practice which did not invade America until the latter part of the eighteenth century. He then shaves, a masochistic rite first developed by the heathen priests of ancient Egypt and Sumer. The process is made less of a penance by the fact that his razor is of steel, an iron-carbon alloy discovered in either India or Turkestan. Lastly, he dries himself on a Turkish towel.

Returning to the bedroom, the unconscious victim of un-American practices removes his clothes from a chair, invented in the Near East, and proceeds to dress. He puts on close-fitting tailored garments whose form derives from the skin clothing of the ancient nomads of the Asiatic steppes and fastens them with buttons whose prototypes appeared in Europe at the close of the Stone Age. This costume is appropriate enough for outdoor exercise in a cold climate, but is quite unsuited to American summers, steam-heated houses, and Pullmans. Nevertheless, foreign ideas and habits hold the unfortunate man in thrall even when common sense tells him that the authentically American costume of gee string and moccasins would be far more comfortable. He puts on his feet stiff coverings made from hide prepared by a process invented in ancient Egypt and cut to a pattern which can be traced back to ancient Greece, and makes sure that they are properly polished, also a Greek idea. Lastly, he ties about his neck a strip of bright-colored cloth which is a vestigial survival of the shoulder shawls worn by seventeenth-century Croats. He gives himself a final appraisal in the mirror, an old Mediterranean invention, and goes downstairs to breakfast.

Here a whole new series of foreign things confronts him. His food and drink are placed before him in pottery vessels, the proper name of which — china — is sufficient evidence of their origin. His fork is a medieval Italian invention and his spoon a copy of a Roman original. He will usually begin the meal with coffee, an Abyssinian plant first discovered by the Arabs. The American is quite likely to need it to dispel the morning-after effects of overindulgence in fermented drinks, invented in the Near East; or distilled ones, invented by the alchemists of medieval Europe. Whereas the Arabs took their coffee straight, he will probably sweeten it with sugar, discovered in India; and dilute it with cream, both the domestication of cattle and the technique of milking having originated in Asia Minor.

If our patriot is old-fashioned enough to adhere to the so-called American breakfast, his coffee will be accompanied by an orange, domesticated in the Mediterranean region, a cantaloupe domesticated in Persia, or grapes domesticated in Asia Minor. He will follow this with a bowl of cereal made from grain domesticated in the Near East and prepared by methods also invented there. From this he will go on to waffles, a Scandinavian invention, with plenty of but-ter, originally a Near-Eastern cosmetic. As a side dish he may have the egg of a bird domesticated in Southeastern Asia or strips of the flesh of an animal domesticated in the same region, which has been salted and smoked by a process invented in Northern Europe.

Breakfast over, he places upon his head a molded piece of felt, invented by the nomads of Eastern Asia, and, if it looks like rain, puts on outer shoes of rubber, discovered by the ancient Mexicans, and takes an umbrella, invented in India. He then sprints for his train — the train, not sprinting, being an English invention. At the station he pauses for a moment to buy a newspaper, paying for it with coins invented in ancient Lydia. Once on board he settles back to inhale the fumes of a cigarette invented in Mexico, or a cigar invented in Brazil. Meanwhile, he reads the news of the day, imprinted in characters invented by the ancient Semites by a process invented in Germany upon a material invented in China. As he scans the latest editorial pointing out the dire results to our institutions of accepting foreign ideas, he will not fail to thank a Hebrew God in an Indo-European language that he is a one hundred percent (decimal system invented by the Greeks) American (from Americus Vespucci, Italian geographer).

From Ralph Linton, "One Hundred Percent American," The American Mercury 40 *(1937): 427–29. Reprinted by permission of* The American Mercury, *Box 1306, Torrance, California.*

Sye figur antzaigt vns das volck vnd infel die gefunden ift durch den chriftenlichen künig zu Portigal oder von feinen vnterthonen. Die leüt find alfo nacket hübfch.braun wolgeftalt von leib.ir heübter.hälß.arm.fcham.füß.frowen vnd mann ain wenig mit federn bedeckt. Auch haben die mann in iren angefichten vnd bruft vil edel geftain. Es hat auch nyemantz nichts funder find alle ding gemain. Vnd die mann habendt weyber welche in gefallen.es fey müter.fchwefter oder freünde.darinn haben fy kain vnterfcheyd. Sy ftreyten auch mit einander. Sy effen auch ainander felbs die erfchlagen werden.vnd hencken das felbig flaifch in den rauch. Sy werden alt hundert vnd fünftzig iar. Vnd haben kain regiment.

Many nineteenth-century theories of cultural evolution built upon European notions of the moral and technological superiority of their own culture. The peoples of the New World were pictured — literally — as savages. This sixteenth-century woodcut represents the indigenous peoples of Brazil according to European stereotypes, particularly in the image of the head and shoulder of a man roasting over a fire as he hangs between two trees, and the figure in the upper lefthand corner who is engaged in making a meal of a human arm. (American Museum of Natural History)

attention to cultural integration. It was with the reemergence of neoevolutionary theory and cultural ecology in the 1950s, and later, cultural materialism, that studies of cultural change and cultural conflict again became central in anthropology.

Since the 1960s, this interest in conflict and change, which had been kept alive on the margins of cultural anthropology by conflict theorists and Marxist anthropologists, moved closer to the center of anthropological theory. **Conflict theory**, and more specifically, Marxist anthropology and feminist anthropology, contribute to our understanding of culture by raising questions about how different aspects of culture serve the interests of various competing groups, such as social classes, ethnic groups, or men and women, and how such conflicts can lead to cultural and social change.

There has also been a renewed interest in the relationship between history and anthropology, focusing on the historical connections between cultures as part of a world system (Wolf 1982). While cultural evolutionists and diffusionists focused on culture contact and change, they treated cultures as if each was a closed, autonomous, integrated unit, set off from other, equally bounded units. The long history of interconnections among human groups, particularly those resulting from the expansion of European capitalism and colonialism, were largely ignored.

In the early 1970s, a growing interest in locating local cultures in the larger economic

Diffusion theorists believed that Mayan temples (left) were derived through culture contact from Egyptian pyramids (right). In fact, though there is a superficial similarity in form, they have different functions, and most contemporary anthropologists believe that these structures were a result of independent invention rather than diffusion. (Serena Nanda)

and political world system was given new impetus by the world systems theory of Immanuel Wallerstein (1974). **World systems theory**, as applied in anthropology, emphasizes that local cultures — the tribes and peasant societies most studied by anthropologists — were products of a specific history of 500 years of "confrontation, killing, resurrection, and accommodation" as Europe reached out to seize the resources and populations of other continents (Wolf 1982:18).

Eric Wolf and others who developed this perspective insist that culture change needs to be examined in European as well as non-European cultures, which have both undergone change as a result of contact over the past 500 years. This world historical approach requires examining the specific processes of historical change both within a culture and outside it. In short, change is seen as a *mutually determined* process of political, social, and economic interaction.

In the ongoing disagreements and debates about culture and culture change that have characterized the history of anthropology as a discipline, we are again reminded of the seven blind men and the elephant, each man arguing for his own definition of the whole, in terms of the piece of the animal he is holding on to. But in spite of the often sharp words between the proponents of one or another theory of culture, these different approaches are not necessarily irreconcilable. As anthropologist Miles Richardson (1984) points out, the aim of seeking explanations and discovering the laws and causes of culture, and the aim of an interpretivist understanding of culture as a system of meaning, "are both useful in understanding the behavior of a species — *Homo sapiens* — that lives in terms of meaning in a physical universe . . . subject to causal law."

Summary

1. Culture, that is, learned and socially transmitted knowledge, is the major adaptive mechanism of the human species. The human species shares many traits with other, nonhuman primates, such as the complex brain, the capacity for learning, and flexibility, upon which adaptation through culture is based.

2. Culture functions to meet human needs. The functionalist theory of Bronislaw Malinowski emphasized that cultural institutions meet the

needs of individuals and societies. The structural functional theory of A. R. Radcliffe-Brown emphasized the ways in which social structures contribute to social solidarity and social stability.

3. Culture is adaptive in that it helps human beings survive and reproduce in specific physical environments. The most clearly adaptive aspects of culture are the ways that humans satisfy their needs for food, shelter, and safety, as indicated in an account of building a house in Thailand.

4. Materialist theories of culture emphasize the technological and economic aspects of culture as the basis of other cultural patterns. The anthropological theories that emphasize this material aspect of culture are cultural evolution, cultural ecology, and cultural materialism. Cultural materialist theories investigate the effect of culturally patterned behavior on the relationship between humans and their physical environments.

5. In contrast to materialist and evolutionary theories of culture are theories that emphasize culture as a system of meaning and symbols, as seen by people within the culture. These theories include French structuralism, symbolic anthropology, and interpretive anthropology.

6. Culture consists of norms, or guidelines for behavior, and values, or ideals. The ambiguity and inconsistency of norms give culture flexibility as people can manipulate norms for their own interests.

7. Culture tends to be integrated. The basic social institutions of a society tend to fit together and the values underlying cultural patterns tend to be consistent: No culture, however, is perfectly integrated, and cultural contradictions exist in all cultures. Ruth Benedict's theory of configurationalism emphasized the integration of cultures. She saw each culture as an interwoven pattern of traits, dominated by a particular theme, or ethos.

8. Culture exhibits both stability and change. Because culture is a system, a change in one part of the culture leads to change and adjustment in other parts. The rate of change is different in different societies; it depends partly on geographical factors, level of technology, and cultural values regarding change.

9. Two important processes in cultural change are innovation and diffusion. Innovation is a new variation on an existing cultural pattern that is accepted into the larger society.

10. Diffusion, a term for any or all of the ways a people take up part or all of another culture, is not an automatic process, but is based on selectivity. The borrowed elements are integrated into existing cultural patterns, not adopted as is. Diffusion theory attempted to account for cultural similarities by the spread of culture traits from one society to another through historical contact.

11. The American historical tradition, led by Franz Boas, was first interested in diffusion and then turned to the study of whole cultures. Boas insisted on the study of particular cultures in their historical and psychological context as the first step toward finding general laws of culture.

12. By the 1960s, anthropology had moved farther away from a functionalist concern with social order to an interest in conflict and change, an interest shared with the early cultural evolutionists. Marxist and feminist anthropologists are particularly interested in conflict within society, as this applies to social classes and male and female differences, respectively.

13. World systems theory, as applied in anthropology, focuses on the connections between cultures as part of a world economic system that has been in the making since the spread of European capitalism in the fifteenth century.

14. Although there is a major difference between anthropologists who view culture as a system of ideas and those who emphasize its material base, each perspective makes a contribution to our understanding of the human experience.

Suggested Readings

Barrett, Richard A.
1984 *Culture and Conduct: An Excursion in Anthropology.* Belmont, Calif.: Wadsworth. A brief, well-written introduction to the concept of culture, covering adaptation, mean-

ing, the persistence of culture, and intracultural variation.

Freilich, Morris, Raybeck, Douglas, and Savishinsky, Joel, eds.
1990   *Deviance: Anthropological Perspectives.* New York: Praeger/Greenwood. A book of readings examining the relationship between nonconformity, or deviance, and culture in a wide range of settings from rural Malaysia to an American hospital.

Harris, Marvin
1974   *Cows, Pigs, Wars and Witches: The Riddle of Culture.* New York: Random House. A witty, fascinating look at such diverse topics as food prohibitions, warfare, messianic cults, and the counterculture in the United States from the standpoint of cultural materialism.

Lewis, William F.
1993   *Soul Rebels: The Rastafari.* Prospect Heights, Ill.: Waveland. An original anthropological perspective on a fascinating culture known to many only for its connections to reggae music and the religious use of marijuana.

Moran, Emilio
1982   *Human Adaptability: An Introduction to Ecological Anthropology.* Boulder, Colo.: Westview Press. A survey of both physiological and cultural mechanisms by which human populations adapt to a wide range of environments — from the tropics to the Arctic.

Romanucci-Ross, Lola
1991   *One Hundred Towers: An Italian Odyssey of Cultural Survival.* New York: Bergin and Garvey. A beautifully written ethnography of cultural survival and adaptation, stressing the interplay of the past and the present in the basic categories of cultural life, including religion, family, language, and economics.

Wolf, Eric
1982   *Europe and the People without History.* Berkeley: University of California Press. An important account documenting with a wealth of historical detail how the expansion of the European economic system transformed cultures in the rest of the world.

The Cultural Context
of Human Behavior

Is there an objective reality, or are there only multiple realities?

How does culture pattern the way we "see" the world?

What is the relationship of intelligence to culture?

What kinds of behaviors come "naturally" to humans?

I have on my table a violin string. It is free. I twist one end of it and it responds. It is free. But it is not free to do what a violin string is supposed to do — to produce music. So I take it, fix it in my violin and tighten it until it is taut. Only then is it free to be a violin string.

Sir Rabindranath Tagore

In the quote that opens this chapter, Sir Rabindranath Tagore, the great Indian poet, writer, and philosopher, suggests an image that is useful in thinking about the relationship between the individual and culture. Because of the emphasis on individualism in the culture of the United States, we often think of culture as something that restrains us and deprives us of freedom. But without culture, human beings would not be human beings. Culture is indeed necessary for humans to become human. Practically everything humans perceive, know, think, value, feel, and do is learned through participation in a sociocultural system. The few well-documented cases on record of children relatively isolated from society in the early years of life bear out this statement.

One of these cases, that of the "wild boy of Aveyron" (Itard 1962; originally published 1806), is of exceptional interest. In 1799, a boy of about twelve was captured in a forest in Aveyron, France. He was brought to Paris, where he attracted huge crowds who expected to see the "noble savage" of the romantic eighteenth-century philosophical vision. Instead, they found a boy whose

eyes were unsteady, expressionless, wandering vaguely from one object to another . . . so little trained by the sense of touch, they could never distinguish an object in relief from one in a picture. His . . . hearing was insensible to the loudest noises and to . . . music. His voice was reduced to a state of complete muteness and only a uniform guttural sound escaped him . . . he was equally indifferent to the odor of perfume and to the fetid exhalation of the dirt with which his bed was filled . . . [his] touch was restricted to the mechanical grasping of an object . . . [he had a] tendency to trot and gallop . . . [and] an obstinate habit of smelling at anything given to him . . . he chewed like a rodent with a sudden action of the incisors . . . [and] showed no sensitivity to cold or heat and could seize hot coals from the fire without flinching or lay half naked upon the wet ground for hours in the wintertime. . . . He was incapable of attention and spent his time apathetically rocking himself backwards and forwards like the animals in the zoo.*

---

*Jean-Marc-Gaspard Itard, *The Wild Boy of Aveyron*. Translated by George and Muriel Humphrey. © 1962, Prentice-Hall, Englewood Cliffs, N.J. Reprinted by permission of the publisher.

This description of the "wild boy of Aveyron" is provided by Jean-Marc-Gaspard Itard, a young psychologist who undertook the education of the boy, whom he called Victor. He believed Victor's apparent subnormality was not due to incurable mental disease or idiocy, but to the lack of participation in normal human society. Itard's account of Victor's education makes fascinating reading. Beyond that, it emphasizes that the human potential can be realized only within the structure of human culture and through growing up in close contact with other human beings. Without the constraints imposed by a specific culture, we are not more free, but rather totally unfree, in that none of our human qualities and abilities can develop.

Cultural Patterning of "Reality"

The ways in which human beings perceive both the physical and the social environment, what they believe to be true about the environment, and how they organize their responses to it are all patterned by culture. Culture is a "codification of reality," a system of meaning that transforms physical reality, what is *there*, into experienced reality. Dorothy Lee (1959), an anthropologist interested in the different ways peoples see themselves and their environments, described her perception of reality as she looked out the window of her house: "I see trees, some of which I like to be there, and some of which I intend to cut down to keep them from encroaching further upon the small clearing I made for my house" (p. 1). She then described the perception of the Dakota Indian, Black Elk, who "saw trees as having rights to the land, equal to his own . . . standing peoples, in whom the winged ones built their lodges and reared their families" (p. 1).

According to Lee, the conceptual frameworks of different cultures provide different ways of perceiving the same physical reality. She believes that all culturally patterned views of reality may contain a different facet of the same truth. These culturally different conceptions of reality also shape our perception of the relationship we have with the natural environment. Thus, continues Lee, "the breaking of the soil in the agricultural process may be an act of violence, of personal aggression, of mastery, of exploitation, of self-fulfillment; or it may be an act of tender fostering, of involvement in the processes of the earth, of helping the land to bring forth in its due time; it may be an act of worship, and the field an altar" (p. 1). The individual may be seen as the center, the mover and master of nature, as in Western culture. Or the person may be seen as in harmony with nature, simply actualizing the potential in both animals and inanimate things, as is true among many native American peoples.

Not only the perceptions of reality but also the ways of proving those perceptions to be "real" are culturally patterned. In many cultures, inner experience can be enough. In Western culture, validation consists of "proof," evidence that can hold up under repeated and objective investigations. The contrasts between these two systems are nicely illustrated in the fictionalized account of an exchange between Carlos Castaneda, writing as a Western-trained anthropologist, and Don Juan, a character modeled on a "sorcerer," or "man of power," among

Among Zen Buddhists, the inner experiencing of reality is achieved through meditation. (Sheldon Brody)

the Yaqui Indians of northern Mexico. Castaneda has been learning Don Juan's "power," which includes the ability to transform himself into various animals. One day Don Juan says that under his commands Castaneda will be transformed into a crow. These are Castaneda's words about the experience:

> I had no difficulty eliciting the corresponding sensation to each one of his commands. I had the perception of growing bird's legs, which were weak and wobbly at first. I felt a tail coming out of the back of my neck and wings out of my cheekbones. The wings were folded deeply. I felt them coming by degrees. The process was hard but not painful. Then I winked my head down to the size of a crow. But the most astonishing effect was accomplished by my bird's eyes. My bird's sight! When Don Juan directed me to grow a beak, I had an annoying sensation of lack of air. Then something bulged out and created a block in front of me. . . . I remember I extended my wings and

flew. I felt alone, cutting through the air, painfully moving straight ahead . . . the last scene I remembered was three silvery birds. . . . I liked them. We flew together.*

A few days after this experience, Castaneda asks Don Juan "the unavoidable question: did I really become a crow?" And what we mean in Western culture by "really" is explained in Castaneda's next question: "I mean would anyone seeing me have thought I was an ordinary crow?" (pp. 172–73). Modern science, which is the core of the Western validation of reality, teaches us to distrust our inner experience as a source of knowledge. We frequently label people whose inner experiences seem "real" as abnormal if those experiences do not match our own culturally patterned definitions of reality.

---

*Carlos Castaneda, *The Teachings of Don Juan: A Yaqui Way of Knowledge.* Berkeley: University of California Press, 1968, pp. 122–24. Reprinted by permission.

Cultural Patterning of Time

In his book *The Silent Language* (1959), the anthropologist Edward Hall presented the theory that perceptions of time and space are different in different cultures and that these perceptions are culturally patterned. Hall called these dimensions of culture "out of awareness," because most people are not conscious of having learned them. In one sense, of course, many aspects of culture are out of awareness. Perceptions of time and space, however, are among the most ingrained of culturally patterned behaviors.

"Time is human; nature knows only change." Telling time is a strictly human invention. Although all cultures have some system of keeping time, in Western industrial societies, time is kept track of in what seems to other peoples an almost ridiculous fashion. We calculate not only the seasons but also the years, months, weeks, days, hours, minutes, seconds, and even thousandths of a second. We are very concerned in the United States with being *on time*; we don't like to *waste time* by having to wait for someone who is late, and we like to *spend time* wisely by keeping busy. All this sounds natural to a North American. In fact, we think, how could it be otherwise? It is difficult for us not to get irritated by the seeming carelessness about time in other cultures, where individuals frequently turn up an hour or more late for an appointment. But "being late" is at least within our cultural framework. How can we begin to enter the cultural world of the Sioux Indians, where there is no word for "late" or for "waiting"? The fact is, of course, we have not had to enter the Sioux culture, but the Sioux have had to enter ours! It is only when we participate in other cultures, on their terms, that we begin to see the cultural patterning of time.

North Americans have a sense of time that is oriented toward the future — not an infinite future, but the foreseeable future. We look back at the past only to measure how far we have come in the present, and we look at the present as a stepping-stone to future accomplishments. The Navajo, in contrast, look skeptically at the promise of benefits in even the foreseeable future. The future among Hindus is conceived of in terms of more than a lifetime; it extends infinitely through many births and rebirths.

Cultural Patterning of Space

Like time, space is organized somewhat differently according to different cultural patterns. Because North Americans are taught to perceive and react to the arrangement of objects, we think of space as "empty." The Japanese, however, are trained to give meaning to spaces. Their perception of shape and arrangement of what is to us emptiness appears in many aspects of Japanese life. There seems to be a similarity between culturally patterned perceptions of time and space. Just as North Americans think of time as being "wasted" unless one is doing something, so we think of space as wasted if it is not filled up with objects.

The cultural patterning of space can be seen in the arrangements of urban space in different cultures. In the United States, most of our cities are laid out along a grid, with the axes generally north-south and east-west. Streets are numbered in order, and buildings are numbered the same way. This arrangement makes perfect sense to us. A city like Paris, which is laid out with the main streets radiating from centers, can be confusing for those who are used to the grid pattern. We tend to "get lost" easily, because walking a relatively short distance in the wrong direction leads us much farther from where we want to go than is true with a grid system. Hall suggests that the layout of space that is characteristic of French cities is only one aspect of the theme of centralization that permeates French culture. Paris is the center of France, French government and educational systems are highly centralized, and in French offices the most important person has the desk in the middle of the office.

Another aspect of cultural patterning of space has to do with the functions of spaces. In

The design of space reflects the culturally patterned need for personal space, which varies in different societies. (United Nations)

middle-class America, we have particular spaces for particular activities. Any intrusion of one activity into a space it was not designed for is immediately felt to be inappropriate. In Japan, this is not the case. Walls are movable, and rooms are used for one purpose during the day and another in the evening and at night. In India, there is yet another culturally patterned use of space. Space in India, both in public and private places, is connected with concepts of superiority and inferiority. In Indian cities and villages, and even within the home, certain spaces are designated as polluted or inferior because of the activities that take place there and the kinds of people who use them. Spaces are segregated so that high caste and low caste,

male and female, sacred and secular activities are kept apart. Archeological evidence uncovered in ancient Indian cities indicates that this pattern may be thousands of years old. It is remarkably persistent even in modern India, where Western influence is strong. Ruth Freed, for example, found this in her study of Chandigarh, a city in North India (1977).

Chandigarh is a modern city designed by the French architect Le Corbusier. Its apartments were built according to European concepts, and the Indians living there found certain aspects of the design inconsistent with their previous use of living space. Freed found that Indian families modified their apartments in a number of ways. Curtains were put up so that men's and women's spaces would be separate. The families also continued to eat in the kitchen, a traditional pattern, and the living room–dining room was used only when Western guests were present. Traditional village living takes place in an area surrounded by a wall. The courtyard gives privacy to each residence group. Chandigarh apartments were built with large windows, reflecting the European desire for light and sun. Many families pasted paper over these windows to re-create the privacy of the traditional courtyard. Freed suggests that the traditional Indian patterns of space use may represent an adaptation to a densely populated environment.

In different cultures, people seem to need different amounts of what Hall calls "personal space." North Americans, for example, seem to require more distance between themselves and others in order to feel comfortable. People from the Arab countries and Latin America appear to want to stand closer to each other than is true for North Americans and people from northern Europe. Whatever the reasons for the different experiences peoples have with space and time, these "out of awareness" cultural patterns are often a source of personal conflict and mutually negative stereotyping.

Cultural Patterning of Perception and Cognition

Cognition refers to the ways in which human beings perceive, understand, and organize their responses to the environment. Interest in the relationships among culture, perception, and cognition has a long history in anthropology. Because they relied on the reports of travelers and missionaries, early scholars were mainly concerned with the *differences* in perception and thought between Europeans and the non-Western peoples they encountered. Some of these scholars attributed the differences to

innate differences in mental processes. They characterized non-Western peoples as mentally deficient, childlike, incapable of abstract thinking, lacking ideas of causality, and unable to differentiate between reality and fantasy. By the turn of the twentieth century, however, anthropologists were arguing that there was a basic similarity in both cognitive and perceptual processes among all human groups.

It is generally taken for granted in modern cross-cultural research on perception, for example, that the uniformities outweigh whatever differences may be found. Given the common experiences with the physical world shared by all peoples, a strong case can be made that physically normal adults in every human society have the same fundamental perceptual abilities: They can recognize familiar objects under varied conditions (object constancy), have depth perception, and have an ability to coordinate information from several sensory sources (intersensory integration) (Munroe and Munroe 1977:64). The most influential contemporary anthropologists and cross-cultural psychologists also hold there is no evidence that different reasoning processes are characteristic of different cultures. That is, there is no evidence for a "primitive" mentality or logic.

As Michael Cole points out in his excellent survey of cross-cultural psychology, the thinking of Don Juan, the Yaqui sorcerer, seems quite different from our own style of thought. Yet in his interpersonal relations, Don Juan demonstrates problem-solving techniques "compelling enough" to greatly influence Castaneda (the anthropologist trained in Western scientific thinking) (Cole and Scribner 1974:169). Cole and the other contemporary anthropologists who believe that basic thinking processes are the same among all humankind emphasize that all peoples employ logic and are concerned with the relationship of cause and effect; furthermore, all classification systems are arrived at by the same processes of abstraction and generalization. It is the content of culture — values, beliefs, and the ways of classifying the world — that differs among different human groups.

Culture and Perception

Research in anthropology and the new field of cross-cultural psychology has shown interesting *differences*, as well as the basic similarities, in specific perceptual and cognitive abilities. One area of research has been on visual perception. Differences among cultures have been found for color differentiation, susceptibility to optical illusions, and pictorial depth perception. A cultural-ecological explanation of the extreme susceptibility of the Arunta of Australia to the illusion in Figure 4.1, for example, relates this to their physical environment. The Arunta live in flat, open desert, and they see great stretches of desert that, on the retina, would be projected as foreshortened planes but that they would learn to interpret as lengthier planes extending into space. Shown Figure 4.1, a person from this environment would tend to perceive the vertical line as representing a plane extending along the line of vision and would therefore perceive it as longer than the horizontal line (Munroe and Munroe 1977). Peoples who do not live in environments with a great deal of vast, open space are less susceptible to this illusion.

Performance on tests of spatial ability (see Figure 4.2) also shows great variation among cultures. Spatial ability means an ability to sort out the different components in an environment, to separate an element from its context, and to locate oneself accurately in relation to environmental features. A number of studies confirm the hypothesis that cultural patterning, particularly ecology and child-rearing practices, has an important impact on the development of spatial-perception abilities (Berry 1974). (See the accompanying box.)

Figure 4.3 illustrates the relationship among ecology, culture, socialization, and individual perceptual and cognitive skills. The figure suggests that the environment is the basic factor in human existence. Culture and child-rearing practices (socialization) are ways in which humans adapt to their environment. Nutrition and disease are also affected by ecology; in these two areas there is an overlap of cultural

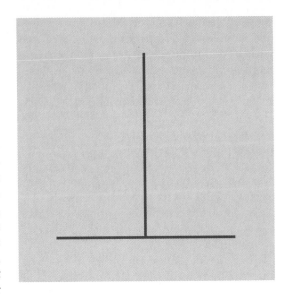

FIGURE 4.1 The horizontal-vertical illusion. Although both lines are the same length, the vertical line appears longer to individuals susceptible to the illusion. Members of some cultures, such as the Arunta of Australia, appear to be extremely susceptible to this illusion; Westerners are moderately susceptible. It has been suggested that susceptibility to this illusion is related to the degree of open space characteristic of particular environments, such as the Australian desert in which the Arunta live.

and biological factors. There are also different gene frequencies for human populations in different environments. All these factors—cultural patterns, including child rearing, what people eat, and what diseases they are subject to, and the specific gene-pool characteristics of their population—influence the perceptual, personality, and adaptive characteristics of the individual. The schematic diagram in Figure 4.3 only begins to suggest the complicated nature of the interaction of culture and biology, group and individual history, in the mental and behavioral outcomes characteristic of any particular individual.

In addition to increasing our understanding of the relationship between the ecological demands placed on a society, various aspects of culture, and the development of specific perceptual and cognitive abilities, Berry's study has a

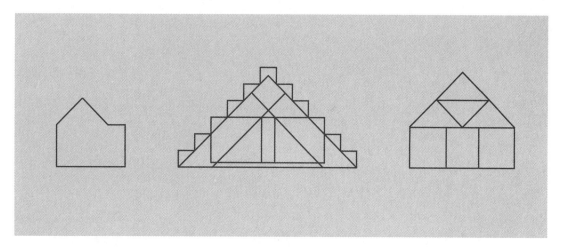

FIGURE 4.2 Items from the Embedded Figures Test. The simple figure on the left is located in each of the other two figures. This test is one measure of spatial perception, and the results appear to differ among different cultures. (From H. A. Witkin, "Individual Differences in Ease of Perception of Embedded Figures," *Journal of Personality*, Volume 19, September 1950–June 1951, pp. 1–15. Copyright 1950 by Duke University Press. Renewed December 1977. Reprinted by permission.)

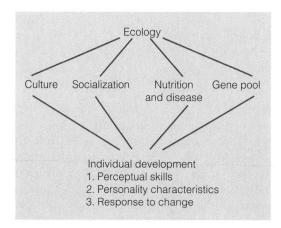

FIGURE 4.3 Individual development in its relationship to ecological and other factors, both biological and cultural. (Berry 1974)

more general relevance. When we see the tiny differences in test scores between the Scottish and the Inuit sample populations, as well as the significant differences between the scores of the traditional and the more urbanized populations *within* each culture, racial factors cannot explain perceptual and cognitive variations. Furthermore, the differences in performance between the Inuit and the African Temne, as well as among other non-Western peoples who have been tested, would seem to finish once and for all any notion of a "primitive mentality."

Culture and Cognition

Cognitive competence, or **intelligence**, consists of many capacities, skills, and adaptive responses to the environment. In our own society, we see intelligence as a particular way of solving problems that involves the ability to abstract, analyze, and reintegrate data into new patterns. This analytic cognitive style is at one end of a continuum; a global cognitive style is at the other. On tests, an individual with the global cognitive style has more trouble separating the different elements in a pattern, taking them from their context, and recombining them in novel ways. Although the analytic cognitive style appears to develop with age, there is some empirical research that shows the

The undifferentiated landscape of the snow-covered Arctic is an important factor in the high degree of visual discrimination found among some Inuit populations. (United Nations/Canadian Government Travel Bureau)

important ways in which culture patterns cognitive skills and style (Witkin 1974). As the accompanying material on the Temne and the Inuit indicates, different perceptual-cognitive skills appear to be adaptive in different ecological situations. One style is not superior to another but rather is more suitable in different environments and life situations. The value of the *analytic* style in our society has an obvious relationship to formal education, the specialized nature of industrial technology, and the rise of scientific thought as a way of understanding the world.

Cross-cultural research is only now beginning to shed some light on the relationship between many different cognitive skills and the cultural patterns and ecological settings in which they exist. It appears, for example, that child-care patterns encouraging freedom and

separation of the child from the family tend to be correlated with, and are assumed in some way to produce, a more analytic style. The high scores achieved by the Tiv, an African people, on Western intelligence tests emphasize the importance of a cultural explanation of intelligence as this applies to human populations. The Tiv, a nonliterate people, stand out in sub-Saharan Africa for their child-rearing patterns. Most other African peoples (like the Temne) teach respect for authority and obedience to elders. The Tiv put less pressure for obedience (vis-à-vis assertiveness) on children. Tiv children also stand out for the extent to which they have spontaneously and enthusiastically participated in intelligence-testing experiences.

The mainstream of anthropology and cross-cultural psychology tries to show that understandings of the universe and of relationships

A comparison of two groups — the Temne, a horticultural tribe of Sierra Leone in Africa, and a group of Inuit from Baffin Island who depend on hunting for their food supply — shows the influence of culture on perception. The Temne score relatively low on tests of spatial ability and differentiation. The Inuit score extremely high, coming very close to a sample of Scottish subjects, which provided a Western population for comparison with these two non-Western groups. The explanation of these test scores is provided by comparing the cultural ecology of the Temne with that of the Inuit.

The physical environment of the Temne is highly differentiated; it is full of colorful vegetation and is naturally structured. The Temne, as farmers, are not very mobile; they tend to "stay put" on their land. Given this particular ecological relationship, it is not necessary to develop spatial discrimination skills. The Inuit are in a completely different position. Their physical environment consists of "endless, uniform snowfields"; theirs is a highly undifferentiated environment. Furthermore, hunting requires the Inuit to travel widely. In this situation, the Inuit need spatial perceptual skills to find their way. They must be aware of minute details in the physical environment and be able to locate themselves in relation to objects around them. These perceptual skills are obviously related to survival among the Inuit.

The Temne and the Inuit have very different child-rearing patterns. Temne parents try to enforce strict discipline through physical punishment, and there is an emphasis on conformity to adult authority.

The Temne mother plays an extremely dominant role in raising the children, and a child is not encouraged to take on adult roles or responsibility. This kind of child rearing is associated with a *field dependent* perceptual-cognitive style, one aspect of which is a less well developed ability in spatial awareness and visual discrimination. Among the Inuit, on the other hand, punishment of children is generally avoided, and the child is given a lot of freedom. Self-reliance, individualism, individual skill development, and curiosity and ingenuity are encouraged. This child-rearing pattern is correlated with a generally high degree of differentiation and leads to a *field independent* perceptual-cognitive style, which in turn is correlated with a high degree of spatial awareness and visual discrimination.

The differences between the two groups in their arts and crafts are also related to their different perceptual skills. The arts and crafts of the Inuit are known for skill in design and execution. Those of the Temne are considered to be of relatively poor quality and tend to be produced by a few specialists in the society. A high quality of arts and crafts engaged in by the general population promotes the early learning of spatial manipulation and discrimination of detail and is positively related to spatial perceptual competence. In language, too, the contrast between the Temne and the Inuit shows the influence of culture on perception. The Temne language contains relatively few terms that express geometrical-spatial concepts, whereas the Inuit language contains many (Berry 1974).

within the universe are learned and do not reflect any innate or biologically inherited differences in intelligence among human groups. No matter what the differences in the ways in which different peoples perform on "intelligence" tests, all human groups studied demonstrate the capacity to remember, generalize, operate with abstractions, form concepts, and reason logically.

Intelligence tests do *not* provide valid information on innate differences in mental capacities among human groups. They *do* predict well the academic success of different groups, which is what they are designed to do. Intelligence tests measure the specific ability to perceive relationships using abstract symbolic material: numbers, forms, spatial relationships, and word meanings. This is just one culturally patterned way of understanding the world. It is because the culture on which intelligence tests are based is the same as the cultural understandings required in the middle-class American school that the tests can predict academic success (Alland 1972:177).

Not only do standard intelligence tests measure just one "codification of reality"; they also measure it in a context that is not equally meaningful for different groups in our society. For middle-class children, who have some reason to believe that their performance on tests is related to success in later life, the motivation for taking them is obviously higher than for children who believe that their fate is sealed by race or ethnicity, no matter how well they may do on a test. The effects of motivation, sophistication in taking tests, and culturally different attitudes toward testing must all be taken into account in interpreting the intelligence test scores of different groups of people.

Doing What Comes Naturally?

The importance of cultural patterning is not easy to understand, particularly in areas of action and emotional response that we assume to be "natural" — sex, eating, feeling, and expressing certain emotions and attitudes. Natural, in the case of every society, is natural according to its own beliefs and customs. In the next section, we examine some of the ways in which basic human behavior patterns and responses are influenced and shaped by culture.

Cultural Patterning and Emotions

The range and quality of human emotions are potentially the same for all human groups. It is in the course of growing up in a particular culture that the range narrows and becomes shaped to a pattern. Fear, love, anger, hostility, shame, guilt, grief, joy, and indifference become channeled by culture so that they appear in different situations, are directed toward different objects and persons, or hardly appear at all. Each culture selects, elaborates, and emphasizes certain emotional possibilities and defines certain feelings about oneself, others, and the world as appropriate or not. This is communicated in direct and indirect ways. A boy who learns not to cry may have been told that "crying is only for girls." He is also surrounded by males who do not cry. Both experiences help pattern his inner responses to situations.

Because human emotions have an "inner" reality, they are felt to be "natural." Drawing on our own experience, we consider it natural for a mother to love her child, for an individual to be jealous of another's success, or for people to be sad when someone dies. The seeming naturalness of human emotions leads us to see them as causes for certain kinds of behavior. War is then explained by humankind's natural aggression, marriage is viewed as the result of love, motherhood is seen as an expression of the maternal instinct, and free-enterprise capitalism is considered the inevitable expression of a natural desire to get ahead in the world. In all this, we have lost sight of the role of culture and its tremendous impact on the human psyche. We project emotions that we have been trained to feel onto peoples in other cultures. We consider our own emotional responses

The flexibility of certain features of the human face, particularly the mouth, means that humans can express a wide variety of emotions in facial expression. Although some of these expressions, such as the smile, which expresses happiness, are considered to be universally human, culture also has a powerful influence on just when and how such emotions are expressed. (Serena Nanda)

"natural" and responses that differ from ours "unnatural."

It becomes hard for us to understand cultures in which several women married to the same man are not jealous of one another or cultures in which mothers neglect their children's health, permit them to die, or even kill them. Every culture sets up expectations not only about how people are supposed to behave but also about how they should feel in different situations. In our own culture, we are taught that it is not good to "carry a grudge," to store up anger or hatred against a person who has hurt us. In cultures where the blood feud exists, not only are people allowed to feel the desire for revenge, but also their very honor will depend on it. A man who does not avenge a hurt loses face for himself and his whole group of kin.

The expression of emotions in body or facial movement is also of interest to anthropol-

ogists, particularly because such expressions are important ways of communicating. A basic issue here is whether there are universal ways of communicating. Evidence that there is a cross-cultural universality in the facial expressions used to convey happiness, surprise, fear, anger, disgust, and sadness raises the issue of whether these expressions may have a biological basis (Ekman 1977). At the same time, it is equally clear that culture and experience have a strong effect on the shaping of facial expression, just as they do on bodily movement. Some emotions, like contempt, seem to have culturally specific facial movements. In other cases, the importance of masking emotions will affect all facial movement in the presence of other people. Where people are taught to be polite and sensitive to the feelings of others, as in Japan, this will affect the facial movements used in the presence of others. In the same situation, Japanese smile more, for example, than Americans do.

The Cultural Patterning of Selfishness and Aggression

One of the characteristic responses of individuals in North American society is to "look out for number one." John Whiting and Beatrice Whiting (1973) studied this "egoistic" attitude in a number of different cultures. They contrasted egoistic behavior, in which the self was the primary beneficiary of interaction, with altruistic behavior, in which another person benefited more. Through carefully controlled observations and comparisons of children, they found that in those cultures where women contributed importantly to the economy and younger children were therefore depended on to help with domestic chores, particularly taking care of a younger sibling, altruistic behavior was more frequent than egoistic behavior. It should not surprise us to discover that the culture rated highest on egoistic behavior was Orchard Town, U.S.A. In Chapter 6, we will study more specifically the ways in which early socialization is related to the development of group-oriented versus individualistic kinds of behavior.

Related to the view in the United States that selfishness is part of "human nature" is the tendency to see aggression as an innate and "natural" human predisposition. The idea that the human species has an aggressive "instinct" most often comes up in connection with warfare. Given the frequency of war throughout human history, it would seem to make sense to believe that humankind has an aggressive, warlike nature. If we examine the matter carefully, however, it can be shown that this theory does not hold up. War is between societies, not between individuals. Many (perhaps most) of the individuals who fight in wars are not there because they are aggressive, but because their society insists that they participate. Furthermore, the degree to which propaganda is used in modern warfare indicates that aggression must be evoked by culturally appropriate means against a culturally approved enemy.

It is true that human beings are among the few animal groups not provided with a biological mechanism that inhibits killing a member of the same species. Humans thus have the potential for intraspecific lethal aggression, and there is no denying that it has frequently been used. Biological interpretations of human aggression are attractive to us because they seem to explain in a simple manner much of the behavior found in Western society. But this kind of explanation fails to take into account the importance of cultural patterning, which can be observed only by looking at the total variety of human cultures.

There are some cultures in which there is little or no organized aggression and in which aggressive behavior by individuals is severely condemned and may almost be nonexistent. One such culture is that of the Semai of the Malay Peninsula (Dentan 1968). The Semai are slash-and-burn agriculturalists who have only recently given up a dependence on a hunting and gathering existence. Under the pressure of the dominant Malays, the Semai have retreated to the hills and mountains of central Malaysia. They consider themselves, and are considered by others, a nonviolent people. They believe that anger is a bad thing, and the ethnographer observed that they rarely do get angry. Semai life is not without conflict, however, and it is usually over the sexual favors of women. When an individual is offended by another, the Semai believe, the offended person will become prone to an accident if he or she stays angry. Thus, one reason that Semai do not want to become angry is that in their culture it is the angry man who gets hurt. If a man feels himself offended by another, he can ask for compensation for his distress. If the offender admits the offense, he will pay the compensation. If not, hostility simmers, leading at the very most to insults and the spreading of rumors. No murder has ever been recorded in Semai society.

The Semai are very gentle, even with animals. A man will not kill an animal he has raised himself, but exchanges it with someone in another village, knowing that it will be killed but not wanting to do it himself. Even under the pressure of military action by the Malayan government during the 1950s, in which some Semai were involved, their nonviolent cultural values prevailed for the most part. Even those Semai who participated in this guerrilla warfare went back to their basically nonaggressive way of life when they returned to their villages. Ethnographic data on the Semai (see Robarchek and Dentan 1987) clearly demonstrate that not only is Semai culture nonviolent but also that nonaggressiveness is an internalized ideal for men and an important component of their self-image.

The variability in the amount, expression, and direction of aggression within human societies testifies to the importance of cultural patterning. In societies in which warfare is a highly valued cultural pattern, males will be taught to be more aggressive than those in cultures in which warfare is absent. Warfare itself does not exist in all societies, and its presence and the form it takes are best explained in terms of ecology and history. Only in specific situa-

The influence of genes on sex roles is a question being intensely discussed in contemporary anthropology. Is the self-sacrificing behavior that human beings often show toward their close kin genetically determined or learned through participation in a sociocultural system? (United Nations)

tions does the human potential for aggression become mobilized in warfare.

A recent study that demonstrates the importance of understanding human emotions in their cultural context is the work of Nancy Scheper-Hughes on what she calls the "lifeboat ethics" of mother love in a region of northeastern Brazil. This area is extremely poor with a very high rate of infant and child mortality. Children are most often raised in single-parent families, where mothers must frequently work, mostly as low-paid laborers on sugar plantations or as domestics in the homes of the rich. In both cases, they are not permitted to bring their children with them to work, and, with their earnings of about a dollar a day, they cannot afford to hire caretakers for their small children. While older children may sometimes watch younger ones, any child of school age who is not in school is expected to be earning some money. In most cases, then, when mothers work, babies are left at home alone.

The subject of Scheper-Hughes's study was the seeming indifference of these mothers to the deaths of their infants. This indifference was articulated as an aversion of the baby to living, making the death seem natural, even anticipated. The high expectancy of infant death, and the ability to face child death stoically, led to a pattern of nurturing that divided infants into those who would thrive and those who were born "wanting to die." The "survivors" were nurtured, while the others were neglected, and the death of these infants was seen as letting nature take its course.

The phenomenon of infant deaths considered inevitable is classified by mothers as "child sickness" or "child attack." This quality is recognized in children who are born small, wasted, weak, and passive. They do not demonstrate any vital force or liveliness. They do not suck vigorously or even cry, and they demonstrate no resistance to diarrhea, respiratory infections, tropical fevers, and other common illnesses of infancy. If these infants develop acute symptoms such as convulsions, they are left alone to die, because it is believed there is absolutely no hope for them. Others die at home, sometimes alone, even before they manifest the symptoms of terminal malnutrition and dehydration.

In this area of Brazil, part of learning how to be a mother is learning when to let go of a child who shows that it "wants" to die by having no "taste" for life, and also learning when it is safe to let oneself love a child. Scheper-Hughes says, "In the absence of firm expectation that a child will survive, mother love as we conceptualize it is attenuated and delayed," resulting in the neglect of already weak infants (1989:33). Thus, the emotional detachment of mothers contributes even further to the high infant mortality rate.

Other cultural patterns provide a context within which this spiral of child neglect and child mortality occurs. The mothers are often very devout Catholics, and allowing "nature to take its course" in child death is seen as cooperating with God's plan, rather than as a sin. The child is believed to become an angel, flying up to a heavenly home. The infant is buried with little ceremony, and no tears. Mothers are told that if they cry, their tears will dampen the little angel's wings so that she or he cannot fly to heaven. Indeed, a mother who cries is thought to be mad, or to demonstrate a profound lack of faith. Other demonstrations of grief are also absent. The graves of infants are not marked and never visited by mothers. They are soon used for other dead infants and the grave quickly becomes anonymous.

This pattern of selective neglect is not limited to this poverty-stricken region of northeastern Brazil, but is found in many societies with a high childhood mortality rate and a high fertility rate. In these cultures, maternal care is organized primarily around survival. It results in a pragmatic recognition that not all of one's children can be expected to live, and that delayed attachment of mother to infant and casual neglect "weed out" the weakest infants so

as to enhance the life chances of healthier siblings and future children. These patterns of child neglect, even unto death, may seem very cruel in the affluent segments of a society in which it is anticipated that all children will live. But, as Scheper-Hughes points out, where there is high child mortality, maternal indifference to some infants may be the most pragmatic survival strategy. Rather than be seen as inhuman and unnatural, the "lifeboat ethic" of mothering can be interpreted as a rational cultural pattern under desperate economic conditions, demonstrating once again the importance of understanding human behavior in its total cultural context.

Sex and Gender

Sex refers to the *biological* differences between male and female, particularly the visible differences in external genitalia and the related difference in the role each sex plays in the reproductive process. **Gender** refers to the *social* classification of masculine and feminine. Every society gives cultural recognition to the sexual division of the species into male and female, but cultures differ in what they consider masculine and feminine. Some male/female differences in behavior appear to be very widespread, however (D'Andrade 1974). Males, for example, have been observed to be more likely to initiate activity than females in various cultures. Females have also been observed to be more altruistic than males.

An important study on the question of whether the characteristics defined as "feminine" in Western culture were universal was carried out by Margaret Mead in New Guinea (1963). Mead studied three different cultures and found that male and female roles and masculine and feminine temperament were patterned differently in each culture. Among the Arapesh, both men and women were expected to act in ways we in the United States consider "naturally" feminine. Both sexes were concerned with taking care of children and with nurturing generally. Neither sex was expected to be aggressive. In the second culture, the Mundugamor, both sexes were what we would call "masculine" — aggressive, violent, and with little interest in children. In the third society, the Tchambuli, the personalities of males and females were different from each other but opposite to our own conceptions of masculine and feminine. Women had the major economic role, showed "common sense" and business shrewdness, and carried out the mundane tasks. Men were interested in esthetics. They spent much time decorating themselves and gossiping. They also had their feelings easily hurt and sulked a lot.

Mead's study showed that the whole repertoire of behavior, emotions, and interests that go into being masculine and feminine are patterned by culture. In the process of growing up, each child learns hundreds of culturally patterned details of behavior that become incorporated into her or his gender identity. In addition to all the direct instructions about being masculine or feminine that every culture imparts, culture unconsciously affects masculinity and femininity by providing different images, aspirations, and adult role models for girls and boys. In assessing the idea that biology determines gender, anthropologists have pointed to the great variability in human societies regarding the behavior, temperaments, and roles of women and men. As always, the anthropologist attempts to deal with the question of the relation of biology to culture by looking outside our own Western traditions, for it is only in this way that we can grasp the variety in human life. What we see is that whatever biological dispositions may be characteristic of one sex or the other, these are responsive to a tremendously wide range of cultural patterning.

Not only are the gender roles of masculine and feminine different in different cultures, but the number and kinds of genders may also differ cross-culturally. Unlike the United States and other Western cultures, many non-Western cultures have had culturally institutionalized roles for people who do not conform to either

The Indians of the North American Plains allowed more variation in gender identity than is true in the United States. The role of the berdache allowed men who did not find the Plains warrior ideal congenial to wear women's clothing and perform women's tasks. This male Crow Indian, "Finds-Them-and-Kills-Them," takes on the female role. (Courtesy of Museum of the American Indian, Heye Foundation)

the male or the female gender role. One such role, the hijra of India, is described in the accompanying ethnography. Among many native American cultures, similar roles existed; sometimes there were three or even more gender roles — women, men, and those who were born of one sex but who wished to live as members of the other sex. Among the Plains Indians, the berdache was a man who dressed in women's clothing, took on women's tasks, and was often considered to have special supernatural powers and privileges in society (Whitehead 1981).

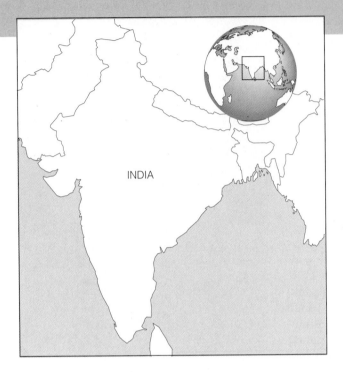

INDIA

Nothing seems more natural, unchangeable, or desirable to us than that human beings are divided without remainder into two biological sexes, male and female, and into two genders, masculine and feminine. This division of humans into two sexes takes place at birth, when sex assignment is made; such sex assignment is assumed to be permanent. The concept of sex and gender as a system of two opposing and nonchangeable categories — male and female; masculine and feminine — is so strong that it is taken for granted by both common sense and most social science. It is difficult for most of us to even think about any alternative to this view of sex and gender.

And yet, a cross-cultural perspective indicates that some cultures include more than two genders. Such alternative, or third, gender roles, which are neither man nor woman, have been described among the Omanis of the Saudi Arabian peninsula (Wikan 1977); among many native American tribes (Williams 1986); in Tahiti (Levy 1973); and in New Guinea and the Dominican Republic (Herdt 1993). I have done fieldwork among one such group in India, called the hijras.

The hijras are viewed as "neither man nor woman." They are born as men, but they dress and live as women. The hijras undergo an operation in which their genitals are surgically removed, but unlike transsexuals in our own culture, this operation turns men into hijras, not into women. Hijras are followers of a Hindu goddess, Bahuchara Mata, and the hijra subculture is partly a religious cult centered on the worship of this goddess. By dressing as women, and especially by having the emasculation operation, which is a ritual expression of their devotion to Bahuchara Mata, the hijras attempt to completely identify with the goddess. Through this operation, the hijras believe that the procreative powers of the goddess are transferred to them.

Traditionally, the hijras earn their living by performing at life-cycle ceremonies, such as the birth of a child — formerly, only for male children, who are much desired in India, but today, sometimes for female children as well — and at marriages, and they also serve the goddess in her temple. It is because the

Hijras performing at a marriage. Note their feminine dress, hairstyles, and gestures. (Serena Nanda)

hijras are vehicles of the goddess' powers of procreation that their presence is necessary on these occasions, when they ask the goddess to bless the newborn or the married couple with prosperity and fertility.

The word *hijra* may be translated as either eunuch or hermaphrodite; in both cases, male sexual impotence is emphasized. In fact, few hijras are born hermaphrodites, and as there are many causes for male impotence, there are many reasons that men may choose to join the hijras. In some parts of India, there is a belief that an impotent man who does not become a hijra, in deference to the wishes of the hijra goddess, will be reborn impotent for seven future lives.

The concept of the hijra as neither man nor woman emphasizes that they are not men because they cannot function sexually as men, though they were assigned to the male sex at birth. Hijras also claim that they do not have sexual

(continued)

feelings for women, and a real hijra is not supposed to have ever had sexual relations with women.

But if hijras, as a third gender, are "man minus man" they are also "man plus woman." The most obvious aspect of hijras as women is in their dress. Wearing female attire is a defining characteristic of hijras. It is required that they be dressed as women when they perform their traditional roles of singing and dancing at births and weddings and whenever they are in the temple of their goddess. Hijras enjoy dressing as women, and their feminine dress is accompanied by traditionally feminine jewelry and body decoration. Hijras must also wear their hair long like women.

Hijras also adopt female behavior: They imitate a woman's walk, they sit and stand like women, and they carry pots on their hips, as women do. Hijras have female names, which they adopt when they join the community, and they use female kinship terms for each other such as "aunty" or "sister." They also have a special linguistic dialect, which includes feminine expressions and intonations. In public accommodations, such as the movies, or in buses and trains, hijras often request "ladies only" seating. They also request that they be counted as females in the census.

But, although hijras are like women in the ways just described, they are clearly not women. Their female dress and mannerisms are often exaggerations, almost to the point of caricature, especially when they act in a sexually suggestive manner. Their sexual aggressiveness is considered outrageous and very much in opposition to the expected demure behavior of ordinary Indian women in their roles of wives, mothers, and daughters. Hijra performances are essentially burlesques of women, and the entertainment value comes from the difference between themselves, acting as women, and the real women they imitate. Hijras often use obscene and abusive language, which again is considered contrary to acceptable feminine behavior. In some parts of India, hijras smoke the hookah (water pipe) and cigarettes, which is normally done only by men.

Sexual Practices

The cultural component in sexual habits is not easily understood. Of all the kinds of human behavior, sexual activity is most likely to be viewed as "doing what comes naturally." But a cross-cultural perspective on sexual practices tells us that every aspect of human sexual activity is patterned by culture and influenced by learning.

Culture patterns the habitual responses of different peoples to different parts of the body. What is considered erotic in some cultures evokes indifference or disgust in others. Kissing, for example, is not practiced in many societies. The Tahitians have learned to kiss from

The major reason hijras are considered not women, however, is that they cannot give birth. There are many hijras who wish to be women so that they could give birth, and there are many stories within the community that express this wish. But all hijras acknowledge that this can never be—that is why they are neither man nor woman.

As neither man nor woman, the hijras identify themselves with many figures in Hindu mythology and Indian culture who are also third-gender figures: male deities who change into females temporarily, deities who have both male and female characteristics, religious roles in which male devotees dress and act as women, male historical figures who temporarily take on the disguise of eunuchs, and also the real class of eunuchs who served in the Muslim courts. Unlike our own society, Indian culture not only accommodates such sexually ambiguous and androgynous figures but also views them as meaningful and even powerful. It is in this cultural context that an institutionalized third-gender role like the hijras "makes sense" in India.

The hijras, and the other third-gender roles such as the *xanith* of Oman, the *mahu* of Tahiti, and the North American *berdache*, force us to rethink our own culture's assumption that there are only two sexes and two genders. Knowledge about intermediate, or third, gender roles also calls attention to both the culturally defined criteria of masculine and feminine and the cultural construction of gender categories. Thinking about sex and gender in its cultural context leads to an awareness that there is no one way of "doing what comes naturally."

From Serena Nanda, Neither Man nor Woman: The Hijras of India. *Belmont, Calif.: Wadsworth, 1990.*

the Europeans, but before this culture contact, they began sexual intimacy by sniffing. The patterns of social and sexual preliminaries leading to sexual intercourse also differ among cultures. The Trobriand Islanders, as described by Malinowski, "inspect each other's hair for lice and eat them . . . to the natives a natural and pleasant occupation between two who are fond of each other" (1929:335). This may seem disgusting to us. To the Trobrianders, the European habit of boys and girls going out on a picnic with a knapsack of food is equally disgusting, although it is a perfectly acceptable custom for a Trobriand boy and girl to gather wild foods together as a preliminary to sexual activity.

Who is considered an appropriate sexual partner also differs in different cultures. The common feeling in the United States that homosexual activity is somewhat shameful or abnormal is not shared universally. In some societies, such as that of the Sambia of New Guinea, a period of obligatory homosexual relationships is part of the initiation for every adolescent male, who as an adult is expected to enter a heterosexual marriage (Herdt 1981). In this culture, and in others in the New Guinea Highlands, it is believed that only men can create men, and this process involves a long period during which boys live away from their parents in a men's cult house and engage in homosexual activity as part of their training to be vigorous, strong warriors. In other cultures, such as those in parts of Samoa, homosexual practices almost never occurred until they were introduced by Europeans. In these cultures, homosexuality is seen as an activity that just does not make much sense if members of the opposite sex are around, but there is no concept that it is a sin, a sickness, or a crime, as has been true in much of European history. In Europe and the United States, the attitude toward homosexuality is changing; in 1974, the American Psychiatric Association dropped homosexuality from its list of mental illnesses, and several states have decriminalized homosexual activity between consenting adults. Homosexuality has also been decriminalized in many European countries, and there has been a movement by activist homosexual groups in the United States to ban discrimination on the basis of sexual preference. For many people in the United States, the aim is to have homosexual relationships considered as just another form of sexual activity that should not be labeled deviant and should not be stigmatized by social, political, or economic sanctions.

In addition to these variations in attitudes toward sex in different cultures, there are many other variations. The ages at which sexual response is believed to begin and end, the ways in which the people make themselves attractive to the opposite sex, the importance of sexual activity in human life—all these are patterned and regulated by culture and affect sexual response and behavior. Partly because anthropology grew up in an age in which sexuality was a forbidden topic and partly because of the difficulty of observing sexual activity, ethnographic descriptions often ignore this topic. What information we do have is enough to show the great contrasts in different societies. A comparison of just two cultures, the Irish of the island of Inis Beag and the Polynesians of the island of Mangaia, who are at opposite ends of a continuum regarding sexual behavior, makes clear the role of culture in this area of life.

John Messenger describes Inis Beag as "one of the most sexually naive of the world's societies" (1971:15). Sex is never discussed at home when children are near, and practically no sexual instruction is given by parents to children. Adults express the belief that "after marriage nature takes its course." (As we shall see, "nature" takes a very different course in Inis Beag than it does in Polynesia!) Women are not expected to enjoy sexual relations; they are a "duty" to be endured, for to refuse to have intercourse is considered a mortal sin. There appears to be widespread ignorance in Inis Beag of the ability of females to have an orgasm, which in any case is considered deviant behavior. Nudity is abhorred by the islanders, and there is no tradition of "dirty jokes." The main style of dancing allows little bodily contact among the participants, but even then, some girls refuse to dance because it means touching a boy. The separation of the sexes begins very early in Inis Beag and lasts into adulthood. Other cultural patterns related to sexual repression here are the virtual absence of sexual foreplay, the belief that sexual activity weakens a man, the absence of premarital sex, the high percentage of celibate males, and the extraordinarily late age of marriage. The differences in sexuality between men and women are expressed by a female informant as "men can wait a long time before wanting 'it' but we [women] can wait a lot longer" (p. 16).

Although the belief that total sexual freedom exists in the South Sea islands is a Western myth, the island of Mangaia, as described by

As economic opportunities for women change, so do conceptions of female sexuality. (Jane Hoffer)

Donald Marshall (1971), presents a strong contrast to that of Inis Beag. In this Polynesian culture, sexual intercourse is one of the major interests of life. Although sex is not discussed at home, sexual information is transmitted to boys and girls at puberty by the elders of the group. For adolescent boys, a two-week period of formal instruction about the techniques of intercourse is followed by a culturally approved experience with a mature woman in the village. After this, the boy is considered a man, by himself and by others. This is an interesting point of comparison with Inis Beag, where a man is considered a "lad" until he is about forty.

Sexual relations in Mangaia are carried out privately, but there is continual public reference to sexual activity. Sexual jokes, expressions, and references are not only common but also expected as part of the preliminaries to public meetings. This pattern of public verbal references to sex contrasts with the public separation of the sexes. Boys and girls should not be seen together in public, but practically every girl and boy has had intercourse before marriage. The act of sexual intercourse itself is the focus of sexual activity. What Westerners call sexual foreplay is generally engaged in by Mangaians after, not before, intercourse. In Mangaia both men and women are expected to take pleasure in the sexual act and to have an orgasm. Female frigidity, male celibacy, and homosexuality are practically unknown. So it is not simply that different societies hold different attitudes about sex but also that these attitudes pattern the sexual responsiveness of males and females in that society.

Like any other aspect of culture, beliefs about human sexuality and sexual practices are integrated into a pattern and functionally related to other aspects of the total sociocultural system. In the absence of artificial birth control, for example, beliefs and practices that limit heterosexual intercourse may be adaptive in contributing to population control.

Human behavior is based on customs and values that develop only in the context of specific social and environmental conditions. Although culture is rooted in human biology, it frees humans from strictly biological controls over behavior to a degree far beyond that of any other animal. An understanding of the cultural context of human behavior — the ways in which specific patterns specify and provide the necessary context for the development of biologically based capacities — is critical to an understanding of what it means to be human.

Summary

1. Human capacities and human behavior develop only within a human sociocultural system. Dramatic evidence of this is demonstrated by the nonhuman behavior of children brought up in isolation from other human beings.

2. Culture patterns the ways in which human beings perceive physical reality. Culture also patterns what people believe to be true about their universe.

3. Keeping track of time is a human invention. The passing of time, the sense of past and present, and the way time is used are different in different cultures.

4. Cultural patterning affects the way humans perceive and see relationships in space, the way in which spaces are used, and how much space people feel they need to be comfortable.

5. One of the basic principles of anthropology is that all human groups have the same capacity for intelligent behavior. Intelligence tests do not measure innate mental capacities of different human groups. Standardized intelligence tests given in North American schools are constructed in terms of only one cultural system: that of middle-class North Americans.

6. Because of the tremendous variability in culture, it is difficult to say what human nature consists of. Every society tends to look at its own ways of behaving as not only right but also "natural." The difficulty in isolating the genetic bases of human behavior is that everything human beings do is patterned by the specific culture in which they live.

7. Body and facial movements are patterned by culture, although evidence from recent research also indicates that some facial expressions may be universal.

8. Culture patterns not only the forms of outward behavior but also the inner life of the individual. How people feel and what motivates them to act are part of a conscious and unconscious teaching process that is culturally variable.

9. In the United States, we are taught to "look out for number one." The equation of individual self-preservation with "human nature" is contradicted by the ethnographic evidence from many non-Western societies.

10. Intraspecies aggression is a potential in the human species. Societies vary greatly, however, in the degree to which individuals act aggressively, and some societies have practically no physical aggression. Aggression is not a human instinct but rather a possibility that is patterned differently in different cultures.

11. The great variety in human sexual behavior indicates that culture plays an important role in patterning and regulating sexual drives and responsiveness. In this sense, we may say that human sexual behavior is learned.

12. *Male* and *female* are biological categories. *Masculine* and *feminine* are cultural creations. By looking at cultures outside Western civilization, anthropologists try to understand the relationship between sex (male and female) and gender (masculine and feminine).

Suggested Readings

Bates, Marston
1971   *Gluttons and Libertines: Human Problems of Being Natural*. New York: Random House. An entertaining and informative book by a natural scientist on such topics as food, sex, rebellion, and the pursuit of happiness.

Herdt, Gilbert, ed.
1992   *Gay Culture in America: Essays from the Field*. Boston, Mass.: Beacon Press. A series of articles refocusing attention away from the "causes" of homosexuality to the lives of gay males and the gay cultures in several large American cities.

Lane, Harlan
1977   *The Wild Boy of Aveyron*. New York: Bantam. Based on original documents, this book about a "wild" child raises provocative questions about human nature.

Nanda, Serena
1990   *Neither Man nor Woman: The Hijras of India*. Belmont, Calif.: Wadsworth. An ethnography examining a unique group of men who dress and act like women, the study raises provocative questions about the possibility of alternative gender roles and their relation to other aspects of society and culture.

Scheper-Hughes, Nancy
1993   *Death Without Weeping: The Violence of Everyday Life in Brazil*. Berkeley, Calif.: University of California Press. A compelling, vivid, compassionate account of the lives and survival strategies of women in one of the most desperately poor areas of Brazil.

Language

What are the special characteristics of human language?

How are human languages similar to and different from one another?

How does language shape the ways we perceive the world?

Do we communicate by how we speak as well as what we say?

. . . the first thing I found strange, even bizarre [in America] was the use and abuse of the word "nice," both in formal conversations and in colloquial language. I participated in the following dialogue at a family party on Thanksgiving Day:

"Nice to meet you. What's your name?"

"Francisco."

"Oh, nice! Do you have a family?"

"Yes, I have two children. . . ."

"Very nice! Do you like America?"

"Yes, but . . ."

"That's very nice! Do you like our weather?"

"It's a little cold for me. . . ."

"But today is a nice day! By the way, did you watch the football game last night?"

"I did, but I don't understand American football. . . ."

"Oh, it's a pretty nice sport!"

Some hours later:

"Bye-bye, Francisco. It was nice to meet you. . . . Have a nice stay in the States."

From Francisco Martins Ramos, "My American Glasses," in Distant Mirrors: America as a Foreign Culture, *p. 3, ed. by Philip R. DeVita and James D. Armstrong. Belmont, Calif.: Wadsworth, 1993.*

Communication is the act of transmitting information that influences the behavior of another organism. Interaction in all animal species depends on a consistent set of signals by which individuals convey information. These signals are channeled through visual, olfactory (smell), auditory (sound), and tactile (touch) senses, which are just a few of the many senses humans and animals have. Among animals such as honeybees, the type of information communicated can be complex. Through stereotyped and patterned movements, a scout bee conveys the direction and distance of a field of pollen-bearing flowers to the others. But although bees can "say" a lot about where flowers are, they cannot "say" much about anything else. Animals use sounds as well as movements to communicate, or share, information. Crows caw as a signal of danger, and crickets chirp when they are ready to mate. Among higher animals, especially primates, far greater amounts of information can be transmitted about many more subjects. Although all animal species exchange information related to the basic requirements of survival, only human language, whether spoken, signed, or written, is capable of re-creating complex thought patterns and experiences in words. Without human language, human culture could not exist.

Origins and Development of Human Language

One of the most important aspects of the plasticity of human adaptation is our language capabilities. Like the communication systems of all animals, our language reflects the particular character of our adaptation. Because it is a creative and open system, it is extremely flexible in that it can communicate new ideas and abstract concepts; most other forms of animal communication are restricted to a set number of signals. Language also makes possible the exchange of abstract and highly complex thoughts, which play a crucial role in the maintenance of the many social relationships within human societies. Without language, it would be impossible to socialize children into the intricate workings of their cultures, to teach others how to make anything but very simple tools, or to pass on the traditions, rituals, myths, and religious beliefs that instill a sense of group identity and maintain social order within human societies.

Like all other aspects of cultural and biological evolution, the development of human speech and language was a long, gradual process. The primary question is not exactly when human speech was "invented" but rather what pressures were at work on our remote ancestors that eventually led to the development of human speech and a human brain and anatomy capable of its production. A number of speculative theories have been proposed concerning the origin of language. For example, in his book *The Emergence of Man* (1972), John Pfeiffer suggests that it was our ancestors' use of tools that made language an especially useful adaptation. Several million years ago the **call system** of our ancestors was probably not too different from that of chimpanzees today; that is, it was triggered by immediate events. It was perhaps in play that new activities and new calls related to these activities developed. Evolutionary pressure increased the fitness of individuals who

Studies of nonhuman primate communication, especially gestures and vocalizations, have been done in the field (e.g., Goodall 1968), among captive groups, and in laboratory settings (Miles 1978; Terrace 1979). Baboons in the wild, for example, constantly transmit information to one another. Lip-smacking, grunts, stares, poses, and screams are all part of their communication system. One long-term study of rhesus monkeys revealed over 120 behavioral patterns that are used in communication.

Because chimpanzees are thought to be humans' closest relations, their communication system is of great interest to social scientists. Wild chimpanzees, like other primates, exhibit a wide variety of communicative behaviors, such as the apparent use of gestures and physical contact to express feelings. For example, when they meet in the forest, "old friends" kiss and hug, pat each other on the head, or rest a hand on the thigh of the other. In addition to gestures, chimpanzees use calls to communicate. These calls are distinctive—a *waa* bark for danger, a series of soft moans for worry, a hooting to communicate excitement caused by the presence of an abundance of food, and screams and squeals of fear. Each kind of call expresses a particular state within the animal, which is perceived by others of its kind and potentially affects the behavior of those who hear it (Reynolds 1965). However, a primate call system is not the same as human language. Although intonation can intensify the meaning of a call—for example, from "danger" to "extreme danger"—a chimp can signal only an immediate danger. A second important limitation is that parts of calls cannot be recombined so as to generate new information: Each call appears to have just one meaning.

A special research strategy involves teaching languages (sign languages or other human-created systems) to higher primates, especially chimpanzees and gorillas. Studies of chimpanzees trained by humans show that chimpanzees are capable of a much more complex level of communication than they demonstrate naturally. The most famous ape language study is that of Washoe, a chimpanzee raised in a human environment since the age of ten months (Gardner and Gardner 1967). Washoe spent all her waking hours in the company of one of a number of researchers who "talked" to her in American Sign Language, which was developed for the deaf. Washoe quickly learned to sign and respond to her human companions. Very significantly, after learning about ten signs, she spontaneously began to produce new combinations of signs. Since Washoe, other studies have been conducted using chimpanzees (e.g., Fouts 1983; Premack 1971; Savage-Rumbaugh et al., 1980), gorillas (e.g., Patterson and Cohen 1978), and even orangutans (e.g., Miles 1983). Besides sign language, apes have been trained using other systems, including colored shapes and specially designed computer keyboards. It is important to note that a controversy exists within the field as to whether the remarkable achievements of the animals, including observations of chimps teaching other chimps to sign, the creative recombination of symbols, the use of grammarlike structuring, and the translation from spoken words to manually produced signs, reflect true language abilities or are simply due to training and unconscious cueing and projecting on the part of researchers. For example, Terrace (1983) notes that his attempt to train a chimpanzee demonstrated the lack of any true human-

Grooming is an important communication pattern among both male and female nonhuman primates. Here an adult female vervet monkey grooms another female, who is nursing her infant. (David Klein)

like language abilities. His widely publicized study has, in turn, been criticized by other researchers, partly on the basis that it was not conducted within a proper social environment and that he used inappropriate research methods.

The theoretical question underlying the ape language studies is whether human language is a completely separate and unique form of communication. The answer depends partly on how we define human language. If we define it very narrowly — "language is human, thus only humans have language" — we can automatically eliminate any possibility of cross-species studies of language behavior. Perhaps it makes more sense to look for a broader definition of

language, by attempting to describe what makes it a special form of communication. Suggestions have been made that the essential features include its creative and open nature, its abstractness, and its learnability. Once such a scheme is devised, it is then possible to look for commonalities between the communication systems of humans and other animals. Thus, similarities to human language are noted among the nonhuman primates, especially chimpanzees and gorillas. However, human language is the result of our own particular evolutionary history. Though a qualitative continuum might exist, human language is unique in terms of its great complexity and the importance of its role as part of our adaptation.

could "reconstruct the past in their minds, and express their images vocally and conceive new sequences of actions to serve as the basis for future plans" (p. 462). The multiplication of new experiences, especially the need for coordination between individuals for hunting and for conveying information to those who remained behind, required a more elaborate form of communication than was possible with a call system. In this scenario, a vocal alphabet developed through a shift of attention from whole calls to parts of calls. With an increase in population, larger settlements, group cooperation for large-scale hunting, and greater complexity in social organization, there was additional pressure for a more structured communication system and therefore for the development of grammatical rules. With each successive phase of human evolution, the world became steadily more complex and thus required more complicated mechanisms to deal with this complexity. It was within this context that human language evolved.

In contrast to the above situation, a number of anthropologists and linguists believe that the original human language was silent and gestural in nature. For example, although Gordon Hewes (1973) agrees with Pfeiffer that the earliest hominids probably had an apelike call system, he feels that the roots of human language are not to be found in this vocal form of communication but within a system of hand, body, and arm gestures. The impetus for developing an early hominid language of signing (which coexisted with the call system) may have had to do with transmitting simple locational information ("Where's the food?" "Which way is home?") and information about the environment among individuals hunting and gathering food within one another's sight. Hewes also contends that the early teaching of toolmaking techniques was done using gestures, noting that a close relationship exists between how the brain is organized for handedness (left-handed/right-handed) and for language behavior. At some point during evolution, cultures became too sophisticated and behaviors too complex to rely on the slower, more ambiguous gestural

system. Brain structures associated with the gestural language went through fairly minor evolutionary modifications so as to accommodate a spoken language, though the vocal anatomy (e.g., lips, throat, mouth) had to evolve simultaneously.

There are many other theories regarding the origins of human language. Only time and more research may eventually prove which of these, if any, are correct. It seems likely, however, that human language must have emerged by the time evolution brought about the first of the genus *Homo* over 1 million years ago. At this point, culture and human behavior necessitated such a grand and powerful system of communication.

Communication and Language

Human Language

Human language is a unique system of communication, distinct from any other animal communication system in three ways. In human language, a limited number of sounds (hardly any language uses over fifty) are combined to refer to thousands of different things and experiences. The association between a meaningful sequence of sounds and what it "stands for" is purely conventional in human language. The animal is no more a *dog* than it is a *chien* (French), a *perro* (Spanish), or a *kutta* (Hindi). Words "stand for" things, and the symbol (the word) is not tied to the thing it stands for. It is **conventionality**, that is, this capacity to separate the vocal symbol from its referent, that is absent in the call systems of nonhuman primates. It is this capacity to recombine sounds to create new meanings that makes human language such an efficient and effective communication system. If we had to use a different sound for every item of meaning, we would wind up with either a very small vocabulary or an impossibly large number of sounds.

Not only is human language efficient, it is also infinitely *productive*: Humans can com-

Where the population of a nation speaks mutually unintelligible languages, as in the People's Republic of China, a common written language is an important means of communication and an instrument of forging national unity. (Joan Gregg)

bine words and sounds into new meaningful utterances they have never heard before. The English sentence below uses words in a combination none of us has probably ever heard before; yet it can be easily made and understood by any English-speaking person: "I don't know the man who took the spoon that Horace left on the table that was lying upside down in the upstairs hallway of the building that burned down last night" (Southworth and Daswani 1974). Speakers of any human language can generate an almost infinite number of such sentences. This productive capacity of human languages makes them extremely flexible instruments for communication, capable of conveying all kinds of new information.

The third distinguishing characteristic of human language is its ability to convey information about something not in the immediate environment. We can describe things that happened in the past, will or may happen in the future, exist only in the mind, and are hypothetical (may not happen at all). This "displacement" characteristic of human languages allows us to think abstractly. Among other animals, communication is always about the present and the particular: A particular threatening object is in a particular place at this particular time. Human language generalizes; it categorizes some objects and events as similar and other objects and events as dissimilar. Humans can talk about a particular tree ("this tree I see in front of my house") and also about trees in general ("trees are standing people with rights to the land"). Language allows trees to be differentiated from bushes, bushes from flowers, and flowers from grass.

Hundreds of thousands of natural and manufactured objects have significance for human beings. Taking command of this incredibly complex world means classifying objects and events in an orderly way. Human language is the most effective means for doing exactly that. These qualities of human language—conventionality, productivity, and displacement—allow humans to make plans, to understand and correct mistakes, and to coordinate their activities. They also give our species a distinct advantage over other animals.

By translating experience into language, humans build up a storehouse of knowledge that can be transmitted to new members of the group. Although some of the things humans teach one another could be learned without language, teaching through language is more efficient and adaptive than relying on the slower and often clumsy process of imitation used by other animals. Furthermore, some human behavior patterns, such as religion, law, and science, would not be possible without the symbolizing capacity of human language. It is through this capacity for accumulating experience and passing it on by teaching others in the social group that human culture has developed.

Although at one time even many anthropologists and linguists believed that contemporary human languages could be classified into "primitive" and "civilized," less complex and more complex, inferior and superior, we know today that this is not so. Although some linguists are coming to believe that the vocabularies of literate urban peoples are richer and more complex than those of nonliterate peoples, all human languages are similar in that they possess a well-defined system of sounds, finite in number and combined to form words, phrases,

and sentences according to definite rules. Although the vocabulary of each language reflects what is important in terms of a particular physical and sociocultural environment, every language has a vocabulary adequate to deal with that environment. Vocabulary can be expanded in any language, with new words added as cultural change requires. All human languages have the capacity to categorize phenomena in the natural environment; the capacity for abstract thought is a property of all human languages. No language limits its references to concrete or individual phenomena, and thus no language as a system of communication can be considered less developed than any other. Nor does any human language reflect a limited mental capacity on the part of its speakers. Languages *do* differ in the specific ways in which they categorize the environment, and these differences affect perception and thinking, as we saw in Chapter 4. We will examine this aspect of language and its relationship to culture later in the chapter.

Acquiring Language

The fact that linguistic symbols are nearly all arbitrary—that is, conventions by which certain sounds are attached to certain objects and events—emphasizes the social aspect of language. In this sense, language is a part of culture. An individual learns a language only by interaction with other human beings who speak that language. An individual from any human population, if taken at birth and brought up in a different society than that to which the parents belong, will grow up speaking the language of the group in which he or she is raised. The normal physical and mental apparatus of human beings everywhere allows them to learn any language with equal ease.

If you are wondering what language a human being would speak if he or she were not taught any particular language, the answer is *none*. In one attempt to determine this, the Egyptian pharoah Psammetichus ordered two infants reared where they could hear no human voices. He assumed that they would "naturally" talk in the language of their ancestors. To his ears, their babbling sounded like Phrygian, which he concluded was the original human language. King James IV of Scotland tried a similar experiment, and he claimed that the two infants spoke Hebrew. This, not surprisingly, coincided with the theory of biblical scholars at that time, who asserted that Adam and Eve had spoken in Hebrew. Because experiments involving isolating human beings at birth are morally unacceptable today, cases of children brought up in isolation, such as Victor, the "wild child" of Aveyron, are always of great interest to the scientific community. In Victor's case, Dr. Itard's training did result in showing that Victor could hear and understand much of what he heard. But although Victor lived in human society until he was forty, he never learned to speak. His case suggests that there may be a critical period of language development in the human animal. It seems that, if speech is not learned at a certain age, the capacity to learn it at all is seriously impaired.

Recent studies of how children learn language indicate that human beings may have an innate (inborn) predisposition or mechanism for learning language patterns or rules, and that all human children go through the same stages of language learning, which appear in the same sequence regardless of the language being learned. Children actually take the initiative in learning language. By six months, the babbling of the infant gives way to consonant and vowel sequences and repetitive patterns. It is apparent that children "discover" language on their own, though this can be done only in the context of a particular social group speaking a particular language. Most adults do not know the rules of the languages they speak, certainly not well enough to teach them to children. What happens is that children are surrounded by a flow of sounds, words, and intonations. They not only imitate these but also take the initiative in forming combinations of words they may have never heard before but that are consistent with the rules of the language. Even when children do not understand the meaning of what they are saying, they can

speak grammatically, using the different parts of speech in correct relation to one another. This understanding of how children learn language has led to an increased interest in the biological basis of human language.

The human brain appears to be uniquely constructed for the development of language. Not only are the visual and auditory areas directly connected to each other, but both areas also are directly connected to the area concerned with touch. Thus, human children are able to make the association between the visible image, the feel of an object, and the sound pattern, or word, used to designate it, even though the word itself is an arbitrary symbol.

Structural Variation in Language

Every language has a structure—an internal logic and a particular relationship between its parts. The structure of any language consists of three subsystems: **phonology,** a system of sounds; **syntax,** the relationship between forms and the rules for combining forms; and **semantics,** a system that relates forms to meaning. Descriptive linguistics, a subfield of linguistics that studies the structure of a given language at a particular time, is the basis of historical linguistics, which studies the change in the structure of a language over time, and of comparative linguistics, which seeks to understand the relationships among different languages based on a comparison of their structures. One of the interests of descriptive anthropological linguistics is to record the structure of as many different human languages as possible. The first thing a descriptive linguist does in studying a language is to record the sounds and regular combinations of sounds in that language. These sounds are usually written in the International Phonetic Alphabet. The IPA was developed to represent all the sounds used in the different languages of the world and allows the linguist to record in writing sounds that are not used in his or her own language. When the linguist figures out how a particular sound is made, that sound can be represented phonetically with an IPA symbol. Let us look now in more detail at these subsystems of language structure.

Phonology

A phone is a sound. All languages use only a limited number of sounds out of the vast range of sounds that can be made by the human vocal apparatus. Sounds used in one language may be absent in other languages. English, for example, does not make use of the "click" sound of the language of the !Kung of southern Africa or many of the tonal sounds of Chinese. Furthermore, combinations of sounds are used in different ways in different languages. For example, an English speaker can easily pronounce the "ng" sound in *thing* at the end of an utterance, but not at the beginning; yet this sound is used in the initial position in Swazi, a language of Africa.

Not every sound used in a language conveys meaning. The smallest sound unit in a language that distinguishes meaning is called a **phoneme.** An example will make clear what is meant by a phoneme. The sound [d] in the English word *day* and [ð] in the English word *they* are phonemes. Their significance is shown by the fact that the words *day* and *they* have different meanings, and this meaning is carried by the initial consonant: [d] as contrasted to [ð]. Spanish also uses these sounds. But in Spanish the sounds [d] and [ð] are not phonemes—that is, they do not serve to distinguish words from one another. These sounds are used in different contexts: [d] at the beginning of words and [ð] when the sound appears in the middle of a word. Thus, the sounds do not create a difference in meaning between utterances. A person who says *nada* using the sound in *dia* will still be understood to be saying "nothing," although people may think the accent is "wrong" or "foreign."

Most languages utilize only about thirty phonemes in their structure. By an unconscious process, the native speaker of a language not

The anthropological linguist is greatly aided by the tape recorder in recording the many sounds of human speech that are part of the phonemic structure of a language. (Raymond Kennedy)

only learns to make the sounds used in the language but also to differentiate between those sounds that are significant (phonemes) and those sounds that are not. The ordinary person does not consciously think about the phonemic pattern of his or her language. It is only when trying to learn another language or hearing a foreigner speak our own language that we become aware of the variation in sounds and phonemes.

Grammar: Morphology and Syntax

A **morpheme** is the smallest unit of a language that has a meaning. In English, -s, as in *dogs,* means plural; un- means negative, as in *undo;* -er means "one who does," as in *teacher.* Because -s, un-, and -er do not occur by themselves, but only in association with another unit of meaning, they are called *bound* morphemes. A morpheme such as the word *giraffe* is called a *free* morpheme, because it can stand alone. A word is the smallest part of a sentence that can be said alone and still retain its meaning. Some words consist of only one morpheme. *Giraffe* is an example of a single-morpheme word. *Teacher* has two morphemes, teach and -er. *Undoes* has three morphemes: un-, do, and -s.

Languages differ in the extent to which their words tend to contain only one, several, or many morphemes. In Chinese, most words have only one morpheme. English, like Chinese, has many single-morpheme words — *dog, house, car* — but also has many words that contain more than one morpheme — plural words such as *dogs, houses, cars* — and words for one who does — *worker, teacher, gambler*. English also has words with three morphemes: *Teachers* consists of the morphemes teach, -er, and -s. English also has words with four morphemes: *undesirables*. The four are un-, desire, -able (a suffix turning a stem word into an adjective), and -s. English might then fall midway on a continuum between Chinese, with its mainly single-morpheme words, and languages like Navajo or Eskimo, which have many words with eight or ten morphemes.

Morphemes combine with other morphemes to make up complex words, phrases, and sentences. The combination of morphemes in any language is fixed by rules. One part of descriptive grammar has to do with formulating the particular rules in a language by which morphemes are arranged to make words. One of the rules of English grammar is that the morpheme for plural, -s, follows the element it is pluralizing. In other languages, the pluralizing morpheme may come before the element it pluralizes. Things are not quite that easy, however. The plural of "dog" is made by adding -s, but the plural of "child" is not made by adding -s. A grammar therefore specifies not only the general rules of morpheme combination but also exceptions to the rules and the rules for different classes of exceptions.

Syntax is the part of grammar that has to do with the arrangement of words to form phrases and sentences. Languages differ in their syntactic structures. In English, word order is important because it conveys meaning. The syntax of the English language gives a different meaning to these two sentences: "The dog bit the man" and "The man bit the dog." In German, the subject and object of a sentence are indicated by word endings rather than word order. In attempting to understand the syntactic structure of a language, the descriptive linguist establishes the different form classes, or parts of speech, for that language. All languages have a word class of nouns, but different languages have different subclasses of nouns. In the Romance languages (Spanish, French, and Italian), as well as in many others, nouns are divided into masculine, feminine, and neuter subclasses. This gender classification applies to verbs, indefinite and definite articles, and adjectives, all of which must agree with the gender classification of the noun. Other languages make class distinctions that we do not use in English; for example, Papago, a native American language, classifies the features of the world into "living things" and "growing things." Living things include all animated objects, such as people and animals; growing things refer to inanimate objects, such as plants and rocks.

All linguists agree that the grammatical categories of one language cannot be used to describe another language. Languages differ in the numbers and kinds of grammatical categories they have and how these categories are indicated. Thus, the information that in English would be expressed as "The dog bit the man" would be "Dog bite man" in Chinese. In China, the tense of the verb need not be indicated, as it must be in English, although it can be brought in by using a time word such as *now* or *yesterday*. In Chinook, an Indian language spoken in the American Northwest, conveying the same information would require the speaker to use morphemes indicating the following: "singular-feminine-subject-dog singular-masculine-object-man singular-feminine-subject-singular-masculine-object directive-bite instantaneous-past." The rules of grammar in different languages not only require different information to be included in a sentence but also differ in the ways they do this.

Although grammatical rules carry meaning, the grammar of a sentence can be understood independently of its meaning. To use a now classic example (Chomsky 1965), consider the following sentences:

> "Colorless green ideas sleep furiously."
> "Furiously sleep ideas green colorless."

Both sentences are meaningless in English. But the first is easily recognized as grammatical by an English speaker, whereas the second is both meaningless and ungrammatical. The first sentence has the parts of speech in English in their proper relation to each other; the second sentence does not.

Transformational Grammar

Traditional descriptive grammars formulate the rules of a language by breaking down sentences into constituents (parts of speech) and analyzing the relationships these parts of speech have to one another and to the sentence as a whole. But this kind of descriptive grammar cannot account for all the features of a language. Traditional descriptive grammars cannot, for example, account for the ambiguity of certain sentences. The sentence "They are flying planes" can be understood to have two meanings: ". . . those specks on the horizon are planes flying in the air," and ". . . those people are flying planes" (Allen and van Buren 1971).

A traditional descriptive grammar that understands sentences by breaking them up into their elements and stops there will not be able to show that the sentence "They are flying planes" has two different meanings. Nor can traditional descriptive grammars account for the differences we feel between the following two sentences: (1) "The picture was painted by

a new technique," and (2) "The picture was painted by a real artist." A traditional grammar would have to represent the structure of these sentences in the same way.

Because of these and other limitations in traditional descriptive grammars, a new approach to understanding language called **transformational generative grammar** was developed by Noam Chomsky in the 1950s. Instead of focusing on the parts of speech in a sentence and their relationship to one another, transformational grammar focuses on the relationship between levels of language structure. According to transformational grammar, languages have two levels: deep structure and surface structure. The deep structure of a language is revealed in basic, or kernel, sentences. These kernels are simple, declarative, affirmative, active sentences: "John loves Mary." They can be transformed by a set of rules into a variety of surface structures. For example, the rule for transforming the positive into the negative would lead to this surface structure: "John does not love Mary." The rule for transforming the declarative into the interrogative would lead to "Does John love Mary?" and so forth. Not all sentences that seem similar — that is, have similar surface structures — have the same deep structure. The two sentences "The picture was painted by a new technique" and "The picture was painted by a real artist" can be shown to have different deep structures and different transformational histories. The first is derived by a double transformation from "John painted the picture by a new technique." The second is the passive of "A real artist painted the picture." Transformational grammar can also account for the surface ambiguity in the sentence "They are flying planes" by showing that the two meanings are generated by different deep structures and can be represented differently at this level.

The excitement created by transformational grammar can be better understood in the context of the theoretical goals of this approach. Here grammar is seen as an account of the competence, or implicit knowledge, of a

A palace guard rushes up to his king in a state of anxiety. In the background, one can see a mob approaching the palace. It is a mob of angry peasants, armed for warfare with clubs and other improvised tools of aggression. The palace guard shouts, "Your majesty, your majesty, the peasants are revolting!" The king is facing away from the window and remains unaware of the tumult among the populace. In a state of regal grace and superiority he answers, matter of factly, "Yes, they certainly are."

The confusion of communication that results from this problem of syntactic ambiguity can be handled by transformational grammar. At the level of deep structure, there are two sentences, each with its own meaning and its own set of rules that transform these different deep structures into the same surface structure.

Guard's communication

Deep structure: The peasants are revolting against you.

Surface structure: The peasants are revolting.

King's communication

Deep structure: The peasants are revolting to me.

Surface structure: The peasants are revolting.

speaker of a language. It describes and attempts to account for the ability of a speaker to understand a sentence in the native language and to produce an appropriate sentence on a given occasion. Ideally, the competence of a speaker-hearer can be expressed as a system of rules that relate signals to their meanings. The problem for the transformational grammarian is to discover and make explicit the system of rules the speaker-hearer knows only implicitly. For the linguist, however, the correct statement of the grammatical principles of a language is of interest primarily for what it tells about the more general question of the nature of universal grammar. A universal grammar, in turn, is of interest primarily for the information it provides concerning innate intellectual structure. The aim of linguistic theory is to understand the nature of mental processes, the ways in which sentences are produced and understood, and the ways in which linguistic competence is acquired. The success with which transforma-tional grammar accounts for linguistic competence has opened up new vistas in the science of linguistics and in our understanding of the workings of the human mind.

Vocabulary

A **vocabulary** is the total stock of words in a language. The relation between culture and language is perhaps most clearly seen in vocabulary. In industrial society, the vocabulary will contain many words reflecting technological complexity and specialization. In a technologically simpler society, the vocabulary will be different. The vocabulary of all cultures is elaborated in the direction of what is most important in that culture. The Subanum of the Philippines, a simple agricultural society, have 132 separate words for the diagnosis of disease (Conklin 1969). This same society possesses over a thousand words for the plants in that environment. The Inuit have many different words for snow: snow on the ground (*aput*), falling snow (*gana*), drifting snow (*piqsirpog*), and so on. This elaboration of Inuit vocabulary has an obvious relationship to the importance of weather conditions for survival.

Because vocabulary reflects the way people with a certain culture perceive their environment, anthropologists use vocabulary as a clue to understanding experience and reality in different cultures. Through vocabulary, anthropologists attempt to get an insider's view of the world not influenced by the anthropologist's own classification system. This perspective has long been used in studying the vocabulary for kinship. In English, for example, the word *brother-in-law* lumps together my sister's husband, my husband's brother, and the husbands of all my husband's sisters. In Hindi, a language of North India, there are separate terms for my sister's husband (*behnoi*), my husband's elder brother (*jait*), my husband's younger brother (*deva*), and my husband's sisters' husbands (*nandoya*). Kinship vocabulary is a good clue to the nature of the most significant family relations in a culture. The single term *brother-in-law* in English reflects the similarity of a woman's behavior toward all the men in those different kinship statuses. The variety of words in Hindi reflects the fact that each of these categories of people is treated differently.

Anthropologists also attempt to discover the criteria for applying a particular label to an aspect of the physical or social environment in order to understand how a culturally specific area of meaning is divided into parts and how these parts are related to one another. One kind of relationship is that of exclusion, or contrast. Thus, going back to our example of kinship, English terminology contrasts *brother-in-law* with *sister-in-law* by the criterion of sex. *Brother* is contrasted with *brother-in-law* by the criterion of blood versus affinal relationship (relation through marriage). But both *brother* and *brother-in-law* are included in *relative*, a more general category that contains people related by both blood and marriage. The category of relatives contrasts with the category of close nonrelatives — friends — and this category contrasts with unknown people, or strangers.

Language and Culture

We have just seen how language, especially in its vocabulary, reflects cultural emphases and the ways in which cultures divide up their physical and social environment. But language does more than just reflect culture: It is the way in which the individual is introduced to the order of the physical and social environment. Language, therefore, would seem to have a major impact on the way an individual perceives and conceptualizes the world. This importance and the special role of language were made clear by Edward Sapir, who wrote:

> Human beings do not live in the objective world alone . . . but are very much at the mercy of the particular language which has become the medium of expression for their society. . . . The fact . . . is that the "real world" is to a large extent unconsciously built up on the language habits of the group. No two languages are ever sufficiently similar to be considered as representing the same social reality. The worlds in which different societies live are distinct worlds, not merely the same world with different labels attached. (1949:162)

If my language has only one term — *brother-in-law* — that is applied to my sister's husband, my husband's brothers, and my husband's sisters' husbands, I am led by my language to perceive all these relatives in a similar way. Vocabulary, through what it groups together under one label and what it differentiates with different labels, is one way in which language shapes our perception of the world.

Anthropologists have long been interested in the ways in which grammatical categories influence the perception of reality. Both Sapir and a student of his, Benjamin Whorf, investigated the ways in which different peoples "see" the universe through the medium of their languages. The **Sapir-Whorf hypothesis**, as it has come to be called, asks these two questions: Are concepts of time, space, and matter given in substantially the same form by experience to all people, or are they in part conditioned by the structure of particular languages? Are there correspondences between linguistic patterns and cultural and behavioral norms? Most anthropologists would probably give a qualified yes to both questions, although we have little actual research to document these answers.

Harry Hoijer (1964) applied the Sapir-Whorf hypothesis to the Navajo, a native American tribe in Arizona and New Mexico. He demonstrated that many aspects of Navajo grammar (for example, the conjugation of active verbs, the reporting of actions and events, and the framing of substantive concepts) emphasize movement and specify the nature, direction, and status of such movement in considerable detail. Where English would say "One dresses," "One is young," and "He is carrying a round object," Navajo would say "One moves into clothing," "One moves about newly," and "He moves along handling a round object." The Navajo language conceives of the universe as being in motion; position is defined as a withdrawal from motion. Where English would say "on," Navajo would say "at rest." Parallels to this linguistic conception of the universe in motion are found in many aspects of Navajo culture. In Navajo mythology, for example, gods and culture heroes restlessly move from one place to another, seeking by their motion to perfect the universe.

Although some correspondences between grammatical categories and cultural themes or world views have been demonstrated, linguistic determinism is not an absolute or established fact. For example, the necessity to distinguish gender in the Romance languages does not correspond to the relative importance of gender in these cultures when compared, for example, to its importance in Chinese and Polynesian cultures, neither of which has gender classes in its language. And the lack of gender classes for nouns and adjectives in English does not correspond to any fact of culturally perceived equality between male and female. This illustrates one of the many difficulties in accepting the Sapir-Whorf hypothesis and illustrates why it is not totally accepted by anthropologists.

The Ethnography of Communication

Anthropological linguistics has mainly been interested in languages as systems of knowledge independent of the ways in which people actually speak. The relatively new field of **sociolinguistics** focuses on speech performance: the actual encounters that involve verbal (and also accompanying nonverbal) communication between human beings. Whereas traditional anthropological linguistics assumes a homogeneous speech community, sociolinguistics is interested in variations in language use as these can be observed by the ethnographer. Whereas the anthropological linguist usually works with one informant and attempts to elicit the ideal pattern of a language, the sociolinguist observes verbal behavior among different individuals and groups in society.

The sociolinguist attempts to identify, describe, and understand the cultural patterning of different speech events within a speech community (society or subsociety). For example, a political speech has different purposes and is limited by different norms from those for a political discussion among friends. The norms regarding political speeches are different in different cultures: who can participate as speaker and audience, the appropriate topics for such a speech, what kinds of cultural themes can be used, where such speeches can take place, the relation between the speaker and hearer in this context, the language used for political speeches in a multilingual community, and so forth. Sociolinguists are interested in the ways in which speech varies depending on an individual's position in a social structure or social

GENDERLECTS: CONVERSATION BETWEEN MEN AND WOMEN

One of the most fascinating recent studies in sociolinguistics is that by Deborah Tannen on conversations between men and women. Tannen's book *You Just Don't Understand* has become a best-seller in the United States because it goes right to the heart of many of the conversational difficulties men and women experience with each other.

According to Tannen, "women speak and hear a language of connections and intimacy while men speak and hear a language of status and independence." Thus, she says, "communication between men and women can be like cross-cultural communication, prey to a clash of conversational styles. Instead of different dialects, it has been said they speak different **genderlects**" (p. 42).

"Where," Tannen asks, "do women and men learn different ways of speaking and hearing?"

Boys and girls grow up in different worlds of words. . . . Boys tend to play outside, in large groups that are hierarchically structured. Their groups have a leader who tells others what to do and how to do it, and resists doing what other boys propose. It is by giving orders and making them stick that high status is negotiated. Another way boys achieve status is to take center stage by telling stories and jokes, and by sidetracking or challenging the stories and jokes of others. Boys' games have winners and losers and elaborate systems of rules that are frequently the subject of arguments. . . . Boys also boast of their skill and argue about who is best at what.

Girls, on the other hand, play in small groups or in pairs; the center of a girl's social life is a best friend. Within the group, intimacy is key: Differentiation is measured by relative closeness. In their most frequent games . . . everyone gets a turn. Many of their activities . . . do not have winners and losers. Though some girls are certainly more skilled than others, girls are expected not to boast about it, or show that they think they are better than the others. Girls don't give orders; they express their preferences as suggestions. . . . They don't grab center stage . . . so they don't challenge each other directly. And much of the time, they simply sit together and talk. Girls are not accustomed to jockeying for status in an obvious way; they are more concerned that they be liked" (pp. 43–44).

Tannen characterizes these differences between the way men and women use words as *report-talk* and *rapport-talk*.

For most women, the language of conversation is primarily a language of rapport: a way of establishing connections and negotiating relationships. Emphasis is placed on displaying similarities and matching experiences. From childhood, girls criticize peers who try to stand out or appear better than others. . . .

For most men, talk is primarily a means to preserve independence and negotiate and maintain status in a hierarchical social order. This is done by exhibiting knowledge and skill, and by holding center stage through verbal performance such as storytelling, joking, or imparting information. From childhood, men learn to use talking as a way to get and keep attention (p. 77).

Tannen gives many examples of misunderstandings men and women have in conversation because of the different ways they use words. Women often want "the gift of understanding" in a conversation, while the man tends to give the "gift of advice." The following misunderstanding arose between a husband and wife after a car accident in which the wife was seriously injured.

Because she hated being in the hospital, the wife asked to come home early. But once home, she suffered pain from having to move around more. Her husband said, "Why didn't you stay in the hospital where you would have been more comfortable?" This hurt her because it seemed to imply that he did not want her at home. She didn't think of his suggestion that she should have stayed in the hospital as a response to her complaints about the pain she was suffering; she thought of it as an independent expression of his preference not to have her at home (p. 50).

Much research supports Tannen's view that men and women speak in genderlects. One study shows how

the difference between public and private speaking . . . explains the stereotype that women don't tell jokes. . . . Although it's not true that women don't tell jokes, it is true that many women are less likely than men to tell jokes in large groups, especially groups including men. . . . Men preferred and were more likely to tell jokes when they had an audience. . . . Unlike men, [women] were reluctant to tell jokes in front of people they didn't know well.

This is consistent with Tannen's view that women are more likely to talk "in a situation that is more private, because the audience is small, familiar, and perceived to be members of a community" than in a more public situation that "requires speakers to claim center stage and prove their abilities" (pp. 89–90).

Men and women also differ in their approaches to conflict, Tannen points out. "Much of what has been written about women's and men's styles claims that males are competitive and prone to conflict whereas females are cooperative and given to affiliation." In a complex way, this is reflected in genderlect. For example, "to most women, conflict is a threat to connection, to

be avoided at all costs. Disputes are preferably settled without direct confrontation. But to many men, conflict is that necessary means by which status is negotiated, so it is to be accepted and may even be sought, embraced, and enjoyed." Thus, male reporttalk "is part of a larger framework in which many men approach life as a contest" (pp. 149–150).

"Differences in attitudes toward conflict show up in daily conversations" says Tannen, and the attitudes of many women emerge as a tendency to hate arguing (p. 159). Women are often in "the role of peacemaker," which "reflects that general tendency among women to seek agreement" as a way of establishing affiliation, whereas men often use competitition to accomplish affiliative ends (p. 167).

In another example, Tannen describes an assignment she gave her students to record an ordinary conversation and transcribe a segment in which someone described personal experiences.

The fourteen stories that men told were all about themselves. Of the twelve stories told by women, only six were about themselves. . . . For the most part, the stories that men told made them look good. . . . Many of the women told stories that made them look foolish (p. 177).

Other research confirmed this pattern, suggesting that "if men see life in terms of a contest, a struggle against nature and other men, for women life is a struggle against the danger of being cut off from their community" (p. 178). These different perspectives are expressed in genderlect.

Deborah Tannen, You Just Don't Understand: Men and Women in Conversation. New York: William Morrow, 1990. Copyright © 1990 by Deborah Tannen, Ph.D. By permission of William Morrow & Company, Inc.

relationship. In some cultures, different speech forms are used depending on whether the speaker and hearer are intimate friends, acquaintances on equal footing with each other, or of distinctly different social statuses. In French, German, and Spanish, among other languages, there are formal and informal terms of address that are lacking in English. Parents in these cultures use the informal term to address their children, but children use the formal term to their parents. In Hindi, the status of a husband is much higher than that of a wife. A wife will never address her husband by his name (certainly not in public), but will use a roundabout expression that would translate into English as something like "I am speaking to you, sir."

It is also clear that in socially stratified societies, speech norms are different in different social classes. Elites and working-class people not only have different vocabularies but also pronounce words differently. Where variation in pronunciation exists, one form will be considered proper, or the "prestige" form, and another will be associated with lower socioeconomic status. Individuals may be aware of these two forms and vary their pronunciation in different contexts. Some people who use the "lower" form in casual speech will switch to the prestige form in more careful speech. For example, William Labov (1972) studied the pronunciation of certain vowels used in ordinary speech in New York City. He found that pronunciation of these vowels (characteristic of a "New York accent") varied with the socioeconomic class, ethnicity, and age of the speaker. The degree of speech variation also correlated with social class. People at the bottom of the social hierarchy did not vary their speech much from casual talk to careful speech. Upper-middle-class people, whose pronunciation normally falls midway between the extreme correct form and the extreme stigmatized form, also showed little variation. The most extreme variations were exhibited by members of the lower-middle class, who used the stigmatized forms in casual speech but the correct forms in careful speech.

This study might be interpreted as demonstrating that those on the bottom do not vary their pronunciation because they have little hope of moving up socially, those at the top do not vary their pronunciation because they are relatively secure in their social position, and those in the middle (lower middle class) vary their pronunciation most because they are "social climbers" and therefore are the most sensitive to behaving in "correct" ways. But in any case, Labov's study makes clear what many of us know but do not like to admit: We do judge a person's social status by the way he or she speaks. The function of speech is not limited to communicating information. What we say and how we say it are also a way of telling people what we are socially—or, perhaps, where we want to be.

The anthropological insight that language use is shaped by cultural values applies to writing as well as speech and helps American writing teachers teach students from other cultures in the American classroom more effectively. The role of cultural values in shaping written communication is seen in a comparison of writing of Chinese and American students (Gregg 1988). In China, for example, where there is a strong sense of group identity and history and an inhibition on questioning authority, it is difficult for students to adopt the Western critical perspective in writing, which is based on values of individualism, experimentation, and an unwillingness to grant past authorities any permanent hold on the truth. When an American writing teacher is faced with work from Chinese students, the students are often penalized because the values underlying their writing style differ from American values. Indeed, it is yet another example of ethnocentrism, in which their style is judged by our stylistic values. When educators become aware of the cultural factors affecting *each* writing style, they can better help students to function in the Western style, required for American schools, without the students feeling culturally inferior.

In many speech communities, the ordinary person knows and uses more than one language. Sociolinguists are interested in the dif-

Sociolinguists are interested in the study of speech performance: how people speak and what choices they make in different social situations. (Serena Nanda)

ferent contexts in which one or the other language would be used. The language a person chooses to use can be a way of solidifying ethnic or familial identity or of distancing oneself from another person or group.

An interesting example of this is the Apache "Whiteman" stories, a speech performance that developed out of the interaction between native Americans and the larger society, and is described in the accompanying ethnography. As "Whiteman" stories are never told to "Whitemen," the ethnography illustrates William Labov's point that the anthropologist must hear people speak in their natural settings in order to grasp their full linguistic creativity.

Black English

Larry H. [is] a 15-year-old core member of the Jets, being interviewed by John Lewis. Larry is one of the loudest and roughest members of the Jets, one who gives the least recognition to the conventional rules of politeness. . . . Contact with Larry would produce some fairly negative reactions on both sides: it is probable that you

would not *like* him any more than his teachers do. Larry causes trouble in and out of school; he was put back from the eleventh grade to the ninth, and has been threatened with further action by the school authorities.

JL: . . . But, just say that there is a God, what color is he? White or black?

Larry: Well, if it is a God . . . I wouldn't know what color, I couldn' say, —couldn' nobody say what color he is or really *would* be.

JL: But now, jus' suppose there was a God—

Larry: Unless'n they say . . .

JL: No, I was jus' saying jus' suppose there is a God, would he be white or black?

Larry: . . . He'd be white, man.

JL: Why?

Larry: Why? I'll tell you why. 'Cause the average whitey out here got everything, you dig? And the [black man] ain't got shit, y'know? Y'understan'? So—um—for—in order for *that* to happen, you know it ain't no black God that's doin' that bullshit.

No one can hear Larry's answer to this question without being convinced that they are in the presence of a skilled speaker with great "verbal presence of mind" who can use the English language expertly for many purposes. Larry's answer to John Lewis is . . . a complex argument. The nearest [standard English] equivalent might be: "So you know that God isn't black, because if he was, he wouldn't have arranged things like that."*

This dialogue also comes from the work of William Labov, this time on Black English. In Labov's work, he criticizes the theories that lower-class African-American children are verbally deficient. According to Labov, much of the seeming verbal deficiency of these children comes from the artificial situation in which psychologists carry out linguistic studies or from studying children's speech in school, a

---

*From William Labov, "The Logic of Nonstandard English," Georgetown University Roundtable on Language and Linguistics 22 (1969): 1–22, 26–31, Linguistics and the Teaching of Standard English to Speakers of Other Languages or Dialects, ed. by James E. Alatis. Washington, D.C.: Georgetown University Press. Reprinted by permission of the publisher.

Scene: It is a clear, hot evening in July. J and K have finished their meal. The children are sitting nearby. There is a knock at the door. J rises, answers the knock and finds L standing outside.

1. J: Hello, my friend! How're you doing? How you feeling, L? You feeling good? (J now turns in the direction of K and addresses her.)

2. J: Look who here, everybody! Look who just come in. Sure, it's my Indian friend, L. Pretty good, all right. (J slaps L on the shoulder and, looking him directly in the eyes, seizes his hand and pumps it wildly up and down.)

3. J: Come right in, my friend! Don't stay outside in the rain. Better you come in right now. (J now drapes his arm around L's shoulder and moves him in the direction of a chair.)

4. J: Sit down! Sit right down! Take your loads off you ass. You hungry? You want crackers? Maybe you want some beer? You want some wine? Bread? You want some sandwich? How about it? You hungry? I don't know. Maybe you sick. Maybe you don't eat again long time. (K has now stopped what she is doing and is looking on with amusement. L has seated himself and has a look of bemused resignation on his face.)

5. J: You sure looking good to me, L. You looking pretty fat! Pretty good all right! You got new boots? Where you buy them? Sure pretty good boots! I glad . . . (At this point, J breaks into laughter. K joins in. L shakes his head and smiles. The joke is over.)*

This joke is one of an inventive repertoire among the Western Apache. It is one of the "Whiteman" jokes, or rather elaborate satirical routines, that the Apache do for one another as a way of expressing their sense of difference from Anglo-Americans. These jokes form part of a process of social criticism and self-definition. In them, the Apache try to "make sense" of the Anglo-Americans with whom they have had to deal for a long time and to confer order on Apache experiences with Anglo-Americans. In these jokes, Apaches play at being "Whitemen," imitating them in speech and nonverbal gestures and behavior.

When Western Apaches stage joking imitations of Anglo-Americans, they portray them as gross incompetents in the conduct of social relations. Judged

*Keith Basso, Portraits of "the Whiteman." New York: Cambridge University Press, 1979. Reprinted by permission of the publisher.

according to Apache standards for what is right and normal, the joke teller's actions are intended to seem extremely peculiar and "wrong." This joke shows the different ways in which Anglo-Americans appear to the Apache to be ignorant of how to comport themselves appropriately in public situations. In line 1, the use of "my friend" indicates the Apache view that Anglo-Americans use this word much too loosely, even for people whom it is clear they hold in low esteem. Among the Apache, a friend is a person one has known for many years and with whom one has strong feelings of mutual confidence and respect. "How you feeling?" as a question to a mere acquaintance indicates a breach of personal privacy for the Apache and indicates an unnatural curiosity about the inner feelings of other people.

In line 2, the joke is criticizing what the Apache view as the unnecessary and embarrassing attention given to the individual in social situations by Anglo-Americans. Among the Apache, both entering and leaving a group should be done unobtrusively to avoid causing anyone to feel socially isolated and uncomfortable. In the use of the personal name L, in lines 1, 2, and 5, the joke teller contrasts the Apache view of a name as an item of individually owned and valued property with the Anglo-American behavior, which uses such names loosely and without propriety. Also, the repetition of the name indicates the Apache view that "Whitemen" must have bad memories and thus must continually remind themselves whom they are talking to. When J slaps L on the back (line 2) and looks him in the eye, the Apache view such behavior as aggressive and insolent. Among the Apache, adult men are careful to avoid touching each other in public, as this is viewed as an unwarranted encroachment on the private territory of the self.

In line 4, the Anglo-American is viewed as being bossy, for to insist that a visitor engage in this kind of behavior implies that he is a person of little account whose wishes may be safely ignored. The rapid-fire questions and repetitions about food in this line are viewed by the Apache as a form of coercion, and the line "Maybe you sick" contrasts with the Apache belief that talking about trouble can increase its chances of happening. In line 5, the attention to L's physical appearance and new boots is another example to the Apache of how Anglo-Americans force others into self-consciousness and embarrassment. Because this kind of remark appears to be well received among Anglo-Americans, however, the Apache conclude that "Whitemen" are deeply absorbed with the surfaces of themselves, an absorption that is related to their need to be regarded as separate and distinct from other people.

To the Apache, "Whitemen" are frequently insensitive in how they conduct themselves in the presence of Indian people. The "Whitemen" stories are a rare opportunity to be on the receiving end of a "native" view of the Anglo-American world.

place often viewed by them as a hostile environment. To be best understood, the verbal capacities of children must be studied within the cultural context in which they were developed. This very anthropological perspective is parallel to that presented in other studies in this chapter. As we will see with the Apache "Whiteman" stories, language use differs depending on its audience and it may be only within the ethnic community that the linguistic capacities of speakers are fully realized.

The dialogue brings together a number of issues involving the applications of anthropology. The verbal exchange between Larry and John Lewis represents a form of speech sometimes referred to as Black English, one of the many diverse patterns of English found in the United States. The specific semantic and grammatical forms characterizing Black English (Burling 1970) demonstrate that this variation on what is considered standard English is governed by rules (as is any language) as orderly as those of standard English and produces verbal utterances as complex.

Yet Black English is not regarded in our culture as just another regional dialect, of which most Americans are generally tolerant. African-American speech patterns have been associated with an inferior social position, and Black English is not merely considered different from standard English, but inferior to it. Black English is linked with "cultural deprivation" and such deficiencies as the inability to do abstract thinking. As the dialogue shows, this is clearly not the case. Larry's logic that God can't be black is impeccable!

The dismissal of Black English by many Americans as inferior burdens African-Americans with a difficult problem. To speak naturally within the family and community, black children must learn one variety of English, Black English, which they first learn is rich and flexible in its own terms and can be used effectively in most of the situations of daily life. But then, when black children enter school, they are confronted with teachers who try to persuade them to abandon this language in favor of what may almost be experienced as a foreign language. Inevitably, many students reject this demand, along with much else of their education.

For some African-Americans, years of classroom drilling, exposure to movies and radio, and the need to work in the world outside the local community have their effect and they become competent dialect-switchers. In their move into the middle class, they are able to use standard English speech patterns where these are called for and use their familiar dialect when speaking with their families or friends. Others, however, do not become fluent in standard English, which becomes a disadvantage in their attempts to operate in a world wider than the local community. The inability of schools to effectively teach African-American children standard English places a burden on these children, who are then at a disadvantage in today's society.

By the late 1960s, with the increasing concern over the educational fate of black children, Black English became a subject of serious linguistic investigation; there was also interest in how *cultural attitudes* toward Black English affected other aspects of black participation in the larger society. Anthropological knowledge was of great use here: Anthropological linguists not only were able to demonstrate the structural and phonological regularities of Black English but were also able to play more active roles in applying their knowledge in practical ways through designing educational materials that would draw on the students' linguistic abilities.

Nonverbal Communication

Ethnographers are also interested in nonverbal communication. In Chapter 4, we noted the work of Edward Hall (1959) on space and time. Think of some of the ways in which, to quote Hall, "time talks" and "space speaks." In our culture, what are we saying to a person when we show up for an appointment forty minutes late? Are we saying something different if we show up ten minutes early? Is a Latin American who shows up late for an appointment saying the same thing?

Part of a nonverbal communication pattern is how close we stand to another person, whether we face him or her directly or stand at an angle, and whether our arms are folded in front of us or hanging down at our sides. All cultures use nonverbal gestures to communicate. Some of these gestures are conscious; some are unconscious. What people say with their facial expressions is a powerful form of communication. Among the Tuareg, a tribal people of northern Africa whose men are veiled, the position of the veil is an important part of nonverbal communication (Murphy 1964). A Tuareg man lowers his veil only among intimates and persons of lower social status. When he is engaged in an encounter in which he does not wish to commit himself to a particular course of action, he will wear the veil very high on the bridge of his nose, so that the other party can read as little as possible from his facial expression. In our culture, as in many cultures, the eyes are considered an important clue to what a person is feeling and thinking. This explains why some people wear dark glasses in the shade. By hiding the eyes, an individual attempts to control the flow of communication and, through this, the entire encounter. Because nonverbal communication is more ambiguous than verbal communication, it leaves the "speaker" with more options. To "say it with flowers" does not involve the same degree of commitment as "saying it with words."

In societies where men wear veils, the height of the veil and the degree to which it exposes the face is an important means of nonverbal communication. (United Nations/AID/Purcell)

Language Change

Language, like other parts of culture, shows both stability and change. The first step in studying language change is to identify it. Historical linguists study different stages of a language in order to identify the kinds of changes that have taken place.

Historical linguistics can be applied to phonology, morphology, or vocabulary. With regard to phonology, linguists have been able to discover certain regularities in the ways in which sounds change. These regularities are called **phonetic laws**. An example of a phonetic law is the change from the accented vowel $\bar{a}$ in Old English to the vowel [ow] in Modern English. This phonetic law is illustrated in the following examples (Sturtevant 1947:65):

Old English	Modern English
bān	bone
bāt	boat
fām	foam
mān	moan
stān	stone
rād	road

TABLE 5.1   Apache Words for Parts of the Human Body and the Automobile

		HUMAN ANATOMICAL TERMS	EXTENDED AUTO MEANINGS
External Anatomy	daw	"chin and jaw"	"front bumper"
	wos	"shoulder"	"front fender"
	gun	"hand and arm"	"front wheel"
	kai	"thigh and buttocks"	"rear fender"
	ke	"foot"	"rear wheel"
	chun	"back"	"chassis"
Face	chee	"nose"	"hood"
	ta	"forehead"	"auto top"
	inda	"eye"	"headlight"
	ze	"mouth"	"gas-pipe opening"
Entrails	tsaws	"vein"	"electrical wiring"
	zik	"liver"	"battery"
	pit	"stomach"	"gas tank"
	chih	"intestine"	"radiator hose"
	jih	"heart"	"distributor"
	jisoleh	"lung"	"radiator"

From Peter Farb, Word Play: What Happens When People Talk. *Copyright © 1973 by Peter Farb. Reprinted by permission of Alfred A. Knopf, Inc.*

This is an example of internal change. Language change can also come about through borrowing. When the Apache borrowed certain words—*loca, rico*—from the Spanish, a new phonemic occurrence was introduced, that of "l" and "r" in initial position, which was not part of the Apache phonemic pattern.

The vocabulary of a language also undergoes both internal and external changes. Words change their meanings, and new words are added. Sometimes, as cultures come into contact, cultural items are borrowed and the original name for the item is kept. Pajama is an item of clothing borrowed from India, and we have kept the original Indian word, incorporating it into the English vocabulary. In other cases, words or combinations of words already present in the language are applied to new cultural items. Some native American groups, upon seeing their first horses (introduced by the Spanish), called them "ten dogs," and North Americans refer to their automobiles in terms of "horsepower." The Apache, who had a particular way of classifying parts of the human body, applied this classification to the automobile, which was introduced to their reservations in the 1930s. This practice resulted in the extended meanings for parts of the automobile that are listed in Table 5.1.

Historical linguists use the data on internal linguistic change to discover the relationships between different languages. If two languages appear related, what is the nature of the relationship? Are the similarities due to historical contact between cultures and resultant borrowing? Or are similarities between certain languages a result of their being derived from the same ancestral language? In other words, do similar languages have a historical or a generic relationship?

When the similarities appear too numerous, too regular, and too basic to be accounted for by borrowing, a generic relationship is assumed. Comparative linguists attempt to work

TABLE 5.2   The Comparative Method

SANSKRIT	GREEK	LATIN	GOTHIC	PROTO-INDO-EUROPEAN
	oinē, 'ace'	ūnus	ains	oinos
duā, dvā	dyō, dōdeca	duo	twa	duō, dwō
trayas	treis	trēs	þreis	treyes
catvāras	tettares	quattuor	fidwor	kwetwōres
panca	pente	quīnque	fimf	penkwe
sat	hex	sex	saihs	sek̂s
sapta	hepta	septem	sibun	septm
aśtāu	octō	octō	ahtau	ok̂tōu
nava	ennea	novem	niun	newn
daśa	deca	decem	taihun	dek̂m

From Edgar H. Sturtevant, An Introduction to Linguistic Science, 1947. *Reprinted with permission of Yale University Press.*

out the relationships between generically related languages. By comparing the basic vocabularies (the words most resistant to change) of the descendant languages, comparative linguists attempt to reconstruct certain features of the ancestral language, or proto-language. Table 5.2 shows the words in Sanskrit, Greek, Latin, and Gothic on which is based the reconstruction of the numbers one to ten in the original proto-Indo-European language (Sturtevant 1947). Some linguists have developed statistical approaches to estimate the date of separation of related languages. One such approach, glottochronology, is based on the rate of change in basic (non-cultural) vocabulary, which is usually retained at 80% per thousand years. Based on this figure, by computing the percentage of shared basic vocabulary words between two related languages, an estimate can be made of how long ago the two separated out from an ancestral language.

Comparative linguistics has been successful in documenting the relationships between many languages and grouping them into language families. Although this has been done in greatest detail for Indo-European languages, the technique has also been applied to non-European languages. Thus, comparative linguistics is an important way of tracing cultural and historical processes. Through reconstruction of a proto-language, comparative linguistics can also tell us something about the culture of the people who spoke that language. For example, because the reconstructed vocabulary of proto-Indo-European contains words for trees and animals that existed in northern Europe, this may have been the home of the original Indo-Europeans.

Traditional linguists have mainly been concerned with internal language change. Sociolinguists are interested in language history, or the study of historical events that affect language change. Some of the contemporary problems here have to do with the impact of industrialization, acculturation, social stratification, and national politics, as these relate to changes in language structure and language use. Sociolinguists are also interested in the social factors within a society that affect changes in both structure and language use. As Labov showed in his study in New York, sound change not only follows phonetic laws; it is also affected by the pattern of social stratification in a society, because different social classes adopt a sound change at different times.

Summary

1. All animals communicate. The main features of true human language are conventionality, productivity, and displacement.

2. Conventionality means that human languages use a limited number of sounds in combination to make an infinite number of meaningful utterances.

3. Productivity means that humans can produce and understand an infinite number of utterances they have never said or heard before.

4. Displacement refers to the ability of human languages to describe things and experiences not immediately present in the environment.

5. Human speech is adaptive: It is efficient and flexible. It allows humans to think, plan, coordinate activities, store up knowledge, and teach others. The complexity of culture depends on the human ability to communicate through speech.

6. All human languages display the same capabilities of conventionality, productivity, and displacement. There are no primitive languages.

7. A child takes the initiative in learning language and learns to speak grammatically without being taught grammatical rules. This suggests that human beings have a precultural, or innate, language-learning capacity. This potential for speech will only be realized, however, through interaction with other human beings speaking a human language.

8. All languages have structure. The three subsystems of a language are a sound system, a grammar, and a vocabulary. Phonemes are minimal sound units that carry meaning; syntax is the combination of morphemes used to produce meaningful utterances; vocabulary links words to their meanings.

9. The grammatical categories of a language are the vehicles by which people think. Grammar and vocabulary influence perception of the environment. The ways in which different cultures perceive reality through the grammatical categories of their language may show relationships to other aspects of that culture.

10. A language is not the same as speech. A language is a system of knowledge independent of the way it is used; speech is what people actually do when they communicate with one another. Sociolinguists are interested in speech behavior as it is culturally patterned and varies according to social factors, including gender.

11. Language changes. Historical linguists are interested in internal linguistic change. Comparative linguists attempt to discover which languages are generically related. Sociolinguists are interested in the historical and social factors in language change.

Suggested Readings

Burling, Robbins
1970   *Man's Many Voices*. New York: Holt, Rinehart and Winston. An excellent introduction to all aspects of language, including topics not usually covered in introductory texts, such as Black English and word games.

Chambers, John, Jr., ed.
1983   *Black English: Educational Equity and the Law*. Ann Arbor, Mich.: Karoma. A collection of articles centering around the Ann Arbor "Black English" case, including some by anthropological linguists.

Farb, Peter
1974   *Word Play: What Happens When People Talk*. New York: Knopf. As is usual with this author, this book is comprehensive, entertaining, and interesting for the nonspecialist.

Gumperz, John J., and Hymes, Dell, eds.
1972   *Directions in Sociolinguistics*. New York: Holt, Rinehart and Winston. A compilation

of interesting articles from a number of different cultures on a variety of kinds of speech performances.

Southworth, F. C., and Daswani, C. J.
1974   *Foundations of Linguistics*. New York: Free Press. This is a good, complete introduction to the study of language and is written in a straightforward, clear manner.

Tannen, Deborah
1990   *You Just Don't Understand: Women and Men in Conversation*. New York: William Morrow. A substantial contribution to the sociolinguistics of gender, this book is a witty, easy to read best-seller that uses research findings and everyday experiences to drive home the point that men and women follow different norms of speaking.

Learning Culture

What are the biocultural bases of human culture learning?

In what ways is child rearing different in India and in the United States?

How does "coming of age" in the United States differ from the same process in other cultures?

What do we learn in school besides the "Three R's"? And how does academic success relate to other aspects of culture?

"Ours is a socialist society; everything is done according to plan." This comment about China, made to an American visitor twenty-five years ago, is attested to by a remarkable uniformity in the care and training of the young. Throughout China there is great consistency in the values and goals in child-care institutions such as nursery schools and kindergartens. The major themes of subordinating personal to social needs, respecting productive labor, altruism, cooperation, and the integration of physical with intellectual labor, describe the kind of citizen China hoped to produce. The techniques used to achieve these values are practiced from infancy.

One quality sure to strike an American visitor in China is the importance of group activities, such as the "cultural performance." Whether they are songs from a revolutionary opera, dances, or folk music, these performances are always presented by groups, and it is impossible to pick out a "star." Many of the child-care facilities seemed to lack the variety of toys and materials which in the United States are considered necessary to "enrich" the child's environment, but the Chinese teachers did not seem to consider this a detriment. Chinese children are generally expected to rely on each other for stimulation, and sharing toys is an approved value. One American visitor noted, for example, that the wooden blocks the children were playing with seemed awfully heavy for a small child to pick up. "Exactly," beamed the teacher. "That fosters mutual help."

Chinese teachers encourage such group behavior as cooperation, sharing, and altruism. "We praise a child when he shows concern for other's interests," said one kindergarten teacher. "For example, at meal time teachers give out bowls and chopsticks. If a youngster gets a nicer bowl and gives it to someone else, we praise him for it." Even in a competitive situation, helping another is more important than winning. "When the children run in a relay race, sometimes one will fall down. . . . If another child stops to help him get up or to see if he is all right, even though his own team might fall behind, we encourage this."

From Bruce Dollar, "Child Care in China," in Society as It Is *(New York: Macmillan, 1980).*

In this description of Chinese child care as it was practiced twenty-five years ago, the Chinese were extremely conscious of trying to raise "revolutionary successors" so that the values and goals informed by the teachings of Mao Tse-tung could be continued in succeeding generations. It may be that as the goals and values of Chinese society change, their child-care practices will also change.

All societies, whether consciously, as in China, or unconsciously, as in other examples throughout this chapter, develop child-rearing practices that aim to produce a person who can fit into the society. As you read, keep in mind the different socialization practices used in different cultures and think about how these are geared to the society's view of its own needs.

Human beings depend on the social, not biological, transmission of knowledge for survival. The importance of learning for humans is related to the prolonged dependency of the human infant and child. Although our complex brain gives us the capacity for learning, it also means we develop more slowly and need the support of others to survive. Human social organization and group living thus provide the basic context in which we can learn from others at the same time that we are being protected by them. Although other animals, particularly nonhuman primates, also have this capacity and live in groups, no other animal species depends as much as we do on learned behavior to meet its needs.

More than any other species, human beings are dependent on others for survival and growth. Human infants cannot survive without the care of other people. They cannot get food, cannot move around, cannot cling, and cannot force adults to respond to their needs. The hu-

man's period of helplessness and dependency on others is the longest in the animal world. It is the price *Homo sapiens* pays for its big brain and its enormous potential for learning. And it is during the long period of infancy that cultural patterning has its strongest effect. The infant simply has no choice about learning to respond in culturally patterned ways.

Human infants become adults only by growing up in a particular human society. Thus, the infant grows up into a child and later into an adult not simply as a human, but as a particular kind of human: a Kwakiutl, Trobriand Islander, Briton, or Tahitian. **Enculturation** is the term anthropologists use to refer to the ways in which human infants and children learn to be adult members of their society; **socialization** refers to the learning processes through which human cultural traditions are passed on from one generation to the next.

Biology, Socialization, and Culture

The human infant, in spite of its helplessness, is not simply an "empty slate" on which culture writes its pattern or a lump of clay on which culture impresses its own shape. Human beings have a biologically based disposition to learn human behavior. The human child actively participates in culture. Human brains and nervous systems are organized to promote social interaction with others, learning, and adaptation to the requirements of a particular sociocultural system. In addition to the biological characteristics of the species, each human being brings a

The dependency of the human infant on human social organization provides the basic context in which infants can learn from others while being protected by them. (United Nations)

Children learn to develop the behavior and attitudes considered acceptable in their society. (United Nations)

unique genetic inheritance to the socialization process. Becoming a human being, therefore, is the result of a complex interaction between universal human capacities and culturally variable child-rearing practices, individual heredity, and the common experiences patterned by culture.

Anthropologists are not in complete agreement about what exactly these innate human capacities and potentialities are. We know that infants have not only physical needs but emotional ones as well. Studies of infants in a variety of situations have demonstrated that "tender loving care" is a prerequisite for healthy emotional development (Spitz 1975). This need also exists among nonhuman primates. Experimental studies demonstrate that infant monkeys who are deprived of the company of their mothers do not develop in the same way as other monkeys. They play less; they are less curious, more hostile, and sexually clumsy. Male monkeys raised apart from their mothers show little interest in female monkeys as adults. Fe-

male monkeys raised apart from their mothers show little interest in their own babies (Harlow 1962).

All human beings also pass through a similar sequence of developmental stages, each characterized by an increase in the capacity to deal with the physical and social environment. At each stage, physical, mental, and psychological potentialities unfold if they are given at least a minimum of encouragement. Physically, the infant increases in muscular coordination; from an immobile creature barely able to focus the movement of eyes and limbs, it begins to be able to lift its head, focus its eyes, sit up, creep on all fours, stand, and then walk by itself. Mentally, it increases its capacity to differentiate and classify objects and people in the environment. Its curiosity increases. Human infants will, if given a chance, take an active role in trying new ways of behaving and exploring the world around them. Psychologically, the infant increasingly develops a sense of itself and others. As the infant grows, it learns to modify its demands so that it will meet with success in its social environment. The infant becomes increasingly able to distinguish what actions will bring gratification and what actions will be met with no response or negative response from others. Cultural variability in child rearing must be seen against the background of universals that grow out of the biological characteristics of the human organism: the needs for physical gratification and for emotional contact with others, and stages of developmental capacities. Thus, socialization must be seen against the different stages of the life cycle.

Every system of cultural transmission takes into account these different stages of life, although the definition of the stages may vary from culture to culture. Infants are treated differently from children; children reach puberty and eventually become adults; adults are distinguished as middle-aged and old. With each of these status changes, different roles are assumed and different kinds of cultural transmission take place. Although in anthropology we have traditionally emphasized early socialization rather than the transmission of culture in later life, we are now paying greater attention to learning in adulthood and among the old.

Not only do societies transmit culture in terms of life stages, but not all people in a society are given the same social conditioning. Status differences and the roles, or behavior patterns, associated with them must be considered in investigating the way culture is transmitted. In societies where social ranking and differentiation are important, what one learns may be largely a function of one's position in the social hierarchy. At the very least, every society treats males and females differently.

Gender-Role Socialization

This process of sex-role socialization frequently begins at infancy or shortly thereafter. The ways in which this is done and its effects on behavior and personality are always of interest to anthropologists. Two important processes associated with sex-role learning are imitation and internalization through identification with a same-sex role model. In play, for example, girls most frequently imitate the domestic activities of their mothers or elder females who stand in this relation to them; boys imitate their fathers or other males. This imitation is subtly encouraged along the lines of sex even when it is not a consequence of direct teaching. Girls and boys are both discouraged from imitating activities culturally considered appropriate for the opposite sex and rewarded for imitating activities considered culturally appropriate for their own sex. The internalization of gender identification — that is, the inner conceptualization of self as being masculine or feminine — is tied up with the playing out of these sex-related activities.

Part of the controversy in the study of sex-role socialization is the extent to which the differences that have been found to be related to sex are based on biology (Draper 1974). Because learning begins at birth, untangling the complex interaction between biology and culture becomes extremely difficult. When adult expectations of children become stereotyped according to sex role, it may be this expectation, even more than possible biological differences, that explains the differentiation in male and female behavior and personality.

The complex way in which biology and culture may interact to produce differences in male and female behavior is illustrated by the findings that girls seem to have greater verbal ability and boys greater spatial ability. It is generally agreed that girls have a better and earlier ability to acquire language than do boys and that they are more sensitive to social cues than are boys. Boys are almost universally shown to have superior spatial ability. If we assume that these abilities have some biological basis, we can also assume that they would be incorporated into parents' expectations of children. Parents would expect little girls to talk more and respond to others and might talk more with them. They would allow, reward, or even initiate activities in which boys can explore their

Sex-role socialization often involves the informal participation of children in the appropriate economic roles of their sex. Here, small boys in Fez, Morocco, hold the golden threads that their tailor fathers are using to make embroidered djellabahs, the local garment. (United Nations)

environment. Subtle but persistent interactions with others based on the initial biological differences may play a large role in explaining some sex role–related patterns in adults — for example, the greater success girls have in school (which rewards verbal ability and social sensitivity) and the superior performance of males on tests of spatial ability.

But the evidence is not clear. In practically all societies, small boys are allowed to roam farther from their home than small girls. This is both consistent with, and may be a cause of, the superior spatial abilities of males. Studies of exceptional girls in one East African society who were allowed to roam farther from home than was typically the case showed they matched their male counterparts on tests of spatial ability. Such findings put us back to a position in which sex-role socialization appears to be best

understood in terms of both biological and cultural components interacting in complex ways. One useful model for understanding this process may be that socialization practices act back upon and intensify possible biological predispositions that are different in males and females.

Early Socialization and Personality

Child-rearing practices in all cultures are designed to produce adults who will be able to function effectively in that culture. In order to be able to do this, adults must learn certain skills, norms, and values; they must learn the cultural *content*. But the transmission of culture involves more than content; in the socialization process, children learn more than just skills and knowledge. The transmission of culture involves patterning children's attitudes and values as well as their outward behavior. The shaping of values and personality, or the inner life of the child, often does not take place consciously. Through unconscious, although culturally patterned, interaction with others, the growing child learns to respond to the world in culturally selected ways. From the vast potential of emotional responses, cultures select out some that are considered appropriate. Through the details of their experience with others, children learn to pattern their emotional responses in culturally approved ways.

The covert aspect of socialization calls attention to culture as a communication process. From this point of view, what is important in cultural transmission is not so much what children are taught or not taught but the ways in which things happen to them and the attitudes of the people around them with whom they are interacting (Schwartz 1976).

Culture and Personality

The field of **psychological anthropology** tries to understand how psychological factors and processes relate to cultural practices, and also how culture may affect psychological processes such as cognition, emotions, attitudes, and personality, much of which is shaped in early childhood. Between 1920 and 1950, some anthropologists were particularly interested in the relationship between culture and personality. This interest grew partly out of Freudian psychoanalytical theory and partly out of the interest in the relationship between culture and psychology formulated by Benedict, Boas, and Edward Sapir, a linguist and cultural anthropologist. Some of the early culture-and-personality studies were done to test specific Freudian theories in non-Western cultures. Malinowski (1953; originally published 1927), for example, attempted to demonstrate that the Oedipus complex (defined by Freud as a sexual attachment of the male child to his mother, accompanied by hatred and jealousy toward his father), which Freud believed to be universal, did not exist in this form in the Trobriand Islands. The Trobriand society was matrilineal (the kinship group was organized around a woman and her descendants), and the mother's brother, rather than the father, was the primary authority in the family. Incest taboos in this society were strongest for brothers and sisters, not mothers and sons, and a boy's major unconscious rivalry was directed toward his maternal uncle, not his father.

Early culture-and-personality studies, having been influenced by Freudian theory, put particular emphasis on child-rearing practices such as feeding, weaning, and toilet training. Although most culture-and-personality theorists were interested in the influence culture had on personality, a group led by Abram Kardiner (1945) wanted to investigate the ways in which personality types might be reflected in patterns of culture. Kardiner and his associates believed that religion, folklore, and political systems might be seen as screens on which the basic personality orientation of a society was projected. They were interested in the relationship between child-rearing practices, the development of basic personality, and other aspects of culture. They saw a basic personality type as an adaptation that grew out of child-rearing practices that were themselves linked to the subsistence patterns of a society.

Later culture-and-personality theorists studied large, complex societies. National character studies, as they were called, appeared for Japan (Benedict 1946), the United States (Mead 1942), and the Soviet Union (Gorer and Rickman 1949), among others. One of the problems with these studies was that it became difficult to generalize about personality in societies composed of several ethnic groups, social classes, and subcultures. Many of these national character studies also made connections between early child-rearing practices and later adult personality traits that were difficult to prove scientifically.

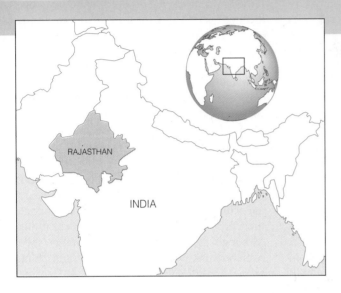

Two basic principles that organize Indian village society are caste and family. Castes, traditionally based on occupation, are ranked as superior and inferior, and individuals cannot change their caste affiliations. Child-rearing patterns differ among castes, and are also conditioned by the patriarchal, patrilineal, and patrilocal nature of the Indian family. Men make most of the important decisions, inheritance is through the male line, and a woman lives in her husband's village after she marries.

. . . Among the Rajput caste in the village of Khalapur in North India, . . . child-rearing practices are directed, both consciously and unconsciously, toward training the child to function effectively within the social framework of family, caste, and village. Three aspects of child-rearing practices related to this are training in emotional unresponsiveness, training in controlling aggression and assertiveness, and the lack of training in self-reliance.

The Rajput caste claims descent from the ancient warrior kings of India. Today, however, they are mostly farmers. Rajput dwellings in the village of Khalapur include separate quarters for males and females, a typical Indian spatial configuration. The women's quarters are within an enclosed courtyard. Rajput women practice purdah: They wear a veil in front of all male strangers and any men in their husband's family who are older than their husband. The life of Rajput women and small children is largely lived within the confines of the courtyard. The men have their own quarters, where they spend most of their time; they socialize, eat, and frequently sleep apart from the women.

Training in emotional unresponsiveness begins at birth. Although Rajput infants will be picked up and attended to when they are hungry or fussing, for the most part they are left in their cots, wrapped up in blankets both to keep off insects and to avoid the evil eye. Except for anxieties about a baby's health, it is not the center of attention. A baby receives attention mainly when it cries. At that time, someone will try to distract it, but when it becomes quiet, the interaction will stop. Adult interaction with babies is generally aimed at producing a cessation of response, rather than stimulation of it. Infants and children of all ages are not shown off to others for fear, parents say, that they will attract the evil eye. Children are also not praised by their parents, who fear that this will "spoil" them and make them disobedient.

Rajput children spend their first two years as passive observers of court-yard life. They are never left alone, yet neither are they the center of interest. The child learns that moodiness will not be tolerated. Few demands are put on Rajput children; they are not pressured or even encouraged to become self-reliant. Weaning, which generally occurs without trouble, takes place at two to three years; but if the mother does not become pregnant, a child may be nursed into its sixth year. There is no pressure for toilet training. Babies are not diapered, and when the baby is being held by someone, it is simply held away from the body when it urinates. . . . When a child can walk, he or she is led outside the courtyard to urinate or defecate; because this is done in public by adults, the child can easily imitate the proper behavior.

Babies are not pressured, or even encouraged, to walk. They learn to walk when they are ready, and mothers say they see no reason to rush this. When a baby can walk alone, it wanders about the courtyard. . . . Village women do little to guide children's behavior by explaining or reasoning with them. There is also little direct instruction to small children, [who] learn the skills, customs, and values of the group through observation and imitation. In the first five years of life, the child moves very gradually from observer to participant in village and family life.

The preschool child plays most of the time. Although some of this play involves imitating adult activities, such as farming and cooking, children are not encouraged . . . to participate in adult activities. The chores a child is given are mainly directed to helping the mother, who is confined to the courtyard. Thus, children may go to the store, carry water, or deliver messages to the men's house. There is little feeling that children should be given chores on principle in order to train them in responsibility. Rajput children take little initiative in solving problems by themselves. Instead, they are taught whom they can depend on for help in the web of social relations of kin group, caste, and village. Children follow the adult pattern of giving aid only when asked and often only if it is insistently demanded. Chores increase as children get older, but it is not a Rajput custom to require children to work if adults can do it. Children are not praised for their work, and a child's inept attempt to do an adult job is belittled. Thus, children are reluctant to undertake what they cannot do well.

This lack of responsibility training is consistent with the pattern of values in a caste society. In the Indian caste system, menial and manual work are considered not only degrading socially but also ritually and spiritually unclean. Many Rajputs are quite wealthy and employ servants to do the menial tasks that in other cultures might be assigned to children. Finally, as a caste of warriors, Rajputs have contempt for farming, although that is how they earn their livelihood. A Rajput family that can afford it will hire laborers to do the farm

(continued)

work. Even if a Rajput man does his own farming, he passes on a negative attitude about this work to his sons.

The third aspect of child rearing in Khalapur related to the requirements of Indian social organization is the inhibition of aggression and assertiveness in small children. There is some ambivalence here. The caste system and the family system require an individual to be submissive to those above but dominant with those below. Also, as a warrior caste, Rajput males feel they ought to maintain an aggressive image. The lack of consistency in training children to control aggression reflects this. On the one hand, mothers *say* a child ought to be passive, submissive, and restrained in the presence of others. Even defensive fighting among children is discouraged. On the other hand, the mothers allow some aggression against themselves, especially on the part of sons. Males learn pretty early that women have a low status in the village and family and can thus be abused, at least verbally. Men are more willing than women to teach a child to be aggressive, and this is reinforced by traditional dramatic performances of Hindu mythology, in which Rajput warrior bravery is an important feature.

Child-rearing practices in Khalapur, which emphasize emotional unresponsiveness and a group orientation, make sense in terms of the context of a caste hierarchy, limited geographical and social mobility, and an extended family: all conditions in which group harmony rather than individualism is the basis of the social order.

For Westerners reading about these North Indian child-rearing practices, the lack of emphasis on self-reliance may strike them negatively, as it is in direct opposition to one of our most important cultural values — and one central in both our formal and informal child-rearing practices. The importance of self-reliance is related to our Western value of individualism and our Western psychological theories of the importance of separation and individuation of the self from the family as the child grows into an adult. The Western yardstick of individuation is the one against which other cultures are judged — and have often been found wanting. Unfortunately, few psychologists have sufficient training in anthropology to make them adequately sensitive to the need for cross-cultural theories of human development — theories that take into account the values of other cultures such as India and Japan where personality is more oriented to other people and where dependence as part of a mature adult personality is much more acceptable than is true in the West. This mode of functioning is not only consistent with the values of these cultures but also with the requirements of their social structures, which emphasize groups and interpersonal relationships.

Adapted from John T. Hitchcock and Leigh Minturn, "The Rajputs of Khalapur," in Beatrice Whiting, ed. Six Cultures: Studies of Child Rearing. © 1963 by John Wiley & Sons. Reprinted by permission of the publisher.

Because of the difficulty of proving many of the ideas of the early culture-and-personality theorists, psychological anthropology took new directions after 1950. There was a greater attempt to use statistics to demonstrate the connections between child-rearing practices, personality, and other cultural patterns. John Whiting and Irvin Child (1984), for example, used a large cross-cultural sample in an attempt to demonstrate some of these interrelationships. One hypothesis they tested was that systems of curing illness would reflect techniques that had been sources of gratification in early child rearing. Thus, a culture in which children were indulged in sources of oral gratification, such as feeding, would tend to use oral medicines for curing illness. Whiting and Child also hypothesized about the reverse of this relationship: They attempted to demonstrate that an aspect of child rearing that was frustrating and promoted anxiety would be used to account for illness. If a culture frustrated a child's oral gratification — by withholding food, for example — that culture might be likely to see disease as something that enters the body through the mouth. Both hypotheses were validated statistically, and the work proved to be a major step toward more refined methods of demonstrating the relationships between child-rearing practices, personality development, and other aspects of culture.

Whiting and his associates also tried to relate child-rearing patterns and subsequent personality development to the basic patterns of culture — food getting, division of labor, and residence. This interest in the relation between ecology and personality has gained importance in culture-and-personality studies. For example, Robert Edgerton (1971) investigated four East African tribes that were divided into farmers and herders. He found personality differences not only among the four tribes but also between the farmers and the herders within each. Herders were more individualistic compared with farmers, who more often felt the need to consult others in making decisions. Edgerton concluded that the more an economy depends on herding, the more that society will value independence as a male personality trait.

Although psychologists are now entering the field of cross-cultural personality studies, anthropologists still tend to take a broader view of personality development. For the anthropologist, biological factors, family relations, cultural images, social roles, and specific situational factors all play a part in shaping personality.

The subtle ways in which personality is shaped through unconscious cultural patterning, as well as conscious training, are illustrated in the accompanying ethnography of child rearing in a village in India.

Socialization throughout Life

Learning one's culture is a process that continues after infancy and early childhood, although most social scientists agree that the earliest years are most crucial. In looking at later socialization, anthropologists have been interested in a number of aspects of the transmission of culture. One is the relationship between early enculturation and later enculturation. As children grow up and move into new and adult roles, is what they have learned in childhood useful for those roles? Is there, in other words, cultural continuity in socialization?

Cultural Continuity and Discontinuity

Ruth Benedict (1938) characterized American culture as containing major discontinuities between what is expected of children and what is expected of adults. Children in our culture are not expected to be responsible; they are supposed to play, not work. Few children in the United States have the opportunity to contribute in any meaningful way to the basic tasks of society. Children take on responsibility only when they become adults. A second major discontinuity is that children are required to be submissive, but adults are expected to be dominant. This is especially true for males. Sons must obey their fathers, but as fathers they must dominate their sons. A third major discontinuity has to do with sex. As children, Americans are not allowed to engage in sexual behavior, and for many people, just the thought of childhood sexuality is repellent. As adults, however, especially as men and women marry, sex is considered to be a normal, even valued, activity.

In contrast to the discontinuities experienced by the individual learning to participate in the culture of the United States is the continuity of socialization among many native American societies as they traditionally functioned. Based on the accounts given to him by elderly informants, E. A. Hoebel described a traditional Cheyenne culture that exhibited a great degree of continuity. For instance, Cheyenne children were not treated as a different order of people from adults. They were regarded as smaller and not yet fully competent adults, although by American standards the competence of Cheyenne children was astounding. The play of small children centered on imitation of, and real participation in, adult tasks. Both boys and girls learned to ride horses almost as soon as they could walk. This skill was related to the importance of the horse in traditional Cheyenne culture, in which buffalo were hunted on horseback. By the time they were six, boys were riding bareback and using the lasso. By eight, they were helping to herd the horses in the camp. As soon as they could use them, boys got small but good-quality bows and arrows. Girls who were just toddlers helped their mothers carry wood and water. Boys and girls learned these activities in play, in which the routine of family life was imitated. Girls played "mother" to the smallest children; boys imitated the male roles of hunter and warrior and even the rituals of self-torture that were part of Cheyenne religious ceremonies.

Control of aggression was an important value among the Cheyenne, and aggression rarely occurred within the group of adults. A chief ruled not by force and dominance but by intelligence, justice, and consideration for others. The needs of the group were more important than the needs of the individual. The Cheyenne learned this lesson at an early age. Infants who cried were not physically punished but were removed from the camp and their baskets hung in the bushes until they stopped. This early lesson in discipline taught that one cannot force one's will on others by self-display. Aggression and lack of control of one's emotions do not bring rewards for either children or adults; rather, they result in social isolation.

The repression of sexuality is another lesson traditionally learned early in childhood and carried through adult life. A Cheyenne girl was considered unchaste if a boy even touched her genitals or breasts, and she could not enter into a respectable marriage. From the time of her first menses, a girl put on a "chastity belt" of rope and rawhide that she took off only at marriage; in fact, she might continue to wear it even during marriage when her husband was away fighting or hunting. Males were also taught to control their sexual impulses, and they could not consider courtship or marriage until they had been in a war party. Sexual control continued to be an ideal even in marriage. The Cheyenne ideal was to space children ten to twelve years apart. A couple that took a vow to refrain from sexual relations for this period after the birth of a child was highly respected in the camp.

Although Cheyenne childhood seems to require a great deal of discipline, responsibility, and competence, these demands were consistent with the demands on adults. There was no discontinuity between Cheyenne childhood, adolescence, and adulthood. The transition to adult status was easy, being a continuum of what was learned in childhood. For a boy, the public recognition of this status came with his first participation as hunter and warrior, which occurred at about age twelve. This was such an important event that his achievement was publicly rewarded by his parents' praise and a feast given in his honor. As Hoebel (1960:93), an ethnographer of the Cheyenne, says: "Cheyenne youths have little reason to be rebels without a cause. They slip easily into manhood, knowing their contributions are immediately wanted, valued and ostentatiously rewarded."

Coming of Age

Anthropologists have looked at later socialization in terms of the ways in which adolescents, who are marginal in some cultures, become fully incorporated into their society. Where there is cultural continuity, as among the Cheyenne, youth are not marginal. There is a gradually increasing social participation from childhood through adulthood. In many societies where there is discontinuity—where a youth must change in order to become an adult—dramatic rituals of initiation ensure that this change is made.

In other societies, as well as our own, there is a discontinuity but no ritual. Young men, particularly, are left on their own to "initiate themselves." This may lead to the formation of youth gangs or to various other informal peer-group activities in which peers socialize one another into the male role. This behavior is frequently rebellious and contrary to society's values, but not always. Among the Xhosa of South Africa, youth groups engage in activities that dramatize the male role, provide an arena for physical and sexual activity, and yet are in full accord with the adult values and roles of the culture (Mayer and Mayer 1970). Here again we are back to the two-faced coin of enculturation: On the one hand, each child must grow up and in doing so achieve the competence and psychological growth necessary for healthy human functioning. On the other hand, each culture must find a way of transmitting its values and knowledge to the growing child and youth so that the basic culture will be continued. As we have seen, and will continue to see, there is great variability in the ways in which this is done.

In the United States, an important part of "coming of age" takes place in college. Anthro-

Among the middle class in the United States, graduation from college is the culmination of a process of coming of age. (Serena Nanda)

pologist Michael Moffatt explored this process through a study of students at a major northeastern public university, in a provocatively titled book, *Coming of Age in New Jersey* (1989). These students, similar to others in the United States, experienced the maturing process that takes place in college as a set of stages, corresponding with the freshman, sophomore, junior, and senior years. College freshmen were foolish and inexperienced; sophomores were "wild men—and women"; juniors saw themselves as suddenly having outgrown the juvenile behavior of the college dorm; and seniors were "burnt out," tired of college, and somewhat anxious about what would happen next.

Students attributed their growing maturity in college to both the formal and informal learning experiences of undergraduate life, but gave most importance to interaction with other students. While it was recognized that the academic aspect of college awarded the credentials needed to progress through a good career, and contributed to broad, general knowledge, most students felt that it was the extracurricular activity that most influenced their personal development. Some of this extracurricular activity was intellectual "fun": long talks with their peers about serious political, philosophical, and morality issues. But what was most influential was the informal "social learning" of skills needed to be a competent adult "in the real world," after graduation.

Foremost among these skills in becoming a competent adult was the ability to take responsibility for oneself. College is a place where teachers and guidance counselors no longer monitored behavior as in high school; living away from home also meant that parents did not know what the individual was doing on a daily basis. With much more free time, a more flexible schedule, and many more distractions and activities available, students had to make their own decisions about how to spend their time between "work" and "play." Another important learning experience for these students was negotiating the complexities of an impersonal university bureaucracy, which built skills of persistence and determination that they believed would be very useful in the "real world." And, although Moffatt noted that the students he studied did not actually have very culturally diverse friendship groups, for many, college was their first experience with cultural diversity — meeting, mixing, and sometimes becoming friends with people from racial, cultural, and religious groups other than their own. Students believed that their ability to, at the very least, "get along" in such a diverse environment was an important social skill and one that contributed to their becoming mature adults.

Not all youths in the United States go to college, and there are also wide differences in college experiences as they relate to coming of age. Moffatt's study indicates that for those American youths who do go to college, these four years give some structure to their coming-of-age process. But his study also confirms what appears to be an important difference between the United States and other cultures; in our society coming of age is largely an informal process that takes place among peers, with little structure or guidance from adults, whereas in many other cultures, coming of age is supervised by adults, and takes place within a ritual structure of formal initiation.

Initiation Rites

A number of anthropologists have suggested that there is more discontinuity in socialization for males than for females (Chodorow 1974). For boys to become men frequently requires an assertion of independence that involves a rejection of both feminine qualities and identification with females. For girls, the transition to adult status is more of a continuation of their early life, which is organized around and involved with the family, primary relationships, and caring for others. The need for boys to break away from identification with and dependence on females may be one explanation of the frequency of male **initiation rites** in many societies. From this perspective, male initiation rites can be seen as bridging the gap where discontinuities exist between early childhood socialization and the requirements of an adult masculine role. Thus, John Whiting and his associates (1967) have shown that male initiation rites are more likely to occur in cultures where there is a strong identification of the boy with his mother and hostility toward the father. This may grow out of sleeping arrangements in which children sleep with the mother apart from the father. In these cases, says Whiting, male initiation rites are necessary to ensure the development of an adequate male role.

In many societies, a boy between the ages of five and twelve must undergo an initiation, after which he is publicly recognized as a man. This "rite of passage" is frequently lengthy, dramatic, and painful, and it often involves circumcision. During this initiation, a boy may be taught tribal lore as well as more practical elements of culture. From this perspective, some anthropologists have seen initiation rites primarily in terms of their educational functions. They are the equivalent of the formal schooling received by children in our own society. Still another explanation offered for male initiation rites is that of dramatizing the values of society in a context outside the intimacy of the home (Hart 1967). By taking the child out of the home, the initiation rite emphasizes the impor-

Male initiation rites are a common feature in the world's cultures and mark the transition from childhood to adulthood. On the eve of his circumcision ceremony, a boy rides a horse accompanied by dancers and musicians in a village in Indonesia. (United Nations)

tance of citizenship—the fact that an individual must be responsible to the whole society and that society as well as the family has an interest in him. Another function suggested for male initiation rites is that of explicitly affirming and maintaining the solidarity of the male bond in society and the importance of male organization to social life. Still other interpretations have focused on the symbolism of the rites themselves. Bruno Bettelheim (1962), a psychoanalyst who studied rites involving circumcision, suggests that they are symbolic of the male envy of the female power of bearing children. The bloodletting associated with the rites is an attempt to imitate and thus participate in these life-creating powers at a symbolic level.

In his autobiography, Tepilit Ole Saitoti, a Maasai, describes his initiation and what it means in his society:

"Tepilit, circumcision means a sharp knife cutting into the skin of the most sensitive part of

your body. You must not budge; don't move a muscle or even blink. You can face only one direction until the operation is completed. The slightest movement on your part will mean you are a coward, incompetent and unworthy to be a Maasai man. Ours has always been a proud family, and we would like to keep it that way. We will not tolerate unnecessary embarrassment, so you had better be ready. If you are not, tell us now so that we will not proceed. Imagine yourself alone remaining uncircumcised like the water youth [white people]. I hear they are not circumcised. Such a thing is not known in Maasailand; therefore, circumcision will have to take place even if it means holding you down until it is completed."

My father continued to speak and every one of us kept quiet. "The pain you will feel is symbolic. There is a deeper meaning in all this. Circumcision means a break between childhood and adulthood. For the first time in your life, you are regarded as a grownup, a complete man or woman. You will be expected to give and not just to receive. To protect the family always, not just to be protected yourself. And your wise judgment will for the first time be taken into consideration. No family affairs will be discussed without your being consulted. If you are ready for all these responsibilities, tell us now. Coming into manhood is not simply a matter of growth and maturity. It is a heavy load on your shoulders and especially a burden on the mind. Too much of this—I am done. I have said all I wanted to say. Fellows, if you have anything to add, go ahead and tell your brother, because I am through. I have spoken." (1986:66)*

Female initiation rites also exist in many societies, although they are not found as frequently as initiation rites for males. Such rites are different from society to society; sometimes the initiate is isolated; sometimes she is the center of attention. Some of the rituals are elaborate and take years to perform; others are performed with little ceremony. Given the great variety, a female initiation rite may be defined as consisting of prescribed ceremonial events, given to all girls in a particular society, celebrated between their eighth and twentieth years. The rite is often a cultural elaboration of menarche but does not include betrothal or marriage customs (Brown 1965). There are a number of possible interpretations of such rites. Brown found that such rites are more likely to occur in societies in which the young girl continues to reside in the home of her mother after marriage. This suggests the rites are a way of announcing a girl's status change, which is made necessary by the fact that she spends her adult life in the same place as she spent her childhood. Though the girl may continue to do the same kind of tasks she did as a child growing up, she now has to do them as a responsible adult. The rites are thus the means by which the girl publicly accepts her new legal role. Where a girl moves to her husband's home after marriage, this move itself signals the change from childhood to adult status.

Another reason, often made explicit in those societies that perform such rites, is that the rites are a way of teaching the girls what they will have to know as adults. Bemba women explain their elaborate girls' initiation rite called *Chisungu* (Richards 1956:125) by saying that they "make the girls clever," using a word that means "to be intelligent and socially competent and to have a knowledge of etiquette."

Although such rites do indeed seem to have a teaching component, this cannot be a full explanation of them, because such rites do not exist in all societies where females perform domestic and subsistence tasks. It is suggested, therefore, that only in societies where women have a central role in subsistence will such rites be performed, in order to assure both the girl and others of her competence and to impress upon her the importance of her adult role.

Finally, Brown also offers an explanation of female rites that inflict a great deal of pain, such as extensive tattooing or a genital operation. These rites are often found in societies with male initiation rites where both a genital operation and seclusion are part of the ritual. Thus, these female rites may be interpreted both as an imitation of male rites and as a way of resolving a conflict of sexual identity, which grows out of the same conditions of infancy that explain the male rites.

Socialization and Formal Education

A child who was asked to recite the multiplication tables for his teacher began "la-di-da-di-da, la-di-da-di-da," at which point the teacher interrupted to ask him what he was saying. He responded that he knew the tune but he did not yet know the words. (Cole et al. 1971)

Although few anthropologists have devoted their attention to the school as an agent of socialization, Jules Henry has been particularly concerned with the kind of learning that

*From *The Worlds of a Maasai Warrior* by Tepilit Ole Saitoti. © 1986 by Tepilit Ole Saitoti. Reprinted by permission of Random House.

goes on in American schools. Henry points out that the school not only formally instructs children in the skills they will need to participate in a highly industrialized society but also transmits some basic cultural values without the students or the teachers being aware of what is going on. In the following incident, "At the Blackboard," Henry observes that competition as a social value is covertly learned along with the overt content of mathematics.

> Boris had trouble reducing "$12/16$" to the lowest terms and could only get as far as "$6/8$." The teacher asked him quietly if that was as far as he could reduce it. She suggested that "he think." Much heaving up and down and waving of hands by the other children, all frantic to correct him. Boris pretty unhappy, probably mentally paralyzed. The teacher, quiet, patient, ignores the others and concentrates with look and voice on Boris. She says, "Is there a bigger number than two you can divide into the two parts of the fraction?" After a minute or two, she becomes more urgent, but there is no response from Boris. She then turns to the class and says, "Well, who can tell Boris what the number is?" A forest of hands appears, and the teacher calls Peggy. Peggy says four may be divided into the numerator and denominator.[*]

Henry goes on to say: "Boris's failure has made it possible for Peggy to succeed, his depression is the price of her exhilaration; his misery the occasion for her rejoicing." Whether Boris has learned math is questionable. Perhaps Boris's "nightmare at the blackboard" was a lesson for him in controlling himself so that "he would not fly shrieking from the room under the enormous public pressure." Boris has learned the fear of failure, which, according to Henry, is one of the things a child must learn in order to get along in the competitive society of the United States.

As formal schooling has been introduced into many cultures through contact with the West, more anthropologists are studying the

role of the school in socialization. Many of these studies address the problems that occur when Western-style middle-class schools and education are imposed on traditional kin-based, non-Western communities. The education in typical Western schools is based on a particular kind of cognitive style: the ability to see abstract relationships that are mediated largely through language. The school atmosphere encourages an active mode of learning, solving problems on one's own, and a situation in which the teacher is involved in an impersonal and impartial role of instructing. Teaching style, educational context, and cognitive skills appear to conflict with traditional informal socialization in non-Western cultures. There, learning takes place in the context of life, teaching is largely by example, verbal instruction plays a minimum role, and many of the problems are posed in terms that require a single solution to a particular case, rather than the ability to generalize. Although numerous studies have shown that with special training children from such traditional learning contexts can develop other cognitive skills and perform well on Western "intelligence" tests, as a rule there is conflict between the two systems, and many children from traditional cultures do not perform well in school.

Cross-cultural studies of schoolchildren indicate a correlation between cultural values and practices, cognition and school performance. For example, a long-term study comparing Mexican and North American schoolchildren found significant differences for both cognitive measures and cognitive-perceptual–style variables (remember, these were discussed in Chapter 4). The authors of the study (Holtzman et al. 1975) attribute these findings, which they characterized as a passive style for the Mexicans and an active style for the North Americans, to the different values in each culture: North Americans value curiosity and independent thinking whereas Mexicans value interpersonal relationships.

The authors of the study also attribute the better performance of North American schoolchildren to such cultural practices as mothers

---

[*] Jules Henry, *Culture against Man*. New York: Random House, 1963, p. 295. Reprinted by permission.

CULTURE CONFLICT AND FORMAL EDUCATION

In a monograph called *The New Mathematics and an Old Culture* (1967), John Gay and Michael Cole present this "culture conflict" as it exists for the Kpelle of Liberia, in West Africa. Traditionally, Kpelle learning is based on the unquestioned acceptance of authority and rote learning. For the Kpelle, the "world remains a mystery to be accepted on authority, not a complex pattern of comprehensible regularities." Kpelle children do not look for patterns in visual stimuli or in words, nor do they think of numbers, measurements, and time in terms of laws and regularities. Among the Kpelle, for example, objects are counted and can be put into sets, but there are no words for independent abstract numerals in their language. Numerals must always be used to modify a noun or pronoun, as in "two of this and two of this make four of them." The abstraction "two and two make four" is not a normal part of Kpelle thinking, and this presents an obvious source of difficulty when multiplication is taught to Kpelle children through rote memorization of the multiplication table.

Although Kpelle learning is functional for traditional Kpelle culture and consistent with the highest Kpelle values of conserving the past and learning to conform to traditional norms, it inhibits learning the scientific culture of the West, which is transmitted through the school. The Kpelle schools try to teach new concepts through old methods. Children are taught Western mathematics, which requires a problem-solving approach, through the old methods of rote learning and imitation. Gay and Cole suggest that teachers must try to break through this authority structure, using material and analogies from the child's daily life and putting them in a framework that will make Western education comprehensible and meaningful. Western culture is impinging on Kpelle life at a fast pace, and the school is one of the most important agents of Western culture. It is the teacher's task to help the Kpelle child cross the bridge from old to new. The teacher must make the classroom a living example of the scientific method, drawing from the child and from the strengths and concepts in Kpelle culture.

reading to their children more frequently, the smaller size of the North American family, the presence of more relatives in the Mexican household, and the Mexican school emphasis on rote learning rather than critical thinking.

It is important to note, however, that these differences are modified by social class. A study using tests similar to those used above but carried out among upper-class Mexican families with children enrolled in an American school in Mexico City shows that most of the cognitive differences between the Mexican and American children disappear. Social class and type of schooling are clearly interrelated, and together they account for differences in group scores on

intelligence tests, success in school, and chances for higher-status professional and managerial positions in the society.

Some anthropologists who have studied public schools among lower-class and minority-group populations in the United States have found in them the same conflict of cultures that occurs when formal schooling is introduced into traditional contexts — and the same failures. In describing a school in Harlem, Gerry Rosenfeld (1971) calls attention to the cultural differences between the black, lower-class students and the white, middle-class teachers, to the different conceptual frameworks that organize life in the school and outside it, to the low expectations teachers have for students, and to the subsequent failure of the children in school. Rosenfeld sees the teacher in the "ghetto school" as a transmitter of a different culture. He or she is an agent of socialization similar to the "outsider" who teaches in a "native" school: largely alienated, even hostile, and ignorant of the culture of the students being taught. Until the teacher learns to understand the cultural context and the life of the student and to get involved with the student as an individual, student performance in such schools will continue to be poor. A common result of the imposition of an alien and irrelevant system of education is that children do not learn what they are supposed to learn; rather, they learn a set of evasive strategies that subvert the intended goals of the teacher and become in themselves the child's primary adaptation to the schoolroom.

These explanations of why minority and non-Western children do not perform well in Western-type schools emphasize cultural differences and conflicts. In the Mexican-American comparison, for example, the authors conclude that Mexican culture does not inculcate values and behavior patterns that are necessary for school success; a "culture-conflict" model is also used to partly explain the failure of schoolchildren in Harlem.

A different explanation for the lack of success of many minority and non-Western children in Western-type schools is proposed by John Ogbu (1974; 1978a), an anthropologist from Nigeria who has done fieldwork in the United States. While Ogbu acknowledges differences in cognitive styles and culture among different social classes in the United States, he holds that formal education, like all forms of socialization, is adapted to the social position of individuals in society. He criticizes socialization and culture-conflict explanations of poor school performance as merely showing *how* cognitive styles are transmitted, not *why* they exist in different parts of the population.

As both an anthropologist and an outsider in the United States, Ogbu's explanation of poor school performance focuses on the larger basic cultural patterns in American society, which many "natives" do not see. He begins with what he calls the "central contradiction" in American life — that between our creed of equality and the fact of racial inequality. Our national creed insists that all children should have an equal chance to succeed in life, and we place great faith in formal education as an equalizer. After more than a century of compulsory, free public education, however, the contradiction between creed and reality has not been erased. African-American, native American, and Hispanic children are still the least successful in our schools and in our adult society.

Ogbu argues that this lack of success occurs because America is still a caste society based on a system of racial stratification and because our ideology of equality does not permit us to see that it is not children's school performance that determines their success or failure as adults in our society, but rather the reverse. It is the barriers to full functioning and success in American society that most cogently explain children's poor performance in school. In his ethnographic study of an ethnically mixed school in Stockton, California, Ogbu shows that racial myths and stereotypes still predominate in our society and are translated into school policy. His data show that minority-group children often reject academic competition with members of the dominant racial and ethnic groups and do not work hard in school partly because educational success has not resulted in the social and occupational rewards that have been available to the dominant groups.

Whereas the white middle-class child perceives a strong correlation between individual ability and effort and postschool rewards, African-Americans, Hispanics, and native Americans — regardless of their social class — tend to perceive their opportunities for social mobility as much more limited *as a group* than for the general population. This perception, for them, is a "socially constructed reality" that negatively influences school performance. If education is supposed to prepare children for their adult roles, racial stratification generates and sustains patterns of school performance compatible with the educational requirements of the social and occupational roles permitted to the different racial, ethnic, and social class groups.

All socialization, formal and informal, is future-oriented. Socialization is adaptive: It prepares children to compete for and successfully perform the typical adult roles in their society by transmitting the necessary motivational, cognitive, and other skills required by social roles. Poor school performance may indeed be an adaptive strategy, not merely to what minority-group children perceive as the hostile environment of the school, as in the case of Harlem, just described, but also, and perhaps more importantly, to racial, ethnic, gender, or other castelike stratification in society.

Ogbu's theory, developed from an ethnographic study of a community in the United States, is supported by evidence on the relation between poor school performance and minority-group status in a variety of cultures, for example, among the scheduled castes (formerly "untouchables") in India, the previously outcaste Burakumin in Japan, the Maori in New Zealand, the West Indians in Great Britain, and the Oriental Jews in Israel. His theory also seems to offer an alternative explanation for the differential performances in school exhibited by the Mexican and North American children, described earlier, as it was noted that when children in the United States were compared with upper-class Mexican children, most of the performance differences disappeared.

The importance of formal education as a means to modernization and upward mobility, both in the United States and elsewhere, has made educational success an important national policy in many countries. Anthropologists have been increasingly involved in these efforts, both at the level of ethnography and in the evaluation of educational programs. Participation of anthropologists in the field of education is consistent with their traditional focus on socialization and culture, as well as their more recent interests in social class in stratified societies.

Summary

1. Developing into a fully functioning adult is the result of the complex interaction between universal human capacities and culturally variable child-rearing practices. Enculturation is the culturally specific ways in which human infants are reared to become functioning members of a particular sociocultural system.

2. Adequate mother-child interaction is necessary for normal human development, both physical and emotional, and it also appears to be of great importance among nonhuman primates.

3. Enculturation proceeds differently for males and females almost from birth. Overt teaching and covert communication patterns and role modeling are the most important factors leading to sex-role differentiation among adult males and females in a particular culture.

4. The enculturation process not only transmits the skills and knowledge of a culture but also shapes the values, attitudes, and personality of the growing child. The expectation is that people who have grown up with culturally patterned experiences will have similar personality tendencies.

5. Between 1920 and 1950, anthropologists developed culture-and-personality studies. These attempted to understand the influence of culture on both normal and abnormal personality. At first done in small, traditional societies, these studies were expanded by the 1940s to national character studies. After 1950, such studies were more oriented toward an ecological approach to personality. They also used more sophisticated methodology, especially statistical analysis of ethnographic data from many societies.

6. An important theory confirmed by much recent research is that personality develops as an adaptation to the requirements of the basic subsistence pattern of a culture. This point is illustrated by the example from Khalapur, India.

7. The major factor that shapes the conforming and dependent personality of the Indian village child is the pattern of joint family living and the need for familial harmony.

8. Enculturation continues past childhood; even adolescents and adults learn new roles and activities. In some traditional cultures, there appears to be greater continuity of enculturation than in our own; adults do not have to unlearn attitudes or skills they have learned as children. The Cheyenne are an example of a culture with major continuities in enculturation.

9. Anthropologists have suggested that males may experience more discontinuities in enculturation than females, because the dependent male child must make the transition to an independent and assertive male role. In many cultures, male initiation rites help the individual make this transition from boy to man.

10. Where cultural continuity is lacking and there are no male initiation rites, young men may "initiate themselves," as exemplified in the American youth gang, informal adolescent peer group, and in college.

11. Although in traditional societies enculturation is largely an informal process, in complex, highly technical societies, formal education (school) plays an increasingly important role. Schools not only teach the formal problem-solving thought processes necessary for competence as an adult but also indirectly communicate the American values of competitiveness and individualism.

12. Western education has not always been successful in non-Western cultures that have values which conflict with those presented in the school.

13. Social class seems to be of great importance in understanding the different levels of success reached by schoolchildren in different racial, ethnic, and social class groups: It may be that the poor performance of lower-class and lower-caste children reflects their low expectations of their future rather than the cultural values of their social class.

Suggested Readings

Edgerton, Robert B.
1971 *The Individual in Adaptation: A Study of Four East African Peoples.* Berkeley, Calif.: University of California Press. Compares the personalities of four different cultures and the farmer and herder divisions within each group.

Freed, Ruth S., and Freed, Stanley A.
1985 *The Psychomedical Case History of a Low-Caste Woman of North India.* New York: Anthropological Papers of the American Museum of Natural History, Vol. 60, Part 2. An excellent example of the use of psychology and culture in the analysis of the life history of a young woman who becomes possessed.

Herdt, Gilbert
1987 *The Sambia.* New York: Holt, Rinehart and Winston. A fascinating account, by a psychological anthropologist, of a culture in New Guinea in which male initiation focuses on ritualized homosexuality.

Holland, Dorothy C., and Eisenhart, Margaret A.
1992 *Educated in Romance: Women, Achievement, and College Culture.* Chicago, Ill.: University of Chicago Press. Another perspective on coming of age in America, documenting the important influences of the informal social life of peer culture in American colleges. A major finding of the study is that the ability to attract men (the romance of the title) is more important for these women than grades or achievement.

Mead, Margaret
1961 *Coming of Age in Samoa.* New York: Dell (first publ. 1928). The classic study of adolescence in a society where the transition from childhood to adulthood is much less turbulent than in our own.

Ogbu, John U.
1974 *The Next Generation: An Ethnography of Education in an Urban Neighborhood.* New York: Academic Press. A Nigerian anthropologist shows how school failure is an adaptation to restricted opportunities for subordinate minority groups in the United States.

Saitoti, Tepilit Ole
1986 *The Worlds of a Maasai Warrior.* New York: Random House. A delightful autobiography by a Maasai who grew up in a traditional society and now straddles his own culture and that of the West.

P A R T

T W O

Sociocultural Adaptations

Making a Living

What is the relationship between environmental and cultural variation?

What are the basic ways in which different societies get their food?

How are various food-getting strategies related to other aspects of culture and social life?

What are the different satisfactions and dissatisfactions related to different ways of making a living?

Until 1958, agriculture was the main occupation for most Taiwanese. Farmers grow rice and sugar, both of which require much labor in very uncomfortable conditions. Wet rice growing involves many hours spent knee-deep in muddy water, and sugar cultivation involves extremely heavy labor with dangers of heat prostration, hernia, back trouble, and snake bite. Most people, therefore, prefer other work when it is available, although many of the new opportunities offered by this industrializing society are also disliked. Hard manual work, such as digging building foundations with shovels, is called "bitter labor" because the hours are long and it is poorly paid. Service work, which includes domestic service; restaurant, hotel, and retail work; and entertainment, including prostitution, which is encouraged by the militarized economy, is also disliked for the long hours and low pay, and the additional "emotional labor" of flattering and cajoling potential customers. Factory work is preferred to bitter labor and service, but even this is not easy, especially for the one-third of the factory work force made up of young women from the countryside. Some young people enjoy the opportunity to leave home, but others become homesick or disillusioned with the dull work routines, the limited opportunities for advancement, and the exploitation. There are also physical dangers in factory work, such as the rapid deterioration of eyesight in assembling microchips, and the exposure to unguarded machinery and toxic substances. Some factories do not have air conditioning, a particular hardship in the hot, sticky Taiwan summers. One valued occupational goal is owning a small business; these typically require little capital, such as the "shoulder pole" noodle sellers, who carry an entire restaurant — stove, cookpot, ingredients, dishes, and stool for the customer — on their shoulders. Other such miniaturized businesses involve mending nylon stockings, recycling light bulbs, and manufacturing bean curd, which is sold to larger factories. Poverty in Taiwan, like in other industrialized countries, punishes weakness, failure, or ill fortune. This is the fear that motivates the industriousness of the Chinese people.

Adapted from Hill Gates, Chinese Working Class Lives: Getting by in Taiwan *(Ithaca: Cornell University Press, 1987), pp. 68–78.*

All human populations must find a way to transform the energy of the environment so that it can support their populations. The variety of occupations described for Taiwan is typical of many societies in the contemporary world, in combining agriculture, industrialism, and service. But this occupational diversity is relatively new in human history. In this chapter we will see the different strategies human populations have used to adapt to diverse environments, ranging from hunting and gathering, through cultivation and pastoralism, to industrialism.

The Environment and Cultural Diversity

A human population and its environment form an interacting **ecosystem**. The environment, or surroundings, of a human population includes both a physical and a social aspect. In its physical aspect, the environment is climate, soil quality, existing plant and animal life, and the presence of vital resources such as water, vitamins, and proteins. In considering the capacity of various environments to support human life, both the quantity and the quality of natural resources must be taken into account. Most environmental zones permit a diversity of food-getting strategies. Some environmental zones are harsher than others and more limiting in the types of cultural adaptations they support. The productivity of any particular zone, however, must be considered in connection with the type of technology used to exploit it.

In considering the effect of environment on culture, including subsistence patterns (food getting), we can say that the environment places limits and provides possibilities but does not determine culture. Each environment always offers some alternatives, and even within culture areas, variation always exists.

The level of technology is the deciding factor in the utilization of a particular environment. In the Midwest of the United States, for example, the complex technology of the industrial age has allowed an adaptive pattern of intensive mechanized agriculture. This region today supports millions of people. In aboriginal America, it supported a much smaller population of hunters and gatherers. In the same way, a desert area that can support very little human life without irrigation can be made to bloom and support much larger populations through an intensive agricultural pattern of adaptation. In explaining the subsistence pattern of a society, the anthropologist must take many factors into account: the nature of the broad environmental zone; variation within the zone, both short-term and long-term; social groups in the environment; and the level of technology and other cultural factors.

Environmental Zones and Food-Getting Systems

The earth contains six major environmental zones, each of which has a particular climate, soil composition, and plant and animal life (Figure 7.1). The major area of the earth's

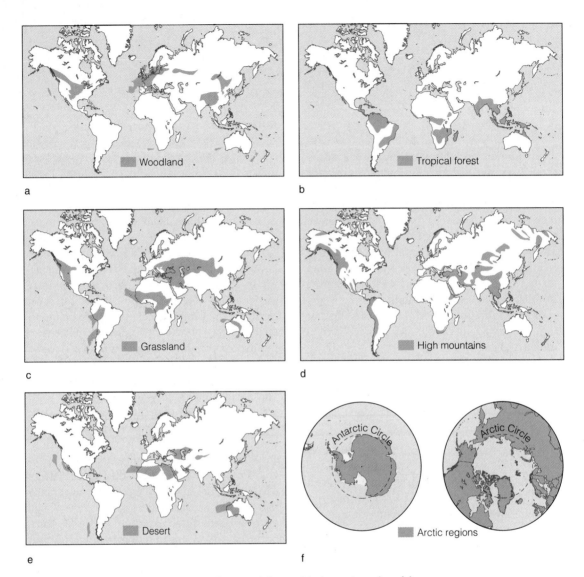

FIGURE 7.1   Six major environmental zones of the world, shown in order of decreasing population.

surface (26 percent) is covered by grasslands, sometimes called steppes, prairies, or savannas. These areas, which can support hunters and gatherers and also populations dependent on herding animals, are inhabited by 10 percent of the world's population. Where complex machine technologies exist, these areas can be made enormously productive for agriculture. Desert regions or dry areas make up 18 percent of the earth's land but contain only 6 percent of its population. Desert areas do not all conform to the popular image of sand dunes and the complete absence of water. Many deserts are covered by brush, and in some areas oases, or fertile concentrations of soil, exist and support small agricultural settlements. Deserts can also support hunters and gatherers, even with simple technology. With extensive irrigation, some can support intensive agriculture and relatively dense populations. The Arctic and subarctic zones cover 16 percent of the earth, but as we would expect, they support only a tiny fraction of the earth's population — less than half of 1 percent — who live mainly by hunting, herding, and trapping.

Almost three-fourths of the world's population lives in the two remaining major environmental zones. The tropical forest zone, with abundant rainfall and luxuriant vegetation, takes up 10 percent of the earth's land mass but supports 28 percent of its population. The typical pattern of subsistence in these areas is extensive cultivation (sometimes called horticulture). The most hospitable environmental zone for contemporary human populations is the temperate forests. Today, 43 percent of the world's population lives in the tropical forest and temperate forest zones. Again, we can see how technology must be taken into account in understanding population distribution. It is only with iron tools that the hardwood trees in these temperate forests could be cut down and the fertile soil used for agriculture. Without iron tools, the trees presented an insurmountable difficulty. Mountains, which vary in climate and other characteristics according to their elevation, occupy 12 percent of the earth's land surface and are inhabited by 7 percent of its population, engaged primarily in pastoralism and extensive cultivation.

Sometimes a number of societies make similar adaptations to a particular environmental zone and through diffusion come to develop similar cultural patterns. Where this happens, anthropologists speak of a **culture area**. Although the concept of a culture area has its uses in explaining certain developments, culture areas also contain cultural variation. Among the American Plains Indians, for example, there were important differences in values and configurations among the different tribes in spite of the basic similarity in the subsistence pattern.

Seasonal Variation and Cultural Response

Due to climatic variation, food resources vary in availability and abundance at different times of the year in any particular local environment. Many aspects of a food-production system will reflect this seasonal variation. Among the Hanunoo of the Philippines, who are horticulturalists, there is an impressive system of intercropping, or planting of different crops at different times of the year when the weather is most favorable for each. Rice, the main crop, is planted in June and harvested in October; in between, a short-season maize crop is planted and harvested. Between October and May, several dry-season crops such as beans, sugar cane, and potatoes are also grown (Conklin 1969). Hunters and gatherers are, of course, also sensitive to seasonal change, because it affects the availability and abundance of game and vegetable foods. Game migrates with the changing seasons, and the hunting groups adjust in size and social organization, as we will see for the Copper Eskimo later in this chapter.

Long-Run Variations in the Environment

Sociocultural systems also develop in response to variations that are unpredictable over the short run — such as drought, floods, or diseases that affect animals — but that are a persistent part of the environment over the long run. Subsistence patterns most directly reflect adaptation to long-run environmental uncertainty. Food habits and preferences, for example, can be adapted to a wide variety of resources, rather than being limited to resources that are not so readily available. Australian aboriginal peoples, such as the Tiwi, have a very simple technology, but they utilize an enormous variety of plant and animal foods in their environment — kangaroos, opossums, mice, wild dogs,

The annual and the long-run variations in the water level of rivers, like the Niger in Mali, are an essential environmental feature to which human cultures must adapt. (Simone LaRive)

whales, frogs, turkeys and smaller birds, lizards, snakes, bird and lizard eggs, fish, roots, fruits, nuts, seeds, flowers—and are thus unlikely to be severely affected if some of these foods become unavailable.

A group can also structure its diet so that, although it uses a wide variety of resources, it also has one that is dependable, that is, in constant abundant supply. The !Kung of the Kalahari, for example, although they know the plants and animals in their seemingly hostile environment well and do use this knowledge to give their diet variety when possible, can always fall back on the protein-rich nuts of the mongongo tree. These nuts are abundant, easily stored, and little affected by environmental variation (Lee 1968).

In addition to using various subsistence strategies to increase survival in a particular environment, a group adapts to the environment by regulating its population. In cultures where the level of technology affords only a limited exploitation of the environment, and where safe and reliable methods of artificial

contraception are unknown, abortion and infanticide are used to limit population growth. Other culturally determined practices and beliefs also result in limiting population. Late weaning and postpartum taboos on sexual intercourse, for example, regulate population by spacing births. Sometimes, methods of increasing a group's survival seem harsh to us, but they are necessary because of extreme food shortages. In particularly hard years when food was scarce, some Inuit groups, for example, would leave old people on the ice to die. Sometimes it was an old person who suggested this course of action. These suicides or "mercy killings" indicate not a lack of concern for human life but rather a commitment to the survival of the group.

In addition to these more obvious ways of adapting to environmental uncertainty, a society can establish trade relations with other groups and thus expand its resource base. This, for example, is always necessary for pastoral groups who do not also do a little farming themselves. Furthermore, some of the ways in

With the introduction of the horse by the Spanish, hunting bison on the American Plains became a more productive strategy than horticulture. This drawing, by Bear's Heart, was made in 1875. A hundred years later, the American bison were extinct. (Photo by Carmelo Guadagno. Courtesy of Museum of the American Indian, Heye Foundation)

which sociocultural systems adapt to long-run environmental uncertainty may not be a part of a group's cultural consciousness, as we saw earlier (Chapter 3) in Marvin Harris's explanation of the Hindu taboo on beef. Frequently, the role such beliefs and practices play in regulating population or increasing the rational utilization of the environment may be understood only through anthropological analysis.

Although increasing technological efficiency is an obvious way of increasing control over the environment, the enormous diversity of sociocultural systems is evidence that technologically simple societies have been able to make satisfactory adaptations even without modern science. Although nonliterate peoples may not express it in the technical terminology

of modern science, they have a much wider knowledge of their environment than they have generally been given credit for. Harold Conklin, who studied the horticulturalist Yagaw Hanunoo of the Philippines, found, for example, that they had forty linguistic categories referring to soil quality and mineral content. They understood what causes soil erosion and had developed techniques to conserve the soil. The Hanunoo distinguish over 1,500 types of plants in their environment and cultivate over 400 in fields and gardens, frequently experimenting with new types. In this sense, their knowledge exceeds that of modern scientific botany, in which plants are grouped into species by grosser criteria than those used by the Hanunoo. The Hanunoo also recognize over

450 animal types in their environment. These people clearly understand the connection between human food-getting activities and their impact on the environment, and they utilize this knowledge in an efficient way to exploit various food resources. Similarly, even where the technology for hunting and horticulture among nonliterate peoples seems primitive compared with our own machine technology, these groups have in fact developed adequate strategies for fulfilling their needs. They make up for the lack of sophisticated technology by human skill, such as in observing the habits of various animals and in stalking them.

The Social Environment and Food-Getting Strategies

Cultural patterns, including how people get their food, are adjusted to the presence of different groups in the environment. Some peoples who originally inhabited a larger area, like the Semai of Malaysia, have recently been pushed back by other groups into marginal areas and have had to change their subsistence patterns. The Mbuti of the Ituri Forest in northeastern Zaire have adapted to the tropical forest as hunters and gatherers, but almost all the Mbuti bands are closely associated with their non-Mbuti neighbors, who are horticulturalists. These other people fear the forest and will not enter it. This has allowed the Mbuti to exploit the forest while making use of their more culturally sophisticated horticultural neighbors, with whom they trade and sometimes live for parts of the year (Turnbull 1961).

Human groups (like other animal communities) tend to engage in specialized adaptations to the environment that, over time, become integrated in their cultural systems and are an important part of their identity. A specialized adaptation to a local environment by a particular group is called its **niche**. Frederik Barth (1956) describes a pattern of social interaction in Pakistan in which three ethnic groups, the Kohistanis, the Pathans, and the Gujars, each have a different niche within the same mountainous area. They are able to live peacefully because each group exploits a different aspect of the environment. The Pathans are farmers, utilizing the valley regions for raising wheat, corn, and rice. The Kohistanis live in the colder mountainous regions, herding sheep, goats, cattle, and water buffalo and raising millet and corn. The Gujars are full-time herders and utilize marginal areas not used by the Kohistanis. The Gujars provide milk and meat products to the Pathan farmers and also work as agricultural laborers during the busy seasons. Such patterns of specialized and noncompetitive interactions among cultures in a local environment are found in many parts of the world and seem especially characteristic of the pastoral peoples.

The Influence of Culture on Environment

The relationship between the environment and culture is not one-way. Although, as just suggested, the environment affects culture, culture also affects the environment. The ways in which people get food and the ways in which they live all have an impact on nature. On the one hand, technology and knowledge can transform deserts into gardens. On the other hand, as we know all too well today, the presence of human populations can have a devastating impact on nature. In industrial societies, factories and automobiles have contributed to polluting the air we breathe. Different methods of getting food, whether hunting, trapping animals, cultivation, or keeping herds of livestock, all affect animal and plant life, quantity of natural resources, the soil cover, and the soil itself. The management of resources is clearly a pressing problem in the world today. One of the contributions of ecologically oriented anthropologists is to show that a wide variety of food-getting strategies makes good ecological sense and that what may at first appear to be a more efficient exploitation of a particular environment may turn out to raise as many problems as it solves.

Major Patterns of Making a Living

There are five basic patterns of utilizing the environment to support human populations (Cohen 1971): hunting and gathering, pastoralism, extensive cultivation, intensive cultivation, and industrialization. Although it is useful to describe basic types, there is a great deal of diversity within each type. Furthermore, any particular society normally has one dominant way of utilizing the environment, but most actually use a combination of patterns in meeting their needs. Each type of adaptation has a characteristic level of productivity (yield per person per unit of land) and efficiency (yield per person per hour of labor invested), though situations vary depending on the particular ecological interaction. Each type of food-getting pattern also seems to have some social correlates (accompanying forms of social organization) and dominant values, though again, many anthropologists are more interested in examining specific cultural adaptations to a particular local environment than in formulating cultural typologies.

For most of human life on earth, people have exploited the environment through hunting and gathering. With the increasing improvement of tools during the last several hundred thousand years, hunters and gatherers were able to spread out into many parts of the world, exploit many kinds of environments, and develop many cultural systems. About 25,000 years ago, humans arrived in Australia and the New World. Population increased in both the Old and New Worlds, even with rela-

tively simple foraging technologies, but this strategy set certain limits on population densities and, consequently, on the complexity of social organization.

About 10,000 years ago, human groups began to domesticate plants and animals in the Old World. About 4,000 years later, similar developments took place in the New World. At one time, anthropologists talked about the transition from a foraging to a food-producing strategy as a "revolution." Increasingly, archeological evidence is demonstrating that this transition was not revolutionary but gradual, although it was revolutionary in the new possibilities it opened up for cultural development. The earliest evidence of plant cultivation and domestication of animals comes from southwestern Asia. It has been suggested that food production developed gradually out of a broad-spectrum foraging economy and resulted from experimentation with different forms of wild plants in new habitats. The domestication of animals, similarly, involved a gradual change in the relationship between humans and the wild sheep, goat, ox, and pig that they hunted (Flannery 1973).

Although archeologists have been able to show that village life is not synonymous with the domestication of plants and animals, increased populations could be supported, and sedentary village life became widespread with the advent of food production. With the increased population pressure, more intensive means of cultivation were developed, and human labor had to be more closely coordinated and controlled. In conjunction with these developments, state societies developed in many parts of the world.

Why intensive agriculture did not arise everywhere — and why, in fact, some populations, such as the Australians, never made the transition from foraging to food production — has to be discussed in terms of the specific relationship between human populations and their environments. In some cases, such as the Arctic, intensive agriculture could not develop. In other cases, such as in the fertile valleys of

California, aboriginal foraging was so productive that there was little pressure to make the transition to food production. Even in contemporary horticultural or pastoral societies, where methods of intensive cultivation are known, the transition to this adaptation is by no means inevitable. In some cases, other strategies may involve less risk and therefore may be more adaptive over the long run. Ideology may also play a role, as different strategies become closely tied up with group identity. This seems to be true for many pastoral peoples, who despise their cultivating neighbors. For many hunting peoples, such as the Mbuti, their whole culture and ideology are intimately associated with exploitation of the forest in which they live. In some cases, the transition to intensive cultivation is not made, because it appears to require too much effort.

The history of humankind as a whole has moved in the direction of developing ways of exploiting the environment that can support greater population densities and require more complex systems of sociocultural integration. With industrialization, which involves the use of machines rather than human or animal energy, we have seen incredible increases in productivity and efficiency. From a typical preindustrial system, in which 80 to 100 percent of the population must be actively involved in food production, we have moved to a situation in industrialized nations in which 10 percent or less of the population can produce food for the other 90 percent. But industrialization, like other systems of adaptation, also raises problems. Industrialization has enormous potential for production and enormous potential for destruction as well. Only time will tell if new cultural forms and values will emerge to allow us to control technology to the advantage of the entire human race.

Hunting and Gathering

Hunting and gathering, or **foraging**, relies on food that is naturally available in the environment. Included in this strategy are the hunting of large and small game, fishing, and the collecting of various plant foods. Hunting and gathering does not involve the production of food, either directly, by planting, or indirectly, by controlling the reproduction of animals or keeping domestic animals for consumption of their meat or milk.

In the past, hunting and gathering occurred in more diverse environments than is true today. For 99 percent of the existence of humankind, life was supported by hunting and gathering. Today, only about 30,000 of the world's people live by means of this strategy. Most contemporary hunters and gatherers occupy marginal areas, having been pushed back by culturally dominant or militarily superior agricultural peoples.

Anthropologists are particularly interested in contemporary hunters and gatherers, because this pattern was such an important part of early human history. The sexual division of labor (males hunting, females collecting vegetable foods), the sharing of food in the group, and the development of language all came into existence as correlates of the hunting and gathering way of life. But although contemporary hunters and gatherers can give us important clues to understanding the early life of humans, these groups do not in any way represent a way of life unchanged from the past. Hunting and gathering, too, has changed and is in fact rapidly disappearing as a way of human life.

Hunting and gathering strategies vary in their productivity. Although it is true that some hunters and gatherers have faced starvation, the marginal existence of contemporary hunters and gatherers may be due to recent effects of culture contact. But even here, some foraging groups make out rather well, thanks to their ingenious technology and their wide knowledge of the environment. Richard Lee (1979) points out that the !Kung actually have a more secure existence than their Herero neighbors, who are horticulturalists and cattle herders. Because the Herero rely completely on water and pasturage for their cattle, they leave themselves open to starvation in years of drought. The Plains Indians also did well with a hunting strategy, especially after the introduction of the horse by the Spaniards in the sixteenth century. Some Plains groups, such as the Cheyenne, gave up an agricultural life for the more productive hunting of bison. But in general, hunting and gathering supports fewer people per unit of land than do other food-getting strategies. Among the !Kung, forty-four people are supported per one hundred square miles of land, but this figure is somewhat higher than is generally true for hunting peoples today.

Hunting technology is simple but not crude, and ingenious methods are used to hunt a wide range of different animals. Because hunting is a prestige activity, it is only recently that much attention has been given to the collecting of vegetable foods. For many foraging groups, vegetable foods make up a substantial part of the diet (up to 80 percent), and it is this rather than hunting that makes foraging a relatively secure way of life. Foraging thus tends to be a generalized pattern of adaptation that utilizes many different aspects of the natural environment for subsistence. The Copper Eskimo described in the accompanying ethnography represent a specialized hunting adaptation to a harsh and limiting environment. Their traditional adaptation, which depends mainly on the hunting activities of the men, is not typical of hunter-gatherer societies, most of which rely much more heavily on the gathering of vegetable foods, which is done by women, as among the !Kung, or even on the hunting of small game by the women, as among the Tiwi of Australia.

Contrary to stereotypes, hunting and gathering is not a particularly difficult and inefficient way of life in terms of the number of hours required to maintain an adequate food supply. Marshall Sahlins (1972) has called hunters and gatherers "the original affluent society." James Woodburn (1968), who studied the Hadza of Tanzania, estimated that they spend less time and energy obtaining their subsistence and appear to be better off nutritionally than neighboring agricultural tribes. Lee estimated that an adult !Kung spends an average of two and a half six-hour days per week in subsistence activities, and a woman can gather enough in one day to feed her family for three days.

There appear to be some typical social correlates of the hunting way of life. Hunters are generally nomadic, with their movements following the availability of game and wild plants. A typical form of social organization among hunters is the small camp made up of kinsmen, coming together when seasonal conditions permit. Recent investigation has shown that the typical hunting band is much more flexible in its membership than was previously believed. Among the Blackfeet bison hunters of the North American Plains, even strangers would be included in the camp. With the notable exception of the Kwakiutl and other fishing and foraging societies of the Northwest Coast of North America, there tends to be little occupational specialization in foraging societies and few differences in power and authority. There is ordinarily a divison of labor by sex — women collect plant foods and men hunt — and by age. Women in these societies also make clothing and contribute in other important ways to the economy, such as by carrying and processing food. There tends to be a higher degree of sexual equality in such societies than in other ways of life — for example, pastoralism or horticulture.

Pastoralism

Pastoralism primarily involves the care of domesticated herd animals. It is a specialized adaptation to an environment that, because of hilly terrain, dry climate, or unsuitable soil, is not sufficiently productive to support a large human population through agriculture. It can support native vegetation sufficient for animals if they are allowed to range over a large area. The main animals herded by pastoralists are cattle, sheep, goats, yaks, or camels, all of which produce both meat and milk. Because the herd animals found in the New World were not of a variety that could be domesticated (with the exception of the llama and alpaca in Peru), pastoralism did not develop as a New World way of life. The major areas of pastoralism are thus found in East Africa (cattle), North Africa (camels), southwestern Asia (sheep and goats),

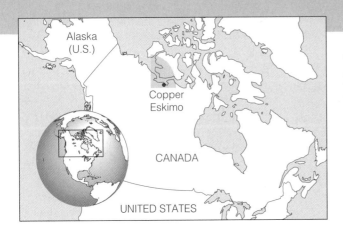

The extreme arctic environment poses many problems that the human populations there must successfully cope with in order to survive. Because the land is unsuitable for cultivation, the Eskimo, or Inuit, must utilize both the rich animal resources of the ocean and land animals such as the caribou. The material culture and technology of the Inuit are admirably designed to cope with their harsh physical environ-

ment. One of their major problems, for example, is keeping warm in cold weather yet not getting overheated during periods of strenuous work. The Inuit design of clothing admirably meets this test. Fur provides warmth, yet there are also many air vents regulated by drawstrings. Further, the Inuit dress in layers, which trap the warm air and act as insulators; in warmer weather, the outer layer can be removed. Boots, gloves, and parkas have an impermeable outer layer, keeping out dampness and wind. Boots and gloves are lined with grass for further insulation. Inuit shelters are also ingeniously designed to hold heat and keep out wind. The snow shelter (igloo), by its shape and composition, provides excellent, warm shelter and can be effectively heated by a seal-oil lamp, which also provides light. The Inuit summer tents, made of two attached layers of sealskin, can also provide warmth during cold snaps by trapping heated air between the layers.

The Inuit also adapt to their environment through a variety of social and cultural practices. Through a bilateral kinship system (which formally recognizes relations on both the male and female sides of the family), adoption, exchange of spouses, a taboo on the marriage of cousins, and meat-sharing partnerships, they extend the social network beyond individual households. The result is a flexible social organization that ensures cooperation, mutual aid, and responsibility for others, thus allowing local populations to expand and contract in response to the fluctuating availability of resources. The socialization of the Inuit, which involves both playing and training in skills such as observing, stalking, and killing game, provides the group with hunters who have both the knowledge and the experience to provide enough food to feed their families. Their religious rituals and ceremonies are effective in providing outlets for the isolation of the long, dark winters, and they serve as safety valves for the release of anxiety and tension. The various Inuit groups of the Arctic actually exploit a number of micro-environments, and this accounts for the cultural differences among them. One of the basic differences is between the coastal Inuit of what is now Alaska, who depend on whaling and sea resources generally, and the in-

The ways in which human populations adapt to their environments through different food-getting strategies are an important factor in cultural variation. The Eskimo are an example of a specialized hunting adaptation. Here two Eskimo women from Coppermine set fishnets under the ice. (Courtesy of the American Museum of Natural History)

land Inuit, who although doing some seal hunting also depend on hunting caribou as an important part of their subsistence strategy (Moran 1979).

The Copper Eskimo, so called by Europeans because of their use of native copper tools, live in the Canadian Arctic. They have lived as hunters in this extreme climate for over 1,000 years (see map). The tundra habitat in which they live contains some trees, moss, grass, and flowers, but many areas are virtual wasteland. The climate is variable, with a long, cold winter and a short,

(*continued*)

cool summer. From around September to June, the water areas become sheets of ice. The main land animal hunted was the caribou, which provided both meat and skin used in clothing. Fish, hare, and fowl were important supplements to the diet. Plant life was scarce, and berries were eaten only during a brief season. When a caribou was killed, the first thing eaten was the half-digested reindeer moss that remained in its stomach. The seal was the most important sea animal hunted, providing a major source of food for people and dogs, fat for fuel, and skins for summer clothing.

The Copper Eskimo culture was adapted to a seasonal cycle in response to the availability of different animals at different times of the year. From late May to November, the Eskimo fished and hunted caribou, often driving them into lakes and harpooning them from kayaks. The caribou migrate in the winter to the richer forest areas to the south. During November and early December, the Eskimo lived on stores of dried and frozen caribou meat and fish, while the women sewed winter clothing. In December, they moved to the sea ice for the winter seal-hunting season. Snow houses were built in from the coast, and a radius of about five miles (considered a convenient walking distance from camp!) was exploited for sealing.

In the winter, seals live in the water under the ice. They make breathing holes by scratching with their flippers on the new ice and have the ability to breathe up through quite a lot of snow. Each seal makes many holes during a winter and may use any one of these. The hunter finds the holes with the aid of specially trained dogs. The method of winter sealing is called "he waits," for that is what a hunter must do. He settles down on a block of ice and waits for an indicator to move, showing the presence of a seal. He may wait for hours or even days. Many men are needed for successful breathing-hole sealing, so the Copper Eskimo winter populations ranged from about 50 to 200 people, with the average group about 100. In spring, the group dispersed into smaller units in response to the lesser requirements of caribou hunting. Caribou are usually scattered into small herds, easily hunted by a few men. Fish were the most important source of food in the spring. They were widely available over the area in numerous lakes, and so did not require communal effort to catch.

Although most ethnographies of the Eskimo concentrate on the activities of the men in providing food through hunting and furs for sale through trapping, women also play an important role in the economy, contributing through their complementary activities to the survival of the group. In addition to caring for children, Eskimo women prepare hides for sale or use, prepare meat for storage, and sew and repair the clothing that is essential for the hunters. In the case of sealskins, the blubber must be scraped off and the skin washed, stretched on a frame to dry, and then, when dry, scrubbed again. Similarly, caribou hides must also be scraped in order to make them flexible enough for use. Meat and fish must be cut up and gutted for storage. Although most of the cloth clothing worn by the Eskimo is bought, women still make fur clothes and boots, which are conceded by all to be much more effective than anything that can be bought in a store. In addition, the women cook, wash, clean the igloo, and may also contribute more directly to the food supply in some Eskimo groups by fishing and hunting small birds (Briggs 1974).

The routine just described was altered somewhat by the introduction of new technology by the whites. By 1925, rifles, traps, and fishnets substantially influenced the Eskimo food-getting pattern. Using rifles to hunt caribou led to a lengthened caribou season and a correspondingly shorter sealing season. More Eskimo stayed inland, not only hunting caribou but also trapping and setting nets in lakes and streams to catch fish. Other aspects of the economy also changed. With the rifle, the kayak hunting of caribou ended, and the kayak fell into disuse. Large caribou drives also became less frequent. With a rifle, one man could succeed at long-range caribou hunting, which then became a much more individual pursuit.

The market for fox furs among whites led to the trapping of foxes. Trapping drew the Eskimo into the marketing system of the outside world, providing them not only with goods that increased the exploitation of the environment but also with food, tobacco, tea, canvas tents, and clothing. With the establishment of fox traps, dog-team travel became more important because mobility was needed to set and watch traps. Where previously a typical family had owned two dogs, many might now own five or six, and the dogs might actually consume more meat than a family consumed.

By the mid-1950s, the decline in caribou due to hunting with rifles led to further changes in Eskimo life. Some Copper Eskimo populations shifted to areas where seals could be hunted year-round, and fishing also became more important. In other areas, the decline of the caribou led to an increased amount of time spent in breathing-hole sealing, a reversion to the aboriginal pattern. Still other Copper Eskimo populations moved to areas where they could be employed by the government, which had established Distant Early Warning radar installations in the Arctic. Trading posts were established and also attracted permanent settlement. Handicrafts and tourism contribute to the present Eskimo economy, and when necessary, the Canadian government provides welfare payments and airlifts of food.

Adapted from David Damas, "The Copper Eskimo," in M. G. Bicchieri, ed., Hunters and Gatherers Today *(New York: Holt, Rinehart and Winston, 1972), pp. 3–50.*

The Kurds of Iraq engage in nomadic pastoralism, in which all members of the group—
men, women, and children—move with their herds throughout the year and there is no
permanent settlement. Women are responsible for the water supply and take care of
the feeding of the fowl that accompany them in their moves. Men herd the animals.
(United Nations)

and central Asia and the subarctic (caribou and reindeer).

Two characteristic patterns of pastoralism are **transhumance** and **nomadism**. In transhumance, herd animals are moved regularly throughout the year to different areas as pastures become available at different altitudes or in different climatic zones. Generally, the men and boys take the animals to the different pastures while the women and children and some men remain at a village site. In a nomadic form of pastoralism, the whole population—men, women, and children—moves with the herds throughout the year. There is no permanent village.

Pastoralism by itself cannot support a human population; food grains are needed as a supplement to the diet. Therefore, either pastoralism is practiced along with cultivation, or trading relations are maintained with cultivators from whom food grains are obtained. In terms of social organization, in most pastoral groups a woman joins her husband after marriage and herds are transmitted from fathers to sons. Recent studies have shown a great diversity in pastoral adaptations, and the very flexibility that has allowed pastoral groups to survive in marginal environments makes this strategy difficult to categorize. Because pastoralism always includes either cultivation or trade, this also leads to rather important variability among pastoralists. Many pastoralists have also been drawn into a market economy, and this too is an important part of contempo-

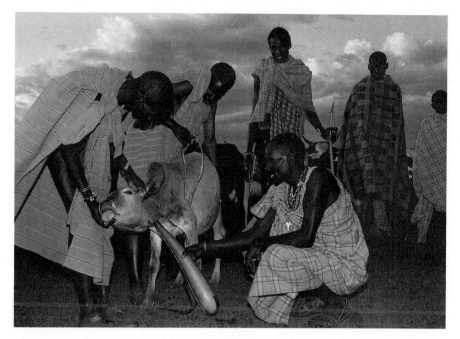

The Maasai of East Africa engage in transhumant pastoralism, in which men take the cattle to different areas as pasture becomes available. The women and children remain in the village. Cattle provide the sole sustenance of the Maasai. In this photograph, some Maasai men are draining the blood from an animal. The basic diet of the Maasai is made up of the blood and the milk of the cattle. They eat meat only occasionally, for a ceremonial feast, or when it is needed for gaining strength, as for a woman after childbirth, or someone recovering from an illness. (Courtesy of Jane Hoffer)

rary pastoralist adaptations. Pastoralism, like hunting, depends on an extensive knowledge of the natural environment. Like hunting, it is also a nomadic adaptation, and the movement patterns of pastoralist groups are of central importance in understanding their culture.

Extensive Cultivation

Extensive cultivation, sometimes called **horticulture**, involves the production of plants using a simple, nonmechanized technology. An important defining characteristic of extensive cultivation is that cultivated fields will not be used permanently, year after year, but will remain fallow for some time after being cultivated. This is one of the important contrasts between an extensive and an intensive cultivation strategy. Horticulturalists plant and harvest with simple tools, such as hoes or digging sticks, and do not use draft animals, irrigation techniques, or plows. Extensive cultivation has a relatively lower yield per acre than intensive agriculture and does not use so much human labor as other forms of farming. Extensive cultivators grow enough food in their fields or gardens to support the local group, but they do not produce surpluses that could involve the group in a wider market system with nonagricultural populations. Population densities among horticultural peoples are generally low, usually not exceeding 150 people per square mile (Netting 1977). There is great variation in horticultural productivity, however. In the highlands of New Guinea, cultivation of the sweet potato supports populations of up to 500 per square mile.

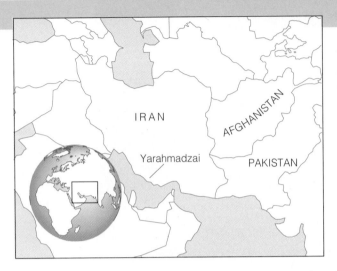

The chief problems presented by human groups adapting to grassland environments revolve around the exploitation of water and pasture. Because of the patchy characteristics of the environment, nomadism is the most common means of securing an adequate supply of these resources. As part of their adaptive strategies, pastoralists have to make important decisions about the size and composition of their herds. These decisions, in turn, reflect both their evaluation of the diet needed to sustain the group and their need to maintain social exchanges with their neighboring cultivators, because some agricultural contribution to the pastoral diet is always required.

The Yarahmadzai are a patrilineal tribe of some several thousand people, living in the area of southeastern Iran known as Baluchistan (see map). The total tribal territory is about 3,600 square miles. The plateau on which the Yarahmadzai live is at 5,000 feet and is cut by high mountains. The winters are cold and the summers hot. Some years there is no rain at all, and the maximum tends to be about six inches a year, most of which falls in the winter. The main natural vegetation is grass, although some areas are completely barren. The area is bounded to the east by a vast desert that contains almost no vegetation.

In winter (December, January, February), each local community of the tribe has a traditional camping area on the plateau consisting of about five to twenty tents. The herds of goats and sheep are taken out together by shepherds, and camels are herded separately by camel boys. At this time, there is practically no vegetation for the animals to eat, and they exist primarily on the accumulated fat of the previous spring. During the winter months, the entire Yarahmadzai area is barren, so there is no point in moving. Their strategy is to "sit tight," protect the animals as best they can, and compensate for the lack of pasturage by feeding the camels with roots, the goats and sheep with grain, and the lambs and kids with dates, processed date pits, and grain. As this is the rainy season, water is normally available. Because no food is produced, the community depends on stores from the previous year.

In spring (March, April, May), grass begins to appear and plants to bud. Because of the variability of the rain and winter runoff water from the mountains, the availability of pasture varies from year to year within the territory. Thus, the community does not know beforehand where it will go. After spending some time gathering information about where the pasture is good, the camp packs up and migrates. In the period observed by Philip Salzman, his camp moved seven times, covering distances of five to twenty-five miles. As even pasturage in a good area is quickly exhausted, all the camps are constantly moving from place to place.

In the first part of summer (June and July), the pasturage begins to dry up. Recently, the Iranian government has introduced some irrigation technology into the area, and many of the tribesmen migrate to these areas to harvest grain. The livestock grazes on stubble and fertilizes the ground with droppings. From March to July, the animals give enough milk both for their young and for heavy consumption by the people. Milk is consumed in many different forms and preserved as dried milk solids and butter. The butter is sold or exchanged for other products, mostly grain.

In late summer and early autumn (August, September, October), the Yarahmadzai migrate to the lowland desert, leaving their winter tents, goats, and sheep on the plateau in the care of young boys. The group makes an eight-day migration to the groves of date palms. During this time, they live in mud huts, harvesting and eating dates and preparing a number of food products for the return journey. Dates, date preserves, and date pits are all needed for consumption in the winter; salt, which is gathered from salt wastes, is consumed year-round; and palm leaves are woven into ropes for tying and packing tents and baggage. The date palms are easily cultivated: A river drains into the desert basin, creating a sandy soil with a five-foot water table into which the date palms sink their roots. Because of the heat, wind, and lack of rain, however, it is not possible for sheep and goats to live there, even for a short time.

In November, the group migrates back to the plateau. Those tribesmen who are also cultivators plant grain at this time, and women go off to work for cash in nearby towns. This labor is a substitute source of subsistence for the extensive livestock raiding of an earlier era, which has since been stamped out by the government. Pastoralism, date cultivation, and additional sources of subsistence are all necessary to an economy that exists in such a marginal and unproductive environment.

Adapted from Philip C. Salzman, "Multi-Resource Nomadism in Iranian Baluchistan," in William Irons and Neville Dyson-Hudson, eds., Perspectives on Nomadism *(Leiden, the Netherlands: E. J. Brill, 1972), pp. 61–69. Reprinted by permission.*

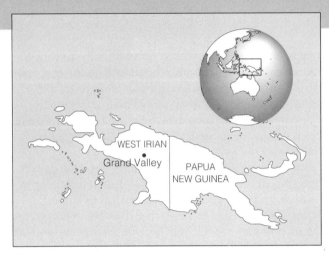

The Dani live in the central mountains of West Irian (western New Guinea), above the tropical jungles of the coast (see map). Because of the altitude, rainfall is evenly distributed throughout the year, and temperature variation is slight. In the tropical forest, there are a few wild animals. Although a few wild foods are collected from the forests and fields, these do not play an important role in the Dani diet. Basically, the Dani rely on the products from their gardens and on their domesticated pigs for subsistence. Like many other highland New Guinea peoples, the Dani make the sweet potato the main item of their diet. Other cultivated plants that are eaten are taro, banana, ginger, sugar cane, and greens. For ordinary meals, sweet potatoes are merely cooked and eaten; ceremonial meals consist of steamed vegetables and pork.

The Dani cultivate three kinds of gardens: great ditched fields on the floor of the Grand Valley, hill slope gardens, and small garden plots behind the houses in their compounds. The bulk of the sweet potato crop is grown on the valley floor. In these gardens, a typical swidden round of activities takes place: The fields are cleared of brush and trees that have grown since the last planting, and the cleared vegetation is burned. The sod is then turned with digging sticks, which are the only agricultural implements among the Dani. Sweet potatoes are planted with vine cuttings from other gardens and spread with the fertile mud that comes from the cleared ditches. A few months later, the gardens are weeded, and about seven months later, the harvesting begins. When the plot is exhausted, pigs are allowed to root over the field. Fields lie fallow from one to twenty years. Since there is no seasonal growing period in the valley, sweet

Although extensive cultivation may be practiced in dry lands, such as among the Hopi Indians, who live in northeastern Arizona and cultivate maize, beans, and squash, it is typically a tropical forest adaptation. As such it is found mainly in Southeast Asia, sub-Saharan Africa, some Pacific islands, and the Amazon Basin in South America. In these environments, a form of cultivation called **swidden**, or **slash and burn**, is practiced. In slash and burn cultivation, a field is cleared by felling the trees and burning the brush. The burned vegetation is allowed to remain on the soil, which prevents its drying out from the sun. The resulting bed of ash acts as a fertilizer, returning nutrients to the soil. Fields are used only for several years potatoes are harvested year-round. Each household maintains several garden plots that are kept at different stages of growth. During the harvesting time for any one plot, enough potatoes are harvested to feed the family for the following day. The valley fields, in contrast to those on the slopes, are cultivated intensively, normally not allowing a chance for heavy vegetation to grow up. The ditching and use of the mud as cover supplies the necessary refertilization of the gardens.

A more extensive slash and burn cultivation is practiced on the slopes. Here sugar cane, taro, cucumbers, and yams are more common than sweet potatoes. In the village gardens, the Dani plant tobacco, bananas, and a few vegetables. Banana plants grown in the compound are used for food but also have other uses; the trees shade houses, the leaves are used as wrappers for food, and the outer stem is softened to use for binding. Pigs provide an essential source of protein. Most men have from one to twenty pigs. Every day, the pigs are taken from their stalls to root in the nearby forest or in fallow gardens. Herding is tedious and means a lot of responsibility. Pigs also play an important role in Dani culture; they are used for exchange and eaten on ceremonial occasions.

The basic division of labor among the Dani is according to sex. Usually, men do the heavy work, women the light work. Men fight, build houses, and clear fields and gardens; women plant, weed, harvest, cook, and make salt. Children frequently herd the pigs. In their basic economy, the Dani are pretty self-sufficient. They provide their own food, shelter, and clothing from materials found or grown in the area. Except for ax and adze blades, needed for felling trees and butchering pigs, the subsistence economy of the Dani is self-contained, and small residential groups are economically independent. The ceremonial economy requires that each Dani group is dependent on a broad trade network.

Adapted from Karl Heider, The Dugum Dani *(Chicago: Aldine, 1970).*

(one to five) and then allowed to lie fallow for a number of years (up to twenty), so that the forest cover can be rebuilt and fertility restored. Swidden cultivators require five to six times as much fallow land as that under cultivation. Swidden cultivation can have a deteriorating effect on the environment if fields are cultivated before they have lain fallow long enough to re-

cover their forest growth. Eventually, the forest will not grow back, and the tree cover will be replaced by grasslands. It is this irreversible ecological deterioration that has caused swidden cultivation to be considered both inefficient and destructive by Western observers.

Recent anthropological investigation has shown, however, that swidden cultivation is

Horticultural peoples supplement their diets by a number of different means. Fishing with a bow and arrow is practiced in Papua New Guinea. (Courtesy of Office of Information, Port Moresby, Papua New Guinea)

not an uninformed, casual, and careless food-getting strategy. Swidden cultivators often have well-developed techniques of clearing, firing, fertilizing the soil, and crop rotation. For example, the Kofyar people of the Jos plateau in Nigeria have an impressive system of stepped terraces that are constructed to deepen the soil, stabilize sloping ground, and prevent runoff and erosion. Among the Tsembaga of New Guinea, planting of several crops is carefully ordered: Sweet potato leaves cover the soil at ground level, taro leaves project over this mat, hibiscus and sugar cane stand still higher, and banana trees spread out above the rest. This ordering results in a garden that has maximum leaf exposure to sunlight, protects the soil, discourages insects, and provides a variety of foods as insurance if one crop fails (Rappaport 1971).

Although some swidden cultivators depend primarily on one crop, many more cultivate several. Because plants grown by swidden cul-

tivators do not provide all the necessary proteins for human health, however, horticulturalists may also hunt and fish or raise some domestic animals. In New Guinea, for example, domestic pigs are an important source of protein, and the Kofyar keep goats, chickens, sheep, and cows.

Because swidden cultivation requires shifting of fields, it has been assumed that horticulturalists shift residences as well. This is not necessarily the case; some swidden cultivators do occupy villages permanently or at least on a long-term basis. In horticultural populations, there is a typical division of labor by sex. The men do the clearing, burning, planting, weeding, and fencing; women harvest, carry plant foods back to the village, and transform raw food into cooked or processed edibles. Where hunting is practiced, it is usually a male task, although either men or women may fish. Females may help plant, weed, and harvest. They also care for pigs, where these are raised.

Intensive rice farming can be enormously productive but is back-breaking work. The greater productivity of intensive cultivation results from more sophisticated technology, such as irrigation, and from intensification of labor. Here women plant rice outside Jogjakarta, Indonesia. (United Nations)

There is great variety in social systems among horticulturalists. The basic unit is most frequently a group of people who believe that they are descended from a common ancestor. This descent group most frequently reckons descent through males, but societies in which descent is reckoned through females occur in greater proportion among horticultural peoples than in any other type of society. This may be related to the important role of women in the cultivation of plants and cooperative domestic activities.

In spite of the generally low population densities, the size of horticultural villages may be quite large, ranging from 100 people up to 1,000. It appears that small, low-density village societies are more egalitarian than those with larger populations and higher density, although generally it can be said that horticulturalists have more formalized group leadership than do hunters and gatherers. These societies also frequently engage in warfare (see pp. 330–332), which may be a way of regulating population size and density.

Intensive Cultivation

Intensive cultivation, or **agriculture,** is characterized by the use of the plow and draft animals and by more effective techniques of water and soil control than are used by horticulturalists. The same piece of land is cultivated permanently and needs no fallow period. Plows are more efficient in loosening the soil than are digging sticks or hoes. In turning of the soil, nutrients are lifted to the surface. Plowing requires a much more thorough clearing of land, but it also allows land to be used year after year. Irrigation is another important pattern in intensive cultivation. Although some horticulturalists do practice some simple methods of water conservation and control, intensive cultivation in dry areas can be carried out only with sophisticated irrigation techniques. In hilly areas,

The following description enables us to see the complicated and sophisticated nature of the role of peasant farmers in modern Egypt, who are active decision makers in their own interests. It also shows how earning a living in certain ways involves constraints and opportunities provided by both the physical environment and the social environment, including the government. The role of government intervention in agriculture described here clarifies the definition of the peasant village as a "part society," integrally intertwined with the larger society.

The village of Musha is located in the Nile Valley, about 400 miles south of Cairo. The Nile Valley consists of three parallel ecological strips. The first strip is a raised bank along the river, which holds back the Nile floodwaters. The villages on the banks contain sandy soil and specialize in growing bananas, palms, and some vegetables. Villagers also fish and trade their catch to villages away from the river. The second strip, where Musha is located, is between the river banks and the desert, which constitutes the third strip. The basin villages, like Musha, are built on mounds raised above the old level of the Nile floodwater. The topsoil is thick and heavy and agriculture predominates.

Musha is larger than the average Egyptian village, containing about 18,000 persons. Most of the village families live in their own houses, which in addition to being used for eating and sleeping are used for storage, stabling animals, raising poultry, and for some agricultural work.

Musha's principal crops are divided into summer crops and winter crops. The main summer crops are cotton, maize, and sorghum. The main winter crops are wheat, beans, chickpeas, and bersim (a variety of millet). There is a two-year crop rotation system. A cycle starts with cotton in the first summer, followed by wheat in the following winter. Maize and/or sorghum follow in the second summer, or the land may be left fallow. The cycle is completed in the second winter with bersim, lentils, and chickpeas. In addition, there are grape and pomegranate orchards, and farmers raise onions, peppers, watermelons, and other vegetables on small patches for home consumption.

Animal husbandry is also important in Musha. Small farmers depend heavily on the water buffalo, which is used for its dairy products of milk, cheese, and butter. Cows, sheep, goats, and poultry are kept by most families for their products (cheese and bread are the most common foods in Musha) as only water buffalo is regularly eaten and sold. Unlike in other Asian peasant systems, water buffalo are not used for traction and other work.

Traditionally, Musha peasants used a simple technology. They relied on either animal power or human effort; their basic all-purpose technological tool was the short-handled hoe, used to weed and irrigate and to prepare the fields for irrigation. Flood irrigation required no special tools. A small sickle was used for harvesting and a digging stick for planting cotton. A shallow plow was pulled by a yoke of cows. Threshing was carried out with a threshing sled pulled around in a circle by a pair of cows. Winnowing relied on the wind and a winnowing fork and sieves for the final cleaning.

Transport was by donkey for small loads and short distances or by camel for larger loads and longer distances. Camels were used to bring the crops in from the field. Winnowing, camel transport, and sometimes plowing were carried out by specialists rather than each household on its own. The tools were mainly wooden and made by carpenters.

In the last twenty years many changes have come to Musha. The number of tractors has increased enormously, and mechanization has almost replaced animal power in agriculture (though some camels and donkeys are still kept for transport). All farmers use machines now, at least some of the time, though animals are still used, too. Tractors have a mechanism for threshing and for pulling four-wheeled wagons, which transport fertilizer and bring crops in from the field. Farmers now depend on chemical fertilizers and pesticides as well as animal manure. Important changes in irrigation were stimulated by the introduction of pumping machines, owned by private farmers, which lift groundwater to supplement the Nile floodwater for part of the year. With pumps, double cropping and the cultivation of cotton became possible. Land values thus increased, leading to the creation of large landholdings and increased demand for labor.

In the 1960s, the completion of the Aswan High Dam brought yet more changes. When the annual flood of the Nile ceased, farmers drew their water from newly constructed, government-owned feed canals, which were linked up to the privately owned pumps in use. The government now supplies water to the canals every other week, and the water raised from the canals to the level of the fields flows through a network of ditches until it reaches the fields.

A farmer who wants to irrigate his fields must arrange with the pump guard to provide water for the ditch that serves his field. The farmer must then provide the necessary labor and open up a break in the ditch band so that the water will flow into his field. The farmer pays the owner of the pump a set fee

(continued)

per watering and also pays the pump guard an annual fee. Pumps are usually owned by several people who share the work of guarding and maintaining the pumps and taking care of the accounts. The government has the responsibility of maintaining the feeder canals and cleans them once a year. The owners of the pumps are responsible for the maintenance of the irrigation ditches that their pumps are used to feed. The organization of the irrigation water within the field is the responsibility of the individual farmer.

The household is a central institution in the labor process, organizing labor from its own members, bringing in extra laborers as needed, or by its own members working outside the agricultural sector. Larger families tend to have more wealth and more land. There is a sexual division of labor, with women doing the housekeeping, caring for animals, and preparing cheese. Women do not work in the fields in Musha as they do in some other parts of Egypt. Children do specific jobs, such as cutting clover for animals, harvesting cotton, and insect control. Most farmers use a labor contractor to recruit children for their cotton-picking gangs. The head of the household plays a key managerial role: He makes sure things are done on time; purchases what is needed for agricultural work; hires labor; and schedules the use of machinery, whether his own, or that he rents.

The two most common crops cultivated in Musha (and Egypt generally) are wheat and cotton. Wheat, normally planted in November and harvested in May and June, is used for both grain and straw; the latter is more profitable because of government-mandated price controls on grain. In order to grow wheat, the farmer must register with the government and follow government rules on crop rotation. The village cooperative records the amount of land a farmer owns and the amount he will plant in wheat. The village (government-owned) bank must then authorize a loan in the form of fertilizer, insecticide, or seed. The farmer then irrigates his land, dealing first with the pump mechanic to make sure the pump is working, next with the pump guard to determine when water will be available for him, then with the pump owner to pay his fee, and finally, with his neighbors to make sure that their land will not be damaged. The farmer must then hire a driver and tractor (if he does not own one, which many small farmers do not) to plow the fields. Fertilizer and seed are hauled from the village bank to his home and from his home to the field. The fertilizer is then broadcast by hand.

Wheat is harvested using a small sickle. The plant is cut at the base or simply pulled up by the roots. For this most farmers hire laborers who are paid piece rates by the amount of area harvested; small farmers also use household members for this work. The reaped wheat is bundled into sheaves, a job done by older men and hired workers, paid piece rates. The sheaves are transported to the threshing ground at the edge of the village, carried there either by camel or by a tractor and wagon. Costs are charged by the trip, and paid in cash. Camels are easier to load and unload, and can go places tractors cannot, but they are also slower.

The grain is threshed using a tractor and drum thresher. Threshing is a long and tedious job, and a threshing gang has five members: one to feed the machine, one to shovel away the threshed crop that has passed through the machine, and the rest to hand sheaves to the feed. The threshed grain is winnowed and sifted by specialists who are paid piece rates. The winnowed grain is measured and sacked by the winnower, an activity which the farmer oversees in person. In the final step the grain and straw are hauled, by animal transport, from the threshing ground back to the storeroom in the farmer's house. The grain is then sold to merchants who sell it in the cities (until very recently, the government was a major purchaser of grain). Some grain will be kept at home to be milled into flour and baked into bread, and some straw will be used by the farmer to feed his own animals. . . .

Musha farmers grow both wheat and cotton for both domestic consumption and, increasingly, for sale, and the latter involves a high degree of government intervention. This mainly takes the form of "forced deliveries" for the basic field crops such as cotton and beans. At one time the farmers were obliged to sell their entire cotton crop to the government; the other crops could be sold at higher, market prices. For cotton, the farmer is paid a base price at delivery, from which the village bank has subtracted the debt of services and products (such as fertilizer) loaned by the government. The cotton price is fixed each year by the government relative to the world-market price. While the government sets a price intended to motivate the farmer to cultivate the cotton properly, the farmers, who know the world-market price, often feel cheated by the notably lower price of the government. The farmer passes on these lower prices in the lower wages he pays his workers.

The profit from farming is uncertain, and most families have several sources of income. Animals are sold in weekly markets through professional brokers who have established and trusted relationships built on personal contact. Fruits and vegetables are sold either in the fields or to merchant brokers. In fact, 70 percent of village households derive their major income from activities other than farming: day labor, government jobs, craft trades, specialist agricultural work, remittances from family members who have migrated, or from rents and pensions.

(continued)

The farming system of Musha is constrained and responds to a number of imperatives. One is the landscape, with its combination of rich soil, no rainfall, and a large river. A second constraint arises from government intervention in the agricultural process. Through the building of the Aswan Dam, the state has remodeled the very landscape on which the farmer works. The state also intervenes in many other direct and indirect ways, providing a framework for agricultural activity and structuring the situation within which the farmer must make choices. The state makes major investments in agriculture through the irrigation system and other infrastructure projects. The state provides agricultural credit for such inputs as seed and fertilizer, relieving the farmers of the necessity of financing each year's crop from the proceeding harvest. The state also is involved in marketing, and state policies, such as importing wheat from the United States, affect the prices it is willing to offer the farmer. The state has a role in setting land-ownership policy and makes rules governing land tenancy, a policy which has made available large pools of labor, who thus have less bargaining power in relation to large landholders. The state also affects the labor market by controlling (and permitting, or encouraging) migration outside the country, which acts as a safety valve for surplus rural labor. The state also benefits from the remittances in hard currency sent back by migrants.

Working within the constraints and possibilities available, the farmer has to interact with a large number of people — government officials, owners of tractors, day laborers, recruiters for child labor, neighbors, contractors for transport animals, and merchants — in addition to supervising a complicated agricultural cycle. The farmer needs to know enough of the traditional skills of farming to supervise the agricultural work and also must know how to manage a wide range of activities, making important decisions at every step. With the increasing monetization of agriculture, farmers now consciously orient themselves to the market and have become sophisticated in dealing with it. No longer does the description of the peasant farmer as one who produces mainly for the subsistence of the household or peasant labor as encapsulated within the village, fit the reality. Increasingly, the peasant farmer must be seen as not only part of a state, but also a world, economy.

Adapted from Nicholas Hopkins, "Mechanized Irrigation in Upper Egypt: The Role of Technology and the State in Agriculture," in B. Turner II and Stephen B. Brush, eds., Comparative Farming Systems *(New York: Guilford Press, 1987), pp. 223–47. Reprinted by permission.*

intensive cultivation requires some form of terracing in order to prevent crops and good soil from being washed down the hillside. Preindustrial intensive cultivation also utilizes techniques of natural fertilization, selective breeding of livestock and crops, and crop rotation, all of which increase productivity. Whereas horticulturalists have to increase the land under cultivation in order to support a larger population, intensive cultivation can support population increases by more intensified use of the same piece of land.

Many more people can be supported per acre of land with intensive cultivation. A comparison of extensive and intensive cultivation in Mexico demonstrated, for example, that with irrigation, which permits two crops a year, a given amount of land can support almost fourteen times as many families as the same area exploited by slash and burn techniques. A dramatic example of the differences in productivity of slash and burn versus intensive cultivation is offered by the island nation of Indonesia. Java, which makes up only 9 percent of the Indonesian land area, supports over two-thirds of the Indonesian population. The "outer islands," which make up almost 90 percent of the land area and support about a third of its population, are mainly exploited by swidden agriculture. In Java, intensive wet rice cultivation using elaborate irrigation terraces supports an average of approximately 1,250 people per square mile. This contrasts sharply with the maximum population density of swidden areas, which has been estimated at about 145 persons per square mile (Geertz 1963:13).

The greater productivity of intensive cultivation results not only from more sophisticated technology but also from greater use of labor. Intensive agriculturalists must work long and hard to make the land productive. In terraced agriculture, for example, ditches must be dug and kept clean, sluices constructed and repaired, and all terraces leveled and diked. It has been estimated that growing rice under a swidden system requires 241 worker-days per yearly crop, whereas wet rice cultivation requires 292

worker-days a year. Intensive cultivation also requires more capital investment than does horticulture. In horticultural societies, the only necessary tool may be a simple digging stick. In intensive cultivation, apart from the cost of human labor, plows have to be bought and draft animals raised and cared for. Although intensive agriculturalists may have more control over food production, they are also more vulnerable to the environment. By depending on the intensive cultivation of one or two crops, they can face disaster in case of a crop failure. Draft animals may be struck by disease, again affecting the cultivator's ability to produce.

Intensive cultivation is generally associated with stable village life and other complex forms of social organization. With the development of intensive agriculture and population increase, we see the rise of cities, an increase in occupational specialization, social stratification arising from great differences in wealth, political centralization, and the development of the state.

Rural cultivators, like those in Musha, who produce mainly for the subsistence of their households, and who are integrated into the larger, complex wholes of state societies, are called **peasants**. In anthropology, the emphasis has been on treating peasant agriculture and peasant labor as encapsulated within the peasant village. In fact, as the description of Musha indicates, peasants are incorporated into larger economic and political systems. In Egypt there is a particularly long (and well-documented) history of state intervention in agriculture — a situation that we see continuing into the present with the introduction of mechanized irrigation techniques, which are controlled by the state. This is, however, characteristic of agricultural peasant societies. Another trend we see in Musha, which is characteristic of other contemporary peasant societies as well, is the importance of labor supply outside the household, and on the other hand, the need of farmers to engage in part-time work outside the village. Peasants are incorporated not only into larger economic structures but also, by definition,

Peasants harvesting barley, one of the main crops, along with rice, grown in Korea. Unlike rice, barley does not demand pesticides, making it cheaper to grow. However, harvesting barley is painful because it must be cut in the summer, when it is very hot, and also barley has pointy growths that severely scratch the skin. Korean peasants, like their Egyptian counterparts, must take many things into account when deciding where to invest their capital and labor. (Courtesy of Soo Choi)

into larger social and political structures, like the state. Much of what peasants produce is taken by others in the form of rent, taxes, or free labor. Whereas horticulturalists produce for the subsistence of the local group and own the land they use for cultivation, peasants have little control over their land and produce to support nonproducing populations. The characteristic of a peasant economy is that part of its agricultural production is commandeered by a politically dominant and non–food-producing class. The peasant must pay for access to land either in cash, a percentage of the harvest, the donation of agricultural labor to the landowner, or tribute to the state. Because modern peasants are required to maintain their own seeds, tools, and animals, they must participate in market economies over which they have no control. In this way also, they are distinguished from horticulturalists and from farmers in industrial societies. Farmers in the

United States, for example, have more control over their land and other means of production and produce for a market in order to maximize personal profit. This distinction should not be taken too literally, however; the small farmer in the United States is faced with many of the same decision-making issues as his counterpart in less industrialized countries. Furthermore, although contemporary peasants do engage in economic practices that seem to limit productivity, most are involved in world markets, and certainly in growing cash crops, they do attempt to maximize their profits.

Industrialism

The basis of industrial society is the use of machines and chemical processes for the production of goods. Although we call the transition from agricultural to industrial society the "In-

A young girl in Pizanou, a village in Upper Volta, West Africa, harvests peanuts while caring for her baby brother. In small-scale peasant economies, and in some segments of industrial economies, children make an important contribution to family income. (United Nations/Ray Witlin)

dustrial Revolution," the change did not come about overnight, as the word *revolution* might lead us to believe. Industrialism began in England in the early 1700s, and within one hundred years, it came into its own as a dominant force with the establishment of mass-production techniques in processing steel and with the invention of the steam locomotive. Compared to the amount of time it took humans to move from hunting and gathering to agriculture, however, a period of many thousands of years, the speed with which industrialism established itself may indeed be called revolutionary. Furthermore, industrialism is a revolution because of the enormous changes it brought about in society, not only in the economic sphere but in all other spheres as well. Industrialism as a way of life, compared with earlier forms of economic organization and production, was "explosive" in its effect on population growth, its consumption of goods and resources, and its need to expand beyond

its own boundaries. Prior to industrialism, for example, the doubling of the world's population is estimated to have taken about 250 years. After industrialism, however, human populations increased much more rapidly. This population growth is in contrast with growth among tribal populations, which, constrained by a variety of social and religious controls, tend to maintain themselves in equilibrium with their resources.

In addition to population growth, industrialism has brought about a tremendous growth in per capita consumption of goods, and industrial economies are based on the principle that consumption must be constantly expanded and that material standards of living must always go up. This pattern contrasts with tribal economies, which put various limits on consumption and thus are able to make lighter demands on their environments. Industrialism promotes resource consumption at so great a pace that it quickly outgrows its own boundaries and results in both export of population and import of resources. In this way, the whole world has been gradually drawn into the market system that has its source in industrialism.

Industrial societies require very large, mobile, skilled, educated, and specialized labor forces, whose activities are well coordinated. They also require the creation of complex systems of exchange between those who supply raw materials and those who use them in manufacturing, as well as between manufacturers and consumers. A central feature of industrial societies is that they are socially stratified. In capitalist industrial societies, there is private ownership of capital and the means of production, whereas in socialist societies, capital and the means of production are controlled by the state. But in both cases, there are at least two social classes: a large labor force that produces goods and services and a much smaller class that controls what is produced and how it is distributed.

Industrialism brought about (and continues to bring about) many changes in society. By the fifteenth and sixteenth centuries, as Europe moved from mercantilism to industrialism, it expanded its economy to incorporate much of the non-European world (Wolf 1982), a process that continues today. As the non-European parts of the world increasingly industrialize, the social changes that characterize industrialization also occur: the movement of people from rural to urban areas, a decrease in the organizing roles of kinship and religion, and the rise of a special kind of formal organization called a bureaucracy. The effects of some of these changes in non-European societies will be discussed in Chapter 15.

Summary

1. Different physical environments present different problems, opportunities, and limitations to human populations. Therefore, the physical environment influences, although it does not determine, culture. There are always at least a few cultural alternatives possible in any environment. The level of technology is the determining factor in the utilization of the physical environment.

2. The subsistence (food-getting) pattern of a society develops in response to seasonal variation in the environment and environmental variations over the long run, such as drought, flood, or animal diseases.

3. Subsistence patterns are adjusted to the presence of different groups in the environment, as well as to physical factors such as climate, soil quality, and availability of water.

4. The five major patterns of using the environment to support human populations are hunting and gathering, pastoralism, extensive cultivation (horticulture), intensive cultivation (agriculture), and industrialism. As a whole, humankind has moved in the direction of using more complex technology, increasing its numbers, and developing more complex sociocultural systems.

5. Hunting and gathering, which relies on food naturally available in the environment, was the major food-getting pattern for 99 percent of the time humans have been on earth. This way of life is rapidly disappearing, although even today it provides a more than adequate living for those groups that practice it.

6. The Copper Eskimo of the Canadian Arctic represent a specialized hunting-gathering adaptation: Unlike other foraging societies, they do not have a large component of vegetable food in their diet.

7. Pastoralism involves the care of domesticated herd animals, which alone cannot provide the necessary ingredients for an adequate human diet. Supplementary food grains are required; therefore, pastoralism either is found along with cultivation or involves trading relations with food cultivators.

8. The Yarahmadzai of Baluchistan are an example of a group that is predominantly pastoralist but also utilizes a variety of other means of obtaining food: wage labor, date cultivation, and trade.

9. Extensive cultivation (horticulture) uses a simple, nonmechanized technology. Fields are not used permanently but are allowed to lie fallow after several years of productivity. Horticulture is typically a tropical forest adaptation and requires the cutting and burning of jungle to clear fields for cultivation.

10. The Dani of New Guinea are horticulturalists, and like others in New Guinea they also have domesticated pigs that provide needed animal protein. Other horticultural groups do some hunting or fishing to provide the protein supplement necessary for human survival.

11. Intensive cultivation uses both land and labor intensively, and a more complex technology involves plows, irrigation techniques, or mechanization. This food-getting pattern supports the largest population densities, and it is thus associated with sedentary village life and the rise of the state.

12. Peasants are cultivators who produce mainly for the subsistence of their households but who participate in the larger political entity called the state. Musha, a village in Egypt, has the typical characteristics of a peasant village: Although agriculture is the main source of subsistence, there is also a well-developed market, participation in the larger cash economy of the state, wage labor, and some occupational spe-

cialization. Unlike farmers in the United States, peasant cultivators have little control over the land they work.

13. Industrialism is a system in which machines and chemical processes are used for the production of goods. It requires a large, mobile labor force and involves a complex system of exchange among all elements of the economy.

Suggested Readings

Applebaum, H.
1981   *Royal Blue: The Culture of Construction Workers*. New York: Holt, Rinehart and Winston. One of the most recent in the popular case-study series about an occupational specialization in the United States.

Cleary, David
1990   *Anatomy of the Amazon Gold Rush*. Iowa City: University of Iowa Press. A timely ethnography on a little known, but important, informal sector of the Amazonian economy, which includes the social and technological aspects of gold mining, set in historical perspective.

Gates, Hill
1987   *Chinese Working Class Lives: Getting by in Taiwan*. Ithaca: Cornell University Press. A readable account of the culture and social organization of a wide range of working-class people in Taiwan that makes interesting use of life histories.

Hopkins, Nicholas
1987   *Agrarian Transformation in Egypt*. Westview Special Studies in Social, Political and Economic Development. Boulder, Colo.: Westview Press. An analysis of an Egyptian village that emphasizes the role of the farmer in relation to the state and examines some of the changes in the social stratification system of the village as a result of changing agricultural technology and government policies.

Lee, Richard
1979   *The !Kung San: Men, Women and Work in a Foraging Society*. Cambridge, England: Cambridge University Press. An extremely detailed yet thoroughly readable book about one of the last human groups that still relies heavily on hunting and gathering.

Spradley, James, and Mann, Brenda
1975   *Cocktail Waitress: Women's Work in a Man's World*. New York: Wiley. An ethnographic study of a bar in an American city using a cognitive anthropological perspective.

Thurston, Clarke
1978   *The Last Caravan*. New York: Putnam's. An engrossing account, interweaving individual stories with a description of the tragic drought in the Sahel of Africa, leading to the near disappearance of the Tuareg pastoral way of life.

Economics

Why are hunters called "the original affluent society"?

How do different societies organize labor?

What are the different principles of distribution and exchange in nonstate and state societies?

What are some major differences among economies associated with the different ways of making a living?

How does the expansion of capitalism affect non-Western societies?

[For the Ik] their violence is there, deep and smoldering, scarring each man and woman, making life even more disagreeable and dividing man against his neighbor even further. There is simply no community of interest, familial or economic, social or spiritual.

With the Ik the family does not even hold itself together, much less serve as a model for a wider social brotherhood of Ik. Economic interest is centered on as many individual stomachs as there are people, and cooperation is merely a device for furthering an interest that is consciously selfish. The . . . old no longer remember . . . that there was a time when people were kind, when parents looked after their children and children looked after their parents. Every one of the Ik who were old today was thrown out at three, and has survived in consequence, and in consequence has thrown his own children out and knows full well that they will not help him in his old age any more than he helped his parents.

The system has turned one full cycle and is now self-perpetuating; it has eradicated what we know as "humanity" and has turned the world into a chilly void where man does not even seem to care for himself, but survives.

From Colin M. Turnbull, The Mountain People *(New York: Simon and Schuster, 1972), p. 15.*
© 1972 by Colin M. Turnbull. Reprinted by permission of Simon and Schuster.

This chilling description of how human love, cooperation, and feeling disintegrate under conditions of extreme food scarcity and are replaced by behavior that is selfish, unfeeling, and cruel, comes from an ethnographic account of the Ik, a tribe of hunters and gatherers living in a remote area of Uganda, who were forced by the government to become sedentary farmers so that their hunting land could be used as a national park. The shift from mobile hunting and gathering to sedentary farming made irrelevant the Ik's entire traditional culture: their beliefs, their habits, their values. Their hunter-gatherer culture was totally inappropriate to farming, and while they seemed to try to adapt, their culture had fitted them for an entirely different way of life. One of the consequences of the change from hunting to farming was that the Ik were suddenly crowded together at a level of density far greater than they had ever experienced. Forced into an intimacy and frequency of contact with each other uncharacteristic of mobile hunter-gatherers, the Ik were then struck by a severe drought, leaving them, in their forced resettlement, near starvation. It is under these conditions that we can try to understand how the Ik lost their "humanity" and what implications this has for understanding the relationships between economics and human behavior.

All human societies have economic systems within which goods and services are produced, distributed, and consumed. It is within these economic systems that economic behavior — the motivations and choices in the production, distribution, and consumption of goods and services — is found. To the extent that economic systems are part of culture, then, different economic systems lead to different economic behavior.

Anthropologists Study Economics

Economic Behavior

A discipline called **formal economics** is a way of looking at human behavior that developed in the context of the Western industrial market economy. The basic assumption of formal economics is that human material wants are unlimited, but the means for achieving these wants are not. All people must therefore make choices about how to use time, energy, and capital in order to achieve desired ends. A further assumption of formal economics is that people **economize** — that is, make choices among alternative courses of action in a rational manner. Here, *rational* means choosing a course of action that will maximize the individual's material well-being and profit.

Economizing is seen as the key to understanding both the production and consumption of goods. Will a business firm cut down or expand its production? Will it purchase a new machine or hire more laborers? Where will it locate its plant? Will it manufacture shoes or gloves? How much will be spent on advertising its product? All these decisions are assumed to be rational — that is, based on the desire to maximize profit. Individuals are also assumed to act rationally, to allocate scarce resources in ways that increase their individual material well-being. How does one allocate one's income, which is limited, among an unlimited number of desires? Will an individual save to buy a new car, send the children to college, fix the roof on the house, take a vacation, or buy a spouse a gift? Or will he or she save it all? Will leisure time be spent playing with the children, getting a second job, or going back to school to get a degree in order to improve one's economic chances in the future?

The definition of economics as the study of economizing made sense in the kind of society in which formal economics developed. Is formal economic theory equally useful in the study of noncapitalist, small-scale, and peasant societies? How much of the behavior in these societies can be understood in terms of maximizing one's individual material well-being?

The data of anthropology show that although people in every society do indeed make choices in terms of rational ends and means, with an eye to their material well-being, they also make choices on the basis of other values. The material on the Ik suggests that in a cultural system which focuses on individual material well-being to the exclusion of all else, the core of our "humanity" may drop away. This emphasis on individual well-being among the Ik derived from their conditions of near starvation. In the United States, also, some anthropologists suggest, rampant individualism derives from abundance, and thus, though the external conditions are different, the Ik may have a message for us all.

In all functioning societies, however, including our own (but perhaps excluding the Ik, whom Turnbull no longer considered as a functioning society), rational cost-benefit analysis is never the sole motivation of behavior. This indicates a note of caution that must be used when we try to analyze behavior in other cultures which appears economic, that is, involves the production, distribution, and consumption of goods, but to Westerners might appear "irrational," that is, not consistent with the maximization of individual self-interest.

Marshall Sahlins (1972), for example, questions whether the idea of scarcity, a basic concept in formal economics, has meaningful application to hunting and gathering societies. Sahlins calls hunters and gatherers the "original affluent societies" not because they are rich but rather because what they desire is limited and their technology is more than enough to meet their needs. According to Sahlins, the assumption that human needs are unlimited and resources are scarce is fundamental to capitalism, under which production units are motivated by profit. It is by no means a condition of all human societies; economizing is not a universal human value. Sahlins says: "We should entertain the . . . possibility that hunters are in business for their health, a finite objective, and that the bow and arrow are adequate to that end" (p. 5). This point of view helps explain some behavior that appears puzzling — for example, "the inclination of hunters to consume at once all stocks on hand, as if they had it made" (p. 5). It also helps explain the economically nonproductive use of leisure time characteristic of many hunting societies.

Among the Hadza of Tanzania, for example, food is obtained without great effort. The Hadza live in an area with an abundance of animal and vegetable food. The Hadza man spends much of his time gambling, and there is no attempt to use leisure time to increase wealth. Surrounded by cultivators, the Hadza have, until recently, refused to give up their hunting way of life, because it "would require too much work." Such behavior seems irrational or "lazy" only if we assume that people have unlimited desires for more than they already possess (Woodburn 1968).

Enjoyable use of leisure time is only one of the ends toward which human effort may be expended. Increasing social status or respect is another value toward which individuals may direct their energies. In our society, prestige is primarily tied up with increased consumption and display of goods and services by the individual. Within the value systems of other societies, individuals also make choices based on the desire to be respected by others. But prestige is associated not with individual display, but rather with generosity and the giving away of

WORK TIME AND FREE TIME: A COMPARISON OF TWO SOCIETIES

For many people in Europe and the United States, modern life offers an unparalleled abundance of material goods. Have these goods made people happy? Have these goods made people happier than people in societies with much less material wealth than ours? The industrial technology and urban living that have made these material goods available also bring a price in the "quality of life." Although some people say that the gains far outweigh the costs, others say the opposite.

The question of how much progress modern civilization represents has been studied by two anthropologists, Allen and Orna Johnson, who compared the working time and nonworking time of people in France and the Machiguenga of the Peruvian Amazon. The Machiguenga have a horticultural and hunting subsistence strategy. They are self-sufficient in that almost everything they consume is produced by their own labor with local resources, the main exception being the simple metal axes used in horticulture, which they get from the Peruvians.

The Johnsons' research indicates that both French men and French women spend more time working than do Machiguenga men and women, the men by one and a half hours, the women by four hours. The French spend three to five times as much time as the Machiguenga in "consumption time" — eating, watching television, participating in sports activities — activities we normally think of as leisure time. In the third category of time, free time — in which the Johnsons include resting, sleeping, "doing nothing," or chatting with other people — the Machiguenga were found to surpass the French by several hours a day.

It appears, therefore, that free time has not increased as a result of technological progress, nor has time spent in working decreased. There *has* been an increase of leisure time at the expense of free time, and we may look at this in two ways. On the one hand, increased consumption of goods seems exciting and a source of pleasure in what would otherwise be "boring" time. On the other hand, the pressure to spend time in consumption increases the sense that "time is short" and may be a source of anxiety or guilt that detracts from our pleasure. People in modern societies increasingly feel that "free time" is "wasted time."

Except that they lack the clearly superior Western medicines for certain sicknesses, such as parasitic diseases or eye infections, the Machiguenga do not suffer from their relatively low level of material affluence, according to the Johnsons. They easily produce more food than they use daily, saving the surplus for periods of crisis or for feeding guests and relatives. They are healthy, and the high quality of their lives is manifest in their warm family ties, integrity, peacefulness, and intimacy with nature.

The Johnsons' research suggests that, although people used to life in the affluent West will probably not want to live in a materially simple society, we should begin to question the costs of industrial technology and society: its harmful effects on the environment, the pressure to consume and the speeding up of time, the alienation of human relations, the mechanization and boredom of work, and the deprivation of unemployment. Studies of people like the Machiguenga can help us question our own goals and address questions about the quality of life in a more balanced way.

Adapted from Allen Johnson, "In Search of the Affluent Society," Human Nature, September 1978. © 1978 by Human Nature. Used by permission of the publisher, Harcourt Brace Jovanovich.

!Kung women filling eggshells with water. Among the !Kung, women play an important role in the economy, but both men and women spend much of their time socializing. (Courtesy Department of Library Services, American Museum of Natural History)

goods to others. Those who have much more than others may be considered stingy, and they may lose rather than gain prestige. "Conspicuous consumers" and stingy individuals become objects of envy and even subject to accusations of witchcraft. In our own society, although we expect to help relatives or close friends who are "down on their luck," we frequently do this only reluctantly, and we often break off social relations with others who continually borrow. In other societies, social relations have priority over economic ones. Friends, relatives, and neighbors are expected to and do help one another out in times of need with little conscious thought of being paid back immediately.

One allocation of resources in traditional societies that often seems excessive to Western-

ers is the investment in expensive ceremonial or ritual occasions that appear to have no direct material benefit to the individual and may even cause a family to go into debt. Although we in the United States also engage in this kind of "uneconomic" behavior, such as spending far more on a wedding than we can "rationally" afford, it is difficult for us to understand such behavior in societies where the material standard of living is below what we consider minimal.

In nonindustrial societies, few aspects of behavior are strictly economic. Most economic activity in such societies is viewed by the people themselves as having social, ceremonial, or moral ends. The anthropological study of economics, called **substantive economics**, must therefore encompass an understanding of the relation of means to ends that goes beyond the maximization of individual material interest. Individuals everywhere make rational choices on the basis of self-interest. But although individuals do the "economizing," culture and society, values and social structures, provide the framework within which these choices are made. Anthropology makes an important contribution to the study of human behavior by demonstrating that rationality has different meanings for different societies. This understanding is of real practical value as nonindustrial societies begin programs of modernization and economic development. People who have never participated in a market economy will not necessarily see its value in the same way that people in the West do. Sudden changes in the economy can have unexpected consequences unless planners and administrators are aware of differences in values.

Economic Systems

An **economic system** is the part of a sociocultural system that deals with the production, distribution, and consumption of goods and services within a particular society. Economics deals partly with things — with the tools used to produce goods and the goods themselves. More important, it deals with the relationship of things to people and with people to one another in the process of producing, distributing, and consuming goods. Anthropologists are interested in understanding the relationship between the economy and the rest of a culture. One aspect of this interrelationship is that culture defines or shapes the ends sought by individuals and the means of achieving those ends. Society and economy are interdependent in other ways. The ways in which production is organized have consequences for the institution of the family and for the political system. Conversely, different types of political organization also have consequences for the modes of production and distribution of goods. How does

a particular level of technological complexity affect the organization of work? How do the processes of production, distribution, and consumption relate to the formation of social classes or the absence of social differentiation? What is the consequence of different economic systems for economic growth and social change?

In preindustrial societies and among peasants, it is often difficult to separate the economic system from the rest of culture. Economics is embedded in the total social process and cultural pattern. Few groups are organized solely for the purpose of production. Rather, production is carried out by groups such as families, larger kinship groups, or local communities. Productive units in traditional societies have many purposes; their economic activities are only one aspect of what they do. The distribution, or exchange, of goods is also embedded in relationships that have primarily social and political purposes, as is consumption. Under these conditions, in order to study the economics of a society, the anthropologist must build a model of a particular system from many activities that are not just economic in that culture.

Production

In order to produce, people must have access to basic resources: land, water, and the materials from which tools are made. Every society has norms or rules that regulate access to and control over these resources as well as labor. After looking at the allocation of land, the basic resource of survival, we will turn to the organization of production — the composition of work groups and the division of labor in society. We will then look at capital — goods that are not directly consumed but are used to produce other goods.

Allocation of Natural Resources: Land

Access to and control over land are basic to every food-getting system. In our own society, most land is privately owned. It belongs to an

In peasant societies, economics is embedded in the total social structure and production is often carried out by families. (Serena Nanda)

individual by right of sale, and the individual who owns it has the right to keep others off and dispose of it as he or she wishes. This system of private ownership is not generally found among hunters and gatherers, horticulturalists, and pastoralists. In these societies, rights to use the land are vested in groups rather than in individuals. An individual acquires the right to use a piece of land by virtue of belonging by birth to the group in whom the right to use the land is vested. But even the group that has rights to use the land may not dispose of it at will; land is "inalienable" and may not be sold. With this type of land "ownership," no individual is deprived of access to basic resources, because every person belongs to a group within the society. Control over land, therefore, is not a means by which one group can exploit another or develop permanent control over other groups. Where rights to land do not include the right to keep others out, we cannot really speak of land "ownership" at all. Let us look at what this means in four types of societies: hunters and gatherers, pastoralists, horticulturalists, and intensive cultivators.

HUNTERS AND GATHERERS The requirements of a hunting and gathering way of life mean that a group of people must spread out over extensive areas of land. The division of land into exclusively defended and privately owned areas would make little sense, because animals roam freely. The adaptive value of flexible boundaries is directly related to foraging strategies, because ranges can be adjusted to a change in the availability of resources in a particular area. Everyone knows where food is located, so there is little concern that one or another group will gain exclusive access to basic resources. Thus, although certain areas are customarily used by particular groups within the society, these areas by no means *belong* to that group.

Among the !Kung of the Kalahari, for example, camps are located near water holes. The traditional area exploited by a local group is measured by one day's round-trip walk (about twelve miles from the camp) in all directions. Thus, each camp has a core area of about six miles surrounding each water hole. By fanning out from the water hole, camp members gain access to food resources within about one hundred square miles. Points beyond this are rarely utilized. Although camps may be moved five or six times a year, they are not moved far. Sometimes the move is only a few hundred yards; the farthest move is about ten or twelve miles (Lee 1968).

Hunters and gatherers require freedom of movement not only as a condition of success in their search for food but also as a way of dealing with social conflict. Hunting bands are kept small in order to exploit the environment successfully. In such small groups, conflict must be kept to a minimum. When arguments break out, individuals can move to other groups without fear that they are cutting themselves off from access to vital resources. If land were individually or even communally "owned" and defended against outsiders, the freedom of movement in hunting societies would be severely limited.

The adaptiveness of flexible relations to the land for hunting groups seems to be demonstrated by recent studies of nonhuman primates in the wild. Gorilla groups, for example, appear to inhabit and use ranges that overlap considerably, and they do not have exclusive territories that they defend. Chimpanzees also appear to constantly change group membership, and even different baboon groups have been observed to come into close daily contact without fighting over territories. Contrary to such popular theories as Robert Ardrey's "territorial imperative," anthropological research on both nonhuman primates and contemporary hunters and gatherers shows no evidence of a human instinct to occupy and defend a geographical area (Alland 1972).

PASTORALISTS   Among pastoralists, access to grassland and water is gained through membership in corporate kin groups, but livestock is owned and managed by individual heads of households. Pastoral tribes have traditionally defined access to pasture and migration routes by arrangements with local authorities who have control over these areas. Within pastoralist camps, all members share equal access to pastures. It is this access rather than ownership that is important. Among contemporary pastoralists, access to land for grazing livestock is frequently established by contracts with the landowners of villages through which the pastoralists move in their migrations. These contracts, which must be renewed every year, specify the rent for the pasture, the borders of the area, and the date by which the area must be vacated.

HORTICULTURALISTS   In horticultural societies, land tends to be communally owned by an extended kin group, although rights to *use* a piece of land may be given to households or even individuals. The users of the land may not sell it or otherwise transfer it, however, because ultimately the land belongs to the larger community. Individual ownership of land does not make sense with a slash and burn horticultural strategy. Usually, plenty of good land is available, and an individual has little use for land that was once farmed but now lies fallow. Once the land goes out of production, the claims to it gradually fade away, although fruit trees that have been planted may remain in private possession (Netting 1977).

Among horticulturalists, the designated elders or officials of the group usually allocate plots to the members of the group or the heads of households. What is important in horticultural societies, therefore, is not exclusive title to land, but rather the work involved in clearing and cultivating. The rights to cleared and productive land and to the products of that land are vested in those who work it, most often the domestic group or household. Because it is possible that the user of the land may die while the land is still productive, some system of inheritance of use rights is usually provided for. Cultivated plots in horticultural societies may be exclusively used and even defended against trespassers, but this system does not deprive anyone of the land necessary for subsistence.

Where population densities are low or great areas of land are available for cultivation, land use and group ownership are not a problem in horticultural societies. But when specific

With the rise of intensive agriculture and later with industrial capitalism, the notion of private land ownership and denying outsiders access to basic resources becomes central to the economic system. (Serena Nanda)

geographical conditions limit the amount of available land, or when population pressure increases, land shortages do occur. Sometimes this is dealt with by warfare, which serves to redistribute populations. Sometimes it is taken care of by the development of more efficient technology. As technology advances and the material base of a society expands, notions of private property develop. It is therefore in systems of intensive agriculture that private ownership of land becomes important.

INTENSIVE CULTIVATORS Under intensive cultivation, the material and labor investment in land becomes substantial. As land remains continually and indefinitely in production, it can feed more people than those who work it. It can support nonagricultural specialists and a

class of landowners. Private or family ownership of rigidly defined fields becomes an economic asset of great value in a society that permits the landowner, not the cultivator, to claim the surplus. That person can then enjoy leisure and command the services of craftworkers. Intensive cultivation therefore tends to be associated with individual land ownership, with the leasing or renting of property, with a political organization characterized by a ruling landowning class, and with occupational specialization. Under such conditions, a peasantry emerges. Peasants, as you may remember from Chapter 7, are agriculturalists who must pay rent on the land they work. Part of what they produce is thus taken by a ruling class.

Individual ownership of land may grow out of population pressures that produce land scarcity and lead to intensified methods of agriculture. Under these conditions, communal control of land creates conflict as people begin to grumble about their share. Those who have improved the land are unwilling to see the investment of their labor revert to a family pool. This may be particularly true when cash crops such as coffee are concerned, because these require long-term care and yield harvests over many years. Individuals thus become tied to particular plots of land. In a study (Brown and Podolefsky 1976) of land use and rights in the New Guinea highlands, it was found that individual ownership of land was correlated with high population density and intensive agriculture. Individual rights to land (though within the framework of "group territory") occurred where plots of land were in permanent use or had a short fallow period (less than six years) and where trees and shrubs had been planted by the owner.

Organization of Labor

In small-scale preindustrial and peasant economies, the basic unit of production is not a group organized solely around economic functions. Most often, the household or some extended kin group carries out production as part of its many activities. These groups produce goods mainly for their own use. Their goals are often social or religious, rather than strictly economic. Labor is not a commodity bought and sold in the market, but rather one aspect of a role that derives its primary meaning and reward from membership in a social group such as the family. Work, therefore, is not a "job"; it is an aspect of social participation (Lee 1959). This pattern is very different from that in industrial societies, where the basic unit of production is the business firm, which is organized only for economic purposes. A firm does not produce goods for the use of its members; the items it produces are sold for profit. Under this system, labor becomes a commodity, bought and sold on the market just like milk and shoes.

Work is carried out in an impersonal setting, and the rewards of work are primarily economic.

But the important difference between the business firm and the household is not the motivations of the actors: Households as well as firms are guided by the desire to maximize, and households also look for profit when they are involved in cash transactions. The point is that the structure of the household as a producing unit limits economic growth, because households have other functions, such as social and ritual functions. Households are also restricted because they can draw labor from only a small group. Nor can a household liquidate if it makes poor choices in the allocation of its resources. Furthermore, it may use resources in economically unproductive ways for ceremonial or social goals (Nash 1967). The business firm, in contrast, is geared toward economic growth and can make its decisions solely on an economic basis. Even when they are not geared solely to the profit of the individual owner (as is true, for example, in the socialist nations), firms are always looking for technological innovation and expansion of productivity. In economies where households are the producing units, then, there can be little expansion and innovation is not a by-product of economic activity. What this means is that large-scale production and the mass distribution systems with which we are familiar tend not to develop where economic systems are made up of households.

DIVISION OF LABOR BY SEX The sexual division of labor is a universal characteristic of human society. In every society, some tasks are considered appropriate only for women and others only for men. The most obvious basis for the division of labor between men and women is that only women can bear and nurse children. Child care is thus a universal female role, with a biological foundation in the physical differences between men and women. Because it is women who get pregnant and nurse, this tends to make them less mobile than men, which may account for the fact that hunting large animals

Among pastoralists, in addition to the processing of daily food, women take care of the water supply and cattle and look after the chickens and turkeys. (United Nations)

and warfare (in nonindustrial societies) are almost exclusively male occupations.

The extent to which biological sex differences are an explanation for sex-role differentiation is a matter of dispute among anthropologists. Ernestine Friedl (1975), among others, points out that the care of small children can be shared by others: older children, neighbors, relatives, old men and women not engaged in food production, and even fathers. Friedl suggests that the division of labor in society is not an inevitable result of the fact that women bear and care for children, but rather that the number of children a woman has is adapted to the division of labor in society and the role women play in getting food. Cultural norms with respect to family size and systems of child care may be arranged to conform with women's productive work, rather than the norms of work being an adaptation to pregnancy and child care. Most anthropologists emphasize the tremendous variation in the sex-related division of labor, and they look for explanations in the

environment, food-getting strategy, and level of sociopolitical complexity of the particular society.

In foraging societies where hunting is done by one or a few individuals, it is always the men who hunt large animals. In most foraging societies, women collect plant foods near the base camp, although among the Hadza and also among the Paliyans of India (Gardner 1966), each man collects most of his plant food himself and women do the same for themselves and their children. Where hunting is a communal activity, as among the Mbuti, women and men from several families collectively drive the animals into some central area, although men do the actual killing. In some societies, men and women also work together gathering nuts or fishing in streams.

In horticultural societies, there is a greater variety in the sexual division of labor, although here too there appears to be a male monopoly — that of clearing the land. Friedl (1975) suggests that men are assigned this task for sev-

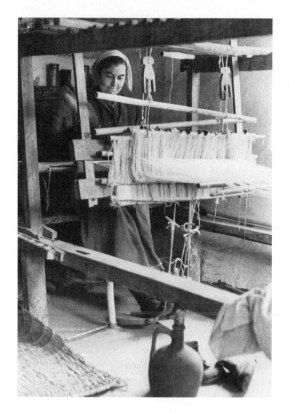 

Sex-role specialization in craft activities varies cross-culturally. In the peasant villages of Greece (left), women do the weaving. In Togo (right), and Africa generally, men do the weaving. (left: United Nations; right: Simone LaRive)

eral reasons. Not only is felling trees and cutting underbrush heavy work; also, new land is often on the frontiers of other groups and may require warfare (a male activity) in order to gain access to it. Furthermore, game is more available in uncleared land, and among horticulturalists, hunting is a male activity. Planting, weeding, harvesting, and carrying produce may be assigned to men or women. The most common pattern among horticulturalists is for men to clear the land and both men and women to cultivate. In some cases, women are responsible for cultivating the basic staples and men raise only the prestige crops used in exchange. In highland New Guinea, for example, women raise sweet potatoes, which are the main food for humans as well as pigs, and men raise sugar, taro, and bananas, which are used only in ex-

change. A common pattern in West Africa is that both men and women cultivate staples and prestige crops and women raise additional staples that they use for trade.

A relatively rare pattern of sex specialization in food production exists among the Yanomamo of the Amazon Basin in South America. Here the men clear and cultivate, with the women giving only minor assistance. Men also hunt and gather honey. Women gather wild plants and both sexes fish, but most of the food supply comes from the gardens cultivated by the men. One explanation of this pattern is that the Yanomamo are constantly engaged in warfare and raiding other villages to capture women to bring home as their wives. This makes it dangerous for women to work unprotected in the forest. Among the Hopi Indians of

The major characteristic of production in industrial society is that labor is a commodity, work is a job, and the production unit is a business firm, or factory, organized solely for profit. (Labor-Management Documentation Center, Cornell University)

Arizona also, men cultivate the staple crops — corn, beans, and squash — with simple irrigation techniques, while the women raise a few vegetables in small gardens near the village.

Wherever hunting and deep sea fishing occur among horticulturalists, these activities are done by men, although women may collect small fish from streams and kill small animals. Where domesticated animals are raised, whether the work falls to men or women seems to depend on the kinds of animals. If pigs are domesticated, as in New Guinea, women usually feed and care for them (though men exchange them); this may be because pigs root in the vicinity of the home and can more easily be taken care of by women who have small children. Sheep, goats, and cattle, which graze at some distance from the home, are usually herded by men or boys.

Carrying food home from the fields is practically always part of a woman's role; a man may or may not also do this. The major daily work of cooking and processing food, which is

a difficult task when it involves grinding grains and pounding root crops, is women's work in all horticultural societies, although the preparation of food for ceremonies is often the task of men.

Sex-role specialization in craft activities varies except for metalworking, which is always a male task and perhaps developed out of the making of metal weapons for hunting and fighting. Weaving is done by women in the North American Southwest, but by men in Africa. In Europe, India, and central Africa, men are the potters, but in West Africa and the Americas, women are the potters. Making bark cloth is a male task in Africa but a female task in Southeast Asia. Baskets are usually made by women if they are for domestic use but by men when they are sold.

In foraging and horticultural societies, women play a very important role in the food-getting strategies. With the transition to intensive agriculture, the female role in food production drops drastically. Wielding the plow is al-

The Abkhasians are a community in which older persons continue to make important contributions to the economy. This inclusion of the elderly in family and community life contributes to their longevity. (Joan Morris)

most everywhere a male task; in addition, because plowing the soil reduces the need for weeding, which is often a woman's task, women's agricultural work is cut back in this way as well. In irrigation agriculture, women still do weeding and transplanting of paddy, but irrigation also increases men's participation in agriculture because they do most of the work of digging irrigation ditches, lifting water from wells and canals, and repairing terraces (Martin and Voorhies 1975:284).

Agricultural societies are a good example of the principle that women lose status in society as the importance of their economic contribution declines; this usually accompanies an increase in their work within the home and an increase in the number of children. As women become increasingly identified with the "domestic" sphere, as happens with the rise of plow agriculture and the introduction of a market economy and wage labor, the value of their role in society declines. This phenomenon, as it is affected by change in the contemporary world, will be discussed in further detail in Chapter 15.

DIVISION OF LABOR BY AGE Division of labor by age is also universal. In our society, childhood is prolonged and young people do not generally engage in productive activities. In other societies, even young children contribute to community life. At the other end of the spectrum, the elderly in our society are often forcibly retired from the work force when they are still in good health. In the United States, where an honest day's work is an important part of people's self-image and their most important connection to the larger society, this forced disengagement of the aged from productive tasks can lead to isolation, loneliness, and diminished feelings of self-worth (Clark 1973).

In many traditional societies, by contrast, the older person continues to make an important contribution to economic life. An outstanding example of this kind of society is the Abkhasians, a people famous for their longevity, who live in an area between the Black Sea and the Caucasus Mountains in the Soviet Union. The Abkhasians were once herders but now live and work on collective farms. Almost everyone in the community works regularly. "Retirement" is unknown. After the age of eighty, and more so after the age of ninety, the workload decreases, but work does not stop. Men who have been shepherds no longer follow the herds up the mountains but instead may tend farm animals. Old men cease plowing and lifting heavy loads but continue weeding. Women of advanced age no longer work in the fields, but they continue to do housework, feed chickens, and knit. One study of twenty-eight Abkhasians over the age of one hundred showed that they worked an average of four hours a day (Benet 1976).

The Abkhasians are an exceptional people. But even in traditional societies where such health and vitality do not exist, older people often contribute to society by taking on the roles of ritual specialists, guardians of cultural traditions, and agents of enculturation. In societies without writing, older people who know and remember are valuable members of society, respected and socially involved even past the time of strictly economic productivity.

SPECIALIZATION IN COMPLEX SOCIETIES
Nonindustrial societies have simple technologies. Although many of their tools and techniques are ingenious and fit the requirements of the environment, toolmaking does not require skills beyond those that can be learned as part of an informal socialization process. The work involved in making the tools of production can be done by every adult and requires no machines or scarce materials. Because there are no specialized operations, there is little need for specialization of labor. Almost everyone can do every job.

In nonindustrial societies, all adult men and women are actively engaged in the quest for food. The few specialists — for example, religious practitioners — are usually part-time specialists and also engage in food production. The characteristic division of labor is not by

Dugout canoes are an important form of capital among the horticultural Paramacca Maroons of Surinam, who also fish in lakes. A man gets his matrilineal kinsmen to help him, and he helps them in turn. (John Lenoir)

job but by age and sex. This contrasts with our own society, in which production is highly specialized.

In addition to the division of labor by sex and age that is found in all societies, complex societies are characterized by a great variety of occupational roles and productive specializations. In the caste system in India, for example, only people belonging to particular hereditary kinship groups are allowed to perform certain services or produce certain kinds of goods. Literally thousands of specialized activities — washing clothes, drumming at festivals, presiding over religious ceremonies, making pots, painting pictures — are traditionally performed by various castes within a village or even by villages as a whole.

The division of labor in society becomes more specialized and complex as population increases and agricultural production intensifies.

Industrialization as an adaptive strategy requires the most specialized and complex division of labor, and only a small proportion of the population is directly involved in producing food. We all know how complicated our mass-production techniques and service delivery systems are, and we are familiar with how specialized jobs have become. Although specialization of production undoubtedly has advantages in terms of efficiency and the ability to produce large quantities of goods, we must also consider what price may have to be paid in terms of other, nonmaterial human values.

Capital

Capital is goods used to produce other goods. Where money exists, capital includes the money used to purchase these goods. In the small-scale economies described so far, capital goods are limited. Among hunting peoples, weapons used in the hunt are capital goods. Among fishing societies, capital goods include water craft and elaborate trapping and netting devices that require great investment of time and labor. In cultivating societies, land, the tools of cultivation, and storage facilities are part of capital. In pastoral societies, the main form of capital is livestock. Animals produce goods that are directly consumed, such as milk, and they are also kept to produce other animals and are used in exchange. Capital goods in nonindustrial and peasant societies are normally owned individually, except for those that are too costly for one individual to buy. In peasant societies, for example, cooperatives may be set up for the purchase of such things as tractors. In every society, some time and energy must be invested in the maintenance of capital goods. Storage facilities must be built and maintained; tools must be made, replaced, and repaired; and animals must be fed and taken care of.

An important point of contrast in economic systems is the extent to which the members of a society have access to capital goods. Differential access to important capital goods develops with more complex political forms, as well as with more complex and specialized technology. In hunting and horticultural societies, where technology is simple and tools are made by hand, every adult has access to capital. No one is deprived of the means of producing food or manufactured items. In politically and technologically more complex societies such as some chiefdoms or states, access to the means of production falls into the hands of a ruling class. Ownership of the means of production may be limited to a small group, whose members thereby gain power over others and control their labor. Capitalist societies are those in which, among other things, capital is invested for profit, rather than used simply for the subsistence needs of the group. Because capitalism is associated with market economies and money, it is discussed in the section on distribution, which follows.

Distribution: Systems of Exchange

In all societies, goods and services are exchanged. There are three main ways in which this exchange occurs: reciprocity, redistribution, and the market. Each system appears to be predominantly associated with a certain kind of political and social organization, although more than one kind of exchange system frequently exists in any particular society (Polyani 1944). Where there is more than one system, each will normally be used for the exchange of different kinds of goods and services. Let us look first at reciprocity.

Reciprocity

The mutual give and take among people of equal status, which is actually a continuum of forms of exchange, is called **reciprocity**. Three types of reciprocity are distinguished from one another by the degree of social distance between the exchanging partners. Generalized reciprocity, which is usually carried out among

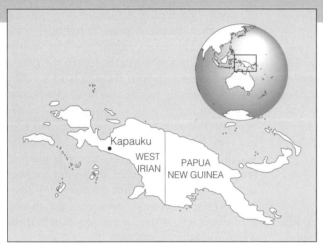

Some technologically simple societies seem to contain many features of stratified, capitalist societies, but there are important differences. The following description of the Kapauku of western New Guinea highlights the workings of a nonstratified society, but one where individual wealth is an important goal. The Kapauku of western New Guinea, described by Leopold Pospisil (1963), are a good example. The Kapauku are basically horticulturalists. The sweet potato, their main staple, is grown to feed both people and pigs. The breeding and trading of pigs is the major source of prestige and political leadership. Although Kapauku technology is simple, the economy is organized around the individual accumulation of wealth, and there are important wealth distinctions within the society.

The economy rests on the use of money. Both cowrie shell and two types of necklaces function as common media of exchange and the common measure of value. The exchange of all kinds of goods — food, domesticated animals, crops, land, and artifacts — is made through purchase. Money is also used for payment for labor in cultivation, for medical and ritual services, and for fines for misconduct. Cowrie shell money comes in various "denominations," and like modern money is easily portable. Cowrie shell is obtained through trade with coastal communities, which is sometimes a difficult enterprise. The value of cowrie shell is fixed by its scarcity and is relatively stable. Market prices for different commodities are thus also relatively stable, and an "ideal" or "fair" price is established by tradition for different goods and services. However, supply and demand can alter the price in any particular situation. Prices may also be affected by the relationship between the trading partners or the social status of the buyer. Prices are usually lower between close relatives, for example. Prices may also be lowered if the buyer is a rich man or a political leader, either in the hope of future favors or as gratitude for past ones. In this respect, the Kapauku market system differs from a true market economy, where — theoretically at least — the price is the same for everyone.

Although buying and selling occur among the Kapauku on a daily basis, most business is transacted on ceremonial occasions, particularly that of the pig feast. Hundreds of animals are killed, and the meat is distributed through sales, loans, and repayment of debts. In addition, the trading of other products, such as native tobacco, bowstrings, salt, bows and arrows, chickens, net bags, and axes, also takes place. The pig feasts are an important institution of interregional trade as well as ceremonial and social functions.

Although practically everything is exchanged among the Kapauku through buying and selling, most of these exchanges take place within local kin groups. In these exchanges, however, the Kapauku are strictly motivated by private profit. Domesticated animals are bought for money and raised for breeding and profit, rather than for domestic consumption. Artifacts are also produced for sale. The extension of credit is an important way in which money is redistributed, although no interest is usually charged on loans. The borrower may promise to pay a few extra cowrie shells for the favor of being lent money, but if he chooses not to do this later, there is no cause for legal complaint. Such a person will, however, lose prestige and be regarded as untrustworthy.

Individualism, and especially the individual accumulation of wealth, has a prominent place in Kapauku society. Every item in the society is individually owned; common ownership is unknown. Money, movable property, houses, canoes, and land thus have only one owner. Even tracts of virgin forest belong to an individual. There is no family, lineage, or village property. When cooperative efforts are needed to build large structures for the benefit of the whole community, such as a drainage ditch, specific individuals own segments of the property and take care of the upkeep of their segment only. Wives and husbands also possess property individually, as do male children who are old enough to work a piece of land. Nor do people like to work cooperatively. A garden plot is divided into individual sections, and even co-wives do not work together.

Every Kapauku man wants to become rich. A young man might begin his career by launching himself as a pig breeder through borrowing a pig from an older, wealthy man. If the young man is successful, the wealthy lender might allow him to buy the desired female piglet, as a way of starting him out in his capital accumulation efforts. As in many societies with wealth distinctions and social stratification, the sons of a rich man have an easier time than the sons of a poor man in starting their "careers." A rich man usually starts his own son out with a few pigs, and the son does not have to "prove" himself as a poor man's son must. The data gathered by Pospisil clearly show an uneven distribution of wealth among the Kapauku; at the time of his study, nineteen of the thirty-eight adult males owned all the pigs. Poor and well-fed households were situated next door to each other.

(continued)

Wealthy Kapauku men parlay their riches into political power and higher social standing, or prestige. Through extending credit to less fortunate men, a rich Kapauku man creates alliances and social obligations, and those in debt to him become his political supporters. Kapauku political organization rests on the shoulders of these "capitalists"; they have much of the authority that is found in chiefs in rank societies. Kapauku society, because of its wealth accumulation in the hands of some men and not others, and because of the association between wealth, prestige, and political power, sounds much like our own socially stratified society. There are some important differences, however.

The first is that, although land is individually owned, in practice it is a kinship unit that controls a "territory." Because there is "mutual affection and a strong sense of unity" within a territory, no one appears to be denied access to the means of subsistence. Furthermore, although "grown men are expected to have gardens of their own" and Pospisil found only two exceptions, the men without gardens helped their brothers and received part of the garden produce. Furthermore, an old man cannot validly sell his land without the consent of his sons. If he tries to, his heirs can repossess the land by giving the purchase price back to the buyer. Although property can be disposed of by the will of a dying man, no sons, brothers, fathers, or nephews can be deprived of their share of the land under any circumstances. Because of the importance of land in providing basic subsistence, this hedging of "individual ownership" is an important difference from our own society, where subsistence depends on selling one's labor and where many individuals have no certain access to the resources needed for survival.

A second important difference is that the Kapauku economic system does not result in the establishment of permanently differentiated social classes. Kapauku wealth is displayed by generosity; a man who has much may lavishly distribute food or be generous in extending credit in order to keep up his reputation as a leader. Because pig breeding and trading is an activity many different people can engage in, the status system is constantly in flux. New men are constantly "coming up," and a rich headman may lose his position to a younger, more successful man. Wealth is therefore tied up with power only temporarily. The culturally prescribed obligation of a "big man" to be generous if he wishes to retain his influence acts to keep wealth fairly evenly distributed among the Kapauku.

Adapted from Leopold Pospisil, The Kapauku Papuans of West New Guinea. *© 1963 by Holt, Rinehart and Winston and renewed 1991 by Leopold Pospisil. Reprinted by permission of the publisher.*

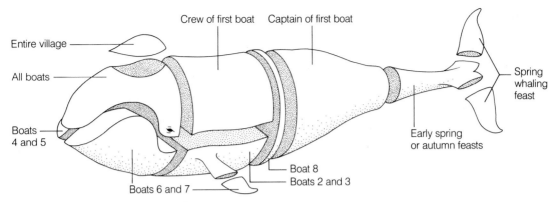

FIGURE 8.1 Hunting of whales by the Inuit involves ten to fifteen boats standing by. The first eight boats to reach and harpoon the whale receive stipulated portions of the meat. The captain of each boat gets his traditional part of the body, and he shares his meat with his crew. The captain of the first boat gives the shaman a narrow strip cut from the belly between the eighth boat's strip and the genitals. The top of the head is cut up and eaten at once by everyone in the village. Portions of the tail are saved for feasting in the spring and autumn. (From Carleton S. Coon, *The Hunting Peoples*. Boston: Little, Brown, 1971, pp. 124–25. By permission of the estate of Carleton S. Coon.)

close kin, has the highest degree of moral obligation. Balanced reciprocity is characteristic of the relationship between friends, or members of different tribes in a peaceable relationship with one another. Negative reciprocity refers to exchanges between strangers or peoples hostile to one another (Sahlins 1972).

GENERALIZED RECIPROCITY **Generalized reciprocity** involves a distribution of goods in which no account is kept of what is given and no immediate or specific return is expected. Such transactions are ideally altruistic, that is, without any thought of economic or other self-interest. Assistance is given and, if possible and necessary, returned. In our own society, we are familiar with generalized reciprocity as it exists between parents and children. Parents are constantly giving things and providing services to their children "out of love" or at least out of a sense of responsibility. What would we think of a parent who kept an account of what a child "cost" and then expected the child to repay this amount? What parents do expect is perhaps some gratitude, love, respect, and the child's happiness.

Generalized reciprocity involving food is an important social mechanism among hunting and gathering peoples. In these societies, a hunter or group of hunters distributes meat among the kin group or camp. Each person or family gets either an equal share or a share dependent on its kinship relationship to the hunter. Robert Dentan (1968) describes this system among the Semai of Malaysia:

> After several days of fruitless hunting, a Semai man kills a large pig. He lugs it back to the settlement. Everyone gathers around. Two other men meticulously divide the pig into portions sufficient to feed two adults each (children are not supposed to eat pork). As nearly as possible each portion contains exactly the same amount of meat, fat, liver, and innards as every other portion. The adult men take the leaf-wrapped portions home to redistribute them among the members of the house group.

Similar systems are used by the !Kung of the Kalahari and the Inuit (Figure 8.1).

A North American might wonder: "What does the hunter get out of it? Aren't some people always in the position of providing and others always receiving?" It is true that the hunter does not gain more from his kill than anyone else in terms of the amount of food he consumes. Still, he is bound by culturally prescribed rules of "generosity" to share. In these small societies, where the good opinion of others is really necessary for survival, the desire not to be thought stingy is a strong motivation to share and to do one's share. Because all men in the society are bound by the same rules, in the long run, the system will provide everyone with an opportunity to give and receive. Generalized reciprocity also has important adaptive functions. One hunter and his family probably could not consume the meat from a large animal at one sitting. Without techniques for storing and preserving food, the meat would go to waste if it were not distributed among groups larger than the family.

BALANCED RECIPROCITY **Balanced reciprocity** involves a clear obligation to return, within a specified time limit, goods of nearly equal value. The fact that balanced reciprocity is most often called "gift giving" obscures its economic importance in societies where it is the dominant form of exchange. We are familiar with balanced reciprocity when we give gifts at weddings or birthdays or exchange invitations or buy a round of drinks for friends. In these exchanges, it is always the "spirit" of the gift and the social relationship between the givers that is verbalized as important. The economic aspect of the exchange is repressed. We also know, however, that an unreciprocated gift or a return gift of very different value will evoke negative feelings. Similarly, accepting an invitation involves the obligation to offer a similar invitation in the future.

The social obligation to give, to accept, and to return is at the heart of balanced reciprocity. A refusal to receive or a failure to return the gift is taken as a withdrawal from a social relationship. Because a gift that is accepted puts the receiver under an obligation to the giver, most people like to "pay off" the debt by giving a return gift. In balanced reciprocity, however, the payoff does not have to be immediate. In

fact, an attempt to return the gift immediately is an indication of unwillingness to be obligated, and therefore also an indication that a trusting social relationship is neither present nor desired (Mauss [1954] 1990).

Balanced reciprocity is often characteristic of trading relations among non-Western peoples without market economies. Such trade, which is frequently carried out over long distances and between different tribes or villages, is often in the hands of trading partners, men who have a long-standing social relationship with each other. Social rules between trading partners permit trade with others not related by kinship where no authority, such as the state, exists for protection.

THE KULA RING The most famous anthropological study of this type of trading is that of the kula ring, described by Bronislaw Malinowski in his ethnography of the Trobriand Islands (1961; originally published 1922). The **kula** is an extensive, intertribal trade among a ring of islands off New Guinea (today part of the nation of Papua). (See Figure 8.2.) From the Trobriand point of view, the most important aspect of the kula was the trading of two kinds of articles, each of which moved in a different direction. *Soulava*, long necklaces of red shell, move clockwise, while *mwali*, bracelets of white shell, move counterclockwise. The exchange of these items took place between trading partners on the different islands that made up the kula ring.

Every detail of the kula transaction is fixed by tradition. In every village on the participating islands, some of the men take part in the kula. They receive the necklaces or bracelets from their trading partners, hold them for a while, and then pass them on. No man keeps any article in his possession permanently. These trading partnerships are permanent, lifelong affairs.

Malinowski showed that the kula was not merely an economic transaction like the impersonal money-goods exchanges in our own market economy, which are separated from other

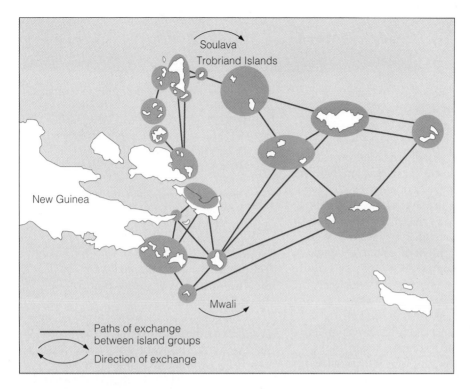

Soulava
Trobriand Islands

New Guinea

Mwali

———— Paths of exchange
          between island groups

⟷ Direction of exchange

FIGURE 8.2 The kula ring. This map shows the islands participating in the trade and the movement of the ritual exchange of necklaces (*soulava*) and armshells (*mwali*).

aspects of culture. In our society, the norms and ethics in economic exchange are not expected to apply to exchanges between friends and kin, nor are the norms of personal relationships expected to apply in the marketplace.

The kula, however, was infused with many extraeconomic cultural norms and values and related to all aspects of Trobriand life: kinship and political structure, magic, prestige, economy, technology, myth, ritual, feasting, and especially friendship and alliance. Although on the surface the kula might appear to be primarily an exchange of goods, Malinowski's intensive fieldwork demonstrated the many complex cultural, social, and psychological meanings the kula had for the Trobriand Islanders.

Participants derived prestige from generous behavior during the exchanges, and the kula gave them an opportunity to display their wealth. Through the preparations and activities, ties between participating local groups were reinforced, contributing to the integration of Trobriand society. Malinowski also noted that the trade of kula valuables was associated with many secondary features and activities. Thus, side by side with the ritual exchange of armbands and necklaces, the natives also carry on ordinary trade, bartering from one island to another a great number of goods, often unprocurable in the district to which they are imported. This suggests that the kula trade has important economic functions that may be recognized by the anthropologist but not necessarily by the people involved, who are motivated by more personal considerations.

The importance of trade and balanced reciprocity in establishing alliances is clearly demonstrated among the Yanomamo. Yanomamo

The **potlatch** of the Kwakiutl Indians of the Northwest Coast of North America is one example of redistribution in action. In Kwakiutl society, social ranking was a primary interest. Every time a chief wanted to demonstrate his prestige in relation to other chiefs, he had to give a potlatch. Potlatches were feasts in which many kinds of wealth were distributed by the chief to the people and to chiefs from other villages who were his guests. They might be held to celebrate births, deaths, marriages, or a youth's coming of age. The number of guests present and the amount of goods given away, or even destroyed, revealed the wealth and prestige of the host chief. The host publicly traced his line of descent and claimed the right to certain symbolic privileges, such as the ownership of a particular song or dance.

Each of these claims was accompanied by feasting and the display and giving away of large quantities of food and manufactured goods, such as blankets, carved wooden boxes, boats, fish oil, and flour.

When there was a competitive potlatch — that is, when two men competed for the same symbolic privilege — one of the rivals might ostentatiously destroy great quantities of property — canoes, blankets, and, in former times, even slaves — in order to show how great he was and how little his possessions meant to him (Rohner and Rohner 1970). During these feasts, the host boasted about himself:

> I am the great chief who vanquishes,
> I am the great chief who vanquishes.
> Oh, go on as you have done!
> Only at those who continue to turn around
>   in this world,

> Working hard, losing their tails (like salmon),
>   I sneer,
> At the Chiefs under the true great chief.
> Ha! have mercy on them! put oil on their
>   dry brittle-hair heads,
> The heads of those who do not comb their
>   hair.
> I sneer at the chiefs under the true great
>   chief,
> I am the great chief who makes people
>   ashamed. (Benedict 1961:192)

The potlatches were thus an expression of the Kwakiutl ethos of social competition and individual rivalry.

Competitive feasts are not always characterized by the boasting and extremes of the Kwakiutl. This feature of potlatching is now believed by anthropologists to have been intensified when the Kwakiutl began to participate in the cash economy of the Canadians. The outside source of income resulted in the "inflation" of potlatching and the "wastefulness" of the destruction of goods described by informants to anthropologists in the late nineteenth and early twentieth centuries. Apparently, traditional potlatches were similar to the feasts that still exist in various parts of New Guinea and the islands of the Pacific.

In Pohnpei, a Micronesian island, for example, the competitive production and display of food at community feasts is not done with boasting, but with modesty. The prestige foods in Pohnpeian feasts are yams and breadfruit, contributed by the guests, and pigs and *kava* (an intoxicating beverage), contributed by the hosts. Those who bring yams and breadfruit are modest about their display. A man who is considered "number one" in terms of the size and

A speaker for the Chief Who Gives Away Blankets, at Fort Rupert on the Northwest Coast of North America. Potlatches were an important feature of the social organization among Northwest Coast peoples. (Photo: Dr. Frang, Courtesy Department of Library Services, American Museum of Natural History)

quality of the foods he brings will always protest that someone else's products are better than his own (Bascom 1970).

The earlier attention anthropologists gave to boasting and rivalry and to the motivations of the individual actors in these competitive giveaways obscures some of their ecologically adaptive functions and their economic importance as means of redistribution. Prestige economies, such as those described for the Kwakiutl and the Pohnpeians, serve as a way of pushing people to produce more than they can immediately consume. It is a way of providing reserves that can be used in times of shortage and is particularly necessary where food-preservation techniques are not well developed. Systems of feasting also provide a way for food surpluses to be distributed among villages that are not in equally good environments. In lean years, such communities could accept the invitations of chiefs from other villages and receive food in return for the diminished status involved in receiving rather than giving. When things got better, the recipients could become hosts, distributing food and goods to others who needed it and thus regaining some of their lost prestige.

society is characterized by hostile relations between different villages. Villages are always looking for alliances, yet at the same time their pride forbids them from openly seeking ties with others. Trading is a good way to begin building up friendly relationships between villages. Each Yanomamo village has one or more products in which it specializes. These include dogs, hallucinogenic drugs, arrows, cotton yarn, baskets, pots, and, recently, steel tools. Napoleon Chagnon, an ethnographer of the Yanomamo, says this specialization cannot be explained by the distribution of natural resources; each village is capable of producing all these things itself. Chagnon explains economic specialization and the "need" to trade among Yanomamo villages as an adaptation to the need for forming alliances. In other words, trade is an adaptation to the sociopolitical environment rather than to the physical one. Trade here functions as a "social catalyst," the "starting mechanism" through which mutually suspicious villages can be brought together over time. These contacts eventually lead to feasting, the exchange of women in marriage, and somewhat stable military alliances (1983).

NEGATIVE RECIPROCITY **Negative reciprocity** is the "unsociable extreme" in exchange between equals. It is conducted for the purpose of material advantage, and it is based on the desire to get something for nothing (gambling, theft, cheating) or to get the better of a bargain (barter or haggling). Negative reciprocity is either an impersonal or an unfriendly transaction. As such, it is generally carried out by those who stand in the position of "outsiders" to each other. Both in our own society and in tribal and peasant societies, outsiders, however they may be defined, are considered "fair game." In a large, complex society, where economic dealings are mainly carried out among strangers, abstract principles of morality develop that should apply to everyone. Tribal and peasant societies are more likely to distinguish between the insider, whom it is morally wrong to cheat, and the outsider, from whom every advantage

may be gained. Among the aboriginal Navajo, for example, the rules vary with the situation; to deceive when trading with foreign tribes is a morally accepted practice. Even witchcraft techniques are considered acceptable in trading with members of foreign tribes. Among pastoralists, negative reciprocity in the form of theft of livestock is an important way in which animals change hands. For the Plains Indians, who hunted buffalo on horseback, horse raids were an important aspect of the economy.

Redistribution

In **redistribution**, goods are collected or contributed from members of a group and then given out to the group in a new pattern. Redistribution thus involves a "social center," to which goods are brought and from which they are distributed. There are many contexts in which redistribution is the mode of exchange. In household food sharing, pooled resources are reallocated among family members. In state societies, redistribution is achieved through taxation, an obligatory payment on the part of the people in return for which various services are provided by a government.

Redistribution is especially important as a mechanism of exchange in societies where political organization includes chiefs or "bigmen." These men act as "social centers" to which goods and food are contributed by the population and from which the goods and food are redistributed back to the people through communal feasting. These feasts, which are sponsored by a chief or big-man, sustain his political power and raise his prestige. At the same time, they reaffirm the values and solidarity of the society.

Leveling Mechanisms

Leveling mechanisms are practices, values, or forms of social organization that result in evening out the distribution of wealth. Leveling mechanisms force accumulated resources or

Pig feasts, at which great quantities of meat and other goods are distributed by a host to his guests, are an important mechanism of redistribution among horticultural peoples of New Guinea. (Courtesy Office of Information, Port Moresby, Papua New Guinea)

capital to be used in ways that do not result in significant or permanent economic differences. They ensure that social goals take precedence over economic ones and thus result in socially stable, though economically static, social systems.

Leveling mechanisms have many different forms. Obligatory generosity as a basis of prestige and political power prevents the formation of social classes. Another leveling device is redistribution through feasting. Manning Nash describes a number of leveling mechanisms that operate in the village of Amatenango, in the Chiapas district of Mexico (1967). One is the organization of production by households. As mentioned earlier, economic expansion and accumulation of wealth are limited where house-

holds, rather than business firms, are the productive units. Another factor in Amatenango is that inheritance is bilateral: All a man's children share equally in his estate. This makes it difficult for large estates to persist over generations. Furthermore, a number of different village offices must be assumed by men in the village. This prevents their holders from working all the time, and the responsibilities of the offices take up some of a family's extra resources. A man must serve in twelve such offices before he can "retire" from public life, so the cost continues throughout adulthood. In addition to these twelve offices, there is the *alferez*, a ritual position filled by a younger man. Part of the requirement of this office is the sponsoring of a community feast, which involves paying for the food and liquor and also renting the costumes. Men are selected for this prestigious office by their ability to pay, and it is an enormous drain on the economic resources of a household. Should a family in Amatenango manage to accumulate more than its neighbors, village sanctions of gossip and accusations of witchcraft come into play. A man who is thought to be a witch is likely to be killed. Such accusations are most often leveled at those who are rich but not generous and who refuse to accept the communal obligations of taking office. Thus, through the interplay of social and economic forces, through the value system of the community, and through informal but powerful systems of control, economic differences are minimized, and the stability of the society as a whole is ensured.

Market Exchange

The predominant feature of **market exchange** is that goods and services are bought and sold at a money price determined by the impersonal forces of supply and demand. Unlike reciprocity and redistribution, in which the social and political roles of those who exchange are important, a market exchange is impersonal and occurs no matter what the social position of the participants. Market exchange is thus the most purely "economic" mode of exchange, the one in which participants are interested only in maximizing material gain. In a society integrated by the market, social or political goals are less important than economic goals. Organization around strictly economic purposes and activities is a dominant feature of social life.

Market exchange is based on the existence of **all-purpose money** — that is, a medium of exchange that is used to purchase a wide range of goods and services and that is a standard of value for stating prices. This feature distinguishes true market systems from societies in which money exists but only certain kinds of goods and services are exchanged for money. Societies with market economies must also be distinguished from those in which reciprocity or redistribution is the primary integrating mechanism, but where marketplaces also exist for the exchange of certain kinds of goods. These societies, which are found in New Guinea and West Africa, may be said to have "peripheral" markets; that is, the important means of production, land, and labor are not exchanged through the mechanism of the market (Dalton 1967).

In systems of market exchange, labor is a commodity; people work for wages that are regulated, like other commodities, by supply and demand. Where, in addition to this feature, we find the private ownership of land and capital goods, and the investment of capital for profit (either in production or through interest on loans), we may talk of a **capitalist society**. A true capitalist society can exist only in connection with the state as a political system, because a powerful central authority is necessary to enforce the contracts on which market exchanges are based. Because the private ownership of basic resources results in denying some people access to these resources, permanently differentiated economic and social classes are also an important feature of a capitalist society. True capitalism is a late development in the history of humankind and in its purest form is best illustrated by the industrial nations of nineteenth-century Europe and the United States.

Accommodation and Resistance to Capitalism

A major effect of the expansion of capitalism was the transformation of non-Western, kinship-based societies. A prominent example of this from our own continent is the fur trade in North America during the eighteenth century. The main target of this trade was the beaver, sought for its fur-wool, which was made into hats. In England, wearing wool caps became the mark of the working classes, and the beaver hat became a symbol of high status, creating a demand that lasted almost 300 years. As beaver populations were hunted out in the eastern part of North America, the fur trade moved rapidly westward, affecting all aspects of the lives of the native Americans who participated in it. Wherever it went, the fur trade brought European-introduced contagious diseases, which had devastating effects on peoples who had no immunity to them. For example, the Abenaki of the Maine Coast were one of the first groups to participate in the trade, around the beginning of the seventeenth century. Within ten years, their population had declined from 10,000 to 3,000. The Southern Kwakiutl, on the Northwest Coast, declined in population from about 8,000 in 1835 to 1,200 in 1911 as a result of European diseases.

As a result of both diminishing numbers and also of the dislocation of smaller native American groups as the fur trade moved west, many native American societies lost their group identity and became incorporated into larger and more successful groups. Many of the Indian "tribes" later recognized as distinct ethnic entities by both government agents and anthropologists did not exist as such prior to European contact and took shape in response to the fur trade.

Equally important in transforming the native American societies was that the fur trade led to increased warfare among these groups as they competed for hunting territories and access to European goods, particularly guns, liquor, metal tools, clothing, and jewelry. In addition, the various European powers, particularly the English and the French, recruited native Americans as military allies in their attempts to gain a larger share of the wealth of the continent. With the introduction of the horse by the Spanish in the late seventeenth and early eighteenth centuries, many tribes that were originally horticulturalists, such as the Cheyenne, became primarily buffalo hunters. This furnished them with another item to exchange for European goods — pemmican, which is dried strips of buffalo meat. This was a useful food for European fur traders, who were now venturing inland to replace native American middlemen. Individuals who could acquire pemmican had greater access to guns and thus could become war leaders. They could then acquire more horses (through war and raids) both for trade and for offensive warfare. This led to a concentration of horses and other valued goods in the hands of the more successful entrepreneurial types in the native American societies and resulted in economic differentiation among what had generally been more egalitarian societies. As the relationship between fur trader and fur trapper became more highly individualized, the fur trade also had the effect of undermining the larger, communally organized hunting aggregates that had previously existed in some tribes.

Different individuals and different native American societies were differentially affected by the fur trade. For some, the seeming advantages of the trade elicited eager and active participation; up until perhaps 1850, the trade might have been characterized as a generally equal and balanced partnership between fur trader and fur trapper. Soon, however, this relationship changed, with native Americans becoming increasingly dependent on trading posts not only for European goods but even for subsistence; so enmeshed had they become in the exchange of furs for consumer goods that they had abandoned their own traditional subsistence patterns. The grave and often disastrous dislocations and adjustments made by hundreds of native American societies as an accommodation to "the profit to be made from trapping a small fur-bearing animal weighing

about 1½ pounds" are among the many examples of how the extension of the European economic system transformed first the economic systems and then the social and cultural systems of almost the entire non-European world (Wolf 1982).

The expanding search for wealth and profit is carried on today, and the extension of the world economic system continues to transform subsistence economies and societies. While the traumatic effect, in terms of cultural and resource loss, of an expanding global economy should not be disregarded, it is also important to keep in mind the resistance to capitalism, which takes varied forms. We have already seen the emergence of the Rastafari as a subculture committed to resisting wage labor and emphasizing noncapitalist networks of reciprocity.

Another example, in a different part of the world, is the Gypsies of Spain (Kaprow 1982). Spanish Gypsies have resisted assimilation and wage labor for hundreds of years, by becoming self-employed in occupations that provided the state with few or no taxes and were difficult to regulate. The Gypsy avoidance of wage labor was part of their larger strategy for resisting state controls, but it has also turned out to be economically successful. In the past, Gypsies were traveling actors, sheep shearers, thieves, and horse traders; today they are scrap dealers, peddlers, contract whitewashers, discount-clothing merchants, and part-time agricultural laborers. Spanish laws trying to force Gypsies to become full-time agricultural laborers have repeatedly failed.

Gypsies earn a good income but stop short of transforming their work into larger, profit-making businesses. The work is labor-intensive, not capital-intensive, and they neither save money nor build up inventories of goods. In short, Gypsies exploit a sector of the capitalist system, but do not fully commit themselves to it. Gypsies, like many peddlers in the United States, work in the informal sector of the economy. They have no permanent stock of goods, no steady clientele, no regular place of business; they carry out all transactions in cash, and pay few or no taxes.

Many Gypsies live in "shacks" that seem unlivable to the outsider, but they are often comfortable and attractive inside. These shacks are another kind of insurance for the Gypsies against future dependence on wage labor. The shacks are self-constructed and rent-free. After they are built, they belong to the builder to rent or sell, and can be an important source of income.

Most Gypsy families Miriam Kaprow studied survived quite well in the period of high unemployment and inflation in Spain from 1974 to 1982, because of the nature and organization of their work. The Spanish government has long realized that the Gypsies' economic organization is crucial to preserving their cultural autonomy and accommodating to the demands of the larger society. By deliberately resisting wage labor, and cultivating an economic status peripheral to the capitalist economy, Gypsies have achieved considerable freedom from bureaucratic control.

Resistance to wage labor and economic marginalization are not always self-chosen, as with the Rastafari or the Gypsies of Spain. Most often, the economic marginalization of certain peoples, whether because of race, ethnicity, or gender, is not voluntary but imposed, a subject that will be explored in Chapter 11, on social stratification.

Summary

1. Formal economics focuses on action that maximizes the individual's well-being and profit (economizing). This approach has limited application to the small-scale, nonindustrial, and peasant economies, in which the production, distribution, and consumption of goods are intricately tied up with other activities and cultural norms that are not solely economic from the people's point of view.

2. Although technological development has resulted in a dramatic increase of material productivity and consumption in Western societies, it also results in changes in the "quality of life," as is suggested by the comparison in the use of time between the modern French and the Machiguenga of Peru.

3. Access to and control over land is basic to every productive system. Among hunters and gatherers, there are few exclusive rights to land; among horticulturalists, land is controlled by the kin group. It is mainly with the rise of intensive agriculture that land becomes subject to private ownership by individuals. Generally speaking, the more the investment of labor and technology and the less land available, the more likely private ownership will be.

4. In tribal and peasant economies, the basic unit of production is a kin group. Resources are produced and used mainly by this group, and production often has social and religious rather than strictly economic ends. This provides an important contrast with Western societies, where the basic unit of production is the business firm, whose interests are almost solely economic.

5. There is little specialization of labor in tribal and peasant societies, compared with the high degree of occupational specialization in industrial societies. Two universal bases of occupational specialization are sex and age.

6. The sexual division of labor has some universal aspects: Hunting, fighting, and clearing the land are done among horticulturalists by men. Women are predominantly responsible for taking care of the children; they also gather crops and do the daily processing of food for domestic use. Beyond this, the sexual division of labor is highly variable; a man's job in one society may easily be a woman's job in another.

7. Capital, goods used to produce other goods, is limited in small-scale economies. In noncapitalist societies, most members have equal access to capital goods and no one group is deprived of the ability to produce.

8. The Kapauku of New Guinea have a society that contains many aspects of capitalism: investment for individual profit, buying and selling, the use of money and credit, and a relation between wealth and rank. But the Kapauku are not real capitalists because no group of people in their society is denied access to the basic resources needed to survive.

9. In all societies, goods and services are exchanged in some way. Three systems of exchange are reciprocity, redistribution, and the market. Reciprocity exists in all societies but is the characteristic system of exchange in band and tribal societies. The kula ring is an example of a system of reciprocity.

10. Redistribution is the characteristic mechanism of integration and exchange in chiefdoms. An example of redistribution is the potlatch of the Kwakiutl of the Northwest Coast of North America.

11. The market system predominates in industrial societies. Systems of exchange function to integrate various elements of a society; they have a social as well as an economic function.

12. Leveling mechanisms are norms and activities that result in an evening out of wealth among a population. The many different kinds of leveling mechanisms — obligatory generosity, witchcraft accusations, gossip, religious obligations to give — all work to force accumulated resources to be used in ways that do not result in significant or permanent economic differences among individuals and groups within a society.

13. The expansion of the European capitalist system has resulted in far-reaching transformations in many non-European societies. One example is the effect of the fur trade on native Americans. Some groups, even today, however, resist full-scale participation in national economic systems. One example is the Gypsies of Spain, who through their choice of marginal occupations retain a large measure of control over their own labor.

Suggested Readings

Cole, Douglas, and Chaikin, Ira
1990   *An Iron Hand Upon the People: The Law Against Potlatch on the Northwest Coast*. Seattle: University of Washington Press. A very readable and objective history of the attempts of the Canadian government to outlaw potlatching, a cultural tradition well known through the anthropological literature.

Dalton, George, ed.
1967   *Tribal and Peasant Economies*. Garden City, N.Y.: Natural History Press. A reader suitable for an introduction to economic systems. Contains many of the most important articles in the field of economic anthropology.

Harris, Marvin
1987   *Why Nothing Works: The Anthropology of Everyday Life*. Orig. title: *America Now: The Anthropology of a Changing Culture*. New York: Simon and Schuster. A provocative analysis of the interlocking of various changes in American society — feminism, violent crime, the rise of cults — from a materialist point of view, written in Harris's usual lively and contentious style.

Jonaitis, Aldona, ed.
1991   *Chiefly Feasts: The Enduring Kwakiutl Potlatch*. New York: American Museum of Natural History. An informative and beautifully illustrated book about this anthropologically famous cultural pattern, which discusses the aesthetic, religious, legal, and social aspects of the Kwakiutl potlatch.

Mauss, Marcel
1954   *The Gift*. New York: Macmillan. The classic on reciprocity in tribal societies, including much information on the ceremonial behavior of the potlatch, showing its many social and economic functions.

Schwartz, Norman B.
1990   *Forest Society: A Social History of Peten, Guatemala*. Philadelphia: University of Pennsylvania Press. A masterful study of the changing economic patterns in this relatively isolated area, particularly as this relates to population increase in the contemporary period.

Toffler, Alvin
1981   *The Third Wave*. New York: Bantam. A readable analysis and best-seller about the sociopolitical consequences of the major economic revolutions in human history: domestication of plants and animals, industrialization, and the computer revolution.

Marriage, Family, and Domestic Groups

What are some of the universal functions of marriage and the family?

Why do some societies prefer that people marry their first cousins?

Why do most societies have parents arrange their children's marriages?

How is the structure of the family in the United States changing?

How does economics influence the shape of the family and the household?

In India, almost all marriages are arranged. So customary is the practice of arranged marriage that there is a special name for a marriage that is not arranged: It is called a "love match."

As a young woman anthropologist in India for the first time, I found this custom of arranged marriage oppressive. It was contrary to everything I had been taught to believe about the importance of romantic love and individual choice as the only basis of a happy marriage.

At the first opportunity, I questioned young people I met on how they felt about the practice of arranged marriage. One of my first informants was Sita, a college graduate who had been waiting over a year while her parents were arranging a match for her.

"How can you go along with this?" I asked her. "Don't you care who you marry?"

"Of course I care," she answered. "That is why I must have my parents choose a boy for me. My marriage is too important to be arranged by such an inexperienced person as myself."

"But how can you marry the first man you meet? You will miss the fun of meeting a lot of different people and you will not give yourself the chance to know who is the right man for you," I countered.

"Meeting a lot of different men doesn't sound like any fun at all," Sita answered. "One hears that in America the girls spend all their time worrying whether they will meet a man and get married. Here we have the chance to enjoy our life and let our parents do this work and worry for us."

"I still can't imagine it," I said. "How can you agree to marry a man you hardly know?"

"But of course he will be known," she replied. "My parents would never arrange a marriage for me without knowing all about the boy and his family background. Naturally we will not rely only on what the family tells us. We will check the particulars ourselves and through our friends and relatives. No one will want to marry their daughter into a family that is not good."

"But Sita," I protested, "I don't mean know the family, I mean know the man. How can you think of spending your whole life with someone you don't love or may not even like?"

"If he is a good man, why should I not like him?" she replied. "With you Americans, you know the boy so well before you marry, where is the fun to get married? There is no mystery and no romance. Here we have the whole of our married life to get to know and love our husband. This way is better, is it not?"

From Serena Nanda, "Arranging a Marriage in India," in Philip R. DeVita, ed., The Naked Anthropologist: Tales from Around the World *(Belmont, Calif.: Wadsworth, 1991).*

The institution of arranged marriage is not likely to have much appeal for young people in the United States. But when we consider our country's high divorce rate, as well as view marriage from the anthropological perspective of its major functions, the practice of arranged marriage can make a great deal of sense. Marriage is an almost universal solution to three problems every human society must face: the regulation of sexual access between males and females, the division of labor between males and females, and the need to assign responsibility for child care. This chapter takes up humankind's solutions.

Marriage and the Family: Functions

The need to regulate sexual access stems from the potentially continuous receptivity of the human female to sexual activity. The human male also has the potential to be sexually aroused continually, rather than just at certain times of the year. Sexual competition could therefore be a source of serious conflict in society if it were not regulated and channeled into relatively stable relationships that are given social approval. These relationships need not be permanent, and theoretically some system other than marriage could have developed. But with the absence of effective contraception and the near certainty that children would be born from such relationships, a relatively permanent union between a male and female that involves responsibility for children as well as economic exchange would seem to be more adaptive than other alternatives. In any case, the near universality of marriage indicates that it is the most common adaptive solution to these human problems.

Earlier, I pointed out that differences in strength and mobility between males and females lead to some universal differences in economic roles in hunting and horticultural societies. Marriage is the way most societies arrange for the products and services of men and women to be exchanged. I have also mentioned the necessity for the intense care of human infants and the prolonged care of children. A relatively permanent relationship between an adult male and an adult female provides a structure (the family) in which the male can provide food and protection and the female can nurse and provide the nurturing needed for the healthy development of the human child. Marriage is a way of assigning responsibility for this care. Still another function of marriage that is important in accounting for its near universality in human societies is its linking of different families and kin groups. Thus, marriage leads to cooperation among groups of people larger than the primary husband-wife pair, which would appear to be of great advantage for the survival of the species.

Marriage refers to the customs, rules, and obligations that establish a special relationship between a sexually cohabiting adult male and female, between them and any children they produce, and between the kin groups of husband and wife. Although marriage and the formation of families rest on the biological complementarity of male and female and on the biological process of reproduction, both

Among the functions of marriage are the regulation of sexual access between males and females, setting up an exchange of goods and services between males and females, and assigning responsibility for the care of infant children. In the United States, marriage is the most important basis for the formation of families; in many other societies, the most important family bond is that between blood relations rather than between husband and wife. (Courtesy of Kathy Clark)

marriage and family are cultural patterns. As such, they differ in form and functions among human societies. In our own society, the marriage tie is the most important in the formation of the family, but this is not true everywhere. In many societies, the most important family bond is between blood relations rather than between husband and wife. In some, it is the blood tie between generations (father and children or mother and children) that is the most important. In matrilineal societies, the tie between brother and sister is the most important. We must be careful, therefore, not to think of the family only in terms of the form it takes in our own society.

From a cross-cultural perspective, it appears that the most basic tie in society is between mother and child. The provisioning and protective male role *may* be played by the husband of the mother, but it may also be played by her brother. Even where marriage is an important emotional relationship, as on the Israeli *kibbutz*, the division of labor and the care of children may not be in the hands of the married couple but in the hands of the community as a whole. Anthropologists are coming to the conclusion that the most useful way to approach the study of marriage and the family is not to establish definitions that will apply to every known group, but rather to look at the different

Among the royal families of ancient Egypt, brother-sister marriage was preferred. This represents a rare exception to the almost universal presence in human societies of taboos against such marriages. (United Nations)

ways in which the basic needs of sexual regulation, infant care, the division of labor, and the establishment of rights and obligations are legitimized in different societies.

Marriage Rules

Incest Taboos

Every society has rules about mating. In all societies, there are some prohibitions on mating between persons in certain relationships or from certain social groups. The most universal prohibition is that on mating among certain kinds of kin: mother-son, father-daughter, and sister-brother. The taboos on mating between kin always extend beyond this immediate family group, however. In our own society, the taboo extends to the children of our parents' siblings (in our kinship terminology called first cousins); in other societies, individuals are not permitted to mate with others who may be related up to the fifth generation. These prohibitions on mating (that is, sexual relations) between relatives or people classified as relatives are called **incest taboos**.

Because sexual access is one of the most important rights conferred by marriage, incest taboos effectively prohibit marriage as well as mating among certain kin. The outstanding exception to the almost universal taboo on mating and marriage among members of the nuclear family is those cases of brother-sister marriage among royalty in ancient Egypt, in traditional Hawaiian society, and among Inca royalty in Peru. Incest taboos have always been of interest to anthropologists, who have attempted to explain their origin and persistence in human society, particularly as they apply to primary (or nuclear) family relationships. Many theories have been advanced, and we will look here at four major ones.

INBREEDING AVOIDANCE The inbreeding avoidance theory holds that mating between close kin produces deficient, weak children and is genetically harmful to the species. The incest taboo is therefore adaptive because it limits inbreeding. This theory, proposed in the late nineteenth century, was later rejected for a number of decades on the ground that inbreeding could produce advantages as well as disadvantages for the group, by bringing out recessive genes of both a superior and an inferior character. Recent work in population genetics has given more weight to the older view that inbreeding *is* usually harmful to a human population. The proportion of negative recessive traits to adaptive recessive ones is very high, and in the human animal, inbreeding has definite disadvantages. Furthermore, these disadvantages are far more likely to appear as a result of the mating of primary relatives (mother-son, father-daughter, sister-brother) than of other relatives, even first cousins. It would seem, then, that the biological adaptiveness of the incest taboo as it applies to the nuclear family must be considered in explaining both the taboo's origins and its persistence.

The question raised here, of course, is how prescientific peoples could understand the connection between close inbreeding and the biological disadvantages that result. But the adaptive results of the incest taboo need not have been consciously recognized in order to persist; rather, groups that had such a taboo would have had more surviving children than groups without the taboo. This reproductive advantage would eventually account for its universality as groups without the taboo died out.

FAMILIARITY BREEDS AVOIDANCE The theory that familiarity breeds avoidance holds that the incest taboo is just a formal prohibition for a natural aversion to sexual relations between people who have grown up together. There are two sources of evidence that such an aversion may develop. Some studies of the Israeli kibbutz show that children "who sit on the potty together" have little sexual interest in one another. Studies of kibbutz marriages tend to show that mates are almost never chosen from the peer group. Most frequently they are chosen from another kibbutz altogether, in spite of the fact that the kibbutz does not discourage marriage between members. Kibbutz members themselves attribute this lack of sexual interest in their peers to the fact of their having grown up together (Talmon 1964).

A study of marriage in Taiwan by Arthur Wolf (1968) makes a similar point. Some Taiwanese practice a form of marriage in which a girl from a poor family may be given away or sold as an infant to a family with a son, with the expectation that she will be his wife. She is brought up with the son as his playmate, and at the proper time they marry. Wolf found that these "daughter-in-law-raised-from-childhood" marriages are much less successful than other marriages, with fewer children and higher rates of sexual difficulties and extramarital affairs.

Although the evidence from Israel and Taiwan may show that familiarity can lead to sexual avoidance, the familiarity-breeds-avoidance theory does not explain why a formal and strongly sanctioned taboo had to arise to prevent what was a natural aversion anyway. Furthermore, as a theory, it is contradicted by evidence showing that in fact incest does occur in many parts of the world. The actual occurrence of incest raises questions about whether familiarity does breed sexual aversion. Some anthropologists (and some psychoanalysts) have suggested the opposite.

PREVENTING DISRUPTION Bronislaw Malinowski and Sigmund Freud believed that the desire for sexual relations within the family is very strong. They suggested that the most important function of the incest taboo is in preventing disruption within the nuclear family. Malinowski argued that, as children grow into adolescence, it would be natural for them to attempt to satisfy their developing sexual urges within the group of people emotionally close to them, that is, within the family. If this were to happen, conflict would occur, and the role relationships within the family would be disrupted; fathers and sons, and mothers and daughters, would compete. This would hinder the family in carrying out the transmission of cultural values in a harmonious and effective way. According to this theory, the incest taboo arose to repress the attempt to satisfy sexual desires within the family and to direct such desires outward.

This theory appears to make quite a bit of sense; unregulated sexual competition within the family would undoubtedly be disruptive. However, an alternative to the incest taboo could be the regulation of sexual competition among the family members. Furthermore, although Malinowski's theory suggests why the incest taboo exists between parents and children, it does not explain the prohibition of sexual relations between brothers and sisters. Regulating sexual activity within the family might solve the problem of disruption through sexual rivalry, but it would not solve the genetic problem. Only the familial incest taboo has both advantages: It prevents disruptions of the family over sexual competition and promotes outbreeding and genetic variability.

FORMING WIDER ALLIANCES Another theory, proposed most recently by Claude Lévi-Strauss (1969), stresses the importance of cooperation among groups larger than the nuclear family. The incest taboo forces people to marry outside the family, thus joining families together into a larger social community. This has undoubtedly contributed to the success of the human species. The alliance theory does not account for the origin of the incest taboo, but alliance between nuclear families certainly seems to be adaptive and can account for the persistence of the familial incest taboo and its extension to groups other than the nuclear family.

In summary, then, it does appear that the familial incest taboo has a number of advantages for the human species. In other animal species, incest is frequently prevented by expelling junior members from family groups as they reach sexual maturity. Because humans take so long to mature, the familial incest taboo seems to be the most efficient and effective means of promoting genetic variability, familial harmony, and community cooperation. These advantages can explain the spread and persistence of the taboo, if not its origins (Aberle et al., 1963).

Exogamy and Alliance

Exogamy specifies that an individual must marry outside particular groups. Because of the association of sex and marriage, prohibitions on incest produce an almost universal rule of exogamy within the primary family group of parents and children and between brothers and sisters. In every society, exogamous rules also apply to some group larger than the nuclear family. Most often, descent groups based on a blood relationship (such as lineages and clans) are exogamous.

The advantages of exogamy are similar to those proposed for the incest taboo. In addition to reducing conflict over sex within the cooperating group, such as the hunting band, exogamy leads to alliances between different families and groups. Alliance between groups larger than the primary family is of great adaptive significance for humans. Such alliances may have economic, political, or religious components; indeed, these intergroup rights and obligations are among the most important kinds of relationships established by marriage. Early humans, living in hunting and gathering bands, undoubtedly exchanged women in order to live in peace with one another and to extend the social ties of cooperation, as they do today.

One outstanding feature of marriage arrangements among contemporary hunters and gatherers is a system of exchange and alliance between groups that exchange wives. These alliances are important among peoples who must move around to take advantage of the availability of a food supply. Different groups take turns visiting and playing host to one another, and this intergroup sociability is made easier by exogamy. One consequence of exchanging women is that each hunting-gathering camp becomes dependent on others for a supply of wives and is allied with others through the bonds that result from marriage. This system contributes to the maintenance of peaceful relations among groups that move around, camp with one another, and exploit overlapping territories. It does not entirely eliminate intergroup aggression, but it probably helps keep it down to a manageable level.

The benefits of exogamy were very clear to the mountain-dwelling Arapesh with whom Margaret Mead (1963) worked. Their attitude about marriage was summed up in the following saying:

> Your own mother
> Your own sister
> Your own pigs
> Your own yams that you have piled up,
> You may not eat.
> Other people's mothers,
> Other people's sisters,
> Other people's pigs,
> Other people's yams that they have piled up,
> You may eat. (p. 92)

Just as hoarding one's own food and not sharing or exchanging with the community is unthinkable for the Arapesh, so is keeping the women of one's group to oneself. In many societies, the very mention of incest is often accompanied by protestations of horror. For the Arapesh, incest simply does not make sense. In answer to Mead's question about incest, an Arapesh informant answered: "No, we don't sleep with our sisters. We give our sisters to other men and other men give us their sisters"

(p. 92). When asked about a man marrying his sisters, the Arapesh answer was:

> What, you would like to marry your sister? What is the matter with you? Don't you want a brother-in-law? Don't you realize that if you marry another man's sister and another man marries your sister, you will have at least two brothers-in-law, while if you marry your own sister you will have none? With whom will you hunt, with whom will you garden, with whom will you visit? (p. 97)

In peasant societies, rules of exogamy may apply to the village as well. In North India, a man must take a wife from outside his village. Through exogamy, the Indian village becomes a center in a kinship network that spreads over hundreds of villages. Because the wives in a typical Indian village may come from many different villages, the village has a "cosmopolitan" character. This also affects the quality of family life in North India. As we have seen in Khalapur (Chapter 6), "peace at any price" can be an important value in a household where brothers' wives are strangers to one another. The potential for conflict among sisters-in-law shapes child rearing and personality and helps explain many rules of conduct in the North Indian family.

Village exogamy is not characteristic of all peasant societies. In Mexico, for example, women tend to marry within, rather than outside, the village. In the village of Tepoztlán, studied by Oscar Lewis, over 90 percent of marriages take place within the village and 42 percent within the same neighborhood. This gives the Mexican village a more cohesive sense of community compared with the Indian village, where caste that cuts across villages, rather than the village community, is the most important unit of identification.

Other Kinds of Marriage Rules

ENDOGAMY The opposite of exogamy, **endogamy** refers to marriage within one's own group, however that group may be defined. In order to keep the privileges and wealth of the

Pictured here is a kin group among the !Kung. A characteristic feature of marriage among contemporary hunters and gatherers is a system of alliances among bands that exchange wives. This allows maximum flexibility among peoples who must move frequently to obtain food. (Courtesy Department of Library Services, American Museum of Natural History)

group intact, blood relations may be encouraged or required to marry. This helps explain endogamy among royalty. In India, the caste is an endogamous group. An individual must marry someone within the caste or within the specific section of the caste to which he or she belongs. Although American society does not have specific named groups within which one must marry, so-called racial groups and social classes tend to be endogamous. In the past, racial endogamy was enforced by law in some states. In the case of social classes, opportunity, cultural norms, and similarity of life-style all contribute to maintaining endogamy. It may be as easy to love a rich person as a poor one, but it is a lot harder to meet one unless you are rich yourself.

PREFERENTIAL MARRIAGE RULES In addition to rules about whom one may *not* marry and the group within which one *must* marry, some societies have rules about the groups or categories of relatives from which marriage partners are drawn. One of the most common is that an individual (Ego) should marry a cross cousin. **Cross cousins** are people related through siblings of the opposite sex at the parental generation—that is, the child of either the mother's brother or the father's sister. In the United States, we do not distinguish our cross cousins from our **parallel cousins**, children of siblings of the same sex at the parental generation—that is, of one's mother's sister or one's father's brother. Both relations are generally excluded from the categories of people from which a mate is selected.

Preferential cross-cousin marriage is related to the organization of kinship units larger than the nuclear family. Where descent groups are unilineal—that is, formed by either the mother's or the father's side exclusively—parallel cousins will be members of Ego's own kinship group, but cross cousins will not. Because unilineal kinship groups are usually exogamous, a person is prohibited from marrying parallel cousins (who are frequently called and treated as "brothers" and "sisters") but will be allowed, or even required, to marry cross cousins, who are outside the kinship group. Preferred cross-cousin marriage reinforces ties between kin groups established in the preceding generation. In this sense, the adaptive value of preferential cross-cousin marriage is the same as exogamy: the establishing of alliances between groups. But where exogamy establishes alliances between a number of different groups, preferential marriage rules intensify the relationship between a limited number of groups generation after generation.

A few societies practice preferred parallel-cousin marriage. Among the Muslim Arabs of North Africa, the preference is for an individual to marry the son or daughter of the father's brother. Muslim Arab culture has a rule of patrilineal descent; descent and inheritance are in the male line. Parallel-cousin marriage may serve to prevent the fragmentation of family property, because economic resources can be kept within the family. A result of parallel-cousin marriage is to reinforce the solidarity of brothers. But by socially isolating groups of brothers, parallel-cousin marriage adds to factional disputes and disunity within the larger social system.

THE LEVIRATE AND THE SORORATE The **levirate** is the custom whereby a man marries the widow of his dead brother. In some cases, the children born to this union are considered children of the deceased man. Among the Nuer, a pastoral people of Africa, a form called "ghost marriage" exists: A man can marry a woman "to the name of" a brother who had died childless. The offspring of this union would be designated as children of the deceased. Thus the levirate enables the children of the dead husband to remain within his descent group, and also keeps them from being separated from their mother. Where the **sororate** exists, the husband of a barren woman marries her sister, and at least some of these children are considered those of the first wife. The term is more commonly used to refer to the custom whereby, when a wife dies, her kin group supplies a sister as a wife for the widower.

The existence of the levirate and sororate attests to the importance of marriage as an alliance between two groups rather than between individuals, as is the case in our own society. Through such customs as the levirate, the sororate, and widow inheritance, not only are group alliances maintained, but the marriage contract can be fulfilled even in the event of death. Because marriage involves an exchange of rights and obligations, the family of the wife can be assured that she will be cared for even if her husband dies. This is only fair if she has fulfilled her part of the marriage contract by providing domestic services and bearing children.

But what if there is no one of the right relationship for an individual to marry? Or what if, as in the case of the levirate or sororate, the preferred marriage partner is already married? The point to note here is that there are often kin who are classified as equals for the purpose of marriage and who can be chosen as marriage partners. For example, if a man is supposed to marry his father's sister's daughter, the daughters of all women classified as his father's sisters, whether or not they are biologically in this relationship to the man in question, will be eligible as marriage partners.

Number of Spouses

All societies have rules about how many spouses an individual may have at one time. **Monogamy** permits only one man to be married to one woman at any given time. Monogamy is the rule in our own society, although it is by no means the most frequent rule in the world's cultures. Given the increasing divorce rate and subsequent remarriage in the United States, perhaps the term *serial monogamy* most accurately describes the pattern in our own society. In this pattern, a man or woman has one marriage partner at a time but, because of the relatively easy divorce laws, will not necessarily remain with that partner for life.

Polygamy is plural marriage. It includes **polygyny**, which is the marriage of one man to several women, and **polyandry**, which is the marriage of one woman to several men. Most societies in the world permit (and prefer) plural marriage. In a world sample of 554 societies, polygyny was favored in 415; monogamy, in 135; and polyandry, in only 4 (Murdock 1949:28). Thus, about 75 percent of the world's societies prefer plural marriage. This does not mean, however, that most people in these societies actually have more than one spouse. Polygyny as

a cultural ideal is related to different factors in different societies. Where women are economically important, polygyny can increase a man's wealth and therefore his social position. Also, because one of the most important functions of marriage is to ally different groups with one another, having several wives from different groups within the society serves to extend an individual's alliances. Thus, chiefs, headmen, or leaders of states may have wives from many different clans or villages. This provides leaders with increased economic resources that may then be redistributed among the people, and it also binds the different groups to the leader through marriage. Polygyny thus has important economic and political functions in some societies.

Polygyny is found most characteristically in horticultural societies in which a high level of productivity is pursued. Although the most obvious advantages in polygynous societies seem to go to men — additional women in the household increase both the labor supply and the productive yield, as well as the number of children — the status of females in such societies is not uniformly low, and in some societies, women welcome the addition of a co-wife because it eases their own workload and provides daily companionship. Furthermore, although when combined with patrilineality, polygyny may mean that women are restricted by patriarchal authority, polygyny can also be combined with a high degree of sexual and economic freedom for women.

Polyandry occurs primarily in parts of Tibet, Nepal, and India. Although the system may be an adaptation to a shortage of females in a society (this has been suggested for the Toda of South India and the Pahari Hindus of the Himalayan foothills), in two of these societies, the Toda and the Tibetan, it is the practice of female infanticide that creates a shortage of women. In a society where men must be away from home for long periods of time, polyandry provides a woman with more than one husband to take care of her. In Tibet, polyandry appears to be related to the shortage of land. If several men

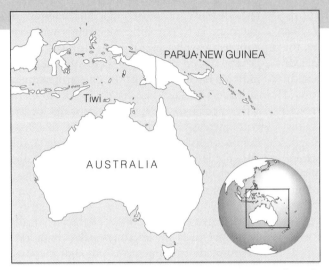

Polygyny appears to be most adaptive in horticultural societies, but there are some foraging societies in which it is also adaptive. The Tiwi of Australia are one such society (Martin and Voorhies 1975).

The Tiwi live in an environment in which there is an ample supply of game and fish and an abundance of vegetable foods. Although kangaroos, lizards, fish, turtles, and geese are hunted by the men, it is the vegetable foods gathered by women that provide the staple of everyday meals. Women also make their own tools and, with their dogs, hunt small game. The major problem in the Tiwi environment is not the shortage of food, but rather the collecting of food that is abundantly available.

Among the Tiwi, as in most human groups, the male-female ratio is about equal, except that in the older age groups, women tend to predominate because they tend to live longer than men. Because the Tiwi require that every single woman must be married but do not require this of men, plural marriage is not only the cultural ideal but a reality for many Tiwi males.

A Tiwi male has the right to betroth his infant daughter to whomever he chooses (within the limits of the kinship system). In choosing a future son-in-law, Tiwi men looked for their own best economic and social advantage. "In Tiwi society daughters were an asset to their fathers and they [the fathers] invested these assets in their own welfare" (Hart and Pilling 1960:15). A Tiwi father might bestow his daughter on a peer who was already a friend or an ally or on someone he wished to become a friend or ally. Or he might bestow his daughter on a man who had already bestowed a daughter on him. If he was looking for "old-age insurance," a father might choose a man much younger than himself who showed signs of being a good hunter and fighter and who seemed likely to rise in influence. When the older man could no longer hunt, his son-in-law would still be young enough to provide him with food.

In all these cases, the future husband would be a great deal older than his young wife. The men on whom infant "wives" were bestowed tended to be in their forties or fifties or perhaps in their late twenties or thirties. As happens in our own society, where "money comes to money," a younger man who looked good to one girl's father would also be an attraction for other fathers. A man who was a "good catch" might have no wives living with him until his late twenties or thirties. Then, as his betrothed wives came of age (around fourteen), he would quickly acquire two or three. As these wives began to have children, he in turn could become an "investor": By betrothing his daughters to other men, he could acquire still more wives for himself. In this system, many younger men, especially those who were not promising hunters, wound up with few or even no wives. These men could acquire wives by marrying older women who had been widowed. Older men who had outlived their contemporaries could marry widows, as could younger men who were not sufficiently attractive to acquire wives by bestowal of other men's daughters. Being an important, influential man required having several wives.

The large, multiple-wife household among the Tiwi can be regarded as an adaptation to the conditions of their existence. The more wives a man had, the more food could be collected. Because of the importance of food collecting, old wives were needed as well as young ones. An older woman knew the environment and was experienced in finding food. Younger wives served as apprentices and reinforcements for older wives. For this reason, every man tried to marry an older woman first. Households in which a man had only one or two wives, especially if both were young, had a much lower standard of living.

Although from this perspective, women appear as little more than pawns in the marriage game, over which they have little control, more recent ethnographic work on the Tiwi by female ethnographers has caused a reexamination of this perspective. The work of Jane Goodale (1971) portrays Tiwi women not simply as wives but rather as women who have a fluctuating inventory of husbands. Early in her married life, the Tiwi girl is introduced to the man who will become the husband of any daughters she may bear. This relationship between a mother-in-law and her prospective son-in-law is very important in Tiwi social structure. The son-in-law must immediately begin to provide food and favors to his mother-in-law, and he often joins her camp at this time. Until a woman has her first pregnancy, she enjoys both sexual and social freedom, and young Tiwi women traditionally engage in several extramarital sexual unions with lovers of their own age, a practice that, although officially not approved of, is tolerated. When a woman gives birth to a girl, who is given to the prospective son-in-law as a wife after a few years, the son-in-law is bound to remain in his mother-in-law's residential group and serve her for life.

As a Tiwi woman gets older, her respect and power increase. As she moves through a series of marriages, she assumes the important role of senior wife, moving into a position of power in the domestic group. Her co-wives and their daughters form a cohesive economic and social unit, and in addition, she has considerable influence over her sons. Goodale's view is that, rather than being socially repressed by male authority as one might assume in a polygynous society, the Tiwi woman has prestige, power, and initiative based on both solidarity with other women and economic complementarity with men.

Polygyny is an ideal in many societies but often cannot be realized except by those of high status. In societies with chiefs, such as this West African society, having many wives is an important economic resource for men of high rank and a way of building alliances throughout the society. (Simone Larive)

marry one woman, this keeps down the number of children a man has to support. If brothers marry the same women, land can be kept within the family rather than fragmented over the generations.

The Toda of South India are a classic case of fraternal polyandry. The Toda female marries one male and at the same time becomes the wife of his brothers. If other brothers are born after the original marriage, they will also share in the marital rights. Sexual access to the wife appears to rotate rather equally, and there is little reported friction or jealousy. When all the brothers live with their wife in one hut, a brother who is with the wife will place his cloak and staff outside as a warning to others. When a wife becomes pregnant, determining the biological father is not considered necessary. Rather, a ceremony called "giving the bow," held in the woman's seventh month, assigns the child a legal or social father. This man makes a ceremonial bow and arrow from twigs and grass and presents these to the wife in front of his relatives. Usually, the eldest brother performs this ceremony, and then all subsequent children are considered his. After two or three children are born, another brother will usually "give the bow." Occasionally a woman will marry several men who are not biological brothers. When these men live in different villages, the wife will live in the village of each husband for a month. The men arrange among themselves who will "give the bow" when she becomes pregnant. Because the practice of female infanticide has largely ceased among the Toda, the male-female ratio has evened out. Due to this, as well as the influence of Christian missionaries, the Toda today are largely monogamous (Queen and Habenstein 1974).

Polygynous societies are much more frequent than polyandrous societies. But even where polygyny is preferred, the ratio of males to females may be such that few men will be able to have more than one wife, if all men are to have at least one. Furthermore, where men must exchange wealth for wives, many men will not be able to afford more than one wife and will therefore have to settle for monogamy.

In our own society, marriage is so closely tied to sexual and emotional exclusivity that it is hard for us to understand how polygynous marriages could exist without conflict and jealousy. The American reader must keep in mind, however, that sexual jealousy among women might not be a problem in societies that do not idealize romantic love and exclusive sexual rights in marriage. In some societies, in fact, sexual intercourse plays a very small role in the marriage relationship. Karl Heider (1970) reports that for the Dani of New Guinea, there is a period of about four to six years of sexual abstinence after the birth of a child. Although polygynous men may have sexual intercourse during this time with any one of their wives other than the new mother, many men appear to prefer to stay with the wife who has just given birth and forego sexual activity. Given Heider's view that the taboo on extramarital intercourse appears to be generally taken seriously, the Dani are a good example of a culture in which interest in sex, even as an aspect of married life, is much lower than in our own. Like people of other cultures in New Guinea, most married Dani men normally sleep in the men's house, sometimes visiting their wives at night.

Even where a low level of sexual interest is not typical in a society, other kinds of mechanisms exist to minimize potential conflict between co-wives. Sororal polygyny, in which a man marries women who are sisters, is one such mechanism. Women who have grown up together may be more willing to cooperate and can get along better than women who are strangers to each other. Also, co-wives usually live in separate dwellings. A husband who wants to avoid conflict will attempt to distribute his economic resources and sexual attentions fairly evenly among his wives so there will be no accusations of favoritism. Where women's work is hard and monotonous, co-wives provide company for one another.

Choosing a Mate

As I have indicated, in most societies marriage is important because it links the kin groups of the married couple. This group interest in marriage frequently overrides any interest the individuals getting married have in each other, and it accounts for the practice of arranged marriages. In our own society, where marriage is primarily an affair of individuals where the married couple tends to make a new home apart from the parents, families have less interest in whom their children marry and certainly less control over marriage than is the case elsewhere. Although choice is not as free in practice as American ideals would lead us to believe, theoretically any individual is free to choose a mate. Furthermore, because sexual compatibility and emotional needs are considered so important in the United States, mates are chosen on the basis of personal qualities largely having to do with physical attractiveness and that whole complex of feelings we call romantic

In some patrilineal societies, especially among Islamic peoples, great emphasis is put on guaranteeing a husband's control over his wife's sexuality. In order to ensure a Muslim woman's honor and that of her family, she wears a fully protective veil when out in public. (Serena Nanda)

love. Ideally, economic considerations are subordinated to the ideal of marrying for love.

In societies where the personal satisfactions of the married couple are subordinate to the needs and interests of the larger group, choosing a mate is much less of an individual, haphazard affair. The kin groups of both bride and groom have a strong vested interest in seeing that both parties fulfill their obligations; therefore, they have much more control over marriage arrangements, including the choice of a spouse for their children.

An important consideration in arranging a marriage is family reputation. In Muslim societies, for example, the honor of a family is a primary consideration in its reputation. This honor is upheld by both men and women, and an individual who is disgraced brings disgrace on the family. This honor is expressed differently by men and women. For men, honor is a public matter involving bravery, piety, and hospitality; it may be lost, but it may also be regained. The honor of women involves one major consideration, sexual chastity. Once this is lost, it cannot be regained. If a woman's loss of virginity becomes known, no one of the appropriate group will want to marry her. Therefore, the family, to the extent that this is possible (and this differs among different social classes), zealously guards daughters, isolating them behind the veil or restricting their movements outside the household. This concern for female sexual chastity is prominent in societies where the children belong to the kin group of the father or where inheritance follows the male line, making the paternity of the child of paramount importance. Only if a woman is a virgin at marriage and is thereafter restricted in her movements and contacts with men can a man be sure the child she is carrying is his own.

In societies with elaborate social hierarchies, such as in India, the family's social status is also important. A marriage will typically be arranged from within the same section of the same caste, although it is the ideal that the family of the boy have somewhat higher social status than the family of the girl. In this patrilineal society, the bride's family must ritually defer and accept a subordinate status to the family of the groom. This is psychologically easier if the social position of the bride's family is a little lower than that of the groom's family. If the bride is expected to move in with her husband's family after marriage, this also shapes the personal qualities considered desirable in a potential marriage partner. Domestic abilities are considered very important—but even more important is the willingness of the girl to be obedient to her elders. A girl who shows signs of having an independent or complaining nature is viewed as a potential source of trouble by her future in-laws.

Where marriages are arranged, go-betweens are frequently used. A go-between, or marriage broker, has more information about a wider network of families than any one family can have. Furthermore, neither the family of the bride nor that of the groom will lose face if its offer is rejected by the other party. Although the arranged marriage system tends to become less rigid as societies urbanize and industrialize, it remains true that in most societies, families and larger kin groups have much more control over marriage and the choice of a spouse than in the United States.

Transfer of Rights and Exchanges of Goods at Marriage

The essence of marriage is that it is a publicly accepted relationship involving the transfer of certain rights and obligations among the participating parties. These rights primarily involve sexual access of husband and wife to each other, rights of the husband over any children born to the wife, obligations by one or both parents to care for children born to the union, and rights of husband and wife to the economic services of the other. Marriage may also give the families or kin groups of the bride and groom certain rights in each other for goods or services. These "relationships of affinity" may be symbolically expressed, as in India, where the family of the wife owes certain forms of deferential behavior to the family of the husband. This is true for all kin. Any person "from the girl's side" will be expected to behave in a ritually respectful manner to a person "from the boy's side."

The transfer of rights in marriage is often accompanied by an exchange of goods and services. Sometimes this exchange may be simply "presents" — that is, items customarily given as a way of winning and preserving the goodwill of those with the power to transfer marital rights, though not necessary to complete the transfer. In other cases, the exchange of goods and services is essential for the transfer of marital rights to take place. If such an exchange is not completed, the rights in marriage can be forfeited.

Three kinds of exchanges made in connection with marriage are bride service, bridewealth, and dowry. **Bride service** refers to the practice whereby a young husband must work for a specified period of time for his wife's family in exchange for his marital rights. This practice tends to be customary in societies where accumulating material goods for an exchange at marriage might be difficult, and it is found among some foraging societies. Among the !Kung, for example, a man may work for his wife's family for as long as fifteen years or until the birth of the third child.

The most common form of exchange of wealth is bridewealth. **Bridewealth** refers to goods presented by the groom's kin to the kin of the bride. A major function of the payment of bridewealth is the legitimation of marriage (Ogbu 1978a). This is confirmed by the fact that in societies where bridewealth is customary, an individual can claim compensation for the violation of conjugal rights only if the bridewealth has been paid. Furthermore, bridewealth paid at marriage is returned (subject to specified conditions) if a marriage is terminated. Another function of bridewealth that has been emphasized by anthropologists is that it entitles the husband to domestic and sexual rights over his wife. Although this is true, marriage confers rights on the wife as well as the husband. By establishing marriage as legal— that is, recognized and supported by public sanctions — bridewealth allows wives to hold their husbands accountable for violations of conjugal rights, as well as the other way around. A third function traditionally ascribed to the payment of bridewealth is that it serves to stabilize marriage.

It is true that the exchange of goods at marriage does indicate the importance of marriage as a social, rather than an individual, affair, and it would seem to give the family of the groom a vested interest in keeping the couple together. A recent examination of cross-cultural data, however, shows that marriage may be stable for reasons other than the payment of bridewealth and that the bridewealth payment itself does not mean that divorce will not occur. Finally,

Among the Medlpa of New Guinea, a marriage is formalized by the family of the groom giving gifts to the family of the bride. The bride's family comes to the groom's village to get the gifts. The big-man of the groom's family (left) praises the quality of the gifts while the big-man of the bride's family denigrates their value. Traditionally, pigs and various kinds of shells were part of the bridewealth. Pigs are still given, but these days cash and pig grease (rendered fat from the pig), which is in the can in the center, have replaced shell money. (Courtesy of Jean Zorn)

the idea that bridewealth is a payment for the loss of the woman to her husband's family is not fully supported by the cross-cultural data either. In some societies, for example, bridewealth is customary even though the husband goes to live with his wife's family or the husband assists his wife's family economically, especially as they get older. This recent reexamination of the conditions under which bridewealth is customary has also led to the reopening of the question of the relationship between bridewealth and women's status. The long-held assumption by colonial administrators, missionaries, and even anthropologists that the payment of bridewealth resulted in a lower status for women can be questioned. John Ogbu (1978a) argues that such payment enhances rather than diminishes the status of women, by enabling both husband and wife to acquire re-

ciprocal rights in each other. The low status of women in parts of Africa where bridewealth is customary has nothing to do with the use of bridewealth in the legitimation of marriage.

Whatever the exact nature of the exchange of goods or services in marriage, the transfer of rights in a marriage is a "public" affair, almost always surrounded by ritual and ceremony. These ceremonies are a way of bearing witness to the lawfulness of the transaction. It is these ceremonies, publicly witnessed and acknowledged, that distinguish marriage from other kinds of unions that resemble it. For example, "living together," a practice in contemporary American society, may have some of the same emotional functions for the two individuals, but it does not involve obligatory economic exchanges or establish relationships between the individual and the partner's kin.

Dowry is less common than other forms of wealth exchange at marriage. Dowry, which is a presentation of goods by the bride's kin to the family of the groom, has somewhat different meanings and functions in different societies. In some cases this transfer of wealth represented a woman's share of her family inheritance, to be used by her and her husband to set up a new household, or to be kept by her for insurance in case she should become a widow, or to invest in her children's future. In other cases, dowry is a payment transferred from the bride's family to the husband's family and not under her control at all. India is a society where dowry, though officially illegal, is still a very important part of the exchanges that take place at marriage.

The functions of dowry in India are a point of some controversy. One point of view holds that the dowry is a voluntary gift, a symbol of filial affection for a beloved daughter leaving home and a way of compensating her for the fact that traditionally she could not inherit land or property. It is also sometimes seen from this point of view as a source of security for her, as the jewelry she gets in her dowry would be hers to keep. Another point of view holds that dowry is a unilateral transfer of resources by a girl's family at her marriage to the groom's family as a recognition of the latter's generosity in taking on what is perceived as an economic liability, because upper-class and upper-caste women in India are not supposed to work. Dowry from this standpoint would be seen as a compensatory payment from the bride's family, who is losing an economic liability, to the groom's family, who is taking one on.

Defining Marriage

In a few societies, sexual rights, economic responsibilities, or socialization of children are not derived from relationships in marriage, but rather are part of the rights and responsibilities of groups other than those formed by husband-wife and parent-child.

A classic case presenting problems to anthropologists attempting to reach a universal definition of marriage is that of the Nayar of South India. They are a landowning caste who live in the state of Kerala. The Nayar "family" was not formed through marriage, but instead consisted of male and female kin descended from a female ancestor. This household group, called the *taravad*, typically contained brothers and sisters, a woman's daughter and granddaughters, and their children. Taravad property was held jointly in the name of the oldest surviving male. This type of family was related to the system of Nayar marriage.

Traditionally there were two kinds of marriage among the Nayar: the *tali*-tying ceremony and the *sambandham* relationship. Every Nayar girl had to undergo the tali-tying ceremony before she reached puberty; this rite marked a girl's transition to womanhood. The man with whom a girl tied the tali had no further rights in her nor did she have any obligations to him (except that at his death she performed certain rituals). After this ceremony, however, a girl could enter into sambandham unions with a number of different men of the proper caste with whom she would have children. The taravad, however, retained rights over a Nayar woman's procreative powers and authority over her children. Even so, for a child to have full birth rights in the taravad, a father had to be acknowledged. Any one of the men with whom the women had had a sambandham union could acknowledge paternity by bearing certain expenses associated with the birth of the child. Where paternity was doubtful, an assembly of neighbors would attempt to coerce the current "visiting husband" to make the payments. If no man of the appropriate caste would take on the role of father, the woman and child were expelled from the taravad and from the caste, because it was assumed that the woman was having sexual relations with a lower-caste man. This was considered "polluting" not only for the woman but for the entire taravad as well.

In the Nayar system, then, a woman had several "husbands" (sambandham unions), but

A primary function of the family — husband and wife sharing responsibility for taking care of children — is illustrated in this yarn painting of the Huichol Indians of Mexico. As the wife struggles to give birth, she pulls on a cord attached to the genitals of her husband so that he, too, may share in the birth pains. (Serena Nanda)

the responsibility and care of children were in the hands of a group of brothers and sisters (the taravad). From the point of view of the polyandrous woman and her taravad, polyandry enhanced both individual and group prestige. Polyandry also gave the Nayar woman access to men who were in many different occupations, and their services could then be accessible to the taravad. The Nayar marriage and family system was well suited to the traditional Nayar occupation of soldiering. Without permanent responsibilities and permanent attachments to wife and children, a young Nayar man was free to pursue a military career. The agricultural land owned by the Nayar taravad was worked by lower-caste landless serfs and managed by an older male, an economic system that also freed younger Nayar men from the necessity of living in the taravad (Mencher 1965).

The data on the Nayar indicate that any universal definition of marriage would have to be very general indeed to cover all the known variations. Anthropologists are not so interested in such a definition as they once were. More important than establishing a definition to cover all known cases is looking at the kinds of rights that are transferred through marriage in different societies and also the kinds of families and domestic groups that marriage creates. Our interest in the Nayar, then, focuses not on whether or not they have marriage, but on the way in which sexual access to women, economic responsibility, and rights over children are legitimized in Nayar society.

Families

Two basic types of families identified by anthropologists are the elementary, or nuclear, family and the extended family. Nuclear families are organized around the conjugal tie, that is, the relationship between husband and wife. The extended family is based on consanguineal, or blood, relations extending over three or more generations.

The Nuclear Family

The **nuclear family** consists of a married couple and their children. This type of family may exist as an isolated and independent unit, as it does in our society, or it may be embedded within larger kinship units. In our own society, in contrast to the Israeli kibbutz, and indeed, in contrast to most of the world's societies, the independent nuclear family is the ideal. A newly married couple is expected to have its own residence, physically removed from that of the parents of either the husband or wife. It functions as a separate domestic and economic unit. Thus, the involvement of parents or other kin in mate selection is marginal. Larger kin groups are not expected to exercise control over or interfere in the affairs of the nuclear family. Although there are some ideals about the different roles that should be played by husband and wife with regard to economic support, sexual activity, and child care, these roles are not rigidly defined. Failure to carry out familial roles may result in dissolution of the nuclear family, but because larger kin groups are not involved in the transfer of rights and obligations in marriage, the dissolution primarily affects only the family members. The nuclear family may also be dissolved by the death of one of the spouses.

This picture of the independent nuclear family in the United States needs to be slightly adjusted, however, to take into account the increasing rates of divorce and remarriage that enmesh nuclear families in ever larger and more complicated kinship networks. As Lionel Tiger (1978) points out, the divorce rate in the United States has jumped 250 percent in the last twenty-five years, and 80 percent of those who divorce remarry. Thus, Tiger says, we seem to be moving to a new system of marriage and kinship that he suggests we call "omnigamy" — the marriage of each to all! When parents divorce and remarry, a situation like the following may occur: A and B divorce; their children

In some Eastern European cultures, when the last child leaves the parental home to get married, the mother dances a muzinka at the wedding. Dancing with the broom symbolizes the sweeping of all troubles out of the house with the departure of the children. (Courtesy of Hadassah Bacaner/ Harvey Shafer)

A_1 and B_1 live with A and her new husband, C, but visit B and his new wife, D, on weekends. C's children, C_1, C_2, and C_3, visit him on weekends, and A and C and their five children sometimes spend the weekends together. D also has children, D_1 and D_2, who become friendly with A_1 and B_1 when they visit their father on the weekends when D_1 and D_2 are not visiting theirs. Add to this the set of grandparents and aunts and uncles that now join these new families and see how complicated it becomes to specify what we mean by the independent nuclear family.

The structure and functions of the family are changing in the United States. With an increase in the number of women working, men are taking a more involved role in child care. (Serena Nanda)

While divorce and remarriage are changing the structure of the family in the United States, other changing demographic features also make nonfamily options more common. In addition to the rise of the divorce rate, the American population is aging, and the age of marriage is rising. As a result, nearly one in four American households are occupied by a single person or unrelated persons (Waite 1991). Many social changes in the United States affect the decision to marry, including the fact that women who live alone, as women increasingly do, are 20 percent less likely to marry than women who remain at home with their parents until marriage. Men who live independently, however, are more likely to marry than women who have lived independently. Also, while both men and women whose parents are divorced are less likely to marry than those from intact families, the likelihood is lower for women than for men. As the divorce rate increases, it will continue to negatively affect the marriage rate. More and more women are working, and many more are finding that they can remain in the work force and achieve an adequate life-style without being married. An-

other factor that can be anticipated to affect the marriage rate is that women, especially those with higher education levels, increasingly desire a family structure in which men and women share more equally in household work. To the extent that the American household is a "gender factory," reproducing traditional gender roles in which boys and girls do different tasks, women who wish to have men take a more equitable share in household tasks may be increasingly reluctant to marry men with more traditional views on marriage and gender assignment of household tasks.

Not only is the number of families in the United States decreasing, but the American family also seems to be declining in the functions it performs for its members. In our society today, many functions formerly belonging to the nuclear family have been taken over by other groups. At one time, the family in Europe and the United States was a productive unit, and this is still true of some farm families. The typical American family, however, has largely lost this function; economically, its most important function is as a unit of consumption. Once, leisure activities and recreation were also carried out primarily within the family group; today, the peer group plays a much more important role in leisure activities and in inculcating values. The state has also, through various kinds of social programs, undermined the importance of caring for the aged or sick person as a family function. Socialization of children, too, takes place in important ways outside the family, in school and through the mass media.

In contrast to this picture of the declining functions of the nuclear family in our own society is the increased expectation that the family will satisfy our needs for affection and intimacy. Critics of the nuclear family in the United States feel that this burden is too much for the family to bear. In an age in which personal happiness has become a primary cultural value, it is perhaps beyond the capacity of any one social group to fulfill these needs. The alienation experienced by many Americans indicates that families often do not carry out their "affective" functions very well (Bronfenbrenner 1974).

The nuclear family is adapted in many ways to the requirements of industrial society. Where jobs do not depend on family connections, and where geographical mobility may be required for obtaining employment and success in a chosen career, a small, flexible unit such as the independent nuclear family has its advantages. This type of family also seems to be adaptive to the requirements of a hunting and gathering life, because more than three-fourths of foraging societies have this type of family unit. In such societies, however, the nuclear family is not nearly as independent or isolated as in our own society; the family unit almost always camps with the kin of the husband or the wife.

Composite, or **compound, families** are aggregates of nuclear families linked by a common spouse. A polygynous household, consisting of one man with several wives and their respective children, would constitute a composite family. In this case, each wife and her children normally occupy a separate residence. The dynamics of composite families are different from the dynamics of a family that consists of one husband, one wife, and their children, all of whom occupy a common residence. In the composite family, for example, the tie between a mother and her children is particularly strong, and the relations between the children of different mothers by the same father is different in a number of ways from the relationship between full siblings in the typical Euro-American nuclear family. Furthermore, in analyzing the dynamics of the composite family, the interaction between co-wives must be taken into account, as well as the different kinds of behavior patterns that emerge when a man is husband to several women rather than just one.

The Extended Family

The **extended**, or **consanguineal, family** consists of two or more lineally related kinfolk of the same sex and their spouses and offspring, occupying a single household or homestead and under the authority of a household head. An extended family is not just a collection of nuclear families. In the extended family system, the ties of lineality — that is, the blood ties between the generations — are more important than the ties of marriage. In more than half of the world's societies, the extended family is the ideal. It should be pointed out, however, that even where it is the ideal — in some peasant societies, for example — it is found much more among the landlord and prosperous merchant classes, and the nuclear or stem family (a nuclear family with a dependent adult added on) is more characteristic of the less prosperous peasants.

Extended families may be organized around males or females. A *patrilineal* extended family (such as the Rajputs of Khalapur, India, described in Chapter 6) is organized around a man, his sons, and the sons' wives and children. A *matrilineal* family is organized around a woman and her daughters and the daughters' husbands and children. The Nayar of South India represent the extreme of the consanguineal family, for the conjugal tie is for most purposes completely absent. Most extended family systems do give some recognition to the nuclear family. Thus, among the Rajputs of Khalapur, women are considered responsible for caring for their own children, and the conjugal tie is clearly recognized, if only as a potential source of trouble for the larger family group.

THE PATRILINEAL EXTENDED FAMILY   A society in which the extended family was the ideal was premodern China. In China, lineal descendants from father to son to grandson were the backbone of family organization. The family continued through time as a permanent social entity. As older members were lost through death, new ones were added through birth. As in India, marriage in China was viewed more as acquiring a daughter-in-law than taking a wife. It was arranged by the parents, and the new couple lived with the husband's family. Again, as in India, the obedient relationship of the son to his father and the loyalty and solidarity of brothers were given more importance than the ties between husband and wife. In fact,

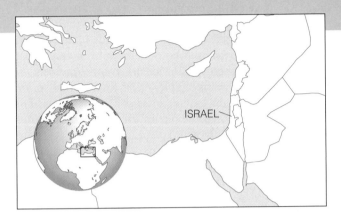

The claim of some anthropologists (Murdock 1949) that the nuclear family is a universal social institution has been disputed on the basis of some exceptional cases, such as that of the Nayar and the Israeli kibbutz. The kibbutz is a collective agricultural settlement. Kibbutzim were created by European Jews who wanted to establish communities built on social justice and the economic principles of "from each according to his ability and to each according to his needs." Private property would be done away with; the community rather than the family would be the most important group. Women, who had been limited to a secondary role in the traditional East European nuclear family, would have a new chance to become full human beings, equal with men, working alongside them, and not limited to the private domestic sphere of family life. Although communal child rearing originally started out as an expedient to allow women to work, it has since grown into an important part of kibbutz ideology. The degree to which communal child rearing is considered essential varies a great deal; some kibbutzim adhere to a communal child-rearing policy much more strongly than others do (Spiro 1974).

In the kibbutzim with strongly communal child-rearing patterns, an infant is raised in an infants' house almost from birth and is cared for, along with several other infants, by a trained nurse. This communal child rearing continues through childhood, and by the age of three, children eat with their peer group, under the supervision of a caretaker. As children grow older, the peer group becomes the main factor of continuity in their life and the major agent of enculturation. Studies of the personalities of kibbutz children seem to indicate that they feel themselves to be "children of the kibbutz" and are regarded as such by adults.

Furthermore, on the kibbutz the basic economic unit, for both production and consumption, is also the whole community, rather than the nuclear family. Eating is a communal activity not only for children but also for adults. Although there is a division of labor between males and females — women tend to predominate in "service" activities, and men dominate in agriculture — the division of labor does not characterize the relationship that exists between couples. Each mate works in some aspect of the economy, each is an independent member of the kibbutz on his or her own, and each, as a member, receives his or her equal share of the goods and services that the kibbutz distributes. Neither en-

gages in economic activities that are exclusively directed to the satisfaction of the needs of the mate. There are no sanctions on sexual relations among adult single members of the kibbutz; two single persons who wish to have a more intimate and permanent relationship request permission to share a room, and the granting of this request is the kibbutz's acknowledgment that they are now "a couple." Becoming a couple, which may often not involve a marriage ceremony until the birth of the first child, does not change any of the communal economic responsibilities of the couple. Thus, it would seem that the kibbutz is a society in which sexual, reproductive, economic, and educational functions are met in the absence of a nuclear family structure.

Yet the issue is more complex. In spite of the absence of formal structure, the nuclear family is a recognizable unit in kibbutz life (Spiro 1974). Affective ties are stronger between men and women who are married to each other than between other kibbutz comrades. Children's affective ties to their own parents

(*continued*)

are also of a different and more intense quality than their ties to other care-takers. Furthermore, although the kibbutz rather than the family provides the basic necessities of life, small luxuries and extras are provided within the nuclear family. More importantly, recent research, some of it by the same anthropologist who did the earliest studies of the kibbutz, Melford Spiro, indicates that the absence of the nuclear family structure is keenly felt by kibbutz women, who are increasingly agitating for more "feminine prerogatives" — in particular, for the right to keep their children in their rooms overnight. This is consistent with the fact that the kibbutz has always seemed to have a "woman problem," in that men are more satisfied as members than women are, and more women than men are likely to want to leave. Women are also more likely than men to violate kibbutz principles regarding the family structure (O'Kelly 1980:308). Can this be explained by pointing to the importance of the nuclear family in meeting the emotional needs of human beings in a way that no other structural unit can?

Although Spiro (1979) and others see the desire to return to more of a nuclear family structure as indicative of some basic biological need in women, other anthropologists have given different answers. It appears, for example, that in spite of the kibbutz ideology of sexual equality, women have not, in fact, participated equally in the high-prestige positions such as agriculture, but have been placed in the more monotonous, low-prestige, nonproductive service sectors. This has resulted in less political influence and participation in kibbutz life. Further, the threat of warfare in Israel has led to a higher value being placed on the male-dominant values that underlie a state in which military combat has assumed a great national importance. The constant threat of war has also led to an increased emphasis on the maternal role for women, who are expected to play a supportive role for their sons. It has also led many mothers to insist on keeping their own children with them at night in response to the tensions engendered by terrorist raids. All of these and other factors are contributing to the lack of success in the arena of sexual equality. Thus, many women on the kibbutz may feel that, because they cannot gain satisfaction from their work or contribution to the community, they should at least be able to have the satisfaction that comes from the maternal role.

In short, we cannot assume that the experiment to do away with the nuclear family has failed because of some inherent factor in human nature that requires it. Rather, the kibbutz research stresses that rigid definitions of family types are not the most useful ways of understanding the family as it exists in specific cultural contexts. It is more useful to examine the different components of the nuclear family "complex" and investigate how these various rights, obligations, activities, and functions are actually distributed — and with what costs and benefits — in different societies.

in both societies, the public demonstration of affection between a married couple was severely criticized. In both systems, it was anticipated and feared that a man's feeling for his wife would interfere with his carrying out responsibilities to his own blood kin.

In such cultures, a good wife is one who is a good daughter-in-law. She must work hard, under the eye of her mother-in-law and her husband's elder brothers' wives. With the birth of a son, a woman gains more acceptance in the household. As the years go by, if she has been patient and played her role well, the relationship between husband and wife develops into one of companionship and a more equal division of power. As her sons grow up, the wife achieves even more power in the household as she begins to arrange for their marriages. When several sons are married, a woman may be the dominant person in the household, even ordering her husband about, as his economic power, and consequently his authority, wanes.

THE MATRILINEAL EXTENDED FAMILY   Extended matrilineal families are found among the Hopi, a Western Pueblo native American group who live in the Southwest. The Hopi household revolves around a central and continuing core of women. When women marry, their husbands come into the household and have important economic functions, though they do not participate in its ritual. Husbands are peripheral, with divided residences and loyalties. When crises arise, the father is often blamed and treated as an outsider.

The father's obligations to his sons are primarily economic. He prepares them to make a living by teaching them to farm and herd sheep, and he may go into partnership with them in herding activities. When a son marries, a father will frequently present him with a portion of the flock and a small piece of land. The economic support a son receives from his father is returned in the father's old age; a son supports his father and takes the responsibility for his funeral rites. In return for this service, the son will receive a larger share of his father's personal property than his brothers. The father's

role is more that of a friend and teacher, and the father-son relationship is characterized by affection and little punishment. A father's relationship to his daughter is generally affectionate but not close, and he has few specific duties in regard to her upbringing.

The mother-daughter relationship is an exceedingly close one based on blood ties, common activities, and lifelong residence together. A mother is responsible for both the economic and the ritual training of her daughters. The daughter behaves with respect, obedience, and affection to her mother and normally will continue to live with her mother and her mother's sisters after marriage. A mother also has a close relationship with her son. He belongs to her lineage and will keep much of his personal and ritual property in her home. A son shows respect for his mother as head of the household and consults her on all important decisions.

The strongest and most permanent tie in Hopi society is between sisters. The foundation of the household group is the relation of sisters to one another and to their mother. The children of sisters are raised together; if one sister dies, another looks after her children. Sisters cooperate in all domestic tasks. There are usually few quarrels, and when they occur, they are settled by the mother's brother or their own brothers.

As in all matrilineal societies, the mother's brother's relation to his sister's sons is a very important one. As head of his sister's lineage and household, his position is one of authority and control; he is the chief disciplinarian and has the primary responsibility for transmitting the ritual heritage of the lineage and clan, which occupies the highest place in Hopi values. He usually selects the most capable nephew as his successor and trains him in the duties of whatever ceremonial position he may hold. A nephew is frequently afraid of his maternal uncle, in contrast to the affectionate relationship with his father. A mother's brother plays an important role at the time of his nephews' and nieces' weddings and is consulted in the choice of a spouse. It is he who instructs his nephew in the proper behavior toward his new relatives

With increasing industrialization, there appears to be a shift to nuclear family households in many societies, such as Japan, although the ideal of the extended family remains strong in many of these societies. (United Nations)

and who formally welcomes his niece's husband into the household.

ADVANTAGES OF THE EXTENDED FAMILY
The extended family is clearly adaptive under certain economic and social conditions. Murdock's (1949) survey indicated that the extended family prevails in all types of predominantly cultivating societies. The main advantages of this type of family are economic; the extended family can provide a larger number of workers than the nuclear family can provide. This is useful both for food production and for producing and marketing handicrafts, which are generally more well developed among cultivators than foragers. Furthermore, in stable agricultural societies, ownership of land becomes important; it is a source of pride, prestige, and power. The family becomes attached to the land, knows how to work it, and becomes reluctant to divide it. A system in which land is divided into small parcels through inheritance becomes relatively unproductive. The extended family is a way of keeping land intact, which

provides additional security for individuals in times of crisis. This relationship between land and family type is supported by evidence from India showing that the higher castes, who own more land and other property, are more likely to have extended families than are the lower castes.

There are also the values of companionship in the extended family as daily activities are carried out jointly by a number of kin working together. A further advantage is that the extended family provides not only economic support but also a sense of participation and dignity for the older person, who lives out his or her last years surrounded by respectful and affectionate kin. This contrasts with the nuclear family, in which the presumed advantages of privacy and personal autonomy are paid for as people grow old and are regarded as a burden and a nuisance if they join the household of one of their children.

Although it may be generally true that old people fare better in societies with extended family systems, the life of individuals past their prime is not always enviable, even in these societies. When sons begin to raise families of their own, extended families frequently split into parts. As the father loses his productive abilities, he is slowly divested of his former status and power. In a Fijian society studied by Marshall Sahlins (1957), the people say "His time is up" — and an old man literally waits to die. Although the Fijian ideal is that an old father should be properly cared for by his brothers and sons, "actually he sinks into a pitiable position. In the old days, he might even be killed. Today he is barely kept alive, his counsel is never sought and he is more often considered silly than wise" (p. 451).

Because the nuclear family appears to be adapted to a modern industrialized society, many social scientists have predicted that the extended family will be modified in the direction of the nuclear family as modernization and industrialization spread. The corollary of this assumption is that, although the extended family has advantages among cultivators or economically marginal populations, these advantages become liabilities with urbanization and industrialization. Milton Singer (1968), an anthropologist who has studied the families of industrial leaders in the city of Madras, India, says no. He points out that the patrilineal joint family as it exists in India is a flexible institution. The principles of mutual obligation of extended kin, joint ownership of property, and an authority structure in which the male household head takes responsibility for making decisions after consultation with junior members can easily be, and have been, successfully transferred to the management of modern corporations.

Domestic Groups and Postmarital Residence Rules

A **domestic group,** or household, is not the same as a family. Although domestic groups most often contain related members, nonkin may also be part of the domestic group. In addition, members of a family may be spread over several domestic groups, or households. The composition of domestic groups is affected by the rules a society has about where a newly married couple will live. **Neolocal residence** exists when it is the norm for a married couple to establish an independent domestic unit. Only 5 percent of the world's societies are neolocal. Neolocal residence is the ideal in our own society. It is related to the high degree of mobility required in an industrial system and to a value system that makes romantic love, the emotional bond between husband and wife, privacy, and independence of primary importance.

Most societies have a rule of **patrilocal residence.** A woman lives with her husband's kin after marriage, either in the same household or in a nearby dwelling or compound. In societies with a **matrilocal residence rule,** the husband lives with the wife's kin after marriage. If a couple has the choice of living with either the wife's or the husband's family, the pattern is one of **bilocal residence.** A fifth and rare residence pattern is called **avunculocal residence.** In this case, the married couple is expected to live with the husband's mother's brother.

In attempting to explain why a society would have a particular kind of residence rule, anthropologists have generally emphasized economic factors. It has been suggested that, where men must work cooperatively, such as in societies dependent on big-game hunting or intensive agriculture, there will be a patrilocal rule of residence. Matrilocality would appear to be adaptive in horticultural societies, where women have an important role in the economy. The cross-cultural data do not prove this reasoning to be entirely correct. Although it is true that most matrilocal societies do practice horticulture, this is also the case for the majority of patrilocal societies.

The importance of male cooperation in warfare is suggested as another reason for a patrilocal rule of residence (Ember and Ember 1971). Where fighting between lineages or villages is common, it is useful for men who will fight together to live together. Otherwise, they might wind up having to make the choice between defending their wife's local group, the one with whom they live, against the families with whom they grew up. Where warfare takes place between societies, rather than within them, and where men must leave their homes to fight, cooperation among women is very important. Because common residence promotes cooperation, matrilocal residence is a functional norm where males engage in warfare that extends beyond local groups.

Residence rules are ideal or preferred norms of behavior; actual behavior is frequently different. The choices couples make about where to live after marriage depend on many individual situational factors, although they are likely to be guided by the ideal norms of the society. Because kinship ideology (to be discussed in the next chapter) is derived from both norms and actual patterns of postmarital residence, residence rules, as well as the actual choices made by individuals, are important in the social organization of a society.

Summary

1. Three major functions of marriage and the family are regulating sexual access between males and females, arranging for the exchange of services between males and females, and assigning responsibility for child care.

2. Although marriage and family are rooted in the biological complementarity of male and female and the biological process of reproduction, they are cultural patterns and differ in different human societies.

3. Incest taboos are prohibitions on mating between relatives or people classified as relatives. Some theories that attempt to account for the universality of such taboos are that the taboos limit inbreeding, that they reflect the natural aversion to sexual relations between close kin, that they prevent disruption within the family, and that they force people to marry out of their immediate families, thus joining people into a larger social community.

4. Exogamy is a rule that requires people to marry *outside* a particular group. This rule is adaptive in forging alliances between families within a society.

5. Endogamy is a rule requiring marriage *within* a specified group. One of its functions is to keep wealth within the group or to maintain the so-called purity of the blood line.

6. All societies have rules about the number of spouses allowed a man or woman. Most of the world's societies allow some form of plural marriage (polygyny or polyandry), whereas our own society has a rule of monogamy (one spouse only).

7. Marriage, which is a publicly sanctioned relationship, most often is legitimated by the exchange of goods between the kin of the bride and the kin of the groom. The most common form of exchange is bridewealth, in which the kin of the groom gives various kinds of goods to the kin of the bride.

8. There are two basic types of families. The nuclear family is organized around the tie between husband and wife (the conjugal tie); the extended family is organized around blood ties extending over several generations.

9. The nuclear family, which is predominantly found in contemporary industrial societies and foraging societies, appears to be adaptive where geographical mobility is important. The extended family predominates among cultivators, because it provides a larger number of workers than does the nuclear family and is also a means by which landholdings can be kept intact over generations.

10. A domestic group is a household; it usually, but not necessarily, contains members of a family. The composition of domestic groups is shaped by the postmarital residence rules of a society.

11. The most widespread rule of residence is patrilocality, by which the wife goes to live with her husband's family. Matrilocality, by which the husband goes to live with his wife's family, is found primarily in horticultural societies. Neolocality, by which the married couple lives independently, is found in a relatively small number of societies, including that of the United States.

Suggested Readings

Fernea, Elizabeth
1965 *Guests of the Sheik: An Ethnography of an Iraqi Village.* Garden City, N.Y.: Anchor Doubleday. An outstandingly readable account of life in a village family from a woman's perspective.

Stack, Carol
1974 *All Our Kin: Strategies for Survival in a Black Community.* New York: Harper & Row. A view of the African-American, lower-class kin group that emphasizes the adaptive nature of extended domestic networks.

Weston, Kath
1991 *Families We Choose: Lesbians, Gays, Kinship.* New York: Columbia University Press. Winner of the Ruth Benedict Award, this provocative study of alternative family ideology and structure is based on participant observation and in-depth interviewing in the Bay Area (San Francisco). It includes chapters on coming out, gay families, the ideology of families as "chosen," parenting, and politics, and is informed by an historical and reflexive perspective.

Wikan, Unni
1980 *Life among the Poor in Cairo.* London: Tavistock. An exceedingly interesting account of how poverty affects marriage, family life, and child rearing in an urban society.

Wiser, Charlotte V.
1978 *Four Families of Karimpur.* Syracuse, N.Y.: Syracuse University Press. Four individual families from different castes in a North Indian village that serves as an excellent introduction to the dynamics of family life in India.

Kinship and Nonkin Bases of Association

Why is kinship so important in nonstate societies?

Can you explain why hunters and gatherers have kinship classification systems similar to those of industrialized societies?

How do kinship terminologies reflect other aspects of a culture?

What are other bases of association than kinship, and how do these function in different societies?

Modern American society and economy emphasize individualism in many ways. The nuclear family is more common than the extended family, and parents and children appear to be close only when the children are very young. Most American parents seem to "lose" their children by the teenage years. . . . [T]he close interpersonal spirit seems to be lacking between the generations. Grandparents have relatively little to do with the grandchildren on any regular basis. The family seems to be graded by age so that grandparents, parents, and children are separated by generational subcultures that are evidently alienated from one another. In one case I knew of, a financially affluent grandmother with Alzheimer's disease was taken care of by hired help in her own home. The (married) daughter visits occasionally to help out, but the mature granddaughter, who has her own family, rarely visits, yet they all live in the same neighborhood. When I asked the granddaughter why she doesn't help care for her grandmother, she said she has her own life. The [North American] value of individualism seems to account for these apparent gaps in family ties and support.

In contrast, in Thailand, older parents with a long-term illness are asked to move in with their children and grandchildren, who take turns attending them. Living together in the same house reinforces moral support among the generations within an extended family, and family relations provide one of the most important contexts for being a "morally good person," traditionally the principal concern in the Buddhist society of Thailand.

Adapted from Poranee Natadecha-Sponsel, "The Young, the Rich, and the Famous: Individualism as an American Cultural Value," in Philip R. DeVita and James D. Armstrong, eds., Distant Mirrors: America as a Foreign Culture *(Belmont, Calif.: Wadsworth, 1993), p. 51.*

The culture shock experienced by a Thai woman who came to live in the United States, described in the opening of this chapter, highlights the importance of kinship in all human societies. The United States, like all other societies, does have a kinship system, although the importance of kin groups, compared with other groups in our society, is not as central as it is in many other parts of the world. In societies traditionally studied by anthropologists, kinship is the most important social bond. Kin relations are the basis of group formation; relationships between individuals are mainly governed by kinship norms; and the extension of kinship ties is the main way of allying groups to one another and incorporating strangers into a group. The importance of kinship in most of the world's cultures provides an important contrast with our own society, in which other principles of social organization, such as work, citizenship, and common economic and political interests, operate to structure behavior and act as the basis on which groups are formed. This does not mean that kinship is insignificant in modern industrialized societies. The nuclear family is, after all, a kin group and a core social institution in the United States. Larger groupings of relatives also become important on various ceremonial occasions. Even in the United States, a person claiming a kin relation is regarded differently from someone who is not a relative, inheritance of property is mainly along kin lines, and there is a strong sentiment that "blood is thicker than water."

Relationships through Blood and Marriage

Kinship includes relationships through blood and relationships through marriage. In every society, the formation of groups and the regulation of behavior depend to some extent on socially recognized ties of kinship. A **kinship system** refers to the totality of relationships based on blood and marriage that link individuals in a web of rights and obligations; to the kinds of groups formed in a society on the basis of kinship; and to the system of terms used to classify different kin (kinship terminology). It is because there is an interrelationship between the formation of kinship groups, the development of kinship ideology, the behavior of different kin toward one another, and the kinship terminology of a society that anthropologists refer to kinship as a system.

Although a kinship system always rests on some kind of biological relationship, kinship systems are cultural phenomena. The ways in which a society classifies kin are cultural, and they may or may not be based on a scientifically accurate assessment of biological ties. The term for father, for example, may refer to the actual biological father (*genitor*) of a child, or it may refer to a man who takes on the responsibility for the child's upbringing and/or is socially recognized as the father (*pater*). In the Trobriand Islands, for example, the biological role of the male in reproduction is not given cultural recognition, and fatherhood is established by marriage; the "father" is the mother's husband. In some polyandrous societies, such as the Toda of India, biological paternity is irrelevant; fatherhood is established by the performance of a ritual. In this and other similar cases, social fatherhood is what counts. Because kinship systems are cultural creations, there is a wide variety of ways in which both consanguineal (blood) and affinal (marriage) relatives are classified in different societies. There are also differences in the kinds of social groups formed by kinship and in the ways in which kin are expected to behave toward one another.

Culturally defined ties of kinship have two basic functions that are necessary for the continuation of society. First, kinship serves to provide continuity between generations. In all societies, children must be cared for and educated so that they can become functioning members of their society. With the possible exception of the kibbutz and other contemporary attempts at collective child rearing in communes of unrelated people, it is a kinship unit that is fundamentally responsible for socialization. Furthermore, a society must also provide for the orderly transmission of property and social position between generations. In most human societies, inheritance (the transfer of property) and succession (the transfer of social position) take place within kin groups.

Second, kinship defines a universe of others on whom an individual can depend for aid in a variety of ways. The minimal group of importance in mutual aid is the domestic group of a woman and her children and an adult male. In most societies, however, kin groups that include relatives beyond this minimum are very important. It is undoubtedly the adaptiveness of social groups larger than the nuclear family that accounts for the fact that expanded kin groups are found in so many human societies.

Rules of Descent and the Formation of Descent Groups

In anthropological terminology, **descent** refers to the culturally established affiliation with one or both parents. In many societies, descent is an important basis of social-group formation. In one sense, of course, the nuclear family is a descent group, but here we use **descent group** to mean those groups of consanguineal kin who are lineal descendants of a common ancestor extending beyond two generations. Where descent groups are found, they have important functions in the organization of domestic life, the socialization of children, the use and transfer of property and political and ritual offices, the carrying out of religious ritual, the settlement of disputes, and political organization and warfare.

Two basic types of descent rule, or kinship ideology, operate in society. In a system with a rule of **unilineal descent**, descent-group membership is based on links through either the pa-

ternal or the maternal line, but not both. Two types of unilineal descent rules are patrilineal descent and matrilineal descent. In societies with **patrilineal descent,** an individual belongs to the descent group of his or her father. In societies with **matrilineal descent,** an individual belongs to the descent group of the mother. (There are some exceptions, as in societies with double descent, which will be described later.)

In societies with a system of **bilateral descent,** both maternal and paternal lines are used as the basis for reckoning descent and for establishing the rights and obligations of kinship. Bilateral kinship systems are found in relatively few societies throughout the world, although they are characteristic of western European culture and of the United States.

Unilineal Descent

The frequency of unilineal descent in the world's cultures is due to two major advantages: (1) Unilineal rules result in the formation of descent groups that can perpetuate themselves over time even though their membership changes (as modern corporations can). Corporate descent groups are permanent units and have an existence over and above the individuals who are members at any given time. Old members die and new ones are admitted through birth, but the integrity of the corporate group as a group persists. Such groups (like lineages) may own property and manage resources (just as a modern corporation does). (2) Such rules provide unambiguous group membership for every individual in the society. In short, where descent is traced through only one line, group membership is both easily and clearly defined. By knowing the descent group to which he or she belongs and the descent group of others, an individual can be sure of his or her rights of ownership, social duties, and social roles. He or she can also easily relate to a large number of known and unknown people in the society.

Although systems of unilineal descent share certain basic similarities throughout the world, they do not operate exactly the same way in

THE KINSHIP DIAGRAM

Kinship diagrams are more convenient than verbal explanations and allow us to see immediately how different kinship statuses are linked. In order to make a kinship diagram precise and unambiguous, all relationships in the diagram are viewed from the perspective of one status, labeled EGO. Terms of reference rather than terms of address are used—that is, terms we would use in talking *about* a relative rather than talking *to* one. In English, for example, we would refer to our "mother" but might address her as "Mom." The symbols used in kinship diagrams are these:

△   Male

○   Female

=   Marital (affinal) tie

——   Blood (consanguineal) tie

Using these symbols, and English terminology, a kinship diagram of the nuclear family looks like this:

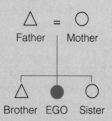

every society. In addition, actual behavior in any society does not correspond exactly to the rules as they are defined in the kinship ideology. Systems of descent and kinship are basically a means by which a society relates to its environment and circumstances. As situations and conditions change, the rules of kinship, like other ideal norms, will be bent and manipulated so that a group may be successful in its environment. The accepted departures from the norm that exist in every society give unilineal systems a flexibility they would otherwise lack—a flexibility necessary for human adaptation. We will look now at some of the different types of unilineal descent groups.

TYPES OF UNILINEAL DESCENT GROUPS   A **lineage** is a group of kin whose members trace descent from a common ancestor and who can demonstrate those genealogical links among themselves. Lineages formed by descent through the male line are called **patrilineages**. Lineages formed by descent through the female line are called **matrilineages**. Lineages may vary in size from one consisting of a male or female, their children, and their children's children to one consisting of more than three generations. Where lineages own land collectively and where the members are held responsible for one another's behavior, the lineage is considered a corporate group. In some societies the lineage functions as a corporate group; in other societies it does not.

Related lineages may form **clans**, whose presumed common ancestor may be a mythological figure, or sometimes no specific ancestor will be known or named. A **phratry** is a unilineal descent group composed of a number of clans who feel themselves to be closely related. Clans are frequently named and may have a **totem** — that is, some feature of the natural environment with which they are closely identified and toward which the clan members must behave in a special way.

Clans and lineages have different functions in different societies. The lineage is frequently a local residential or domestic group, and its members therefore cooperate on a daily basis. The lineage is also important in regulating marriage; in most societies, an individual must marry outside his or her lineage or the lineage of either parent. Clans are not generally residential units but tend to spread out over many villages. Clans therefore often have political and religious functions, rather than primarily domestic and economic ones.

One of the most important functions of a clan is to regulate marriage. In most societies, clans are exogamous. The prohibition on marriage within the clan strengthens its unilineal character. If a person married within the clan, his or her children would find it difficult to make sharp distinctions between maternal and paternal relatives. Robert H. Lowie (1948:237) says of the Crow Indians of North America, among whom clans are very important, that in case of marriage within the clan, "a Crow . . . loses his bearings and perplexes his tribesmen. For he owes specific obligations to his father's relatives and others to his mother's, who are now hopelessly confounded. The sons of his father's clan ought to be censors; but now the very same persons are his joking relatives and his clan." Not only would this person not know how to act toward others, but others would not know how to act toward him. Clan exogamy also extends the network of peaceful social relations within a society as different clans are allied through marriage.

PATRILINEAL DESCENT GROUPS   In societies with patrilineal descent groups, an individual (whether male or female) belongs to the descent groups of the father, the father's father, and so on (see Figures 10.1 and 10.2). Thus, a man, his sisters and brothers, his brother's children (but not his sister's children), his own children, and his son's children (but not his daughter's children) all belong to the same group. Inheritance moves from father to son, as does succession to office.

The degree to which a woman is incorporated into the patrilineage of her husband varies in different societies. In some cases, a woman may retain rights of inheritance in her father's lineage. In general, however, in a patrilineal system a man gains some degree of control over his wife and children. Great care is taken in patrilineal societies to guarantee the husband's rights and control over his wife (or wives) and children, because the continuity of the descent group depends on binding the wife and children to the husband. Patrilineal systems most often have patrilocal rules of residence, so a wife may find herself living among "strangers" (this of course would not be the case in societies where cousin marriage is practiced), and this undermines female solidarity and support. Because marriage in patrilineal systems is generally surrounded by strict sanctions and tends to be more stable than it is in matrilineal systems, anthropologists have tended to neglect the potential for disruption that derives from the discontent of women in these societies. In fact, women are not always as submissive as they have been portrayed in the anthropological literature on patrilineal societies, and their struggles against control by the husband's group are an important theme both in the reality of domestic life and in mythology and literature (Denich 1974).

The Nuer, a pastoral people who live in the Sudan in East Africa, are a patrilineal society. Among the Nuer, all rights, privileges, obligations, and interpersonal relationships are regulated by kinship; one is either a kinsman or an enemy. Membership in a patrilineal descent group is the most significant fact of life, and the father, his brothers, and their children are considered the closest kin. Membership in the patrilineage confers rights in land, requires participation in certain religious ceremonies, and determines political and judicial obligations, such as making alliances in feuds and warfare.

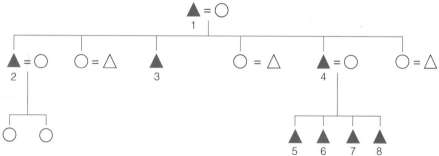

FIGURE 10.1 In India, the patrilineal rule of descent forms the basis for the patrilineal joint family, which is a corporate group in that property is owned conjointly by male members.

The patrilineage has important political functions among the Nuer. Lineage membership may spread over several villages and thus help create alliances between otherwise independent villages that contain members of several different lineages. Related lineages form still larger groups, or clans. Clans are viewed as composed of lineages, not of individuals. Each Nuer clan has its members spread out over many villages. Because an individual cannot marry someone from within his or her own lineage or clan or from the lineage of the mother, kinship relations extend widely throughout the tribe. In the absence of a centralized system of

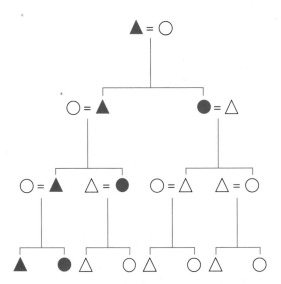

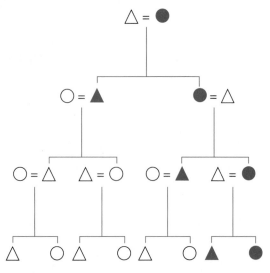

FIGURE 10.2 Membership in a patrilineal descent group. In societies with patrilineal descent groups, membership is based on links through the father only. Sons and daughters are members of their father's descent group (shown in color), as are the children of sons, but *not* of daughters.

FIGURE 10.3 Membership in a matrilineal descent group. In a society with matrilineal descent groups, membership in the group is defined by links through the mother. Sons and daughters are members of their mother's descent group, as are the children of daughters, but *not* the children of sons.

political control, kinship-based alliances are an important mechanism for keeping the peace, in view of the Nuer belief that kin should not fight with one another.

MATRILINEAL DESCENT GROUPS Two fundamental ties recognized by every society are that between a woman and her children and that between siblings (brothers and sisters). In all societies, males have the responsibility of providing for and protecting the mother-child unit, and they have control over women and their children. In patrilineal societies, this control falls to the man who is designated as the child's father. In matrilineal societies, however, the major protecting, providing, and controlling male is the brother of a woman rather than her husband. A man gains sexual and economic rights over a woman when he marries her, but he does not gain rights over her children. Children belong to the mother's descent group, not the father's. Thus, the membership of a matri-

lineal descent group consists of a woman, her brothers and sisters, her sister's (but not her brother's) children, her own children, and the children of her daughters (but not of her sons) (Figure 10.3).

Matrilineal systems tend to be correlated with a matrilocal rule of residence; a man goes to live with or near his wife's kin after marriage. This means that in the domestic group, it is the man who is among "strangers," whereas his wife is surrounded by her kin. The inclusion of a husband in the household is of less importance in a matrilineal system than in a patrilineal one, and marriages in matrilineal societies tend to be less stable than those in other systems. As we saw among the Nayar of India, it is possible for a matrilineally organized group to do away with the presence of husbands and fathers altogether, as long as there are brothers who assume responsibilities. It is important to remember that, although women usually have higher status in societies where there is a matrilineal reckoning of descent, matrilineality is not the same as matriarchy, a society in which the formal positions of power are held by women. With a few possible exceptions (Wallace 1970), the most important resources and highest political positions are in the control of males, although the male with the most power and control in matrilineal societies is not the husband (father) but the brother (uncle). The role of the mother's brother is an important or special one even in patrilineal societies, but in matrilineal societies it is particularly important. The mother's brother is a figure of authority and respect, and it is the children of a man's sister rather than his own who are his heirs and successors.

In a matrilineal society, the relationship between a man and his son is likely to be affectionate and loving, because it is free of the problems of authority and control that exist between fathers and sons in a patrilineal society. A man may feel emotionally close to his sons, but he is committed by the matrilineal kinship ideology to pass on his knowledge, property, offices, and so on to the sons of his sister. With these individuals (his "nephews"), he may have less friendly relations or even conflicts, as they are subject to his control. Thus, in a matrilineal system, a man's loyalties are split between his own sons and the sons of his sister; in a patrilineal system, this tension does not occur as part of the kinship structure.

The Hopi, a Pueblo group in the American Southwest, are a matrilineal society. The matrilineage is conceived of as timeless, stretching backward to the beginnings of the Hopi people and continuing into the future. Both male and female members of the lineage consider their mother's house their home, though men move out to reside with their wives after marriage. They return to this home for many ritual and ceremonial occasions, however, and also in the case of separation or divorce. The relationship of a man with his father's lineage and household is affectionate, involving some economic and ritual obligations but little direct cooperation or authority.

In addition to lineages, the Hopi also have matrilineal clans that extend over many different villages. A Hopi man must not marry within his own clan or the clan of his father or his mother's father. Marriage thus results in a wide range of relatives in addition to those an individual acquires through birth through the clan he (and his mother) belongs to. A Hopi has obligations to the clan of the father as well as to that of the mother and also to the clans of the person designated as the ceremonial father. Kinship terms are extended to all these individuals, leading to a vast number of potential sibling relationships and a lateral integration of a great number of separate lineages and clans. This extension of Hopi kinship relates a Hopi in some way to almost everyone in his or her village, in other villages, and even to individuals in other Pueblo groups who have similar clans. While the lineage group is particularly important to women, these larger clan groups are the arena of male activities. Here men play important political and religious roles, in contrast to the marginal positions they have in domestic life. The Hopi also extend kinship ideology to the world of nature. The sun is called "father," and the earth and corn are called "mother." These phenomena in nature such as plant and animal species that serve as clan names are also referred to by kinship terminology, such as "mother" or "mother's brother" (Eggan 1950).

A number of explanations have been given by anthropologists in their attempts to understand the evolution of unilineal descent groups. Many of these explanations fail to take into account the diversity of the systems that have been lumped together as unilineal. The contemporary anthropological approach is not so much to ask "What kind of kinship system exists in a particular society?" but rather to ask "What are the common interests that give people a reason for joining together and defining themselves as a collective entity justified by reference to kin ties?" These interests *may* be economic, such as land or cattle or gardens; they may also be political or religious or involve

DOUBLE DESCENT: THE YAKO OF NIGERIA

When descent is traced through a combination of matrilineal and patrilineal principles, a system of **double descent** exists. In societies with double-descent systems, the individual belongs both to the patrilineal group of the father and the matrilineal group of the mother. Such societies are rare, about 5 percent of the world's known cultures. In double descent, matrilineal and patrilineal descent both operate as principles of affiliation, but the descent groups operate in different areas of life.

The Yako of Nigeria have a system of double descent. Cooperation in daily domestic life is strongest among patrilineally related kinsmen who live with or near one another. These men jointly control and farm plots of land, and membership in the patriclan is the source of rights over farmland and forest products. Patriclan obligations include providing food at funerals. Inheritance of membership in the men's associations and the right to fruit trees are also transmitted in the male line. The arbitration of disputes is in the hands of senior patriclan members, and cooperation in ritual and succession to some religious offices are also derived from clan membership.

Matrilineal bonds and clan membership are also important in Yako society, despite the fact that matriclan members do not live near one another and do not cooperate as a group in everyday activities. The rights and duties of matrilineal kinship are different. Practical assistance to matrilineal kin, the rights and obligations of the mother's brother and his sister's sons, and the authority of the priest of a matrilineal clan are based on mystical ideas regarding the perpetuation and tranquillity of the Yako world. The Yako believe that the fertility of crops, beasts, and humans, and peace between individuals and within the community as a whole are associated with and passed on through women. Life comes from the mother; it is by a wife that children are produced. The children of one mother are bound to mutual support and peaceful relations. The matrilineage is thus held together by mystical bonds of common fertility, and anger and violence between its members are considered sinful. These sentiments are reinforced in the cult of the matriclan spirits, whose priests are ritually given the qualities of women.

Despite their isolation from one another by the rule of patrilocal residence, matriclan relatives have specific mutual obligations. Rights in the transfer of accumulated wealth, as opposed to basic economic resources, belong to the matrilineal kinship group. It is the members of a matriclan that supervise a funeral and arrange for the disposal of the dead person's property. All currency and livestock customarily pass to matrilineal relatives, who also receive the greater share of tools, weapons, and household goods. The movable property of women passes to their daughters. Matriclans also have the responsibility for the debts of their kin, for making loans to one another at reasonable rates, and for providing part of the bridewealth transferred at the marriage of a sister's son. Thus, for the Yako, paternity and maternity are both important in descent; each contains inherently different qualities from which flow the rights, obligations, and benefits, both practical and spiritual, by which individuals are bound to one another and through which the continuity of the society is ensured.

Adapted from Daryll Forde, "Double Descent among the Yako," in A. R. Radcliffe-Brown and Daryll Forde, eds., African Systems of Kinship and Marriage *(London: Oxford University Press, 1967 [first publ. 1950]), pp. 285–332.*

warfare within the society or with other societies. As older theories of kinship lose their explanatory power under the weight of new data, rethinking kinship has become an important new focus in anthropology.

Nonunilineal Kin Groups

About 40 percent of the world's societies are nonunilineal. Two types of nonunilineal kin groups, the bilateral kindred and bilineal, or double descent, are discussed in the accompanying box. In systems of bilateral descent, an individual is considered to be related equally to other kin through both the mother's and the father's side, although in our own society, which is bilateral, the patrilineal principle is dominant in the handing down of family names. In a unilineal kinship system, an individual is affiliated with a large number of lineally extended relations through time, but only on one side of the family. A bilateral group extends along lines established by links through both males and females, but it incorporates only close biological relatives.

In bilateral (or cognatic) systems of descent, there are no clear descent groups formed in the way described for unilineal systems. The kin network formed by a bilateral reckoning of descent is called a **kindred.** With the exception of brothers and sisters, every individual's kindred is different from every other individual's. Kindreds are actually overlapping categories of kin (which is why the term *kin network* rather than *group* is used), so they cannot be the basis for the formation of corporate groups. This is the major functional weakness of the kindred as a cooperative, kin-based collectivity. Because it is not a group but rather an ego-centered network, it cannot own land or have continuity over time. But bilateral systems have great flexibility. An individual can mobilize a number of relatives from either the father's or the mother's side (or both), depending on the particular enterprise being undertaken. Bilateral kinship systems appear to be particularly adaptive in societies where mobility and

independence are important, and they predominate among hunters and gatherers and in modern industrial societies.

The Classification of Kin

In all societies, kin are referred to by special terms. The total system of kinship terms and the rules for using these terms make up a kinship classification system. No kinship classification system has a different term of reference for each position in the kinship structure. This would require far too many terms to remember. In every system of kinship terminology, therefore, some relatives are classed together — that is, referred to by the same kinship term, while other relatives are differentiated from each other, that is, called by different terms.

The ways in which kin are classified are associated with the roles they play in society. If, for example, an individual refers to his father and his father's brothers by the same term, the roles he plays in relation to all of these relatives will tend to be similar. By the same token, if an individual's father and the father's brothers are referred to by different terms, it is expected that an individual will act differently toward each of them and that they will act differently toward him. Furthermore, kinship systems, like other aspects of culture, have an ideal and a real component; while kinship terms call forth expectations of certain kinds of behavior, actual behavior is modified by individual personality differences and special circumstances.

Principles for Classifying Kin

Societies differ in the categories of relatives they distinguish and the principles by which kin are classified. The seven important principles for separating and grouping together (classifying) different categories of kin are the following:

1. *Generation.* This principle distinguishes ascending and descending generations

A *pumashi*, or reciprocal work group, in rural Korea. This group consists of male cousins and their wives. Cousins are called "brother" (as in North India), and perhaps because of the potential for conflict among brothers, they often avoid each others' company, whereas male cousins are not only close kin but also "true blue" friends. (Courtesy of Soo Choi)

from Ego. For example, in English we call relatives in the parental generation by such terms as *aunt* or *uncle*, and kin in the descending generation *nephew* or *niece*.

2. *Relative age*. In a kinship system that uses this principle there are different kinship terms, for example, for one's older brother and one's younger brother. English kinship terminology does not recognize this principle.

3. *Lineality vs. collaterality*. **Lineal kin** are related in a single line, such as grandfather-father-son. **Collateral kin** are descended from a common ancestor with Ego, but are not Ego's direct ascendants or descendants. For example, our brothers and sisters (siblings) and our cousins are collateral kin: We and they are descended from the same ancestors, but they are not in our direct ascendant or descendant line. In many societies, collaterality is not distin-

guished in the kinship terminology, so that Ego refers to both his father and father's brother as *father*. Both the mother and her sisters may similarly be referred to as *mother*. In these systems, parallel cousins (but not cross cousins) may also be referred to by the same terms as those for brother and sister.

4. *Gender*. In English, some of our kinship terms differentiate by gender, for example, *aunt, uncle, brother;* the term *cousin*, however, does not differentiate by gender. In some other cultures, all kinship terms distinguish gender.

5. *Consanguineal vs. affinal kin*. People related to Ego by blood (consanguinity) are distinguished from similar relationships by marriage; for example, English kinship terminology distinguishes *sister* from *sister-in-law*, and *father* from *father-in-law*, and so on. The English term *uncle*,

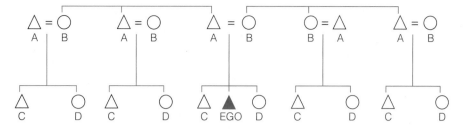

FIGURE 10.4 Hawaiian kinship terminology. Symbols with the same letters underneath are referred to in the same way by Ego.

however, does not distinguish between consanguineal and affinal relationships: It is equally applied to the brother of our father or mother, and to the husband of our father's or mother's sisters.

6. *Sex of linking relative.* In societies where distinguishing collateral relatives is an important principle of kinship classification, the sex of the linking relative may be important in the kinship terminology. For example, parallel cousins may be distinguished from cross cousins and may further be distinguished by the gender of the linking relative (for example, matrilateral as opposed to patrilateral cross or parallel cousins). This is particularly important where Ego is prohibited from marrying a parallel cousin but may, or even must, marry a cross cousin.

7. *Side of the family.* Under this principle of classification, called **bifurcation**, kin terms distinguish between relatives from the mother's side of the family and those from the father's side. An example would be those societies where the mother's brother is referred to differently from the father's brother. This principle is not used in English kinship terminology.

Understanding kinship classification systems is not just an interesting anthropological game. Kinship classification is one of the important regulators of behavior in most societies, outlining each person's rights and obligations, and specifying the ways in which the

individual must act toward others and they toward him or her. Kinship classification systems are also related to other aspects of culture: the types of social groups that are formed, the systems of marriage and inheritance, and even deeper, and broader, cultural values. The following ethnography illustrates how the differences in kinship classification systems between North America and North India reflect many other cultural patterns in those two societies.

Types of Kinship Terminologies

Systems of kinship terminology reflect the kinds of kin groups that are most important in a society. Anthropologists have identified six systems of kinship terminology: Hawaiian, Eskimo, Iroquois, Omaha, Crow, and Sudanese.

HAWAIIAN   As its name suggests, this system is found in Polynesia. It is rather simple in that it uses the least number of kinship terms. The Hawaiian system emphasizes the distinctions between generations and reflects the relative equality between the mother and the father's sides of the family in relation to Ego. All relatives of the same generation and sex — for example, father, father's brother, and mother's brother — are referred to by the same kinship term. Male and female kin in Ego's generation are distinguished in the terminology, but the terms for sister and brother are the same as those for the children of one's parents' siblings (Figure 10.4). This system correlates with *ambilineality* and *ambilocality*, which means that

KINSHIP CLASSIFICATION SYSTEMS IN ACTION:
A COMPARISON BETWEEN NORTH AMERICA
AND NORTH INDIA

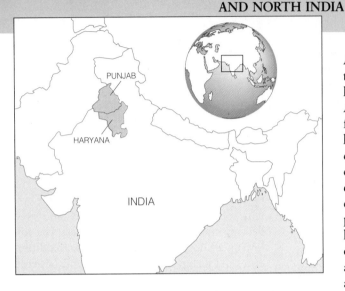

As an anthropologist, I have had the traditional professional interest in kinship classification systems. As an American woman married to a man from North India, however, I have had a more personal interest in understanding how the principles of classification in my own culture differ from those of my husband's culture. In order for me to behave properly with the members of my husband's family, I had to learn each of the North Indian kinship terms and the expected behaviors associated with them. At first, I made a lot of mistakes but as I continued to meet new family members I learned to ask the relevant questions about their relationship so that I could act appropriately. My anthropological experience in making and interpreting kinship diagrams was very helpful in this respect.

As the two diagrams indicate, one immediately apparent difference between the North American and the North Indian kinship classification systems is the number of terms: In North India there are forty-five terms, while in the United States there are only twenty-two. This is because the North Indian system distinguishes several kinds of kin that we, in North America, group together. Thus, although my husband also had to learn a new cultural classification of kinship, it was somewhat easier for him because of the smaller number of categories of relatives, and the correspondingly greater flexibility in behavior that is acceptable in North America as compared to North India. For me, learning the many different North Indian kinship terms and the many corresponding "rules" of kinship behavior seemed quite a burden. But when I understood the cultural patterns upon which these terms and rules of behavior were based, they made more sense to me and I could more easily fit new relatives into the system and act accordingly.

Many of the North Indian cultural patterns that underlie kinship terminology are based on the importance of the patrilineal and patrilocal joint family (see p. 243): the importance of the male principle in inheritance and seniority; the lower status of a family of the bride compared to that of the groom; the obligations a male child has toward his parents, including specific ritual obligations of the eldest son; and the ritual roles played by various kin in life-cycle ceremonies such as marriage and death. These patterns are based on two major principles of Indian culture and social organization: the values of hierarchy and the importance of the group. These values contrast with the Western values of equality, individualism, and the nuclear family, which are expressed in our kinship terminology. While space limitations prohibit examining all of the ways in which the contrasts between the Indian cultural values of hierarchy and group orientation, and our own values of equality and individualism, are reflected in the kinship classification systems, several examples will make this clear.

The principle of relative age, which is an aspect of hierarchy, is critical in the Indian kinship system but absent in our own. Thus, my husband uses different terms to refer to his father's elder brother (*tau*) and his father's younger brother (*chacha*) and this carries over to their wives; his father's elder brother's wife is *tai* and his father's younger brother's wife is *chachi*. This terminological difference reflects the importance of respect attached to seniority. My relationship with my husband's brothers and their wives is also regulated by this same principle of seniority. I was instructed that my husband's elder brother is my *jait* and his wife is my *jaitani*, and that both these relations must be treated with deference, similar to that shown to my father-in-law, by adding the suffix "ji" to their kinship terms, by touching their feet when I meet them, and by refraining from using their first names in either referring to or addressing them. But my husband's younger brother, who is my *deva*, and his wife, who is my *devrani*, may be treated with the friendly informality more characteristic of sister and brother-in-law relations in the United States. On our trips back to India, I can greet my husband's younger brother with an embrace, and talk with him in a joking, familiar manner, but I must never embrace my husband's elder brother, even though I feel equally friendly toward him and like him equally well. Because Indians understand that Americans are generally friendly people who do not recognize these status differences in their own culture, my husband's relatives were very tolerant of my sometimes forgetful lack of deference. For an Indian woman, however, such lapses would be much more serious and her relations with her husband's elder and younger brothers would be much more strictly differentiated. Indeed, were I an Indian woman, out of respect for the principle of hierarchy, I would probably have to cover my hair, if not my face, in the presence of both my father-in-law and my husband's elder brother.

A second principle that complicates the Indian kinship system from the point of view of a Westerner is the differentiation of kin according to which side of the family, male or female, the relationship is based on. This principle, bifurcation, is absent in English kinship terminology. In North India, the father's brothers and the mother's brothers are called by different terms, as are the father's and mother's parents: *dadi* and *dada* are the "grandparents" on the

(*continued*)

father's side, and *nani* and *nana* are the "grandparents" on the mother's side. These terminological distinctions reflect the Indian principle of respect and formality that is associated more with the male side of the family and the more open show of affection permitted with the maternal side of the family.

In India, social interaction with one's mother's parents is very different from that with one's father's parents also because, ideally, the Indian household is based on the patrilineal joint family, composed of a man, his brothers, his father, and his sons. Thus, a son interacts with his father's parents on an everyday basis, whereas his mother's parents will live some distance away. Visiting his mother's parents has more of the nature of an exciting pleasure trip, and

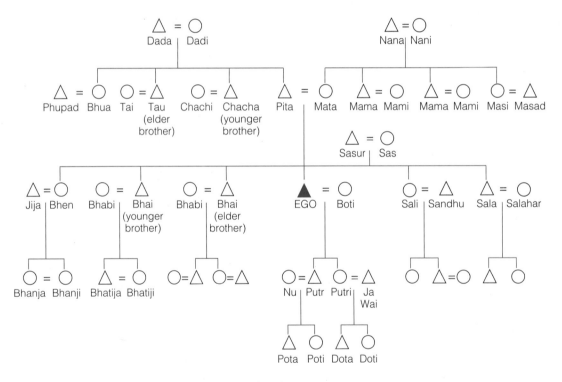

Kinship Classification in North India

Note: There is no term for a man's nieces and nephews on wife's side. They are referred to descriptively as wife's sister's daughters or sons. Not shown on this diagram are the terms a wife uses for her husband's sister, her husband's sister's husband, her husband's elder brother, his wife, her husband's younger brother, and his wife, which adds six terms to the thirty-nine used by EGO.

increased fondness and absence of conflict seem to come with distance. In addition, because the parents of a daughter are expected to give gifts, both to her and to her husband, when she visits, this extends to her children, who thus have an additional reason to look forward to such visits.

The patrilineal joint family structure also accounts for another terminological difference between India and the United States, in this case, their grouping together terminologically kin that we distinguish. In order to highlight the importance of the nuclear family in the United States, our kinship system distinguishes between our siblings (brothers and sisters) and our cousins, both of

(*continued*)

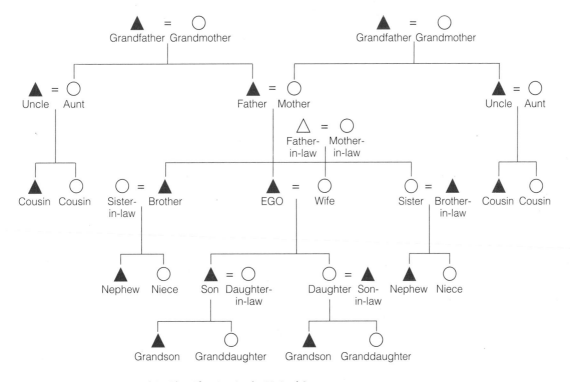

Kinship Classification in the United States

which are collateral relations. But in India, this distinction is not made. There is no word for cousin, and what we call cousins they refer to by the terms for "brother" and "sister."

The Indian principle of hierarchy turns up again in the higher status accorded the family of the husband relative to that of the wife. This status inequality is reflected in a number of ways in Indian kinship terminology and behavior. For example, in the terminological distinction between Ego's wife's brother (*sala*) and his sister's husband (*jija*), both relations are called "brother-in-law" in the English system, reflecting the general equality in North America of the husband's and wife's sides of the family. In India, a man's sister's husband is in a higher position relative to him than is his wife's brother. Correspondingly, a sister's husband is treated with great respect, while a wife's brother may be treated more ambivalently and may be the target of jokes. The behavioral expectations of this unequal relationship between the bride's and groom's families extend even further. When my husband's sister's husband's sister's husband first visited our home, we treated him with the extra respect due to a man who had taken a "daughter" from our family (the "daughter" referring to both my husband's sister and her husband's sister).

A last example I use to illustrate the importance of kinship terminology in regulating behavior involves the ritual role that different relatives take in life-cycle ceremonies, a form of behavior familiar in the United States. For example, in the United States, a woman's father accompanies her down the aisle when she marries. In India, the marriage ceremony is much more complex. Each part of the ceremony involves a person in a specific kinship relation to the groom or bride, reflecting all of the important principles by which kin are classified there: relative age, lineality, collaterality, bifurcation, gender, generation, consanguineality, and affinity. Thus, when my husband's sister's son got married, my husband, as the brother of the groom's mother, tied the turban on the groom. However, when my husband's sister's daughter marries, he, as the mother's brother, will give her the ivory and red bangle bracelets that she will wear for one year, and the special piece of red cloth that is used in the marriage ceremony. These rituals are concrete symbolic expressions of the continuing warmth and support a girl can expect to find among her mother's male kin, a very important expectation in a culture where a woman is otherwise separated from her own family and incorporated into her husband's joint family household. This ritual role of the mother's brother in an Indian marriage ceremony also symbolizes the very important kinship tie in India between brother and sister, which is ritually affirmed every year. These rituals, like other aspects of culture involving kinship, reflect the underlying values of a society.

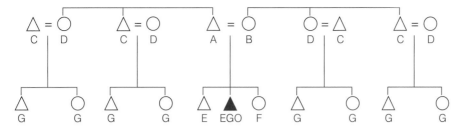

FIGURE 10.5 Eskimo kinship terminology.

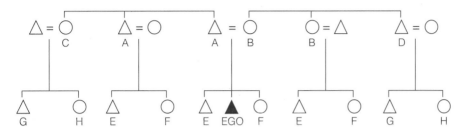

FIGURE 10.6 Iroquois kinship terminology.

an individual may choose which descent group he or she wishes to belong to and will live with after marriage. By using the same terms for parents and their siblings, a closeness is established with a large number of relatives in the ascending generation, allowing a wide choice for Ego in deciding which group to affiliate and live with.

ESKIMO The Eskimo terminology is correlated with bilateral descent. It is found among hunting and gathering peoples and also in our own society. The Eskimo system emphasizes the unit of the nuclear family by using terms for its members (mother, father, sister, brother, daughter, son) that are not used for any other kin. Outside the nuclear family, many kinds of relatives that are distinguished in other systems are lumped together. We have already given the examples of aunt and uncle. Similarly, all children of our kin in the parental generation are called cousins, no matter what their sex or who the linking relative is. The Eskimo system singles out the biologically closest group of relations (the nuclear family) and treats more distant kin more or less equally (Figure 10.5).

IROQUOIS The Iroquois system is associated with matrilineal or double descent and emphasizes the importance of unilineal descent groups. In this system, the same term is used for mother and mother's sister, and a common term also applies to father and father's brother. Parallel cousins are referred to by the same terms as those for brother and sister. Father's sister and mother's brother are distinguished from other kin, as are the children of father's sister and mother's brother (Ego's cross cousins) (Figure 10.6).

OMAHA The Omaha system is found among patrilineal peoples, including the native American group of that name. In this system, the same term is used for father and father's brother and for mother and mother's sister. Parallel cousins are equated with siblings, but cross cousins are referred to by a separate term. A man refers to his brother's children by the same terms he applies to his own children, but he refers to his sister's children by different terms. These terms are extended to all relations who are classified as Ego's brothers and sisters (Figure 10.7). In this system, there is a merging of generations

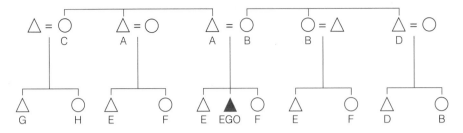

FIGURE 10.7 Omaha kinship terminology.

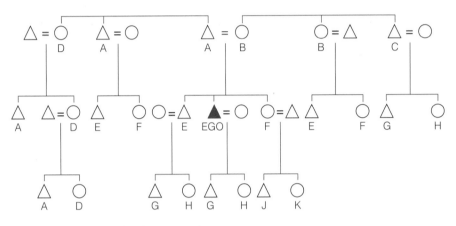

FIGURE 10.8 Crow kinship terminology.

on the mother's side. All men who are members of Ego's mother's patrilineage will be referred to as "mother's brother" regardless of their age or generational relationship to Ego. Thus, the term applied to mother's brother is also applied to the son of mother's brother.

This generational merging is not applied to relations on the father's side. Although father and his brothers are referred to by the same term, this does not extend to the descending generation. The differences in terminology as applied to the father's patrilineal and the mother's patrilineal group reflect the different position of Ego in relation to these kin. Generational differences are important on the father's side, because members of the ascending generation are likely to have some authority over Ego (as his father does) and be treated differently than patrilineage members of Ego's own generation. The mother's patrilineage is relatively

unimportant to Ego in this system, so this is reflected in lumping them all together in the terminology.

CROW   The Crow system, named for the Crow Indians of North America, is the matrilineal equivalent of the Omaha system. This means that the relations on the male side (Ego's father's matrilineage) will be lumped together, whereas generational differences will be recognized in the mother's matrilineal group (Figure 10.8). In both the Omaha and Crow systems, the overriding importance of unilineality leads to the subordination of other principles of classifying kin, such as relative age or generation.

SUDANESE   The most descriptive terminology systems are sometimes called Sudanese systems, after the groups in Africa, primarily in Ethiopia, that use them. The terminological

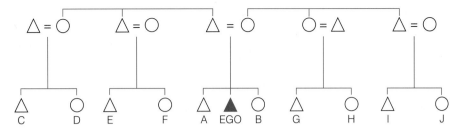

FIGURE 10.9 Sudanese kinship terminology.

types included here use different terms for practically every relative — siblings, paternal parallel cousins, maternal parallel cousins, paternal cross cousins, and maternal cross cousins. Ego refers to his or her parents by distinct terms and uses separate terms for father's brother, father's sister, mother's sister, and mother's brother (Figure 10.9). Although most groups using this system tend to be patrilineal, there is also evidence of ambilineality. This distinguishes these kinship systems from other patrilineal systems described here and may account for this distinctive and rare type of terminology.

The great variety in kinship terminologies calls attention to the fact with which we began this chapter: Kinship systems reflect social relationships and are not based simply on biological relations between people. Kinship classification systems are part of the totality of a kinship system. Each type of classification just described emphasizes the most important kinship groupings and relationships in the societies in which it is found. Thus, the Eskimo system emphasizes the importance of the nuclear family, setting it apart from the more distant relations on the maternal and paternal sides. The Iroquois, Omaha, and Crow systems, found in unilineal societies, emphasize the importance of lineage and clan. In the Hawaiian system, the simplicity of terms leaves the way open for flexibility in choosing one's descent group. At the other extreme, the Sudanese system, with its highly descriptive terminology, may in fact have the same function. In making sense out of kinship, including our own system, anthropol-ogists attempt to understand the relationship between terminologies, rules of descent, and the formation of groups based on kinship and the particular ecological, economic, and political conditions under which different kinship systems emerge.

Nonkin Forms of Association

Although kinship is of great importance in structuring social relations and as a basis for forming groups in all societies, other principles of association are also important. Here we will look at groups and relationships that are not based on kinship but rather on other social principles.

Groups Based on Age

All societies recognize at least three social categories based on age: children, adults, and the elderly. Each category has its own role, and in some societies, groups based on age are extremely important. Age as a basis of social groups reaches its most elaborate development among some cultures in Africa. Some of these societies are (partly) organized through **age grades,** that is, categories of persons who fall within a particular, culturally distinguished age range. In societies that contain **age sets,** a group of persons of similar age and sex move through some or all of life's stages together. Age-set organization has been described for a variety of cultures in Africa, Melanesia, South America,

Taiwan, and the North American Great Plains. Age sets cross-cut kinship ties and are the basis for important social bonds. Many of these age-based groups are made up of males and have military and political functions.

The occurrence of age sets in some kinds of societies, but not others, has raised questions about their functions. It would appear from some cross-cultural studies that age sets develop in societies which have frequent warfare and nonstable local groups. Men cannot rely on their kin as allies in warfare because their kin may not be nearby. Age sets provide a more dependable source of allies (Ritter 1980).

Although in our society age is not as important a principle of organization as in the societies just described, age is becoming a more important basis of association here, as there are more older people, living to more advanced ages, whose incomes permit them to build a life-style congenial to their stage of life. Indeed, even American courts have recognized the relevance of age as a principle of social organization and residence, and they have in some cases upheld the rights of older people to live in communities that exclude people because of (their younger) age (Norgren and Nanda 1988: 213–15).

Association Based on Sex

Sex — that is, being male or female — provides an obvious basis for solidarity. In some societies sex is a very important principle upon which associations are formed. Most anthropological attention has been paid to male associations, probably because more societies have such groups than have comparable ones for females. Age grading, for example, is largely a male phenomenon, with women apparently "tacked on" through marriage.

In Melanesia, Australia, and among some South American Indian groups, men's associations and cults are prominent in social and religious life. Adolescent boys are initiated into the men's cult and thereafter spend most of their lives in the men's house, only visiting their wives, who live with the children in their own huts in the village. These men's cults are closed to women and surrounded by great secrecy. The men's house itself is usually the most imposing structure in the village, and in or near it are kept the sacred musical instruments and paraphernalia of the cult. The musical instruments, which are often flutelike (shaped like the male genitals), are the symbolic expressions of male dominance and male solidarity in opposition to women. Often, and especially in Australia, these cults are associated with circumcision rites for newly initiated boys, after which the initiates are considered men and introduced to the secrets of the cult. Frequently associated with these cults is a mythology of how the cults came into being and an "explanation" of why women are not allowed in them. These myths may also "explain" why women are considered socially inferior to men and why men and women have different roles in these societies.

Some social scientists give psychological interpretations of these cults. The cults are viewed as unconscious defenses against the males' recognition of their own vulnerability in relation to women. Men, after all, are born of women and nurtured by them; only women have the creative power of childbirth. Many of the rituals associated with men's cults appear to be reenactments of childbirth. The very secrecy with which men's cults are surrounded, the phallic shape of the musical instruments, and the associated mythology seem to make sense as an expression of the ambivalence men have toward women, who give them life and from whom they must ultimately break away if they are to become truly men (Bettelheim 1962; Murphy and Murphy 1974). The solidarity of women in these societies is not formalized in cults or associations but is based on the cooperation of domestic life and strong interpersonal bonds among female kin.

In many native American societies, particularly those of the Great Plains, associations based on sex were prominent. Some of these associations were age graded, others were not. Some of them were ritual cults that had the function of controlling nature and the healing of mind and body. These cults consisted of both

A men's house in Pohnpei, Micronesia. In societies with men's cults, the men's house is often the most imposing structure in the village. (Raymond Kennedy)

priests and doctors, and they were always concerned with the physical and mental well-being of the tribespeople. The cults were associated, like much else in Plains Indian life, with visions and were said to originate in a vision in the form of an animal "helper," which the vision seeker then used for the benefit of the tribe. The membership of the cults was made up of persons who had dreamed of the same objects, which might be stars, stones, animals, or birds. The dream, or vision, endowed the dreamer with a supernatural power that could be put to use for the tribe through the performance of rituals and medicine practices.

Another kind of association among Plains tribes was the warrior society, whose primary functions were defending the tribe and policing actions within the tribe. An example of this kind of society was the Black Soldiers Society among the Blackfoot. All such societies had

their special regalia and costumes: Each Black Soldier wore a narrow headband made of wolf skin with an upright tail feather attached to each side of it, plus wolf-skin anklets and wristbands. His entire body was painted red, and wide black bands were drawn across the forehead and chin. Two vertical black lines representing wolf's teeth were painted on his cheeks. Each man carried a long staff painted red, to which strips of wolf skin were attached. The leader also wore a wolf skin draped across his shoulders, and he carried a wooden club.

The Black Soldiers Society often served as camp police during the large annual encampments of the tribe. The society members imposed severe sanctions on their own members who failed in their responsibilities to the society. For example, if a member were absent from a ceremony, the other members attacked and destroyed his tipi and possessions. The Black

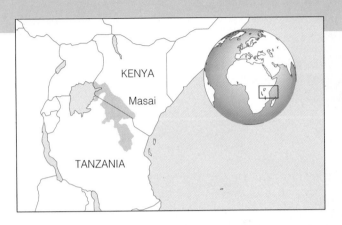

Male age sets are important among the Maasai, an East African herding people living in Kenya and Tanzania. Unlike females, who move through their life stages individually as lovers, wives, and mothers, a traditional Maasai male follows a well-ordered progression through a series of age grades in groups. The entry into each stage requires a formalized rite of passage, and the preparation of and participation in these rituals are at the heart of Maasai culture.

Among the Maasai today, a new age set is open for recruitment every fourteen years. After childhood, boys are initiated into the warrior stage, which is the highlight of a Maasai male's life and lasts about fifteen years. The warriors then graduate, in another ceremony, to a less active status during which they can marry. Finally, about twenty years after the age set was formed, and another age set created, the age set retires to elderhood in another great ceremony. The sequence of ceremonies serves to bring together Maasai from different sections of the tribe periodically, renewing their shared identity, sense of unity, and cooperation and confirming a system of leadership under age-set spokesmen. This lends political coherence to a people who live dispersed from each other and have no centralized government.

Age organization provides an ethic of behavior for the Maasai. Age mates must provide hospitality to one another, as when a visitor to a village is presented to the home of a member of the same age set, where he is given food and shelter. If desired by both parties, sharing may even extend to the favors of an age mate's wife. This relation is not considered adultery because the woman is considered to have "married the age set." The relations between members of an age set are warm and intimate, and age mates are free to tease and compete with each other and even fight. This contrasts with the relations of respect due from members of an age set to their sponsors, who are two age sets senior to them. In this relationship, obedience is required and behavior or speech that might suggest intimacy must be avoided. Sexual relations with sponsors' wives, who are like mothers, and with the daughters of age mates (who are like one's own daughters) are strictly forbidden.

The central focus of the Maasai age-set system is the warrior stage, and warriorhood is a central theme in Maasai culture. As warriors (literally, the circumcised), young men enjoy certain privileges and have certain obligations.

A Maasai senior warrior. (United Nations)

They are relieved from daily herding activities, which occupied them as uninitiated boys, and are paired with cohorts of uninitiated girls with whom they
may have sexual relations (a warrior is forbidden to have sexual relations with
an initiated girl). Warriors are forbidden to eat meat that has been seen by
mature, initiated women or to drink milk outside the presence of their age
mates. These restrictions underline the solidarity of warriors and their social
separation from normal domestic life, because they spend much of their time in
meat camp retreats or warrior villages and they live and travel in groups.

Warriorhood is a period of training, of gaining social, political, and military skills, and of forming cohesive units traditionally geared to cattle raiding
or warfare. Much time is spent on bodily adornment, including the fixing of the
elaborate hairstyles that Maasai warriors wear. There are many opportunities

(*continued*)

for singing and dancing, group praise for bravery, and displays of trophies of the hunt and of military achievements. Young boys (naturally enough) are eager to become warriors, and warriors (also naturally enough) are not eager to give up this status that brings them so much prestige.

But ultimately, the warriors must pass on to the next age grade, which involves the responsibilities of getting married and building up one's cattle herds. It may also be that after so many years of warriorhood, they grow tired of the mobile life, isolated habitation, male companionship, and relations with girls who cannot become their wives. As warriors pass into the next age grade, marriage approaches and there is a gradual withdrawal from age-set life and increasing involvement in herding and domestic family life.

In the contemporary world, the Maasai are under great pressure to change, and some of the restrictions of the Kenyan and Tanzanian governments have particularly undermined age-set organization. The British colonial governments of Kenya and Tanzania (then Tanganyika) outlawed Maasai cattle raiding, an important warrior activity, and tried to stifle the initiation ceremonies. Traditionally, the Maasai test of manhood was the killing of a lion, which is now outlawed by both the Kenyan and the Tanzanian governments. The *manyatta*, or traditional warrior villages, are now also forbidden, and this has left the warriors without a place to live, as they cannot live with their mothers and they do not yet have wives.

Some Maasai of the warrior age grade have gotten jobs in cities, while others live off the land or steal cattle. The governmental compulsory education laws, with which the Maasai long resisted complying, now offer some alternative opportunities for both Maasai males and females. The Maasai appear to have accepted the necessity of formal schooling, which brings its own age grading oriented to a new set of values; this acceptance is their acknowledgment that they no longer live in a traditional world. In the face of the drastic reduction of land available to the Maasai for herding their cattle, and the laws undermining their social organization, the Maasai continue to celebrate their culture. Although without land and without cattle there will be no Maasai, Tepilit Ole Saitoti, in his autobiography, *The Worlds of a Maasai Warrior* (1986), is confident that if change can come gradually, rather than abruptly, the Maasai will adapt and survive.

Adapted from "Introduction" by John G. Galaty, in Tepilit Ole Saitoti, The Worlds of a Maasai Warrior *(New York: Random House, 1986), pp. xiv–xxi.*

A drawing by Jesse Cornplanter of the False Face Society among the Iroquois. Such associations had important curing, religious, and political functions among many native American peoples. (Courtesy of Museum of the American Indian, Heye Foundation)

Soldiers knew that to achieve their best results as camp police they had to set a high standard among themselves, so that people would understand their orders were not to be taken lightly.

While most of the sex-based societies among native Americans were for men, a few also existed for women, and in some cases women could join men's societies. Among the several types of women's societies were the cult groups made up of women whose dreams led to participation in rituals connected with buffaloes and other animals, and the raising of crops, aimed at fertility and abundance. For example, among the Gros Ventre there was a Buffalo Cow Society only for women. Its ceremony was performed when a member dreamed of the dance or pledged to perform it as part of a vow for an ill relative. When the sick person recovered, the ritual was performed (under the guidance, one must add, of an old man who was a ritual leader). The women dressed in various parts of the buffalo — skin, horns, etc. — and in dancing

they did not lift their feet but swayed from side to side to imitate the movement of a buffalo. At one point, the women, imitating a herd of buffalo, went to the river and drank. Here, a man lay in wait for them with a gun. They acted afraid, like buffaloes do, but the hunter always managed to "kill" one of the buffaloes. As the woman fell to the ground, the tribe was assured of good hunting for the season (Mails 1973).

In West Africa, many kinds of associations with important social functions existed for both males and females. Two of the most well documented of these societies are the Poro and the Sande, which are the male and female associations among the Kpelle of Liberia and many other tribes of that region. Both societies had the initiation of the young as one of their primary purposes, but they had many other functions as well. The Poro (male) society had important political functions beyond the local community, and it extends even today into national politics. Although Sande power was more limited, there was in the past a female head of the entire tribal Sande. In Sierra Leone, where the Sande organization includes over 90 percent of rural women, men are discouraged from marrying uninitiated women. The Sande organization has power through its transformation of girls into marriageable women. Madam Yoko, a woman who became very powerful in Sierra Leone in the late nineteenth century, effectively utilized her role within the Sande organization to build the political network on which her leadership was based. Sande dancers achieve great prestige, and Madam Yoko was an outstanding dancer. She also sponsored the initiation of many girls into Sande and arranged marriages for them in ways that would advance her own political career. Even today, women in Africa use the Sande organization to establish alliances and further their political careers (Hoffer 1974).

In small and technologically simple societies, associations such as I have been describing appear to be organized for recreation and the distinction of rank. They also may have religious functions. In some cases, these societies are for healing; only individuals who have recovered from serious illness can become members and are then called upon to practice their arts on others. In tribal societies, associations that go beyond kinship as a basis for membership have important political functions. Among the Plains Indians, they keep the peace during communal hunts and also provide entertainment. In other cases, associations resolve disputes, protect members against both supernatural and human harm, and integrate different segments of a tribe beyond the local level. The presence of societies in West Africa, for example, corresponds with an absence of age-group organizations; where one is absent, the other fulfills similar political and social functions. Many of these associations are based on ascribed statuses such as sex or age, but others are voluntary, and still others require certain achievements for membership. It is under conditions of modernization and urbanization that voluntary associations increase dramatically and play important roles in social change.

Summary

1. Kinship systems are cultural creations that define and organize relatives by blood and marriage. A kinship system includes the kinds of groups based on kinship and the system of terms used to classify different kin.

2. The functions of kinship systems are to provide continuity between generations and to define a group of people who can depend on one another for mutual aid.

3. In traditional societies, kinship is the most important basis of social organization. This contrasts with industrial societies, in which principles of social organization, such as citizenship, social class, and common interests, become more important than kinship.

4. In many societies, descent is important in the formation of corporate social groups. In societies with a unilineal rule of descent, descent-group membership is based on either the male or female line. Unilineal systems are found among pastoral and horticultural societies.

5. A lineage is a group of kin whose members can trace their descent through a common ancestor. A clan is a group whose members believe they have a common ancestor but cannot trace the relationship genealogically. Lineages tend to have domestic functions, clans to have political and religious functions. Both lineages and clans are important in regulating marriage.

6. In patrilineal systems, a man's children belong to his lineage, as do the children of his sons but not of his daughters. Husbands have control over wives and children, and marriage is surrounded by strong sanctions.

7. In matrilineal systems, a woman's children belong to her lineage, not that of their father. The mother's brother has authority over his sister's children, and relations between husband and wife are more fragile than in patrilineal societies.

8. Patrilineality grows out of patrilocality, which is based on the common economic interests of brothers. Matrilineality grows out of matrilocality, which arises under special circumstances; when these conditions disappear, the kinship system tends to change.

9. In systems of double descent, Ego belongs to both the patrilineage of the father and the matrilineage of the mother. Each group functions in different social contexts. The Yako of Nigeria have a system of double descent.

10. In bilateral systems, Ego is equally related to mother's and father's kin. A bilateral rule of descent results in the formation of kindreds, which are Ego-centered kinship networks, rather than a permanent group of kin. Bilateral kinship is found predominantly among foragers and in modern industrialized states.

11. Kinship terminology groups together and distinguishes relatives according to various principles such as generation, relative age, lineality or collaterality, sex, consanguinity or affinity, bifurcation, and sex of the linking relative. Different societies may use all or some of these principles in classifying kin. A comparison of kinship terminology in North India and the United States illustrates these differences.

12. The six types of kinship classification systems defined by anthropologists are the Hawaiian, Eskimo, Iroquois, Omaha, Crow, and Sudanese. Each reflects the particular kinship group that is most important in the society.

13. Although kinship groups dominate in most structurally simple societies, other forms of association are also found. Some of the nonkin groups in tribal societies are based on age. One example is the age-set system of the Maasai.

14. Groups based on sex may also be important. In many parts of Melanesia and South America, men spend most of their time in association with other men and live in a special men's house. In many native American societies, both men's and women's associations are found, having the functions of keeping social order and caring for the physical and mental well-being of the tribe. In West Africa, men's and women's associations are important in religious, political, and social life.

Suggested Readings

Bohannan, P., and Middleton, J., eds.
1968   *Kinship and Social Organization*. Garden City, N.Y.: The Natural History Press.

Classic articles on kinship and kinship terminology.

di Leonardo, Micaela
1984   *The Varieties of Ethnic Experience: Kinship, Class, and Gender among California Italian-Americans*. Ithaca: Cornell University Press. A lively account of ethnicity that emphasizes variability in ethnic experience among different social classes, and between women and men. Kinship and family are prominently discussed from the perspective of individual life histories and in the context of regional, national, and global change.

Pasternak, Burton
1976   *Introduction to Kinship and Social Organization*. Englewood Cliffs, N.J.: Prentice-Hall. Just what it says—a good introduction for the beginning student.

Schneider, David M.
1968   *American Kinship: A Cultural Account*. Englewood Cliffs, N.J.: Prentice-Hall. A look at kinship in the United States and what it suggests about our culture.

Schneider, David M., and Gough, Kathleen, eds.
1961   *Matrilineal Kinship*. Berkeley: University of California Press. An examination of a variety of matrilineal systems and how matrilineality may be related to subsistence, productivity, and political organization.

Trawick, Margaret
1990   *Notes on Love in a Tamil Family*. Berkeley: University of California Press. A sensitive, insightful, and skillful interweaving of the author's own life situation with an ethnography of Tamil (Indian) family relationships. This book gives both a picture of culturally patterned relationships and a vivid experience of the individuals in the family.

Wilson, Monica
1963   *Good Company: A Study of Nyakyusa Age-Villages*. Boston: Beacon Press (first publ. 1951). An interesting study of an African society with an unusual form of social organization.

Social Ranking and Stratification

Are there any societies in which all people are equal?

What are the differences between a class and a caste system?

What are the characteristics of the American social-stratification system?

What is the relation between race, ethnicity, and social stratification?

Tally and I were in the Carry-out. It was summer, Tally's peak earning season as a cement finisher, a semiskilled job a cut or so above that of the unskilled laborer. His take-home pay was well over a hundred dollars for those weeks — "a lot of bread." But for Tally, bread was not enough.

"You know that boy came in last night? I ought to be in his place . . . dressed nice, going to [night] school, got a good job."

"He's no better off than you, Tally. You make more than he does."

"It's not the money. It's position, I guess. When he finish school he gonna be a supervisor. People respect him. . . . Thinking about people with position and education gives me a feeling right here" [pressing his fingers into the pit of his stomach].

"You're educated, too. You have a skill, a trade. You're a cement finisher. You can make a building, pour a sidewalk."

"That's different. Look, can anybody do your job? Well, in one week I can teach you cement finishing. Anybody can do what I'm doing. You remember at the courthouse, when you and the lawyer was talking in the hall? You remember? I just stood there listening. I didn't say a word. You know why? 'Cause I didn't even know what you was talking about. That's happened to me a lot."

"Hell, you're nothing special. That happens to everybody. Nobody knows everything. One man is a doctor, so he talks about surgery. Another man is a teacher, so he talks about books. But doctors and teachers don't know anything about concrete. You're a cement finisher and that's your specialty."

"Maybe so, but when was the last time you saw anybody standing around talking about concrete?"

From Elliot Liebow, Tally's Corner *(Boston: Little, Brown, 1967), p. 61.*

One important difference in the way societies are organized is the degree to which individuals within the society have equal access to prestige, power, and the resources necessary to sustain life. Although it is clear that not all human beings are equally endowed with talents, physical attractiveness, and skill, not all societies formally recognize this inequality. In approaching this aspect of social organization, anthropologists have distinguished three basic types of societies: egalitarian societies, rank societies, and stratified societies. Each of these three principles of social organization has its own economic and political organization. The economies of egalitarian societies are primarily organized through reciprocity, although some have very active trading systems and some do have the kind of redistribution through a central figure that is normally associated with chieftainships. The economies of rank societies are organized primarily through redistribution and those of stratified societies through market exchange. Similarly, as we will see in Chapter 12, egalitarian societies have little specialization of political roles; rank societies are characterized by chiefs as the ruling powers; and stratified societies are correlated with a particular kind of political organization known as the state. Although for some purposes, economics, social status systems, and politics can be separated, they are in fact all interrelated.

Egalitarian Societies

In **egalitarian societies,** no individual or group has more access to resources, power, or prestige than does any other. This does not mean that in such societies all members have equal prestige. In addition to age and sex differences, individual differences in skill at a variety of tasks will always be recognized. Some individuals are better hunters; others are regarded as more skilled at a craft; others are singled out for their healing ability; still others are acknowledged as knowing more or speaking in a more expressive manner than does the ordinary person. In an egalitarian society, however, no individual, no matter how high or low in esteem in the group, is denied the right to make a living or is subject to the control or exploitation of others. Furthermore, whatever prestige an individual gains on the basis of ability is not transferable to his or her heirs or relatives. There is no fixed number of positions that are ranked and for which individuals must compete. The prestige attached to being a good hunter, for example, will go to as many good hunters as there are in the group.

Hunting and gathering societies are characteristically egalitarian. Factors preventing any permanent and unequal distribution of wealth are the lack of land ownership; the low technological level, which inhibits storing up large quantities of food; the need for mobility, which inhibits the accumulation of material goods; and the obligation to share food. The activity of hunting and foraging itself does not require a permanent leader, and food-getting activities are often carried out individually or in groups in which individuals are organized as equal, cooperating members. Even when hunting societies have a headman, this position carries no real power or economic advantage and is not inherited or inheritable. But not all foraging societies are equally egalitarian. Among some Inuit groups, for example, differences in wealth did develop. In groups where whaling was

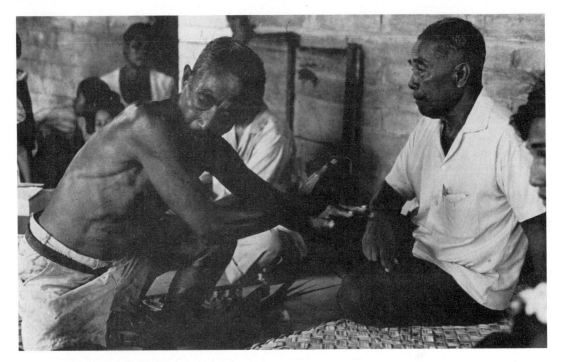

In rank societies, the chief is a source of supernatural power. Here, a chief on the island of Pohnpei, Micronesia, is being served kava, a ceremonial drink. The server's head is turned away, as no one may look directly at the chief. (Raymond Kennedy)

important, a successful whaler, who also owned the whaling boats, harpoons, and lines, accumulated more wealth than others did and often distributed it in such a way as to control the less successful men. The fishing groups along the Northwest Coast of America were not egalitarian at all; in fact, they exhibited a higher degree of ranking than did many horticultural societies.

Rank Societies

In **rank societies,** there are formal differences in prestige but no important restrictions on access to basic resources. There is an inherited position of chief, and his prestige is linked to the redistribution of goods, frequently in the form of competitive feasts and religious cere-monies. But although chiefs in such societies may have great prestige and certain privileges, they do not accumulate food and goods for their own use. Their basic standard of living does not differ from that of the ordinary members of the society. Rank societies have not only the high-prestige position of chief but also ranking of kin groups. Kin groups closest to the chief genealogically have the most prestige, and in some rank societies order of birth is important as a criterion of social status.

Rank societies are mainly found among cultivators and herders, though simple ranking also exists among some hunting groups. The most complex ranking systems were found in Polynesia and among indigenous societies of the Northwest Coast of America. These societies consisted of a series of individual positions, all ranked in order; no two individuals were precisely equal. Among the Nootka, rights to man-

Facial and body designs are an important means of artistic expression and indications of social status in many societies. Facial tatooing was particularly important in denoting rank in traditional Maori (New Zealand) culture. (Serena Nanda)

age all economic resources, such as fishing, hunting, and gathering grounds, were held by individuals, although a relative could not be prevented from using them. Inheritance of these rights passed only through the line of the eldest sons. The same was true for the office of chief. The line that went through lesser sons was ranked lower than that of eldest sons, and these differences in rank were typically expressed in terms of wealth. This wealth consisted only partly of important economic resources; it was also symbolic, as in the right to use special names, perform certain ceremonial functions, sponsor potlatches, and wear certain items of clothing and decoration. Only chiefs, for example, were allowed to wear abalone shell jewelry and sea otter fur on their robes. The right of directing the use of economic re-

sources supported the symbolic ranking system. As manager, a chief of a kin group received resources that formally acknowledged his rank — the first of the salmon catch, the best parts of sea mammals that had been killed, blankets, and furs. It was from this source that a chief could sponsor a potlatch at which most of these goods were given away.

A similar ranking system existed in Tahiti, although that society could be divided into the Ari'i, who were the immediate families of the chiefs of the most important lineages in the larger districts; the Ra'atira, who were the heads of less important lineages and their families; and the Manahune, which included the remainder of the population. Social rank in Tahiti had an economic, political, and religious aspect. Mana, a spiritual power, was possessed by all individuals, but in different degrees depending on rank. The Ari'i had the most mana because they were closest to the ancestral gods from which mana comes. An elaborate body of taboos separated those with more mana from those with less and also regulated social relations between individuals in the three ranks. Higher-ranked people could not eat with those of lower rank; and because men had higher rank than women and children, they could not eat with them. The highest-ranking Ari'i was so sacred that anything he touched became poison for those below him. Thus, in some Polynesian islands, the highest chief was kept completely away from other people and even used a special vocabulary that no one else was allowed to use.

Rank societies, then, are organized by kinship. Rank is based on position (birth order and genealogical closeness to the chief) within the kinship system, and membership in the kinship group entitles each individual to access to basic resources. No one group of people is exploited in order to maintain a ruling class exempt from food production. Even in ranked societies where slaves existed, they were actually individuals attached to wealthier families and not an exploited class on which the economy depended. In these ways, rank societies are distinguished from societies with social stratification. The ethnography on the Kapauku, in Chapter 8, gives an example of the relationship between wealth and rank in a nonstratified society.

Stratified Societies

A **stratified society** has formal, permanent social and economic inequality. Some individuals and groups (over and above those defined by age and sex) are denied access to the basic resources necessary for survival and well-being. Stratified societies have relatively permanent and wide differences between groups in terms of standard of living, security, prestige, political power, and opportunity to fulfill one's potential in society. These major dimensions of **social stratification** are usually analyzed in terms of power, wealth, and prestige. Anthropologists are interested in studying the relationships among these dimensions within a society and in comparing stratification systems in different cultures.

One important distinction that is made in comparing systems of social stratification is whether they are based on ascription or achievement. In a stratification system in which ascription is important, an individual's status, or position in the system, is mainly determined by birth. **Ascribed statuses** are those social positions to which an individual is born. Sex, race, and ethnic group are examples of ascribed statuses in the United States. Kinship group and caste membership are other examples of ascribed statuses. In a stratification system based on achievement, an individual's position is largely determined by his or her own efforts. **Achieved statuses** are those an individual chooses or achieves on his or her own. Wife, doctor, criminal, and artist are examples of achieved statuses in the United States. In simple societies most statuses are ascribed, although in some of them individual achievement plays an important role, and there are some opportunities for moving up in society through a combination of skill and hard work.

Although different systems of social stratification can be described as based primarily on ascription (closed systems) or achievement (open systems), most societies contain both. Anthropologists are interested in the many kinds of statuses, both ascribed and achieved, and the ways in which individuals are chosen to fill social positions.

The stratification system in the United States includes elements of both ascribed and achieved status. Color is an ascribed status, which affects an individual's placement in the system no matter what other status he or she *achieves*. The position of shoeshine man is an achieved status that places an individual low in our class hierarchy. (Serena Nanda)

Power, Wealth, and Prestige

Power is the ability to produce intended effects on oneself, on other human beings, and on situations. Another way of defining power is as the control of access to resources; that is, anything one wants, needs, or thinks one needs. Power thus means the ability to make and carry out decisions affecting one's own life, to control the behavior of other human beings, and to transform objects or resources. Power used with the consent of the members of a society is called **authority** and is legitimate. Power may also be illegitimate, exercised without the approval of society. The powerful individuals or groups in a society are best able to act on their perceptions of where their self-interest lies. In stratified societies, this frequently means at the expense of the goals of other individuals and groups. From an anthropological standpoint, our interest is in knowing who has the power in a society, through what channels it is exercised, and what its sources are. As one example, we might compare power in the United States as it rests with corporation presidents, elected public officials, movie stars, or the heads of organized crime families. From a cross-cultural perspective, we might compare the sources and management of power of an American president, a Bantu chief, and the head of the Communist party in the People's Republic of China.

Wealth as an aspect of social stratification is the accumulation of material resources, or access to the means of producing these resources. Many social scientists believe that wealth is the most important aspect of social stratification and the foundation on which the other dimensions, such as power and prestige, rest. For Karl Marx and those who follow his thinking, the basic principle of social organization is the system by which resources are produced and allocated to provide for the satisfaction of basic human needs. Marx differentiated between two main strata in society: the capitalists, who own the means of production, and the workers, who are employed by others. According to Marx, it is this relationship to the means of production that is important in determining not only how much power and prestige one has but also one's chances to survive. One need not be a Marxist to see the obvious ways in which wealth can translate into power. Rich men are

more likely to run for political office and win than others, and wealthy capitalists can influence government in ways that are in their own self-interest.

Prestige, or social honor, is a third dimension of social stratification. Complex societies, which are occupationally specialized, contain a number of different positions that are ranked high or low in relation to one another. Occupations are ranked somewhat differently in different societies. We will see, when we look at the Hindu caste system, that one criterion for ranking occupations in India has to do with the level of ritual purity or pollution. Although this exact concept does not exist in the United States, we do have the idea of a "dirty job" ranked lower than jobs that are not dirty. Generally speaking, white-collar occupations carry more prestige than do blue-collar occupations. As socioeconomic conditions change, the value system that supports a particular system of prestige will also change. Different occupations may gain or lose prestige. In ancient China, for example, the intellectual had high status; in modern China, an attempt is being made to raise the prestige of the worker, and the once highly valued traditional Confucian intellectual is now regarded as a parasite.

In the dialogue that opens this chapter, between Elliot Liebow, an anthropologist, and Tally, an African-American man in Washington, D.C., Tally notes that "bread is not enough" and that a man's pride in his work is also important. That pride is related to the prestige which the occupation has in society. In his book, Liebow gives an interpretation of unemployment among lower-class African-American males that contradicts the popular explanation that they don't work because they are "lazy." Liebow shows that it is not unwillingness to work that explains high male unemployment but rather a combination of the exploitation of these men when they do find work, the lack of self-esteem that stops them from taking work opportunities, and the culture of the street-corner group, which gives emotional support only for failure.

In the United States, a person is "worth" what he or she is paid. The self-worth of the street-corner man is constantly under attack because he cannot often get work and because much of the work he is offered is low-paying, psychologically unrewarding, physically difficult, and intermittent. Those who hire the street-corner man often justify the low wages they pay on the ground that these men steal from them, thus making the material rewards of the job actually much higher than the standard salary. But it is in terms of salary that an American measures his or her self-worth. What is stolen from the job does not count in society's terms, and it also leaves workers vulnerable to the wishes of an employer who might want to fire them or exploit them in other ways. The poor, inner-city male is seen by himself as a failure; in this he reflects society's view of him as a failure because of his marginal work role, in low-prestige, low-paying, nonsteady jobs.

The prestige given different occupations is related to the power inherent in such occupations, the income derived from them, and their importance to the society, among other factors. Although income is a basis for prestige in American society, the ways in which that income is earned and wealth is accumulated also have to be taken into account. Generally speaking, people who earn their incomes illegally have less prestige in the community than do those whose incomes are legally earned. Who do you think has more prestige in our society: a baseball player who signs a $2 million contract, a heart surgeon who earns $400,000 a year, or the head of an illegal gambling syndicate whose profit runs to millions? However, money eventually buys high social position, at least in our society. Sending one's children to the best schools, buying a home in the best neighborhood, joining the right clubs, and so on give individuals the chance to interact socially with others in high social positions. All of these opportunities cost money. The social status of a family can thus improve dramatically over just a few generations. The ancestors of some families now prominent in United

States political life, for example, made their fortunes in ways that today would be considered deviant or illegal.

The question of whether prestige or class is more important as a basis for protecting one's self-interest has long been argued by social scientists. Two opposing views on this question are those of Karl Marx and Max Weber, a German sociologist of the late nineteenth century. Whereas Marx saw people as conscious of themselves as a group mainly in terms of similar economic interests, Weber believed that people may value prestige and the symbolic aspects of status even more than money. Weber further argued that political action can be motivated by a group's desire to defend its social position as well as, or even in opposition to, its economic self-interest. For example, poor whites in the American South did not join poor blacks in working for improvement of their common economic position because they were more interested in maintaining the status differences based on color.

Social Class

The two basic forms of social stratification are class and caste. In a **class system**, the different strata (classes) are not sharply separated from one another but form a continuum. **Social mobility** (movement from one class to another) is possible. An individual born into one social class can, through various means (education, marriage, good luck, hard work), move up into another. Social mobility can also be downward, and as the accompanying ethnography indicates, this is becoming a more frequent occurrence in the United States.

Social Class in the United States

The United States is said to have an open class system: One's position depends largely on achieved statuses such as occupation, education, and life-style, and there is a good chance for upward mobility. The open class system of our society is part of our mythology and is based on the democratic principle of equality and opportunity for all. Many people in the United States find it difficult to accept the evidence that this equality has not yet been fully realized and that, in fact, social class is an important aspect of social organization in our nation. Many studies have shown that social class membership does appear to correlate with various attitudinal, behavioral, and life-style factors, testifying to the reality of social classes.

Anthropological research indicates that social class is more than an economic phenomenon. A social class is also a subculture; its members share similar life experiences, occupational roles, values, educational backgrounds, associational affiliation, leisure activities, buying habits, and political views. Beyond being linked by these shared traits, members of a social class tend to associate more with one another than with people in other classes. Studies of social stratification in many societies show that informal social interaction such as visiting most frequently involves members of the same class. Thus, the life-style and interactional dimensions of social class reinforce one another. Through interaction based on common residence and schooling, for example, individuals learn the life-style of their social class. Because life-style is an important part of sociability, people with similar life-styles tend to associate with one another.

Social Class and Life Chances

Some social scientists argue that approaches to social stratification emphasizing life-style, cultural patterns, and prestige obscure important economic and power differences in American society. Another way to look at social class that brings economic factors and power into sharper focus is to examine the differences in life chances among social classes. **Life chances** refers to an individual's opportunity to fulfill or fail to fulfill his or her potential in society.

An individual's life chances include the chance of survival, opportunities to obtain an education that will help maximize intellectual and creative potential, opportunities to participate in associations and cultural life, and opportunities to live in comfort and security.

An individual's life chances are linked to his or her position in the stratification system. Although the American myth of equality includes the belief that "anyone can become president," the relationship between life chances and social mobility does not uphold this idea. Social mobility is also a life chance that depends on where one already is in the class system. Individuals born into positions of wealth, high status, and power strive to maintain those positions, and because of their high social class frequently have the means to keep others from achieving mobility. People born into the middle class have a better chance of improving their life chances than do people born into a poor class. The very poor and those who belong to minority groups that are discriminated against in our culture have lower life chances than does the middle class. Low social position tends to negate not only one's own life chances but also those of one's children. Poverty tends to perpetuate itself through generations, calling into question the openness of the American class system.

The interactional and life-style commonalities associated with social class are reinforced by kinship links, particularly among elites, who use these links both as a basis for exclusive interactional networks and as a way of improving their life chances. As part of the cultural denial of the relevance of class in the United States, we tend to associate kinship links in the elite class with other cultures and nations, not our own. And yet the expression "It's who you know, not what you know that counts" suggests we are aware of the contradiction between the ideal of our class system that bases success on merit, and the reality, in which personal relationships play an important role in improving one's life chances. According to Jack Weatherford, an anthropologist who has studied the

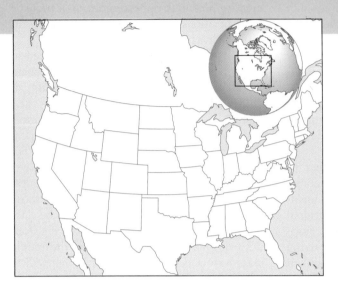

In most discussions of social class in the United States, the openness of the class system, and the opportunities for upward social mobility — either within one's lifetime, or for one's children — occupy a central place. This upward mobility is, indeed, the core of "the American Dream" for both the native-born and the millions of immigrants who come to our shores. The belief in opportunities for upward mobility is built into our national mythology and intricately tied up with the "core" American values: individualism, meritocracy, the work ethic, optimism, a "national faith in progress and achievement," and a belief in the ability of individuals to control the circumstances of their lives. The American Dream is based on the belief that if an individual works hard and makes personal sacrifices to acquire skills, knowledge, and competence, the material standard of living for the individual and his or her family will improve.

This widespread belief in the American Dream leads many people in the United States to deny that there is such a thing as a class system here, in spite of the reality of millions of people in poverty, and of the great, persistent inequalities among different segments — racial, gender, ethnic, and regional — of the population. One way in which Americans characteristically deny the existence of class is the application of the label "middle class" to a very wide range of occupations, incomes, and life-styles, ignoring the diversity of cultures that make up the American middle class. Another way in which the denial of class operates is the lack of focus on downward, as opposed to upward, mobility.

Katherine Newman defines the downwardly mobile middle class as people who had secure jobs, comfortable homes, and reason to believe that the future would be one of continued prosperity for themselves and their children. Through job loss, they experience not only economic decline, but also a decline in prestige: They have lost their *place* in society, and with it their sense of honor and self-esteem. In spite of the very high numbers of Americans who have become downwardly mobile, and in spite of its high toll on both individuals and the economy, downward mobility is almost institutionally invisible. The media more often focus attention on upward mobility, and the lives of the rich and famous. These images reflect implicit, but nevertheless dominant assumptions that life gets better from year to year. While American culture provides many rituals and symbols of upward mobility and success in the form of displays of wealth and status, there are no such occasions to mark status deterioration. As Newman says, "Downward mobility is a hidden dimension of our society's experience because it . . . does not fit into our cultural universe."

Because of the glorification of economic success in the United States, and the consequent lack of discussion of failure, the economic burdens of downward mobility in the middle class are intensified by the psychological burdens. First, because we put so much emphasis on the individual's ability to control his or her life, failure to do this quickly turns into self-blame. We tend to "blame the victim," rather than assume or investigate possible causes in systemic economic conditions, such as the flight of manufacturing jobs and capital investment to foreign countries, the transition from a manufacturing to a service economy, the recurring downturns that have been part of the capitalist economy for over two hundred years, and changing demographics. This "blame the victim" syndrome, which is an outgrowth of our particular culture, means that our government is less responsive to victims of downward social mobility than is true in Japan and many nations of Europe. These governments, for example, spend more money on retraining workers who have lost their jobs, require substantial warning periods to workers who will be losing their jobs from plant closings, and have better and longer unemployment benefits.

While economists and sociologists can provide statistical data on downward mobility among the middle class in the United States, anthropologists have a unique contribution to make in understanding the *meanings* downward mobility has for the people who experience it. Using the anthropological perspective that culture shapes our interpretations of experience, Newman shows that downward mobility means different things to — is experienced differently by — different segments of the middle class. She compares this experience among middle managers fired from large corporations, air traffic controllers who lost their jobs as a result of a strike, a town of blue-collar workers who became unemployed when their major factory closed, and middle-class women, who primarily suffer downward mobility as the aftermath of divorce. A most interesting comparison is presented between the middle managers, who experience downward mobility as a personal failure and an emotionally debilitating experience, and the contrasting experience of air traffic controllers. While both groups were influenced by American cultural values in interpreting their experience, the collective nature of the air traffic controllers' occupation led to a very different psychological position than that of the middle managers and executives.

(continued)

The middle-class managers and executives, mainly white men in their late forties and early fifties, married, suburban dwellers with teenage children, typically lost their jobs as a result of corporate shrinkage in response to declining sales or prices. They intensely experienced their unemployment as a personal failure resulting in demoralization, self-blame, and shame, and an excruciating sense of social isolation. Their social networks disappeared rapidly as they were increasingly unable to afford the reciprocity upon which social interaction depends; they were isolated in their large suburban homes where there was rarely a sense of neighborly community; and their economic contacts shrank as their peers were similarly vulnerable and, in fact, became their competition in the job market. Prolonged inability to find a managerial job similar to the one they lost, or even any job, brought home the "stigma" of unemployment as a part of American middle-class culture. Keeping up appearances was critical to these men; some managers did not even tell their wives and families about their firing till long after the fact. Their unemployment and subsequent downward mobility negatively affected all of their family life and routine; many leisure activities had to be abandoned; the father's role as the "person in charge" declined as wives and children saw him as the person "who had got them into this mess"; and the families were forced into the unfamiliar situation of having to talk to each other more than previously. The major interpretation of their downwardly mobile experience for these managers was a feeling of worthlessness, as their self-esteem was so significantly tied to their prestigious and high-paying occupations, upon which they had built an extremely comfortable life-style: When they lost their jobs, and their incomes, their self-esteem was drastically affected.

The air controllers' interpretation of job loss was different: Although also hit hard by the difficulties of job loss, they saw themselves as paying a hard price for standing up for what they believed in and their self-esteem was less severely affected. Air traffic controlling requires teamwork within the workplace, and indeed, between different regions of the country. Air traffic controllers had forged many personal friendships and a sense of brotherhood through their occupation, and this collective sense of pride and principle carried over to the initiation of the strike and its aftermath. The air traffic controllers were mainly employed by the federal government; many of them had achieved upward social mobility from working-class backgrounds through military service, rigorous training, and selection for this high-paying, highly selective, prestigious, and challenging occupation. They were confident that their strike, which took place in August 1981, would be successful, partly because it involved demands for safety measures as well as higher wages. When the strike failed, through successful government efforts to decrease aircraft traffic and hire substitute workers, and a media focus on the higher wages rather than safety demands, which led to indifference by the public and organized labor, these workers did not, like the managers, experience paralyzing self-blame, self-doubt, and a sense of loss of control over their lives. Indeed, in their collective struggle against the government, they found dignity and comradeship that survived long after most of them found other, less prestigious and economically rewarding jobs, and after the public had largely forgotten the strike.

Unlike the managers and executives, who could not make sense of their experiences except in terms of individual failure, the air traffic controllers drew on themes in American culture that gave dignity to their actions and made sense of their suffering. They saw their struggle against what they perceived as injustices by a vengeful government as a new kind of patriotism and their strike as a moral protest. In the collective act of the strike, they found self-respect in their loss of occupation, rather than experiencing a sense of individual failure. The search for meaning in suffering, which is part of every human disaster, led them to tie their strike to other "honorable rebellions" in American history, giving their actions a moral character: The strike became less an effort to gain personal benefits than a struggle for human rights and professional altruism. The downward mobility that resulted from the strike — few of the air traffic controllers were able to get jobs with anywhere near the prestige or income of their former positions — was interpreted as a tragedy of conflict between the government and the people, not as a personal rejection.

Katherine Newman's anthropological analysis of one aspect of the American class system indicates that social class is defined by more than economic statistics. People interpret their place in society in different ways, even if they label these different experiences as an aspect of being "middle class." Her work shows that there are cultural themes in the United States that can be used to interpret the same experience in very different ways. In her conclusion, Newman notes that downward social mobility has a cost not just for individuals, but also for society. The lack of an ethos of loyalty and commitment to workers on the part of American companies and the government contrasts, as previously noted, with attitudes in other nations. Newman suggests that downward social mobility is a monumental waste of intelligence and motivation; that it undermines confidence in business and government; that it leads to a decline in the quality of manufacture and service; and that it ultimately, as has already happened, will leave the United States far behind as a competitor in a global economy.

Adapted from Katherine S. Newman, Falling from Grace: The Experience of Downward Mobility in the American Middle Class *(New York: Random House, 1989).*

One characteristic of the poor in many developing nations is the high percentage of female-centered families with large numbers of children. This helps form a large potential pool of surplus labor and thus has a depressing effect on wages. (Bernard Krauss)

U.S. Congress in a book with the intriguing name of *Tribes on the Hill* (1981), it is kinship connections that often "determine who gets the chance to play the game" and which players stand the best chance of winning.

Among the families Weatherford lists as "political perennials" are the Byrds of Virginia; the Adamses, Cabots, and Lodges of Massachusetts; the Fish family of New York; the Tafts of Ohio; the Roosevelts of New York; and, most recently, the Kennedys of Massachusetts. There are also many other lesser known, but nevertheless important, families who are active in U.S. politics. Weatherford criticizes those who would see the relationship between kinship and politics as somehow atypical in American life, or perhaps limited to certain parts of the country like the Old South or New England. He demonstrates that this family connection in politics is part of an overall pattern, not only in

the fact that Congress is full of members of the same families, but that these kinship ties are also important in influencing who gets the real power positions within the Congress. Weatherford's analysis illustrates one of the important ways, though certainly not the only way, that political, social, and economic elites maintain their power in a society.

Caste

In contrast to class systems, which are based primarily on achieved statuses, a caste system is based on birth. An individual belongs to the caste of his or her parents and cannot move from one caste to another. In a class system, individuals from different classes may marry

Apartheid, or separateness, was for many years the official state policy of the Republic of South Africa, and it illustrates the extremes to which caste stratification may lead. Here, workers in the Elsies River Plant of the Chrysler Corporation were required to leave their work by segregated exits. (United Nations)

(and marriage is one route to upward social mobility). In a caste system, an individual can marry only within his or her caste. Caste, in other words, is hereditary and endogamous. The castes, however many there are, are ranked in relation to one another and are usually associated with a particular occupation. A **caste system,** then, consists of a ranked and culturally distinct number of interdependent endogamous groups. Unlike class systems, in which no clear boundaries exist between the different classes, a caste system has definite boundaries between castes. Many of the social rules in a caste system are directed toward maintaining social distance between castes.

The Caste System in India

The unique elements of the Indian caste system are its complexity, its relation to Hindu religious beliefs and rituals, and the degree to which the castes (or, more properly, subcastes) are cohesive and self-regulating groups. The Hindu belief about the division of society is that there are four caste categories, called *varna.* The varna are ranked according to their ritual purity, which in turn is based on their traditional occupations. The Brahmins, who are ranked highest, are priests and scholars; the Kshatriyas, or warrior caste, are second; the Vaishyas, or merchants, are ranked third; and the shudras, or menial workers and artisans, are ranked fourth. Below these four varna is a fifth group, called the untouchables. The untouchable castes, who perform the polluting work of cleaning latrines or working with leather, are considered so ritually impure that just their mere touch contaminates the purity of the higher castes. An individual's birth into one of these varna is said to be a reward or punishment for the quality of his or her actions in a previous life.

Many traditional rules of behavior in India are designed to maintain the boundaries between castes. Members of different castes do not eat with one another, and a higher-caste person will not accept most kinds of food or drink from a lower-caste person. Untouchable castes are segregated in their own part of the village and are not allowed to drink water out of the same wells as higher castes. Before recent laws establishing legal equality, marriage and sexual relations between castes were forbidden. Each caste has distinguishing cultural features, and the higher castes more nearly approximate Hindu religious ideals in their behavior. This includes vegetarianism, a taboo on alcohol, and the prohibition of remarriage for widows. Only high castes are allowed to perform certain rituals, such as the tying of the sacred thread on young boys, which symbolizes a second birth. Formerly, Brahmin priests would not minister to the religious needs of the untouchables and lower castes, and untouchables were not allowed to enter village temples.

Caste in India is tied up, especially in the village context, with the exchange of goods and services. Families of various artisan and serving castes, such as carpenters, potters, blacksmiths,

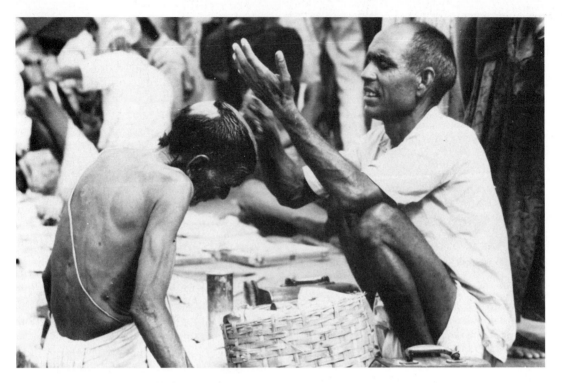

In India, the caste system is an important means of regulating the exchange of goods and services. Barbering, for example, is an activity traditionally performed in exchange for grain and clothes, rather than cash. (Serena Nanda)

water carriers, leather workers (who remove dead cattle from the fields), barbers, and washermen, perform necessary services for families of high-caste landowners and in return receive food from them. In addition, landowning families may pay serving-caste families with grain, clothing, fodder for animals, and animal products such as butter and milk. The landowning castes may also give the serving castes small amounts of cash, free rent, or the use of tools. This client-patron, or *jajmani*, relationship is often carried on over several generations between the same families. The serving castes also exchange goods and services among themselves. Thus, at the village level, the different castes form an interdependent whole.

This view of the caste system emphasizes its integrative function and the way caste bene-fits society as a whole, showing how it provides benefits to both the high-caste landowning families and the serving castes. Landowners get a steady supply of workers and can maintain a high-status life-style; they need not perform menial and ritually polluting work. The serving castes, in turn, are assured economic security. This description, however, is a somewhat idealized one; it is given mainly by Brahmins, and anthropologists have perhaps too often taken it at face value. More recently, many anthropologists have argued that the benefits of the system are much greater for the high castes than for the low castes and that social integration in the Indian village is due as much to physical coercion and the absence of alternatives for the lower castes as it is to the integrating force of reciprocity.

This woman is a sweeper, a member of one of the formerly called untouchable castes in India. Although the Indian government has taken a strong stand on affirmative action and reserved places in schools and jobs for members of these oppressed castes, they still suffer economic and political burdens derived from their low status in the caste and class hierarchy. (Serena Nanda)

The Dynamics of Caste

Idealized views of the caste system, which emphasized its stability, were obtained by anthropologists mainly from high-caste Hindus. New studies of caste in rural and urban areas reveal a dynamism that earlier studies overlooked. Lower- and middle-ranked castes frequently do not accept their position and use a number of strategies to rearrange their rank. Efforts by untouchable castes to change their rank often bring a violent reaction from the higher castes, who want to preserve their own prestige, wealth, and power.

Social mobility in the caste system is a group rather than an individual effort. A caste that has achieved a certain amount of economic success might try to raise its prestige by adopting the customs of a higher-caste group and claiming a new rank for itself. An upwardly mobile caste attempts through its caste council to change the behavior of its members, getting them to conform to higher-caste behavior patterns. A lower caste might also, as part of its strategy, invent a myth for itself showing that it originally came from one of the higher-ranked varna.

With the achievement of Indian independence in 1948 and the creation of a democratic constitution, caste in India has both weakened and gained strength. The Indian government, in an attempt to make up for past discrimination and suffering, has reserved special jobs and places in the universities for members of untouchable and lower castes. The advantages to be gained by claiming membership in one of these castes may therefore be substantial, and a number of caste associations have grown up to help members use these new opportunities. Discrimination against untouchables was also outlawed, although as we have seen with race relations in the United States, this is difficult to enforce at the local level. The vote has been extended to all castes, and low castes now have a potential for political power through elected representation. These factors have somewhat altered the strategies of upward mobility for some low castes.

Owen Lynch (1969) has described these changes in strategy for the Camars, an untouchable caste of leather workers in the city of Agra. Camars have traditionally been shoemakers, and because of the increased demand for shoes both in India and abroad, some of them have become fairly wealthy. Changes in the economic conditions of the Camars, as well as their political circumstances, have stimulated them to try to raise their position in the caste system. They claimed to be Kshatriyas (the warrior caste), and in an effort to get this claim accepted by the higher castes, they outlawed the eating of beef and buffalo and adopted some high-caste rituals, such as the tying of the sacred thread. These efforts, however, were not successful. Under the leadership of an untouchable, Dr. B. R. Ambedkar, who was educated in England and the United States, the Camars are now trying a different strategy, that of conversion to Buddhism. Unlike their earlier attempts to raise their status within the caste system, this move is an attempt to improve their position by putting themselves outside the caste system altogether. At the same time, they wish to retain their status as a special caste in order to be eligible for the benefits of affirmative action undertaken by the Indian government.

The Camars of Agra offer a good example of the dynamics of caste and how it is both weakened and perpetuated in modern India. The study also invites comparison with similar efforts by other groups in other societies — for example, among African-Americans in the United States.

Although Indian castes are ranked on the basis of prestige rather than wealth, the gains of high-caste position are not just symbolic. The higher castes also benefit materially from their higher status and are in a better position to exercise political power in their own self-interest. The lower castes appear to accept their low position without question, but their conformity actually hinges a great deal on their awareness that economic sanctions and physical force will ultimately be used against them if they dare to try and break out of their low caste. Members of the upper castes, whether in India or the United States, have long used the rationalization that the lower strata of their society are "happy where they are." That this is not the case is clear from the protest movements by the poor and oppressed in both India and the United States.

One of the problems with much of the social science work done on caste in India is that most studies, unlike Lynch's, cited above, are done from the viewpoint of members of the highest castes. Joan Mencher (1980) is another anthropologist who has studied the Indian hierarchy from the point of view of untouchables, or Harijans, to use the word coined by Gandhi,

which means "children of God." Mencher's work suggests that the untouchable castes are caught in a circular bind of stigmatized identity (that is, they are viewed as polluting) and economic exploitation. Although the Indian constitution outlaws untouchability, there has not been the kind of radical economic reform that would eliminate the economic barriers to their mobility, and without economic improvement there can be no change in the stigmatized aspect of their identity. At the same time, without a change in their stigmatized identity as untouchables, it is difficult for any radical economic change to take place. Furthermore, although high-caste Indians frequently refer to the religious basis of caste as a justification for the social hierarchy, lower-caste informants almost universally explain their low status by referring to economic factors, such as the concentration of land or capital in the hands of the elite.

In examining the contemporary political/economic scene in India, Mencher raises the question of why caste has continued to play such an important role in social identity and politics. Her conclusion is that richer members of the high castes emphasize the importance of caste status in order to inhibit poorer members of the high castes from uniting economically with members of lower castes and thus threatening the dominance of richer, capital- and landowning upper-caste members. As long as members of untouchable castes continue to be socially stigmatized, this will inhibit the formation of classes and class consciousness in India, an obvious advantage to those at the top.

Race and Social Stratification

In Chapter 1, I noted that race has fallen into disuse as a scientifically valid way of classifying human diversity. It is nevertheless important to understand race as a cultural and social category and the role that racial classifications play in social stratification. Many cultures use some visible physical differences to categorize people into "races"; these labeled categories may then be, and often are, used as a basis for social stratification and discrimination. In the United States, race, defined largely by attribution of skin color based on presumed ancestry, is culturally significant. In the United States we culturally divide people into "blacks" and "whites," despite the fact that this opposition in no way reflects the reality of the skin color spectrum, which includes many shades in-between and, indeed, places many people in the "black" category whose skin shades are actually lighter than that of some people in the "white" category. This calls attention to the fact that our cultural category of race is really based on presumed ancestry, not on any objectively measured physical characteristics.

The culturally constructed definition of race in the United States, as based on parentage or "blood," which shows up in skin color, was the basis of many state laws incorporating legal definitions of race; in many Southern states individuals were defined as black if they had one-thirty-second "Negro blood," even if they "looked" white. Louisiana had such a law, and in 1982, a woman named Suzie Phipps, who had been classified as black because her great-great-great-great-grandmother was an African-American, went to court to have herself declared white, a categorization that more accurately reflected her skin color. As a result of anthropological testimony that the Louisiana law was "nonsense," it was dropped from the books (Dominguez 1986:3). The case is one of many examples of the ways in which cultures construct racial categories which have social, but no scientific, validity.

Highlighting the cultural construction of racial categories as relevant to social stratification is a conversation I had in Malaysia, a nation that has three primary cultural groups — Chinese, Indian, and Malay — as well as a small population of Portuguese descended from those who came in the sixteenth century as traders and later dominated Malay society politically for one hundred years. A Malay acquaintance, trying to describe for me the diversity of Malaysia, began by saying, "The Indians are the black people," referring to the dark skin color of the Indians in Malaysia, who are mainly from South India. Joking with him a little, from my own cultural frame of reference, I asked, "If the Indians are the black people, who are the white people?" "Oh," he answered, without missing a beat, "the Portuguese used to be the white people, but now the Chinese are the white people."

To understand this conversation, it is necessary to know Malaysian history and to understand the particular system of racial classification and social stratification. The Portuguese were powerful and wealthy; they no longer are. When the (white) British, who colonized the area, left, the Chinese moved into many of the commercial and professional positions in Malaysia and now dominate the economy. Having taken over the economic position of the British, the Chinese are now defined as having taken over their "racial" category as well.

Cultures are different, not only in their recognition of *racial* categories, but also in the physical criteria that may become the basis for those categories. Huang Shu-min, a Chinese anthropologist, reported his confusion when, during his first stay in the United States, someone referred to a classmate as "the little redhead." His discovery that "Americans frequently divide their hair into color categories" and refer to people in terms of hair color came as a surprise. Such classifications are totally foreign to Chinese culture, where all of the people have black hair, except for the aged and the bald (1993:41).

Gerald Berreman, an anthropologist who has studied both caste in India and racial stratification in the United States, points out that race, like caste, is a birth-ascribed dimension of social stratification and therefore functions like caste, and like caste is an "invidious" distinction (1988). By "invidious," he means something that the individual is born with, cannot change, and that is viewed as a source of inherent inequality. Invidious distinctions categorize persons by a particular ascribed group identity — whether that identity be claimed as one of caste, ethnicity, race, or sex. Invidious distinctions assign people to groups and stereotype them on the basis of the group characteristic, which overrides any of their individual qualities or achievements. In a birth-ascribed situation of social stratification, such as the caste system in India, or Japan, or parts of Africa, and the system of racial stratification in the United States, "Everyone is sentenced for life to a social cell shared by others of like birth, separated from and ranked relative to all other social cells."

Indeed, Berreman points out that the system of racial stratification in the United States, particularly as it operated in the American South, is structured and functions very much like the caste system in India. The castelike aspects of this social system included membership based on birth (one was born white or black and remained in that category for life), marriage within the caste, cultural distinctiveness of the two groups, traditional occupations each group could enter or was prohibited from entering, and a rank order in which white was superior. Many of the norms of behavior in the Old South revolved around "keeping blacks in their place" and preventing blacks and whites from mixing except under certain conditions. Like a caste system anywhere, this system had a full-fledged mythology associated with it, an attempt to "explain" and justify the inferior position of the lower caste. Ultimately, this system, like other caste systems, was maintained by physical force, which came into the open whenever the status quo was threatened. In writing of the South in the 1930s, John Dollard, in his *Caste and Class in a Southern Town* (1937), demonstrated that, although social classes existed within the two castes, a castelike line was drawn between blacks and whites. No matter how high a position a black reached, he or she could not cross the caste barrier. In his comparison of caste in India and the United States, Berreman (1959) demonstrated convincingly not only that castelike features operated in the United States but also that classlike features operated in the Indian caste system.

Berreman strengthens his argument that race must be understood as a social concept, functioning in the same way as other birth-ascribed criteria (such as caste), with the ex-ample of the Japanese Burakumin. The Burakumin are a category of people in Japan who have been historically stigmatized and oppressed, and indeed are still so treated today, in spite of their official emancipation in 1871 (DeVos and Wagatsuma 1966). They are called a "race" in that the Japanese believe that the Burakumin are physically and morally distinct, although, in fact, they are not so at all. Burakumin are only recognizable by their ancestry as manifested in their family name, occupation, place of residence, and life-style. They are thus an example of a sociological race, but in no way a genetic one. Hence, they are sometimes referred to as an "invisible" race.

The discrimination and stigmatization of the Burakumin indicate the seemingly universal fact that all systems of birth-ascribed stratification include the belief that the social distinctions are reflected in biological, that is, "racial" differences. These so-called racial differences, that is, differences in physical appearance, are then associated with "traits of character, morality, intelligence, personality, and purity" that are also seen as natural, inherited, and unalterable. As the Japanese case demonstrates, where *no* observable physical differences exist between the majority and minority populations, "races" will still be invented. The point of associating supposedly unchangeable physical characteristics with equally unchanging cultural and moral characteristics is to rationalize birth-ascribed systems of social stratification. It is perhaps because such systems are in some deep way felt to be so unfair that so much energy goes into finding elaborate justifications for them, whether those justifications are built upon criteria of race, sex, ethnicity, or spiritual purity.

Regardless of the specific ideology of a birth-ascribed system of social stratification, Berreman calls attention to their important consequences, both negative psychological ones for the individuals harmed by such systems, and a condition of latent instability for societies based on birth-ascribed stratification. He compellingly points out that such systems are kept in place by outward conformity, but not consensus; by sanctions of coercion and force, often naked violence, not by agreement. While the oppressed in such situations may not openly resist, though that also happens when the risk seems worth taking, such groups will, in many ways, big and small, subvert the system, even as they may display outward compliance. Thus, inherent in birth-ascription systems are conflict and disorder, and occasionally, when the balance of power is perceived as having changed sufficiently, outright revolt. Where the dominant group has overwhelming power and insists on uncompromising enforcement, the subtlety of subversion often goes unnoticed, giving the false impression of a social order based on legitimacy.

Ethnicity and Social Stratification

The term **ethnicity** probably is familiar to the readers of this book. Many of us might identify ourselves as belonging to one or another ethnic group, citing such cultural elements as language, customs, dress, or foods that are part of a tradition we inherited from our parents or grandparents. In much of social science thinking, ethnicity has indeed been defined in terms of shared cultural characteristics and an unreflecting, yet emotionally charged, sense of collective selfhood. Anthropologist Clifford Geertz, for example, has defined ethnicity in terms of what he calls "primordial bonds," those ties which stem from common blood, religion, language, attachment to a place, or customs (1973:277). For Geertz and others, these ethnic ties, which are passed down from one generation to the next and differentiate group members from nonmembers, are the expression of a basic self and group identity. This "primordialist" definition of ethnicity views ethnic ties as natural and even spiritual. Ethnicity and ethnic groups are seen as inherent in human social life, exerting an independent force on behavior and accounting for collective mobilization in

the political or economic interests of the ethnic group. The highly emotional nature of ethnic ties is given as the reason why such ties persist despite the many trends of modernization — urbanization, education, the mass media — which might be expected to weaken them. In this view, the importance of ethnic groups and ethnic-group conflict in contemporary societies is explained as "a clinging to old loyalties" or, in the case of Third World societies, as an example of traditional societies' "resistance to change."

Although the nonrational, or even irrational, aspect of ethnicity seems to capture an undeniable component of ethnic-group behavior in the contemporary world (Stack 1981), a major criticism of the primordialist definition is that it does not sufficiently take either history or social structure, particularly class conflict, into account. Treating ethnic ties as inherent in human social life, for example, does not explain why ethnicity appears and disappears in different historical periods nor why ethnic ties are manifested differently under varying social, political, and economic conditions. Just as anthropology is moving away from a view of cultures as holistic, isolated entities, so too does a definition of ethnic groups emphasizing their closed, static nature seem inadequate.

In introducing an expanded view of ethnic groups, Frederik Barth (1969) pointed out as too simplistic the "primordialist" view that geographic and social isolation is the critical factor in sustaining cultural diversities. Barth's major contribution to the study of ethnic groups was to show that ethnic boundaries persist *despite* the fact of interaction among ethnic groups and that, in fact, there are often vitally important social relations across ethnic boundaries. While Barth agreed that ethnicity has an important cultural content, he demonstrated that there is no simple one-to-one relationship between ethnic units and "objectively defined" cultural differences. Rather, Barth and others emphasized that ethnicity is *emergent* in the very process of social interaction; that is, ethnicity is not merely inherent in a social environment but rather emerges in a particular form under particular circumstances.

Headgear is frequently an important symbolic ethnic marker, which carries cultural meanings but also symbolizes position in an economic, social, and political hierarchy. (Sarah Grossman)

This approach led anthropologists to ask new questions about the kinds of circumstances that call forth, or mobilize, ethnicity as a relevant identity and basis for association and group action. No longer was ethnicity seen merely as a "survival" or continuation of an earlier cultural tradition. It became apparent that an ethnic group's culture had as much to do with a contemporary situation as it did with a cultural continuity from the past. Studies of ethnicity in Africa, for example, indicated that the tribal identities which formed the basis of ethnic mobilization were often constructs created by colonial governments who found these tribal identities useful to control indigenous populations through indirect rule. Similarly, the ethnic groups and their pattern of interaction in African cities could be traced specifically to the nature of urbanization in the colonial and postcolonial setting (Cohen 1969). This new understanding of ethnicity as a con-

struct, or artifact, of group interaction in specific circumstances opened the way for anthropologists to investigate the origins of newly emergent ethnic identities, where previously such ethnic origins had been regarded as inherent in a particular cultural group.

An ethnographic approach to ethnicity has shown that ethnic identities and ethnic groups are fluid rather than static. They appear, undergo transformation, and disappear in response to changing conditions in the economic and social environment. Ethnicity, in short, is a historically constituted social identity. With the increasing acceptance in the last twenty years of a more dynamic, materialist, and conflict-oriented perspective in anthropology, the study of ethnicity is currently embedded in the study of social relations within and *between* groups, especially in situations where social relations are characterized by inequality. Ethnic and class analyses have been linked in an attempt to understand the complex dynamics of modern ethnic processes. Currently, class and power relations are accepted as essential to understanding ethnicity; at the very least, ethnicity is viewed in the context of competition between groups in society for political or economic access or dominance. As one anthropologist has put it, "Ethnicity is a mask for confrontation" (Vincent 1974:377).

An example of the complex ethnic dynamics of contemporary society — particularly of the emergence of ethnicity as a response to changing material conditions of life — is presented by Jay O'Brien's study of agriculture in the Sudan, in Africa (1986).

In 1925 the British, who then occupied the Sudan, wanted to expand cotton production there. In order to have sufficient labor for the peak agricultural season, they encouraged local peasants and pastoralists to become part of a seasonally migrant wage-labor force. But this local labor force was not sufficient, so the British encouraged immigration of poor peasants from West Africa into the Sudan. These peasants, who were mainly Muslim Hausa speakers, were given incentives to settle in the Sudan and served as a stable, year-round, cheap labor force. Other groups of West Africans were also encouraged to settle in other areas of the Sudan, where they were given their own land to farm, but could be drawn upon as seasonal wage laborers for the cotton scheme. There was considerable cultural diversity among these West Africans. Even among the Muslim Hausa-speaking group, there were many distinct, named ethnic identities, speaking different (second) languages and having different customs.

From the beginning, the local Sudanese people resented the West Africans, who were used by the British to discipline the local labor force. Many of the native Sudanese, who had only recently become cultivators, held agricultural work in low esteem, avoided it when possible, and worked at it only very indifferently, when necessary. The West African immigrants, on the other hand, had a long history of disciplined agricultural work under exploitative conditions and were more productive.

Within a short time, the immigrants came to be known in Sudan as "Fellata," or Fulani (many had come from the West African Fulani Sultanates). This term was applied indiscriminately to all of the immigrants from West Africa, and it took on negative connotations stereotyping the West Africans as hard-working and slavish. Thus, this one element of West African behavior became, for the local people, the dominant element of their "ethnicity," and the many important cultural differences among the immigrants were glossed over by the local Arabs.

The West African immigrants responded to hostile treatment and confinement to the lowest rungs of the social ladder through a process of cultural realignment. While on the one hand they adopted some of the customs — dress and house type, for example — of the local people, on the other hand they elaborated some key cultural symbols to which they attached a positive meaning to differentiate themselves from the Arabs. In particular, the immigrants emphasized their more fundamentalist Islamic practices such as abstaining from alcohol and secluding their women, forbidding them, for example, to work in the fields as local women did. They also articulated an ethic of hard work and moderate consumption, which gave dignity to their labor.

Gradually, the term *Takar* replaced the term *Fellata*. Takari is a respectful term generally applied to Muslim pilgrims from West Africa. With the emergence of the label Takari, there was a tendency for the subgroup differences — for example, between the Hausa and the non-Hausa — among the West Africans to be submerged, and the ethnicity of these diverse peoples is now Takari. Thus, partly in response to local hostility and the lumping together by others, these diverse cultural groups combined some commonalities of their past heritage and of the present, specifically Sudanese situation, to form a new ethnic identity. As this study illustrates, the emergence of new ethnic identities — and more specifically, the emergence of ethnic hierarchies — must be seen in the context of a particular system of social stratification.

Sexual Stratification

Sexual stratification refers to one aspect of the relations between the sexes: equality (or inequality). Because we live in a society in which sexual inequality predominates, we may tend to assume that male dominance is universal; and we may think it is inherent in either biological or role differences between men and women. Thus, it is important for us to look at other cultures in which this aspect of male-female relations is different, in order to see the culturally determined nature of sexual stratification and the conditions under which it arises and is maintained. Furthermore, a cross-cultural perspective will uncover societies that are much more egalitarian than our own and reveal the conditions under which such egalitarianism exists.

There are some societies, including our own, that we can call male dominated. In this type of society, both people's ideology and practices, or behavior, involve sexual stratification. Males have control over the most important resources in society, and they are believed to be both different in nature from and superior to women. Some societies considered to be clearly male dominated are India, Muslim Middle Eastern societies, and some Mediterranean societies — for example, Sicily.

Even in societies that appear to be strongly male dominated, however, women do not simply or easily adapt to their subordinate status but attempt to check male dominance in some way and thereby achieve a measure of autonomy or even influence of their own (Cronin 1977). For example, in many of the lower strata of male-dominated societies — such as among the lower castes in India, in Sicily, or among the Ladinos of Guatemala (Maynard 1974) — there are existential conditions that ameliorate the actual power men have. In the case of India, lower-caste women work. In Sicily, the men's farm work keeps them too busy to deal with the bureaucratic authorities, so women have to take over this job. Furthermore, the cultural

ideal of male infallibility makes men especially sensitive to the humor that women use to undermine their egos. Among the Guatemalan Ladinos, the frequency with which lower-class men abandon their families leaves the wives in control of the household. Where male dominance is rigid, men and women often have separate spheres of activity, and this means that there are female domains — notably the household and even certain kinds of economic activities — where women derive social and emotional satisfaction. This is true, for example, of high-caste Indian women in villages. Although they may be subject to male control, they can exercise some substantial power as mothers-in-law and mothers.

In a second type of society, which has qualified, or modified, male dominance, women have some important political roles or some access to resources of their own. They can use these to advance their position in the home and the position of their kin and to extend and enhance their own social networks. This type of society is characteristic of many cultures of West Africa, where women not only produce but also market and control the resources from certain crops. Women in West Africa may also be politically active through their control of female initiation societies, similar to those of young men.

In a third type of society, the egalitarian, the ideology of male dominance is absent or very weak. Women have the means to gain access to important economic resources and to occupy decision-making roles and positions. Egalitarianism between men and women may be based on a complementarity of roles; it does not necessarily mean, as we tend to mean in the West, that women and men do the same things. Thus, in some foraging societies, such as the !Kung, the fact that men hunt and women gather does not mean a system of male dominance. A more recent look at some societies, such as the Inuit, that on the basis of male ethnographies were held to be male dominated suggests that they, too, may be egalitarian in practice, in spite of a slight ideological bias to-

In many parts of West Africa, women both produce and sell their products in the marketplace. This control over important economic resources improves their position in society. (United Nations)

ward male dominance based on hunting of big-game animals (Briggs 1974). In socialist societies, such as China and the Israeli kibbutz, there is a strong ideology of sexual egalitarianism. Although the reality may not have matched the ideal, women in these societies make important contributions to the economy and hold political office, and behavioral equality is upheld by law and by social norms.

An important factor in sexual stratification is the relation of women to the production and distribution of goods. A major question affecting women's status is "Who will care for the children?" In no society have men taken over child care, or even a substantial proportion of it. Where governments have made communal child care available, women's ability to involve themselves productively in the economy has raised their status; where child care is not addressed, no ideology of equality alone can be sufficient for egalitarianism.

Another factor affecting sexual stratification is the nature of the social institutions. Where the household organization is the central social unit and social groups beyond the household are weak, women's position is likely to be higher than in societies where there are well-organized groups outside the household. The household tends to be the most important unit in a society where production is for subsistence or small-scale exchange and the society's members are not engaged in complex and

This infant and child-care center is part of the International Instruments factory in Bangalore, India, which employs many female workers. The availability of economically feasible child-care centers is an important factor in allowing women to participate in and benefit from economic development in a society. (Serena Nanda)

long-distance trade networks. Furthermore, where the needs of defense or military expansion require male-centered military organizations, or where there are important civil or religious bureaucracies, women's status tends to be lower than otherwise. The influence of Westernization, including European missionary activity and the international market economy, has almost always had the effect of undermining women's status in previously more egalitarian societies (Leacock 1981).

Finally, it must be understood that the particular relationship of the sexes in any society is an outcome of the mingling of many forces—political, economic, social, and ideological—over time. It is through ethnographic detail and analysis of these forces that we can come to see that sexual stratification is not a biological, or even cultural, universal in human societies, but rather a problem to be analyzed and explained.

Perspectives on Social Stratification

Social stratification results from the unequal distribution of goods and services within a society. The basic questions here—who gets what and why—depend on cultural values, the organization of production, and the access different individuals and groups within a society have to societal goals. Social scientists approach the understanding of social stratification from two major theoretical perspectives: functionalism and conflict theory.

A functionalist view stresses the integrative functions of social stratification and the contribution such systems make to social order, stability, and social functioning. Functionalists hold that the existence of every complex society depends on the regular performance of specific tasks that require special training and intelligence. If the most intelligent, talented, and best-trained individuals are to perform these tasks, they must be motivated by a system of rewards. The assumption is that, if you pay a surgeon the same as a sanitation worker, no one will be a surgeon, because it takes long years of training and involves enormous responsibilities. Thus, a major function of social stratification is that it provides a system of rewards, both material and symbolic, so that all the necessary jobs in society will be filled. From a functionalist perspective, social stratification also contributes to the social order by integrating groups that have common economic and political interests when kinship no longer plays an important integrating role. A system of social stratification is seen as inhibiting social conflict between individuals and groups; social inequality is the price of social stability.

Critics of functionalism point out that societies do not always reward individuals who fulfill the most essential roles. Such vital roles as nurse and schoolteacher, for example, do not carry material or symbolic rewards equal to those of a baseball player or television personality in our own society. Furthermore, a stratification system prevents many intelligent and talented people who are members of low-prestige and powerless groups from gaining access to the training and opportunities that lead to the more highly rewarded occupations and positions in society.

Gerald Berreman eloquently states his opposition to this point of view:

> The systematic ranking of categories of people, especially in their access to livelihood and power . . . is humanly harmful in that it is painful, damaging, and unjust, and it is consistently experienced as such by those who are deprived and oppressed. . . . It is responsible for hunger even when there is plenty, for high mortality, high fertility, and low life expectancy, for low levels of education, literacy, political participation, and other measures of quality of life. Stratification is also dangerous in that the poverty, oppression, hunger, fear and frustration inherent in it result in resentment among the deprived and anxiety among the privileged, with the result that overt, perhaps catastrophic, conflict is inevitable. Much of the source of crime in the streets, terrorism, ethnic conflict, civil war, and international war is inequality so organized. . . . Inequality between peoples and nations is a major threat to societal and even human survival. (1981:4–5)

A conflict perspective holds that the natural condition of society is change and conflict, not order and stability. From this perspective, social stratification results from the constant struggle for scarce goods and services that takes place in all complex societies. Stratification exists because those who have acquired power, wealth, and prestige exercise their power to keep what they have. This is accomplished not only by the threat of force or the use of force but also by social values and beliefs that justify the present system of inequality in the minds of those in the lower social positions. Conflict theorists contend that stratification not only results from but *generates* conflict, because the interests of the different social classes are opposed. They tend to view conflict and change in a more positive light than do functional theorists, because they see progress that results from conflict as better for a society than maintaining the status quo. Thus, conflict theory is useful in calling attention to conflict and change as universal aspects of human life and society. In examining social phenomena such as class and caste, for example, we can look at them from two perspectives: (1) How do such systems contribute to social integration and social order? (2) How do they reflect conflict and stimulate social change?

Summary

1. Social ranking is an important feature of variation in social organization. Anthropologists have identified three types of social systems:

egalitarian, rank, and stratified. Egalitarian systems, which are found among hunters and gatherers, give every individual and group in society equal access to basic resources, power, and prestige.

2. Rank societies, or chiefdoms, recognize differences in prestige among individuals and groups, but no one is denied access to the resources necessary for survival. Like egalitarian societies, rank societies are still organized along kinship lines. The ruling family maintains its position largely through the distribution of goods and food throughout the entire society, rather than through force.

3. In stratified societies, social, political, and economic inequality is institutionalized and maintained through a combination of internalized controls, political power, and force. Kinship ties between the upper and lower strata are no longer recognized, and there is a wide gap between them in standard of living. Some of the productive efforts of the lower strata go to support the life-style of the upper strata, who control the basic resources but are themselves exempt from food production.

4. The three major dimensions of social stratification are power, wealth, and prestige. Power refers to the ability to control people and situations, wealth to accumulation of economic resources, and prestige to the way in which an individual is socially evaluated by others. The particular value system of a culture determines the ways in which power, wealth, and prestige interact to determine where a person will be placed in the stratification system.

5. Two major types of stratification systems are class and caste. In a class system, social position is largely achieved, though it is also determined partly by the class into which a person is born. People may move between social classes, which form a continuum from bottom to top. Social classes are characterized by different life-styles and different life chances.

6. In the United States, the emphasis has been on upward social mobility, the improvement of one's material standards and life chances within one's lifetime and for one's children. But downward mobility among the middle class is now also becoming a widespread feature of the American class system. Downward mobility is experienced differently depending on one's occupation and values.

7. Racial categories are culturally constructed as groups of people who share similar physical and moral traits transmitted by heredity. Such categories are scientifically invalid but play an important role in many cultures, where they are used by elites to justify unequal distributions of economic and social resources.

8. Ethnicity is an important aspect of social hierarchy in the contemporary world. Although ethnic groups are bound together by cultural ties and a sense of "we-group," ethnicity primarily emerges in the context of struggles for economic resources and power.

9. In a caste system, social position is ascribed (based on birth). Boundaries between castes are sharply defined, and there is no intermarriage. The Indian caste system is the most complex and is based on Hindu ideas of ritual purity and pollution. Aspects of a caste system are also said to exist in the relations between blacks and whites in the traditional social system of the United States.

10. Both sexual stratification and sexual egalitarianism can be explained by a complex mix of social, economic, political, and cultural institutions. Sexual stratification tends to develop where societies are engaged in complex economic relations with outsiders and in expansionist military activities.

11. Social stratification can be viewed as functional for the social order, because it motivates people to undertake all the jobs necessary for the society to survive. Social stratification can also cause conflict, however; different social strata, with opposing interests, can clash with one another over goals and resources.

Suggested Readings

Leacock, Eleanor Burke
1981   *Myths of Male Dominance.* New York:
        Monthly Review Press. An excellent collec-
        tion of articles which cogently and persua-

sively make the case that the perspective that women are universally subordinate to men is derived from the sexual stratification of Western society.

Newman, Katherine S.
1989   *Falling from Grace: The Experience of Downward Mobility in the American Middle Class.* An original perspective on the study of social class in the United States, comparing the loss of status, money, and identity among laid off middle managers, factory workers, air traffic controllers, and divorced women.

Perin, Constance
1988   *Belonging in America: Reading between the Lines.* Madison: University of Wisconsin Press. An insightful and sophisticated approach to American culture and personality, including an emphasis on categories of inclusion and marginality as central to our culture.

Steinberg, Stephen
1989   *The Ethnic Myth: Race, Ethnicity, and Class in America.* Updated and expanded edition. Boston: Beacon Press. An exceptionally readable book whose thesis is that much of what is called ethnic in the United States today is really related to social class, locality, and other social conditions.

Valentine, Betty Lou
1978   *Hustling and Other Hard Work.* New York: Free Press. A valuable and readable work with case studies of three families in a poor African-American neighborhood in the United States. Based on five years of fieldwork by a sensitive and perceptive ethnographer.

Wiser, William, and Wiser, Charlotte
1971   *Behind Mud Walls, 1930–1960.* Berkeley: University of California Press. A classic description of an Indian village, showing the workings of the *jajmani* system. An epilogue follows the changes up until 1970.

Political Systems
and Social Control

What happens when people break the rules of their society?

How do different societies resolve conflicts?

Why do so many tribal societies engage in warfare?

How can we account for the origin of the state?

In Pebvil [Mexico] the ceremony by which a new chieftain took office was remarkable. At six o'clock in the morning all the members of the barrio marched into an open space, bringing the elected chief with them. . . . A few men ran ahead to ring the church bells. . . . Fireworks were set off to the accompaniment of music, dancing, frolic, and noise.

The retiring chief made a speech. The new chieftain replied politely and modestly. Now a chair was brought up. It was a low chair woven of wickerlike twigs. The seat had a hole in the middle.

The new chieftain pulled down his white cotton trousers and sat on the chair, while all the men who had crowded around to watch the ceremony laughed and made ribald jokes. Holding the ebony staff with its silver knob in his right hand, the chief sat solemnly in the chair, his face turned to all the men. . . . Now three men came up carrying an earthenware pot with holes bored into its sides. The pot was filled with glowing charcoal, glowing brightly because of the holes.

One of the men explained the purpose of the pot. When he concluded, he put this pot of glowing charcoal under the seat of the new chief. He said in his speech that the fire under the chief's posterior was to remind him that he was not sitting on this seat to rest himself but to work for his people. He was not to forget . . . that it was done to remind him from the outset that he could not cling to the office but had to give it up as soon as his time was up, so as to prevent any risk of a lifelong rule, which would be injurious to the welfare of his people. If he tried to cling to his office they would put a fire under him that would be large enough to consume both him and his chair.

As soon as the pot of glowing charcoal had been placed beneath the chair, rhymed sayings were recited. . . . The new chief had to remain seated until these recitals were at an end. Whatever the chief might feel, he would not show. . . . Quite the opposite. When the sayings were done, [he] remained sitting to show he had no intention of running away from the pains and troubles which his office might hold in store for him. When the charcoal died down the chief got up slowly. Great blisters had been raised on his skin. A friend smeared his backside with oil and applied a compress of crushed herbs, while another poured him a huge glassful of tequila.

The new chief would not forget for weeks what he had had under his seat. It helped him considerably during his period in office to carry out his duties as his nation had expected of him when it had elected him.

From B. Traven, Government *(New York: Random House [Schocken], 1971), pp. 173–77.*

In the ethnographic description of local government in Mexico in the nineteenth century, we see that there are many different concepts of legitimate power and many different ways of governing. **Political organization** refers to the patterned ways in which legitimate power, or authority, is used to regulate behavior. All cultures have some form of political organization. While most of us might not approve the custom of instituting a new leader in the way just described, we would nevertheless recognize the spirit of democratic values that underlies it. In the first part of this chapter, we will look at some of the aspects of coordinating and regulating human behavior that fall into the realm of politics. We will also look at **law,** another way in which human societies regulate the behavior of their members and make and enforce decisions. Both politics and law often come in guises not recognizable to us, because law and political organization take different forms at different levels of social complexity: bands, tribes, chiefdoms, and states.

Regulating Human Behavior

Political Organization

In most societies, the authority to make decisions that affect the public interest is placed in some part of the social system, such as kinship, economics, or religion. Group leaders can rule by virtue of their positions as heads of families, lineages, or clans. In other cases, rulers base their claim on divine ancestry. In some societies, the coordination and regulation of behavior are in the hands of a religious practitioner.

If supernatural intervention is an important aspect of the decision-making process — where to hunt, when to move camp, how to find a thief — those who have access to supernatural power will have important political roles in society. If political authority is based on the distribution of goods and services, as it frequently is, leadership will be embedded in economic roles and modes of exchange.

Legitimate power, or authority, means power exercised with the approval of the community. In cases of the legitimate use of power, people obey because they expect that eventually they will benefit from the exercise of that power. We may not like to pay taxes, but we do recognize the right of our government to collect taxes and consider it one of the prices we have to pay for the benefits of government in general. The shared values and beliefs that legitimize the distribution and uses of power in a particular society make up its **political ideology.** If power is not legitimate, it is coercive; people obey because they are afraid of some immediate, direct, and specific punishment. Although some political systems rest more on coercion than others, both coercion and political ideology play a role in maintaining order in a society.

Up until 1940, anthropologists were primarily interested in how political institutions — the structure of status roles through which legitimate power is exercised in a society — worked to maintain stability. More recently, they have turned their attention to **political processes,** the ways in which groups and individuals mobilize support and use power to achieve a variety of public goals. These goals include changing the relationships between groups in society — for example, the redistribution of material resources or the right of access to political

Political leaders surround themselves with elaborate symbols of office in order to help legitimize their control. (United Nations)

office. Another goal may be changing the relationship of the group to its environment, such as building a road or clearing public land. Political goals may also involve changing the relationship of the group to other groups, such as waging war, making peace, or gaining independence from a colonial power. The motivations behind these goals are many; although all political behavior affects the public interest, it is not always in the public interest. Groups and individuals may be motivated by self-interest, a desire for economic gain, or a need for prestige; they may also be motivated by altruism and idealism.

The study of political processes focuses on political activities and events and the ways in which groups compete with one another for control. Anthropologists look for sources of power outside formal political institutions. One is factions, or informal systems of alliance within well-defined political units such as lineages or villages. Another is leadership, which may depend partly on political office but also on the manipulation of kinship networks or wealth in order to build a following. The study of political processes emphasizes how power changes hands in society and how new kinds of political organization develop.

Political processes are thus not just activities that support the social order, avoid or resolve conflicts, and promote the general welfare. The political goals of a group within a

Political processes are the ways in which different, and often conflicting, interest groups mobilize resources to achieve their goals. Shown in this photograph is the peaceful protest by homosexuals in New York City aimed at getting passage of a gay rights bill. The Hassidim, an orthodox Jewish sect, along with other conservative religious groups, demonstrate against the bill. (John McCabe)

society may, in fact, be to promote conflict, change some of the basic aims of existing political institutions, or even destroy the existing social order. Groups or factions within a society may use illegal or informal means to gain their ends — terrorism, for example — but this does not make these activities any less political. But conflict and violence are not *necessarily* destructive. In many societies, violence is a legitimate means of dealing with conflict, as in the case of blood feuds in tribal societies. Conflict may actually support the social order; competition for legitimate goals makes those goals seem worth fighting over. The violent conflict that may occur over succession to office does not destroy the power of the office being sought. The struggle itself emphasizes that the conflicting groups see the office as something worth struggling for. Thus, there is a difference between **rebellion,** the attempt of one group to reallocate resources *within* the existing political structure, and **revolution,** an attempt to

overthrow the existing form of political structure and put another type of political structure in its place.

Law

In no human society does life move along in peace and harmony at all times. Individuals do not always do what they are supposed or expected to do, and they frequently act in ways that disrupt the social order. For a society to function satisfactorily, there must be some conformity among its members. An important — perhaps major — basis for conformity in most societies is the internalization, or learning, of norms and values. Most people comply with authority, and most societies do not rely on force to maintain order.

But what happens when people do not want to conform or, rather, want to do things that do not follow the norms and values of their society? Every society has developed mechanisms to deal with this situation. Many of these mechanisms are informal; gossip and ridicule, for example, are important ways of regulating human conduct. Most individuals value the esteem of others, so the fear of being gossiped about or made fun of is a powerful way of ensuring conformity. Witchcraft accusations are another control mechanism. Anyone who stands out in society, is malicious, or has a nasty temper may be accused of being a witch and suffer punishment. Just the fear of being accused exerts pressure on individuals to conform. Avoidance is another informal way of dealing with social deviants. In small societies, where activities are cooperative, an individual who is shunned by others is at a great disadvantage, both psychologically and economically. Even in our own society, avoidance is a powerful way to get people to conform. One of the strongest expressions of anger, and one often used by small children who have few resources at their command with which to control others, is to say, "I'm not going to talk to you anymore."

Supernatural sanctions are also important in regulating human behavior. A sin is a deviant

The village court in Sierra Leone is administered by a tribunal of local leaders headed by the chief. The defendant (center, with shaved head) faces the tribunal on charges of possessing stolen goods at the time of his arrest. The chief's police officer (left, with white skull cap) acts as defender for the accused. In this case, the defendant was given three months at hard labor and a fine. (United Nations)

behavior that is believed to call forth punishment by supernatural forces. In the Trobriand Islands, incest is a sin; an individual who engages in this behavior is punished by a divinely imposed skin affliction. Supernatural forces that punish social deviants are found in every culture; there are ghosts, spirits, giants who eat little children—even a Santa Claus who does not give presents to children who do not behave.

But what of those who just will not conform? Every society has such people. What is to be done with them? This is where law comes in. In *The Law of Primitive Man*, E. Adamson Hoebel (1974) defines law as "those social norms whose neglect or infraction is regularly met, in threat or in fact, by the application of force by an individual or group who have the socially recognized privilege of acting this way" (p. 28). In every society, some offenses are considered so disruptive that force or the threat of force will be applied. It may be applied by

official representatives of the community, such as judges, courts, police, and jails. It may also be done by individuals with community approval; kin of a murdered man may be allowed, or even expected, to revenge him by killing someone from the murderer's kin group. The control of deviant behavior is therefore a major function of law in all societies.

Another major function of law is to resolve conflicts that would otherwise be disruptive to community life. In politically complex societies such as contemporary nations, crimes against the state are differentiated from grievances that individuals have against one another, though both are addressed by law. In structurally simple societies, disputes between individuals may be handled by the community in the interests of maintaining order. Conflicts between individuals may involve the whole community as judge, as in Inuit song duels. Or a go-between may try to get the complainants to settle. In some societies, go-betweens have the authority to enforce their decisions; in others, they can only persuade the parties to resolve their differences peaceably. In still other cases, supernatural powers are called upon — for example, in cases of trial by ordeal.

The anthropology of law, like political anthropology, has also redefined its emphasis in the last twenty years. Now the focus is more on the informal and formal ways in which behavior is regulated and conflicts are resolved in a society than on the formal legal institutions with which we are familiar. At one time, there were heated arguments over whether primitive societies, with no formal institutions for regulating behavior, could be said to have law. Such questions are no longer of interest to most anthropologists. All societies have "trouble cases," incidents of individual behavior that contradict important social norms or conflicts between individuals that cannot be settled informally between themselves. Every society includes patterned ways of responding to these cases, and it is in this response that law is found. Because political organization includes both the ways in which public policy is made and the ways in which it is enforced in a society, our study of political organization also includes the study of law.

Kinds of Political Organization

Political organization and law exist in all societies, but not all societies have specialized, formal mechanisms through which authority is exercised and law is enforced. The main point about variation in political organizations is, in fact, the degree to which political roles, institutions, and processes are differentiated from other aspects of social organization. A second important aspect of variation is the degree to which authority is centralized or diffused throughout society. Both aspects of political variation, in turn, are related to social complexity: the number of different *kinds* of groups in a society and the ways in which they are connected to one another. Using social complexity

as a standard, anthropologists have defined four major types of political organization (Service 1971). In order of increasing complexity, these are bands, tribes, chiefdoms, and states. Each type tends to be correlated with a particular way of making a living, population size and density, economic system, and pattern of social ranking. Of course, these exact types are not always found in the real world; many societies have some but not all the characteristics of an ideal type. In the sections that follow, the types of political organization are sharply differentiated from one another as a teaching device; in reality, these types overlap with each other, and few societies fall exactly into one or another category.

Band Societies

Band organization, which is the least complex type of society, is characteristic of hunters and gatherers. Reciprocity is the dominant economic pattern in band societies. There is seldom any concept of private ownership of basic resources, such as land or water, although bands may be loosely identified with certain territories. Band societies are egalitarian: There is little role specialization and little difference among the members in terms of wealth, prestige, or power.

Political Integration

A **band** is a small group of people (twenty to fifty) made up of nuclear families who live together and are loosely associated with a territory on which they hunt and gather. Bands are relatively independent of one another. There are few higher levels of control or centralized mechanisms of leadership.

Bands tend to be exogamous (members must marry outside their band), and ties between bands are established mainly by marriage. Because a bilateral kinship system is characteristic of band societies, an individual is linked to many different bands through ties of blood and marriage. Bands may also be linked through the trading relations of some of their members. Membership in bands is flexible, and individuals may change their residence from one band to another fairly easily. The flexibility of band organization is particularly adaptive for the hunting and gathering way of life and low population densities.

Leadership

There is no formal leadership in band societies. Leaders in foraging bands are usually older men whose experience, knowledge of group traditions, and success in hunting are the source of their respect by others. Leaders have no way of enforcing their views; decisions are usually made by all adult men in the group, and leaders can only persuade. Others follow them if they have been successful in the past. Among Inuit groups, for example, the local level leader is called "The One to Whom All Listen," "He Who Thinks," or "He Who Knows Everything Best." Successful Inuit whaling captains who do not generously distribute their accumulated wealth among the group are called merely "rich men" and are distinguished from those whose superior ability and generosity make them respected leaders in the village.

Social Control

In band societies, social order is maintained informally by gossip, ridicule, and avoidance. In extreme cases, an individual may be killed or driven out of the community. Among the !Kung, for example, the sharing of meat is so strongly established that they can hardly conceive of an individual's not doing this. When anthropologist Laura Marshall tried to suggest that an individual could hide with his family in order not to share meat with others, the !Kung "howled with laughter. They said that a man

would be very bad to do that. He would be like a lion. They would have to treat him like a lion by driving him away or teach him manners by not giving him any meat . . . not even a tiny piece" (1967:23). Stealing is another crime among the !Kung, although it occurs rarely. An individual's footprints are as recognizable as his face, and a thief can easily be detected. In the one case of stealing recounted to Marshall, a man who stole another's cache of honey was killed by the owner.

Although theft and the refusal to share food are serious offenses in most band societies, not all are as successful as the !Kung in regulating them. The Siriono, a hunting society of the Amazon Basin in Bolivia, have a similar norm, but it is recognized more in the breach. Siriono frequently attempt to hide food, and families steal off to the forest in the night to eat in order to avoid sharing. Unlike the !Kung, however, the Siriono live in a difficult environment and are constantly on the brink of starvation (Holmberg 1969). Where food is very scarce, social norms about sharing may break down altogether, as illustrated by the selfishness of the Ik of Uganda, described by Colin Turnbull (1972). Theirs is a truly frightening story of a society in which almost perpetual starvation led children to take food from the mouths of their old parents, and people who shared were ridiculed as fools.

Among the Inuit, supernatural sanctions are an important means of social control. Violations of norms are considered sins, and offenders may be controlled through ritual means. Public confessions are directed by the shaman. The offender is defined as a patient, rather than a criminal, and is led to confess all the taboos he or she has violated. The local villagers form the audience and participate as a background chorus. These confessions are mainly voluntary, although a forceful shaman may denounce a member of the community he feels has engaged in acts repulsive to the spirits and is therefore dangerous to the whole group. A person who fails to obey the orders of the shaman may be driven from the community.

Conflict Resolution

Although the need for cooperation and reciprocity minimizes conflicts between individuals in band societies, they do occur and may even become violent. Under the conditions of band society, where the effective social unit is a small group of persons in face-to-face contact, quarrels and conflicts between individuals have a way of involving many other group members. Though few formal institutions exist for resolving conflicts, social mechanisms do operate to prevent the quarrels from seriously threatening the social order.

The Mbuti of the Ituri Forest, for example, have a process called flux (Turnbull 1968). Among the Mbuti, there is great flexibility in the composition of local groups; individuals may change their residence easily, and bands regularly break up into smaller units and re-form into larger ones throughout the year. Breaking the band down into smaller units always separates individuals who have been in conflict with one another, thus preventing prolonged hostilities.

Among some Inuit groups, disputes between individuals are resolved through various kinds of contests. Some of these are physical, such as head butting or a kind of boxing. Others are verbal, such as the famous song duels, where the weapons are words — "little, sharp words like the wooden splinters which I hack off with my ax" (Hoebel 1974:93). Although murder is normally resolved by killing the murderer, a man may choose to revenge his kin in a song duel if he feels too weak to kill his opponent or if he knows he will win the song contest. Each contestant in a song duel tries to deliver the traditional compositions with the greatest skill. The one for whom the audience claps the loudest is the winner. Winning the song duel has little or nothing to do with the facts of a dispute. But it does resolve the quarrel and restore normal relations between those who have become hostile toward each other. The original complaint is laid to rest, and a "judgment" is laid down that is accepted by the contestants.

There is fighting in band societies, both verbal and physical. Violent aggression of an individual nature is not infrequent, and it can result in death or serious injuries. But warfare or armed conflict between socially defined groups of people is not formalized in most band societies, because of the low level of technology and simple political organization. Among band-level hunting and gathering societies, war usually takes the form of family feuding that may continue for generations. There is no formal organization for war and no position of warrior. Military activity is contained within the patterns of kinship. There is little production for warfare and little organized social mobilization to support armed combat. In band societies, the primary objectives of war are likely to be personal; the motivations for fighting are the personal grievances of one individual or a small group of people. Fighting takes place in short skirmishes. Where band societies come into contact with technologically and culturally more dominant groups, the bands tend to retreat into marginal areas rather than fight. They isolate themselves or form peaceful relations with their neighbors (Harrison 1973:42).

Tribal Societies

A **tribe** is a culturally distinct population whose members think of themselves as descended from the same ancestor or as part of the same "people." Tribes occur primarily among pastoralists and horticulturalists, and they are integrated economically by both reciprocity and redistribution. Like bands, tribes are basically egalitarian, with no important differences among members in wealth, status, and power. Also like bands, tribes do not have a separate and distinct set of political roles and institutions. Tribes are usually organized by unilineal kin groups. It is these groups that are the units of political activity as well as the "owners" of basic economic resources. The emergence of local kin groups larger than the nuclear family

In social systems based on complementary opposition, such as that of the Swat Pukhtun of northern Pakistan, brothers and cousins are often pitted against each other in the struggle for power. In Pukhtun society, therefore, friendship between two unrelated males is highly idealized. (John Gregg)

goes with the larger populations that develop in horticultural and pastoral societies.

The effective political unit in these societies is a shifting one. For most of the time, local units of a tribe operate independently. They come together in response to external conditions — either the threat of attack or the opportunity to attack others. Otherwise, little tribal-level organization exists. In fact, under certain conditions, segments of a tribe may be in a state of perpetual violent conflict. As is the case with bands, tribal political organization and mechanisms of social control are embedded in institutions such as kinship or religion. Political functions and roles are not specialized.

Political Integration

The major difference between band and tribe is that a tribal society contains mechanisms that integrate the local segments of the society. Age

sets (p. 273) are one kind of association that serves to integrate different local segments; these are particularly important in many East African tribes. Military societies, such as existed among some Plains Indian tribes in North America, and secret societies, such as those described earlier for West Africa, also cut across and integrate the local segments that make up a tribe. The clan is a form of tribal association based on kinship, and clans may even link members of different tribes.

Another form of tribal integration, which is based on both kinship and locality, is the **segmentary lineage system,** which has been described for the Nuer (Evans-Pritchard 1968) and the Tiv of Nigeria. Among the Nuer, for example, there are about twenty clans, each of which is divided into lineages. Below the level of the clan are segments called maximal lineages, which are broken down into major lineages. Major lineages are, in turn, subdivided into minor lineages, and minor lineages are

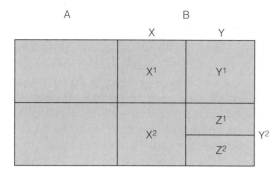

FIGURE 12.1 Complementary opposition functions in the following way: When Z^1 fights Z^2, no other section gets involved. When Z^1 fights Y^1, Z^1 and Z^2 unite as Y^2. When Y^1 fights X^1, Y^1 and Y^2 unite, and so do X^1 and X^2. When X^1 fights A, X^1, X^2, Y^1, and Y^2 all unite as B. When A raids the Dinka (another tribe), A and B may unite. (After Evans-Pritchard in Marshall Sahlins, "The Segmentary Lineage: An Organization of Predatory Expansion." *American Anthropologist* 63:332–45.) Reprinted by permission of Oxford University Press.

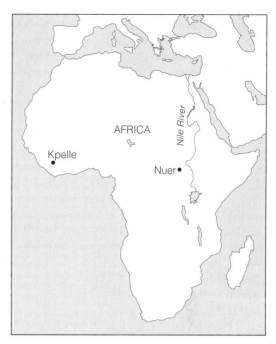

FIGURE 12.2 The location of the Nuer.

made up of minimal lineages. The minimal lineage contains three to five generations and is the basic descent group that functions in day-to-day activities. Members of a minimal lineage live in the same village and regard one another as close relatives. Minimal lineages are politically independent, and there is no formal or centralized leadership above this level. The higher-order lineages function mainly in the context of conflict — they are not groups and do not live together. Rather, they are the basis of an alliance network that emerges only when lower-order segments come into conflict. In a serious dispute between members of different lineages, the higher-order lineage members take the side of their nearest kin (see Figure 12.1). This kind of political structure is called complementary opposition.

Marshall Sahlins (1961) suggests that the segmentary system allows stronger tribes to expand into nearby desirable territories held by weaker groups. Complementary opposition directs the energies of the society upward, away from the competition between kin, to the outside enemy. Lineage segments on the borders of other tribes know that, if they attack an enemy, they will be helped by other lineages related to them at the higher levels of organization.

Tribes with segmentary lineage systems are expanding populations. The Nuer have expanded at the expense of the Dinka, a neighboring pastoral group that originally inhabited the grasslands desired by the Nuer for pasturing their livestock. Because the Dinka were the first in this area and had neither enemies to fight nor neighbors to push back, they did not develop strong mechanisms of tribal integration. The Nuer were the invaders in this area. Their segmentary lineage system developed in response to the need for expansion, and they have, in fact, been successful in pushing the Dinka off much of their land (Figure 12.2).

Leadership

Like bands, tribal societies have leaders but no centralized leadership and no formal offices that are a source of political power. Among the

Nuer, for example, the head of the minimal descent group can use his authority to threaten members of the local group with banishment if they do not agree to settle a dispute. Among many native American populations, there were different kinds of leaders for different kinds of activities. The Cheyenne had war chiefs and peace chiefs. Among the Ojibwa of Canada, there were war leaders, hunting leaders, ceremonial leaders, and clan leaders. Europeans who first came in contact with the Ojibwa frequently misinterpreted the system and imposed on the Ojibwa the concept of a supreme leader or chief. A much better translation of tribal leader in many of these groups is "big-man." When the Canadian government insisted that the Ojibwa must have a chief, the Ojibwa coined a native word, *okimakkan*, which is best translated as "fake chief."

Under certain ecological and social conditions, a more substantial kind of political leadership may emerge in tribal societies. In areas with predictable climate and abundant resources, strong authority roles or true chiefs emerge. The Basseri of southern Iran are a tribe of pastoral nomads with a strong chieftaincy. On their migrations, the Basseri move through areas used by other tribes. To avoid exhaustive grazing of an area, famine of the flocks, and intertribal fighting, the Basseri must stick to their migration schedules and fixed routes. One of the important functions of the Basseri chief, therefore, is to coordinate the movements of the tribe.

The Basseri chief's strength rests not only on the need for a strong authority to coordinate migration movements but also on the role he plays in mediating between the tribe and the settled agricultural populations with whom the Basseri interact. The Basseri must pass through land inhabited by farmers under centralized bureaucratic control. They negotiate contracts with these agriculturalists for using pastureland, and they also exchange products with them. These interactions can result in conflicts; for example, a nomad's herds may damage a farmer's crops.

Because the nomad and the farmer operate within two different social systems, informal mechanisms of conflict resolution cannot be used to settle their differences. Furthermore, the nomad, because he must be on the move, cannot take the time to become involved in lengthy court proceedings, which are a regular way of settling disputes among farmers. The nomad may not even be able to respond to a court summons without hardship. Violence is, of course, a solution, one that has been used frequently in the past. But for peaceful resolution of farmer-nomad conflicts, other political mechanisms must come into play. This is provided by the institution of centralized chieftaincy. The chief represents a fixed point in the nomadic community on which the farmer can fix his grievance. Because a chief has a domestic staff and is relieved from the actual duties of pastoralism, he has the time to work at conflict resolution and can represent the interests of his tribe. Nomads recognize the need for a chief in these situations and have a great feeling of respect for him and awareness of their dependence on him, all of which strengthen his power (Barth 1964).

Another kind of tribal leader is characteristic of societies throughout Melanesia and New Guinea. This is the big-man, a self-made leader who gains power through personal achievements rather than through holding office. He begins his career as the leader of a small, localized kin group. Through a series of public actions, such as generous loans, the big-man attracts followers within the community. He skillfully builds up his capital and increases the number of his wives. Because women take care of pigs, he can increase the size of his pig herds. He distributes his wealth in ways that build his reputation as a rich and generous man: by sponsoring feasts, paying subsidies to military allies, purchasing high ranks in secret societies, and paying bridewealth for young men seeking wives. By giving generously, he places many other people under obligation to him. Big-men command obedience from their followers through this personal relationship of gratitude and obligation.

The activities of big-men do provide leadership above the local level, but this integration is fragile. It depends not on the creation of permanent office but rather on the personality and constant striving of an individual. Big-men rise and fall. With their deaths, their factions may dissolve, or other ambitious men may undermine their power. Most important, however, the big-man must spur his local group on to ever greater production if he is to hold his own against other big-men in the tribe. To maintain prestige, he must give his competitors more than they can give him. This means the big-man must begin to withhold gifts to the followers who are producing for him. The discontent this brings may lead to the defection of the followers or even the murder of the big-man. A big-man cannot pass on his status to others; each individual must begin anew to amass the wealth and forge the internal and external social relationships on which big-man status depends (Sahlins 1971).

Social Control and Conflict Resolution

Tribes, like bands, depend a great deal on informal ways of controlling deviant behavior and settling conflicts, but they have also developed more formal mechanisms of control. The Cheyenne were particularly successful in peacefully resolving intratribal conflict and in controlling individual behavior when this was necessary for the common good. Their relatively formal structure of social control came into play during the summer season, when Cheyenne bands came together for great communal buffalo hunts and tribal ceremonies. Order was necessary to prevent disputes, and strict discipline was required on the buffalo hunt. An individual hunter could ruin the hunt for others by alarming and scattering the buffalo. These tribal gatherings and communal hunts were policed by members of military associations. The associations not only punished offenders but also tried to rehabilitate the guilty parties by bringing them back within the tribal structure.

The function of the police was not revenge, but getting the deviant to conform to tribal law in the interest of the welfare of the tribe. Individuals were punished by a variety of methods. Sometimes their teepees were ripped to shreds, or the ears of their horses were cut off, a mark of shame. Offenders might also be whipped. If they resisted, they might be killed on the spot. If, however, they accepted the punishment and appeared to have learned a lesson, they were accepted back into the group, and their belongings were often replaced. But the Cheyenne military societies operated only during the hunt period. At other times, more informal sanctions and leadership operated at the band level.

Another means of regulating behavior in tribal societies is through the use of go-betweens. Among the Nuer, a Leopard Skin chief acts as a mediator, particularly in cases where a killing takes place. As in other tribal societies, when one person kills another, retaliation can be expected from the dead person's kin and may begin a true feud. After a killing, the killer may seek sanctuary in the home of the Leopard Skin chief. The chief goes to the home of the slayer's family and gets the family to promise to pay a certain number of cattle to the dead person's family. He then goes to the family of the victim and tries to get them to accept this compensation. The Leopard Skin chief can only mediate, however; he cannot compel either of the families to accept the settlement. In the case of other kinds of disputes, such as that over ownership of cattle, the chief and perhaps other respected elders in the community may attempt to get the two sides to make a settlement through public discussion. There is no means of enforcing their suggestions, however. Although go-betweens have little or no authority to enforce their decisions, they express the general interest of society in ending tension, punishing wrongs, and restoring social stability. Go-betweens, with the power of public opinion behind them, are usually effective. But if a settlement cannot be agreed upon, a feud will begin, undertaken by the aggrieved party.

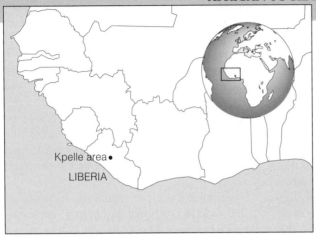

Many traditional societies in West Africa are known for their high development of law and legal procedures. In addition to these formal procedures and courts, however, there are informal, quasi-legal procedures for settling disputes. One such procedure, found among the Kpelle of Liberia, is called the moot, or "house palaver." The Kpelle are rice cultivators who live in central Liberia. The most important kinship group is the patrilocal polygynous family; several of these families form the core of a residential group, known as a village quarter, headed by a quarter elder.

In Liberia the highest official court is that of a paramount chief; there are also official courts of the district chief. There are also unofficial town chief, or quarter elder, courts, and in addition, grievances are settled informally at moots. Kpelle courts are basically coercive and handle best those types of cases, such as assault or theft, in which the litigants are not linked in a relationship that must continue after the trial. The courts are not effective, however, in the many matrimonial cases brought before them, because the courts' harsh and official tone tends to drive spouses apart rather than reconciling them. Kpelle courts customarily treat matrimonial cases by granting the couple a divorce. The moot, on the other hand, tends to reconcile the couple; it is successful in doing this because it is not only conciliatory but also therapeutic.

The Kpelle moot takes place before an assembled group that includes kinsmen of the litigants and neighbors from the quarter where the case is being heard. The cases before it are usually domestic matters: alleged mistreatment by a spouse, an attempt to collect money from a kinsman for a job not completed, or a quarrel among brothers over the inheritance of their father's wives.

The moot is most often held on a Sunday — a universal day of rest among the Kpelle — at the home of the complainant, the person who calls the moot. The mediator at the moot is selected by the complainant. He is a kinsman who also holds an office, such as quarter elder, and thus has experience in handling disputes. The proceedings begin with one of the group elders pronouncing a blessing on the complainant and his relations. The elder does this dramatically, walking up and down, waving a fly whisk, and demanding that the assembled group join him. The effect is to unite those attending in common action before the hearing begins and to focus attention on the concern with maintaining harmony and the well-being of the group as a whole. The litigants and spectators, including the elders, sit crowded together, in sharp contrast to the spatial separation between litigants and judges in a courtroom. The mediator, though a chief, wears ordinary clothing.

The complainant speaks first and may be interrupted by the mediator or anyone else present. After he or she has been thoroughly questioned, the accused answers and is also questioned by those present. The two parties question each other directly and question others in the room. The meeting is spirited and lively, but order is maintained by the mediator. The mediator and others point out the various faults committed by both parties. After everyone has been heard, the mediator expresses the consensus of the group. The person held to be mainly at fault then formally apologizes to the other person. This apology takes the form of giving token gifts such as clothing, a few coins, or some rice to the wronged person. The winning party, in accepting the gifts of apology, is expected to give, in return, a smaller token to the loser to show goodwill. The losing party must also present beer to the mediator and the spectators, and it is then consumed. The elder again pronounces a blessing, offers thanks for the restoration of harmony within the group, and asks that all continue to act with good grace and unity.

A comparison with a court case highlights the therapeutic effectiveness of the moot. Whereas in a courtroom, grievances can be only partially aired, in the moot, there is a much fuller airing of the issues, and the range of relevant material is very broad. This fuller airing results in catharsis; if the solution to a dispute reached in the moot is to be lasting, it is important that there should be nothing left unsaid that will embitter either party and undermine the decision.

Secondly, the resolution of the case is not a solution imposed by a judge, but is based on consensus. There is no unilateral ascription of blame but rather an attribution of fault to both parties. The ritualized apology symbolizes concretely the consensual nature of the solution. The public offering and acceptance of the tokens of apology indicate that neither party has any further grievances. The parties and the spectators drink together to symbolize the restored solidarity of the group and the rehabilitation of the offending party.

This group support, which is heightened by the opening and closing blessings, is very important in indicating to both parties that they have a real problem but that others are concerned and willing to help them. This support motivates the participants to speak freely and thus move toward a lasting resolution of their problems. Furthermore, in the moot, the litigants are allowed to say things to each other that would probably result in a citation of contempt and possible jail sentence if they were in a court. In hurling recriminations, litigants invite response from the spectators, who frequently gently reprimand them for being in the wrong. Thus, the litigants are able to see that their own perspective may not be based in reality and are moved to reconsider their position.

Finally, just as the patient is coaxed to conformity by the granting of re-

(*continued*)

wards in the therapeutic situation, so the reward of group approval is granted publicly in the moot, both to the wronged person who accepts an apology and to the person who is big enough to make one. In this way, the wrongdoer is restored to good grace; because blame is typically spread around, he or she is not singled out and isolated in being labeled deviant. Moreover, the "fines," or token gifts, are not so expensive as to give the loser additional reason for anger directed at the winning party.

The rewards of the moot are positive, in contrast to the negative sanctions of the courtroom. The deviant is pulled back into a relationship with the wider group; if the moot is successful, reconciliation will be achieved with no residue of bitterness or resentment. In the case of married couples, then, the successful moot results in reconciliation, not divorce; in other relationships that must continue outside the case, it is hoped that the moot will finish off people's quarrels and abolish bad feeling.

The moot and similar institutions in other societies are mechanisms of social control that break the progressive alienation of the deviance cycle — something that is normally not achieved in a more formal court proceeding. The model of the West African moot has become the basis for a reexamination of many court procedures in the United States. As courts become more crowded and inaccessible for various kinds of disputes between parties who are in long-term relationships, the process of mediation, or informal dispute resolution, has mushroomed all over America (Tomasic and Feeley 1982). Legal and social reformers are hoping that these new neighborhood justice centers, which utilize the "house palaver" model, will make justice more responsive to people's needs.

Adapted from James L. Gibbs, Jr., "The Kpelle Moot: A Therapeutic Model for the Informal Settlement of Disputes," in Johnnetta B. Cole, ed., Anthropology for the Eighties *(New York: The Free Press, 1982).*

Formal, complex, and specialized systems for resolving conflicts and regulating behavior are particularly well developed in West Africa. Among the Ibo, for example, the body of elders met in a central council to act as mediators and referees in settling disputes. In these courts, or councils, the senior elder opened the proceedings by a prayer to the gods to enable them to come to the right decisions and punish anyone who attempted to pervert justice or any witness who gave false evidence. In some towns, a council elder was first made to swear that he would not make decisions in secret, take sides in disputes, appropriate communal or other property by force, or use public monies for his own purposes.

Not every offense resulted in a trial. A criminal might be punished by the family or by the person against whom he or she had committed the crime. Murderers could hang them-

Many native American tribal "chiefs" were created by Europeans who projected their own systems of centralized political office on groups with whom they came in contact. Dealing with one leader was easier than dealing with a collective body. (Photo: Rodman Wanamaker. Courtesy Department of Library Services, American Museum of Natural History)

selves or get a relative to substitute, and the case would be considered closed. Trials were held when a case was in doubt. The elders who tried cases took into account the social position of those accused, the strength of their kin relations, and whether they were useful members of society, as well as the seriousness of the offense. If after the evidence was heard, the case was still in doubt, it was decided by an oath or an ordeal. An **ordeal** is a means of determining guilt or innocence by having those who are accused submit themselves to dangerous or painful tests believed to be under supernatural control. Among the Ibo, the drinking of poison was

an ordeal. The use of ordeals means that judges do not have to put their own prestige on the line in every judgment. Where there is no central political authority to enforce decisions, mediators need the extra weight of supernatural backing to ensure that people will comply (Meek 1972).

In many New Guinea societies, and other Melanesian horticultural tribes, violent solutions to conflict are replaced by compensation payments to aggrieved parties. The payment demanded is thought to be proportionate to the severity of the act that precipitated the dispute, and it is usually proportionate to the extent to

WARFARE AMONG THE YANOMAMO

While feuding and warfare appear to be constant in many tribal societies, among the Yanomamo in the Amazon areas of Venezuela and Brazil both personal and organized violence seem to reach extreme levels. For the "fierce people," as they are described and most widely known through the ethnography of Napoleon Chagnon (1983), violence by men against women, violence among men in the same village, and warfare between villages are part of their daily life and the focus of their culture. Anthropologists have long tried to answer the question "Why are the Yanomamo so violent?" According to the Yanomamo themselves, warfare among villages is not for land, but to steal each other's women. In a Yanomamo raid, as many men as possible are killed and as many women as possible are captured. Chagnon's explanation is that the constant warfare and militant ideology of the Yanomamo are a way of preserving village autonomy (1983). Because the Yanomamo have not been able to control conflict within villages, fights often break out among individuals. This leads to the division of villages into independent and hostile camps. In order to be able to survive as an independent unit in an environment of constant warfare, members of a village adopt a hostile and aggressive stance toward other villagers. Yanomamo aggressiveness is encouraged from childhood and reinforced by a cultural pattern that demands a display of ferocity on the part of males. This ferocity is demonstrated not only in the fights between men but also in the way husbands treat their wives.

Another explanation for Yanomamo violence and warfare is offered by William Divale and Marvin Harris (1976). According to Divale and Harris, Yanomamo war-

fare (and warfare in other horticultural tribes) is a way of controlling population. Divale and Harris argue that war regulates population indirectly by leading to female infanticide, not by causing deaths in battle. In societies where warfare is constant, there is a cultural preference for fierce and aggressive males who can become warriors. Because male children are preferred over females, female infants are frequently killed. Among the Yanomamo, the shortage of women that results from female infanticide appears as a strong *conscious* motivation for warfare, thus providing a continuing "reason" for the Yanomamo to keep fighting among themselves. In the absence of reliable contraception and abortion, the most effective and widespread means of regulating population growth is reducing the number of fertile females, by female infanticide.

A more recent analysis of Yanomamo violence and warfare focuses on a historical factor that Chagnon, Divale, and Harris do not sufficiently take into account: the effect of European contact on the Yanomamo (Ferguson 1992). According to Brian Ferguson, the "fierce people" immortalized by Chagnon were studied at a particular moment in history in which Yanomamo culture was "pushed into an extreme conflict mode" because of the intensification of a Western presence (p. 200). Ferguson emphasizes depopulation due to European-introduced disease epidemics and the availability of European manufactured goods as two major factors that directly and indirectly have resulted in a heightened level of Yanomamo violence and warfare. Although some Yanomamo had experienced some Western contact for hundreds of years, it was in the quarter century before Chagnon did his fieldwork in the mid-1960s that this impact was intensified and thus the level of Yanomamo violence reached extreme heights.

Since the 1940s the Yanomamo had experienced a severe increase in mortality as a result of both various epidemics and warfare. Because many of those stricken were adult food providers, malnutrition compounded the effects of disease and contributed to the high death rate. These deaths and the consequent disruption of family life resulted in a significant tear in the Yanomamo social fabric. Yanomamo social order is intertwined with the alliances formed by family life, kinship, and marriage. These relationships are built on complex exchanges and take years to develop. Indeed, one of the paramount concerns of a senior

Yanomamo man is to find wives for his sons, younger brothers, and other related men in his village. The negotiation of marriage arrangements has been made far more difficult by the lethal effects of epidemics and warfare. While it is true that a scarcity of women among the Yanomamo is linked to both female infanticide and polygyny (themselves linked to warfare), the death rate from epidemics, particularly as this affects the youngest generation of women, means that arranging new marriages becomes more difficult, even chaotic. With this breakdown of the marriage system, the stage is set for increasing violence both within and between villages.

Undoubtedly, a major impact on Yanomamo culture was created by the Yanomamo desire for European manufactured goods, particularly metal tools — machetes, axes, and knives — and firearms. Metal tools are highly prized for their effectiveness and, until the last thirty or so years, for their scarcity. Metal tools not only are more effective and efficient in a horticultural economy, but firearms give a substantial advantage in warfare. A direct effect of the introduction of guns has been an increase in both the amount and the lethal result of warfare. A village with even a few shotguns is not only more effective on the offensive, but is also less likely to be attacked. Metal tools are also useful for military purposes, such as in building barricades around a village to resist attack. European-manufactured metal tools and weapons, therefore, have an unquestionable role in directly sustaining Yanomamo militarization, in addition to other uses.

A central problem for the Yanomamo is how to acquire these European goods.

(continued)

Previously, European goods were traded at long distance, but in recent times, the surest way to obtain European goods was to live in more settled villages, relatively close to the European outposts. This made European goods available through gifts from missionaries and others, in return for services, such as acting as guides or interpreters, or as payment for goods the Europeans need, such as garden produce, meat, or firewood. The increasing preference of some Yanomamo to live relatively close to European outposts, in order to secure a supply of Western goods, as well as to benefit by Western medicine (which is particularly useful in patching up the wounded in warfare), has also indirectly led to increased levels of conflict and violence.

As forest horticulturalists who also hunt, the Yanomamo consider meat an important and prized source of protein. Sharing meat is an important basis of village solidarity and, thus, social control in Yanomamo villages. In indigenous circumstances, when a village depleted the game supply in its immediate vicinity, either the men would extend their hunting trips deeper into the forest, or the village would relocate in a more remote area where game was more plentiful. But as the perceived benefits of European contact make the Yanomamo reluctant to leave the European outposts, villages now more often remain in locations even where the game has been depleted. As a result, meat becomes very scarce in these "settled" villages, and it is no longer shared among everyone in the village, but is kept and consumed by individual families. This breakdown of village reciprocity and the atomization of families that results increases social conflict within villages. Village fissioning is more likely, and these villages become potential enemies.

In addition the indigenous strategy of relocating deeper into the forest in response to a decreasing food supply avoided potential conflict and aggression between villages. With this "flight" response no longer so attractive, villages are more likely to fight when conflict arises.

Still other effects of Western contact help maintain a high level of Yanomamo violence. The high intensity of warfare reinforces the low status of Yanomamo women and helps perpetuate male violence against them. The wars, in turn, reflect the unequal distribution of Western goods among Yanomamo villages. One way to address this imbalance is plunder: Those who don't have use force to take from those who do. While this occurs infrequently, as it is a high-risk enterprise, it does contribute to a high level of violence. More indirect routes, also using force, however, are more common: A village may ambush another village to motivate it to move further away from a European outpost, or on a more personal level, men may engage in club fights and other violent confrontations as a way of securing valued material goods in an exchange relationship.

Ferguson's analysis, which introduces the historical element into an understanding of why the Yanomamo are so violent, is not in contradiction to, so much as a necessary complement to, the theories of Chagnon and Divale and Harris. Ferguson and others, who apply a world historical perspective to an understanding of tribal warfare, locate it in the larger context of European contact. The effects of this contact will not be the same in each situation, but with regard to the Yanomamo, it seems that the "fierce people" are so fierce partly because we helped make them so.

which the dispute involves other kinsmen as allies, who must get part of the payment. Payment of compensation generally implies acceptance of responsibility by the donors and willingness to terminate the dispute by the recipients (Scaglion 1981). Recently in some parts of New Guinea, very inflated compensation payments were being demanded in homicide cases, and the size and distribution of these payments became the basis for further disputing, rather than facilitating conflict management.

The government of Papua New Guinea viewed this situation as a problem and invited anthropologists who had worked in the area to apply their knowledge of customary law to the government's attempt at law reform. With the emergence of Papua New Guinea as a nation, the government is trying to reform its law and courts to integrate both Western law, a legacy of its Australian colonial era, and tribal customary law (Ottley and Zorn 1983). As is often the case in applied anthropology, the anthropologist's position is that matters are not as simple as they might seem: Compensation and customary law are complex issues and vary among social groups. They are also part of a wider, interlocking social and cultural system and cannot easily be tampered with. While the New Guinean administrators who seek the anthropologist's advice are often impatient with the caution implied in the academic approach, the anthropologist must resist giving "hard and fast answers," providing instead the knowledge upon which only elected legislators can make decisions.

Nomadic pastoralist tribes, like horticulturalists, have a tendency to engage in feuding and warfare. Warfare among pastoralists is most frequently associated with raiding other groups for animals, a way of bringing about a balance between population and resources. The approach to warfare that stresses the interrelationship among ecology, social structure, level of sociocultural complexity, and conflict is a good example of the kinds of understanding anthropologists seek. Anthropological studies indicate that warfare can be explained *not* by a human instinct for aggression but rather by its relationship to ecological, historical, and sociocultural factors—that is, as part of a total sociocultural system.

Warfare in Tribal Societies

Anthropologists have long been interested in explaining the high frequency of warfare in tribal societies. In the absence of strong mechanisms for tribal integration through peaceful means, and the absence of strong motivations to produce food over and above immediate needs, warfare may serve to regulate the balance between population and resources in tribal societies. Andrew Vayda (1976) has suggested that a critical factor is that most tribal societies practice slash and burn horticulture. Because it is much harder to clear forest for cultivation than to work land that has already been used, a local group may prefer to take land from other groups, by force if necessary, rather than expand into virgin forest. This sets up a condition in which warfare is a way for societies that have experienced a decrease in food supplies due to population increase, or that have reached the limits of expansion into unoccupied land, to expand. Where there are effective nonwarlike ways in which population can be redistributed within the total territory of the tribe, tribes may not be warlike or may direct their aggressive activities outward toward other tribes. According to Vayda, the Maori of New Zealand are an example of the first model, and the Iban of Sarawak are an example of the second.

Warfare within tribes may also be linked to aspects of social structure. Structural features such as patrilineality and patrilocality, by promoting male solidarity, make the resort to force to resolve conflicts more feasible than in matrilineal and matrilocal societies, which undermine fraternal solidarity and engender conflicting loyalties among males. However, patrilocality and matrilocality may develop out of societies that have different types of warfare.

When warfare is carried out over long distances, for example, matrilocality favors domestic harmony when the warriors are away.

Although anthropologists may not agree about the specific causes of warfare, one area of wide agreement is that war is grounded in material, or ecological, conditions. This aspect of warfare has greatly increased with Western contact. As pointed out earlier, for example, warfare among native American tribes intensified after contact with Europeans as a result of competition through the fur trade over access to European manufactures. The most recent anthropological thinking on warfare among tribes highlights the role of Western contact and colonialism as major factors in generating or transforming tribal warfare (Ferguson and Whitehead 1992). While each case needs to be explained in terms of its own historical context, some generalizations about the connections between Western contact and tribal warfare are useful.

One well-documented outcome of European culture contact was depopulation as a result of the epidemic spread of diseases for which indigenous peoples had no immunity. This population loss disrupts indigenous social structure and relationships, contributing to intertribal violence. European contact also modifies the environment substantially by the more rapid depletion of subsistence resources. While even the simplest foraging society always modifies its environment, the European drive for wealth and profit greatly intensifies this process. For example, indigenous native American buffalo hunting, even after the introduction of the horse, did not seriously affect the food supply. Only as a result of the large-scale trade in buffalo skins stimulated by European demand did the buffalo disappear. One effect of this depletion of resources is the competition for food among and within tribal groups, heightening the possibilities for warfare.

A third important factor in increasing tribal warfare was the desire of indigenous peoples for the metal manufactures, and particularly guns, that were introduced by the Europeans on a large scale. Metal tools are very useful in horticultural tribal societies, and guns, obviously, have an additional impact in both increasing warfare and intensifying its lethal results. In the box discussing warfare among the Yanomamo (pp. 330–332), we can see the working out of these factors in a particular cultural situation.

Chiefdoms

Two main characteristics distinguish chiefdoms from tribes. Unlike a tribe, in which all segments are structurally and functionally similar, a **chiefdom** is made up of parts that are structurally and functionally different from one another. A ranking system means that some lineages, and the individuals in them, have higher or lower social status than others. As we saw for Polynesia and the Northwest Coast of America, rulers, nobles, and commoners may be distinguished from one another by genealogical closeness to the chief. There may also be geographical units within a chiefdom, each of which has its own chief or council.

The second difference between tribes and chiefdoms is that a chiefdom has a centralized leadership that consists of an *office* of chief (as opposed, for example, to the individualistic and self-made leadership provided by a Melanesian big-man). The rise of a centralized governing center—that is, the chief and his political authority—is closely related to redistributive exchange patterns. Goods move into the center (the chief) and are redistributed through the chief's generosity in giving feasts and sponsoring rituals. The economic surplus created by the chief level of organization is used to benefit the whole society, though at the same time it is the primary support of the chief's power and prestige.

The economic surplus in a chiefdom provides more security than in a tribal society without chiefs. The chief distributes labor as well as food. In addition, centralized authority prevents the outbreak of violence between segments of the society, and at the same time it

Native American societies relied on "peace" chiefs, like Judge Wolf Plume of the Black-foot, to resolve disputes and conflicts within the society and between different tribes. (Courtesy of the American Museum of Natural History.)

gives the society a greater degree of military power vis-à-vis other societies than tribes are able to muster. Chiefdoms are found mainly in pastoral societies or those in which intensive cultivation is practiced, though they also existed among the hunting and fishing societies of the Northwest Coast of America and Polynesia.

Regulation of Behavior and Conflict Resolution

Compared to tribes, internal violence within chiefdoms is reduced, because the chief has authority to make judgments, to punish deviant individuals, and to resolve disputes. In the Trobriand Islands, the power of a chief to punish people is achieved partly by hiring sorcerers

to kill the offender by black magic. The greatest power of the Trobriand chief lies in his power to control garden magic. As "garden magician" he not only organizes the efforts of the villagers under his control but also performs the rituals considered necessary for success at every step: preparing the fields, planting, and harvesting. The ultimate power of the chief is his magical control of rain; if he wishes he can produce a prolonged drought, which will cause many people to starve. This power is used when the chief is angry as a means of collective punishment and enforcement of his will.

Among the Basseri, the chief, or *khan*, has great power in settling disputes. Disputes come to the chief only after informal methods within the camp have failed to achieve a settlement. Once a dispute is brought to the chief, he can dispose of the case at his will. His decisions must be obeyed, and an individual who does not comply is beaten with a pole. In other societies, even where chiefs have equally strong powers, they choose to rule with tact and kindness, rather than by the use of force. Clellan Ford describes the actions of a wise Fijian chief in the following case:

> A woman had gotten angry at her husband, who had failed to fix their leaky roof. One rainy night she threatened to kill him with a knife. She chased him around the room and finally aimed a blow at his head. The husband grabbed a mat from the floor to use as a shield. The knife struck the mat and rebounded on the woman's head, resulting in a deep cut. On hearing of this, the chief called both parties together, and listened with great seriousness to their arguments. The wife complained her husband was lazy and spent all his time drinking *kava*. The husband complained his wife neglected her duties and seldom cooked for him. The chief could easily have disposed of the matter by fining the husband and the wife for causing trouble. Instead, he sensed an underlying tension in the relationship, of which this fight was only a symptom. He called members of the village and heard their testimony. It appeared that the woman thought herself too good for her husband, and he felt and resented this. The chief got the husband and wife to admit this. He then ordered the woman to be a better spouse and sent the man off to work in his garden, warning him that any future trouble would result in his exile from the village. The chief then gave a gift to the male members of the village and asked them to repair the roof. After settling the dispute, the chief held a feast for the village. (1938:545)

Social order in chiefdoms is maintained through fear and through genuine respect for and loyalty to the chief. As our examples illustrate, the chief's authority is backed by his control of symbolic, supernatural, administrative, economic, and military power. This permits more stability in chiefdoms than in tribes, though sometimes violent competition for the office of chief occurs. Chiefs generally suppress any attempt at rebellion or threats from competitors and deal harshly with those who try to take their power. To emphasize the importance of this office for the society, offenses against the chief are punishable by death.

State Societies

The most complex political organization is the state. A **state** is a hierarchical, centralized form of political organization in which a central government has the legal monopoly over the use of force. In addition, states are characterized by social stratification. In most cases, state societies rest on a system of intensive agriculture, the productivity of which allows the development of cities, economic and occupational specialization, and extensive trade. One of the most important characteristics of the state is its ability to expand indefinitely without splitting, through the incorporation of a variety of political units and ethnic groups. Thus, states can become much more populous, heterogeneous, and powerful than any other kind of society.

Social Stratification

As it does with chiefdoms, the rise of a centralized ruling authority creates an economic surplus. But in state societies, only a part of the surplus created by intervention in the economy goes back to the people directly; some is used to support the activities of the state itself, such as maintaining administrative bureaucracies, standing armies, artists and craftworkers, and a priesthood. Part of the wealth produced in states is also used to support the ruling class in a luxurious style. Only the ruling class has unlimited access to basic resources. The power of the state is used to maintain this unequal access and to collect food surpluses through taxation.

In chiefdoms, ranking is based on kinship. In state societies, kinship does not regulate relations between the different social classes. Instead, each class marries within itself, and kin ties no longer extend throughout the whole society. This contributes to the widening of the gap between the classes.

Centralized Government

The state as a form of political organization is characterized by a high degree of functional specialization. Social order is maintained through government — an interrelated set of status roles that became separate from other aspects of social organization, such as kinship. The components of a state are no longer kinship groups; other kinds of groups and relationships, particularly those based on territory, become more important. A person becomes a member of the society through citizenship rather than kinship, and the sense of being "one people" is no longer limited to those who recognize ties of blood and marriage. The administrative divisions of a state are territorial units, cities, districts, and so on. Each unit has its own government, though these governments are not independent of the central government.

In state societies, **government**, a social institution specifically concerned with making and enforcing public policy, performs the functions that keep the society going. The state, for example, intervenes in every aspect of the economic process. Through taxation, it stimulates the agricultural production of households. It also controls labor; it can order people to work on roads and buildings and to serve in armies, thus affecting the work force available for agriculture. The state also intervenes in the exchange and distribution of goods and services through complex market networks. It protects distribution by making travel safe for traders as they move their goods from one place to another and by keeping peace in the marketplace. The state may also intervene in the consumption process. It can pass laws regarding which people are allowed to use which goods — for example, by reserving for the elite such items as gold, silk, or other costly symbols of high status. These complicated exchanges and rules brought a need for record keeping. Systems of writing arose in some states, as well as systems of weights and measures. In some states, cities

In a state society, the legal monopoly over the use of force rests in the hands of the state. (United Nations)

arose as administrative, religious, and economic centers. It was in these centers that important cultural achievements in science, art, architecture, and philosophy were stimulated.

The Monopoly of Force

The major defining characteristic of state societies is the government's monopoly over the use of force. A state uses a code of law to make clear how and when it will use force and forbids individuals or groups to use force. Written laws are passed by authorized legislative bodies and enforced by formal and specialized institutions of law enforcement. Courts and police forces, for example, have the authority to impose all kinds of punishments: prison, confiscation of property, fines, and even death.

In state societies, the fact that only the state has the authority to use force does not mean that force is used only by the state. In fact, many states are plagued by the illegal use of force and violence, which may take many different forms.

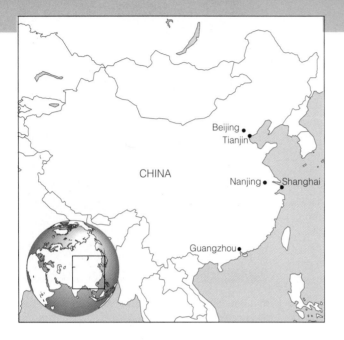

Dorothy Bracey, an anthropologist who has studied the criminal justice system in the People's Republic of China, describes how the current Chinese government's system of social control is built upon a concept of human nature different from that underlying the system of social control in the United States. As part of this system, the Chinese government runs Reform-Through-Education Farms. Residents of the Reform-Through-Education Farm have not had a trial, nor have they been sentenced by a judge. They are undergoing "administrative punishment" for periods of up to three years, a punishment suggested by the police and approved by the city's Reform-Through-Education Bureau. In addition, the punishment must be approved by the offender's neighborhood or workplace committee. Petty theft, hooliganism, fighting, disturbing the social order, and swindling are the activities likeliest to land a Beijing resident among the orchards, grapevines, and wheat fields that comprise most of the farm's acreage and consume much of the inmate's time. Six to eight hours of agricultural work each day are followed by evenings spent studying Chinese history, politics, and party ideology. The staff proudly reported a recidivism rate of less than 8 percent.

The Chinese attribute this low rate of recidivism to the farm program, which involves "helping people confess from their hearts that they have committed offenses. Then they will try to reform themselves and develop correct moral attitudes." This comment clearly indicates that the North American and Chinese systems of justice and social control are based on entirely different concepts of human nature. Americans accept as a given that human beings are basically selfish, that even though the worst of them may have moments of spontaneous generosity, they are motivated primarily by self-interest. They avoid vice in favor of virtue only because they believe that although vice brings pleasure immediately, it brings pain eventually. Perhaps this view rests on the concept of original sin; certainly teachings of twentieth-century Freudian and Skinnerian psychology are consistent with a vision of human nature as intrinsically self-centered, demanding, and controlled only by commands and prohibitions, punishments and rewards.

Confucius taught that people were born without innate defects, and therefore their moral growth depended upon education. The primary aim of education was to cultivate permanent and correct mental attitudes toward social norms. Social control, in other words, could be internalized; it did not have to depend upon the promise of rewards or the threat of punishments from outside the individual. All people have this innate capacity to be good, but not all have been equally fortunate in receiving the education that would allow them to develop that capacity to its fullest extent. In the words of Confucius, "By nature, men are nearly alike; by practice, they become very different."

Chinese Marxism has perpetuated much of this traditional view. Human nature is regarded as plastic and malleable at any age; although it is corruptible, it is also improvable. The Chinese believe that, given the choice between good and evil, people will deliberately choose good. If they do not, they possibly do not see the choice as clearly as others see it, or their education has not equipped them to make the correct choice, or they have been corrupted by bad teachers, leaders, parents, or companions. Society owes it both to these people and to itself to reeducate them so that they will be capable of choosing good in the future.

The Chinese have no doubts about the best technique for reeducation: Present people with a model. Confucius urged virtue on the ruler largely because a ruler should be a model for others. His disciple Mencius was so convinced that people emulated the behavior of others, he urged people to examine the morality of village or neighborhood inhabitants before deciding to move, as their own behavior would inevitably be influenced by that of their new neighbors.

Models for emulation may be living or dead, national or local. A model may exhibit general virtues, such as "selflessly serving the socialist motherland," or particular ones, such as doubling one's output in a factory. The model's example helps to develop an entrenched attitude, which the Chinese feel is far more stable than is a fear of punishment. It is not that coercive methods do not exist but rather that they are regarded as being second best. The obverse side of this emphasis on the model as a teaching device is the tendency to encourage people to become models. Praise as a model citizen or worker — just as the chaste widow or filial son was proclaimed by the Confucian emperor — leads to imitation and to group respect, the most legitimate and desirable forms of reward.

All of these observations have implications for Chinese social control in general and criminal justice in particular. They help to explain much that Americans find striking in the Chinese criminal justice system, such as the Reform-Through-Education Farm. The "farm" is based on the belief that hu-

(continued)

man nature is basically good but corruptible, that education is the best tool for both systemic and individual reform, and that people are malleable throughout their lives. These beliefs explain the evening "study sessions," which are devoted to gaining a better understanding of Chinese history and society as interpreted by the Chinese Communist party. This understanding, in turn, will lead to an offender's recognition of the nature and cause of his misdeeds and a sincere desire not to repeat them.

The insistence on "confession from the heart" and the belief in its redemptive qualities provide the rationale for the Reform-Through-Education Farm and its practices. Farm directors are convinced that models of proper behavior provide the most desirable mode of learning. The residents are urged to "learn from the good performers." They are also exhorted to act as models for others. Those chosen as models of neatness, productiveness, helpfulness, or some other virtue are lauded at meetings and study sessions, while others are encouraged to follow their example. The good performers are singled out and rewarded by having small red banners placed by their names on the list of occupants posted outside each dormitory.

The belief that all people have at least the potential for good also explains the wide variety of social control devices available to Chinese society; these range from informal and formal criticism during neighborhood committee mediation, public self-criticism, and Reform-Through-Education Farms, to prison and reform-through-labor camps. The Chinese believe that it is important to intervene early, before deviance has become extreme or caused too much damage. To refrain from correcting minor expressions of deviance on the grounds that such correction interferes with the individual's civil rights strikes the Chinese as analogous to withholding early treatment of a disease on the grounds that the disease has a right to develop until it proves to be lethal. This is particularly true because society (through bad education) is at least partially to blame for the deviance; it thus has a corresponding duty to correct it.

Mao himself made this comparison of deviance to illness under the rubric of "curing the sickness to save the patient." It has also been suggested that this version of the redemptive process can be seen as a partial substitute for conventional civil liberties because, just as a patient cured of a disease is again treated as a healthy person, a properly repentant sinner may again gain grace.

This raises the issues that many Americans find hard to accept. Residents of the Reform-Through-Education Farm are incarcerated for up to three years for offenses that would be classified as violations or misdemeanors under the American legal system. Their sentences are not the result of a trial. Although the police recommendations have to be approved by a number of bodies — including one that is intimately familiar with the offender and his actions — the offender has no formal opportunity to present a defense, nor is there any procedure that bears even a slight resemblance to due process.

The Chinese belief in the redemptive process helps to justify some of this. The farm's regime of reeducation allows an offender to recognize his misdeeds and attain the correct moral attitudes that create a happy and productive member of society. There is also the belief that society is both the cause and the victim of crime; therefore, society has the right and the duty to prevent future crimes. The smaller the deviance and the earlier it is treated, the more confident one can be of success. It follows that society should apply its most efficacious treatment while the offender is young and the offenses relatively trivial. As some Chinese scholars have pointed out, the Chinese justice system is, however, very harsh toward individuals it views as "class enemies." With regard to these persons, the criminal process is viewed as an official inquiry into an evil that must be stamped out. In these circumstances, China's leaders feel it would be absurd to have the judiciary act as merely an umpire to make sure rules are obeyed: They do not view the role of the state as that of a neutral in the struggle against evil.

Similar assumptions probably led to the government's June 1989 crackdown against the students and workers demonstrating in Beijing's Tiananmen Square. The demonstrators' desire for a greater say in government was perceived not only as the demands of individuals who presumed to set their own wishes against the well-being of the state but also as the posturing of potential bad models for the rest of the population. For this reason, government officials may have felt that they could not afford to ignore the demonstrations while allowing them to continue; from their point of view the danger of emulation was too great. Just as minor deviation on the part of an individual may, if unchecked, lead to serious crime, so may small but highly visible rebellions against the legitimacy of the state lead to sweeping revolution.

From Dorothy H. Bracey, "The System of Justice and the Concept of Human Nature in the People's Republic of China," Justice Quarterly 2 (1), March 1985, pp. 139–44. *Reprinted by permission.*

Sometimes force occurs as disputes between individuals; sometimes, as the terrorizing of the population by bandits or outlaws; sometimes, as rebellion directed at overthrowing those who control the government; and sometimes, as revolutionary attempts to overthrow the entire structure of government. The state is constantly on the alert to ward off threats to depose the government or outbreaks of violence that might result in civil war. To the extent that a state wins the loyalty of its people by its ideology and effective protection of their economic and political rights, the constant use of force will not be necessary. It is always there in the background, however, as an instrument of social control. In addition to suppressing internal disorder, the state also defends itself against external threats. More than any other form of political organization, the state can mobilize to carry out military action or war for both defensive and offensive purposes.

The Rise of State Societies

The formation of a state is the result of a number of interrelated events feeding back on one another in complex ways. Ecological and historical circumstances, population pressure, long-distance trade, warfare and military organization, conquest, internal competition between groups, the maintenance of private property and the privileges of elite classes, and the necessity for more integrated management of public works such as irrigation all may play a role in the emergence of the state (Cohen and Service 1978).

Theories of state formation tend to emphasize either conflict or integration as the dominant factor. A conflict theory proposed by Morton Fried (1967) focuses on the centralization of government power as a response to social stratification. In Fried's view, as population increases, different parts of a population begin to compete for access to scarce resources. Ultimately, one group becomes dominant, and that group then wants to protect its superior position. In order to do this, it centralizes the insti-

tutions of government, particularly those that give a monopoly on the use of force. For Fried, the function of the state is first and foremost to protect the system of social stratification.

Elman Service (1971) stresses the integrative functions of the state. He emphasizes the positive benefits of the state as a form of sociopolitical integration and points out that all its citizens tend to regard it as legitimate and even good. There are many examples in history of states ruled by a monarch who was despotic and even cruel and who nevertheless was perceived by the people as deserving of respect and loyalty. For Service, the main functions of the state are protecting the rights of citizens, providing effective mechanisms for the peaceful settlement of disputes, and promoting the ability to substantially increase food production, thus offering a greater measure of economic security than do other forms of organization. Social stratification, in Service's view, is a result rather than a cause of state formation; conditions leading to centralized government bring with them the development of a ruling class.

Within this opposition between the conflict and integrative approaches to state formation are theories that emphasize more specific factors. V. Gordon Childe (1951), an archeologist, sees the state developing automatically with the invention of agriculture. As the domestication of plants increases the surplus of food, some individuals are able to take on full-time occupational specialties. This creates a more complex division of labor, out of which develops the complex form of political integration called the state. One criticism of this view is that increased food production does not automatically create a surplus. Rather, a food surplus tends to be created by social mechanisms, such as the rise of centralized political institutions or the introduction of a cash economy.

Another theory stresses large-scale irrigation as the main factor leading to development of the state. This theory attempts to demonstrate that under certain ecological conditions, large-scale irrigation is perceived as conferring definite economic advantages on a population. But building irrigation projects and keeping

A view of Machu Picchu, the site of a pre-Columbian Peruvian state. Like other indigenous states, this one arose in an area of circumscribed agricultural land. (United Nations/A. Jongen)

them in repair require much coordination as well as more complex decision-making processes, because conflict can easily arise over who receives what benefits. The need to regulate rights to water and to manage human labor leads to the centralization of political power and ultimately results in the formation of a state. Critics of this theory point out that, although large-scale irrigation does lead to some political centralization, it does not necessarily lead to formation of a state. On the whole, however, centralized political authority does seem to be adaptive in an economy dependent on irrigation.

Another theory (Carneiro 1970) sees the state developing as a result of warfare where there is a limit on the agricultural land available to expanding populations. An example is state formation in pre-Columbian Peru. The independent, dispersed farming villages of Peru were confined to narrow valleys bounded by sea, desert, or mountains. As the population grew, villages split and population dispersed until all the available agricultural land was

used up. At this point, more intensive methods of agriculture were applied to land already being farmed, and previously unusable land was brought under cultivation by means of terracing and irrigation. As population continued to increase, more pressure was brought on the land, and war over land was the result. Because of the environment, villages that lost wars had nowhere to go. The price of a defeated population remaining on its land was acceptance of a politically subordinate role. As a number of villages were defeated, the political organization of these areas became more complex and developed into chiefdoms. The warring units were now larger. As conquest of larger areas continued, centralization of authority increased, until finally the entire area was under the control of one chief. The next step was the conquest of weaker valley chiefdoms by stronger ones until powerful empires emerged. The Inca Empire of Peru is a notable example of this process of state formation.

As a form of sociopolitical organization, the state is one of humankind's most important cultural achievements. Philosophers as well as anthropologists have been fascinated by what induces human beings to give up part of their freedom to the control of the state. In seeking the answer to this question, anthropologists have examined the available evidence, for both ancient and contemporary states, and have developed various theories. It is now generally agreed that no theory limiting state formation to one single chain of cause and effect is a sufficient explanation. A newer approach sees the origin of the state as involving a different interaction of factors in different circumstances. Prestate societies in various situations respond to different selective pressures by changing some of their internal structures, by subduing a competing group, by gaining control of water resources, or by establishing themselves as politically dominant in a region. This initial shift sets off a chain reaction of other changes that leads ultimately to the state. The state thus emerges as a cultural solution to various kinds of problems that demand more centralized coordination and regulation of human populations.

Warfare in State Societies

A comparison of warfare in various kinds of societies raises the question of the relationship between political evolution and warfare and, particularly relevant to our own culture, questions about the relationship of warfare to the state. Warfare can be examined as part of the process of political evolution; it often, though not inevitably, tends to lead to increased political centralization through the increased need to regulate daily life, especially the suppression of internal conflicts. Further, because waging war is costly, it often leads to increasingly centralized control over production. In contrasting war in tribal, egalitarian societies with war in our own society, a major issue is that warfare in tribal societies must essentially be carried out by the voluntary contribution of adult males. In a state society, coercion replaces voluntariness. Furthermore, although in tribal societies, it is possible that some individuals benefit more than others from going to war, in state societies, it becomes clear that there are divergent interests in going to war, and that some economic and political groups benefit much more than others. It is when this fact is perceived that coercion replaces voluntarism.

The view that warfare is not universal or inevitable but arises from a complex interaction of factors, including competition over scarce resources, need not mean that modern states are destined to wage war over raw materials and cheap labor. In modern states, we need to direct our attention to the economic and political interests of those who decide military policy. The costs and benefits of warfare in modern states are unequally distributed. The myth of instinctive and inevitable human aggression as a cause of warfare is an important prop of militarism in the United States, and it is congenial to some of our most important cultural values. Anthropologists, in uncovering the "hidden agenda" in warfare in a wide range of societies, including our own, can make a real contribution to understanding what circumstances engender in people the motivation to go to war and perhaps, ultimately, contribute to controlling warfare in the future by illuminating its causes in the past.

Summary

1. Political systems, which include law, function to solve the problems of coordinating and regulating human behavior. The major political processes in any society are making and enforcing decisions affecting the common good and resolving conflicts.

2. Both informal and formal mechanisms of social control regulate human behavior. Informal social control is achieved through gossip and ridicule. Formal sanctions include exile, death, and punishment as meted out by judges, courts, and police.

3. Political organization varies according to the degree of specialization of political functions and the extent to which authority is centralized. These, in turn, vary with the degree of social complexity. Four basic types of political organization are bands, tribes, chiefdoms, and states.

4. In a band society there is little integration of groups at a level higher than the band and no centralization of leadership or social control. Band-level political organization is characteristic of hunting and gathering societies.

5. Tribal organization occurs mainly among horticulturalists and pastoralists. Most frequently, localized kin groups, which are the typical political units in tribal society, act independently. But under certain social conditions, such as the threat of attack, these units may come together in collective action. Tribal societies contain some mechanisms of organization, such as age groups, clans, and associations, that integrate all the local segments of the tribe.

6. Although tribal societies often have some centralized form of social control that inhibits violent conflict between segments, warfare is frequent. Warfare may be adaptive in these societies as a way of limiting population growth or redistributing land, or it may grow out of competition for European goods.

7. In a chiefdom, kinship is the most important principle of social organization. Unlike the tribe, this form of society has an office of chief, which is a socially recognized position of leadership and authority. An important support of the chief's power is his role in the redistribution of goods through feasting.

8. A state, which is a hierarchical, centralized form of organization in which a central government has a legal monopoly over the use of force, is the most complex of the four types of political organization. States are characterized by social stratification. But unlike chiefdoms, in which social ranking is based on kinship, the state incorporates groups and classes that have no kinship ties with one another.

9. A number of theories deal with the rise of the state. Some emphasize the conflict created by the existence of social classes; others emphasize the integrative functions of the state, such as protecting the rights of citizens, providing for the peaceful resolution of conflict, and promoting increased food production.

10. If we examine the various factors associated with the rise of states in different parts of the world and at different times, it appears that the state is a cultural solution to a number of *different* problems, all of which demand more centralized coordination and regulation of human populations.

Suggested Readings

Anderson, Benedict
1991 *Imagined Communities: Reflections on the Origin and Spread of Nationalism* (Rev. Ed.). New York: Verso. A thought provoking look at the relationship between the growth of nationalism and such diverse factors as the development of vernacular language, religion, colonialism, and concepts of time.

Cohen, Ronald, and Service, Elman R.
1978 *Origins of the State: The Anthropology of Political Evolution*. Philadelphia: Institute for the Study of Human Issues. A series of articles on the rise of the state in different parts of the world. A good introduction summarizes anthropological theories of state formation.

Harris, Marvin
1977 *Cannibals and Kings: The Origins of Cultures*. New York: Random House. In his usual interesting style, the author discusses, among other things, the rise of states and warfare in nonindustrial societies.

Hoebel, E. A.
1974 *The Law of Primitive Man*. New York: Atheneum (first publ. 1954). Interesting ethnographic material showing the relationship of law to other aspects of society among groups at different levels of sociocultural integration.

Kuper, Hilda
1986 *The Swazi: A South African Kingdom*, 2nd ed. New York: Holt, Rinehart and Winston. One of the popular anthropological monograph series that examines the Swazi in transition from a kingdom, through the colonial period and independence, and for the period after, discussing some of the problems of culturally based nationalism.

Lindholm, Charles
1982 *Generosity and Jealousy: The Swat Pukhtun of Northern Pakistan*. New York: Columbia University Press. A fascinating account of a society where husbands and wives, fathers and sons, brothers and cousins all are opposed to each other, and the guest and the friend are idealized.

Meggitt, Mervyn
1977 *Blood Is Their Argument*. Palo Alto, Calif.: Mayfield. A very interesting, readable ethnography of warfare among the Mae Enga of the New Guinea highlands from the excellent Explorations in World Ethnology series.

Nader, Laura
1990 *Harmony Ideology: Justice and Control in a Zapotec Mountain Village*. Stanford, Calif.: Stanford University Press. An extension and expansion of Nader's earlier ethnography of a Zapotec Mountain village in Mexico, which also reexamines some theoretical questions in legal anthropology, as well as issues of methodology and cross-cultural comparison.

Religion

Why is religion a universal human institution?

What are some of the religious beliefs and rituals found in different cultures?

What are the differences between shamans and priests? cults and congregations?

How is religion adaptive in human societies?

What are the characteristics of religion in an affluent society like the United States, and how are these both similar to and different from religion in other kinds of societies?

Mapletown has a population of almost 5,000 people, who depend on farming, labor, business, service, the professions, and industry. Every Friday, the local newspaper publishes a Durkheimian statement: "Strong Church makes strong communities." The theme is further elaborated as follows: The Church is the greatest faith on earth for the building of character and good citizenship. It is a storehouse of spiritual values. Without a strong Church, neither democracy nor civilization can survive. These messages say much about the place of formal religion in the community, yet about one-fourth of the community does not belong to any church, and another one-fourth does not attend church regularly. Most of the unchurched come from the lower-income groups, yet these people do believe in God and want a minister to preside over their funeral ceremonies.

In the ritualistic (Catholic and Episcopal) and fundamentalist churches, the services are nonsecular. The numerous esoteric symbolic elements, such as the figure of Jesus on the cross, candles, and symbolic gestures of the minister, create an atmosphere of sanctity quite distinct from ordinary life. The fundamentalist churches effect the separation from day-to-day life by their emotionalism, while the "rationalist" Protestant churches give the impression of being social clubs with special emphasis on sober moralizing.

The theme of hypocrisy in religious behavior and divergence between what is practiced and what is preached is widespread in the community. Among the educated, there is a decline of "supernaturalism," and "Heaven" and "Hell" are considered states of mind rather than places. The Devil and angels are ruled out as mythical symbols. God is invisible and is an abstract principle symbolizing what is best in humans. Although reliance on God seems on the decline, religion is sustained because it makes community life vivid, follows the contours of the social structure, sanctifies events like death and marriage, and bolsters the shared image of America as the best nation in the world and the one with the highest ethical standards.

Adapted from Surajit Sinha, "Religion in an Affluent Society," in Johnetta Cole, ed., Anthropology for the Nineties *(New York: Free Press, 1988), pp. 429–47.*

Religion may be defined as "the beliefs and practices concerned with supernatural beings, powers and forces" (Wallace 1966). *Supernatural* refers to those powers, events, and experiences that are beyond ordinary human control and the laws of nature and are outside reality as normally experienced. Every society has some set of beliefs and practices that center on the relationship of humans to the supernatural. It is important to understand, however, that many cultures do not separate the natural and the supernatural and that the consideration of religion as a separate category of thought and action is rooted in our own Western tradition.

Religion, which goes back to the beginnings of the human species, is a cultural universal. The antiquity and universality of religion have led many anthropologists to speculate about its origins and functions. Although the search for origins no longer dominates anthropological thinking as it once did, anthropologists are still interested in the many functions religion serves in human society. Some of the most important functions of religion are discussed in the following section. They will come up again as we look at the variety of religious beliefs and practices throughout the world's cultures.

The Functions of Religion

The Search for Order and Meaning

One of the most important functions of religion is to give meaning to and explain those aspects of the physical and social environment that are important in the lives of individuals and socie-

ties. Religion deals with the nature of life and death, the creation of the universe, the origin of society and groups within the society, the relationship of individuals and groups to one another, and the relation of humankind to nature. Anthropologists call this whole cognitive system a **cosmology,** or world view. Human societies create images of reality in symbolic ways that serve as a framework for interpreting events and experiences, particularly those that are out of the ordinary. These "different realities" emerge as a way of imposing order and meaning on the world within which humans live and of giving humans the feeling that they have some measure of control over that world.

Science and religion, which are often opposed in Western thought, are similar in that both involve "the quest for unity underlying apparent diversity; for simplicity underlying apparent complexity; for order underlying apparent disorder; for regularity underlying apparent anomaly" (Horton and Finnegan 1973). But where science provides explanations that are open to new data and explicitly acknowledges a possibility of various alternatives, religious systems tend not to be open to empirical testing.

The separation between religion and science in our own society corresponds to our sharp separation of the supernatural and the natural. In other societies, these two concepts are less sharply separated. The supernatural can be seen as part of the natural and as intervening in all aspects of life. Thus, the kin group includes both living relatives and dead ancestors; power and leadership are often believed to have divine origins; rules of behavior are given divine sanction; and breaches are punished by the gods. The success of even ordinary undertakings in the physical world is ensured by enlisting the help of supernatural powers. Natural disasters, illness, and misfortune are believed to be caused by extrahuman or supernatural spirits. Natural and supernatural; human and natural; past, present, and future, may be perceived as a unity in a way that violates the logic of Western thought. This makes it difficult for us to understand many non-Western religions and accounts for our ethnocentric labeling of them as "irrational," "contradictory," or the products of faulty thinking.

Reducing Anxiety and Increasing Control

Many religious practices are aimed at ensuring success in carrying out a wide variety of human activities. Prayers and offerings are made to supernatural beings in the hope that they will aid a particular individual or community. Rituals are performed to call on supernatural beings and to control forces that appear to be unpredictable, such as those in the natural environment upon which humans depend for survival. One of the widespread practices used to control supernatural forces is magic. Although magical practices exist in many societies, magic seems to be more prominent in those in which there is less predictability in the outcome of events and thus less feeling of being in control of the social and physical environment. In the Trobriand Islands, for example, magic is not used for ordinary canoe trips within the lagoons, but only when the Islanders undertake the long-distance and dangerous canoe trips to other islands in their kula trade. Magic is also prevalent in sports and games of chance.

Even if magic cannot "work" from the standpoint of Western science, it may be effective in achieving results indirectly, mainly by reducing the anxiety of the individuals and groups that practice it. This reduced anxiety allows them to proceed with more confidence, and the confidence may lead to greater success. Where technological advance and science are able to increase predictability and control over events and human relations, magic tends to become less important.

Maintaining the Social Order

Religion has a number of important functions that either directly or indirectly help maintain the social order and the survival of a society. To begin with, religious beliefs about good and evil are reinforced by supernatural means of social control. Thus, religion is a powerful force for conformity in a society. Furthermore, through myth and ritual, social values are given sacred authority and provide a reason for the present social order. Religious ritual also intensifies solidarity by creating an atmosphere in which people experience their common identity in emotionally moving ways. Religion is also an important educational institution. Initiation rites, for example, almost always include the transmission of information about cultural practices and tradition.

By supporting the present social order and defining the place of the individual in society and in the universe, religion also provides people with a sense of personal identity and belonging. When individuals have lost a positive identity, or when life has no meaning because of the disintegration of a traditional culture, religion can supply a new and more positive identity and become the basis for a new adaptation. Religion can also provide an escape from reality; in the religious beliefs of an afterlife or the coming of a savior, powerless people who live in harsh and deprived circumstances can create an illusion of power through the manipulation of religious symbols. Religion in these circumstances is an outlet for frustration, resentment, and anger and is a way of draining off energy that might otherwise be turned against the social system. In this way, religion indirectly contributes to maintaining the social order.

In summary, religion has both instrumental and expressive functions. The instrumental aspect of religion has to do with actions performed in the belief that, if people do certain things, they can influence the course of natural or social events to their advantage. The expressive aspect of ritual refers to the ways in which religious symbolism is used to express ideas about the relation of humans to nature, self to society, or group to group. In its expressive aspect, religion is an important force for social integration.

Religion and Symbolism

Because religious ideas are always expressed through symbolism, anthropologists today are also interested in studying the meanings of religious symbolism and the logic that connects symbols to religious beliefs. Religious symbols may be verbal, such as the names for gods and spirits, and certain words, phrases, or songs that are believed to contain some supernatural power. **Myths,** or sacred narratives that tell how the world came to be created through the agency of semidivine heroes, are powerful symbolic communications of religious ideas. Myths are not merely explanatory stories of the cosmos but rather have a sacred power in themselves that is evoked by telling the myths or acting them out ritually. Myths may recall historic events, though they are clothed in poetic and sometimes esoteric language.

Myths tell of natural beings and heroes and of the origin of all things. By explaining that things came to be the way they are through the activities of sacred beings, myths validate or legitimize beliefs, values, and customs, particularly those having to do with ethical relations. As Bronislaw Malinowski pointed out over half a century ago, there is an intimate connection between the sacred tales of a society, on the one hand, and its ritual acts, moral deeds, and social organization on the other (1954). "Myth is not [merely] an idle tale," wrote Malinowski, "but a hard-worked active force; the function of myth, briefly, is to strengthen tradition and endow it with a greater value and prestige by

tracing it back to a higher, better, more supernatural reality of initial events" (p. 146).

A clear example of what Malinowski meant is provided by the origin myth of the Yanomamo described by Napoleon Chagnon. The Yanomamo call themselves "the fierce people." Not only do warfare and other forms of violence such as club fights and wife beating play an important role among them; they also make frequent reference to their masculine cultural ideal as one of aggressiveness and fearlessness. They justify both this ideal and the violent activity in which they engage in terms of their origin myth.

According to the Yanomamo belief, Periboriwa, the spirit of the moon, had a habit of coming down to earth to eat the souls of children. One day, two brothers, Uhudima and Suhirina, who lived on earth, got so angry at Periboriwa for doing this they decided to shoot him. One of the brothers shot a bamboo-tipped arrow at Periboriwa while he was overhead and hit him in the stomach. Blood spilled from the wound, and as it hit the earth, it changed into men. This was the beginning of the Yanomamo population; it is because they have their origin in blood that they are so fierce and are continuously making war on one another (Chagnon 1983:95). It is easy to see how this myth functions as a "social charter" for society. In the telling of such myths and in the ritual reenactments that often accompany them, social tradition is reinforced and solidarity enhanced.

Religious symbolism may also be expressed in material objects—in masks, statues, paintings, costumes, body decorations, or objects in the physical environment.

Religious ideas are also acted out, in dance, drama, and physical movements. In religious ritual, all of these symbolic means are used to express religious ideas. It is because religious ideas are so complex and abstract that they require symbolic representation in order to be grasped by the ordinary person. The Christian ritual of the communion service, for example, symbolizes the New Testament story of the Last Supper, which communicates the difficult idea of "communion with God." This idea is present

In Hinduism, the classic theme of the God and Goddess is expressed in many artistic forms. The God, or male, symbolizes the passive aspect, or Eternity; the Goddess, or female form, symbolizes the activating energy, or dynamism of time. They appear to be opposites but are in essence one. Just as the God has his living counterpart in every man, so does the Goddess have her living counterpart in every woman. The two together represent the unity of the divine essence. This sculpture is from the temples of Khajuraho in India. (Serena Nanda)

in other religions but is represented by different symbolism. In Hinduism, for example, one of the most popular representations of communion with God is the love between the divine Krishna, in the form of a cowherd, and the gopis, or milkmaids, who are devoted to him. In the dramatic enactment of the stories of Krishna, and in the singing of songs to him, the Hindu religion offers a path to communion with God that ordinary people can understand.

Anthropologists interested in culture as a system of meaning, such as, for example, the French and other structuralists (see Chapter 3), most frequently analyze myth and ritual because it is there where much creative human thought takes place. From the structuralist perspective that sees human experience as contrasts, the function of myth, ritual, and other cultural elements, particularly religion, is to reestablish a bridge between opposite elements. This bridge is established by the introduction of a third category, which partakes of both of the oppositions and is thus in itself abnormal. It is this mediating category that is the focus of religious awe and all ritual and taboo. A structural analysis of the Hebrew taboo on pork, for example, centers on the pig as an animal that partakes of two animal categories; it has cloven hoofs, as do cattle, but does not chew cud. Being neither here nor there, it is unclean (in a spiritual or symbolic sense) and thus tabooed (Douglas 1970). The structuralist approach also helps explain the widespread use of such symbols as hair (which is part of the human body but can be separated from it), ashes (which are both matter and nonmatter), the color white (which is all colors and no color), and the mythological use of "monsters," or figures with bodies of animals and heads of humans.

Structure and Anti-Structure

Victor Turner (1969) has extended the concept of structuralism to explain the function and symbolism of a wide variety of roles and activities in different societies. Turner goes back to the work of Arnold van Gennep (1961), who noted a similarity in many rituals in human societies, particularly those rituals he called "rites of passage." **Rites of passage** are rituals that accompany every change of social status by individuals or groups. Van Gennep identified three phases in such rites: The first phase is separation, which serves to detach the individual or group from a former status. The second, or liminal, phase is one in which the person subjected to the ritual is "in limbo," having been detached from the old status but not yet attached to a new one. The third stage is reincorporation, where the passage from one status to another is symbolically consummated. Now the ritual subject is in a new status by virtue of which he or she takes on rights and obligations binding on incumbents in the new position. We shall see further on in the chapter how these phases are applied to the transitions from childhood to adulthood in many societies.

Turner is most interested in the liminal stage. The symbols of this stage are often those of "nothingness," or ambiguity, representing things that are "neither here nor there," betwixt and between. This stage is often associated with danger or supernatural power and sacredness. A main characteristic of the liminal stage is that it involves a dissolution of many of the structured and hierarchical classifications that normally separate people in society — for example, caste, class, or kinship categories. Another characteristic of the liminal stage is that it involves the ritual subjects in a relationship of oneness, or what Turner calls "communitas." Communitas is a human bond that puts all persons in the same, relatively undifferentiated category. Communitas can be expressed in different ways in different societies, in a variety of activities in which the low become high and the high become low, or structure is dissolved temporarily for a festival or ceremony, or through certain kinds of performances in which mediating figures are dominant. Communitas, or anti-structure, alternates with structure in the form of communal rituals.

As society becomes more complex and differentiated, some institutionalized liminal statuses emerge in society. These statuses are part of the anti-structure and function as representatives of communitas, or as the medium for bringing it about. These sources of communitas are most often persons or groups that share the characteristics of liminality; they are outlaws, or of low status, or of ambiguous nature. It is their very marginality or low status or ambi-guity that is, paradoxically, the source of their power. For example, the *hijras* of India, discussed in Chapter 4, are in between the classifications of male and female; it is because of their sexual ambiguity that they are believed to have the power to confer blessings for fertility. The restoration of political or economic equilibrium in society is often brought about by outlaws, such as Jesse James, who stole from the rich to give to the poor. Similarly, in Western fairy tales we hear of simpletons, or "little tailors," who strip off the pretensions of the powerful and bring them down to common humanity. Turner views the hippies and other counterculture groups of the 1960s as emphasizing their marginality as a way of enhancing their own sense of communitas, as well as a way of undermining the structure of society.

Turner explains a great many seemingly diverse roles in different cultures by the concept of communitas: the Catholic monastic orders, Hindu mendicants, medieval court jesters, prostitutes with a heart of gold. All of these roles marginal to the structure of society represent humanity or communitas versus the special interests of high-placed groups within the normative structure. All of these structurally marginal roles represent an open morality or anti-structure in contrast to the closed morality and structure of the larger society. In representing communitas, these individuals and groups attempt to capture the spontaneous, immediate, and concrete nature of the human bond, as opposed to the norm-governed institutionalized, and abstract nature of society. If structure is a set of classifications into, for example, male and female, then communitas breaks in at the margins of the classification system, in the form of bisexuals or transvestites, who are sacred and have power because they transgress or dissolve structure.

Communitas is the source of much myth, art, symbol, and ritual. Turner concludes from his cross-cultural study of communitas that humans need this bond and that social life is a process of moving between structure and anti-structure. Humans need structure to provide order, but as Turner says, "Beyond the structural lies not only the Hobbesian 'war of all against all' but also communitas . . ." (1969:131), the dissolution of structure aimed at transcending structure and thus helping people to more fully realize the oneness of the self and the other.

Kinds of Beliefs: Animism and Animatism

A basic distinction in types of religious beliefs is that between animism and animatism. **Animism** is the belief that not only living creatures but also inanimate objects have life and personality; these supernatural persons are referred to as spirits, ghosts, or gods. Such beings are believed to behave as people do: They are conscious, they have will, and they feel the same emotions as human beings feel. Such spirits may reside in features of the physical environment, such as trees or stones, or they may reside in animals. In hunting societies—for example, the Lele of Africa and the Inuit—the spirits of animals are worshipped because it is believed that a hunt will be successful only if an animal allows itself to be killed. Souls, which may also reside in human bodies, are believed to be able to leave the body at will, temporarily during sleep or permanently as in death. Spirits or souls that leave the body at death turn into ghosts, which come in a variety of forms and relate in various ways to the living in different cultures.

The distinction between a spirit and a god is mostly one of scale. A god is a supernatural being of great importance and power; a spirit is a lesser being. **Polytheism** is the term used for a religion with many gods, and **monotheism** refers to a religion with only one god. Whether a religion is polytheistic or monotheistic is not so clear-cut in real cultures, however. In so-called polytheistic religions, the many gods may be just so many aspects of the one god. In India, for example, it is said that there are literally millions of gods; yet even an uneducated Indian will understand that in some way (which does not confuse him or her, though it may confuse us), these are all aspects of one divine essence.

The Nuer are another culture in which the distinction between the Great Spirit and lesser spirits is fuzzy to the outsider. The Nuer, of course, have no difficulty in understanding the different contexts in which different aspects of the Great Spirit are invoked. E. E. Evans-Pritchard (1968) describes a ceremony held to end a blood feud. All the speakers, representing both clans and including the Leopard Skin chief, addressed the various gods: Great Spirit, spirit of the sky, spirit of our community, spirit of the flesh (this refers to the divine power of the Leopard Skin chief), and spirit of our fathers. Each clan representative appealed to God not only as God but also as God in relation to the group he represented. The Leopard Skin chief referred to God in his special relation to his religious role as mediator, as well as to the priestly lineage he belonged to.

Just as in polytheistic religions, in which all gods and spirits may be reflections of one god, so in monotheistic religions, the one god may have several aspects. In the Roman Catholic religion, for example, there is God the Father, the Son, and the Holy Ghost, in addition to a number of lesser supernatural spirits such as the saints, ghosts, the devil, and the souls of people in heaven, hell, and purgatory, as well as the souls of those living on earth.

Animatism is the belief in an impersonal supernatural power. *Mana* is perhaps the most widely known term for this power. **Mana,** or supernatural power, may be inherent in the universe but may also be concentrated in individuals or in objects. We have seen earlier that Polynesian chiefs had a much higher degree of mana than ordinary people did. Mana is the key to success, but it can also be dangerous. That is why the belief in mana is so frequently associated with an elaborate system of taboos, or prohibitions. Mana is like electricity; it is a powerful force, but it can be dangerous when not approached with the proper caution.

A cross-cultural approach seems to indicate that mana, or power, is often found in those areas (spatial, temporal, verbal, or physical) that are the boundaries between clear-cut categories. Hair, for example, is believed to contain supernatural power in many different cultures (remember the Old Testament story of Samson and Delilah). Hair is a symbol of the boundary between the self and the not-self. It is both part of a person and can be separated from the person. Hence its ambiguity and its power. Doorways and gates are also familiar symbols of supernatural power. They separate the inside from the outside and can thus serve as a symbol of moral categories such as good and evil, pure and impure. Because these symbols of boundaries contain supernatural power, they are frequently part of religious ritual and are surrounded by religious taboos.

Practices and Rituals

A religious **ritual** is a patterned act that involves the manipulation of religious symbols. Most religious rituals use a combination of the following practices to contact and control supernatural spirits and powers: prayer, offerings and sacrifices, manipulation of objects, telling or acting out myths, altering the physiological state of the individual (as in trance and ecstatic experiences or through drugs), music, dance, and drama (Wallace 1966).

Prayers and Offerings

Prayer is any conversation held with spirits and gods. Prayer can involve a request or a pleading; it can be in the form of a bargain or consist of merely praising the deity. In many religions, it is common to make a vow in which the individual promises to carry out a certain kind of behavior, such as going on a pilgrimage or building a temple, if the gods will grant a particular wish. Other forms of prayer are less familiar to the Westerner. In some cultures,

gods can be lied to, commanded, or ridiculed. Among the many Northwest Coast tribes of North America, the insulting tone used to one's political rivals was also used to the gods. In these ranked societies, the greatest insult was to call a man a slave; when calamities fell or their prayers were not answered, people would vent their anger against the gods by saying, "You are a great slave" (Benedict 1961:221).

Making offerings and sacrifices to supernatural beings is also a widespread religious practice. Sometimes these offerings consist of the first fruits of a harvest—grain, fish, or game. Sometimes the offering of food is in the form of a meal for the gods; among the Hindus, the gods are given food that they eat behind a curtain. After the gods have eaten, this food is distributed among the worshippers.

In some societies, animals or humans may be sacrificed as an offering to the gods. Among cattle pastoralists of East Africa, such as the Nuer and the Pokot, cattle sacrifices are an important part of religious practices. The essence of the East African "cattle complex" is that cattle are killed and eaten only in a ritual and religious context, which seems to be an inefficient use of resources. This ritual use of cattle in sacrifice has always been of interest to anthropologists, and at one time it was given as a common example of how religious practices interfere with rational exploitation of the environment. More recent research has shown, however, that the sacrifice of cattle in a ritual context may be quite adaptive. Cattle sacrifices are offered in community feasts that occur on a fairly regular schedule, averaging once a week in any particular neighborhood. The feasts are thus an important source of meat in the diet. Furthermore, the religious taboo that an individual who eats ritually slaughtered meat may not take milk on the same day has the effect of making milk more available to those who have no meat, or conserving milk, which can be consumed as sour milk on the following day. In addition, the Pokot prefer fresh meat, which is also healthier than meat that is not fresh. Because one family could not consume a whole steer by itself, the problem of how to utilize

Offerings to the gods are frequently used to gain their helpful intervention in human affairs. Here a Pohnpeian pounds the root for making kava, a ceremonial drink that is offered to the deities. (Raymond Kennedy)

beef most efficiently without refrigeration techniques is solved by offering it to the community in a ceremonial setting. In this way, meat can be shared without fighting over the supply, because the portions are distributed according to age and sex by a rigid formula (Schneider 1973).

In cultures where animal sacrifice occurs, only certain animals are considered appropriate offerings. Among the Nuer, for example, only animals that have been neutered, particularly oxen, are used in religious ritual. In sacrificing an ox, a parallel is being made between symbolic and social categories. Among the Nuer, certain problems involve the restraint of sexuality and the role of women. The ideal norms of Nuer society require loyalty of brothers to the patrilineage. In reality, however, it is the brothers by the same mother who are most

loyal to one another and may be in competition with their half-brothers (the Nuer are polygynous). An important source of conflict in Nuer society thus centers on women. Furthermore, there is conflict between the cooperation demanded by loyalty to the patrilineage versus the individual ambitions a man can realize through his wife and his sons. Thus, Nuer women are divisive on two counts — as wives and as mothers. These conflicts are projected onto women, and women are blamed for the conflicts between men. The aggressive aspects of sexuality are seen as responsible for the failure of Nuer men to live up to their moral obligations. Cattle are important religious symbols for sexuality and social relations. Bulls represent the attributes of maleness and vitality, which are admired but which, it is recognized, contain elements of ambition and aggression that are socially disruptive. The castrated ox, on the other hand, represents the subordination of sexuality and disruptiveness to social ends and thus symbolizes the Nuer moral ideal. This makes the ox the most suitable animal for ritual sacrifice (Beidelman 1966).

Human sacrifice has also been a widespread practice, although it was often stamped out by European colonial governments. The Aztecs of Mexico, for example, had a religion in which human sacrifice was an important element. The Aztec gods, such as the jaguar and the serpent, were bloodthirsty and fierce and required human victims to appease their appetites. The victims, most of whom were captured in war, were ritually killed at the top of a pyramid built for this purpose. Although Aztec cannibalism was limited to the ruler, nobles, and those who had captured victims in a war, it was practiced on a rather grand scale, perhaps totaling about 20,000 victims a year.

A wide-ranging debate has occurred in anthropology over the meanings and purposes of Aztec cannibalism. Michael Harner (1977) proposes an ecological interpretation of Aztec sacrifice and cannibalism. He holds that human sacrifice was a response to certain diet deficiencies in the population. In the Aztec environment, wild game was getting scarce, and the population was growing. Although the maize-beans combination of food that was the basis of the diet was usually adequate, these crops were subject to seasonal failure. Famine was frequent in the absence of edible domesticated animals. To meet essential protein requirements, cannibalism was the only solution. Although only the upper classes were allowed to consume human flesh, a commoner who distinguished himself in a war could also have the privilege of giving a cannibalistic feast. Thus, although it was the upper strata who benefited most from ritual cannibalism, members of the commoner class could also benefit. Furthermore, as Harner explains, the social mobility and cannibalistic privileges available to the commoners through warfare provided a strong motivation for the "aggressive war machine" that was such a prominent feature of the Aztec state.

A more symbolic approach to understanding Aztec cannibalism has been suggested by Marshall Sahlins (1978) and Peggy Sanday (1986). According to Sahlins, materialist anthropologists such as Harner have focused too much on Aztec cannibalism and have not paid enough attention to the context of human sacrifice. For the Aztecs, the consumption of human flesh was less emphasized than the sacred character of the sacrificial rite, the aim of which was to bring humans into communion with the gods. Without the proper nourishment of human hearts and human blood, the gods could not work on behalf of humans. The gods depended on human sacrifice for energy, without which the sun would not come up, the sky would fall down, and the universe would return to its original state of chaos. The sustenance given to the gods in the sacrificial offering and to humans in their houses ensured the regeneration of every individual and of Aztec society.

Sanday's cross-cultural study, appropriately named "Divine Hunger," emphasizes the ritual context of Aztec and other forms of cannibalism, viewing it "as a system of symbols and ritual acts through which human beings explore their relationship to the world, to other beings, and to being itself" (1986:31). Thus she, like Sahlins, sees Aztec cannibalism as making a statement about the sources of life and death and how these sources can be controlled by human beings. While both Sanday and Sahlins agree that the practice of cannibalism involved political and economic factors, as well as relations of the Aztec state with its enemies, both see Harner's materialist approach as too simplistic and partly as a projection of the American cost-benefit ideology.

Other criticisms of the materialist approach have also been offered. To begin with, some anthropologists question whether the Aztecs even practiced ritual cannibalism, and there is no agreement about the extent of this practice. Harner, for example, bases his arguments on the evidence from early Spanish chroniclers such as Cortez, who wrote journals and letters describing Mexican customs. But as one critic (Ortiz de Montellano 1978) points

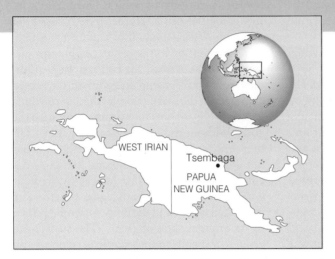

Recent research has shown that religious belief and ritual not only indirectly contribute to the survival of a society but may also directly affect the relationship between a social group and its physical environment. A study by Roy Rappaport (1967) of the Tsembaga of New Guinea shows how religious belief and ritual may produce "a practical result on the external world."

The Tsembaga, who live in the valleys of a mountain range in New Guinea, are swidden cultivators who also raise pigs. Small numbers of pigs are easy to keep, as they eat anything and help keep residential areas free from garbage. Although pigs can ruin gardens in the early stages of planting, after the trees are well established, pigs are allowed to root in the gardens, where they actually help cultivation by eating seeds and tubers (sweet potatoes). If pig herds grow very large, however, feeding them becomes a problem, and it becomes necessary for extra food to be harvested just to feed the pigs. Furthermore, when pig herds become too large, they are more likely to invade gardens and require more supervision. The Tsembaga kill pigs only on ritual occasions — either at pig feasts or in times of misfortune such as illness, death, or warfare.

The Tsembaga have a ritual cycle that they perform, they say, in order to rearrange their relationships with the supernatural world. This cycle can be viewed as beginning with the rituals performed during warfare. In Tsembaga warfare, opponents generally occupy territories next to each other. After hostilities have broken out, each side performs certain rituals that formally designate the other group as the enemy. Fighting may continue on and off for weeks, sometimes ending with one group's being routed. In this case, the survivors go to live with their kinsmen, and the victors destroy the losers' gardens, slaughter their pigs, and burn their houses. The victors do not occupy their land, however, as this is believed to be guarded by the ancestors of the defeated group.

Most Tsembaga warfare ends in truce, however, with both groups remaining on their territory. When a truce is declared, each group performs a ritual called "planting the rumbin." The rumbin is dedicated to the ancestors, who are thanked for helping in the fight. At this ritual planting, there is a wholesale slaughter of adult pigs. Some of the meat is eaten by the local group itself, and the rest is distributed to other groups that have helped it fight. After this feast, there is a period in which the fighting groups are still considered to be in debt to their allies and their ancestors. This period will not end until the rumbin plant is uprooted. This ritual also requires a pig feast and occurs when there are sufficient pigs.

The question is: How many pigs are sufficient? It is when pig herds reach over four per woman caretaker that they become too troublesome to manage and begin to compete with humans for food. Thus, it is the wives of the owners of large numbers of pigs who begin agitating for the ritual to uproot the rumbin. This ritual, which is followed by a pig festival lasting about a year, involves much entertaining among villages. Food is exchanged, and hosts and guests spend the nights dancing. At this time, future alliances may be set up between hosts and guests. At this time, also, much trade takes place, involving such items as axes, bird plumes, and shell ornaments. For one festival, Rappaport observed that between 4,500 and 6,000 pounds of pig meat were distributed over 163 occasions to between 2,000 and 3,000 people in seventeen local groups. The pig festival ends with another pig slaughter and the public presentation of a salted pig belly to one's allies. This concludes the ritual cycle. A local group would now consider itself free to attack its neighbors, knowing that assistance from both human allies and ancestors would be forthcoming because their obligations to feed them pork had been fulfilled.

This ritual cycle among the Tsembaga shows a number of functions of religion. It adjusts the man-land ratio, as survivors in a defeated group seek refuge in other local groups. It also facilitates trade through the markets and exchanges that take place during the year of the pig festival. Most directly in terms of survival, however, it ensures the distribution of local surpluses of pig meat, which is a source of high-quality protein, throughout the whole Tsembaga region. The ritual cycle also helps to maintain an undegraded environment, as pigs are killed when there get to be too many of them and when they threaten the source of human food.

out, the Spanish conquistadors did not necessarily write straightforward accounts of what they saw; they slanted their descriptions to make the Aztecs seem like barbarians in order to convince the king of Spain to support the conquest and undertake a large conversion effort by the Roman Catholic church. Bernard Ortiz de Montellano further argues that Aztec cannibalism can be fully explained by religious ideology and the desire to achieve status. He holds that neither the need for a dietary supplement nor the significance of the dietary contribution of human flesh has been convincingly demonstrated by Harner. The point here is not to prove one side of the argument or the other but to indicate some of the ways in which anthropologists have tried to "make sense" out of (to us) seemingly bizarre religious practices, by relating them to the sociocultural systems of which they are a part.

Magic

Magic is an attempt to mechanistically control supernatural forces. In performing magic, human beings are expressing their belief that they may directly affect nature and one another, for good or ill, by their own efforts. Magic is thus different from other religious practices, such as prayer and offerings, in which the gods are *asked* to help bring about some condition. Magic involves specific ritual procedures that, if done correctly, will compel a specific and predictable result. In imitative magic, the procedure performed resembles the result desired. Imitative magic may go back thousands of years; pictures of bleeding animals painted on cave walls suggest that imitative magic was used to ensure success in hunting. Imitative magic may make use of verbal elements as well. Among the Cherokee, a spell for minor burns is:

> Water is cold
> Ice is cold
> Snow is cold
> Rime is cold
> "Relief!" I will be saying.

Here the spell invokes four cold things. Along with saying the spell, cold water is also blown onto the burns, and this probably has some healing power of its own. Contagious magic uses something that has been in contact or will be in contact with whatever the magician wishes to influence. In contagious magic, the part may represent the whole; for example, sorcerers use the hair or fingernails of their intended victims to work their magic against them.

In many cultures, magical practices are part of most human activities. Among the Asoro of New Guinea, when a child is born, its umbilical cord is buried so that it cannot later be used by a sorcerer to cause harm. In order to prevent the infant's crying at night, a bundle of sweet-smelling grass is placed on the mother's head, and her wish for uninterrupted sleep is blown into the grass. The grass is then crushed over the head of the child who, in breathing its aroma, also breathes in the mother's command not to cry. When a young boy kills his first animal, his hand is magically "locked" into the position of the successful kill. When he later tries to court a girl, he will use love magic, which in a particularly powerful form will make him appear in front of her with the face of another man to whom she is known to be attracted. Both magical and technical skills are used to make gardens and pigs grow. One technique is to blow smoke into the ear of a wild pig to tame it. This is based on the belief that the smoke cools and dries the pig's "hot" disposition. Magical techniques are used to treat serious illness—blowing smoke over the patient to cool a fever (which is hot) or administering sweet-smelling leaves with a command for the illness to depart.

Divination, a magical practice directed toward obtaining useful information from a supernatural authority, is found in many societies. Flipping a coin is an example of divination in our own culture. Divination is magical in that it is a mechanical procedure for picking one of a set of alternative solutions, no one of which appears on the basis of available evidence to be preferable to the other. The practice

A Korean shaman chanting for a woman who was losing her eyesight. Traditional healers are often preferred to Western medical treatment, although shamans can be expensive. This shaman charged the equivalent of $500 but the treatment did improve the client's eyesight, and she was well satisfied. (Courtesy of Soo Choi)

of divination makes people more confident in their choices when they do not have all the information they need or when several alternative courses of action appear equal. Divination may also be practiced when a group decision has to be made and there is disagreement. If the choice is made by divination, no member of the group feels rejected.

Among the Naskapi, who hunt caribou on the Labrador peninsula, a form of divination called scapulomancy is used for hunting. In the divination ritual, a shoulder blade (scapula) of a caribou or other animal is scorched by fire. The scorched bone is used as a map of the hunting area, and the cracks in the bone are read as giving information about the best place to hunt. Naskapi scapulomancy may be adaptive because it randomizes the choices of location, a strategy that modern game theorists know results in the least chance of repeated failures.

Some farmers in the United States use a divination technique called "water witching" or "dowsing" to find sources of well water

where scientific opinion offers no certainty about where water will be found. In one technique, the dowser holds a forked willow branch (a willow is a tree found by river banks and is "sympathetic" to water) in his hands as he walks over a property. When he stands above water, the wand is supposed to bend downward. The effect of this ritual is to help a homesteader make a decision and be able to move forward confidently in developing his farm. In fact, because of the great variability of the water table, the method of the dowser appears to be no more or less reliable than scientific techniques in determining which spots will have water.

Sorcery

Magic may be used to benefit the community or an individual, or it may serve antisocial purposes. **Sorcery** is the use of magic with the intent of harming another person. Bone pointing is a magical technique of sorcerers in Melanesia and is described by Malinowski for the Trobriand Islands. The sorcerer ritually imitates throwing a magical stick, either an arrow or the spine of some animal, in the direction of the person the magic is intended to kill. For the magic to work, the sorcerer must perform the procedure with an expression of hatred. He thrusts the bone in the air, twists it in the ground as if angry, and then pulls it out with a sudden jerk. Both the physical act and the emotional state of passion have to be imitated to achieve results.

Cases of magical death, or death from sorcery, have been observed by anthropologists in a number of parts of the world. A classic case is that described by Walter Cannon (1942), in which he observed an Australian aborigine who sickened and died after believing himself the victim of sorcery. Sorcery, like the other forms of magic discussed earlier, achieves its results indirectly by affecting the individual's emotional state. The effectiveness of sorcery depends on the victim's awareness that a magical ritual is being performed against him or her. If the victim is psychologically vulnerable to begin with and believes in the effectiveness of sorcery, he or she may exhibit a stress reaction that consists of the disordering of various physiological functions. The intended victim may despair, lose his or her appetite, and slowly starve to death, unable to overcome the inertia caused by realizing he or she is a victim.

The use of magic and sorcery appears to be attracting an increasing following in our own society, where it also achieves its results through exploiting the vulnerability of people who feel they have little control over their lives. It may also be that people have lost faith in their previous religions but have not lost faith in the powers themselves.

Witchcraft

Witchcraft, like sorcery, is an attempt to harm another person through supernatural means. Unlike sorcery, which requires material substances, witchcraft is a quality of an individual, and witches operate only through psychic means. Sorcerers consciously undertake the kinds of actions they know will harm another; the power of witches may be an involuntary one. Our understanding of witchcraft will best be furthered by looking at the way it operates in a particular human society, in this case the Azande of Africa, who have been intensively studied by the anthropologist E. E. Evans-Pritchard (1958).

The Azande believe witchcraft to be a physical condition of the intestines that allows the soul of the witch to go out at night and harm others. Although the Azande believe that witchcraft can enter into every misfortune that befalls them, they do not live in constant terror of witches. After some misfortune occurs, they blame it on a witch. The Azande know that misfortunes are part of life: Canoes are overturned, people become ill, houses burn down. The questions the Azande ask, which are the basis of the belief in witchcraft, are "Why me?" and "Why now?" Witchcraft in one sense is thus a theory of causation; what Americans might attribute to coincidence or bad luck, the Azande blame on the activities of a witch. Where a belief in witchcraft pervades a society, it becomes the first explanation when misfortune occurs. The Azande understand perfectly well that sometimes a lack of skill or a lack of morality is the cause of misfortune. A careless potter whose pots break will have a hard time getting others to accept witchcraft as the cause. Similarly, the Azande do not believe that witchcraft causes a person to lie or steal, and they hold the individual responsible for such moral lapses.

The Azande believe that witches are motivated by hate, envy, and spite against a specific person. Thus, an Azande man who believes that witchcraft has been worked on him looks around for the person with whom he has quarreled or who may have reason to be jealous of him. If the misfortune is a significant one, such as an illness or blight on his crops, the man takes action in a number of ways. He may try using magic to stop the witchcraft or call in a

The popularity of astrology and fortunetelling, as a way of predicting and thereby controlling the future, can be seen as an indication that many persons feel they have little control over their lives. (Serena Nanda)

diviner to find out who the witch is so that he or she can be persuaded to call off the evil. In extreme cases, he may kill the alleged witch.

Witchcraft as it operates among the Azande indirectly helps to maintain the social order. It provides an explanation for what would otherwise be unexplainable and therefore gives support to the established pattern of culture. The procedures involved in handling witchcraft also help prevent the open disruption of established social relations, because an oracle must be consulted to divine who the witch is. Action is taken only with the support of the group; one person does not carelessly accuse another of being a witch. Witchcraft also serves as a leveling mechanism among the Azande, as it does in other societies. Because the most likely target of witchcraft is a man who has repeated good fortune or who acquires more than the normal amount of wealth, individuals rarely attempt to outdo their neighbors by producing more than

what is required for their own needs. Furthermore, witchcraft helps reinforce Azande ideas about morality; it defines the good man and the evil man. The person who is jealous, spiteful, and envious knows that he is most likely to be accused as a witch, and this expectation will bring his behavior more into conformity with the norms. In this way, witchcraft is a means of controlling behavior considered harmful and disruptive to the society. These functions of witchcraft are not unique to Azande society; they have been found to operate in many other societies as well.

The Organization of Religion

Like other human behavior, religious behavior is patterned and organized. A useful way of examining religious organization is in terms of the degree of specialization of religious personnel—those who conduct ceremonies and perform rituals. On this basis, Anthony Wallace (1966) identifies four patterns of religious organization: individualistic cults, shamanistic cults, communal cults, and ecclesiastical cults. Although all patterns can be found in complex societies, simple hunting and gathering societies may have only individualistic and shamanistic cults. Communal cults are characteristic of horticultural and tribally organized societies, and ecclesiastical cults are found in state societies.

Individualistic Cults

In **individualistic cults**, each person may be a religious specialist, seeking contact with the supernatural directly according to his or her own experience and psychic needs. An example of an individualistic religious cult is the *vision quest*, a pattern of seeking contact with the supernatural found among many Indian groups of North America. In these cultures, an individual was able to develop a special relationship with a particular spirit that would give the person power and knowledge of specific kinds. The spirit acted as a personal protector, or guardian. The vision seeker was under a strong emotional impulse and by various means, such as fasting, isolation in a lonely spot, or self-mutilation, intensified his or her emotional state.

The Thompson Indians of western Canada had a vision quest that included most of the traits typical of this pattern. When a boy, usually between the ages of twelve and sixteen, became old enough to dream of an arrow, a canoe, or a woman, he began his search for a guardian spirit. Before the actual quest itself, the boy had to run, with bow and arrow in his hands, until he was exhausted. Then he was made to plunge into cold water. He did this four times a day for four days. His face was painted red, and he put on a headband of cedar bark and tied ornaments made of deer hoof to his knees and ankles. He also wore a skin apron decorated with symbols of the life occupation for which he sought the spirit's assistance. The

nights prior to undertaking the quest were spent in dancing, singing, and praying around a fire on some nearby mountain peak.

The boy then went on lonely pilgrimages into the mountains, eating nothing for several days on end. He intensified his physical suffering by sweating himself with heated rocks over which he threw water and also by whipping his body with nettles. During all this time, he also threw rocks and ran for miles to ensure against disease, laziness, and bad luck. This strenuous regimen continued until the boy had a dream of some animal or bird and received the inspiration for a spirit song that he would then always use to call upon his protector. He also prepared a medicine bag of the skin of the spirit animal and filled it with a variety of objects that had taken on symbolic significance for him during his quest. These became the symbols of his power (Pettitt 1972).

Although the vision quest was an intensely individual experience, it was nevertheless shaped by culture in a number of ways. Among the Crow Indians, for example, several informants related the same vision and interpretation to the anthropologist Robert Lowie (1963). They told of how on their lonely vigil they saw a spirit or several spirits riding along and how the rocks and trees in the neighborhood turned into enemies who attacked the horsemen but were unable to inflict any harm. They interpreted this to mean that the spirits were making the visionary invulnerable. This motif is part of Crow mythology and is unconsciously worked into their experience by the vision seekers. Another cultural influence is that most Crow Indians obtained their spiritual blessing on the fourth night of their seclusion, and four is considered a mystical number among the Crow.

Shamanistic Cults

A **shaman** is socially recognized as having special supernatural powers that are used on behalf of clients for a variety of activities: curing, divination, sorcery, and reading fortunes, among others. Among Inuit coastal communities, the shaman's most important service is to make a yearly spiritual trip to the bottom of the sea to persuade the sea goddess (Sedna), who is the keeper of the sea animals, to release the game so that the Inuit can live through one more year. Inuit shamans are also frequently called upon to cure illness; this is done by discovering which supernatural being has been offended by a broken taboo and caused the illness. Frequently, the illness is treated by extracting a confession from the victim, and through a ritual procedure, the possessing spirit is then exorcised.

A typical shamanistic curing performance among the Netsilik Inuit is described by the ethnographer Asen Balicki:

> The shaman, adorned with his paraphernalia, crouched in a corner of the igloo . . . and covered himself with a caribou skin. The lamps were extinguished. A protective spirit called by the shaman entered his body and, through his mouth, started to speak very rapidly, using the shaman's secret vocabulary. While the shaman was in trance, the *tupiliq* (an evil spirit believed to be round in shape and filled with blood) left the patient's body and hid outside the igloo. The shaman then dispatched his protective spirits after the *tupiliqs*; they, assisted usually by the benevolent ghost of some deceased shaman, drove the *tupiliqs* back into the igloo through the entrance; the audience encouraged the evil spirits, shouting: "Come in, come in, somebody is here waiting for you." No sooner had the *tupiliqs* entered the igloo than the shaman, with his snow knife, attacked them and killed as many as he could; his successful fight was evidenced by the evil spirits' blood on his hands. (1963:385)

In case the patient died, it was said that the *tupiliqs* were too numerous for the shaman to kill or that after the seance evil spirits again attacked the patient.

Shamanistic activity has important therapeutic effects for individual clients, who are often relieved of illness through the cathartic effects of the ritual. Shamanism also has important integrating functions for the society. Through a wide variety of symbolic acts, shamanistic performances bring together various beliefs and religious practices in a way that dramatically expresses and reinforces the values of a culture and the solidarity of a society. Such performances frequently involve participation by the audience, whose members may experience various degrees of ecstasy themselves. These performances are cathartic in the sense that they release the anxiety caused by various disturbing events affecting individuals or the community as a whole. The forces of nature and the supernatural, which have the power to do evil in a society, are brought under control; seemingly inexplicable misfortunes are given meaning within the traditional cultural pattern; and the community is better able to carry out its normal activities.

Communal Cults

In **communal cults,** groups of ordinary people hold rituals or ceremonies for the entire community or parts of it — for example, age groups, sex groups, kinship groups, castes, or neighborhoods. These ceremonies may use ritual specialists, but the basic responsibility lies with ordinary people who on this occasion take on specialized sacred roles and perform sacred acts. Communal cult institutions include many different kinds of rituals. Some are not connected with the supernatural, such as Fourth of July celebrations in the United States. Most of these rituals can be conveniently divided into rites of passage and rites of intensification.

RITES OF PASSAGE Rites (rituals) of passage mark the transition of an individual from one social status to another. One of the most important functions of religion is to help individuals and society deal with the crises of life. In almost all societies, transitions in social status — conception, birth, puberty, marriage, death — are surrounded by religious ritual. As I mentioned earlier in the chapter, rites of passage tend to have three phases: separation, transition, incorporation. In the separation phase, the individual is removed from his or her old group or status. The rituals of this phase symbolize the loss of the old status or personality — having the head shaved or casting off one's old name. In the transition stage, the individual is between stages; although cut off from the old status, he or she has not yet been incorporated into the new one. At this point, the individual may be treated as sacred, in recognition of the power and the danger of this in-between position. In the third stage, the individual is incorporated into the new group or status. The rituals and symbols of this stage frequently are those of rebirth.

The Kaguru, a matrilineal tribe living in East Africa (Beidelman 1971), have initiation rites for both boys and girls. The Kaguru view initiation as necessary in order to convert irresponsible, immature minors into morally responsible adults. Kaguru male initiation includes both circumcision and moral instructions. Kaguru initiates learn how they will be expected to conduct themselves as adults. The physical distress of initiation makes the difference between the old life of the child and the new life of the adult more dramatic and leads to a greater acceptance of a new code of behavior.

Ideally, a group of boys is initiated together, both to increase the prestige of the ceremony and to divide the costs; also, it is felt that the boys will bear the pain of circumcision and learn better if they are in a group. The most important persons in charge of putting the boy through initiation are his father and his mother's brother, who plays an important role in all matrilineal societies. A professional circumcisor is hired for the operation. He is chosen for his skill in cutting and the effectiveness of his medicines, which protect the boy from both physical and supernatural dangers.

The themes of danger and vulnerability are dominant in the ritual. On the announced day, the boys, some senior male kin, and their circumcisor are led into the bush. The boys are stripped of their clothing and shaved of all body and head hair. This symbolizes the separation from their previous statuses. The boys are told that they may die from the circumcision. The boy's elder kinsmen hold him down in a sitting position while he is circumcised. It is consid-

When a Torajan, from Indonesia, seems about to die, his or her soul may begin to wander. This wandering soul, as well as the soul of the dead, is called *bombo*. During a funeral, the bombo is believed to hover in the area. For Toraja who can afford the full funeral ritual, effigies of the bombo are made to house the soul of the deceased, and the bombo watches the funeral from a special stand. At the end of the funeral the effigy is put into a cliffside balcony (pictured here) so that it may travel to the Land of the Souls and not hover to pester the living. (Courtesy of Kathleen Adams)

ered admirable not to flinch or cry out, but those who do so are not condemned. The cutting is accompanied by songs and ritual. The foreskin is cut off, removing the "low, dirty," femininelike part of the boy. The bloodied objects are buried secretly. The boys are led to a shed to rest and be fed by elders. During the healing time, they are considered to be helpless, like babies.

When the boys recover physically, each day they are allowed to go farther back into the

Funerals as rites of intensification are participated in by the entire community. Here, guests at a funeral among the Toraja of Indonesia participate in an all-night song and dance that involves a recital of the life history of the dead person. (Courtesy of Kathleen Adams)

camp. The boys are told that if they reveal the secrets of initiation, they will be devoured by wild beasts. During this time, the kin of the boys are also on their best behavior, because their actions may supernaturally endanger the boy's life. When the boys have finally recovered, they are sent out into the forest to perform some task. Everything in the initiation camp is then burned or buried. When the boys return, they are told that the elders have swallowed everything. After staying up all that night, the youths, singing to show they have "conquered" the bush, are led out of the camp the next morning by their friends and kinsmen. After a feast and dance, the boys will be considered fully initiated. During this feast, the boys are blessed and given new names associated with certain kinsmen, both living and dead. The youth is now considered a fully responsible member of society. He may engage in an adult sex life, court girls, and consider marriage. He will require a full funeral when he dies and will become a true ancestral ghost.

RITES OF INTENSIFICATION   **Rites of intensification** are directed toward the welfare of the group or community, rather than the individual, and have explicit goals: increasing the fertility of the land in agricultural societies or the availability of game among hunting and fishing groups. These rites are also performed when there is a crisis in the life of the group, as in the transfer of power or in the loss caused by death. Funerary rites directed at moving the deceased individual from death to a new life have corresponding rituals that must be observed by the survivors. In the first stage, the survivors ritually express their bereavement for the loss of the deceased; in the interim stage, they are in a period of limbo (mourning); finally, with the performance of rituals that end the mourning period, they resume normal social activity. Rites of intensification are also carried out to maintain the ties between the dead and the living, as in the case of ancestor worship, or to express the unity between humans and nature, as in the case of totemism.

Initiation rituals use many kinds of religious symbolism. Here, white pipe clay is being applied as part of an Australian ritual. (Courtesy Department of Library Services, American Museum of Natural History)

Totemism is a prominent feature of the religion of the Australian aborigines, who believe that people and nature share a common life and belong to one moral order. Just as human society is divided into mutually dependent and reciprocating groups, so too is nature. Each human group is linked with some species or object in the natural environment, which is its totem and with which it is mutually interdependent. By rules of birth and locality, people are grouped into "societies" or "lodges," each of which is associated with a different totem. This totem is their Dreaming. The Dreaming refers to the name of the totem species, to a cult hero, to the myths that tell of the deeds and sacred places of the totem species or hero, and to the rituals organized to represent the myths. In order to join the cult for which he is eligible, each male must undergo an initiation symbolizing death and rebirth. Only after this initiation is knowledge of the myth, ritual, and sacred objects that

make up the Dreaming gradually given to him. The chief object is the bull-roarer, the symbol and voice of the sky hero or of the totemic Dream Time heroes.

In desert areas of Australia, the most important aboriginal rites are for the increase of the totemic species. These rites are connected with centers associated with the cult heroes. Natural objects, mostly rocks, are said to be transformed bodies or parts of heroes or totemic species that appear in the cult myths. Myths are sung, actors recreate the heroic scenes, and human blood is applied to the stone symbol. As a result, the natural species increases, as the spirits of the species go forth to be reincarnated. Except for an annual ritual occasion, the members of a totemic group do not eat its totem species, although members of other totem groups are allowed to do so. Thus, each group denies itself one type of food and depends on other groups for the ritual increase of foods it does eat. In addition to increasing rites, there are also ceremonies held at temporarily sacred places. Here, the past of the Dream Time heroes is reenacted. As they realize the presence of the Dreaming, onlookers and performers become carried away in a state of ecstasy. Through these rituals, the community maintains continuity with the past, enhances the feeling of social unity in the present, and renews the sentiments on which cohesion depends (Elkin 1967).

The totem rites of the Australians clearly point up the social functions of religion. According to Emile Durkheim (1961; originally published 1915), a French sociologist, it was this function of religious ritual that was most important. When people worship their totem, which is a symbol of their common social identity, they are actually worshipping society — the moral and social order that is the foundation of social life. Durkheim believed that totemism was the origin of religion, because the aboriginal populations of Australia are technologically among the world's simplest societies. Although this aspect of his theory is no longer considered correct, his analysis of the social function of religious rites in terms of heightening social solidarity is an important contribution to anthropology.

Religious ritual can also promote social solidarity by channeling conflict so that it does not disrupt the society. In all societies, there are conflicts of interest and unconscious hostility between groups who are in unequal power relationships. Many societies have *rituals of reversal* during which people in the different groups ritually reverse their relationships. In the Zulu society in Africa, one day in the year women act as men and men act as women. The women chase and beat the men and act sexually aggressive toward them. In India, the celebration of Holi, which is primarily a harvest festival, includes a ritual reversal between dominant and inferior castes, as well as between men and women.

We are familiar with such reversals in Sadie Hawkins Day and Leap Year rituals, when in our own society it is considered permissible for women to ask men to marry them. In many high schools and colleges, one day is set aside when freshmen are allowed to harass the senior class, or students take over the classrooms and teachers take the role of students. Rituals of reversal contribute to social stability by allowing the channeled release of tensions that build up when one group of people is in a permanently subordinate position to another.

Ecclesiastical Cults

An **ecclesiastical cult** has a professional clergy that is formally elected or appointed and that devotes all or most of its time to a specialized religious role. These people, called priests, are responsible for performing certain rituals on behalf of individuals, groups, or the entire community. Individuals have access to supernatural power only through these intermediaries. Where ecclesiastical cults exist, there is a clear-cut division between the lay and priestly roles. Laypeople participate in the ritual largely as passive respondents or audience, rather than as managers or performers. Ecclesiastical cults are most frequently associated with gods who are believed to have great power; these cults may be part of a religion that worships several such high gods, as in the religion of the ancient Greeks, Egyptians, and Romans, or just one high god, as in the Judeo-Christian tradition and Islam. Ecclesiastical cults are usually found in politically complex state societies. In these socially stratified societies, the elite may invoke religious authority in order to control the lower classes. The priesthood and religion act not only as a means of regulating behavior, which is a function of religion in all societies, but also as a way of maintaining social, economic, and political inequalities.

In societies where an ecclesiastical cult is the established religion of the state or the upper classes, the religious practices and beliefs of the poor or lower classes may be different from those of the elite. Powerless segments of society may use religion to rationalize their lower social position, and they may place more emphasis

In ecclesiastical religions, priests and other kinds of intermediaries are required to carry out religious ritual. These specialists are also more knowledgeable than the ordinary person and act as teachers, as does the Buddhist priest in Katmandu, Nepal. (United Nations)

on an afterlife in which they will receive more rewards than will those who had power. Sects and cults among the poor may have a millenarian outlook — they may be focused on the coming of a Messiah who will usher in a utopian world. In many of these cults, members participate in rituals that give individuals direct access to supernatural power by experiencing states of ecstasy heightened by singing, dancing, handling of dangerous objects such as snakes, or using drugs. There are many such sects and cults in the United States.

One of the most well known is that of the serpent handlers, whose churches are spread over southern Appalachia. Serpent handling is justified in these fundamentalist congregations by reference to Mark 16:17–18, in the King James Bible:

> And these signs shall follow them that believe: In my name shall they cast out devils; They shall speak with new tongues; *They shall take up serpents;* and if they drink any deadly thing, it shall not hurt them; They shall lay hands on the sick, and they shall recover.

For those who are members of these churches, the above signs are demonstrations of the power of God working in those individuals who, through their belief, become his instrument. When a person receives the power of the Lord, he or she is able to handle poisonous snakes without being bitten. In these church services, members of the congregation pick up handfuls of poisonous snakes, thrust them under their shirts or blouses, hold on to them while dancing ecstatically, and even wrap them around their heads and wear them like crowns. The ritual of serpent handling takes up only part of the service, which includes in addition the singing of Christian hymns, dancing, spontaneous sermons, faith healing, and "speaking in tongues," all of which are part of the holiness movement in Appalachia.

Male villagers in Korea carry the coffin of a widow. Korean village funerals are a syncretic ritual composed of Confucian and local customs. This sometimes angers the Christianized peasants, who are seen here in Western clothes. At the close of this funeral, the Christians sang hymns as a protest against the traditional, "heathen" burial practices. (Courtesy of Soo Choi)

Weston LaBarre, writing about these churches in *And They Shall Take Up Serpents* (1969), suggests that to the extent that these religious experiences create an illusion of power and stop people from making real changes in their lives, these sects and cults are maladaptive. They are adaptive at the level of the whole society, however, because they channel dissatisfaction and anger so that the larger social structure is left intact.

Religion in Resistance and Revitalization

Religion has been an important element in the resistance of indigenous populations to domination, and continues to play an extremely important role in the contemporary world for groups resisting domination, whether in the form of Westernization, socialism, or other forms of **secularism**. As religion is used to resist the imposition of cultural domination, religious forms emerge that are syncretic, that is, they combine the belief and ritual systems of two or more different religions into a new religious system.

Religious Syncretism: Santeria

Santeria is an African-based religion that originated in Cuba, and has spread through Latin America, the Hispanic Caribbean, and among Latino populations in the United States. It grew out of the slave society in Cuba, where almost one-third of the slave population came from areas of West Africa influenced by Yoruba culture. Santeria is a **syncretic religion**, an amalgam of the religious beliefs of the Yoruba from southwestern Nigeria and Spanish Catholicism. Santeria is not the same as the original

Yoruba religion, from which it derives many beliefs and practices; like all syncretic religions it joins together different belief and ritual systems to come up with something new and different from the religions on which it is based.

The term *santeria* comes from the Spanish word *santo* and means "the way of the saints" (Murphy 1989). Santeria is based on belief in *orichas*, or *santos*, who are supernatural beings, and the core of Santeria ritual and belief is the honoring of these African spirits in order to gain both worldly success and heavenly wisdom. *Olodumare*, the omnipotent supreme deity in the Santeria cosmology, is not much involved in daily life. It is the orichas, or saints, who are lower divinities, that act as intermediaries between Olodumare and humans, who are at the center of Santeria ritual. Each oricha-saint is identified with certain specific attributes and is believed to control a specific aspect of human life. The *santeros* and *santeras*, or priests and priestesses, are the instruments of the orichas on earth.

Ritual practices in Santeria revolve around relationships with the orichas and the work they do in healing, cleansing, and individual spiritual development. These practices involve offerings, divination, and different kinds of spiritual communication, through chanted prayers in Lucumi, the Cuban-Yoruba ritual language, as well as drumming, dancing, and spirit possession; they also sometimes involve animal sacrifice, a practice that has brought the followers of Santeria into conflict with local law enforcement agencies. Daily ritual takes place at an altar and shrine in the home; larger, more public organized meetings, rituals, and celebrations are held in a house made sacred for that purpose.

The emergence of Santeria as a syncretic religion is related to its birth in slave resistance. The attempts of the Spanish to suppress many aspects of African culture among their slaves in the New World led these slaves to carry out their religious practices in hidden ways. Toward this end, they performed some of their rituals, particularly those of the initiation of the santeros, under strict vows of secrecy, in isolated locations. In addition, they identified their deities with the saints of the Catholic church. It is this identification that most clearly illustrates the syncretic nature of Santeria. When the Yoruba orichas became identified with the Catholic saints, the saints became invested with the same supernatural powers the African deities possessed, and were invoked to effect the same functions of curing, casting spells, and influencing a particular aspect of a worshipper's life.

For example, Orunmila is an oricha who knows the ultimate destiny of each individual and can therefore give guidance about how to improve one's fate; in addition, he knows what the orichas desire from humans and can therefore help in propitiation and communication. Orunmila is identified with Saint Francis of Assisi and his special day is celebrated on October 4, the day of Saint Francis in the Catholic church.

Another important oricha, probably the most popular of them, is Chango, who is identified with power, whether of a procreative, authoritative, destructive, medicinal, or moral nature. Because Chango has the potential for violence, santeros recognize the danger of offending him. In Santeria, Chango is depicted as a lover of food, dance, and women. Chango has identifications with many Catholic saints, and Saint Barbara is one of his most popular identifications. It is not unusual for a male oricha to be identified with a female saint, and the associated symbolism reflects the dual gender identification. Saint Barbara was probably identified with Chango because she has a cup in one hand, similar to the mortar that Chango carries, and a sword in her other hand, which is identified with the axe carried by Chango. Sometimes Saint Barbara is represented in Santeria with the point of her sword up, in a warrior's attitude of defense, and as an invocation of Chango's protection against evil, rather than in the Catholic image with the sword down. Like Chango, whose authority as a legendary ruler in Nigeria is represented by a castle at his feet, Saint Barbara also has a castle at her feet.

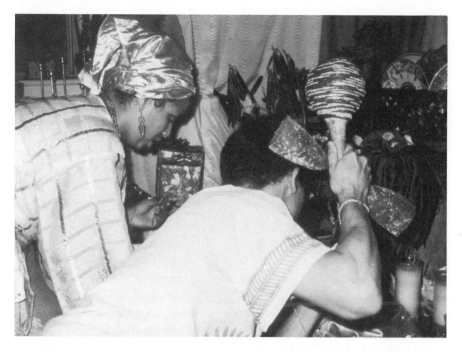

Santeria is a spiritist tradition that incorporates African spirits, called "orichas," into the spirit hierarchy. These orichas are associated with Catholic saints, and each has its own associated symbols and celebrations. This photograph illustrates a priestess, Chief Olumeto Agbomola of Imota, giving salutation to Yemoya, in New York City. (Serena Nanda)

Saint Barbara, whose red and white clothes carry the colors of Chango, is also traditionally identified with thunder and lightning; Chango is invoked during severe thunderstorms and at such times it is recommended that one burn some of the palm leaves given by the Catholic church on Palm Sunday, which pacifies Chango, another of the many identifications between Santeria and Catholic symbolism. Chango's feast day in Santeria is celebrated on the same day, December 4, as that of Saint Barbara in the Catholic church. Chango is the patron saint of firefighters because of his control over fire.

Santeria, as it has diffused throughout Latin America, takes on different aspects in different cultural milieus. In Brazil, it has emerged as *candomble*, where it is also syncretized with Catholicism in the identification of the orichas with the Catholic saints. Candomble offers so-lutions for many different types of human problems: business deals, political campaigns, love affairs, and illnesses. The attitude of the Catholic church toward candomble is ambivalent. Although many of the rituals and magical practices are condemned by the church, the clergy may actually allow other rites to be performed inside the church, and a major initiation may be held as part of a Sunday mass. Church officials acknowledge the similarity of some values in Catholicism and candomble — for example, that on authority — and also acknowledge that the divine power of Santeria and candomble is the same as the Christian state of grace (Gonzalez-Wipler 1989). Since Santeria is most widely found in Catholic countries, it is clear that many Catholics find no contradiction between the two religions, and feel comfortable practicing both.

The anthropologist Peter Worsley describes cargo cults as they have operated in Melanesia (1959). For the last 400 years, Western culture has been spreading through the islands of Melanesia. Initially, the Melanesians were receptive to Western culture, which primarily reached them through trade goods, called "cargo" in Pidgin English, and Christianity, which was introduced by missionaries. They believed they would receive cargo and the riches of the Europeans through the missions, but they found that accepting Christianity did not bring the cargo any nearer. The Melanesians were discriminated against because of their color, and they realized that the preaching of Western religion was different from its practice.

With the expansion of the plantation economy in the islands, the enthusiasm of the Melanesians for Western culture began to wane. The Europeans removed men from their villages to work on plantations in Fiji and Australia. This trapped them into a worldwide community market in copra and rubber in which the prices, and thus wages, changed every month. These tribal peoples searched for an answer to the power of the white man and concluded that it rested on magic, which was the basis of power in their own societies. This made sense in terms of their observation of the whites: Whites did not work; they merely wrote "secret signs" on scraps of paper for which they were given shiploads of goods, whereas the Melanesians, who worked so hard, got nothing. Plainly, the whites who knew the secret of cargo were keeping it from the islanders.

Cargo cults began to appear in all parts of Melanesia. The central theme of the cults was based on the Christian idea of the millennium; in native belief, the world was about to end in a terrible catastrophe. Then God (or the ancestors or some local culture hero) would appear, and a paradise on earth would begin. The riches (cargo) of the white man would come to the Melanesians. When Australian government patrols arrived in one part of the New Guinea highlands in 1946, they found themselves viewed as the fulfillment of a prophecy — the sign that the end of the world was at hand. The natives butchered all their pigs in the belief that after three days of darkness, "great pigs" would appear from the sky. Food, firewood, and other necessities were stockpiled to see the people through until the great pigs arrived.

In other places, native prophets announced that Europeans would soon leave, abandoning their property to the natives. In Guadalcanal, native peoples were preparing airfields, roads, and docks for the magic ships and planes they believed were coming from America. In Dutch New Guinea, where the Dutch had been driven out by the Japanese, it was believed that on the return of Mansren, the native culture hero, the existing world order would be reversed. White men would turn black like the Papuans, Papuans would turn white, root crops would grow in trees, and coconuts would grow on the ground. In some cults, the believers sat around tables dressed in European clothes, making signs on paper, in the belief that these mysterious customs were the clue to the white man's extraordinary power over goods and people.

Worsley emphasizes that, although the Europeans viewed these cult activities as "madness," they were rational attempts to

Copra is one of the important cash crops of New Guinea. The involvement of native New Guinea populations in processing raw materials for colonially dominated markets led to the emergence of cargo cults. As indigenous peoples gain more control over their own economies, it is likely that the cargo cults will become less important as an element of religious life. (Office of Information, Port Moresby, Papua New Guinea)

make sense out of a seemingly chaotic and senseless social order, whose economy, politics, and society were beyond the comprehension of the tribal peoples caught up in them. The cargo, of course, never arrived, and old cults and leaders gave way to new ones.

Anthropologist Pem Davidson Buck (1989) moves the discussion of cargo cults even beyond Worsley's. Buck suggests that the analytical category of cargo cult was developed as part of the discourse of colonialism, whereby the irrationality it seemed to represent was used as yet another justification for colonial Australian rule over New Guinea. Labeling these behaviors as irrational, and even self-defeating, permitted Europeans to suppress some kinds of activities and encourage others, as this suited their own purposes under colonialism. For Buck, then, cargo cults are not merely "native" myths but also functioned as myths for the colonial power.

Santeria is one of the many forms of spiritualism that are popular in Latino communities within the United States, and it makes an important contribution to mental-health care among Latino populations (Harwood 1977). *Espiritismo*, or spiritism, centers on the belief that human distress has spiritual as well as social causes and that distress can be treated by the removal of harmful spiritual influences through the intervention of mediumistic communication. Spiritists visit mediums regularly or in times of crisis, either privately or at public sessions held in spiritist centers (*centros*). Spiritists also perform certain rituals in their homes to cleanse the premises of harmful spiritual influences.

Among Puerto Ricans in New York, spiritism is an important community mental-health resource. In addition to operating as a form of psychotherapy, it also contributes to the social and psychological well-being of its adherents by functioning as a voluntary association, a religion, and an important source of ethnic identity.

As a voluntary association, for example, the spiritist center operates as a job-referral network and offers assistance to members during life crises. It helps socialize its members, many of whom are recent migrants to New York City, to new urban ways and provides recreational activities for both members and nonmembers. As a religion, spiritism fulfills a wide range of cognitive and psychological functions; in addition, the role of spiritist medium provides one of the few opportunities for a Puerto Rican woman to achieve formal leadership in a group composed of males and females. Spiritism also provides a basis for building relationships with strangers in a new situation, as adherents of the religion form social networks.

Basically, however, spiritism is a form of treatment and rehabilitation of psychological disorders. Most people consult spiritist mediums on a short-term basis. Clients' problems most often involve relationships with spouses, in-laws, other kin, or people on the job; the death of a close relative; life transitions, such as puberty or terminal illness; vague anxiety; and physical complaints for which the person has not received satisfactory medical attention. The treatment consists of improving the client's relationships with his or her spiritual protectors and also of direct counseling to the client regarding his or her social relationships. These activities may take place at private sessions between medium and client, in family groups, or in larger groups at the spiritist centers, where the medium works with the client before an audience. Here, others besides the client benefit because members of the audience can use the medium's counsel to the client as a way of coping with similar problems in their own lives.

Revitalization Movements

In many parts of the world, groups of people have experienced rapid disintegration of their culture through contact with the West. Culture loss, and the subsequent loss of a positive personal identity, have led to the emergence of **revitalization movements,** consciously organized efforts to construct a more satisfying culture. Some of these movements aim to restore a golden age believed to have existed in the past; others look toward a utopian future in which roles will be reversed and the lowly will be in power. Sometimes, these movements reject all elements of the old cultural systems under which they suffer; in other cases, they attempt to combine new customs with the old and dissolve the social boundaries between the dominant groups and the powerless groups in society. Even when a revitalization movement may be relatively ineffectual in bringing about the desired changes, it can still bring a sense of salvation and a more positive identity to people afflicted with feelings of conflict, inadequacy, and alienation from themselves and society.

In our own society, cultural loss, economic oppression, and powerlessness experienced by different lower-class and minority groups have also led to religious revitalization movements, such as the ghost dance among the native Americans in the 1880s and the Black Muslim movement in contemporary America. Two hundred years of slavery and a hundred and fifty years of prejudice and discrimination have left African-Americans economically deprived and burdened with a sense of racial inferiority. Various religious revitalization movements have appeared from time to time in the black community as a response to the stress of deprivation and the inability to forge a positive identity within American culture and society. The Nation of Islam, also known as the Black Muslims, is a revitalization movement that appears to be successful both in attracting members and in improving their lives (Parenti 1967).

The Black Muslims advocate racial separation in a nation of their own and obedience to the messianic and authoritarian leadership of the "messenger," Elijah Muhammad. The movement contains many religious elements drawn from Islam and rejects many cultural patterns that are part of black life in the United States. The Black Muslims do not for the most part seek violent confrontations with whites in order to create their new world; rather, they attempt to change the behavior of African-Americans in a way that will endow their life with meaning and purpose. The movement offers hope in a future in which blackness will no longer be despised.

The success of this movement with those for whom all hope of rehabilitation had been dismissed — drug addicts, criminals, alcoholics, unemployed slum dwellers — has been impressive. They have become obedient to the teachings of Elijah Muhammad, abstaining from drink, drugs, tobacco, gambling, promiscuity, stealing, and idleness. Muslims are forbidden to spend money frivolously and are committed to pooling their resources to help themselves and one another. They have created Muslim-owned schools and businesses. Muslim men must dress conservatively in suits and ties. Muslim women are supposed to wear a full white robe covering their arms and legs and a white headdress. The dress of both men and women represents a break with the stereotype of the flamboyantly dressed lower-class black in America. The woman's dress in particular symbolizes a new relationship between Muslim men and women: Women are protected, secluded, and obedient to men and are expected to be devoted to their homes and families.

The foods prescribed by the Nation of Islam are wholesome (whole wheat rather than white bread), and those that are forbidden include both the traditional Islamic taboos on pork and seafood, as well as "soul food" — the standard Southern fare reminiscent of the past, such as corn bread, black-eyed peas, collard greens, and opossum. There is only one daily meal, which the family eats ceremoniously together. These patterns do not merely symbolize a new and positive identity for Black Muslims; they also have had a strengthening effect on health and family life.

The Black Muslim movement is a clear example of the ways in which the construction of a collective identity through the use of myth, symbol, and organization revitalizes the identity of the individual. The movement suggests that the seeking of change through secular political organization has not made a sufficient impact in restructuring American society to include a positive identity for all its citizens. Where politics fails, religious revitalization movements fill the gap.

This discussion of the Black Muslims indicates that religion is adaptive in different ways for different groups in society. Where religious myths justify social stratification, elite groups obviously benefit more than others. Where the resentment of oppressed or subordinate groups is drained off in religious ritual, the resulting social stability would seem to be most advantageous to those already in the dominant positions. Although religion allows an illusion of control, this illusion may not be adaptive for many peoples in the long run. It remains to be seen whether political revitalization and participation will undermine the power of religious beliefs and rituals to alleviate the stresses caused by culture contact, modernization, and social inequality in the contemporary world.

Summary

1. Religion is the beliefs and practices of a society concerned with supernatural beings, powers, and forces. Religion is a universal culture pattern and goes back to the beginnings of the human species.

2. Religion has many functions. Some of the most significant are explaining aspects of the physical and social environment, reducing anxiety in risky situations, increasing social solidarity, educating, ensuring conformity, maintaining social inequalities, and regulating the relationship of a group of people to their natural environment.

3. Religious ideas are always expressed through symbols in which things stand for other things. Religious ideas are also acted out in ritual, and ritual reinforces beliefs.

4. Two widespread kinds of religious beliefs are animism and animatism. Animism is the belief that inanimate objects as well as living creatures have life and personality. Animatism is the belief in an impersonal supernatural power.

5. Many kinds of religious rituals are used to manipulate and control supernatural powers: prayer, offerings and sacrifices, telling and acting out myths, music, and altering physiological states through physical suffering or drugs.

6. Magic is an attempt to control supernatural forces mechanically. Magic may be used for benevolent or antisocial purposes; sorcery, however, is the use of magic with the intent of harming another person.

7. Beliefs about witchcraft have a number of functions in society. They ensure conformity, explain unpredictable events, prevent open social conflict, and act as a leveling mechanism.

8. Religious behavior is almost always organized. Four types of organization have been defined, based on the degree of specialization of religious personnel.

9. In individualistic cults, each individual may be his or her own religious specialist and have direct contact with supernatural power.

10. Shamanistic cults involve the use of shamans, who are socially recognized as having special powers that they exercise on behalf of their clients and groups in society.

11. In communal cults, groups of ordinary people hold rituals for the welfare of the whole community or of groups within the community. Two kinds of communal rituals are rites of passage, which mark the transition of individuals from one social status to another, and rites of intensification, which are directed toward the welfare of the community.

12. Ecclesiastical cults are characterized by a professional group of religious specialists who are responsible for performing rituals on behalf of individuals or the community. Only these specialized practitioners have access to supernatural power. This kind of religious organization is characteristic of complex and socially stratified societies.

13. Religion is often used to resist cultural domination. Such religious resistances are often syncretic, that is, combining features of two or more religions so that a new, syncretic religion emerges. Santeria, a syncretism of Yoruba religion and Spanish Catholicism, is an example of a syncretic religion originating in resistance.

14. Religious revitalization movements are consciously organized efforts to construct a new culture and personal identity. These movements arise in situations in which a group of people has been oppressed and has suffered cultural loss and loss of personal identity.

Suggested Readings

Brown, Karen McCarthy
1991   *Mama Lola: A Vodou Priestess in Brooklyn*. Berkeley: University of California Press. An outstanding person-centered account, illustrating that ethnography is a human relationship, and introducing a fascinating religion to the reader.

Faris, James C.
1990   *The Nightway, a History: And a History of Documentation of a Navajo Ceremonial*. Albuquerque: University of New Mexico Press. This text is among the best ethnographies on Navajo religion, representing Na-

vajo knowledge, using biographical, linguistic, and behavioral data to convey the Navajo world view.

Myerhoff, Barbara

1976   *Peyote Hunt: The Sacred Journey of the Huichol Indians.* Ithaca, N.Y.: Cornell University Press. A fascinating account of the search for peyote, which figures prominently in the annual rituals of the Huichol Indians of northern Mexico.

Thompson, Judith, and Heelas, Paul

1988   *The Way of the Heart: The Rajneesh Movement.* San Bernardino, Calif.: Borgo Press. An anthropological approach — sympathetic yet detached — of the followers of Bhagwan in England and the United States. A well-researched and well-told story of a religious group that attracted many members and much controversy.

Turner, Victor

1977   *The Ritual Process: Structure and Anti-Structure.* Ithaca, N.Y.: Cornell University Press. A discussion of the roles and rituals that represent communitas in different societies, with a case study from the Ndembu of southcentral Africa by a leading figure in symbolic anthropology.

Wafer, Jim

1991   *The Taste of Blood: Spirit Possession in Brazilian Candomble.* Philadelphia: University of Pennsylvania Press. A winner of the Victor Turner Prize in Ethnographic Writing, this ethnography conveys the personal experiences of candomble and calls into question some traditional anthropological divisions of experience into oppositions such as rational and irrational.

Expressive Culture

What does Ice Age art suggest about the earliest human societies?

Is music a universal language with many dialects?

How is dance an adaptive aspect of human culture?

What does folklore communicate about human society and social status?

How do sports express cultural values?

[When compared to the Navajo] . . . it seems to us that people in our culture can make movies of people living somewhere else or being somewhat different much more easily than we can make movies of ourselves. The Navajo [on the other hand] were extremely loath to photograph those distant from themselves, and conversely always sought the closest kin as their subjects. . . . They also felt extremely uncomfortable photographing anybody else's land, sheep, hogans, or horses. If they had no alternative, they always asked elaborate permission or tried to "borrow" the needed person or object from someone related to them. Their attitude toward photographing an animal or a house was similar to the attitude we would have of "borrowing" it. We would feel most comfortable in borrowing houses (for use during a vacation, for example) from our nearest relatives or perhaps from our dearest friends.

The filmmakers, as members of Navajo society, were subject to broad moral strictures which tend to regulate their interpersonal behavior. One such stricture concerns property rights. Property for the Navajo is not just the ownership of real estate, silver jewelry, sheep, and other wealth, but extends even to the rights of a medicine man to conduct a curing rite; he may not do so until he has paid his medicine man teacher from whom he learned the ceremony.

During an interview, [we asked Mike] why he had chosen to take a picture of [a] particular horse, when there were so many horses down by the lake. Mike explained that this particular horse was his brother's and that he didn't know who the other horses belonged to and "had better not [shoot] them because the people who owned the horses might not like it."

Mike had a problem getting a picture of sheep. No self-respecting Navajo would want their home environment shown without sheep, and no apprentice Navajo filmmaker would want to deprive a relative of such respect. [But] neither Mike nor his family owned sheep. There were lots of sheep around but Mike would have had to get permission from the owners to film them, as he wouldn't do it without their permission — and he might have to pay them for it. . . . So he found a much better solution. He borrowed a piece of film from Susie with sheep on it; these were sheep that belonged to her mother which she had photographed for her film on weaving. While [in our culture] to "borrow" a "piece of film" means to borrow the celluloid, not the image on it, the Navajo student filmmakers were borrowing the image — from Susie. This was acceptable, but borrowing the image of the sheep — in filming it without permission — was not.

From Sol Worth and John Adair, Through Navajo Eyes: an Exploration in Film Communication and Anthropology *(Bloomington, Indiana University Press), pp. 181–89.*

In every society, human beings have developed ways of expressing themselves that go beyond the need for mere survival. Thus, every culture has characteristic forms of creative expression that give personal satisfaction as well as express cultural values and attitudes. The forms of this expressive activity are sometimes referred to as the arts and do include the graphic and plastic arts, such as painting, sculpture, carving, pottery, and weaving. But the expressive aspects of culture are not limited to art: They also include the structured use of sound as in music, song, poetry, and folklore, and the movements of the human body in dance, sports and games, and play. In short, expressive aspects of culture, or **art**, involve the application of imagination, beauty, skill, and style to matter, movement, and sound in a way that goes beyond the merely practical. In this sense, for example, tea drinking is an art form in Japan and cockfighting is an art form in Bali; neither are art forms for most people in the United States.

Anthropological Perspectives on Art

Because art is a universal aspect of human experience, it is worthy of study by anthropologists and by those who wish to understand our species more completely. It is also humans' great variety of artistic forms and styles that makes the study of the arts so rewarding. Because artistic endeavors express some of the basic themes and values of a culture, they are an important way to gain insight into cultural patterning in different societies and into the different ways in which peoples perceive reality. In fact, it was this very aim that motivated anthropologists Sol Worth and John Adair to teach filmmaking and editing to a group of Navajo in order to enable them to make motion pictures depicting themselves and their culture. They believed that if the Navajo were given a free hand in making motion pictures, they could focus on whatever interested them and that this would be an excellent way to follow the anthropological injunction to "grasp the native's point of view." The resulting films did indeed indicate that the Navajo have a different view of reality and concepts of continuity and time than that of the non-Navajo culture of the United States.

Anthropological discussion of the arts ordinarily divides them into five types: graphic and plastic arts, music, dance, folklore, and sports and games. Certain general approaches in cultural anthropology can be applied to the study of all these arts, but because of their different natures, they are usually studied by specialists. Some of the generalized approaches to the study of the various arts consider (1) content, themes, or subjects; (2) style; (3) changes over time; (4) social and psychological functions; (5) relationships with other aspects of culture and society; and (6) the creative process and the interaction of artists and their audience. Before looking at the various forms of art, we will examine the functions of art in society and the place of art within culture.

The Symbolic Nature of Art

One way of analyzing art is in terms of how it functions as a form of symbolic communication in society. In the first place, art can be seen

Masks are an important art form in parts of Africa. When used in rituals, they are believed to take on the supernatural power of the spirits they represent. By confining supernatural power in a mask, or other material form, such power is more easily controlled and manipulated. (Serena Nanda)

is not the actual spirit; they consider it a confinement of the spirit. The point of confining, or localizing, the spirit in material form is to manipulate it for human ends.

A second way in which art is symbolic is that particular artistic elements reflect particular emotions or meanings. In this case, the symbolism is culturally specific, and one needs a knowledge of the particular cultural meanings assigned to a particular artistic element. In Western music, for example, the use of the minor scale conveys the emotion of sadness, and various other musical forms are traditionally associated with particular emotions. The traditional element is important in evoking the emotion, because individuals in that culture have been taught the association. In our own culture, the phrase "Once upon a time" signals to us that this is not going to be a story about "real" events and people, and sets the stage for us to respond emotionally in certain ways.

A third way in which the arts are symbolic is that they reflect certain kinds of social behavior or social structure. The totem poles of the Northwest Coast Indians reflect the importance of social hierarchy. Stories of traditional dance dramas deal with religion. The organization of ritual using dance and music reflects the division of society into various kinship units or ethnic groups. Art styles may also reflect cultural values or patterns. In a study of Navajo music, for example, David McAllester (1954) showed that it reflected values in several ways. The characteristic Navajo cultural value on individualism is reflected in the attitude that what one does with one's music is one's own affair. Second, the Navajo are essentially a conservative people and believe that "foreign music is dangerous and not for Navajo." Third, the Navajo value of formalism is expressed in the belief that there is only one right way to sing every kind of song (one can contrast this with the value of innovation expressed in improvisation in music—for example, jazz).

The arts may also be symbolic on a deeper level; that is, they represent certain universal aspects of human thought, needs, and emotions. Freudian psychology, for example, as-

as communicating direct meaning. For example, some dance movements attempt to imitate the movements of animals, and the contents of some paintings are believed not merely to represent, but to *be*—to partake of the spirit of—the thing visualized. Masks used in ritual are often believed to take on the supernatural power of the spirits or beings they represent. By being given a form, as in a mask, a painting, or a sculpture, the spirit can be more easily manipulated and controlled by humans. Among the Kalabari of Africa, for example, spirit beings are represented by sculptures. Offerings are made to them, and the sculptures are the center of ritual action. The more sophisticated individuals in the culture recognize that the statue

Tourists watching Törajan carvers at work in the village of Ke'te' Kesu', Tana Toraja Regency, Indonesia. With the increase of tourists into the area, Torajans have now turned their exceptional carving skills toward the making of souvenirs, as well as continuing their tradition of carving religious figures. (Courtesy of Kathleen Adams)

signs certain universal meanings to certain kinds of symbols. The widespread plots of myths having to do with incest might appear to reflect the unconscious working out of the Oedipal complex. The shape of the flute as a musical instrument and its association with men's cults in many culture areas have been interpreted as having phallic significance. And certain colors have been interpreted as expressing universal physiological processes: red for blood or white for semen or breast milk.

The Integrative Function of the Arts

The symbolic nature of the arts in communication is related to what is undoubtedly their most important function — that of integration. Through the arts, the beliefs, values, ethics, knowledge, emotions, and ideology and world view of a culture are expressed and communicated. The art forms of a society do not merely reflect culture and society. Participation in cultural performances fosters the unity and har-

mony of a society in a way that is intensely *felt* by its members. It is perhaps the primary social function of the arts to produce this condition. The art forms of a society take up cultural themes and individual emotions — death, masculinity, pride, chance, relations between male and female, aggression, social cooperation — and present them in ways that make their essential nature understandable, even if it cannot be consciously articulated. Art makes dominant cultural themes visible, tangible, and thus more real. Thus, art is a means of expression that not only heightens emotions associated with cultural themes, values, and goals but also serves to display them in ways that are emotionally compelling.

The Arts in Cultural Context

The study of art largely divorced from its cultural context reflects to some extent an ethnocentric point of view that "art for art's sake" exists in all cultures. In fact, the opposite is true. Art in most societies is in fact *not* manufactured (or performed) solely for the purpose of giving pleasure. The separation of art from other activities and the separation of a class of objects or acts labeled "art" is characteristic only of modern societies. It is an extension of their tendency toward less cultural integration than is generally found in nonindustrial societies. In modern societies, for example, even bad art is distinguished from other cultural products. In nonindustrial societies, art is embedded in all aspects of culture; no separate class of material products, movements, or sounds is created solely to express esthetic values.

The Inuit, for example, who are considered by anthropologists to have a highly developed artistic skill, do not have a separate word for art. Rather, all "artificial" objects are lumped together as "that which has been made," regardless of the purpose of the object. This does not mean that Inuit do not have esthetic values, but rather that their plastic art is applied to the manufacture of objects that have primarily instrumental value, such as tools, amulets, or weapons. It should not surprise us, then, that the Inuit, like most other nonindustrial societies, traditionally did not make a distinction between artist and craftworker, a distinction that does exist in our society. Similarly, many skills—dancing, weaving, singing, playing a musical instrument—that in our own society are performed as a special category of behavior called the arts are in other societies skills that most people use in everyday life. In all societies, some individuals are recognized as more competent in these skills than others, but this competence does not necessarily translate itself into the specialized role of artist.

Because art is so embedded in cultural traditions, many anthropologists tend to believe that it may be difficult to measure esthetic values and styles according to any universal standard. What is beautiful in one culture may not be in another. Each culture has developed its own traditions of content and style, to which individuals in that culture conform in their application of creative imagination and skill. The appreciation of art in terms of values and forms

A typical house style with elaborate decoration in a Paramacca Maroon village in Surinam, South America. Each man carves his own house decoration, and the excellence of the craftsmanship is a source of prestige. (John Lenoir)

that are not our own is difficult to achieve, although this can partly be overcome by attempting to understand the cultural context of art. One of the difficulties is that in the United States today, originality and innovation are an important part of our artistic standards. But art, which is a creative process, is not necessarily an innovative one. Artists in other societies may be very conservative, and archeologists provide evidence that the artistic styles of cultures remain stable over very long periods. Furthermore, the integration of art with religion in non-Western societies may limit the range of variation that individual artists display. Where religion and art have become separated, as is now true in much of the contemporary world, experimentation, innovation, and real change in artistic endeavor are much more likely to occur.

Cultures differ not only in their esthetic preferences but also in the attention they give to various types of art. In some cultures, masks

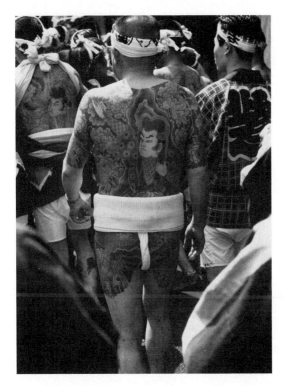

Tattooing in Japan may have begun with fishermen who believed that tattoos of dragons and demons would scare off sharks, or it may have its origins in the branding of criminals. Swashbucklers of feudal times adorned themselves with a more terrifying air. Ultimately, this practice spread to other social classes, including, today, wrestlers and members of organized crime associations. (Sheldon Brody)

groups, we find that art has an important place in the culture and that skill in a variety of art forms is of a very high level. We may thus speculate that art is essential in human society and may even have important adaptive functions.

Graphic and Plastic Arts

Many skills come under the heading of graphic and plastic arts: painting; sculpture and carving in wood; work in precious metals, bone, ivory, and horn; pottery and work in clay; basketry; weaving and embroidery; architecture; the tailoring of skins and other materials for clothing; and tattooing and other kinds of body ornamentation. The major anthropological emphasis on the arts in small-scale societies has been on the study of graphic and plastic arts. This may be due to the fact that such arts result in products that can be dealt with on their own, removed from their cultural setting, in a way that nonmaterial products such as dance or musical performance cannot. Plastic and graphic forms of art, for example, can be collected and exhibited in museums and art galleries, illustrated in books, and photographed easily. This allows them to be fairly easily compared with one another—in chronological sequences, in terms of stylistic variation, or as representative of the work of individual artists. An artistic product has a permanence that a performing art does not have, and this also makes it easier to study.

Style and Society

Interpreting Ice Age art (see accompanying box) is just one example of how art can lead us to an understanding of culture and how culture can influence art. Another fascinating attempt in this direction is the work of John Fischer (1961). Fischer's theory is that certain aspects of artistic style "say something" about sociocultural reality and that this reality in turn shapes

and painting are the most important media for the expression of esthetic values and technical skill. In other cultures, verbal skills are more important, with a wealth of myths, folktales, and word games and relatively little painting, sculpture, or pottery. Although every culture has dramatic performances as part of its religion, some cultures have developed this skill more than others have. We do not know of any human culture, no matter how simple its technology or how difficult its environment, that does not have any form of art. In fact, when we look at cultures in which making a living is not easy and in which social structure is relatively simple, such as Inuit and aboriginal Australian

One early anthropological interest in the graphic and plastic arts was an attempt to apply to them the evolutionary perspective that was being applied by nineteenth-century anthropologists to other aspects of culture. One of these evolutionary theories held that there was a progression of abstract art, characteristic of "primitive" cultures, to the naturalistic or realistic art found in Western civilizations. This theory was undermined by the discovery of Paleolithic, or Ice Age, art, much of which consists of paintings of animals on cave walls. The images are realistic and complex and show a high degree of delicacy, skill, and stylistic variation. When this art was first discovered in France and Spain, it was hard to believe it had been created by human beings living 30,000 to 15,000 years ago. The fact that this art was in no way primitive and yet was made by the earliest modern ancestors of our species underlines the difficulty of trying to establish an evolutionary perspective in the development of art styles. Contemporary anthropologists have thus attempted to study this art from a different perspective: that of what it can tell us about the ideology and life-styles of the humans who created it.

Although it is impossible to know for certain, comparison with the art of contemporary hunting and gathering societies suggests that some Ice Age art had a close association with hunting ritual and with a world view that is particular to hunting societies (Levine 1957). In these societies, dependence on nature leads to an intense and intimate relationship with the natural setting. Given the technology of hunting peoples, the hunt is difficult, and killing big animals may even be dangerous. Although hunting peoples are extremely knowledgeable about their environment, unexpected natural phenomena can produce crises in their lives. Even when the food supply is abundant, unpredictability and the resistance of game to the hunter's purpose create anxiety. This anxiety and uncertainty are expressed by an ideology that perceives nature as active and personal. The peopling of the universe with gods or spirits that can take helping action allows hunting societies to have some control over their situation. It is believed that nature can be appealed to, by humans. One of the ways this is done is by ritually compensating nature for what humans must take from it.

These themes are associated with certain attitudes and patterns of behavior toward art. The main belief in this connection is that a work of art *is* what it represents. From this belief stems the idea that art objects themselves have *mana*-like power. Thus, hunting peoples who make artistic products often do so ritually — that is, as a way of satisfying and appealing to nature. Some aspects of Ice Age art may be interpreted in this way. Many of the drawings of animals, for example, show signs of having been superimposed; it is possible to inter-

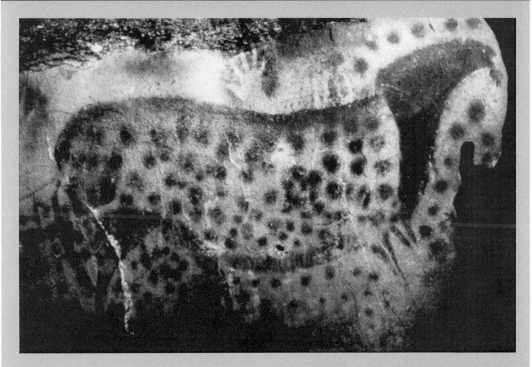

Analysis of a horse, found in a cave in France and dated about 14,500 B.C., indicates that the outline was filled with spots over a period of time and that the handprints above the horse, and more spots, were added later. These superimpositions support the argument that such paintings had ritual value for the peoples who made them.

pret this superimposition as being part of a restitution ritual. Whenever an animal was killed, its essence was restored to nature by a ritual drawing of the animal's image at a sacred spot. If restitution to nature is believed not only possible but also necessary, drawing images is one way that this can be accomplished. Taking a life is dangerous; ritual art, dedicated to the powerful spirits who protect life, is one way of lessening the danger.

Traditional art forms may use contemporary subject matter. Here, a woman driver is expressed in the "X-ray" style characterstic of much of Australia and New Guinea. Note the repetition of simple elements in the art of egalitarian societies. (Serena Nanda)

the kinds of fantasies that provide psychological security and thus esthetic satisfaction for the artist. Using a cross-cultural sample of homogeneous societies, Fischer tested several hypotheses relating artistic style to the development of social hierarchy. First, he distinguished two major types of societies: authoritarian (hierarchical) and egalitarian.

In authoritarian societies, social hierarchy is positively valued. Society is viewed as divided into groups in higher and lower statuses. Each group has a set of rights and responsibilities in relation to those above and below. Those lower than Ego serve him, and he must help and protect them; Ego must serve those higher than he, who will in turn help and protect him.

The opposite ideal type is the egalitarian society, in which hierarchy as a principle of organization is rejected. Although differences of prestige do exist, these are not emphasized or even explicitly recognized. Work is seen as cooperative, rather than involving power differences among people working together. Individuals who attempt to control others are not valued as leaders; in fact, they are likely to be seen as a threat to society.

Fischer hypothesized that hierarchical and egalitarian societies would have different art styles, and he specifically related four aspects of style to emphasis on social differentiation:

1. Designs that included the repetition of a number of simple elements would be characteristic of egalitarian societies, whereas designs integrating a number of unlike elements would be characteristic of hierarchical societies. This hypothesis was based on the idea that security in egalitarian societies depends on the number of comrades (equals in social status) that Ego has. The multiplying of the same design elements is the symbolic representation of peers. In hierarchical societies, security depends on relationships with individuals in a number of differentiated positions. In design, these are symbolized by the integration of a variety of distinct elements.

2. Designs with a large amount of empty (irrelevant) space should characterize egalitarian societies; designs with little irrelevant space should characterize hierarchical societies. This hypothesis was based on the assumption that in egalitarian societies people relate to others as equals or do not relate at all. Security in egalitarian societies is found in isolation from other groups. In hierarchical societies, security is produced by incorporating strangers into the hierarchy in a position of relative dominance or submission. This tendency for incorporation would be expression in designs having little empty space.

3. Symmetrical designs should characterize egalitarian societies; the designs of hierarchical societies should tend to be asymmetrical. Symmetry is a special case of repetition; asymmetry expresses difference.

4. Figures without enclosure should characterize egalitarian societies; enclosed figures should predominate in the designs of hierarchical societies. The lack of enclosure in egalitarian societies symbolizes their face-to-face interaction on an equal

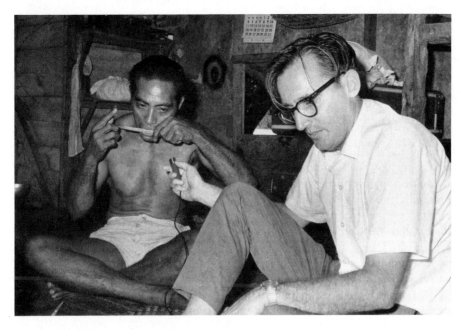

Anthropologists use a variety of techniques to gain information about a culture. Here, Raymond Kennedy, a specialist in ethnomusicology, elicits musical information in Pohnpei. (Raymond Kennedy)

basis. The enclosures in the designs of hierarchical societies symbolize the importance of social boundaries between individuals of different ranks.

Fischer's hypotheses were all supported, which suggests that he is indeed on to something in his view that in the field of visual design, at least, art styles may be seen as "cognitive maps" of a sociocultural system.

Music

The Conceptual Basis of Music

All cultures have their own traditional way of using the voice and instruments in structured ways to produce song and music. But the variety in musical systems is not limited to the different ways in which sound is structured; different conceptualizations underlie and shape musical systems. Although music is sound, not all human sound is music. Intimate knowledge of a culture is required to understand the culture's conceptualizations, which are part of its musical behavior. A description of the conceptual basis of music of the Basongye people of the Republic of the Congo by Alan Merriam (1964) serves as an excellent example. The Basongye see music as something uniquely human. They do not consider as music the sounds made by birds or animals or such natural sounds as the wind whistling through the trees. But all human sound is not music either. The Basongye say: "When you are content, you sing; when you are angry, you make noise. When one shouts, he is not thinking; when he sings, he is thinking. A song is tranquil; a noise is not" (p. 64). Furthermore, the Basongye consider that sound, in order to be music, must be organized. Thus, a single tap on a drum is not considered music, but drums played together in the traditionally patterned form drummers use are making music. For sound to be considered music, it must continue over time. Thus, striking all drums once together does not produce music.

Focusing on the conceptualization of music in a particular culture leads us to understand why some avant-garde or controversial music elicits such resistance, even in our own culture. In a book significantly called *Silence* (1961), John Cage, a composer who is original, even "shocking," in his conception of music, advocates some new understandings. Cage, unlike the Basongye, wants to work out compositions according to the idea that "nothing takes place but sounds"; he wants to include in musical compositions those sounds that just happen to be in the environment. A composer who makes a musical composition out of twelve radios playing simultaneously challenges us to consider our own conceptualization of music in the same way that musical behaviors from another culture do.

Variation in Culture Areas

Although the variety of conceptualizations of music has not been explored by anthropologists, the variety of musical forms and instruments has been well documented. We are fond of saying that music is a universal language, but it may be more correct to say that music is a language consisting of a number of dialects, some of them mutually unintelligible. Several musical culture areas of the world can be differentiated, though all culture areas show significant internal differences in details and have several rather than only one musical tradition.

The East Asian area includes China, Mongolia, Korea, and Japan. The music of this area is essentially melodic rather than harmonic. Melodic instruments in the early Confucian orchestra consisted of sets of like units: a set of tuned metal bells for chimes, stone slabs for stone chimes, a set of strings on a zither. In contrast to the Western idea of an ensemble in which all instruments sound together as one, each instrument in this music maintains its own identity. Divergence in time, pitch, and

ornamentation of several instruments simultaneously playing the same basic melody gives the music a highly stylized quality.

In the Southeast Asian area, percussion, made with gongs, xylophones, cymbals, and bells, predominates. Here, the orchestra is not a group of musicians but rather a set of instruments unified by their physical appearance and common tuning system. In Indonesia, for example, the *gamelan* (orchestra) is unified by the proper relative sizes of the instruments, the themes and motifs of the decorative carving, and the particular color combinations of paints on the instruments. There is no standard tuning; only instruments belonging to the same orchestra or made by the same person are in tune with one another. Thus, unlike in the West, musicians do not bring their own instruments to a concert. Each instrument has a function in the orchestra: Some lead, others carry the theme, and others accentuate the theme. This is also in contrast to the Western symphony orchestra, in which one instrument may do several of these things at various times during the performance.

In South Asia (India and Sri Lanka), there are many traditions: tribal music, folk music, commercial film music, and a classical tradition that grows out of religion and philosophy of the Vedic period, going back several thousand years. In the classical tradition, music is seen as a path to self-realization; the texts of classical songs are prayers to the gods. The human voice is the primary instrument. Vocal style is basic to all melody, whether sung or played on an instrument. If an ensemble includes a vocalist, her or his role is preeminent. What is sung is more important than how it is sung. The music is essentially melodic, and improvisation has a significant place in performance.

Music in Africa is part of community life. The most important general characteristics of African music are its rhythmic complexity, a call and response pattern, the constant use of percussive devices such as hand clapping and foot stomping, improvisation, interesting vocal effects such as falsetto, and the simultaneous sounding of different pitches by singers or in-

Music, dance, costume, and song all are part of the rich ceremonial life of the cultural groups of West Africa. (United Nations)

strumentalists. A great variety of materials is used for musical instruments — clay, metal, gourds, bamboo, tortoise shells, hides, skins, seeds, stones, and palm leaves. Wind and string instruments are found in Africa, but it is the drum that has always attracted the attention of students of African music. Drums are used to talk to spirits, to communicate between people, and to provide accompaniment for dancing. The important factor in the "talking drums" for which Africa is famous is that the drums create a sound that will carry for long distances. Although in some tribes arbitrary signals are used to symbolize words and concepts, more frequently the sound system of the drum is tied into the pitch structure of a language. Most African languages are tonal, which means that each syllable of a word has a prescribed tone or pitch. In order to be understood, a speaker must use the proper pitch and syllable. With drums on which the pitch can be changed, the tones and rhythms of these languages can be played and understood.

Among native Americans, music is essentially used in connection with religious ceremonies. It is largely vocal, with flutes, drums, and rattles used to accompany the voice. There is a wide variety of vocal styles. The Pueblos of the Southwest prefer deep male choruses; Plains tribes and the Navajo have a piercing falsetto tradition. In South America, where complex civilizations developed, orchestras and musical drama predate the Spanish conquest. Some of these forms spread into the countryside in the form of folk versions of urban music. Orchestral and choral effects are quite unlike anything in North America. Contemporary urban music often includes aboriginal influences in both melody and instruments.

In contemporary music in the Americas, the influence of the African tradition is important, particularly rhythmic sophistication, call and response patterns, and the use of improvisation. African musical styles have continued with the least change in the dance and cult music of Brazil and the Caribbean, and they blend in with Hispanic styles in the rhumba and conga of Cuba. In the United States, spirituals and blues and jazz, from which rock and roll is derived, also have their origins in African-American music.

The music of the islands of Polynesia shows great variation, with a few common stylistic features. For the most part, traditional music was restricted to chantlike recitations and employed relatively few pitches. The complex manner of singing used trills, different tempos, shouts, and variations in breathing that were often more significant than tonal range or song structure. Traditional chant songs consisted of genealogies, accounts of mythological events, war songs, and love songs. The number of instruments was relatively small: drums, slit-gongs, and bamboo pipes. For making the rhythm of dance movements audible, shells or animal teeth were strung together and worn on the body. Before European contact, stringed instruments were scarce; today, two imported string instruments — the ukulele and the guitar — are among the most popular in all Oceania.

Music and Human Adaptation

Documenting the wide variety of musical styles and instruments is, of course, only the beginning in the science of ethnomusicology. Music, like the other arts, can be said to represent the "soul," or cultural identity, of a people in a highly condensed and emotional form. An important aspect of studying music, then, is an attempt to understand the culture of a particular people. And like other art forms, music plays an important indirect role in human adaptation, primarily perhaps by contributing to the integration of society.

One of the most ambitious attempts to document the more direct ways in which music enters into human adaptations has been carried out by Alan Lomax and his colleagues (1968). One obvious relationship is the way in which music is used as an accompaniment for the procurement of food and natural resources and the processes of preparing them for human use. Lomax demonstrates that there is a direct correlation between the ways in which people work and their song style. Individualized song performances are correlated with several work situations, such as the voluntary and temporary work teams found in simple band societies and the small family work teams found in societies with plow agriculture. In horticultural societies — where work groups are relatively permanent, cohesive groups of age mates, clan brothers, or extended families — group singing predominates. Thus, the individualism characteristic of many aspects of life in hunting societies has its correlate in individualized song performance. The solidarity and cohesiveness of kin groups in horticultural societies is reflected in the communal or group nature of their singing. In industrial societies, where the individual or individual family is separated from the others, individualized song performance again emerges as important.

Dance

Dance is a form of human behavior composed of culturally patterned, purposeful, and intentionally rhythmical body movement and gestures that are not part of ordinary motor activities and that have an esthetic value. Dance appears in every human culture and is also universally combined with other kinds of media — music and song, for example. It also involves supplementary materials added to the human body, such as decoration, costume, and masks.

Dance, like the other arts, is also symbolic behavior. It carries meanings that are arbitrary and culturally specific in the same way that human speech does. In dance, as in other kinds of human behavior, social learning is important. It is this aspect of human dance that differentiates it from biologically programmed ritual movements among nonhuman animals, such as the "dance" of honeybees or the mating movements of birds. Dance in human societies is used to communicate a variety of ideas and emotions (information), but the meaning of human dance is not self-evident; it depends primarily on the meanings assigned to it in different societies.

Because of its physical nature and its ability to elicit intense emotions, dance is often associated with the kind of excitement that signals special events in the lives of individuals or groups. Thus, dance is often involved in rites of passage, which mark changes in social status. Because the physical behavior involved in rhythmic and energetic dance may alter various physiological processes, such as the production of adrenaline, dance is also an important way of altering states of consciousness. In this connection, it may be part of rituals that involve trance and other states of emotion that transcend everyday experience. Through dance, an individual and a group can *feel* the qualitative shift in the normal pattern of mental functioning through a disturbed sense of time, a loss of control, perceptual distortion, a feeling of rejuvenation, a change in body image, or hypersuggestibility.

Music and dance are often combined to produce trance experience, which is one mode of gaining supernatural powers. At the Bab Segma in Fez, Morocco, on Sundays, hundreds of people gather to watch and listen to storytellers and boys who fall into a trance after hours of dancing. (United Nations)

The study of dance suggests that it appears to be rooted in human capabilities for imposing order on the universe and may be adaptive for human societies as a way of conveying information about this universe (Hanna 1977). Dance may also be adaptive in that, like the other arts, it is a form of exploratory, novel, even playful behavior. Novelty and play are also important adaptive aspects of other primate species. Dance teaches coordination and the skills that are involved in hunting, agriculture, and war. Ordinary movements used in procuring food may be incorporated into dance. Dance (and music) are used in many cultures to stir up feelings that can then be directed toward dealing more effectively with one's environment or coping with social problems. War dances, for example, may rouse men to the proper pitch of excitement and confidence so that they can act more effectively in battle. Dance also provides a protected situation in which human beings can experience forms of disorientation that could not be tolerated in everyday life. These opportunities may keep alive the capacity for new orientations to reality that at some point may be critical in a group's ability to adapt and thus to survive.

The Artist in Society

In studying the artist in society, anthropologists have been somewhat limited by the lack of ethnographic data. Part of the reason for this is that in many small-scale societies, the artist as a specialist does not exist. Even if certain individuals are recognized as exceptionally skilled, they may not be full-time artists but rather combine artistic specialties with other kinds of activities. As already noted, artistic skill may be applied to the manufacture of objects for everyday use. Various other artistic skills, such as in dance and music, are usually embedded in the role of religious specialist.

Furthermore, in Western society, we tend to define the artist as an innovator. The importance we place on being "original" has blinded us to some extent to the role of the artist in societies where the artistic product appears to conform much more to cultural tradition and is less likely to stand out. The emphasis on innovation and difference has led us, in general, to see the artist as a special person, often a deviant, working alone and often in opposition to rather than in harmony with society.

Artists in other societies do not always have this deviant or marginal status; their personalities may also be much closer to the cultural norm than is true in the West. The importance of designating a particular individual as the creator of a particular work of art is also not universal. Much artistic production in non-Western societies has a collective and thus anonymous quality. Folk art has traditionally been defined, in fact, as productions in which the individual creator is not known or has faded out of memory. As folk art becomes commercialized, however—as is the case all over the world today in places where there are tourist markets—individual artists emerge as specialists. They have been created by market forces; the work of certain individuals is in greater demand than that of others.

In an ambitious attempt to explore the role of the artist in society, Dennison Nash (1968) developed a model that raises some questions which lend themselves to cross-cultural research. Although Nash was specifically interested in the role of the composer in society, his framework can be applied to other kinds of artists as well. Nash concentrated on the social factors operating in recruitment to the artistic role, personality, and the role of the audience.

Although people with artistic talent may appear in either sex and in any social class, societies, through their cultural definitions of ascribed status, may inhibit or prevent these talents from developing and thus not use the gifts of talented individuals to their full potential. Art, for example, is often limited to either males or females in a particular society. Kinship status may define who fulfills artistic roles. Artistic roles may be inherited in families, clans, or castes. Where art is family property, such as in the songs owned by kinship groups among Northwest Coast Indians, the singing of these songs is limited to members of the group. In India, to give another example, certain art forms are practiced only by the members of certain castes. For a long time in India, certain forms of a classical dance called *bharatanatyam* could be performed only by women of a particular caste. These women were called *devadasis*, and they were attached to temples and ceremoniously married to temple deities. Their female children also became devadasis, whereas their male children became musicians and music teachers. Often people who are marginal in a culture are its performers. In Europe and Asia, for example, Gypsies play an important role in musical performances. It is possible that marginal peoples are more able to be innovative because of their marginality.

Where religious activity, such as shamanism, incorporates artistic performance, it may be that essentially unstable personalities are attracted to artistic roles. The idea of the artist as separated from, and at odds with, the world is a Western conception. We might expect to find, therefore, that the personality of the Western artist does differ in important respects from that of the nonartist. A study of avant-garde painters in the United States in the 1960s showed that they had a variety of personality characteristics, but a common thread was a profound quest for autonomy and alienation from middle-class life. Perhaps only when music or the other arts become vehicles for altered states of consciousness do the arts attract particularly unstable personalities, although they may always attract those with an exceptional innate talent and a drive that sets them apart from others in the culture.

The Western idea that the very essence of art resides in artists "expressing themselves" in some unique and innovative way appears to

In tribal and peasant societies, the artist seeks not so much to express herself in a unique and individualistic way as to re-create traditional designs that are pleasing but well within the traditional limits of the group. (United Nations)

contain a culturally specific value of individualism. Certainly, the situation for some kinds of art among the Tiv of Africa would be very foreign to us. According to Paul Bohannan (1971), art among the Tiv is a secondary aspect of other facets of life — play, religion, social status. Much of Tiv art is communal; the artist, as an individual, is unimportant. In making various products out of wood, such as walking sticks or stools, one man may start a design or carving. If for some reason he has to leave it for a while, another person may add a few strokes and then in turn hand the object to a third person. It may take several people to finish the design or carving. In Tiv society, then, the audience, or critics, of some kinds of art may also play a role in creating it. This situation contrasts with the Western view that art should be individually created.

In music, dance, and drama, the communal nature of the arts is much more apparent in traditional, small-scale societies than in modern, industrial nations. Creation, performance, and audience reaction tend to merge and feed back into one another. For a performer's activity to be socially significant, it must carry some meaning to an audience, and thus such performances are always carried out within certain cultural traditions. Even in the West, however, where innovation is an important artistic value, composers and artistic performers have written and performed largely for their own times and within the framework of the musical conventions of their culture. If there is no writing system for recording or notating music, dance, and drama, this is even more likely to be true. If the audience does not understand or like one's artistic activity, there will be little chance for it to become part of the culture; and without becoming part of the culture, there is little chance of its being preserved for posterity.

Sports and Games

In many cultures, including our own, games and sports are emotionally compelling and symbolic in a way that makes us think of them, at least in their function, as like traditional art forms. It has been suggested, for example, that the popularity of football in the United States derives from the fact that it contains characteristics particularly important in our society: technological complexity, coordination and specialization, as well as the tendency to violence, although that violence is expressed within the framework of teamwork, specialization, and mechanization (Arens 1976). From this view: "The football team looks very much like a small scale model of the American corporation: compartmentalized, highly sophisticated in the coordinated application of a differentiated, specialized technology, turning out a winning product in a competitive market" (Montague

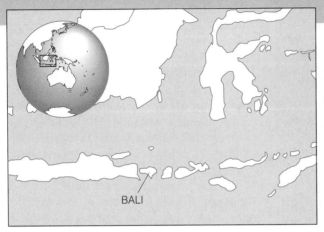

Cockfights are a consuming passion of the Balinese. In his symbolic analysis of cockfighting, Clifford Geertz illustrates that in the cock ring, much of Bali culture is revealed. For, as he says, "It is only apparently cocks that are fighting there. Actually it is men."

Balinese men have an intense identification with their fighting cocks and spend much time caring for them, discussing them, and looking at them. At the same time that the cocks are a magnification of the owner's masculine self, they are also expressions of what the Balinese regard as the direct inversion — esthetically, morally, and metaphysically — of human status: animality. The Balinese have a great revulsion for anything that is animal-like, so that in identifying with his cock, the Balinese man is not just identifying with his ideal masculine self but also, and at the same time, identifying with what he most fears, hates, and is fascinated by — "the powers of darkness."

In the cockfight, man and beast, good and evil, the creative power of aroused masculinity and the destructive power of loosened animality, fuse in a bloody drama of hatred, cruelty, violence, and death. It is little wonder that in seeking analogues for heaven and hell the Balinese compare the former to the mood of a man whose cock has just won, the latter to that of a man whose cock has just lost.

Cockfight programs run about three to four hours and include ten matches. The matches are arranged on an ad hoc basis. Owners of cocks move into the ring, trying to find an opponent, and when a match is made, the selected cocks have their spurs affixed. The spurs are razor-sharp, five-inch-long, pointed steel swords. Affixing the spurs is a delicate, almost ritualistic, job and is done only by specialists.

After the spurs are affixed, the two cocks are placed by their handlers in the ring. The cocks almost immediately fly at each other in an explosion of animal fury. Within moments, one or the other drives home a solid blow with its spur. The cock that has landed the blow is immediately picked up so that it will not get a return blow, for otherwise the match is likely to end in a mortal tie as the cocks hack each other to pieces. After a short interval the cocks are again placed in the ring, where the cock who landed the first blow usually finishes off his opponent. What counts is which cock dies first: The cock that lasts longer wins the match.

The cockfight — as rage untrammeled and form perfected — is a sociological event and has an intimate relation to the collective life of the Balinese. The pivot of cockfighting around which all other aspects turn is gambling.

There are two kinds of bets: one bet in the center between the owners of the cocks and the side bets around the ring between members of the audience. The center bets are large and collective — the bet is never raised simply by the owner in whose name it is made, but by him together with four to eight allies (kin, neighbors, close friends). This bet is a matter of deliberate arrangement by the coalition members with the umpire as witness. The audience bets are smaller and individual — between two men — and are made through shouting offers and acceptances among the excited audience. The center bets are always even money; the audience bets are never for even money.

The side betting takes place after the center bet has been made and its size announced. Then in a rising crescendo of shouts, backers of the underdog offer their propositions to anyone who will accept them, while those backing the favorite also try to find takers. In a large-bet, well-made match, there is a mob scene atmosphere — a sense of sheer chaos about to break loose — as all the waving, shouting men try desperately to find a last-minute partner. This frenzy is heightened by the intense stillness that falls as the cocks are put down in the ring and the battle begins. When the fight ends, all bets are immediately paid. There are no IOUs.

It is this distinction between the balanced center bets and the unbalanced side bets that is the key to an analysis linking cockfight betting to the wider world of Balinese culture.

When the center bet is large, every effort is made to ensure that the cocks are as evenly matched as possible. From this follows two facts: The higher the center bet, the shorter the odds of the side bets and the greater the volume of side betting. A more evenly matched fight is not merely considered more "interesting" in that such a match is less predictable, but more crucially, more is at stake in such a fight — in terms of money, fighting ability of the cocks, and especially, social prestige. It is these large-bet matches that Geertz calls "deep play."

In deep play, the stakes are so high that, from a utilitarian standpoint, it is irrational for men to engage in it at all. And yet, men do engage in such play — frequently, and with great passion. For the Balinese, the explanation lies in the fact that in such play, much more is at stake than material gain, namely, esteem, honor, dignity, respect — in a word, status. This does not mean that the money at stake is not important; to the contrary, it is important because so much money is involved that risking it — publicly — is also risking one's status, especially one's masculinity. It is this irrationality that increases the meaningfulness of the cockfight to the Balinese.   (*continued*)

The importance of the deep play aspect of the cockfight to the Balinese is attested to by the sociomoral hierarchy of betting. Lowest in this hierarchy are the women, children, adolescents, and extremely poor and socially despised people, who bet at a penny ante level at the various games of sheer chance that go on around the cockfighting arena — roulette, dice throw, coin spin, pea-under-the-shell, and so on. Cockfighting men would be ashamed to go anywhere near these people. Slightly above these people are those who do not themselves fight cocks but who place side bets on smaller matches. Next are those who fight cocks in small or medium matches but do not have the status to join in the large matches, though they may bet on them. And finally, there are those substantial members of the community, around whom local life revolves, who fight cocks in the larger fights and bet on them around the side.

What makes Balinese cockfighting deep play is thus not money in itself but rather what money causes to happen: the migration of the Balinese status hierarchy into the body of the cockfight. The cockfight is not merely a symbolic contest between male egos; it also is deliberately made to be a simulation of the social matrix — the villages, kin groups, "castes" in which its devotees live. And because prestige is the central driving force in Balinese society, so also is prestige the central driving force of the cockfight, turning this sport into a "status bloodbath." The more a match is between men of nearly equal status, or between personal enemies, or between high-status individuals, the "deeper" the match is felt to be. The deeper the match the more other things follow: The more a man will advance his best cock and the one he most closely identifies with; the finer the cocks involved and the more exactly they will be matched; the greater the emotion that will be involved and the more absorbed the audience will be with the match; the higher the center and side bets and the more overall betting; the less an "economic" view and the more a "status" view of gambling will be involved; and finally, the more substantial the citizens who will be doing the gaming.

The Balinese themselves are aware of what their involvement in cockfighting reveals about their status concerns and social hierarchy, and they talk about cockfighting as "playing with fire without getting burned." It activates village and kin group rivalries and hostilities, but in "play" form that comes dangerously and entrancingly close to the expression of open and direct interpersonal and intergroup aggression (something that almost never happens in the course of normal, ordinary Balinese life), but which is not quite the same, because after all "it is only a cockfight."

Adapted from Clifford Geertz, "Deep Play: Notes on the Balinese Cockfight," reprinted by permission of Dædalus, Journal of the American Academy of Arts and Sciences, Winter 1972, Vol. 101, No. 1, 1–37.

Games and sports often convey important cultural values. Like the cockfight in Bali, falconing in many Middle Eastern societies encode masculine values and are surrounded with rules and rituals. (Joan Gregg)

and Morais 1976:39). Thus, the football game is a model of the most important productive unit in our society—the business firm. By watching football, we are watching a model of the way our world works. It is because football is a small-scale model of our world that it allows us to understand that world. It "renders visible and directly comprehensible a system that is far too large and complex to be directly comprehended by any individual" (p. 39). How many of us can understand the interconnections among all aspects of the American economic system?

Beyond this, however, football is a model of the traditional route to success in our society. Dedication, hard work, and self-sacrifice for the good of others (here, the football team) are held up as the basic principles on which success is based and are the characteristics most praised in individual players. Football is the staging of a real event in which the principles of success are shown to work. The success model is also illustrated in football commen-

tary or sportscasting. The accomplishments of each player are compared with those of others, and the rewards of the system—money and recognition—are then extended to the players on the basis of their performances. To the extent that football is a model of the real world, the audience sees the actors being evaluated according to objective criteria and rewarded according to performance. It is this process that is at the ideological core of the traditional culture of the United States and that is ultimately related to the productive process in our society. Surely football is an example of the statement that "art" serves to display the cultural themes of a society in ways that make them emotionally compelling. As for its integrative function, Arens notes at the very beginning of his article that 79 percent of American households were tuned in to the first Super Bowl game on TV, indicating that this entertainment cuts across all the divisive aspects of our social structure—race, ethnicity, income, political affiliation, and regionalism.

Folklore: Forms and Functions

Folklore includes stories about supernatural characters and events; legends, which concern historical persons and events; and other kinds of oral traditions, such as riddles, proverbs, epic poems, and word play. Folklore has many functions, such as the transmitting of cultural knowledge and oral traditions, and serving as a means of moral instruction. Thus, folktales and stories are an important element in socialization in all societies.

Folktales

Although folktales may contain a supernatural element, they are not sacred in the same way as myths. Folktales are told mainly for enjoyment, although they often have important educational functions. Most folktales and other verbal arts, such as riddles and proverbs, have a moral. Oral traditions are thus important in the socialization process of every society, especially in societies without writing. Folklore can tell us much about the cultural values of a society, because it reveals which actions are approved and which are condemned. The heroes in folktales give us clues to characteristics considered admirable in a particular culture. The audience is always led by the way the tale is told to know which characters and attributes are a cause for ridicule or scorn and which are to be admired. Thus, in studying folklore, the cultural context of its telling is an important clue to understanding the tale itself.

Folklore and Social Protest

Another important way of understanding folklore is in terms of its psychological and social functions in society. Folklore provides a socially acceptable outlet for emotions that might otherwise be disruptive to the social order. Through humor, fantasy, and the creative use

Be good, loyal and work hard
and you will get your just reward !!!

Humor in folklore is one way of releasing tension when protest cannot be expressed openly. This anonymous bit of folklore from urban life is a protest against the unfairness of the system of rewards in contemporary bureaucracies.

of imagination, oral traditions provide a channel through which hostility, ambivalence, distress, and conflict can be released. Thus, folklore is an important channel of social protest.

Folktales often embody conflicts that are part of a shared experience; the conflict of heroic folk figures symbolically touches on and communicates what the audience feels but cannot articulate. Folklore resolves in fantasy issues that are problems in real life. This function is illustrated by the studies of Roger Abrahams (1970) of the various oral traditions among urban blacks in the United States. One of the most common figures in this oral tradition is the "trickster," or "clever hero." The trickster, who is usually smaller and weaker than those against whom he is matched, triumphs through his wits rather than through force. This folklore hero is known in the United States through the Br'er Rabbit tales — a set of stories in which small animals are constantly getting the better of larger ones. The popularity of trickster tales in the Old South seems to have an obvious relationship to social relations between blacks and whites before the Civil War. The trickster tales can be seen as a veiled reaction or protest against domination and as a way of presenting feelings of protest in a nonthreatening way. For African-Americans, the trickster may represent the hero who can be in control of his world only through cleverness. The humor of these tales serves to release tension in a situation in which open rebellion seems futile.

Abrahams points out that, as the social situation has changed for African-Americans, their folklore has also changed. In urban black areas, the "badman" has supplanted the trickster as a hero. The badman, unlike the trickster, is consciously rebelling against authority. He is arrogant and virile, and unlike the manipulative and sly trickster, the badman is manliness openly displayed. The emergence of the badman hero would appear to relate to the recognition of a more open environment in the urban North and of the greater possibility of resisting authority than was true in the Old South.

Summary

1. Art refers to both the process and products of human skill applied to any activity that meets the standards of beauty in a particular society. For convenience, the arts can be divided into the graphic and plastic arts, music, dance, folklore, and games and sports.

2. Art is a symbolic way of communicating. One of the most important functions of art is to communicate, display, and reinforce important cultural themes and values. The arts thus have an integrative function in society.

3. The arts should be studied in their cultural context; the separation of a class of objects or activities labeled "the arts" is mainly characteristic of modern societies and reflects the general tendency toward the separation of many kinds of activities from one another.

4. The comparative evaluation of esthetic values and artistic styles is difficult, if not impossible. Each culture has its own standards of beauty and its own artistic traditions. Cultures also differ in the degree to which they have developed various art forms. It is thus generally agreed by anthropologists that art should be studied in its cultural context.

5. Because they are easily separated from their cultural context, most attention has been given to the study of the graphic and plastic arts. These arts can be examined in terms of their stylistic variation, as a way of understanding a particular culture, or as a cognitive map of a sociocultural system.

6. Music is a universal language with many different dialects. Each musical culture area of the world has its own characteristic way of structuring voice and instrument sound. Music has many functions in culture, and it may have a directly adaptive role in its relation to the nature of work in different societies.

7. Dance is a universal form of human behavior in which meaning is attached to specific movements. Dance and music are frequently associated with altered states of consciousness and are used in ritual and other performances that mark exceptional events in the life of the individual and the group. Both are frequently associated with religion.

8. Dance may also be directly adaptive in teaching physical coordination and in building skills necessary in productive work and in warfare.

9. In small-scale societies, the artist is rarely a full-time specialist, and art is much more of a communal or anonymous endeavor. The importance of innovation as a part of artistic judgment is more characteristic of Western culture than of other cultures.

10. Although people with artistic talent may appear in any segment of society, most societies restrict the artistic role to certain individuals, using criteria of sex, kinship status, or social class. Sometimes those who fill artistic roles are cultural outsiders or members of culturally marginal groups.

11. Where art is a vehicle for altered states of consciousness — for example, where it is tied in with religion — the artist may have a personality that is strikingly different from that of other members of society. Even where the artist is an exceptional personality, however, he or she tends to operate within the traditions of society.

12. Expressive culture includes sports, games, and "deep play." These activities, too, go beyond the merely practical, express important cultural themes, and are performed with an application of skill and stylistic forms. The Balinese cockfight and American football are examples of deep play.

13. Folklore refers to oral traditions, particularly myth and folktales. Myths are sacred narratives that function as social charters, validating the beliefs and social structure of a society. Folktales, though told primarily for entertainment, also have important functions in society. They serve to educate, to release tension and act as a channel for social protest, and to integrate society by displaying cultural themes in a dramatic setting.

Suggested Readings

Dundes, Alan, and Pagter, Carl R.
1975   *Work and You Shall Be Rewarded: Urban Folklore from the Paperwork Empire.* Austin, Tex.: American Folklore Society. A very funny book that looks at the visual and written folklore of modern bureaucracies.

Hanna, Judith Lynne
1988   *Dance, Sex and Gender.* Chicago: University of Chicago Press. A comprehensive and well-written work on the relationship between dance and sexual identity, structures of dominance and defiance, and sexual desire and behavior from a wide range of cultures, including Western theater dance.

Harris, Janet C., and Park, Roberta J., eds.
1983   *Play, Games and Sports in Cultural Contexts.* Champaign, Ill.: Human Kinetics Publications. An important and interesting book using various theoretical perspectives — materialist, functional, and symbolic, among others — to study play, games, and sports in a diversity of cultures, including our own.

Klein, Alan M.
1991   *Sugarball: The American Game, The Dominican Dream.* New Haven, Conn.: Yale University Press. A skilled historical and ethnographic analysis of a fascinating subject — the significant impact this relatively small country has had on the American game of baseball, employing the dual concepts of U.S. dominance over the game along with Dominican resistance to that dominance.

Manuel, Peter
1993   *Cassette Culture: Popular Music and Technology in North India.* Chicago: University of Chicago Press. A clearly written and important book that examines the impact of tape cassette technology on various forms of folk and popular music in India. It pays particular attention to the ways in which this new technology has also affected religious and political relationships in India.

Marre, Jeremy, and Charlton, Hannah
1985   *Beats of the Heart: Popular Music of the World.* New York: Pantheon. An interesting and readable account of different kinds of popular music performances from a wide range of societies.

Waterman, Christopher Alan
1990   *Juju: A Social History and Ethnography of an African Popular Music.* Chicago, Ill.: University of Chicago Press. A scholarly treatment of a non-Western African performance tradition, examining the urban and colonial context, social relations, and esthetic aspects of a popular musical form in contemporary Nigeria.

Whiting, Robert
1989   *You Gotta Have Wa.* New York: Macmillan. Another example of deep play: a study of the particular Japanese values that are incorporated into the game of baseball as played in Japan.

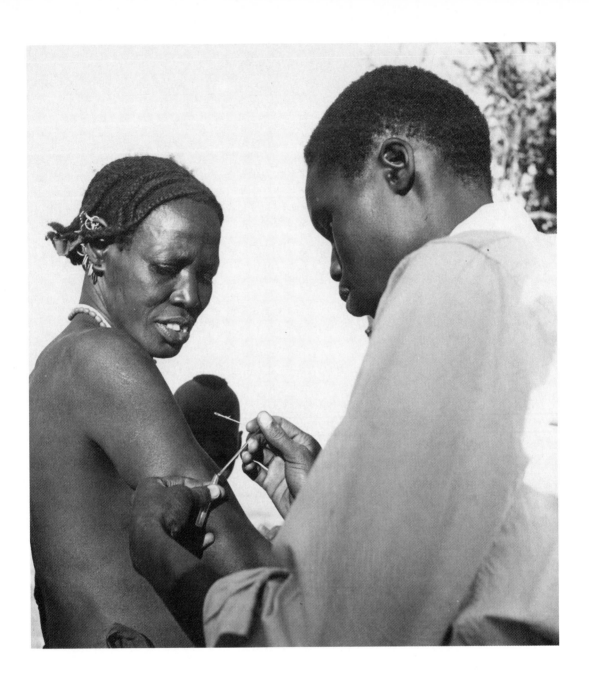

Change in the Contemporary World

What are the most important sources of cultural change in the contemporary world?

How are economic changes related to other changes in society?

Because things change, does it mean they are getting better?

How does change affect women's roles?

THE UNITED FRUIT CO.

When the trumpets had sounded
  and all
was in readiness on the face of
  the earth,
Jehovah divided his universe:
Anaconda, Ford Motors,
Coca-Cola Inc., and similar entities:
the most succulent item of all,
The United Fruit Company
  Incorporated
reserved for itself: the heartland
and coasts of my country,
the delectable waist of America.
They rechristened their properties:
the "Banana Republics" —
and over the languishing dead,
the uneasy repose of the heroes
who harried that greatness
their flags and their freedoms,
they established an opera bouffe:
they ravished all enterprise,
awarded the laurels like Caesars,
unleashed all the covetous, and
  contrived
the tyrannical Reign of the Flies —
Trujillo the fly, and Tacho the fly,
the flies called Carias, Martinez,

Ubico — all of them flies, flies
dank with the blood of their
  marmalade
vassalage, flies buzzing drunkenly
on the populous middens:
the fly-circus fly and the scholarly
kind, case-hardened in tyranny.

Then in the bloody domain of the flies
The United Fruit Company
  Incorporated
unloaded with a booty of coffee
  and fruits
brimming its cargo boats, gliding
like trays with the spoils
of our drowning dominions.

And all the while, somewhere, in
  the sugary
hells of our seaports,
smothered by gases, an Indian
fell in the morning:
a body spun off, an anonymous
chattel, some numeral tumbling,
a branch with its death running out
  of it
in the vat of the carrion, fruit laden
  and foul.

From Pablo Neruda, Selected Poems *(New York, Grove Press). Reprinted by permission of Grove/ Atlantic Monthly Press. Translation © 1961 by Ben Belitt.*

The contemporary world is characterized by connectedness and change. Americans get the Hong Kong flu; a shutdown of oil wells on the Persian Gulf halts generating plants in Ohio; the AIDS epidemic crosses the continents; a rancher in South America encroaches into the Amazon rain forest to raise cattle to produce meat for a hamburger in the United States; thousands of Indians and Koreans build cities in the Middle East; a woman from the Philippines works in an Israeli restaurant. These connections and the changes that come about through culture contact have always been part of human history, but with today's global economy, they are occurring at a faster rate than ever before. While the connections between cultures have always resulted in change, the age of European exploration, the expansion of capitalism, and colonization of the non-European world have wrought transformations over the last 500 years that have been particularly rapid and intense, and as Pablo Neruda's poem vividly reminds us, very often with unequal benefits to the cultures involved.

tion, expansion of Christianity and Western-style education, and access to mass-produced consumer goods. Indeed, culture loss and victimization were frequently the case. Less often discussed were the ways in which indigenous peoples and peasants took an active role in change, or actively resisted it; also less discussed were the detailed historical circumstances and the specific processes by which change took place. This historical approach is now being addressed and there is increasing anthropological interest in the study of the expansion of European capitalism and colonialism, as well as a greater attempt to study local cultures within a world systems context. There is, in addition, a greater willingness to acknowledge that culture contact produced culture conflict, undermining the myth that European culture was passively, willingly, or even eagerly embraced by all those non-European cultures that came into contact with it.

Another view of change that was, and is, important within and outside of anthropology is the model of change as modernization.

Models of Change

Anthropological models of culture change have most often focused on the destructive impact that non-Western societies experienced as they came into contact with Europeans or were drawn into the European colonialist and capitalist orbit. This view, sometimes called **acculturation,** documented change as a process of culture loss and victimization, as non-European, small-scale societies faced the maws of industrialization, mechanized agriculture, urbaniza-

Modernization Theory and Its Critics

Between the 1950s and the 1980s, the model of change that perhaps dominated the Western view of the non-Western world, regarding both tribal and peasant societies, was that of "modernization." **Modernization** models of change envision an ideal modern/traditional dichotomy in which (non-Western) societies move from tradition to modernity. Modernity is defined as the technological and sociocultural systems of industrialized nations. It includes advanced machine technology, industrialization of the production process, urbanization, a market economy, centralized and bureaucratic structures of political administration, a decline in the importance of kinship and a growth of nonkinship social groupings, and an attitude that favors innovation and change.

This process of change as modernization was used — by anthropologists and others — both as a description of "reality" and as a prescription for what should happen in order for economic development to take place. The theory assumed that change in "traditional" societies would follow the pattern of development of the Western European nations, and it was expected that foreign aid from Western Europe and the United States to many societies and new states in Asia, Africa, and Latin America would help hasten this process, which was considered desirable: Modernization was equated with progress and development. It is from this model that the division of the world into the "developed" and the "undeveloped" or "developing" nations emerged.

Development models of change try to identify the structural, cultural, and psychological features of traditional societies that "stand in the way of" modernization, particularly of economic development. For example, because most traditional societies are agrarian, modernization models envision that these societies will change from using "simple" traditional technology and intensive human and animal labor, to using machine technology. Economically, modernization assumes a shift from subsistence economies to cash economies, as indigenous peoples move into the world-market economy by increasing their cultivation of cash crops and move from agriculture into industrial wage labor; both of these shifts are presumed to result in economic development and a higher standard of living.

Politically, modernization refers to the growth of centralized and bureaucratic structures of political administration and law that extend down to local levels, both undermining local and traditional mechanisms of social control and filling in where such control mechanisms have been eroded by other processes of social change. New political ideologies emerge as the nation-state becomes the overriding structure of social integration. Previously autonomous cultural groups are drawn into national networks and brought (with varying degrees of success) under control by the state.

On a psychological level, modernization models picture traditional peoples as "backward," fatalistic, and resistant to innovation. In this view, so-called traditional societies, in order to become modern, must develop a more open attitude toward change and the achievement orientation that characterizes the "developed" Western societies.

In spite of the political power of modernization models, which continue to shape development efforts and programs, much of what the theory predicted just did not happen. It was partly the failure of many development programs at the local level that led to new approaches in conceptualizing change in the so-called underdeveloped parts of the world. In the first place, modernization theorists envisioned the various changes associated with modernization as taking place more or less together, as they had in the West, but this has not been the case. For example, industrialization can, and has, taken place without large-scale urbanization, and conversely, large-scale urban migration sometimes occurs even when there is little industrial employment to absorb the migrants. As another example, the entry of tribal and peasant societies into world markets has not always led to local development; indeed, it has often resulted in a deterioration of local economies with few corresponding benefits, as economic benefits may well depend more on world-market prices for a commodity than on whether or not the people producing it are "modernized." Thus, one important failure of modernization theory was that it did not take into account the relationship of local cultures to the global economy.

Modernization theory also foundered on the ethnocentric assumption that all "underdeveloped" peoples would necessarily view the modernization package as progress, and that they would eagerly want to adopt, part and parcel, the whole bundle of economic, social, and cultural changes involved. The theory clearly underestimated the ability of peoples to resist this impact, whether in the form of religious syncretism as a response to Christianity, a seemingly stubborn decision to stick to older technologies and methods of subsistence in the face of "modern" (but often ineffective) technology or, more recently, political resistance by ethnic groups and indigenous peoples to the dominance of the nation-state.

In addition, while most elite groups that control new nation-states in Asia, Africa, and Latin America are committed to Western ideas of progress and development and are deliberately trying to transform their rural populations through programs of planned change, the ways in which this happens are extremely variable, and precise formulas are not very useful. As Clifford Geertz points out, modernization is not just the replacement of the traditional and obsolete with the imported and up-to-date. The new nations of the world have the double goal of seeking to retain parts of their traditional culture and at the same time adapting to the requirements of the twentieth century: "There is no simple progression from 'traditional' to 'modern,' but a twisting, spasmodic, unmethodical movement, which turns as often toward repossessing the . . . past as disowning [it]" (Geertz 1973:319).

By viewing modernization, as it occurred in the West, as the best—or only—model of change, development theorists overlooked many of the negative effects of development on non-European peoples, and ignored much of the local knowledge and technology by which these societies had successfully adapted to their environments. Nor were the benefits of modernization equally distributed within local communities, as development theorists assumed. Indeed, in many cases, development turned out to benefit only a small number of local people, and was disastrous for many others, a result development theory programs did not sufficiently take into account.

From a more theoretical standpoint, modernization theory perpetuated a misleading dichotomy between "traditional" and "modern" cultures, by ignoring the variety of creative adaptations that local cultures had been making for centuries. It was in recognition of these flaws in both the theory and practice of modernization and development that the world systems approach to culture change emerged.

World Systems Theory

One critique of modernization that reflects a world systems approach was dependency theory. Dependency theory holds that underdevelopment is not a result of traditional culture patterns which need to change, but rather an outcome of the incorporation of non-Western societies and nations into a world economic system that creates, and depends on, economic inequality among nations (Nash 1981). Dependency theory holds that as some countries, specifically those of the West, expand and advance economically, others, frequently lumped together as the "Third World," which interact with them within the global economy as dependents, can only expand (develop economically) as a reflection of the dominant countries (Dos Santos 1973:76–77). This emphasis on relations of dominance and subordination among different nations can also be applied within nations, for example, in the unequal distribution of wealth and power between rural and urban sectors. The action programs generated by dependency theory focus on the liberation of dominated groups or classes from relations of exploitation, a perspective which modernization theory and programs ignore. While dependency theorists emphasize the economic aspects of the world system, some anthropologists ernments and international aid agencies. In this chapter we will discuss some of the effects of both planned and unplanned change on local communities, and in Chapter 16 we will look at the role of anthropologists in planned change and development.

Changing Economies and Changing Cultures

An essential aspect of change in the contemporary world is economic factors such as the expansion of the world-market economy, and the introduction of scientific knowledge and machine technology to the production process. Along with these economic changes come changes in the traditional patterns of work: an increase in occupational specialization, the separation of production from kinship units, and the substitution of cash wages for traditional forms of exchange. As a result, social inequalities frequently develop where they had not existed or been important. In socially stratified societies, technological improvements often lead to even wider gaps between different segments of the population — whether men and women, or social classes — as the benefits of economic change are not equally realized by all groups within the society.

Entry into World Markets

Through the imposition of agricultural wage labor by governments and multinational companies, as well as through the desire for manufactured goods made available by industrialization, many nonindustrial peoples are drawn into worldwide market economies. Consumer goods such as electrical appliances, new clothing, bicycles, and many other gadgets become available to tribal and peasant populations, stimulating them to look for new economic opportunities. The market economy, with its commercialization of exchange and the use of

War has also played a role in culture change, both directly, by disrupting traditional economic and political life of peasants, and indirectly, by the introduction of Western values, behavior patterns, and the disruption of traditional social institutions. These changes are suggested here by the differences between two generations in Vietnam. (John Lenoir)

have characterized the unequal relationship between industrialized Europe and the "disinherited," which divided the world into the rich and the poor, as a "world-order founded on conquest and maintained by force" (Worsley 1959).

In spite of the many flaws of modernization theory, and the approaches of anthropologists that have gone beyond it in analyzing cultural change, it is an important theory to understand because it continues to inform many, if not most, programs of planned change in tribal and peasant communities initiated by national gov-

Many non-Western nations have become dependent on one crop that is produced for a world market. Coffee is one of the most important cash crops in Rwanda, and most of it is grown by individual farmers. The farmer shown here is putting coffee beans out to be dried by the sun. (United Nations)

all-purpose money, penetrates the tribal and peasant household or subsistence economy. Soon, even the most geographically remote peoples become caught up in market networks that extend not only to nearby urban centers but also to other societies thousands of miles away. In order to obtain the cash necessary for participation in the market economy, these societies commercialize agriculture. Production of cash crops equals or even outdistances production for use. We have already seen that participation in world markets they neither controlled nor understood was one of the factors that led to the rise of cargo cults among various peoples of New Guinea. This is but one of many examples of the effects of such participation on local cultures.

Another example, with somewhat different effects, was the introduction of the growing of sisal in the Sertao in northeastern Brazil (Gross 1973). Peasants had traditionally subsisted on cattle raising and small-scale growing of beans and maize. In the 1930s, sisal, which is used

to make rope, was introduced as a cash crop. When World War II cut off the supply of hemp from the Philippines, the price of sisal rose dramatically in the world market. Sisal was hailed as "green gold," and both large and small landholders planted all their land with sisal in the expectation of great profits.

Sisal crops take four years to harvest, however. The world price for sisal dropped dramatically after the war, and many small landholders found that they could not realize a profit on their harvest. As they no longer had any land to use for the growing of traditional crops with which to feed themselves, many small landowning peasants were forced to work for wages processing sisal for the large landowners who had bought processing machines and thus could still make a profit. Machine processing of sisal involves enormous amounts of manual labor, including shifting thousands of pounds of fiber per hour. Because the workers were paid on a production basis, they worked long hours to make ends meet in order to buy the food they could no longer grow. Food had to be imported into the region, which now produced only sisal, and a new social class of well-to-do shopkeepers grew up upon whom the peasants were economically dependent. Furthermore, once established as a crop, sisal is extremely difficult to root out and the land is ruined for growing other crops without the investment of a tremendous amount of labor. This becomes no longer feasible for most peasants because they now must put their effort into earning money so they can buy food.

A study of the economic and social changes resulting from sisal growing was made by Daniel Gross, an anthropologist, in collaboration with a nutritionist (Gross 1973). These researchers studied household budgets and caloric intake and measured physical growth and health among peasant families. They found that households which depended on wages from sisal work spent nearly all of their money on food, most of which was needed to sustain the energy level of the wage earner so that he could adequately perform his demanding job. As a result, children in the households of sisal workers were being deprived of sufficient calories to maintain good health and normal rates of growth. In contrast, the economic gains of the higher social classes were manifested in a marked improvement in their nutritional state and that of their children. Sisal had brought prosperity to only a favored few; for most peasants, it only increased their poverty and intensified their misery.

Economic Changes and Gender Roles

As small societies with subsistence economies become transformed by their contact with expanding European market economies, one important change that takes place is in the work roles of men and women, and the value attached to them. These changes, which most often work to the disadvantage of women, are illustrated on the Polynesian atoll of Nukumanu, studied by anthropologist Richard Feinberg (1986).

Before European contact, the Nukumanu atoll depended on the abundant marine life and a few indigenous plants, such as the coconut, pandanus, and taro (a starchy root), as its major food resources. Women's primary responsibilities were domestic; their economic contributions took place close to home, whereas men contributed food acquired some distance from the home through fishing, hunting for shellfish, and collecting and husking coconuts. Men also made the canoes and constructed the new buildings, while women cooked, and collected and prepared leaves for thatch.

Women's and men's roles were both highly valued in Nukumanu society. Women were (and are) exclusively responsible for the cultivation of swamp taro, and taro swamps were controlled by groups of sisters and passed to their female descendants. Residential units also included a woman and her daughters, who shared an oven house and cooked together as a unit. In addition to the considerable social and political influence of women, based on their residential solidarity and control of an important food resource, women also gained prestige as storytellers, singers, and healers. Men's power came from their economic contribution, which included the control and working of the coconut groves, and all formal positions in the chiefly hierarchy were held by men.

In the 1880s, under German colonial dominance, most of the Nukumanu land was appropriated by a European company and turned over to production of copra (dried coconut meat). Wage labor was introduced, with many laborers imported from nearby New Guinea and the Solomon Islands. Although the land was turned back to the Nukumanu in the 1950s by the Australians, who had assumed control from the Germans, the major cultural and economic changes that had taken place over the past one hundred years were irreversible.

The economic changes were particularly pervasive. Though marine life continues to be important both as a food source and a commercial item, wheat flour and rice have replaced taro as a major food. Coffee, tea, and sugar, once luxury items, have become necessities for which cash must be paid; this has had a major impact on work in Nukumanu. While women still work a few hours a week in the subsistence gardening of taro, the major income-generating labor, that of collecting and processing *bêche-de-mer* (sea cucumbers) and copra production, are primarily male activities.

The decline of the dependence on taro, combined with the importance of copra, has meant that women's traditional sphere of influence has declined while men's sphere has expanded. In addition, the traditional dichotomy between the worlds of men and women has intensified. With the introduction of *kareve* (sap of the coconut tree fermented to make a potent alcoholic beverage) in the 1950s, men's economic activities, for example, canoe building, took on a social aspect involving drinking. Since the production and consumption of kareve is a male activity that takes up a great deal of men's leisure time, and excludes women, sexual segregation has increased.

In the changes that have taken place over the past century, women appear to have lost more than men. The important contribution that women make to the well-being of Nukumanu society through their exclusively feminine domestic activities in cooking, mat making, preparing thatch for houses, and washing clothes, is recognized but does not have the excitement or prestige of the men's activities related to the sea and to drinking kareve. And a major source of women's influence in precontact Nukumanu, their control over taro, has been drastically devalued. With the decline of the importance of taro, women's collective activities have also become more individualized and women more isolated and dependent on their husbands and brothers than they were in the past. Male-female tensions have also increased, partly as a result of kareve drinking, which many women now vehemently oppose.

These changes began with the introduction of European commodities and wage labor superimposed on a division of labor in which men dealt more with the outside world, through their sailing activities, and women's concerns remained mainly within the community. Thus wage earning and money handling seemed logically to become male responsibilities. The traditional tendency for men to travel off the island more than women has also negatively affected women's status as it is now mainly men who go overseas for wage labor and higher education.

But more recently, the introduction of a Western egalitarian influence is also having an effect, as some women have gone off the atoll to school and to pursue careers. The gender division of labor, relations between men and women, and women's status in society need to be examined in several cultural contexts: In precontact Nukumanu, women and men were separate but more or less equal; with the nineteenth-century entry of Nukumanu into the world-market economy, women remained culturally separate, but became unequal. Now, with the influence of a new kind of egalitarianism, women may become more equal and less separate, partly returning Nukumanu culture to its tradition of sexual egalitarianism.

Technology and Change

Changes in technology are undoubtedly one of the most important kinds of changes a society can experience, and they often have the most profound and unanticipated effects. Two very different kinds of technological changes in two very different kinds of places are described below. Although the first of these examples, the introduction of the snowmobile among the Skolt Lapps, was an unplanned change, while the introduction of the tractor into Indian peasant villages was part of a government-sponsored development program, the unanticipated and longer-term consequences of both the changes turned out to be a mixed blessing for different individuals in society, and for the cultures as a whole.

The Skolt Lapp economy of northern Finland (Pelto 1973) is based on reindeer herding, and reindeer were traditionally important for both subsistence and transportation in this Arctic environment. Skolt Lapp males took great pride in their abilities as reindeer herders.

The society was basically egalitarian: Most individuals had equal access to basic economic resources, and there was little opportunity for social and economic differences to develop. Although the Lapps had obtained some material goods, such as flour, sugar, and various metal objects, from the outside world for centuries, the energy sources on which their subsistence depended were locally available and they were essentially an autonomous society.

Snowmobiles were first introduced in Finland in 1962. They caught on swiftly, and by 1971, practically all Lapp households owned at least one snowmobile and used it for transportation, hauling, and herding reindeer. Reindeer-drawn sleds, the traditional means of transportation, had completely disappeared. Many families sold their sled reindeer to finance the purchase of snowmobiles. Mechanized reindeer herding appeared to be a success; it made herding physically easier and economically more productive for the families who were the first to take advantage of the new technology.

The snowmobile has brought significant changes in Skolt life. From being economically independent, the Skolt Lapps are now dependent on external and commercially distributed sources of energy for transportation, which is the critical factor in the reindeer-herding economy. The management of resources now requires new skills, including reading and writing, and the use of money, as well as the technical skills involved in repairing and maintaining the snowmobiles. These skills are not equally present in all Skolt Lapp families.

Because of the initial cash outlay required to purchase a snowmobile, the families who were somewhat better off had a head start in making the transition to mechanized herding. They also gained additional income by providing transportation to families without snowmobiles. This initial advantage was a critical factor in subsequent economic success. The accumulation of resources could be used to expand into other opportunities, such as acting as tourist guides or even freeing adult males for wage work.

Not all families are equally able to keep up in the snowmobile revolution. Those with lesser skills, cash, and flexibility dropped out of herding altogether and became dependent on the Finnish government for welfare payments and training for new kinds of employment. The social differentiation between successful snowmobile herders and families marginal to the herding economy will probably become greater.

The snowmobile revolution brought some economic advantages for some families, but it substantially increased dependency for all families. Even those that succeeded are dependent on external sources of credit, for example. With the loss of the old skills involved in nonmechanized reindeer herding, the diminished prestige accorded traditional herding activities and skills, the abandonment of sled reindeer for transportation, and the loss of control over the reindeer themselves (which have become more fearful of humans as a result of the noise and speed of the snowmobile), a complete return to the presnowmobile economy is not feasible.

The Skolt Lapps themselves are somewhat divided on how they view the changes in their society. Those in the younger generation and those older men who have been successful tend to regard the snowmobile revolution positively. Looking at it in a more objective light and with an eye to the long-run changes, another conclusion is that the snowmobile substantially decreased the autonomy and adaptive flexibility of the Skolt Lapp sociocultural system as a whole.

Tractors against Women

The much-heralded "green revolution" of North India, referring to the increased productivity of Indian agriculture, was based on the introduction of modern, heavy equipment, such as pumpsets, tractors, and threshers, and chemical fertilizers. What is not often said about the green revolution, which began in the late 1950s, is that it also resulted in the marginalization of many small landholders who were not so easily able to take advantage of the modern technology, and it also increased the inequality between the sexes (Frankel 1971; Dasgupta 1980).

In many rural development programs, women are perceived as basically peripheral to the agricultural economy, and their work roles are generally ignored in planning and policy making. In addition, in the transformation of agricultural production through machine technology, there is a reduction in the overall labor force, and this particularly affects women, whose traditional jobs in cultivation do not include working with this kind of technology. Women are disproportionately excluded from the productive process as their jobs are replaced by labor-saving technology. The inequality between the sexes is also apparent in the lower wages paid to women as agricultural laborers and in the concentration of women in the labor-intensive aspects of agriculture such as weeding, transplanting, and harvesting. Although the wages in North India, the location of the green revolution, are generally higher than in other parts of India, the disparity of income between men and women workers is actually increasing (Kelkar 1985).

In spite of the important domestic and productive roles that women have in rural India, their work is ignored by government planners as unpaid household work and their contribution to agricultural production is regarded as secondary, or supplementary, to men's contributions. This raises the value of males — sons — as potential contributors to the family income and accounts for the greater amounts of money spent on their food, clothes, health care, and general well-being. Although the ideology of the better-off Indian peasant villagers is that women do not work in the fields, this is not borne out in practice. Women do engage in agricultural production, especially at the time of transplanting paddy, weeding, threshing, harvesting, and processing of food grains. Indeed, as males are caught up in urban and industrial wage labor, the agricultural work falls even more on women. In spite of this, both men and women still perceive women's work as nonspecialized, which supports the "houseworker ideology" that views women's agricultural work as an extension of housework and thus devalues it.

With modernization, many of the avenues previously available to women to improve their economic position are now closing. For example, traditional crafts, in the face of competition from urban industry, are often unable to survive. Earlier, village women of the artisan castes contributed equally to craft production. Likewise, in the traditional organization of agriculture, women participated in every activity except plowing. With the increased cultivation of cash crops that is part of the modernization and development process, women have lost their roles in decision making about grain distribution; this has contributed to a decline of their domestic authority as well. Thus, much planned economic development results in more women and children becoming more dependent on men.

In the ideology of work in rural India, the greatest importance in agriculture is given to the core productive activity over which women have no control: plowing. They are prohibited from touching the grip of the plow, which is regarded as representative of the phallic symbol signifying fertility. A similar practice is found in pottery making, where women are engaged in the collection, watering, and beating of clay but may not touch the potter's wheel, the symbol of phallic masculinity.

The second major activity in agriculture, next to plowing, is preparing the land for irrigation. Previously, when fields had no direct access to water and water had to be collected in little ditches where it would be thrown out via a bucket system, women were very active in irrigating the fields. However, now, with development schemes in effect, better-off landowners have acquired diesel pumpsets and manual labor is no longer required for this activity, which results in women being excluded from irrigation. Where the traditional system of irrigation exists, however, women still participate in it.

In efforts at modernization, traditional forms of communication are used to convey new ideas. Here, a traditional Balinese song and dance drama presents the theme of family planning. (United Nations/Ray Witlin)

Although women do weeding, this is considered an unimportant job and is done in between the day's housework and cooking the evening meal. Women are actively engaged in grain processing, both for the family's use and for the market. Cleaning, drying, and storing grain are done entirely by women. Yet, the core activity of marketing the grain almost always excludes women from any decision-making role.

Even in traditional Indian society, women's roles in the household and in agriculture were not culturally acknowledged as valuable. Economic development has largely reinforced the inequality between men and women and even increased it: Now only men have access to the prestigious new technology, while women's productive roles and their cultural value are decreasing. Indeed, very often the ideology of development programs explicitly views the "backwardness" of peasant women as an obstacle to development, implicitly stigmatizing their resistance to change as irrational.

The development planners' view of agriculture as an exclusively male activity is unrealistic. The only realistic basis on which to plan development programs is to recognize women's work in agriculture as valuable and to include them in economic planning and policy making. The aim of development programs should be to fully integrate women into the agricultural process, not diminish their economic roles through household industries such as silkworm breeding or cigarette making. Development programs that do not fairly distribute development benefits among the well-off and the poor, and among men and women, are likely to increase inequality and injustice, not erase it. In the green revolution in North India, tractors worked, not for women, but against them!

Planned Change

With the dismantling of colonialism after the Second World War, the new independent nations of Africa and Asia became committed to programs of economic development and, with the aid of various European nations and the United States, as well as the then Soviet Union, attempted to bring modernization to their indigenous and peasant populations through programs of planned change, or development. At the same time, these nations, as well as those with a longer national history, such as Brazil, were developing ideologies and political strategies aimed at enhancing both their legitimacy and their control over their populations. As part of their strategies in attaching all sectors of the population to national goals and national identities, such governments forcefully introduced strong measures for cultural assimilation, as well as for economic expansion. An example of these kinds of programs is the one for the Bakairi of Brazil, described in the accompanying ethnography.

Revolutionary Change in Peasant Societies

In some cases, the social changes planned by modern governments may take place through peaceful, democratic means. The transformation of peasant societies may also occur through more violent alternatives, as in the case of revolutionary movements in China, the former Soviet Union, North Korea, North Vietnam, and Cuba, in which peasants took an active part. In modern peasant revolutions, which are supported by a coherent ideology and an effective organizational framework, the social structures of some traditional societies have been almost completely destroyed and new socialist states created in their place.

The most dramatic example of revolutionary changes is provided by the People's Republic of China (Potter 1967). In 1949, when the Chinese Communist party took power, China was an overpopulated, poverty-stricken country with more than 80 percent of its people living in rural villages. Many farms were small and inefficient, and technology had changed little in 2,000 years. Most villagers made hardly enough money to meet their basic needs, and any surplus went into the ceremonial activities — funerals and marriages — necessary to maintain a family's status. Much of the surplus capital was siphoned off by landlords in the form of rents and exorbitant interest rates on loans. The landlord-scholar-government official class dominated the entire society. Traditionally, government intervened little in village life; its primary functions were maintaining order and collecting taxes. China was exploited economically by foreign powers and almost totally disrupted by the Japanese invasion in the late 1930s. An important basis of the achievement of the Communist government in reorganizing the society was the view that only through modernization and industrialization could China regain its national dignity.

The new government intervened in every aspect of peasant life in order to control the peasants and mobilize them to work in the interest of the state. The first order of business was land reform. Through government-supervised peasant associations, land and property were taken from wealthy landlords and redistributed to the peasants. The destruction of the landlord class, which had been the main buffer between the peasants and the government, now left the way open for direct government intervention in the villages.

The ultimate aim of the new government was to totally collectivize village life. This process was to be achieved by stages. In every stage of reorganization there were heavy propaganda campaigns and educational meetings in order to commit the peasants to the goals of the government and a collectivized society.

The Bakairi Indians live on a reservation in the central Brazilian state of Mato Grosso. They are slash and burn horticulturalists, growing bitter manioc, rice, corn, bananas, and melons in their gardens, which are laid out along the banks of the rivers in the tropical forest that covers part of their reservation. They also fish and hunt with guns, and the men frequently work as unskilled labor on the nearby Brazilian ranches in order to earn cash to purchase Western goods.

The Bakairi live in extended families, and related males and females work together; the men help each other clear and burn gardens and the women process food and wash clothes together. Kinsmen also share resources, including cash, when necessary. The Bakairi live in villages whose egalitarian social structure is sustained by the fact that, in their subsistence economy, the technology, necessary knowledge, and access to resources are available to people equally. Older men, and some women, may be more influential than others, but there are no formal status positions.

The Bakairi live on a reservation quite removed from other settlements, and are somewhat isolated from the nearest towns by poor roads. Their reservation of 50,000 hectares was set aside in the early twentieth century when their population numbered about 150. While part of the reservation land was quite fertile forest, reasonably productive under slash and burn horticulture, most of the reservation was arid, infertile land, called *cerrado*, which cannot be used for horticulture but can be used for hunting and cattle raising.

The earliest contact between the Europeans and the Bakairi was recorded in 1723, when the Indians were being enslaved to work in the local gold mines. As gold mining declined in the early nineteenth century, some Bakairi were absorbed into the spreading cattle-raising economy, which resulted in some loss of cultural traditions. By 1920, when their reservation was laid out to its present size, the relative isolation of the Bakairi diminished, as the Brazilian government aggressively pursued a policy to assimilate them into the national culture and economy. The Indians were forced to dress in European clothes and to abandon their traditional longhouses for new-style huts housing individual families. They were also forced to cultivate crops and care for a small cattle herd, which supplied food for the representatives of the Brazilian government in charge of their assimilation. Later, forced acceptance of government teachers, agents, and missionaries, and contact with Brazilian ranchers, also had their influence. One of the effects of this cultural contact was a series of devastating epidemics, of syphilis and malaria, which almost resulted in the Bakairis' extinction; by the 1950s, the Bakairi population had recovered its numbers and, indeed, was growing rapidly.

By the late 1970s, when the Brazilian government introduced a program of planned change, the Bakairi numbered 260 people, living mainly in single-family houses in one village that was located at the intersection of three rivers, providing water for drinking, fishing, bathing, and washing clothes. The current government development project is carried out by FUNAI (the National Brazilian Indian Foundation) and has the objectives of improving food sources for the Bakairi, teaching them new skills, and increasing their participation in the Brazilian socioeconomic system, most centrally, the cash economy. By these means, the Brazilian government hopes to strengthen the links by which the Bakairi would be bound to the national society.

The primary focus of the development project is to increase the production of rice as a cash crop, through the introduction of mechanized agriculture. The government supplied a tractor, disk plow, row planter, and dispenser for insecticide and fertilizer, along with rice seeds, barrels of diesel fuel, insecticides, and fertilizer.

The project has been largely unsuccessful in achieving its objectives, partly because the Bakairi at first lacked experience with, and understanding of, the mechanized production process. They did not know, for example, how much fertilizer to use. The project, indeed, suffered from all of the pitfalls of modernization projects just described. Although this "development project" has led to many changes in Bakairi culture and social structure, it is not clear whether these changes can be called "development."

The Bakairi gain most of their protein intake from the vegetable produce from their gardens; this source of protein is not as rich as that provided by their cattle, which they raise in the area of the cerrado close to their village. This is the same area that the government chose for mechanized rice farming: The intention was good — to make it convenient for the Bakairi to cultivate the rice without having to travel too far to their fields — but the result was competition for resources needed for cattle.

(continued)

FUNAI introduced technology and organization of work that also affected the Bakairi in unforeseen ways. Although — or perhaps because — FUNAI decreed that the cerrado rice land be communally owned and the responsibility of the entire village, the Indians believed that the land was *really* owned by FUNAI, who had provided the technology. Since most Bakairi had no experience in mechanized rice agriculture, and since the participation of women and children was limited, rice field production was an activity isolated from the community. In addition, since those few men who were familiar with the technology worked more than the others, quarrels broke out about how the rice should be distributed.

Within their subsistence economy, each member of the Bakairi community participated in complementary, but important, ways; whatever small excess of wealth occurred was distributed through leveling mechanisms in the form of rituals or kin networks so that families were typically equal in wealth and status. Since kinship was the basis of work groups, work had social as well as economic meanings.

The FUNAI project changed this. It undermined the vitality of the household and family by shifting the economic focus from the family garden to the FUNAI rice fields. Work was redefined so that its economic value dominated over its social value; instead of being an activity that implied social reciprocity, it was defined as an activity performed for an outside group (FUNAI) for which one gets paid. With this redefinition, the social solidarity functions of work for the community attenuated. And while previously, the labor of each person was equally valuable, under the new program, the experience and skills in mechanized agriculture that some men had, as well as the fact that these men could drive tractors, speak Portuguese, and read and write, made them more valuable to the project. This set the stage for social differentiation and, as noted, led to conflict.

Bakairi autonomy was also reduced as a result of the growing importance of the national market and the cash economy; the self-sufficiency of the village was threatened by the new, increasingly important interactions of the community on the reservation with the world around it. Prior to the FUNAI project, the Bakairi were involved in the cash economy — men had left the reservation to work on cattle ranches, and government pensions had been paid to widows and the elderly. This cash income was used to buy basic necessities such as clothes, soap, flashlights, fishing lines, and hooks. Then FUNAI itself became an additional source of cash, paying salaries to Bakairi it employs to maintain the schoolhouse and the FUNAI agent's house. In addition, FUNAI provided a truck that the Bakairi could use to go to the nearest city. The total cash payment to the village has become substantial, and now much of it is invested in buying bicycles, guns, expensive knives, and watches, all of which can be sold later. Whereas previously the cash links between the Bakairi and non-Indians were not central to the Bakairi economy, now they are vital to their survival.

The rising cost of energy also negatively affects Bakairi autonomy because mechanized agriculture depends on fuel, oil, and fertilizers; when this is added to the enormous rate of inflation in Brazil, the changing national and international market prices for rice, the Bakairis' lack of experience in accurately estimating market prices, and the indefinite need for the Bakairi to depend on FUNAI financing of loans and credit, it becomes apparent just how far the Bakairi have moved from self-sufficiency. All of these changes will intensify in the future, making the Bakairi increasingly tied to the national economy.

While the FUNAI project has allowed gradual assimilation by permitting the Bakairi to stay on their own lands, and thus retain some of their traditional culture, a high price will be paid. If the results of incorporation into national economies of other indigenous Indian populations in South America are an indication, the Bakairi can look forward to a less protein-nutritious diet, the spread of such diseases as diabetes, the rise of class differences, the decline of community solidarity, and an increase of proletarianization and pauperization. Like other development projects, the FUNAI project suggests that reliance on complex industrial machinery that requires skill and expensive fuel is not the most appropriate way to bring change to indigenous communities.

Many development projects reflect national political and economic priorities, and even international (funding) priorities; even those that represent a sincere commitment to the well-being of indigenous peoples will not succeed, however, if they are not based on more realistic models of change. Anthropological expertise in the form of detailed, ethnographically based knowledge of local communities can be immensely valuable in helping governments develop programs that more sensibly integrate subsistence economies and local patterns of production, and build upon local culture. Anthropologists can also contribute to short-term and long-term evaluation of such programs through qualitatively and quantitatively measuring their effects on the health and culture of the recipients.

A work brigade on a commune in Yunnan Province, People's Republic of China. The thresher is collectively owned and would be too expensive for any individual farmer to buy. More recently, the Chinese government has acknowledged that individual initiative is also an important factor in agricultural productivity. (John Gregg)

By 1958, when almost all Chinese peasants had been organized into socialist cooperatives, the Great Leap Forward into the commune stage began. These communes were multifunctional organizations covering an area including about twenty villages. The communes operated small factories and ran banks, commercial enterprises, schools, and the local government. In this stage, houses, trees, domestic animals, and garden plots, which the peasants had earlier been allowed to own and work privately, were confiscated. Women were mobilized to work alongside men, and common mess halls, kindergartens, and old-age homes were built to take over many functions previously performed by the family.

The Great Leap Forward is now acknowledged to have failed. The labor resources devoted to industry left a shortage of agricultural labor; confiscation of garden plots substantially decreased production by reducing incentive on the part of peasants; communal family activities demoralized the population. The government began a retreat to less radical forms of collective organization, and since the end of 1960, private garden plots have been returned to the peasants along with their houses and kitchens and domestic animals. Industry is giving greater attention to producing consumer goods.

The increased emphasis on individual incentives has been accompanied by an effort to reduce bureaucratic control over economic planning and distribution. Free markets continue to expand, and the amount of "private plot" land allowed in a village has increased. China's political leadership is seeking an approach to rural development that links economic benefit more directly to the efforts of the individual family and the small work group, rather than the large collective, though collective forms of ownership are still being maintained. Individual incentives, in the form of bonuses, are also being used in urban factories.

The government hopes that this will lead to increasing production while acknowledging that it also leads to less "egalitarianism."

It appeared throughout the 1980s that the Chinese government was becoming more open to those features of society necessary to develop technologically, and to raise the standard of living of the people, even if this meant allowing more individual material incentives (Chance 1984). However, the quick suppression of student and other demonstrations in 1989 in Tiananmen Square in Beijing has led observers to wonder what direction China will move in next.

The thoroughness of the Chinese revolution involved total social reorganization and ideological commitment that were mutually reinforcing, and resulted in violence, coercion, and interference with basic freedoms. While planned development in other nations may involve less violence, a disturbingly frequent violation of the rights of indigenous peoples has accompanied modernization efforts by purportedly democratic nation-states, as well as by multinational corporations that seek to develop natural resources located on lands reserved to indigenous peoples. Such peoples often become the "victims of progress" (Bodley 1990). The coercive measures and human rights violations often associated with planned economic change raise important questions about the price of change and who should pay it.

Tourism and Change

Since World War II, there has been an enormous increase in the number of Europeans and Americans visiting what were previously remote areas of the world. With greater accessibility, primarily through the development of airports, islands in the middle of the Indian Ocean, villages in the center of deep jungle in South America, and Inuit villages in the Canadian and American Arctic are feeling the impact of tourism. Although 90 percent of the world's tourists both come from and visit countries in Europe, the United States, and Japan, tourist spending is often a major part of the economy in developing nations.

On the positive side, it is maintained that tourism can have a beneficial impact on developing nations through providing foreign exchange to pay for needed imports; creating jobs; generating taxes; stimulating activity, particularly in the commercial and industrial sectors of the economy; and fostering foreign and local investment and capital formation. Some of the noneconomic advantages claimed for tourism are that it contributes to international understanding and peace and respect for other cultures. On the negative side, tourism that is unplanned and is controlled by outsiders can lead to overcrowding in tourist areas, rapid urbanization, labor shortages in nontourism sectors, prostitution and other demoralizing forms of "hustling," hostility toward tourists' affluence, and an increase in crime and violence. Although tourism can support and reaffirm cultural identities by reviving respect for traditional art forms, it can also degrade and parody cultural differences, lead to envy for Western goods and a Western life-style, and intensify cross-cultural conflict. Perhaps one of the inevitably damaging aspects of tourism is that it "remains a statement of fundamental inequality, whereby the 'haves' can travel halfway around the world for pleasure, while the 'have nots' struggle for subsistence beneath their noses" (Callimanopulos 1982:5). The control of tourism can thus be seen as another aspect of a fundamental issue: minorities' rights to self-determination.

Anthropologists have only recently begun to look at the effects of tourism on traditional cultures and economies. Consistent with the anthropological approach of examining cultural change in depth and, as much as possible, from the point of view of the recipients of change, research on tourism's impact often raises issues ignored by foreign investors interested only in their own profits. The economic benefits of tourism, first of all, often do not go to local people. Secondly, although it is true that tourism brings in hard currency, it is also true that much of this money has to be spent in order to import things that tourists want and that are not available locally. In the Seychelles, an island nation in the Indian Ocean where tourism is the main industry, food imports increased 1,400 percent over a period of fifteen years, during which the number of tourists rose from a little over 500 to about 80,000. Because of the tourist demand for seafood, coastal waters have been fished out, and fish imports nearly doubled in one year, from 1978 to 1979.

Tourism almost invariably results in harm to the environment, some of it irreversible. In Bali, for example, many coral reefs are being destroyed as coral is used for building roads and making concrete. The reefs used to break up the surf, but now they are being taken away, and pollution is preventing new ones from replacing them. Thus, a severe storm would probably have a devastating effect on the economic system as well as on nearby inhabitants (McKean 1982). In the American Southwest, giant hotels use more water in one month — for swimming pools, lawn sprinklers, washing machines, and the like — than a local town and the hinterland formerly used in a year (Smith 1982). As a result, water for agriculture is disappearing or becoming so costly that small farmers and ranchers cannot afford to sink deeper wells, and many must give up their livelihood. In the mountains and forests, thousands of acres are burned annually by careless tourists. In the desert of the Sinai, which became a popular tourist destination for campers, many palm trees have died because ignorant tourists built fires in their midst, burning their roots. This has adversely affected the life-style of the Bedouin nomads, for whom these date palms are an important part of the traditional economy (Zito 1982).

Although it is true that tourism does initially create jobs, many of these are low-skilled jobs in the service sector of tourism. The local population is expected to serve the personal needs of the tourists by cleaning their hotel rooms or waiting on tables or to amuse them in exotic ways. Thus, a class of "beach boys" has developed on some Caribbean Islands to "cater to North American women who have been steeped

The advertising copy for this photo reads: "Aloha from Hawaii — That's the message behind the warm smile of Rose Marie Alvaro, the Hawaii Visitors Bureau poster girl. This five-foot four-inch beauty, a beguiling blend of Hawaiian, Portuguese, Chinese, and English ancestries, is an accomplished hula dancer and Island entertainer." Critics of the effect of tourism on indigenous populations point to the denigrating effects tourist imagery creates as it tries to capture the fantasies, often sexual, of Western, industrialized nations. (Courtesy of Hawaii Visitors Bureau)

in the myth of black virility and come to the Caribbean to experience it" (Manning 1982). In Bangkok, tourist publicity geared to the "single man" of both Europe and Japan advertises the availability of females for sexual companionship in massage parlors, teahouses, nightclubs, and disco-restaurants (Phongpaichit 1982). Granted that these "jobs" offer a source of income, they would not seem to fit the aim of the World Tourism Organization to "create jobs that are not mechanical or alienating but based on reciprocal relations and help in integrating the individual in a more balanced society" (Callimanopulos 1982:4). Neither would such intercultural relations seem to foster "international understanding and respect for other cultures."

From a cultural perspective, tourism is selling fantasy, which often involves turning a traditional culture into a spectacle for the benefit of a tourist audience. Frequently, in order to increase the flow of tourist revenue, artificial and inauthentic "folk culture" performances are invented for the tourist. Among the Eastern Cherokee of North Carolina, for example, during the tourist season a certain number of males

> are self-employed in the colorful business of "chiefing." These men dress in pan-Indian garb and post themselves in front of the tourist shops as an attraction. They specialize in having their pictures taken. . . . Tourists seem willing to accept the vulgar Indian stereotype the "chiefs" present for it fits in with their own preconceived ideas of what an Indian is. (Hodge 1981:127–29)

Not all of the impact of tourism is so negative on indigenous culture. In Bali, for example, the interest of tourists in cultural performances has stimulated an improvement in the artistic quality of some of the dance and dramatic performances. The economic boost from tourist patronage of these performances has allowed local troupes to buy new instruments for their gamelan orchestras and new costumes, and it has encouraged the opening of schools and institutes throughout Indonesia for training in traditional art forms. An expert and professional group of Indonesian artists has maintained tight control over performances and is acting to conserve the quality of the arts. Similarly, the interest in tourism as a source of income among the Inuit of Greenland has led to a revival of ethnicity, which had almost disappeared, and to a desire to establish cultural ties with other Inuit throughout the United States and Canada.

Anthropological research seems to suggest that tourism is like all other forms of social change. When it is introduced gradually and controlled by local people, it can serve indigenous needs and improve some aspects of life. Mass tourism is an element of life that many non-Western cultures are having to deal with,

whether they like it or not. It would seem to be in their interest to gain control of this process of "development" so that they can use it to serve their ends and not be manipulated by it.

Multinational Corporations and Change

For several hundred years, the most important factor in change for many non-European societies was their colonization by the Western nations. It was in this context that anthropology emerged, yet much of anthropology tried to ignore this colonial context as it described cultures in the "ethnographic present" (Sanjek 1991), an "as if" anthropological fiction that tried to capture an authentic, precontact and precolonial culture. The legacy of the colonial era remains important as it affects both cultural change and the representations of culture, and indeed, some cultures are still under Western colonial rule. Anthropology, from the perspective of the historic world system, is now examining that legacy.

At the same time, another globalizing phenomenon, that of the spread of multinational corporations, intensifies. This "invasion" of multinational corporations, and the conversion of non-Western societies into economic colonies serving the needs of outsiders, have important effects both on local communities in the developing nations and on the industrial societies themselves. In the United States, the impact of multinational corporations has produced rising unemployment of U.S. workers, plant closings, "cheap imports," loss of company loyalties to workers and their communities, and a new phenomenon of widespread downward social mobility and skepticism about the promise of the American Dream (Newman 1989).

Multinational corporations affect the environment as they attempt to develop natural resources for profit, cause worldwide shifts in population as economic opportunities open up in some societies and decline in others, and are implicated in the transformation of agricultural populations into wage labor on a huge scale, as

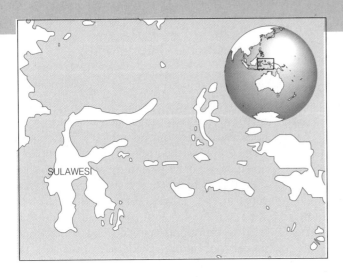

Toraja is the name used for the people who live in the northern part of South Sulawesi, the island formerly known as Celebes, located north of Bali and now part of Indonesia. The term *Toraja* was not used indigenously to designate these people until the 1930s, but it is now completely accepted. The Toraja are mainly subsistence cultivators who also raise water buffaloes, pigs, and chickens; all of these animals are killed and eaten on ritual occasions.

Toraja society, today as in the past, centers on ancestral houses and the rituals associated with them. The houses represent links among ancestors, living kin, and future kin; thus, the rituals associated with them are important expressions of both social and spiritual life.

In the 1950s, over 50 percent of the Toraja were converted to Christianity. While the Christian missionaries succeeded in suppressing some of the Toraja rituals, particularly those given for supernatural spirits, they did not suppress the mortuary rituals dedicated to ancestors, and these have actually expanded and grown more elaborate among both Christian and non-Christian Toraja. In fact, Toraja culture has been increasingly defined in terms of these rituals both in the minds of outsiders and among Toraja themselves. In this process, two factors involving change have been particularly important. One is the out-migration of Toraja to other parts of Indonesia, and the other is the influx of Western tourists.

In the traditional, precolonial Toraja society, the main source of group consciousness was expressed in kinship terms: ties of blood and marriage and shared ancestral houses. Houses in different villages were linked through marriage and descent and participated together in rituals in which water buffaloes and pigs were slaughtered and the meat exchanged. These ritual exchanges also defined each person's place in the social hierarchy, as nobles, commoners, and slaves participated in the rituals according to well-established customary rules. To fulfill one's ritual obligations and to extend the social network by creating and fulfilling social debts was the major way of establishing one's honor. It is this participation in animal sacrifice rituals that today is such an important theme in the construction of Toraja culture.

These *tongkonan*, or traditional Torajan houses with their spectacular shapes and carved figures, are an important draw for tourists. (Courtesy of Kathleen Adams)

Traditionally, the Toraja were not a migrating people (unlike some other Indonesian peoples), and the house rituals provided a strong center, both spatially and spiritually, for the individual. By the late 1960s, a number of factors led to large-scale migration to other parts of Indonesia. Rebellions in the area, which made travel difficult and dangerous, were suppressed at this time. Also, the Indonesian government decided to welcome foreign investment, and many multinational corporations set up operations on some nearby islands.

Many Toraja youth, especially those from low-status families, left to take the jobs opened up by foreign investment. Toraja are hard workers and they earned a great deal of cash. Though some of their money went to buy Western-style consumer goods, much of it was used to sponsor mortuary rituals, far in

(*continued*)

excess of what was traditionally allowed for families of low status. Both the quantity and the elaborateness of these rituals expanded tremendously, a fact that caused some resentment among upper-class Toraja.

At the same time that the wealth of the migrants was expanding the number and the quality of Toraja mortuary rituals, tourism began in the Toraja area. Almost all of this tourism was oriented toward viewing the Toraja rituals; in fact, organized tourism to view the animal sacrifices was an important part of the tourist strategy of Indonesia's first five-year plan. Among the early tourists was a British film crew, so the Toraja became known throughout Europe in connection with their rituals. Indeed, for many Europeans the ritual was *the* Toraja cultural marker. Tourism increased rapidly, and the presence of so many wealthy foreigners, with their expensive cameras, filming every aspect of the Toraja rituals, reinforced the rituals' cultural significance for the Toraja.

While tourism brings in money, the tourist trade thrives on the image of the Toraja as exotic pagans, an image that many Toraja themselves have rejected or at least feel ambivalent about. They are understandably reluctant, however, to give up this economically profitable image, particularly as it is focused on a cultural pattern that is important to them. Proponents of tourism claim that tourism and Toraja cultural identity based on traditional values, that is, the giving of mortuary feasts, are mutually beneficial: Tourism promotes economic growth and also pride in Toraja culture, and it is this very culture that promotes tourism.

But the "traditional" Toraja culture which attracts tourists is not the culture of precolonial times: It is a contemporary culture that is self-consciously being constructed as an image through which the outside world can come to know the Toraja. This contemporary Toraja culture construction is an attempt to create meaning in the present, while giving coherence to a past that has rapidly changed, primarily through out-migration and tourism. By radically expanding their world outward, Toraja have become aware of the distinctiveness of their culture, increasingly defined in terms of its rituals, in relation to other groups and peoples. The strength of Toraja culture clearly rests not on a resistance to change, or a survival of past loyalties, but rather on a contemporary economic situation in which a particular cultural definition of Toraja is a resource to be used in adapting to a changing world.

Adapted from Toby Alice Volkman, "Great Performances: Toraja Cultural Identity in the 1970s," American Ethnologist *11, no. 1 (1984): 152–68. Used by permission of the American Anthropological Association. Not for further reproduction.*

Industrialization spreads through the expansion of the global factory, as Western corporations take advantage of lower wages in non-Western parts of the world. This photograph is of an industry set up in Singapore with the aid of the United Nations Development Program in conjunction with the International Labor Organization. (United Nations/R. Witlin)

these corporations shift their operations to areas of ever lower wages. Since much of the "cheap labor" that multinational corporations depend upon for their profits is women and children, there is a clear link between feminist concerns in anthropology and the extension of the global economy. The operations and decisions of multinational corporations affect land rights in many countries, as national governments, including our own, attempt to persuade or coerce indigenous populations to give up their land so as to make it available for the economic investments that only multinational corporations can afford.

The activities of multinational corporations raise important questions about the entitlements of different people to a share of the benefits that accompany their economic activi-

ties (Bonsignore 1992) as well as questions about how the social, cultural, and health costs of their operations should be borne. These questions become particularly urgent in the face of major disasters such as the Exxon oil spill in Alaskan waters and the accidental release of a lethal gas in December 1984, in Bhopal, India, in which at least 1,700 people were killed and as many as 50,000 were injured.

For anthropologists studying change, an important new challenge is to apply ethnographic strategies to the study of local communities as these are being reconstructed symbolically — reinvented as it were — in the face of the transformations introduced by the forces of the global economy. Our ethnographic, holistic, cross-cultural perspective gives anthropologists a unique view on the global economy and on the local communities that participate in it. To address the processes of change that derive from this newest source of global expansion is to do what we have been committed to all along: describing and analyzing cultures in their local contexts, and illuminating how people make sense, through symbolic constructions, of the economic and political changes in their world.

Urbanization and Change

In many of the nations of Asia, Africa, and Latin America, migration of peasants to urban centers is one of the most important mechanisms of change. Although cities had important cultural roles in preindustrial societies, in the contemporary world urban migration has increased dramatically. Rural people come to cities seeking jobs and the social, material, and cultural advantages they perceive to be related to urban living. There are many different ways in which urbanization affects traditional societies. One anthropologist has characterized the adaptations of traditional societies to urbanization as a "three-ring circus," referring to the three arenas within which adaptations to urbanization take place: among the members of the home community left behind, among the urban migrants themselves, and within the urban host community to which the migrants go (Graves and Graves 1974).

Many of the migrants who leave their local communities do so only temporarily. They return to their places of origin to participate in a variety of economic or social activities and maintain important ties with those left behind. The degree to which urban migration is permanent depends partly on the personal involvements of the migrating individual within the local rural community, partly on the ability of the local community to reabsorb its returning migrants, and partly on the barriers to assimilation the migrant group meets in the urban area.

In a study of out-migration from Vasilika, a Greek village, Ernestine Friedl (1974) showed how a variety of factors led to a high degree of permanent migration to Athens, the Greek capital. Vasilika, like other peasant villages all over the world, had a labor surplus. At the same time, there were job opportunities in Athens. Furthermore, Vasilikans had a positive view of living in Athens; city living carried more prestige than village life did. Rural families would support one of their sons who went to Athens to get an education, a usual first step toward obtaining a job in government service. In return for the family's support, the migrant generally gave up his rights to his share of village land, an economic benefit for those who remained. This loss of one's share in village property is a strong factor in permanent migration. Furthermore, because Vasilikans were not an ethnic or racial minority group in Athens, there were few barriers to assimilation. The Vasilikans lived throughout the city and had a wide range of social contacts with urban people. Many of them married nonvillagers, which also contributed to the permanence of urban migration.

Whether temporary or permanent, however, urban migration is both a direct and an indirect source of change in traditional societies. Not only are urban migrants themselves changed in the process of adapting to urban life, but the communities of origin are also changed. Most modern influences enter the countryside through urban centers, either by mass communication, as radios and movies become available in villages, or through the links between urban migrants and those who remain at home. Not only modern consumer goods but also new ideas, knowledge, and values are passed on to villagers through urban migrants. These modern influences permeate the village only slowly, however; material culture is affected first and then social organization and ideology.

Ruth and Stanley Freed (1978), who studied a village close to New Delhi, the Indian capital, found that in spite of the large numbers of villagers who worked in the city, village social organization and culture remained largely traditional. Although some urban-oriented men were more relaxed about requiring the isolation and *purdah* (veiling) of women, role behavior in the family did not change substantially nor were the basic features of the caste system changed much. Two important changes that did occur were a decrease in prohibitions on lower-caste use of public facilities and a transformation of *jajmani* (client-patron) relationships into "fee-for-service" arrangements. The prohibitions on untouchability were due more to new laws passed by the national government than to urbanization itself, but the transformation of the jajmani system was clearly the result of the alternative of urban jobs for landless laborers who preferred to work for cash.

In summing up the trends they believed were due to urbanization in this Indian village, the Freeds listed the following factors, which would probably apply in a general way to other urbanizing societies as well: (1) an increasing modernization of material culture; (2) an increase in the number of villagers earning a living from modern industrial and commercial jobs instead of traditional crafts and farming; (3) less dependence of landless laborers on large landowners; (4) more casual social interactions across caste boundaries; (5) an emphasis on various features of Hinduism that were more in accord with city life than rural life; (6) a rising level of education; and (7) more exposure to the wider world through mass communications.

Urbanization and Voluntary Associations

With urbanization, a great variety of social groups based on voluntary membership develops. These groups are generally called **voluntary associations.** Voluntary associations are adaptive in helping people organize to achieve their goals in complex and changing societies, especially in helping migrants make the transition from traditional, rural-based society to a modern, urban, industrial life-style. Although not all voluntary associations formed in newly urbanized societies have goals that are directly economic or political, these associations frequently serve as vehicles through which such goals can be achieved.

Voluntary associations that emerge among newly urbanized populations may serve as mutual aid societies, lending money to members, providing scholarships for students, arranging funerals, and taking care of marriage arrangements for urban migrants. Some of these voluntary associations develop along kinship or tribal lines that were relevant in the traditional culture, but others, such as labor unions, are based on relationships deriving from new economic contexts and have no parallel in traditional rural society. Voluntary associations help migrants adjust to city living, and they provide the basis for political organization through which the interests of different groups in newly emergent states can be served. Such associations are also training grounds for new skills that are useful in industrial and urban contexts, such as electing officials, speaking before a group, and using a language other than one's native tongue. Because these associations often award prestige based on modern rather than traditional role achievements, they ease the transition from traditional to modern identities.

Voluntary associations can also help members move beyond narrow local identities based on kinship, village, caste, and tribe to wider identifications more relevant in modern nation-states, such as those of citizen or worker. Some urban voluntary associations are based on traditional statuses. These include tribal and regional associations found in West Africa, caste associations in India, and the kinship-based associations found among the Batak peoples who have migrated to cities in Indonesia. These associations have a dual function, however. On the one hand, they provide continuity with traditional sources of identity and culture; on the other, they also socialize their members into city ways, serving as a link between traditional and modern structures.

During my fieldwork in India, I studied a voluntary association in Bombay formed by women who had originally come from villages and small towns in North India. These women were drawn together by their common language and culture, which was distinct from that of the majority ethnic group in Bombay. They belonged to the same category of high castes and were upper middle class; their husbands were professionals and businessmen. The women began their group about twenty-five years ago, meeting once a week mainly for the purpose of holding religious ceremonies and participating in the devotional singing that is an important feature of contemporary Hinduism. In their ritual activity, they attempted to re-create the social and religious life of their native region. Although this is the reason they organized, their association now has other purposes and functions as well. Through the informal exchange of gossip in the group, new patterns of behavior are introduced, discussed, evaluated, and diffused. For example, if a woman's son marries a Westerner, the group will discuss this and its implications for their own lives. In this way, the association provides a kind of emotional support system that helps the women adjust to change. Through informal discussion, new fashions and new ideas are introduced and slowly become part of an upper-middle-class urban life-style.

Because high-caste Indian women are not encouraged to work, women's associations play an important role in widening their cultural horizons and their social circle within the appropriate caste, ethnic, and class groups to which they belong. Women's groups in North India tend to be age-graded; through participation in such a group, a young daughter-in-law can escape, at least temporarily, from the supervision of her mother-in-law and find solidarity with other women of her own age. For older women whose sons and daughters are ready to be married, these associations provide access to a network within which marriages can be arranged with some confidence.

Voluntary associations are an important part of the adaptive strategies of urban migrants, because they can be based on an almost infinite number of interests and serve a wide

In complex societies, informal relationships become important as frameworks for social activity. Network analysis is useful for studying urban life, pictured here in San Juan, Puerto Rico, where both friendship and kinship are important factors in social life. (Bernhard Krauss)

range of purposes. In West Africa, for example, urban women's associations are much more directly concerned with political goals and economic interests, reflecting the fact that their membership is made up of working women. The importance of these associations reflects the important economic and political roles women in West Africa traditionally play. The importance of voluntary associations in the nations of Asia, Africa, and Latin America is paralleled by the importance of similar associations among immigrant groups in the urban centers of the United States.

Informal Social Networks

A **social network** refers to a set of both direct and indirect links between an individual, who is at the center of a network, and other people. Unlike a social group, such as the voluntary associations discussed above, a social network is a framework for understanding social relationships imposed by the outsider. Networks are a useful way to study social organization in

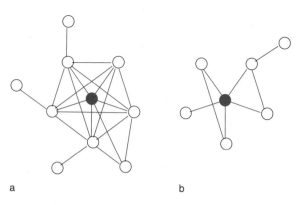

FIGURE 15.1 A comparison of a highly connected network (a) and a dispersed network (b).

cities and in complex societies, where social organization consists less of closed, kin-based, corporate groups and more of links between individual actors who share only a part of their lives with a great many other individuals in a number of situations.

One of the important points of comparison among networks is the degree of connectedness or density of the network. In a highly connected, or dense, network, the individuals with whom Ego is connected are also connected to one another. In a low-density, or dispersed, network, Ego is connected to other people who do not know one another (see Figure 15.1). Comparison of network density and structure has been used to explain a number of kinds of social behavior — for example, communication of gossip, diffusion of norms, and pressures for social control. One of the earliest uses of social networks was in the study of urban families in England (Bott 1957). Among other things, **network analysis** showed that, although many urban families are not contained within organized groups (such as a corporate kin group), they do have many external relationships with individuals and institutions who are not, however, linked. Network analysis opens up a new perspective on the urban family; it allows us to see that the urban family is not necessarily isolated, as is often claimed, but rather is involved

in a more or less dispersed network of social relations without which it could not survive.

Not all the individuals with whom Ego is connected have the same relationship to him or her. In some of the relationships, Ego will be related to an individual in a number of ways — friend, kin, neighbor, co-worker. In other relationships, Ego may be linked to an individual in one role only — say, as a co-worker. Furthermore, Ego uses different parts of his or her network depending on the situation. Some individuals may be mobilized when it comes to finding a job, others in times of personal crisis, still others in building up a power base.

A recent interesting use of the kin network concept is in Micaela di Leonardo's (1984) study of Italian-American families in California. She recognized that with the dispersal of this ethnic community in different towns, cities, and suburbs, the traditional anthropological methodology of the ethnographic study of a spatial community would not be appropriate. She followed the kin and nonkin networks of key informants to yield more relevant material. Analysis of kin networks revealed important information about the social functioning of different individuals within the context of class and ethnicity. For example, di Leonardo found that Italian-Americans who worked in professions where ethnicity was irrelevant had more individuals in their social networks who were not Italian-Americans. Social network analysis also revealed the importance of gender: Because "kin work" is left to women, women had more family members than did men in their social networks. Similarly, because part of women's kin work was to mediate between family members of different social classes, women's social networks had more individuals from different social classes than did men's networks.

As people in traditional societies move out of their self-contained communities of kinship and local groups and expand their social ties in new situations, new methods of anthropological analysis become appropriate. Network analysis is one of these methods. Its increasing use is an example of the ways in which anthropology itself is adapting to change in the contemporary world.

Summary

1. Earlier anthropological models of change that emphasized the one-way impact of the West on the non-West have given way to more complex models of change, such as world systems theory, which emphasize the connectedness of cultures in a world economic system.

2. Modernization theories of change, widely accepted in the 1950s and 1960s, are now criticized because they were based on a too simple (and ethnocentric) dichotomy between so-called traditional and modern society, and did not sufficiently take into account the many paths along which change occurs, the resistance to change, and the effect of the world economic system on change.

3. Entry into worldwide market systems is another powerful factor of change in the contemporary world. Although such participation may increase the number of consumer goods available to tribal and peasant peoples, it does not necessarily raise their basic standard of living. Furthermore, it leads to a dependence on often unstable world markets over which traditionally autonomous populations have no control.

4. The Bakairi of Brazil illustrate both the ideology that underlies planned change by national governments, and the many cultural and economic reasons why such programs are often unsuccessful among indigenous peoples.

5. Tourism is a special kind of entry into world markets. Although many economic advantages are claimed for tourism, these are often more apparent than real. Tourism, although it may promote cultural identity and intercultural understanding, may also promote a loss of cultural integrity and intercultural conflict.

6. The Toraja of Indonesia are an example of an important economic and cultural factor in the contemporary world: tourism. As a result of tourism and other economic and political factors, the Toraja seem to have been able to successfully incorporate some of the elements of their traditional culture with the new source of tourist wealth. In doing so, a new Toraja ethnic identity has emerged.

7. Sometimes the results of development programs have the effect of increasing inequalities, such as those between men and women, and of marginalizing the poorer members of the community. In the case of women, their traditional work roles are often not acknowledged by development policy and they are also excluded from using modern technology.

8. Where governments are not successful in bringing about change voluntarily, there may be peasant revolutions, as in the People's Republic of China. The new socialist government intervenes in every aspect of the people's lives in order to increase productivity and, through modernization and industrialization, restore China to a respected place in the world community of nations.

9. Urbanization is yet another important process of change. The migration of rural peasants to cities affects not only the lives of those who migrate but also the culture and social structure of the rural areas they leave. Because of the rapid rate of urbanization in the contemporary world, the study of urban adaptations has become an important subject of anthropological research.

Suggested Readings

Bodley, John H.
1990   *Victims of Progress*. 3rd ed. Mountain View, Calif.: Mayfield. An outstanding book that persuasively details the ways in which autonomous tribal societies have become the victims of industrialization and the expansion of the state.

Gewertz, Deborah, and Errington, Frederick
1991   *Twisted Histories, Altered Contexts: Representing the Chambri in a World System.* New York: Cambridge University Press. Through chapter-length accounts of individuals caught up in situations that reflect aspects of the encounter between the Chambri of Papua, New Guinea, and representatives of the larger world, the authors show how world processes of social and cultural change operate.

Kottack, Conrad Phillip
1992   *Assault on Paradise: Social Change in a Brazilian Village.* 2nd ed. New York: Random House. An excellent and readable account designed for use in introductory anthropology courses that sets the social changes of a Brazilian village in a national and global context.

Kriger, Norma J.
1992   *Zimbabwe's Guerrilla War: Peasant Voices.* New York: Cambridge University Press. An important and stimulating book based on the rarely heard voices of peasants about their experiences of the Zimbabwean revolution of the late 1970s.

Potter, Sulamith Heins, and Potter, Jack M.
1990   *China's Peasants: The Anthropology of a Revolution.* New York: Cambridge University Press. A book based on a field trip to China during 1979 to 1980. The first half of the book gives a detailed description on agricultural development and rural industry, and the last half deals with the more anthropological subjects of the cultural patterning of emotions, marriage, and family with a particularly interesting discussion of birth planning and state-sponsored abortion from the Chinese cultural perspective.

The Uses of Anthropology

What are some of the ways anthropologists have contributed to solving human problems?

What roles can anthropologists play in shaping and implementing public policy?

What special insights do anthropologists bring to the solving of human problems?

Anthropologists want to have greater impact on the conduct of public affairs . . . and are searching for new ways to bring anthropology into the public eye and for new paradigms to assure the growth of our discipline into the twenty-first century. Two keys to successful anthropological influence over policy initiatives stand out. One key includes the distinctive features of anthropological practice, especially the linkage and translation functions provided. In each case, knowledge and empathy earned through community-based fieldwork addressed to concrete problems of local concern provide anthropologists with critical understandings and, frequently, solutions to obstacles to policy goals. In applied anthropology, holistic ethnological understanding becomes a means to interpret the significance of behaviors rather than the end of analysis. Other special orientations of anthropology that can play a role in the success of a policy include the tracing of dynamic lingages between the local decision-making unit and the larger socioeconomic milieu, recognition of the differences between "real" and "ideal" behavior, and attention to past experiences. Ethnographic skills produce results not easily duplicated by quantitative data. Anthropologists, used to wrestling with complex, partial patterns of data, are in some ways better equipped to produce reliable, actionable results than are colleagues in other disciplines. In many successful cases of applied anthropology, anthropologists have come down on the side of the poor and disempowered and adopted a client-driven goal structure within broader policy contexts.

Adapted from Eric J. Arnould, "Anthropology and West African Development: A Political Economic Critique and Auto-Critique." Human Organization 48, 2 (1989):135–48.

Anthropologists are too often exclusively identified with the study of remote cultures that seem, at first glance, to have little to do with the problems of the contemporary world. In fact, anthropology, as the chapter-opening selection indicates, is very concerned with human problems, and it was conceived of by its founders as a "reformer's science." To the extent that knowledge is power, all of anthropological research has the potential for improving the human condition. Throughout this text, we have considered some of the general ways that anthropology relates to human problems: By its emphasis on culture as learned behavior, anthropology heightens awareness of how human behavior can be changed and why resistance to change may arise. In this chapter, we consider more specifically answers to the question "What knowledge can anthropologists contribute that may be used to solve problems in our own and other societies?" The urgent necessity for humanistic social planning in the contemporary world calls for increased awareness and use of anthropological knowledge and perspectives, and increasing numbers of anthropologists are applying their work toward the important task of solving human problems.

Anthropology and Public Policy

As societies become more complex and heterogeneous, their segments tend to become increasingly isolated from one another — ethnic group from ethnic group; occupational specializations from one another; elites from poor people; and, particularly, bureaucratic, policy-making, and policy-implementing public agen-

cies from the populations at whom policies are directed (Spicer and Downing 1974:1). Public policies, however well intentioned, have not been and cannot be successful when they are based on ignorance of the populations affected by them. This is an arena in which anthropological knowledge can make important contributions. Anthropologists are uniquely qualified, because of their ethnographic training, not only to gather data from groups on the receiving end of government policies of intervention and change but also to act as "cultural brokers" between policy makers and "target populations," many of whom are traditionally powerless groups that have little access to power centers where such policies are made. Thus, most often the populations at whom public policies are directed have little to say about those policies, and the policy makers have little knowledge about the real behavior patterns of such populations. Anthropologists can help fill this vacuum.

Drug Use and Abuse

One example of the kinds of research that anthropologists engage in that relates to contemporary social problems is the area of drug use and abuse.

In the United States, cannabis, or marijuana, has been treated in public policy as a lethal, socially dangerous substance, lumped together with heroin, cocaine, and other narcotics and hallucinogens. Recreational use of cannabis first gained popularity in the United States during Prohibition, and it was not made illegal until 1937. At that time, the director of the newly created Federal Bureau of Narcotics waged an intense publicity campaign to convince Congress and the public that cannabis was a lethal drug and that its users were potential murderers and maniacs. Congress was convinced, and the result was the passage of the Marihuana Tax Act of 1937. From that time, federal and state penalties for possession, cultivation, or sale of cannabis have increased in severity. The Federal Bureau of Narcotics has insisted that cannabis users are criminals who support themselves by preying on society and that cannabis use is related to deviancy, parasitism, and marginality (Partridge 1978). Evidence from studies of prison populations has been used to support this view. In fact, the laboratory and clinical studies of captive populations can contribute little of use to social policy formulation, because often the social and psychological behavior of such subjects is as much the product of the expectations of the institutions as of the drug use itself.

The few ethnographic studies of cannabis use in natural cultural contexts show that the effects of drugs are not merely chemical but vary dramatically according to their cultural and situational settings. In recognition of this important finding, the National Institute of Mental Health sponsored anthropological investigations of cannabis use in a variety of cultures: Jamaica, South Africa, Costa Rica, Greece, and Colombia. These studies clearly demonstrated that cannabis use and its effects do vary according to cultural circumstances and that the view of the cannabis user as a parasite on society and a criminally inclined deviant is not accurate in those societies. As part of this cross-cultural project, William Partridge studied cannabis use among agricultural workers in Colombia. Here, he found, cannabis use is an integral part of the mutual exchanges that cement social relations among workers, and cannabis use begins among adolescent males when they begin to adopt adult work patterns. Cannabis is smoked in the context of work and out in the fields and is perceived by its users to make them better workers. Workers' perceptions that cannabis is an energizer were found in Jamaica and other cultures as well. Thus,

Partridge concludes from his ethnographic study that in this coastal subculture of Colombia, cannabis is used in conditions that promote conformity, social alliance, and productivity and is linked to labor recruitment and achievement of adulthood. This finding stands in dramatic contrast to the North American perception, which, while perhaps having some truth for our culture, is nothing more than ethnocentric when applied to other cultures.

In Latin America, for example, coca has for centuries been an integral part of life for many indigenous groups, and its importance cannot be understood in isolation from the total culture (Pacini and Franquemont 1986). Indeed, in some parts of the high Andes, the use of coca is central to the cultural identity of the peasants who use it in many rituals (Allen 1989). In addition, while some indigenous peoples are using the income from illicitly grown drug crops to support local independence movements, in other cases, indigenous peoples are finding it difficult to keep their land in the face of increased pressures for expanded production of coca for the world drug market.

Anthropologists, unlike law enforcement and policy officials, are sensitive to both the outsider's view of substance abuse and the effects that the illicit world market for drugs has on indigenous peoples. Anthropological data on substance use and abuse indicate that we have a special contribution to make to the field through our traditional ethnographic methodology and comparative and cultural perspective on human behavior. Through the anthropologist's holistic understanding of drug cultures, they can identify the constellation of constraints and incentives that surround the choice either to use or not to use a drug. Certainly this methodology can serve as a basis for distinguishing between the facts and the fictions on which public policy is based and can help government leaders to formulate a more rational and effective policy than the one now in effect in the United States.

Recently, anthropologists' work on drug abuse has turned from an interest in marijuana use to the use of crack, a cocaine derivative.

Anthropologist Ansley Hamid talking with a crack addict in New York as part of his ethnographic work on the economics of substance abuse. (Don Hogan Charles/NYT Pictures)

Ansley Hamid (1992), Philippe Bourgois (1989), Terry Williams (1989), and others show, for example, that not only does the "culture" of substance use (and abuse) differ according to the particular substance but also the production, distribution, and consumption of each substance are interrelated in different ways with other aspects of culture and have different impacts in different geographical regions, ethnic groups, and class strata.

Medical Anthropology: A Growing Field of Applied Anthropology

Inadequate health care is undoubtedly a major contemporary human problem and an important area of government planning and intervention. Theories of disease and healing practices are part of the culture of all human groups, and medical systems are one of the adaptive responses that humans make to disease and illness. Anthropologists have long studied healing systems in nonliterate societies and have always been interested in the behavioral as well as the medical aspects of health problems.

Not until the 1940s and 1950s did anthropologists begin to apply their research to national and international problems of health care (Hill 1985). In the 1970s, health-care planning underwent a shift from a medical approach to health, which focuses on the treatment of disease, to a broader approach, more concerned with the prevention of disease and the promotion of health. This shift in interest led to increased funding for programs of comprehensive health care, which sought to provide affordable and culturally appropriate care, preventive as well as curative, to populations that traditionally had less access to modern health-care facilities.

Initially, models of health-care intervention were based on the assumption that modern Western medical practices and institutions were clearly superior to other, indigenous systems and that when these were introduced, people would drop their traditional practices and turn to the newer systems. It gradually became clear to planners that this assumption was incorrect;

modern facilities were not being used extensively, and traditional practices and specialists remained influential. Here is where it seemed that anthropologists could be useful, both in identifying the cultural, social, and psychological barriers inhibiting acceptance of new health-care measures and in designing programs that would be more in accord with different cultural expectations in developing nations, where many of the health-care programs were being implemented (Pillsbury 1985).

The importance of cultural variables in explaining the use or nonuse of professional medical services also has relevance for health-care interventions in the United States. Research has shown that both the demand for and the supply of health-care services vary according to social class and ethnic background. Not only are the health-care facilities supplied to the poor of lesser quality than those provided to the rest of society, but also the patterns of use of these facilities differ among social classes and ethnic groups.

Anthropology and AIDS

The AIDS (Acquired Immune Deficiency Syndrome) epidemic is one urgent area of health care where anthropologists are applying their knowledge. This epidemic is so deadly that some anthropologists view it as the greatest contemporary challenge to our discipline (Singer 1992). In the United States, the two highest-risk populations for AIDS are homosexual males and intravenous drug users; in other parts of the world, for example, Africa and parts of Asia, AIDS is mainly spread by heterosexual intercourse. Since a vaccine for preventing AIDS has not yet been discovered, the most effective intervention at this time involves changing people's behavior to minimize the risk of contracting HIV, the virus that causes AIDS, through sexual activity or through drug-use patterns, specifically, sharing of needles with infected persons.

Changing people's behavior requires, first of all, knowing how they behave and what meaning they attach to their behavior. Only then can culturally appropriate intervention strategies be developed that are effective because they can be incorporated into ongoing behavior patterns. Designing such strategies for AIDS-related behavior is particularly difficult because such behavior is carried out in intimate and private settings, hidden from the public eye. This difficulty of observing AIDS-related behavior is compounded by the stigma attached to much of it, and in the case of intravenous substance abusers, the criminal penalties attached to it. Anthropologists, with their participant-observation, nonjudgmental methodology, can make a particularly valuable contribution to our understanding of AIDS-related behavior, to forming realistic and effective policies to combat it, and to implementing such efforts in local communities.

An early attempt by applied anthropologists to respond to the AIDS epidemic was the work of Douglas Feldman among gay males (1986). Feldman's study examined the degree of concern about AIDS within the New York gay community and explored how the spreading AIDS epidemic was affecting the high-risk sexual behavior of homosexual men. Using a questionnaire that elicited information on the number of sexual partners an individual had before and after learning about AIDS, Feldman's study revealed that knowledge about AIDS had indeed affected behavior: Almost 50 percent of the respondents indicated that they had decreased the number of their sexual partners, and also decreased their higher-risk sexual activities. Since Feldman's work, many more anthropologists are doing research on the cultural meanings and behavior patterns related to AIDS, and applying that knowledge in creating and evaluating a variety of intervention efforts aimed at stopping the spread of AIDS.

In the last ten years, as gay men were responding in some measure to decrease high-risk behavior, AIDS was spreading fast among another population, that of intravenous drug users, who were becoming infected with AIDS through using unclean needles and sharing needles with infected drug users. Needle-sharing behavior is very common among intravenous drug users, especially among African-Americans and Latinos, who, correspondingly, have a higher proportion of AIDS and HIV infection (Singer et al. 1991:143). Indeed, AIDS appears to be fast becoming the leading cause of death for people of color in the United States, and the percentage of cases among African-Americans and Latinos will soon be more than double their proportion of the U.S. population (Singer 1992:89). As of 1992, 51 percent of women who have AIDS are African-American, and another 20 percent are Latinas. Among children, over 75 percent of the AIDS cases are in minority groups. Heterosexual transmission of AIDS disproportionately affects minority adolescents and young adults.

Anthropological fieldwork among intravenous drug users indicates that a high percentage use unclean needles because their dominant concern is their need to inject drugs, and clean needles are not available. Many drug users do not own their own "works" (syringes and related paraphernalia) because they cannot afford to buy them. In addition, where it is illegal to be in possession of a needle without a prescription, as it is in many states, drug users may prefer to borrow a needle from a friend, or even a stranger, or to rent one in a "shooting gallery." Injecting drugs in places where sharing needles is more likely, as in "shooting galleries," rather than in one's home, is very likely to lead to exposure to the AIDS virus, unless the sharing is done among a closed group of uninfected users (which is not very likely among street users) or unless the needles are effectively cleaned after use, a practice not, as yet, widely engaged in by intravenous drug users (Singer et al. 1991). Although illicit needle sellers (using needles obtained with forged prescriptions, stolen from hospital emergency rooms, or purchased from diabetics) do make some clean needles available, many of these sellers just repackage used (and possibly infected) needles and sell them as new.

Applied anthropologists, with their unique ethnographic understanding of the social and cultural aspects of AIDS-related behavior, have begun advocating government-funded intervention programs of clean needle distribution in the United States. Several European countries either have or are considering needle distribution programs (where addicts would turn in a used needle and receive a new, sterilized one) in order to break the link between substance abuse and HIV infection. In spite of research that indicates many intravenous drug users would take advantage of such a program, a policy of distributing clean needles meets strong opposition from government officials and others in the United States because it appears to condone intravenous drug use and is, in addition, in conflict with those state laws which make possession of a hypodermic needle without a prescription illegal.

Anthropological efforts to make an impact on needle-sharing behavior among intravenous drug users have exposed a cultural contradiction in our society: Public policies that appear to condone what our culture designates as immoral behavior (drug use) are resisted, even when those policies might successfully change behavior in a desired direction, that of stopping the spread of AIDS. Exposing these cultural contradictions is a necessary first step in educating the public, including policy makers, who often resist acknowledging that such contradictions exist.

The educative role is an important part of applying anthropology to solving social problems through effective policy making, but applied anthropologists are active in other ways as well, both in implementing substance-abuse programs and evaluating them. Anthropologically directed interventions and evaluations of substance-abuse programs (and other medical interventions) are distinguished by their long-standing commitment to community-based models. Two principles underlie this model: The first is that the needs and goals of a particular community-based group are being served, and this "target group" has the initiative in seeking changes. Second, in this model, the applied anthropologist is taking an active role in trying to change people's behavior. The community-based action model is thus based on the value that democratic self-determination at the local level is the most effective and constructive means of change, both for the community group concerned and for the larger society (Barger and Reza 1989, in Singer 1992:143).

Program Evaluation

Evaluating programs of change is another important role anthropologists play in responding to societal problems. Evaluation of substance-abuse prevention and intervention programs has generally followed impact or outcome evaluations using quantitative, experimental designs, depending largely on statistically analyzed survey instruments (of the type referred to in Feldman's study) that link behavior or attitude change to a specific intervention aimed at only one part of the community, for example, schools, or family, or law enforcement. Research demonstrates, however, that prevention efforts in substance abuse — whether alcohol or drugs — are most effective when they integrate all parts of the community, that is, when they are conceived holistically. Thus, more government efforts are being aimed at community-based intervention programs, an approach very congenial to anthropologists with their holistic methodology of ethnography and their concept of culture as a whole.

With a new emphasis on community-based, holistic action programs, anthropologists have an increasing role in evaluating these programs with qualitative, ethnographic methodology (Brooks 1992). Where traditional statistical or quantitative designs tend to focus only on the "impact" of a program after it is completed, ethnographic models of evaluation use description and interpretation to illuminate the complex cultural and social context of a program's implementation. And where the traditional quantitative design usually assesses the relative success or failure of a program without illuminating the causes of that success or failure, ethnographically based evaluations are better able to "reveal the many interrelated variables that create the everyday reality for real people"

(Brooks 1992). This descriptive, holistic, ethnographic approach, which is at the core of anthropology, effectively contributes in showing what programs are working, and how those that are not can be improved. Ethnography can also be used to analyze the process of implementing the program, that is, the relationship between the program's staff and the members of the target community. This "process ethnography" is yet another way in which anthropologists can apply their knowledge to helping solve human problems.

Anthropologists as Advocates

Cultural Survival

Another important way that anthropologists are involved in change is as advocates on behalf of indigenous peoples whose cultures are destroyed and whose rights are violated when they are perceived as standing in the way of economic development and political priorities of the nation-states of which they are a part. A key organization in this effort is Cultural Survival, established by a group of anthropologists at Harvard University in 1972.

Cultural Survival is directed toward increasing the abilities of tribal peoples and ethnic minorities to improve their adaptive capacities within the multiethnic or culturally pluralistic nation-state. It helps indigenous peoples retain their cultural identities while accommodating more gradually to the changes accompanying national economic development. The advocacy by anthropologists for tribal peoples and ethnic minorities is based on the conviction that such societies have been wronged over the past centuries and that anthropologists can, and should, help right those wrongs (Maybury-Lewis 1993). One way anthropologists can help is to analyze the nature of these injustices and the possible strategies for fighting them. It is this emphasis on action that distinguishes the work of Cultural Survival.

As David Maybury-Lewis and others involved in Cultural Survival point out, the historical wrongs committed against these societies began with the conquest of the New World and continue today in the name of development and modernization (see Chapter 15). Indigenous peoples are often stigmatized as clinging to a backward or primitive way of life and obstructing economic development, nation building, and development. These national political and economic policies are often aimed at, or result in, appropriation of the lands of indigenous peoples, upon which the survival of their cultures depends. Such nations often engage in culturally repressive assimilation policies, which they rationalize by saying that the assimilation of ethnic or cultural minorities is not only good but inevitable in any case. This view is often uncritically accepted both by international funding agencies and by the public, in spite of formal United Nations declarations about guarding the rights of indigenous peoples.

In addition to educating the public as to the falsity of these arguments and the harm they do, Cultural Survival is involved in trying to create models of culturally diverse states that would permit the gradual accommodation of indigenous peoples and ethnic minorities to national cultures in a way that they wish. Thus, Cultural Survival does not insist that peoples hold on to every aspect of their "traditional" culture; in the recognition that culture is always changing, Cultural Survival helps people who request help to maintain those aspects of their culture *they* think are important.

Land is critical to the survival of indigenous cultures, and the loss of land and land rights is a constant threat, as nations and international corporations expand their operations in the search for new resources and profits. An important part of the work of Cultural Survival is to help indigenous peoples understand the implications of changes in their land tenure systems from communal to individual ownership (in which the land becomes more vulnerable to sale) and become more effective in their negotiations and strategies to protect their land base. Indigenous peoples will not be left alone by national and international organizations, such as national governments and the United States Agency for International Development (AID), but these policy makers can be educated and pressured by international public opinion and political activism to be more sensitive to the needs of indigenous peoples. The anthropological community has a long and strong commitment to preserving cultural diversity, and is currently joined in that effort by many conservationist groups. Applying anthropological knowledge as a basis for advocacy does not mean preserving indigenous peoples in some mythical original state of culture. Rather it means supporting the rights of a society to have a say in its own future. Cultural Survival thus tries to help create conditions under which such societies can maximize their autonomy and make decisions about their own future. This may be done through legal, political, and economic strategies, and an important part of what Cultural Survival does is help develop and sustain satisfactory alternatives to traditional subsistence economies that are being transformed by development policies and programs.

An example of the kind of program supported by Cultural Survival is that of assistance to the !Kung San. As we have read, the !Kung San are the peoples of the Kalahari desert who have lived for thousands of years as hunter-gatherers. Within twenty years after the South African government brought them under administrative control in 1960, the !Kung San hunting and gathering way of life had collapsed; they became dependent on menial government jobs, and welfare replaced their former self-sufficiency. Social disintegration, increasing alcoholism, and a rising infant mortality rate followed. In 1978, when the South African government began recruiting !Kung San for its war against a people's liberation movement in neighboring Southwest Africa, many !Kung San were attracted by the cash wages, leading to economic inequalities in what had been an egalitarian society. The land area of the !Kung San has been drastically reduced, and with the plan of the South African government to turn their remaining land into a game reserve, the

!Kung San nomadic hunting and gathering way of life seemed irretrievably doomed.

Based on the desires of the !Kung San themselves, Cultural Survival has mounted an international campaign to help them reorient their economy around cattle husbandry and subsistence farming supplemented by hunting and gathering. Direct assistance will take the form of providing livestock, medicine and medical services for livestock, and tools for improving the water holes around which !Kung San bands have traditionally settled and which can become the core of their new economies (Lee 1992a).

Cultural Survival advocates for a wide variety of programs — from legal aid to Indians in Colombia to demarcating lands for indigenous peoples in Amazonian Ecuador. Its view is that "development" is inevitable and that anthropologists should be actively involved in the development process so that programs of change can be implemented in ways that protect the rights of indigenous peoples, help them maintain their cultural integrity, and benefit them in ways that they desire.

Not all anthropologists agree with Cultural Survival's approach to the issue of how anthropologists can best serve the interests of indigenous peoples or be most usefully involved in the development process. Because many more anthropologists are finding work in national and international development efforts, this topic has become one of increasing discussion within the profession.

Anthropologists as Expert Witnesses

Another application of anthropological knowledge on behalf of cultural diversity and autonomy takes the form of anthropologists serving as expert witnesses in legal battles between governments or corporations and indigenous peoples and ethnic minorities. Such expert testimony is often critical in the outcome of these cases. An early example of this concerned the use of peyote in the Native American Church. In this church, whose membership primarily consists of native Americans from many different tribes, peyote use plays a central, sacramental role. Because peyote is not addictive, it does not come under federal narcotics laws, but it has been proscribed by several state health codes. The Bureau of Indian Affairs had long tried to stamp out its use, claiming that Indians substitute it for modern medical care, that there is a connection between peyote use and the use of other, more harmful drugs, that it was used to indoctrinate minors, that it was associated with sexual immorality, and that its use "obstructs enlightenment" and "shackles the Indian to primitive conditions" (*People* v. *Woody* 1964).

In 1951, a group of anthropologists challenged the government's efforts to have peyote declared illegal. Based on their own experiences with peyote, they claimed that "it does not excite, stupefy, or produce muscular incoordination; there is no hangover; and the habitual user does not develop an increased tolerance or dependence." They totally dismissed the government's charge that peyote use was accompanied by immorality, that it was given to children, or that it was used for medical purposes. The anthropologists further claimed that the moral standards of members of the Native American Church were probably higher than those of other Indians because, for example, the church forbids the use of alcohol (Farb 1978:304–5).

In 1962, a group of Navajo using peyote in a church ceremony in California were arrested for violation of California's health code. They appealed their conviction in the trial court to the California Supreme Court (*People* v. *Woody* 1964). Incorporating the anthropologists' expert testimony on peyote, the supreme court reversed the earlier decision and declared that denying the members of the Native American Church the right to use peyote in their rituals was a violation of their constitutional rights under the First Amendment.

Although a more recent case (*Oregon* v. *Smith* 1990) found against peyotists, there was an outcry against this decision from the legal community and others, and it remains to be seen whether the positive views toward cultural pluralism expressed in the Woody case will be revived by the courts, or whether the Oregon case is an indication of the narrowing of rights of religious minorities for the future.

An entirely different kind of case involved the efforts of Glenn Petersen (1985), an anthropologist who has done ethnography in Pohnpei, one of the islands in the American Trust Territory of Micronesia. The United States has attempted to retain major control over the trust territory, which it views as having high strategic military value. Our government has offered various units of the territory the opportunity to participate in a compact of free association, which falls short of full independence and which was rejected in a plebiscite by the Pohnpeins. Petersen has testified before the U.S. Congress and the United Nations (under whose guidelines trust territories are controlled) that the contract of free association deprives the territories of self-determination and violates a major Pohnpeian cultural value that runs through their family, community, and political life: that of autonomy and the importance of people being responsible for their own welfare. Petersen holds that no amount of development aid can substitute for self-determination and that self-determination for Pohnpei can be meaningful only with full political independence.

As one last example, we may look at expert testimony in another context, that of a 1976 court case involving educational equity for African-American children. In that year, a federal district court in Ann Arbor, Michigan, ruled that the city's public schools were denying black elementary-school students their civil rights by failing to teach them to speak, read, and write standard English as an alternative to the Black English that was their native dialect. The court said that failure on the part of the schools to recognize and use Black English as a basis for teaching standard English denied black children an equal opportunity to succeed in school and thus in later life.

An important part of the expert testimony was that of William Labov, a sociolinguist who has conducted extensive ethnographic research in the language patterns of speakers of nonstandard English in the United States. Labov's research showed that Black English is a distinct linguistic system, but not a foreign language; that it has many features in common with southern dialects because blacks lived in the South for several centuries; and that it also has distinct marks of an Afro-Caribbean ancestry, reflecting earlier origins of the African-American community (Labov 1983:31). Because the judge wanted to narrow the issues to linguistic, rather than cultural, barriers to the children's learning, Labov's testimony focused on the specific structural features in Black English that interfere with reading in standard English. The judge charged the Ann Arbor school district to find ways to provide its teachers with this kind of information so that they could more adequately teach children who speak Black English in their homes and neighborhoods how to read and function in standard English as well. Labov's research, which is based on the study of children's speech in natural settings, as discussed in Chapter 5, demonstrated that Black English is not an impoverished and *deficient* language but that it is a *different* linguistic system, which is as capable as standard English of expressing complex and abstract ideas. Through the use of his research in both civil rights litigation and educational program design, Labov has made an exceptionally important contribution to a problematic area of American life—that of educational equity for minority groups.

Planned Change and Development Anthropology

As noted in Chapter 15 and earlier in this chapter, economic development based on modernization models is being pursued by national governments and international development agencies. An important component of these programs is the idea of community development, a concept endorsed by the United States

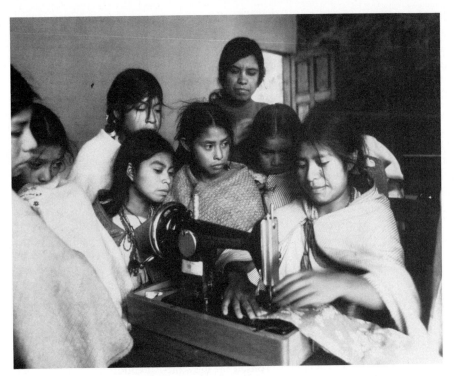

Modernization involves the use of machine technology, often as a substitute for traditional hand labor. The sewing machine, which has been introduced as part of community development programs in Mexico, is regarded as a useful tool in many peasant villages and lessens their dependence on buying goods from outside merchants at high prices. (United Nations)

and other Western nations as well as the United Nations, to promote economic growth and Western-style political democracy throughout the world. The rationale of community development is that people can improve the material and nonmaterial conditions of their lives through community autonomy and self-sufficiency. One assumption underlying many community development programs is that the behavior, values, and beliefs — in short, the cultures — of local communities engaging in basically subsistence economies are resistant to change and that this resistance is the primary obstruction to economic development. This model has been applied to indigenous peoples, peasants, hunters and gatherers, and pastoral peoples who make up the less economically developed, or most economically unproductive, sector of the larger societies of which they are a part.

Government-sponsored community development projects are aimed at changing behaviors of local communities so that they become more economically productive and also at changing people's attitudes so that they may develop the confidence and the competence they need to help themselves. Ideally, development aims at helping a community realize its own goals by using its own human resources, while recognizing that some outside support, both financial and technical, will be needed along the way. Part of the officially sanctioned methodology of community development is to discover the "felt needs" of the population at the local level and work through these to achieve improvements. The assumption of this model is that local communities are homogeneous and that development will benefit the whole community, as well as the larger society.

A SUCCESSFUL APPLICATION OF ANTHROPOLOGY IN ECONOMIC DEVELOPMENT: HAITI

Throughout the Third World there is a growing shortage of wood for fuel and construction, particularly in densely populated areas with a long history of agriculture. Because forests take such a long time to grow and such a short time to cut down, reforestation is a worldwide ecological problem. In Haiti, the deforestation problem is closely related to problems of poverty and overpopulation. Anthropologist Gerald R. Murray had an opportunity to help Haitians work on this problem using the unique methods and perspectives of anthropology.

Based on ethnographically gained knowledge about the cash-oriented foundation of Haitian peasant horticulture, Murray suggested wood as a market crop; because of this same knowledge, fast-growing wood trees were chosen rather than fruit trees, which are commercially vulnerable because of the perishability of the crop. Ethnographically gained knowledge of Haitian peasant land tenure also suggested to Murray that a collective or community forest scheme would not work even though such schemes are often preferred by development planners. The ethnographic elicitation of folk taxonomies led to the realization that whereas fruit trees are classified as a crop by Haitian peasants, wood trees are not, and so the program was able to see the need to explicitly get the message across that wood can be a crop just like coffee or corn. Furthermore, Murray's familiarity with Haitian peasant attitudes, gained through his anthropological fieldwork, enabled him to understand that the most productive way for peasants to engage in reforestation was to have them think about trees not in conservationist terms but rather in terms of being a harvestable crop.

As Murray so ably points out, had anthropological knowledge not been fed into this project, the Agency for International Development (AID), which funded the project, would probably have been based on the traditional — and in Murray's view, highly unsuccessful — model of trees as an instrument in soil conservation, involving educational programs to teach peasants about the value of trees. This value model, characteristic more of government elites and middle-class Western thinking, does not match the world view of Haitian peasants or fit in with their culture. Because of anthropology, Murray was able to revisit Haiti and see the fruits of successful development: Several houses had been built using wood from the trees planted through the project, charcoal made from the project trees was being sold in local markets, and poles of wood from the trees were bringing in cash in markets. As Murray says, "I felt a satisfaction at having chosen a discipline [anthropology] that could give me the privilege of participating, even marginally, in this . . . transition."

Adapted from Gerald F. Murray, "Seeing the Forest While Planting the Trees: An Anthropological Approach to Agroforestry in Rural Haiti," in D. W. Brinkerhoff and J. C. Garcia-Zamor, eds., Politics, Projects, and Peasants: Institutional Development in Haiti *(New York: Praeger, 1986), pp. 193–226.*

Many anthropologists work in development projects; the official policies of the community development approach are consistent with anthropological emphasis on community initiative, autonomy, and development "from the bottom up." Community development projects are also consistent with the view that local communities are integrated wholes and that, without the major emphasis on culturally appropriate interventions, development projects were bound to fail.

While anthropologists are still committed to some of the values of community development, such as increasing local autonomy, local self-initiative, and the importance of local culture, the earlier emphasis on local communities as self-contained, relatively isolated wholes, based on traditional, static culture, is changing (Schwartz 1981). The major conceptual criticism of the community development approach of the 1950s and 1960s is that the focus on the detailed, holistic, local context directed attention away from the impact of external forces. Community structures were viewed as if they were explanations for behavior when, in fact, many of the community structures and constraints on local behavior come from the interaction of the local community with its physical environment and with the larger political forces of the nation and the world market. A new emphasis in development anthropology stresses the economic and ecological context of local decision making and its political links outside the community. The focus in this new approach is less on the local community as a closed, integrated, culturally stable system than on the links between the community and larger structures. The diversity within and between local communities, hierarchical differences and conflicts within communities, and national systems of power are emphasized.

Economic, social, and other decisions made by local communities are now seen not merely as a matter of cultural tradition but rather as rational and necessary, given available economic resources and environmental constraints. For example, it had frequently been assumed in developing nations that traditional pastoral economies were wasteful and that pastoralists were lacking in innovation, which is why they continued with an economy that appeared, in the eyes of development experts, to consist of "a herder seated in the shade of a tree while his animals graze; of women poking at a desperately poor piece of ground to raise a few uncertain crops and of an almost total lack of the outward material show associated with more settled cultures" (Baker 1981:66). We are now becoming more aware that pastoral societies have developed patterns of animal management over long periods of time, which are adaptive in minimizing most of the risks of overgrazing in the marginal physical environments in which pastoralists live. Attempts at "development," which increase herd sizes with an eye to commercialization and build water tanks and wells without considering the potential effects of increased numbers of animals on limited grazing areas, have upset, sometimes irreversibly, the delicate ecological balance that traditional pastoral cultures have achieved.

The stress on the rational, adaptive, or opportunistic calculations of local communities tends to emphasize that people will take risks and make changes if *better* economic and political opportunities are offered to them. It suggests that any attempt to help people "from the bottom up" must then also take into account the larger political and economic structures and processes that limit the access of people to such opportunities. Thus, the new development anthropology gives prominence to power and coercion and the impact these dimensions have on different kinds of local communities. In the previous community development view, the failure of local communities to solve their own problems was attributed to a lack of solidarity and motivation within the community. Yet it can also be said that development is inhibited at the local level because of a lack of national resources and national bureaucratic mismanagement.

The new approach also stresses the importance of peasants and indigenous peoples as social classes, rather than merely isolated subcul-

Community development often works through local elites, who are often the major beneficiaries of planned change. Here, local chiefs in Libya meet to plan community development projects, including wells, roads, and schools. (United Nations)

tures. It argues that power is an essential factor in sociocultural change and that this must be recognized if local communities are to take control of their own lives. Toward this end, conflict has a positive effect, as it can be used to heighten a shared class consciousness among peasants. Similarly, the concept of Indian, in the Latin American context, is used as a culturally differentiating and stigmatizing term and may be seen as a way national elites maintain control over Indians. Recent development theory holds that Indians and mestizos should also be regarded as economic classes as well as ethnic groups. This point of view would tend to undercut the traditional development view that cultural integrity must always be attended to and furthered.

Finally, the newer development anthropology focuses on intracommunity differences rather than assuming community homogeneity. Empirical work has shown that responses to new economic opportunities in some local communities depend on one's wealth and rank in the stratification system, which relates to the willingness to take the economic risks that development requires. For example, as part of the "green revolution," which involved the introduction of new, high-yield wheat strains into peasant villages in India, it soon became apparent that these new strains were superior only if planted in heavily irrigated fields and intensively treated with chemical fertilizers and pesticides. It was thus mainly those richer farmers, who already owned the more heavily irrigated fields and could afford to pay for the expensive chemical fertilizers, that benefited from this development project. The attempt to introduce these wheat strains, produced in the West and capable of fulfilling their potential only with Western chemicals and the hardware necessary to run large farms, was of major benefit to the multinational companies that produced the chemicals and the hardware and to the richer farmers and merchant classes (Mencher 1974).

ANTHROPOLOGISTS AND AGRICULTURE:
A SUCCESSFUL INTERVENTION IN BOLIVIA

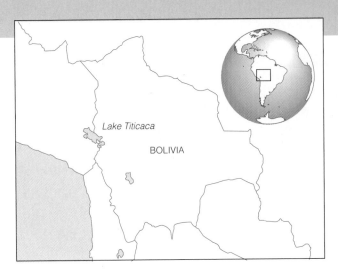

The applications of anthropological knowledge cover diverse fields, but given the long interest of anthropologists in tillers of the soil — horticulturalists and peasants — they have not had the impact one might expect in the area of planned agricultural change (Rhoades 1984). The anthropologist and the agronomist working together can help solve some of the crucial problems in the interactions between humans and their environments. One current project being undertaken by anthropologists and agronomists in a high plateau region of the Andes mountains in Bolivia illustrates this point well.

In this area, a system of ancient agriculture is being revived, with experts and local farmers working together. This region, on the shores of Lake Titicaca, was the site of an ancient culture called the Tiwanaku. Around 1500 B.C. local farmers had developed a system of agriculture that was ingenious in taking advantage of the particular resources of this area while compensating for its deficiencies.

Lake Titicaca, which has the highest elevation of any lake in the world, is slightly salty. It is fed by rivers and springs and receives intense sunlight during the day, but during the growing season it is subject to severe drops in the evening temperature. Successful farming in this area had to cushion the growing area from these temperature extremes and also prevent the seepage of brackish water into the cultivated area.

To adapt to the opportunities and drawbacks of the region, the Tiwanaku farmers constructed a system of raised-bed agriculture. They made a series of platforms, beginning with a foundation layer of cobblestones; above this they constructed a level of clay that prevented the salty lake water from seeping into the topsoil. Above the clay was a layer of sand and gravel that promoted drainage, and above that was the fertile soil in which the crops were grown. Surrounding the platforms, or levels, were canals, filled with water from a river that the farmers rerouted from its natural bed. This water trapped the radiant energy from the intense Andean sunlight so that an insulating blanket of warm water seeping into the growing soil from the canals could protect, or insulate, the crops from the evening frosts. These canals of standing water also became an environment for plants, insects, and other organisms that enriched the soil.

After the Spanish Conquest in the sixteenth century, these raised fields fell into disuse, as the farmers adopted European farming methods. The platforms

Thick cobblestone base

Layer of clay prevents slightly salty lake water from seeping into fields

Large, coarse gravel

Finer grade of gravel

Topsoil

Irrigation channels positioned to take maximum advantage of sun's heat to encourage algae growth and to prevent frost damage

600 ft

50 ft

5 ft

deteriorated into marshy pasture, though the mounds were still visible around the lake. In 1979 anthropological archeologist Alan Kolata noted the mounds when carrying out a project to investigate the remains of the ancient culture in the area. His research indicated that this area once had supported a much larger population than it presently did, and this led Kolata to think about whether reviving this earlier system of agriculture might prove more productive for contemporary local farmers than their present methods. Kolata's idea was positively received by local development experts, who were beginning to question industrialized, capital-intensive, irrigation-based agriculture as the only solution to problems of food production in developing nations and were looking for new alternatives more suited to local conditions. By 1987 Kolata was supervising five experimental raised-bed fields to compare current agricultural yields with those produced by traditional (since the sixteenth century) farming methods.

The potato yield in the experimental fields was much higher than in the traditional plots, and the experimental fields survived a further crucial test: When potatoes and other crops were nearly destroyed by a frost late in the growing season, the crops raised in the experimental raised-bed fields escaped almost undamaged. Kolata is now spearheading a project to reclaim more land on which to revive this ancient system of agriculture that has proven to be so effective (University of Chicago 1989). In such ways does basic research in anthropology demonstrate its use when applied to human problems.

The contemporary anthropological perspective on planned change requires looking beyond the local community to regional, national, and even supranational levels. In asking questions about the role of inequality, dissent, conflict, power, and coercion, the conflict model implies that change proceeds from the top down and that the village or local community may not be the most relevant site for initiating change. Development anthropology poses some significant problems for anthropologists. To the extent that they locate the sources of change and stagnation outside the local community, it logically follows that the solutions they would recommend would entail some radical changes in the seats of power, something that development program administrators are not likely to want to act on (Schwartz 1981:319).

A major constraint on the effectiveness of development anthropologists involves the conflict between what is needed from the point of view of the local community, whose interests are primary for the anthropologist, and the perceived needs of national politicians and governments. In spite of this important constraint, as well as others that come from both the culture of anthropology (for example, discouraging anthropology students from pursuing managerial skills), anthropologists can be important, even crucially so, in the success of development projects (Arnould 1989; van Willigen 1993), as the two examples in Haiti and Bolivia indicate.

Key features of anthropological success in contributing to development programs are the knowledge and empathy that link anthropologists to local communities as a result of their relatively long-term involvement in fieldwork. This degree of understanding gives anthropologists an ability to address concrete problems of local concern that other project staff may not have. This local knowledge also makes anthropologists effective evaluators of what solutions might be created. Anthropological data on differences between ideal and real behavior, on a people's past experiences, and on the complex, interpretive nature of behavior in people's "lives on the ground" are as critical, if not more

critical, to the success of intervention programs than data gathered by other, more quantitative methodologies (Stull and Schensul 1987).

Intercultural Communication: The Use of Anthropology in International Business and Conflict Resolution

As we have seen in Chapter 4 and Chapter 5, one of the important differences between cultures is the ways people perceive time and space, and the ways in which people communicate with each other both verbally and nonverbally. These differences in cultural communication patterns take on new significance in the global economy and the global polity; intercultural communication is thus an important area in which anthropologists can make — and are making — an important contribution. One of the best-known anthropologists in the field of intercultural communication is Edward Hall (1959), whose work emphasizes the many ways in which what he calls "out of awareness" cultural patterns play a role in intercultural communication.

The dimensions that seem to operate cross-culturally in affecting people's behavior in communicating with each other include differences between direct- and indirect-dealing cultures; cultural attitudes toward cooperation, competition, and conflict; different cultural attitudes toward task-versus-affective elements in human relationships; different cultural attitudes toward authority and social ranking; high-context and low-context cultures and their effects on information sharing; and cultural differences in time management (Moore 1993).

Direct-dealing cultures, such as the dominant cultures in the United States and Western Europe, are those that prefer direct, face-to-face interaction, and even debate, in communication and problem solving, even if this means making opposite points of view explicit. Indirect-dealing cultures, such as Japan and many other cultures in Asia, stress the maintenance of harmony, and prefer to avoid face-to-face dealing where conflicting views would be expressed or "face" would be lost or damaged. Indirect-dealing societies make significant use of third parties, or go-betweens, in their social interactions, as a way of preventing the overt conflict or loss of face that occurs in direct dealing.

Cultures also differ in their attitudes toward cooperation, competition, and conflict. Cultures that place a high value on harmony try to avoid an outward show of conflict or competition in problem solving, and thus tend to prefer outcomes in decision making that involve consensus and accommodation, rather than adversarial, win-lose outcomes. In these kinds of cultures, found in Asia and other parts of the non-Western world, the affective, or emotional, aspect of relationships is very important. This contrasts with the task orientation of much of Western culture, where achieving substantive agreement, or impersonal contractual outcomes, outweighs the value of preserving social relations between parties.

Another culturally variable aspect of social relationships is the attention paid to social status in interpersonal interaction. Whereas in some Western cultures, perhaps most in the United States, people of different social statuses feel some measure of comfort in stating their needs and interests in direct interaction — such as the negotiations between labor and management which are a central part of our economic structure — in other, more highly stratified cultures, establishing dominant and subordinate relationships is an accepted cultural pattern and those in subordinate positions are expected to be deferential to those in superior positions.

Another dimension of cultural communication that varies around the world is the degree to which members of a culture are similar in their shared meanings about the world. High-context societies have high levels of assumed or commonly understood information because of a high level of common experiences, backgrounds, and widely held cultural assumptions or values. These cultures, which include those of the Japanese, Arabs, and many Mediterra-

nean peoples, often do not provide the level of detail in their communication that would be provided in low-context cultures, where commonality is not assumed. Thus, in low-context cultures, such as the United States, information sharing involves much more explicit detail. In high-context cultures, people may speak in more general terms and communicate in subtle ways, with an emphasis on building long-term relationships within which specific details will be worked out later. In contrast, communication in low-context cultures contains much more explicit communication, focus on details, and a highly defined, clear, final agreement as the major way of making sure both parties carry out their obligations in a relationship.

Finally, as noted in Chapter 4, the management of time also differs among cultures. Cultures with highly linear orientations toward time see it as a limited resource to be used efficiently, and work toward quick methods of problem solving or coming to agreement. In cultures with a less linear view of time, there is less pressure to come to a quick solution to problems. With respect to time, cultures also differ in how many things are expected to happen at the same time: Monochronic cultures expect things to happen one at a time, in sequence; for example, people are expected to take turns in talking and to discuss one issue at a time. This differs from polychronic cultures, where a lot of different things go on at one time and, from an outsider's perspective, "everyone is talking at once."

Two important areas where this anthropological emphasis on cross-cultural differences in communication are critical for success are international business and conflict resolution. Edward Hall's primer, *Hidden Differences: Doing Business with the Japanese* (1987), gives advice to Americans on how these cultural differences can get in the way of successful business outcomes. Just to give one example, when Americans meet with Japanese businesspeople, they try to make rigid time commitments, expressed in schedules and deadlines, even if this means cutting short human interactions, such as long, elaborate dinners or long, recreational weekends, which they would view as a distraction from the main business at hand. The Japanese, on the other hand, consider time commitments as a goal to be achieved if possible, but never at the expense of building a personal relationship. While the American businessman tries to adhere rigidly to a preplanned schedule, the Japanese businessman is willing to remain more flexible, and changing plans is less problematical for him. He perceives the Americans' rush as an insult. Similarly, American businesspeople, coming from a low-context culture, have a need to ask for and receive much detailed information as part of the negotiation process; in contrast, the Japanese make it a point to learn what they need to know *beforehand*, so that they have all the information they need and can communicate in a more general, subtle, and unspoken manner. These, and many other cultural differences in both communication patterns and the relationship between employers and employees (Trice and Beyer 1993), frequently mean that international business negotiations become stalled or ultimately unsuccessful, because of a lack of awareness of cultural differences, or an inability to adjust behavior to different cultural patterns.

Another area where an awareness of cultural differences is crucial for success is in the field of conflict resolution. The description of the Kpelle moot in Chapter 12 introduced the idea that the goals and methods of handling conflict and disputes are different in different cultures. The successful application of nonadversarial methods of conflict resolution has led to an expansion of these approaches on an international scale, ranging from local communities where national forms of law are not working, to international disputes on such topics as the environment. Successfully applying conflict-resolution techniques in different cultures, or between parties who come from different cultures, means paying attention to the same kinds of factors that affect international business relationships. To give one example, in the United States, the use of third parties, such as mediators or arbitrators, is based on the assumption that these third parties have no prior relationship with the parties to a dispute, and thus can and will be neutral. In many cultures, this assumption does not hold true; rather, third parties are viewed as either enemies or allies, or conversely, the best and fairest third party is one that has long-standing relationships with both parties to a conflict.

These two briefly described applications of anthropological data and insights illustrate another way in which anthropology can be used to solve human problems, whether those problems are based on self-interest, such as that of an American corporation that wants to expand its market in Japan, or in a peace-making effort to deescalate violence on an international scale.

Problems in Making Use of Anthropology

It is clear that anthropologists do indeed work on problems that have direct implications for policy making in a wide variety of fields. And yet, it is equally clear that anthropological research is often overlooked when policy is made. The role of anthropologists in policy formation has been very uneven and probably hit its high point during World War II, when about 25 percent of anthropologists were employed in research and consultation directly related to the war effort. Margaret Mead, one of the anthropologists deeply involved in this effort, says of that period: "We had, in every government agency, people who were prepared to use what those of us who were outside . . . were producing" (1975:13). This is perhaps less true today, as the preceding discussions indicate. The question raised here is why problem-oriented or applied anthropological research has not made more of an impact than it has. Part of the answer has to do with the fact that the formulation of policy is a political process and does not proceed on the basis of available scientific evidence alone. Clearly, simply publishing their research findings is not an adequate way for anthropologists to change public policy. Anthropologists recognize that they must become more involved in the political process for their findings to be used.

Although the number of applied, or practicing, anthropologists is growing, there are still barriers to their widespread participation in policy formation. One is that the anthropological values of cultural relativity and holism appear to be in conflict with the partisanship required if one is employed by a government agency. Another conflict is that anthropologists, as scientists, see their main responsibility as illuminating the complexity of reality, whereas administrators feel the need to make decisions even when *all* of the evidence is not in. Third, anthropologists feel a conflict between the rational ethic of science and the pragmatic concerns central to the politician. The policy maker and politician are subject to political pressures that run counter to the scientist's ethic of basing conclusions on the facts, wherever they may lead, or however politically unpalatable they may be (Hinshaw 1980).

Now that so many more anthropologists are working in problem-oriented or applied research, the profession is beginning to examine more seriously the ways in which anthropologists can begin to overcome some of the barriers that keep their data from being constructively used in policy making and implementation. Clearly, one of the directions suggested by this chapter is the necessity to "study up," that is, to turn our attention to the study of power structures in the United States, in other societies, and on an international scale. This task has not yet been undertaken in a large way by anthropologists, but beginnings have been made. The anthropological perspective and methodology, which has proven so important in the study of small-scale societies, will undoubtedly prove equally significant and revealing when turned on elites, government bureaucracies, and corporations.

Because of the rapidly changing world and increasingly complex fieldwork situations in which anthropologists find themselves, those in this profession have also become more aware of the ethical dilemmas that confront them as a group and as individuals. Anthropologists are involved with their discipline, the individuals and groups with whom they do fieldwork, governments, and the study of issues affecting human welfare. Such complex involvements require making choices among conflicting values, and they generate ethical dilemmas. In some cases, these dilemmas may be so intense as to lead to a decision to drop a piece of research altogether. The statement of ethics adopted by the Council of the American Anthropological Association in May 1971 holds anthropologists responsible for the policies that may be formulated by governments on the basis of their research and for considering how these policies may affect various groups in the society. Their obligations to the public include a positive responsibility to speak out, both individually and collectively, in order to contribute to an "adequate definition of reality" that can become the basis of public policy and public opinion.

Just as all cultures change, the culture of anthropology is also changing, meeting the challenge of the founders of the discipline who saw in anthropology a means of leaving the world a better place than they found it.

Summary

1. Anthropologists can make important contributions to public policy formation by providing data on the groups toward which policies of change are directed. Examples of this are the anthropological studies on drug use and abuse and AIDS.

2. Anthropologists also act as advocates for populations they have studied — for example, by writing, testifying before policy-making bodies, being expert witnesses in court cases, and helping to protect the rights of indigenous peoples whose cultures are threatened by national development programs.

3. An important area of anthropological involvement has been in programs of planned change or development in peasant or village com-

munities. Although anthropological theory at one time emphasized a holistic and functional view of such communities, it has now moved to a conflict perspective, emphasizing economic and political constraints that come from the larger society.

4. Because policy making is a political process, anthropological data have not always been used to their fullest potential. Therefore, anthropologists need to turn their attention to the study of centers of power, where policy decisions are made.

Suggested Readings

Bodley, John H.
1984   *Anthropology and Contemporary Human Problems.* Palo Alto, Calif.: Mayfield. A work for the introductory student that attributes many contemporary problems to the culture pattern of modern, industrial civilizations, including problems of war, hunger, and destruction of the natural environment.

Feldman, Douglas, ed.
1990   *Culture and AIDS.* New York: Praeger. A valuable collection of articles written by anthropologists actively involved in AIDS research and activities, which emphasizes the importance of looking at AIDS as a cultural phenomenon, including suggesting culture-specific interventions that can lower risk.

Fiske, Shirley J., and Wulff, Robert M.
1987   *Anthropological Praxis: Translating Knowledge into Action.* Boulder, Colo.: Westview. A collection of short, readable papers on award-winning projects showing the wide range of things anthropologists are doing outside of academia.

Hall, Edward T., and Reed Hall, Mildred
1987   *Hidden Differences: Doing Business with the Japanese.* New York: Anchor/Doubleday. A primer on Japanese cultural values and attitudes that need to be understood for successful business dealings in a country vital to the interests of the United States.

Podolefsky, Aaron, and Brown, Peter J.
1989   *Applying Anthropology: An Introductory Reader.* Mountain View, Calif.: Mayfield. A wide-ranging and accessible reader with articles on the contemporary relevance of archeology, biological anthropology, and cultural anthropology.

Sheehan, Brian
1984   *The Boston School Integration Dispute: Social Change and Legal Maneuvers.* New York: Columbia University Press. An outstanding example of "studying up." Sheehan analyzes the factors in the Boston school integration controversy of the 1970s, paying particular attention to how changes in educational policies are related to political and economic interests and class structure.

Trice, Harrison M., and Beyer, Janice M.
1993   *The Cultures of Work Organizations.* Englewood Cliffs, N.J.: Prentice-Hall. A comprehensive account, useful for anthropologists and those in business, which integrates an enormous amount of data from many fields on cultures of the workplace.

van Willigen, John
1993   *Applied Anthropology: An Introduction* (Rev. Ed.). Westport, Conn.: Bergin and Garvey. An excellent primer for undergraduates in applied anthropology that addresses questions of research techniques, social impact assessment, evaluation research, action anthropology, community development, and ethics, as well as some practical points on job hunting.

A Chronology of Theories of Culture

The purpose of this annotated chronology of theories of culture, which is keyed to Chapter 3, "The Culture Concept and Anthropological Theory," is to provide a more complete listing of major works, set in their historical context, to help the interested student understand the relation of anthropology and theories of culture to some of the larger intellectual issues of the times in which they emerged.

The Enlightenment

In eighteenth-century Europe, the intellectual foundation of the culture concept and the discipline of cultural anthropology emerged through the following works:

1690 John Locke, *An Essay Concerning Human Understanding*. Oxford: Clarendon Press. This is a seminal Enlightenment work emphasizing the role of the environment as a conditioning factor in human thought and action.

1725 Giambattista Vico, *The New Science*. T. G. Bergin and M. H. Fisch, trans. Ithaca: Cornell University Press (1948).

1748 Baron Montesquieu, *The Spirit of Laws*. T. Nugent, trans. New York: Hafner (1949). Vico and Montesquieu's theories that social life and history are governed by regularities that are a consequence of natural law later became incorporated into anthropological theories of cultural evolution, in which the orderliness of human history was associated with the progressive perfection of humankind's rationality, cultures, and societies.

1795 Marquis de Condorcet, *Outline of the Intellectual Progress of Mankind*. Paris: Masson (1822). This work describes the progressive stages of human history, a precursor to the stages outlined by the early cultural evolutionists.

The Nineteenth Century: Classic Cultural Evolutionary Theories

Among the nineteenth-century intellectual trends that provided a lasting foundation for the emergence of anthropology were positivism, an attempt to approach the study of humankind with the same objective perspective as that used in the study of other natural phenomena; Darwinism, which laid bare the processes of biological evolution, through the principle of natural selection; and the political economy perspectives of Karl Marx.

The ideas of racial determinism, racism, and the application of the biological evolutionary process of "survival of the fittest," associated with the "social Darwinism" of Herbert Spencer, to explain social stratification within nations and the inequalities among nations, were convenient rationales for early industrial capitalism and European imperialism (Harris 1990).

1859 Charles Darwin, *Origin of Species*. New York: New American Library, Mentor (1958).

1859 Karl Marx, *The Critique of Political Economy*. I. N. Stone, trans. Chicago: International Library Publication Co. (1904). The preface to this work contains Marx's outline of the evolutionary stages of class society. The scheme of world historical stages outlined by Marx and by Friedrich Engels in his *Origin of the Family, Private Property and the State* (Ernest Untermann, trans. Moscow: Foreign Languages Publishing House, 1947 [orig. 1884]) examine how different concepts of property are associated with various modes of production.

1861 Henry Maine, *Ancient Law*. London: J. Murray. Maine presents cultural evolutionary theory emphasizing kinship as the basic principle of organization in nonindustrial, non-Western societies.

1871 Edward Tylor, *Primitive Cultural: Researches into the Development of Mythology, Philosophy, Religion, Language, Art and Custom*. London: J. Murray (New York: Harper Torchbooks, 1958). Tylor applies the comparative method to study religious beliefs as they evolved from animism to monotheism.

1977 Lewis Henry Morgan, *Ancient Society*. New York: Gordon (1974). Morgan foreshadows the anthropological concepts of the importance of kinship in prestate societies and the role of property in the development of social stratification.

The First Half of the Twentieth Century

Reactions against classic cultural evolution theory took several forms. There was greater explicit interest in diffusion in both Europe and the United States; the American historical school, under the leadership of Franz Boas, rejected the search for laws of culture and emphasized the uniqueness of cultures and the importance of fieldwork; an emphasis on the synchronic study of cultures as wholes, which rejected the study of history, emerged in Britian; and interest in cultural materialism waned.

Historical Particularism

Franz Boas and his students rejected cultural evolutionary interests and emphasized the study of particular cultures (in Boas's case, the Kwakiutl of the Pacific Northwest) and, later, the study of the relationship of culture to personality.

1911 Franz Boas, *The Mind of Primitive Man*. New York: Macmillan. Boas explicates the position that there are no laws of cultural development, while at the same time, he reaffirms the importance of psychic unity in human culture. His *Race, Language and Culture* (Chicago: University of Chicago Press, 1988 [first published in 1940]) presents a full range of his work, beginning in 1887.

1915 Alfred Kroeber, "The Eighteen Professions." *American Anthropologist* 17:283–89. This is the most explicit statement of Boas's historical particularism. Kroeber's insistence that culture has influence above the psychology of individuals ("The Superorganic," *American Anthropologist* 19:163–213 [1917]); his contribution to the development of the idea of culture areas ("Cultural and Natural Areas of Native North America." *Univer-*

sity of *California Publications in American Archeology and Ethnology* 38 [1939]); and his work *Configurations of Culture Growth* (Berkeley: University of California Press, 1944) both reflected and influenced Boasian anthropological interests.

1917   Clark Wissler, *The American Indian: An Introduction to the Anthropology of the New World*. New York: D. C. McMurtrie. Wissler uses the concepts of diffusion and cultural areas to explain cultural similarities and differences among North American Indian groups.

1920   Robert Lowie, *Primitive Society*. New York: Boni and Liveright. Another Boasian-type critique of cultural evolution, which also emphasizes the Boasian interest in the psychological meanings that members of a culture attach to their behavior.

Culture and Personality

Freudian theory and Boas's interest in the meaning of culture led to the study of the relationship between the individual and culture, particularly during the 1920s and 1930s.

1927   Bronislaw Malinowski, *Sex and Repression in Savage Society*. London: Routledge and Kegan Paul (1953). This ethnographic study of the matrilineal Trobriand Islands culture is presented as a refutation of Freud's theory of the universality of the Oedipus complex.

1928   Margaret Mead, *Coming of Age in Samoa*. New York: Morrow (1971). A student of Boas and Ruth Benedict, Mead, in her study of adolescence in Samoa, was influenced by Boas's cultural determinist position in the nature/nurture controversy.

1934   Ruth Benedict, *Patterns of Culture*. New York: Houghton Mifflin (1961). Benedict's presentation of cultures as unique configurations is based on psychological concepts.

1949   *Selected Writings of Edward Sapir*. David Mandelbaum, ed. Berkeley: University of California Press. Sapir is an American anthropologist who wrote on patterns in language, culture, and personality, and was an important influence in the American culture-and-personality field.

1953   John Whiting and Irving Child, *Child Training and Personality: A Cross-Cultural Study*. Westport, Conn.: Greenwood (1984). This culture-and-

personality study was influenced by the reemergence of cultural materialism.

Functionalism

Functionalist theory is mainly associated with British Social Anthropology, and was a dominant perspective in the first half of the twentieth century. It emphasized the ways in which cultural elements serve the needs of individuals or society.

1893   Émile Durkheim, *Division of Labor in Society*. G. Simpson, trans. New York: Macmillan (1933); **1895** *The Rules of the Sociological Method*. S. Solovay and J. Mueller, trans. New York: Free Press (1938); **1912** *The Elementary Forms of the Religious Life*. J. W. Swain, trans. London: Allen and Unwin (1915). Durkheim is the French sociologist whose positivism and views of society as an organism influenced functionalist theories in anthropology.

1922   Bronislaw Malinowski, *Argonauts of the Western Pacific*. New York: E. P. Dutton (1961). This masterful ethnography introduces Malinowski's theory of functionalism, which maintains that culture is the instrument that serves to meet the biological, psychological, and social needs of human beings.

1952   A. R. Radcliffe-Brown, *Structure and Function in Primitive Society*. London: Oxford University Press (1965). The British school of structural functionalism emphasized how cultural elements contribute to the ongoing functioning of society. Developed in ethnographies of African tribal societies in European colonies from the 1930s to the 1950s, structural functional theory provided a convenient rationale for the British colonial policy of indirect rule.

Cultural Idealism

Several theories of culture, developed in Europe and the United States, explain culture as collective ideas existing in the minds of members of a society. Growing out of Emile Durkheim's concept of culture as a "collective consciousness" and influenced by structural linguistics, French structuralism emphasized the meaning of cultural ideas and, later, their foundation in the structure of the human mind. In the United States, this perspective is represented by the cognitive theories of the "new" ethnography, componential analysis, and ethnosemantics.

1924 Marcel Mauss, *The Gift*. I. Cunnison, trans. New York: Norton (1990). The focus is on reciprocity in non-Western, non-industrial society.

1956 Ward Goodenough, "Componential Analysis and the Study of Meaning." *Language* 32: 195–216.

1974 Claude Lévi-Strauss, *Structural Anthropology*. Vol. I, New York: Basic; Vol. II, Chicago: University of Chicago Press (1983).

Cultural Materialism

The revived interest in the material basis of culture began in the 1940s and continues to the present.

1955 Julian Steward, *The Theory of Culture Change*. Urbana: University of Illinois Press (1972). Steward presents the ecological, materialist, and evolutionary perspectives of the cultural materialist revival, as well as the return to the classic evolutionists' interest in theories of causality and regularity in culture.

1959 Leslie White, *The Evolution of Culture*. New York: McGraw-Hill.

1968 Marvin Harris, *The Rise of Anthropological Theory: A History of Theories of Culture*. New York: Harper (1990). The most prominent contemporary cultural materialist evaluates anthropological theories' contributions to cultural materialism.

1982 Eric R. Wolf, *Europe and the People without History*. Berkeley: University of California Press. Wolf presents an influential world systems approach to cultural change, which has been significantly responsible for reviving the current interest in political economy in cultural anthropology.

Interpretive Anthropology

Influenced by postmodernism and the concept of culture as a system of meaning, interpretivist anthropology represents, along with cultural materialism, the dominant contemporary approach to the study of culture.

1973 Clifford Geertz, *The Interpretation of Cultures*. New York: Basic Books. This is a collection of essays by the most eloquent spokesman for the view that anthropology is the study of culture as a system of meaning.

1986 George E. Marcus and Michael M. J. Fischer, *Anthropology as Cultural Critique: An Experimental Moment in the Human Sciences*. (Chicago: University of Chicago Press). A discussion of the postmodern "crisis of representation" places contemporary views of ethnography and interpretivist anthropology in a historical context.

Glossary

Acculturation   The process that takes place when contact between two societies is so prolonged that one or both cultures change substantially.

Achieved status   A social position that an individual chooses or achieves on his or her own.

Adaptation   The ways in which living populations relate to the environment so that they can survive and reproduce.

Age grade   Categories of persons who fall within a particular, culturally distinguished age range.

Age set   A feature of social organization in which a group of persons of similar age and sex move through some or all of life's stages together.

Agriculture   See **Intensive cultivation**.

All-purpose money   Money that serves as a means of exchange, a standard of value, and a means of payment for a wide variety of goods and services.

American historical tradition   The collective referent for the anthropologists in the United States who, under the influence of Franz Boas, turned away from the attempt to discover laws of culture and focused instead on understanding particular cultures.

Animatism   The belief in impersonal supernatural power (sometimes called *mana*).

Animism   The belief that living creatures and inanimate objects have life and personality, referred to as spirits, ghosts, or gods.

Anthropology   The comparative study of humankind.

Applied anthropology   The organized interaction between professional anthropologists and both private and public policy-making bodies; the application of anthropology to the solution of human problems.

Archeology   A specialized field of cultural anthropology focused on human cultures that have existed in the past and for which there are no written records.

Art   The process and products of human skill applied to any activity that meets standards of beauty in a particular society.

Ascribed status   A social position an individual is born into.

Authority   Power exercised with the consent of the members of the society (legitimate power).

Avunculocal residence rule   System under which a married couple resides with the husband's mother's brother.

Balanced reciprocity   An exchange of goods of nearly equal value, with a clear obligation to return them within a specified time limit.

Band   The basic social unit in many hunting and gathering societies, made up of fewer than one hundred people related to one another through blood ties or marriage.

Bifurcation   A principle of classifying kin under which different kinship terms are used for the mother's side of the family and the father's side of the family.

Bilateral descent rule   System under which both maternal and paternal lines are used in reckoning descent.

Bilocal residence rule   System under which a married couple has the choice of living with the husband's or wife's family.

Binary oppositions   Dualistic contrast between categories, such as male/female and light/dark, associated with French structuralist theory.

Biological (or physical) anthropology   The study of human evolution and the biological processes involved in human adaptation.

Bride service   Work that the groom performs for his bride's family for a variable length of time either before or after the marriage.

Bridewealth   Goods presented by the groom's kin to the bride's kin to legitimize a marriage.

Call system   Form of communication among non-human primates composed of a limited number of sounds that are tied to specific stimuli in the environment.

Capital   Goods used to produce other goods, or wealth invested to purchase capital goods.

Capitalist society   A society in which people work for wages, land and capital goods are privately owned, and capital is invested for individual profit.

Caste system   A system of stratification based on birth and in which movement from one stratum (caste) to another is not possible.

Chiefdom   A society with social ranking in which political integration is achieved through an *office* of centralized leadership.

Clan   A unilineal kinship group whose members believe themselves to be descended from a common ancestor but who cannot trace this link genealogically.

Class system   A form of social stratification in which the different strata form a continuum and in which social mobility is possible.

Cognition   The ways in which human beings perceive, understand, and organize their responses to the universe.

Cognitive anthropology   A theoretical approach that defines culture in terms of the rules and meanings underlying human behavior, rather than behavior itself.

Collateral kin   Kin related through a linking relative, such as a man and his father's brother.

Communal cult   A type of religious organization in which ordinary people hold rituals for the community or segments of it.

Communication   The act of transmitting information that influences the behavior of another organism.

Composite (or compound) family   An aggregate of nuclear families linked by a common spouse.

Configurationalism   The theory which holds that each culture is a unique configuration or pattern of elements and values.

Conflict theory   A theory of social stratification which holds that the natural condition of society is constant change and conflict. The inequality in systems of social stratification is considered evidence of this conflict.

Consanguineal family   Individuals who are related by birth and descent.

Controlled cross-cultural comparison   An anthropological method that uses comparable ethnographic data from many societies and tests particular hypotheses.

Conventionality   Refers to the feature of human language that words are only conventionally or arbitrarily connected to the things for which they stand.

Cosmology   The system of beliefs that deals with fundamental questions in the cosmic and social order.

Cross cousins   Individuals related through siblings of the opposite sex at the parental generation.

Cultural anthropology   The study of human behavior that is learned, rather than genetically transmitted, and that is typical of a particular human group.

Cultural ecology   A theoretical approach that regards cultural patterns as adaptive responses to the basic problems of human survival and reproduction.

Cultural evolution   The process by which new cultural forms emerge out of older ones.

Cultural integration   The tendency of the parts of a culture to be consistent or in harmony with one another.

Cultural materialism   A theoretical perspective which holds that the primary task of anthropology is to account for the similarities and differences among cultures and that this can best be done by studying the material constraints to which human existence is subjected.

Cultural relativity   An attempt to understand cultural patterns from the "inside" and to see the traits of a culture in terms of the cultural whole.

Culture (general)   The learned and shared kinds of behavior that make up the major instrument of human adaptation.

Culture (particular)   The way of life characteristic of a particular human society.

Culture area   A broad geographical area in which a number of societies make similar adaptations to a particular ecological zone and through diffusion come to develop similar cultural patterns.

Descent   The culturally established affiliation between a child and one or both parents.

Descent group   A group of kin who are lineal descendants of a common ancestor, extending beyond two generations.

Deviance   Departures from cultural norms regarded negatively by society.

Diffusion   The spread of cultural elements from one culture to another through cultural contact.

Divination   A magical practice directed at obtaining useful information from a supernatural authority.

Domestic group   A household unit that usually, but not always, consists of members of a family.

Double descent   The tracing of descent through both matrilineal and patrilineal links, each of which is utilized for different purposes.

Dowry   Presentation of goods by the bride's kin to the family of the groom or to the couple.

Ecclesiastical cult   A type of religious organization in which access to supernatural power is mediated by a professional and specialized clergy.

Economic system   The norms governing production, distribution, and consumption of goods and services.

Economizing   Choosing a course of action that maximizes the well-being and material profit of the individual.

Ecosystem   Term referring to the interaction between human populations and their environment.

Egalitarian society   A society in which no individual or group has more privileged access to resources, power, or prestige than any other.

Ego   The kinship status from which a kinship diagram is constructed.

Emic (perspective)   A perspective that uses concepts, categories, and distinctions that are meaningful to participants in a culture.

Enculturation   A term referring to the specific ways in which human infants and children learn to be adult members of their society.

Endogamy   The rule prescribing that marriage must be *within* a particular group.

Ethnicity   A group identity based on culture, language, religion, or a common attachment to a place or kin ties.

Ethnocentrism   Perceiving and judging other cultures from the perspective of one's own culture.

Ethnography   The major research tool of cultural anthropology; includes both fieldwork among people in society and the written results of fieldwork.

Ethnology   Refers to the comparative statements about cultural and social processes that are based on cross-cultural ethnographic data.

Ethos   The dominant theme or value of a culture.

Etic (perspective)   A perspective using concepts, categories, and rules derived from science; an outsider's perspective, which may not be meaningful to native participants in a culture.

Exogamy   A rule which specifies that an individual must marry *outside* the group covered by the rule.

Extended (or consanguineal) family   Family based on blood relations extending over three or more generations.

Extensive cultivation   See **Horticulture**.

Fieldwork   The firsthand, systematic exploration of a society. It involves living with a group of people and participating in and observing their behavior.

Folklore   Primarily oral traditions that have anonymous authorship and include at least two variations of the same form.

Foraging   See **Hunting and gathering**.

Formal economics   Theory holding that human material wants are unlimited but the means for achieving these wants is finite and that people make choices among alternative courses of action in a rational manner.

Functionalism   The anthropological theory that culture functions to serve the needs of individuals in society.

Gender   The social classification of masculine and feminine.

Genderlect   Refers to the consistent variations in private and public speaking patterns between males and females.

Generalized reciprocity   A distribution of goods with no immediate or specific return expected.

Government   A social institution specifically concerned with making and enforcing public policy.

Horticulture   Production of plants using a simple, nonmechanized technology; fields are not used continuously (also called extensive cultivation).

Hunting and gathering   A food-getting strategy that does not involve food production or domestication of animals (also called foraging).

Ideology (political)   The shared values and beliefs that legitimize the distribution and use of power in a particular society.

Incest taboos   Prohibitions on sexual relations between relatives or persons classified as relatives.

Independent invention   The process whereby similar cultural features develop without involving cultural exchange.

Individualistic cult   A form of religious organization in which each person may be her or his own religious specialist.

Initiation rite   A ritual that marks the passage from childhood to adult status.

Innovation   A new variation on an existing cultural pattern that is subsequently accepted by other members of the society.

Intelligence   The many skills and capacities that are part of the adaptive responses human beings make to their environment.

Intensive cultivation   A form of food production in which fields are in permanent cultivation using plows, draft animals, and techniques of soil and water control (also called agriculture).

Interpretive anthropology   A theoretical approach that emphasizes that culture is a system of meaning and that the aim of cultural anthropology is to interpret the meanings of cultural acts for their participants.

Invention   New combinations of existing cultural elements.

Kindred   A descent group made up of all the people related to an individual.

Kinship   A culturally defined relationship established on the basis of blood ties or through marriage.

Kinship system   The totality of kin relations, kin groups, and terms for classifying kin in a society.

Kula   A pattern of exchange among trading partners in the Trobriand Islands and other islands that are part of the kula ring.

Law   Those social norms whose neglect or violation is regularly met by the application of force by those in a society who have the socially recognized privilege of doing so.

Leveling mechanism   A practice, value, or form of social organization that results in an evening out of wealth within a society.

Levirate   The custom whereby a man marries the widow of a deceased brother.

Life chances   The opportunity of an individual to fulfill or fail to fulfill his or her potential in society.

Lineage   A group of kin whose members trace descent from a known common ancestor.

Lineal kin   Blood relations linked through descent, such as Ego, Ego's mother, Ego's grandmother, and Ego's daughter.

Linguistics   A field of cultural anthropology that specializes in the study of human languages.

Magic   An attempt to mechanistically control supernatural forces.

Mana   Sacred force, associated with Polynesian nobility, causing individuals to be taboo.

Market exchange   A system in which goods and services are bought and sold at a money price determined by the impersonal forces of supply and demand.

Marriage The customs, rules, and obligations that establish a special relationship between a sexually cohabiting adult male and female, between them and any children they produce, and between the kin of the bride and groom.

Matrilineage A lineage formed by descent in the female line.

Matrilineal descent A rule that affiliates an individual to kin related through the mother only.

Matrilocal residence rule System under which a husband goes to live with his wife's family.

Modernization The process in which traditional societies move technologically and socially in the direction of industrialized nations.

Monogamy The rule that permits a person to be married to only one person at a time.

Monotheism The belief in one god.

Morpheme The smallest unit of a language that has a meaning.

Myth A narrative that tells of the creation of the universe through the agency of supernatural beings.

Negative reciprocity Exchange between equals conducted only for the purpose of material advantage and the desire to get something for nothing.

Neolocal residence rule System under which a couple establishes an independent household after marriage.

Network analysis An approach to understanding the informal and fluid social relations that are typical in complex societies by mapping the links individuals have with others.

Niche Specialized adaptation to a local environment by a group of people.

Nomadism The constant mobility of human groups in pursuit of food (as in foraging) or a form of pastoralism in which the whole social group (men, women, children, and animals) move in search of pasture.

Norm An ideal cultural pattern that guides human behavior in a particular society.

Nuclear family The family organized around the conjugal tie (the relationship between husband and wife). A nuclear family consists of a husband, a wife, and their children.

Ordeal A means of determining guilt or innocence by having an accused party submit to tests believed to be under supernatural control.

Paleontology The discipline that traces the evolution of humankind in the fossil record.

Parallel cousins The children of siblings of the same sex at the parental generation.

Pastoralism A food-getting strategy that depends on the care of domesticated herd animals. It occurs in areas where, for a variety of reasons, large human populations cannot be supported through agriculture.

Patrilineage A lineage formed by descent in the male line.

Patrilineal descent rule A rule that affiliates children with kinsmen of both sexes related through males only.

Patrilocal residence rule System under which a bride goes to live with her husband's family.

Peasants Food-producing populations that are incorporated politically, economically, and culturally into nation-states.

Phoneme The smallest significant sound unit in a language. A phonemic system is the sound system of a language.

Phonetic laws Regularities in sound changes that can be traced by linguists.

Phonology The sound system of a language.

Phratry A unilineal descent group composed of a number of clans who feel themselves to be closely related.

Political ideology See **Ideology (political)**.

Political organization The patterned ways in which authority is used to coordinate and regulate human behavior in the public interest.

Political process The ways in which individuals and groups use power to achieve public goals.

Polyandry The rule permitting a woman to have more than one husband at a time.

Polygamy The general term for the rule allowing more than one spouse.

Polygyny The rule permitting a man to have more than one wife at a time.

Polytheism The belief in many gods.

Potlatch   A form of competitive giveaway practiced by the Kwakiutl and other groups of the Northwest Coast of North America.

Power   The ability to produce intended effects on oneself, other human beings, and situations.

Prayer   Any conversation held with spirits or gods.

Prestige   Social honor or respect.

Primate   The *order* within the mammalian *class*, which includes monkeys, apes, and humans.

Psychic unity   The anthropological proposition that all human groups have the same mental capacities and ability to think logically.

Psychological anthropology   A specialization in cultural anthropology that seeks to understand the relation between psychological processes and cultural practices.

Racism   The belief that some human populations are superior, or inferior, to others because of inherited, genetically transmitted characteristics.

Rank society   A society in which there are institutionalized differences in prestige but no important restrictions on access to basic resources.

Rebellion   The attempt of a group within society to force a redistribution of resources and power.

Reciprocity   A mutual give and take among people of equal status.

Redistribution   A form of exchange in which goods are collected from or contributed by members of the group and then redistributed to the group, often in the form of ceremonial feasts.

Reflexivity   The idea that anthropological fieldworkers, as observers of behavior, need to analyze their own personal and cultural experience as a source of influence on their observations and as a resource in the analysis of their own and other cultures.

Religion   The beliefs and practices concerned with supernatural beings, powers, and forces.

Revitalization movement   A consciously organized effort to construct a more satisfying culture.

Revolution   An attempt to overthrow the existing form of political organization.

Rites of intensification   Religious rituals directed toward the welfare of a group or society.

Rites of passage   Rituals that mark the transition of an individual from one social status to another.

Ritual (religious)   A patterned act that involves the manipulation of religious symbols.

Sapir-Whorf hypothesis   The hypothesis that perceptions and understandings of time, space, and matter are in part conditioned by the structure of a language.

Secularism   A trend in cultural beliefs and/or practices emphasizing nonreligious or nonsupernatural elements.

Segmentary lineage system   A form of sociopolitical organization in which multiple descent groups (usually patrilineages) form at different levels and function in different contexts.

Semantics   The subsystem of a language that relates form to meaning.

Sex   The biological difference between male and female.

Sexual stratification   The system of inequalities between men and women in a particular culture.

Shaman   A person who is socially recognized as having special supernatural power used on behalf of human clients.

Slash and burn   See **Swidden**.

Social function   The contribution a cultural trait makes to the maintenance and solidarity of a social system.

Socialization   The learning processes through which human cultural traditions are passed on from one generation to the next.

Social mobility   Movement from one social class to another.

Social network   A set of direct and indirect links between an individual and other people.

Social stratification   A system of institutionalized inequalities of wealth, power, and prestige.

Society   A group of people who are dependent on one another for survival or well-being and who share a particular way of life.

Sociolinguistics   An anthropological specialty interested in speech performance.

Sorcery   The use of magic with the intent of harming another person.

Sororate   The custom whereby, when a man's wife dies, her sister is given to him as a wife.

State A hierarchical and centralized form of political organization in which the central government has a legal monopoly over the use of force.

Status A social position within a social structure; a role is the behavioral norms associated with a social status.

Stratified society A society with formal, permanent social and economic inequality, in which some individuals are denied access to basic resources.

Structural functionalism An anthropological theory developed by A. R. Radcliffe-Brown that emphasizes the ways in which different structural elements in a social system contribute to social solidarity.

Structuralism (French) A theoretical perspective in anthropology that attempts to analyze the deep meanings underlying cultural elements and the rules by which cultural meanings are produced.

Subculture A system of perceptions, values, beliefs, and customs that are significantly different from those of the larger, dominant culture, yet which also shares some aspects of that culture.

Substantive economics The study of economic systems as part of a total sociocultural system.

Swidden A form of cultivation in which a field is cleared by felling the trees and burning the brush (sometimes called slash and burn cultivation).

Syncretic religion A syncretic religion is one that emerges from the combining of elements of two or more other religions.

Syntax The part of grammar that has to do with the arrangement of words to form phrases and sentences.

Theory A general idea that attempts to explain and ultimately predict the interrelationships among phenomena in any scientific discipline.

Totem A plant or animal considered to have an intimate relationship with a human group, sometimes as an ancestor.

Transformational generative grammar A model of language that focuses on the relationship of deep structures of sentences to surface structures, and the rules that relate the two.

Transhumance A pastoralist pattern in which herd animals are moved regularly throughout the year to different areas as pasture becomes available.

Tribe A culturally distinct population, the members of which consider themselves to be descended from the same ancestor.

Unilineal descent rule A rule that specifies that membership in a descent group is based on links through either the maternal or paternal line, but not both.

Values Culturally defined ideals of what is true, right, and beautiful.

Vocabulary The total stock of words in a language.

Voluntary association A social group based on voluntary membership, typically found in complex and modernizing societies.

Wealth The accumulation of material resources or access to the means of producing these resources.

Witchcraft The attempt to harm people through supernatural means and powers, using only psychological processes and not any material objects.

World systems theory A model of global relationships emphasizing the integration of all people and cultures within a world capitalist system.

Bibliography

Aberle, David F., et al.

1963 "The Incest Taboo and Mating Patterns of Animals." *American Anthropologist* 65:253–65.

Abrahams, Roger D.

1970 *Deep Down in the Jungle*. Chicago: Aldine.

Abu-Lughod, Lila

1987 *Veiled Sentiments: Honor and Poetry in a Bedouin Society*. Berkeley: University of California Press.

Alland, Alexander, Jr.

1972 *The Human Imperative*. New York: Columbia University Press.

Allen, Catherine

1989 *The Hold Life Has: Coco and Cultural Identity in an Andean Community*. Washington, D.C.: Smithsonian Institute.

Allen, J. P. B., and van Buren, Paul, eds.

1971 *Chomsky: Selected Readings*. London: Oxford University Press.

Altorki, Soraya, and El-Solh, Camillia Fawzi, eds.

1988 *Arab Women in the Field: Studying Your Own Society*. Syracuse, N.Y.: Syracuse University Press.

Arens, W.

1979 *The Man Eating Myth: Anthropology and Anthropophagy*. New York: Oxford University Press.

1976 "Professional Football: An American Symbol and Ritual." In *The American Dimension*. W. Arens and Susan P. Montague, eds. Pp. 3–14. Port Washington, N.Y.: Alfred.

Arnould, Eric J.

1989 "Anthropology and West African Development: A Political Economic Critique and Auto-Critique." *Human Organization* 48(2):135–48.

Baker, Paul T., ed.

1978 *The Biology of High-Altitude Peoples*. Cambridge: Cambridge University Press.

Baker, Randall

1981 "'Development' and the Pastoral People of Karamoja, Northeastern Uganda: An Example of Treatment Symptoms." In *Contemporary Anthropology: An Anthology*. Daniel Bates and Susan Lees, eds. Pp. 66–78. New York: Alfred A. Knopf.

Balicki, Asen

1963 "Shamanistic Behavior among the Netsilik Eskimos." *Southwestern Journal of Anthropology* 19:380–96.

Barth, Frederik

1969 *Ethnic Groups and Boundaries*. New York: Allen and Unwin.

1964 *Nomads of South Persia*. New York: Humanities Press.

1956 "Ecologic Relationships of Ethnic Groups in Swat, North Pakistan." *American Anthropologist* 58:1079–89.

Bascom, William
1970 "Ponapean Prestige Economy." In *Cultures of the Pacific: Selected Readings*. Thomas G. Harding and Ben J. Wallace, eds. Pp. 85–93. New York: Free Press.

Basso, Keith
1979 *Portraits of "the Whiteman."* New York: Cambridge University Press.

Baum, A., and Epstein, V. M., eds.
1978 *Human Response to Crowding*. New York: Wiley.

Beidelman, Thomas O.
1971 *The Kaguru: A Matrilineal People of East Africa*. New York: Holt, Rinehart and Winston.
1966 "The Ox and Nuer Sacrifice." *Man* (new series) I:453–67.

Benedict, Ruth
1961 *Patterns of Culture*. Boston: Houghton Mifflin (first publ. 1934).
1946 *The Chrysanthemum and the Sword*. Boston: Houghton Mifflin.
1938 "Continuities and Discontinuities in Culture Conditioning." *Psychiatry* 1:161–67.
1934 "Anthropology and the Abnormal." *Journal of General Psychology* 10:791–808.

Benet, Sula
1976 *How to Live to Be 100: The Life Style of the People of the Caucasus*. New York: Dial Press.

Berreman, Gerald D.
1988 "Race, Caste, and Other Invidious Distinctions in Social Stratification." In *Anthropology for the Nineties: Introductory Readings*. Johnetta Cole, ed. Pp. 485–518. New York: Free Press.
1981 *Social Inequality: Comparative and Developmental Approaches*. New York: Academic Press.
1962 "Behind Many Masks: Ethnography and Impression Management in a Himalayan Village." Society for Applied Anthropology, Monograph 4. Ithaca, N.Y.: Cornell University Press.

1959 "Caste in India and the United States." *American Journal of Sociology* LXVI: 120–27.

Berry, J. W.
1974 "Ecological and Cultural Factors in Spatial Perceptual Development." In *Culture and Cognition: Readings in Cross-Cultural Psychology*. J. W. Berry and P. R. Dasen, eds. Pp. 129–40. London: Methuen (first publ. 1971).

Bettelheim, Bruno
1962 *Symbolic Wounds*. Rev. ed. New York: Collier.

Boas, Franz
1988 *Race, Language and Culture*. Chicago: University of Chicago Press (first publ. 1940).

Bodley, John H.
1990 *Victims of Progress*. 3rd ed. Mountain View, Calif.: Mayfield.

Bohannan, Paul
1971 "Artist and Critic in African Society." In *Anthropology and Art*. Charlotte M. Otten, ed. Pp. 172–81. Garden City, N.Y.: Natural History Press.

Bonsignore, John J.
1992 "Multinational Corporations: Getting Started." *Focus on Law Studies* 7(1):10–11.

Bott, Elizabeth
1957 *Family and Social Network: Roles, Norms and Extended Relationships in Ordinary Urban Families*. London: Tavistock Publications.

Bourgois, Philippe
1989 "Crack in Spanish Harlem: Culture and Economy in the Inner City." *Anthropology Today* 5, 4.

Bracey, Dorothy
1985 "The System of Justice and the Concept of Human Nature in the People's Republic of China." *Justice Quarterly* 2(1):139–44.

Brady, Ivan
1982 The Man Eating Myth. Review article. *American Anthropologist* 84:595–610.

Briggs, Jean
1974 "Eskimo Women: Makers of Men." In *Many Sisters*. Carolyn J. Matthiasson, ed. Pp. 261–304. New York: Free Press.

Brody, Hugh
1981   *Maps and Dreams*. New York: Pantheon.

Bronfenbrenner, Urie
1974   "The Origins of Alienation." *Scientific American* 2:53–61.

Brooks, Charles R.
1992   "Using Ethnography in the Evaluation of Drug Prevention and Intervention Programs." *International Journal of the Addictions*, vol. 27. In press.
1989   *The Hare Krishnas in India*. Princeton, N.J.: Princeton University Press.

Brown, Judith
1965   "A Cross Cultural Study of Female Initiation Rites." *American Anthropologist* 65:837–55.

Brown, P., and Podolefsky, A.
1976   "Population Density, Agricultural Intensity, Land Tenure, and Group Size in the New Guinea Highlands." *Ethnology* 15:211–38.

Buck, Pem Davidson
1989   "Cargo-Cult Discourse: Myth and the Rationalization of Labor Relations in Papua New Guinea." *Dialectical Anthropology* 13:157–71.

Burling, Robbins
1970   "Black English." In *Man's Many Voices*. Robbins Burling, ed. New York: Holt, Rinehart and Winston.

Cage, John
1961   *Silence*. Middletown, Conn.: Wesleyan University Press.

Callimanopulos, Dominique
1982   "The Tourist Trap — Introduction." *Cultural Survival Quarterly* 6:3–5.

Cannon, Walter B.
1942   "The 'Voodoo' Death." *American Anthropologist* 44:169–80.

Carneiro, Robert
1970   "A Theory of the Origin of the State." *Science* 169:733–38.

Castaneda, Carlos
1968   *The Teachings of Don Juan: A Yaqui Way of Knowledge*. Berkeley: University of California Press.

Caudill, William
1973   "Psychiatry and Anthropology: The Individual and his Nexus." In *Cultural Illness and Health*. Laura Nader and Thomas W. Maretski, eds. Pp. 67–77. Washington, D.C.: American Anthropological Association.

Chagnon, Napoleon
1983   *Yanomamo: The Fierce People*. 3rd ed. New York: Holt, Rinehart and Winston.

Chance, Norman A.
1984   *China's Urban Villagers*. New York: Holt, Rinehart and Winston.

Childe, V. Gordon
1951   *Man Makes Himself*. New York: Mentor (first publ. 1936).

Chodorow, Nancy
1974   "Family Structure and Female Personality." In *Women, Culture, and Society*. Michelle Rosaldo and Louise Lamphere, eds. Pp. 43–66. Stanford, Calif.: Stanford University Press.

Chomsky, Noam
1965   *Syntactic Structures*. London: Mouton.

Clark, Margaret
1973   "Contributions of Cultural Anthropology to the Study of the Aged." In *Cultural Illness and Health*. Laura Nader and Thomas W. Maretski, eds. Pp. 78–88. Washington, D.C.: American Anthropological Association.

Cohen, Abner
1969   *Custom and Politics in Urban Africa*. London: Routledge and Kegan Paul.

Cohen, Ronald, and Service, Elman R., eds.
1978   *Origins of the State: The Anthropology of Political Evolution*. Philadelphia: ISHI.

Cohen, Yehudi, ed.
1971   *Man in Adaptation: The Institutional Framework*. Chicago: Aldine.

Cole, Michael, et al.
1971   *The Cultural Context of Learning and Thinking*. New York: Basic Books.

Cole, Michael, and Scribner, S.
1974   *Culture and Thought*. New York: Wiley.

Conklin, Harold C.
1969   "An Ethnoecological Approach to Shifting Agriculture." In *Environmental and Cultural Behavior*. Andrew P. Vayda, ed. Pp. 221–33. Garden City, N.Y.: Natural History Press.

Coon, Carleton S.
1971   *The Hunting Peoples*. Boston: Little, Brown.

Cronin, Constance
1977   "Illusion and Reality in Sicily." In *Sexual Stratification*. Alice Schlegel, ed. Pp. 67–94. New York: Columbia University Press.

Dalton, George
1967   "Primitive Money." In *Tribal and Peasant Economics*. George Dalton, ed. Pp. 254–81. Garden City, N.Y.: Natural History Press.

Damas, David
1972   "The Copper Eskimo." In *Hunters and Gatherers Today*. M. G. Bicchieri, ed. Pp. 3–50. New York: Holt, Rinehart and Winston.

D'Andrade, Roy G.
1974   "Sex Differences and Cultural Conditioning." In *Culture and Personality*. Robert A. LeVine, ed. Pp. 16–37. Chicago: Aldine.

Dasgupta, B.
1980   *The New Agrarian Technology and India*. New York: Macmillan.

Denich, Betty
1974   "Sex and Power in the Balkans." In *Women, Culture, and Society*. Michelle Rosaldo and Louise Lamphere, eds. Pp. 243–62. Stanford, Calif.: Stanford University Press.

Dentan, Robert
1968   *The Semai: A Nonviolent People of Malaya*. New York: Holt, Rinehart and Winston.

DeVita, Philip R., ed.
1992   *The Naked Anthropologist: Tales from around the World*. Belmont, Calif.: Wadsworth.

DeVita, Philip R., and Armstrong, James D.
1993   *Distant Mirrors: America as a Foreign Culture*. Belmont, Calif.: Wadsworth.

DeVos, George and Wagatsuma, Hiroshi, eds.
1966   *Japan's Invisible Race: Case Studies in Culture and Personality*. Berkeley: University of California Press.

di Leonardo, Micaela
1984   *The Varieties of Ethnic Experience*. Ithaca, N.Y.: Cornell University Press.

Divale, William Tulio, and Harris, Marvin
1976   "Population, Warfare and the Male Supremacist Complex." *American Anthropologist* 78:521–38.

Dollar, Bruce
1980   *Child Care in China: Society as It Is*. New York: Macmillan.

Dollard, John
1937   *Caste and Class in a Southern Town*. New Haven, Conn.: Yale University Press.

Dominguez, Virginia
1986   *White by Definition*. New Brunswick, N. J.: Rutgers University Press.

Dos Santos, Teotonio
1973   "The Crisis of Development Theory and the Problem of Dependence in Latin America." In *Underdevelopment and Development*. Henry Bernstein, ed. Harmondsworth, England: Penguin.

Douglas, Mary
1970   *Purity and Danger*. Baltimore: Penguin.

Draper, Patricia
1974   "Comparative Studies of Socialization." In *Annual Review of Anthropology*. Bernard J. Siegel, ed. Pp. 263–78. Palo Alto, Calif.: Annual Reviews.

Drucker, P., and Heizer, R. F.
1967   *To Make My Name Good*. Berkeley: University of California Press.

Dumont, Louis
1970   *Homo Hierarchicus: An Essay on the Caste System*. Chicago: University of Chicago Press.

Durkheim, Emile
1961   *The Elementary Forms of the Religious Life*. New York: Collier (first publ. 1915).

Eaton, S. Boyd, and Konner, Melvin
1989   "Ancient Genes and Modern Health." In *Applying Anthropology: An Introductory Reader*. Aaron Podolefsky and Peter J. Brown, eds. Pp. 43–46. Mountain View, Calif.: Mayfield.

Edgerton, Robert
1992   *Sick Societies*. New York: Free Press.
1971   *The Individual in Adaptation*. Berkeley: University of California Press.

Eggan, Fred
1950   *The Social Organization of Western Pueblos*. Chicago: University of Chicago Press.

Ekman, Paul
1977   "Biological and Cultural Contributions to Body and Facial Movements." In *Anthropology of the Body*. John Blacking, ed. Pp. 34–89. New York: Academic Press.

Elkin, A. P.
1967   "The Nature of Australian Totemism." In *Gods and Rituals*. John Middleton, ed. Pp. 159–76. Garden City, N.Y.: Natural History Press.

Ember, Melvin, and Ember, Carol R.
1971   "The Conditions Favoring Matrilocal vs. Patrilocal Residence." *American Anthropologist* 73:571–94.

Evans-Pritchard, E. E.
1968   *The Nuer*. Oxford, England: Clarendon Press (first publ. 1940).
1967   "The Nuer Concept of Spirit in Its Relation to the Social Order." In *Myth and Cosmos*. John Middleton, ed. Pp. 109–26. Garden City, N.Y.: Natural History Press.
1958   *Witchcraft, Oracles, and Magic among the Azande*. Oxford, England: Clarendon Press.

Fallers, Lloyd
1955   "The Predicament of the Modern African Chief: An Instance from Uganda." *American Anthropologist* 57:290–305.

Farb, Peter
1978   *Man's Rise to Civilization*. New York: E. P. Dutton.
1974   *Word Play: What Happens When People Talk*. New York: Knopf.

Feinberg, Richard
1986   "Market Economy and Changing Sex-Roles on a Polynesian Atoll." *Ethnology* 25(4):271–82.

Feldman, Douglas
1986   *The Social Dimensions of AIDS: Method and Theory*. New York: Praeger.

Ferguson, Brian, ed.
1984   *The Ecology and Political Economy of War: Anthropological Perspectives*. New York: Academic Press.

Ferguson, R. Brian
1992   "A Savage Encounter: Western Contact and the Yanomamo War Complex." In *War in the Tribal Zone: Expanding States and Indigenous Warfare*. R. Brian Ferguson and Neil L. Whitehead, eds. Santa Fe, N. M.: School of American Research Press.

Ferguson, R. Brian, and Whitehead, Neil L., eds.
1992   *War in the Tribal Zone: Expanding States and Indigenous Warfare*. Santa Fe, N. M.: School of American Research Press.

Fischer, John
1961   "Art Styles as Cognitive Maps." *American Anthropologist* 63:79–93.

Flannery, K.
1973   "The Origins of Agriculture." In *Annual Review of Anthropology*. Bernard J. Siegel, ed. Pp. 271–310. Palo Alto, Calif.: Annual Reviews.

Ford, Clellan S.
1938   "The Role of a Fijian Chief." *American Sociological Review* 3:542–50.

Forde, Daryll
1950   "Double Descent among the Yako." In *African Systems of Kinship and Marriage*. A. R. Radcliffe-Brown and Daryll Forde, eds. Pp. 285–332. London: Oxford University Press.

Fouts, Roger
1983   "Chimpanzee Language and Elephant Tails: A Theoretical Synthesis." In *Language in Primates*. Judith de Luce and Hugh T. Wilder, eds. Pp. 63–75. New York: Springer-Verlag.

Frankel, Francine R.
1971   *India's Green Revolution: Economic Gains and Political Costs*. Princeton, N. J.: Princeton University Press.

Freed, Ruth S.
1977   *Space, Density, and Cultural Conditioning*. Annals of the New York Academy of Sciences 285:593–604.

Freed, Stanley A., and Freed, Ruth S.
1978   "Shanti Nagar: The Effects of Urbanization in a Village in North India. 2. Aspects of Economy, Technology and Economy." *Anthropological Papers of the American Mu-*

seum of Natural History, Vol. 55, Part I. New York: American Museum of Natural History.

Freeman, Derek
1983   *Margaret Mead: The Making and Unmaking of an Anthropological Myth*. Cambridge, Mass.: Harvard University Press.

Fried, Morton
1967   *The Evolution of Political Society*. New York: Random House.

Friedl, Ernestine
1975   *Women and Men: An Anthropologist's View*. New York: Holt, Rinehart and Winston.
1974   "Kinship, Class and Selective Migration." In *Family in the Mediterranean*. J. Peristiany, ed. London: Cambridge University Press.

Gardner, B. T., and Gardner, R. A.
1967   "Teaching Sign Language to a Chimpanzee." *Science* 165:664–72.

Gardner, Peter
1966   "Symmetric Respect and Memorate Knowledge: The Structure and Ecology of Individualistic Culture." *Southwestern Journal of Anthropology* 22:389–413.

Garn, S. M.
1969   *Human Races*. Springfield, Ill.: Charles C. Thomas.

Gay, John, and Cole, Michael
1967   *The New Mathematics and an Old Culture*. New York: Holt, Rinehart and Winston.

Geertz, Clifford
1973   *The Interpretation of Cultures*. New York: Basic Books.
1963   *Agricultural Involution: The Process of Ecological Change in Indonesia*. Berkeley: University of California Press.

Gonzalez-Wippler, Migene
1989   *Santeria: The Religion*. New York: Harmony Books.

Goodale, J.
1971   *Tiwi Wives*. Seattle: University of Washington Press.

Goodall, J.
1968   "A Preliminary Report on Expressive Movements and Communication in the Gombe Stream Chimpanzees." In *Primates: Studies in Adaptation and Variability*. P. Jay, ed. New York: Holt, Rinehart and Winston.

Goodenough, Ward
1956   "Componential Analysis and the Study of Meaning." *Language* 32:195–216.

Gorer, G., and Rickman, J.
1949   *The People of Great Russia*. London: Cresset.

Graves, Nancy B., and Graves, Theodore D.
1974   "Adaptive Strategies in Urban Migration." In *Annual Review of Anthropology*. Bernard J. Siegel, ed. Pp. 117–51. Palo Alto, Calif.: Annual Reviews.

Gregg, Joan
1988   "Contrastive Rhetoric: An Exploration of Chinese and American Expository Patterns." Temple University Working Papers in Composition. Spring. Philadelphia: Temple University.

Gross, Daniel
1973   "The Great Sisal Scheme." In *Man's Many Ways*. Richard Gould, ed. Pp. 371–79. New York: Harper and Row.

Hall, Edward
1959   *The Silent Language*. Greenwich, Conn.: Fawcett.

Hall, Edward T., and Hall, Mildred Reed
1987   *Hidden Differences: Doing Business with the Japanese*. New York: Doubleday.

Hamid, Ansley
1992   "The Developmental Cycle of a Drug Epidemic: The Cocaine Smoking Epidemic of 1981–1991." *Journal of Psychoactive Drugs*, 24(4) 337–48.

Hamilton, James W.
1987   "This Old House: A Karen Ideal." In *Mirror and Metaphor: Material and Social Constructions of Reality*. Daniel W. Ingersoll, Jr., and Gordon Bronitsky, eds. Lanham, Md.: University Press of America.

Hammar, Lawrence
1989   *Gender and Class on the Fringe: A Feminist Critique of Ethnographic Theory and Data in Papua New Guinea*. Working Papers on

Women in International Development. East
Lansing: Michigan State University.

Hanna, Judith
1977   "To Dance Is Human." In *The Anthropology of the Body*. John Blacking, ed. Pp.
        211–32. London: Academic Press.

Harlow, Harry
1962   "Social Deprivation in Monkeys." *Scientific American* 206:1–10.

Harner, Michael
1977   "The Ecological Basis for Aztec Sacrifice."
        American Ethnologist 4:117–33.

Harris, Marvin
1990   *The Rise of Anthropological Theory: A History of Theories of Culture*. New York:
        Harper (first publ. 1968).
1974   *Cows, Pigs, Wars, and Witches: The Riddles of Culture*. New York: Random House
        (Vintage).
1966   "The Cultural Ecology of India's Sacred Cattle." *Current Anthropology* 7:51–66.

Harrison, Robert
1973   *Warfare*. Minneapolis: Burgess.

Hart, C. W. M.
1967   "Contrasts between Pre-pubertal and Post-pubertal Education." In *Personality and Social Life*. Robert Endelman, ed. Pp.
        275–90. New York: Random House.

Hart, C. W. M., and Pilling, Arnold R.
1960   *The Tiwi of North Australia*. New York:
        Holt, Rinehart and Winston.

Harwood, Alan
1977   *Rx: Spiritist as Needed: A Study of a Puerto Rican Community Mental Health Resource*. New York: Wiley.

Heider, Karl
1970   *The Dugum Dani*. Chicago: Aldine.

Henry, Jules
1963   *Culture against Man*. New York: Random House.

Herdt, Gilbert H.
1981   *Guardians of the Flutes: Idioms of Masculinity*. New York: McGraw-Hill.

Herdt, Gilbert H., ed.
1993   *Third Sex, Third Gender*. Paris: Zone.

Hewes, Gordon W.
1973   "Primate Communication and the Gestural
        Origins of Language." *Current Anthropology* 14:5–12.

Hill, Carole I., ed.
1985   *Training Manual in Medical Anthropology*.
        Washington, D.C.: American Anthropological Association.

Hinshaw, Robert E.
1980   "Anthropology, Administration, and Public Policy." In *Annual Review of Anthropology*. Bernard J. Siegel, ed. Pp. 497–545.
        Palo Alto, Calif.: Annual Reviews.

Hockett, C. F., and Ascher, R.
1964   "The Human Revolution." *Current Anthropology* 5:135–68.

Hodge, William
1981   *The First Americans: Then and Now*. New York: Holt, Rinehart and Winston.

Hoebel, E. Adamson
1974   *The Law of Primitive Man*. New York: Atheneum (first publ. 1954).
1960   *The Cheyennes: Indians of the Great Plains*. New York: Holt, Rinehart and Winston.

Hoffer, Carol
1974   "Madam Yoko: Ruler of the Kpa Mende Confederacy." In *Women, Culture, and Society*. Michelle Zimbalist Rosaldo and Louise Lamphere, eds. Pp. 173–88. Stanford, Calif.: Stanford University Press.

Hoijer, Harry
1964   "Cultural Implications of Some Navajo Linguistic Categories." In *Language in Culture and Society*. D. Hymes, ed. Pp. 142–60.
        New York: Harper and Row.

Holmberg, Allan R.
1969   *Nomads of the Long Bow: The Siriono of Eastern Bolivia*. Garden City, N.Y.: Natural History Press.

Holtzman, Wayne H., Diaz-Guerrero, Rogelio, and Swartz, Jon D.
1975   *Personality Development in Two Cultures*.
        Austin: University of Texas Press.

Hopkins, Nicholas
1987   "Mechanized Irrigation in Upper Egypt: The Role of Technology and the State in Agriculture." In *Comparative Farming Systems*. B. Turner II and Stephen B. Brush, eds.
        Pp. 223–47. New York: Guilford Press.

Horton, Robin, and Finnegan, Ruth, eds.
1973   *Modes of Thought: Essays on Thinking in Western and Non-Western Societies.* London: Faber.

Huang, Shu-min
1993   "A Cross-Cultural Experience: A Chinese Anthropologist in the United States." In *Distant Mirrors: America as a Foreign Culture.* Philip R. DeVita and James D. Armstrong, eds. Belmont, Calif.: Wadsworth.

Hunt, George T.
1940   *The Wars of the Iroquois.* Madison: University of Wisconsin Press.

Hymes, Dell
1972   *Reinventing Anthropology.* New York: Random House (Vintage).

Itard, Jean-Marc-Gaspard
1962   *The Wild Boy of Aveyron.* George and Muriel Humphrey, trans. Englewood Cliffs, N.J.: Prentice-Hall (first publ. 1806).

Johnson, Allen
1978   "In Search of the Affluent Society." *Human Nature*, September, pp. 50–59.

Kaprow, Miriam Lee
1982   "Resisting Respectability: Gypsies in Saragossa." *Urban Anthropology* 11(3–4):399–431.

Kardiner, Abram, et al.
1945   *The Psychological Frontiers of Society.* New York: Columbia University Press.

Keesing, Roger M.
1987   "Anthropology as Interpretive Quest." *Current Anthropology* 28(5):161–76.

Kelkar, Govind
1985   "Tractors against Women." In *Development* 3:18–23.

Kinsey, Alfred C., Pomeroy, Wardell B., and Martin, Clyde E.
1948   *Sexual Behavior in the Human Male.* Philadelphia: W. B. Saunders.

LaBarre, Weston
1969   *And They Shall Take Up Serpents.* New York: Schocken Books.

Labov, William
1983   "Recognizing Black English in the Classroom." In *Black English: Educational Eq-uity and the Law.* John Chambers, ed. Pp. 29–55. Ann Arbor, Mich.: Karoma Publishers.
1972   "On the Mechanisms of Linguistic Change." In *Directions in Sociolinguistics.* John J. Gumperz and Dell Hymes, eds. New York: Holt, Rinehart and Winston.
1969   "The Logic of Nonstandard English." *Georgetown Monographs on Language and Linguistics* 22:1–22, 26–31.

Langness, L. L., and Frank, Geyla G.
1981   *Lives: An Anthropological Approach to Biography.* Novato, Calif.: Chandler and Sharp.

Leacock, Eleanor Burke
1981   *Myths of Male Dominance.* New York: Monthly Review Press.

Lee, Dorothy
1959   *Freedom and Culture.* Englewood Cliffs, N.J.: Prentice-Hall.

Lee, Richard B.
1992a "The Ju/wasi and Us: 1959–91." *Symbols*, September, pp. 5–14.
1992b "Art, Science, or Politics? The Crisis in Hunter-Gatherer Studies." *American Anthropologist* 94:31–54.
1979   *The !Kung San: Men, Women and Work in a Foraging Society.* Cambridge, England: Cambridge University Press.
1974   "Eating Christmas in the Kalahari." In *Conformity and Conflict.* James Spradley and David W. McCurdy, eds. Pp. 14–21. Boston: Little, Brown.
1968   "What Hunters Do for a Living, or, How to Make Out on Scarce Resources." In *Man the Hunter.* Richard B. Lee and Irven DeVore, eds. Pp. 30–48. Chicago: Aldine.

Lessinger, Hanna
1983   "Why the Right Wants to Discredit Her Work — *Sociobiologists v. Margaret Mead.*" *The Guardian.* February 23, 1983, p. 7.

Levine, Morton
1957   "Prehistoric Art and Ideology." *American Anthropologist* 59:949–62.

Lévi-Strauss, Claude
1974   *Structural Anthropology.* Vol. I, New York: Basic; Vol. II, Chicago: University of Chicago Press (1983).
1969   *The Elementary Structures of Kinship.* Boston: Beacon Press (first publ. 1949).

Levy, Robert
1973   *Tahitians: Mind and Experience in the Society Islands.* Chicago: University of Chicago Press.

Lewis, Oscar
1966   *La Vida.* New York: Random House.
1960   *Tepoztlán, Village in Mexico.* New York: Holt, Rinehart and Winston.

Lewis, William F.
1993   *Soul Rebels: The Rastafari.* Prospect Heights, Ill.: Waveland.

Liebow, Elliot
1967   *Tally's Corner.* Boston: Little, Brown.

Lindenbaum, Shirley
1979   *Kuru Sorcery: Disease and Danger in the New Guinea Highlands.* Palo Alto, Calif.: Mayfield.

Linton, Ralph
1937   "One Hundred Per Cent American." *The American Mercury* 40:427–29.

Lomax, Alan
1968   *Folk Song Style and Culture.* American Association for the Advancement of Science Publication No. 88. Washington, D.C.

Long, Norman
1977   *An Introduction to the Sociology of Rural Development.* London: Tavistock Press.

Lowie, Robert H.
1963   *Indians of the Plains.* Garden City, N.Y.: Natural History Press (first publ. 1954).
1948   *Social Organization.* New York: Holt, Rinehart and Winston.

Lynch, Owen K.
1969   *The Politics of Untouchability.* New York: Columbia University Press.

Lynd, Robert, and Lynd, Helen
1937   *Middletown in Transition.* New York: Harcourt, Brace and World.

Mails, Thomas E.
1973   *Plains Indians: Dog Soldiers, Bear Men and Buffalo Women.* New York: Bonanza Books.

Malinowski, Bronislaw
1967   *A Diary in the Strict Sense of the Term.* New York: Harcourt, Brace and World.
1961   *Argonauts of the Western Pacific.* New York: E. P. Dutton (first publ. 1922).

1954   *Magic, Science, and Religion.* Garden City, N.Y.: Doubleday (first publ. 1926).
1953   *Sex and Repression in Primitive Society.* London: Routledge and Kegan Paul (first publ. 1927).
1944   *A Scientific Theory of Culture and Other Essays.* Chapel Hill: University of North Carolina Press.
1929   *The Sexual Life of Savages.* New York: Harcourt, Brace and World.

Manning, Frank E.
1982   "The Caribbean Experience." *Cultural Survival Quarterly* 6:13–15.

Marcus, George E., and Fischer, Michael M. J.
1986   *Anthropology as Cultural Critique: An Experimental Moment in the Human Sciences.* Chicago: University of Chicago Press.

Marshall, Donald
1971   "Sexual Behavior on Mangaia." In *Human Sexual Behavior: Variations in the Ethnographic Spectrum.* Donald S. Marshall and Robert C. Suggs, eds. Pp. 103–62. New York: Basic Books.

Marshall, Laura
1967   "!Kung Bushman Bands." In *Comparative Political Systems.* R. Cohen and J. Middleton, eds. Pp. 15–44. Garden City, N.Y.: Natural History Press.

Martin, M. K., and Voorhies, Barbara
1975   *Female of the Species.* New York: Columbia University Press.

Mauss, Marcel
1990   *The Gift.* New York: Norton (first publ. 1924).

Maybury-Lewis, David H. P.
1990   "A Special Sort of Pleading: Anthropology at the Service of Ethnic Groups." In *Talking About People: Readings in Contemporary Cultural Anthropology.* William A. Haviland and Robert J. Gordon, eds. Pp. 16–24. Mountain View, Calif.: Mayfield.

Mayer, Philip, and Mayer, Iona
1970   "Socialization by Peers: The Youth Organization of the Red Xhosa." In *Socialization: The Approach from Social Anthropology.* Philip Mayer, ed. Pp. 159–89. London: Tavistock Publications.

Maynard, Eileen
1974   "Guatemalan Women: Life under Two Types of Patriarchy." In *Many Sisters.* Caro-

lyn J. Matthiasson, ed. Pp. 77–98. New York: Free Press.

McAllester, David P.
1954   *Enemy Way Music*. Cambridge, Mass.: Peabody Museum, Harvard University.

McKean, Philip
1982   "Tourists and Balinese." *Cultural Survival Quarterly* 6:32–34.

Mead, Margaret
1975   "Discussion: The Role of Anthropology in International Relations." In *Anthropology and Society*. Bela C. Maday, ed. Pp. 13–18. Washington, D.C.: The Anthropological Society of Washington.
1971   *Coming of Age in Samoa*. New York: Morrow (first publ. 1928).
1963   *Sex and Temperament in Three Primitive Societies*. New York: Dell (first publ. 1935).
1942   *And Keep Your Powder Dry: An Anthropologist Looks at America*. New York: Morrow.

Meek, Charles K.
1972   "Ibo Law." In *Readings in Anthropology*. Jesse D. Jennings and E. Adamson Hoebel, eds. Pp. 247–58. New York: McGraw-Hill.

Meggitt, Mervyn
1977   *Blood Is Their Argument: Warfare among the Mae Enga Tribesmen of the New Guinea Highlands*. Palo Alto, Calif.: Mayfield.

Mencher, Joan P.
1980   "On Being an Untouchable in India: A Materialist Perspective." In *Beyond the Myths of Culture, Essays in Cultural Materialism*. New York: Academic Press.
1974   "The Caste System Upside Down: Or the Not-So-Mysterious East." *Current Anthropology* 15:469–94.
1965   "The Nayars of South Malabar." In *Comparative Family Systems*. M. F. Nimkoff, ed. Pp. 162–91. Boston: Houghton Mifflin.

Merriam, Alan P.
1967   "The Arts and Anthropology." In *Horizons of Anthropology*. Sol Tax, ed. Pp. 224–36. Chicago: Aldine.
1964   *The Anthropology of Music*. Evanston, Ill.: Northwestern University Press.

Messenger, John C.
1971   "Sex and Repression in an Irish Folk Community." In *Human Sexual Behavior: Vari-*

ations in the Ethnographic Spectrum. Donald S. Marshall and Robert C. Suggs, eds. Pp. 3–37. New York: Basic Books.

Miles, H. Lyn
1983   "Apes and Language: The Search for Communicative Competence." In *Language in Primates*. Judith de Luce and Hugh T. Wilder, eds. New York: Springer-Verlag.

Miles, Lyn W.
1978   "Language Acquisition in Apes and Children." In *Sign Language and Language Acquisition in Man and Ape*. Fred C. C. Peng, ed. Pp. 103–20. Boulder, Colo.: Westview Press.

Moffatt, Michael
1989   *Coming of Age in New Jersey*. New Brunswick, N. J.: Rutgers University Press.

Montague, Susan, and Morais, Robert
1976   "Football Games and Rock Concerts: The Ritual Enactment." In *The American Dimension*. W. Arens and Susan P. Montague, eds. Pp. 33–52. Port Washington, N.Y.: Alfred.

Moore, Christopher W.
1993   "Have Process, Will Travel." Reflections on Democratic Decision Making and Conflict Management Practice Abroad. *Forum*, Winter, pp. 1–12.

Moran, Emilio F.
1979   *Human Adaptability: An Introduction to Ecological Anthropology*. Boulder, Colo.: Westview Press.

Morgan, Lewis H.
1974   *Ancient Society*. New York: Gordon (first publ. 1877).

Munroe, Robert L., and Munroe, Ruth H.
1977   *Cross-Cultural Human Development*. New York: Aronson.

Murdock, George
1949   *Social Structure*. New York: Free Press.

Murphy, Joseph M.
1989   *Santeria: An African Religion in America*. Boston: Beacon Press.

Murphy, Michael Dean, and Johannsen, Agneta
1990   "Ethical Obligations and Federal Regulations in Ethnographic Research and Anthropological Education." *Human Organization* 49(2):127–34.

Murphy, Robert
1964   "Social Distance and the Veil." *American Anthropologist* 66:1257–73.

Murphy, Yolanda, and Murphy, Robert
1974   *Women of the Forest*. New York: Columbia University Press.

Murray, Gerald F.
1986   "Seeing the Forest While Planting the Trees: An Anthropological Approach to Agroforestry in Rural Haiti." In *Politics, Projects, and Peasants: Institutional Development in Haiti*. D. W. Brinkerhoff and J. C. Garcia-Zamor, eds. Pp. 193–226. New York: Praeger.

Myerhoff, Barbara
1978   *Number Our Days*. New York: Simon and Schuster.

Nanda, Serena
1992   "Arranging a Marriage in India." In *The Naked Anthropologist: Tales from Around the World*. Philip R. DeVita, ed. Belmont, Calif.: Wadsworth.
1990   *Neither Man nor Woman: The Hijras of India*. Belmont, Calif.: Wadsworth.

Nash, Dennison
1968   "The Role of the Composer." In *Readings in Anthropology. Vol. II: Cultural Anthropology*. Morton H. Fried, ed. Pp. 746–48. New York: Thomas Y. Crowell.

Nash, June
1981   "Ethnographic Aspects of the World Capitalist System." *Annual Review of Anthropology* 10:393–423.

Nash, Manning
1967   "The Social Context of Economic Choice in a Small Society." In *Tribal and Peasant Economies*. George Dalton, ed. Pp. 524–38. Garden City, N.Y.: Natural History Press.

Netting, Robert
1977   *Cultural Ecology*. Menlo Park, Calif.: Cummings.

Newman, Katherine S.
1989   *Falling from Grace: The Experience of Downward Mobility in the American Middle Class*. New York: Random House.

Norgren, Jill, and Nanda, Serena
1988   *American Cultural Pluralism and Law*. New York: Praeger.

O'Brien, Jay
1986   "Toward a Reconstitution of Ethnicity: Capitalist Expansion and Cultural Dynamics in Sudan." *American Anthropologist* 4:898–907.

Ogbu, John
1978a   "African Bridewealth and Women's Status." *American Ethnologist* 5:241–60.
1978b   *Minority Education and Caste: The American System in Cross-Cultural Perspective*. New York: Academic Press.
1974   *The Next Generation: An Ethnography of Education in an Urban Neighborhood*. New York: Academic Press.

O'Kelly, Charlotte G.
1980   *Women and Men in Society*. Belmont, Calif.: Wadsworth.

Oliver, Symmes C.
1965   "Individuality, Freedom of Choice, and Cultural Flexibility of the Kamba." *American Anthropologist* 67:421–28.

Oregon v. Smith
1990   494 U.S. 872.

Ortiz de Montellano, Bernard R.
1978   "Aztec Cannibalism: An Ecological Necessity?" *Science* 200:611–17.

Ottley, Bruce L., and Zorn, Jean G.
1983   "Criminal Law in Papua New Guinea: Code, Custom and the Courts in Conflict." *American Journal of Comparative Law* XXXI(2):251–300.

Pacini, Deborah, and Franquemont, Christine, eds.
1986   *Coca and Cocaine: Effects on People and Policy in Latin America*. Cultural Survival Report 23. Cambridge, Mass.: Cultural Survival Publications.

Parenti, Michael J.
1967   "Black Nationalism and the Reconstruction of Identity." In *Personality and Social Life*. Robert Endelman, ed. Pp. 514–24. New York: Random House.

Partridge, William
1978   "Uses and Nonuses of Anthropological Data on Drug Abuse." In *Applied Anthropology*. W. L. Partridge and E. M. Eddy, eds. Pp. 350–72. New York: Columbia University Press.

Patterson, F., and Cohen, R.
1978 "Conversations with a Gorilla." *National Geographic* 154:454–62.

Pelto, Pertti
1973 *The Snowmobile Revolution: Technology and Social Change in the Arctic.* Menlo Park, Calif.: Cummings.

People v. Woody
1964 61 Cal. 2d 716, 394 P. 2d 813.

Petersen, Glenn
1985 "A Cultural Analysis of the Ponapean Independence Vote in the 1983 Plebiscite." *Pacific Studies* 9(1):13–51.

Pettitt, George A.
1972 "The Vision Quest and the Guardian Spirit." In *Readings in Anthropology.* Jesse Jennings and E. Adamson Hoebel, eds. Pp. 265–71. New York: McGraw-Hill.

Pfeiffer, John
1972 *The Emergence of Man.* New York: Harper and Row.

Phongpaichit, Pasuk
1982 "Bangkok Masseuses." *Cultural Survival Quarterly* 6:34–37.

Picchi, Debra
1991 "The Impact of an Industrial Agricultural Project on the Bakairi Indians of Central Brazil." *Human Organization* 50(1): 26–38.

Pilbeam, David
1972 *The Ascent of Man.* New York: Macmillan.

Pillsbury, Barbara L. K.
1985 "Anthropologists in International Health." In *Training Manual in Medical Anthropology.* Washington, D.C.: American Anthropological Association.

Polyani, Karl
1944 *The Great Transformation.* New York: Holt, Rinehart and Winston.

Pospisil, Leopold
1963 *The Kapauku Papuans of West New Guinea.* New York: Holt, Rinehart and Winston.

Potter, Jack M.
1967 "From Peasants to Rural Proletarians: Social and Economic Change in Rural Communist China." In *Peasant Society: A Reader.* Jack M. Potter, May N. Diaz, and George M. Forster, eds. Pp. 407–18. Boston: Little, Brown.

Premack, D.
1971 "On the Assessment of Language Competence in the Chimpanzee." In *Behavior of Nonhuman Primates,* Vol. 4. A. M. Schrier and F. Stollnitz, eds. New York: Academic Press.

Queen, Stuart, and Habenstein, Robert W.
1974 *The Family in Various Cultures.* New York: J. B. Lippincott.

Radcliffe-Brown, A. R.
1965 *Structure and Function in Primitive Society.* New York: Free Press (first publ. 1952).
1964 *The Andaman Islanders.* New York: Free Press (first publ. 1922).

Rappaport, Roy A.
1971 "The Flow of Energy in an Agricultural Society." *Scientific American* 225:116–32.
1967 "Ritual Regulation of Environmental Relations among a New Guinea People." *Ethnology* 6:17–30.

Rathje, William, and Murphy, Cutten
1993 *Rubbish! The Archaeology of Garbage.* New York: Harper Perennial.

Redfield, Robert
1971 "Art and Icon." In *Anthropology and Art.* Charlotte M. Otten, ed. Pp. 39–65. Garden City, N.Y.: Natural History Press.

Reynolds, Vernon
1965 *Budongo: An African Forest and Its Chimpanzees.* Garden City, N.Y.: Doubleday.

Rhoades, Robert E.
1984 *Breaking New Ground: Agricultural Anthropology.* Lima, Peru: International Potato Center.

Richards, Audrey I.
1956 *Chisungu: A Girl's Initiation Ceremony among the Bemba of Northern Rhodesia.* New York: Grove Press.

Richardson, Miles
1984 Personal communication.

Ritter, M. L.
1980 "The Conditions Favoring Age-set Organization." *Journal of Anthropological Research* 36:87–104.

Robarchek, Clayton A., and Dentan, Robert
1987   "Blood Drunkenness and the Bloodthirsty Semai: Unmaking Another Anthropological Myth." *American Anthropologist* 89: 356–63.

Rohner, Ronald, and Rohner, Evelyn
1970   *The Kwakiutl: Indians of British Columbia.* New York: Holt, Rinehart and Winston.

Roland, Alan
1988   *In Search of Self in India and Japan.* Princeton, N.J.: Princeton University Press.

Rosaldo, Michelle Z., and Lamphere, Louise, eds.
1974   *Women, Culture, and Society.* Stanford, Calif.: Stanford University Press.

Rosenfeld, Gerry
1971   *Shut Those Thick Lips: A Study of Slum School Failure.* New York: Holt, Rinehart and Winston.

Sahlins, Marshall
1978   "Culture as Protein and Profit." *New York Review of Books* 25(18):45–53.
1972   *Stone Age Economics.* Chicago: Aldine.
1971   "Poor Man, Rich Man, Big Man, Chief." In *Conformity and Conflict.* James P. Spradley and David W. McCurdy, eds. Pp. 362–76. Boston: Little, Brown.
1961   "The Segmentary Lineage: An Organization of Predatory Expansion." *American Anthropologist* 63:332–45.
1957   "Land Use and the Extended Family in Moala, Fiji." *American Anthropologist* 59:449–62.

Saitoti, Tepilit Ole
1986   *The Worlds of a Maasai Warrior.* New York: Random House.

Salzman, Philip C.
1972   "Multi-Resource Nomadism in Iranian Baluchistan." In *Perspectives on Nomadism.* William Irons and Neville Dyson-Hudson, eds. Pp. 61–69. Leiden, the Netherlands: E. J. Brill.

Sanday, Peggy Reeves
1986   *Divine Hunger: Cannibalism as a Cultural System.* New York: Cambridge University Press.
1981   *Female Power and Male Dominance.* New York: Cambridge University Press.

Sanjek, Roger
1991   "The Ethnographic Present." *Man* (new series) 26:609–28.

Sapir, Edward
1949   "The Status of Linguistics as a Science." In *The Selected Writings of Edward Sapir in Language, Culture and Personality.* David Mandelbaum, ed. Pp. 160–66. Berkeley: University of California Press.

Savage-Rumbaugh, E. S., Rumbaugh, D. M., and Boysen, S.
1980   "Do Apes Use Language?" *American Scientist* 68:49–61.

Scaglion, Richard, ed.
1981   *Homicide Compensation in Papua New Guinea: Problems and Prospects.* Law Reform Commission of Papua New Guinea Monograph 1. Papua, New Guinea: Office of Information.

Scheper-Hughes, Nancy
1989   "Lifeboat Ethics: Mother Love and Child Death in Northeast Brazil." *Natural History* 98(10):8–16.

Schlegel, Alice, ed.
1977   *Sexual Stratification: A Cross-Cultural View.* New York: Columbia University Press.

Schneider, Harold K.
1973   "The Subsistence Role of Cattle among the Pokot in East Africa." In *Peoples and Cultures of Africa.* Elliott P. Skinner, ed. Pp. 159–87. Garden City, N.Y.: Natural History Press.

Schumacher, William
1975   *Small Is Beautiful.* New York: Harper and Row.

Schwartz, Gary
1972   *Youth Culture: An Anthropological Approach.* Reading, Mass.: Addison-Wesley.

Schwartz, Norman B.
1981   "Anthropological Views of Community and Community Development." *Human Organization* 40(4):313–22.
1978   "Community Development and Cultural Change in Latin America." In *Annual Review of Anthropology.* Bernard J. Siegel, ed. Pp. 235–62. Palo Alto, Calif.: Annual Reviews.

Schwartz, Theodore
1976   *Socialization as Cultural Communication.* Berkeley: University of California Press.

Service, Elman
1971   *Profiles in Ethnology.* New York: Harper and Row.

Singer, Merrill
1992   "AIDS and U.S. Ethnic Minorities: The Crisis and Alternative Anthropological Responses." *Human Organization* 51(1): 89–95.

Singer, Merrill, Irizarry, Ray, and Schensul, Jean J.
1991   "Needle Access as an AIDS Prevention Strategy for IV Drug Users: A Research Perspective." *Human Organization* 50(2):142–53.

Singer, Milton
1968   "The Indian Joint Family in Modern Industry." In *Indian Society: Structure and Change.* Milton Singer and Bernard Cohn, eds. Pp. 432–52. Chicago: Aldine.

Sluka, Jeffrey
1990   "Participant Observation in Violent Social Contexts." *Human Organization* 49(2):114–26.

Smith, M. Estelli
1982   "Tourism and Native Americans." *Cultural Survival Quarterly* 6:10–12.

Southworth, F. C., and Daswani, C. J.
1974   *Foundations of Linguistics.* New York: Free Press.

Spicer, Edward H., and Downing, Theodore E.
1974   "Training for Non-Academic Employment: Major Issues." In *Training Programs for New Opportunities in Applied Anthropology.* Eleanor Leacock, Nancie Gonzalez, and Gilbert Kushner, eds. Pp. 1–12. Washington, D.C.: American Anthropological Association.

Spiro, Melford
1979   *Gender and Culture: Kibbutz Women Revisited.* Durham, N.C.: Duke University Press.
1974   "Is the Family Universal? — The Israeli Case." In *The Sociological Perspective.* 3rd ed. Scott G. McNall, ed. Pp. 509–20. Boston: Little, Brown.

1958   *Children of the Kibbutz.* Cambridge, Mass.: Harvard University Press.

Spitz, Rene A.
1975   "Hospitalism: The Genesis of Psychiatric Conditions in Early Childhood." In *The Human Life Cycle.* William C. Sze, ed. Pp. 29–44. New York: Aronson.

Spradley, James
1970   *You Owe Yourself a Drunk.* Boston: Little, Brown.

Stack, Carol
1974   *All Our Kin: Strategies for Survival in a Black Community.* New York: Harper & Row.

Stack, John, Jr., ed.
1981   *Ethnic Identities in a Transnational World.* Westport, Conn.: Greenwood Press.

Steadman, Lyle B., and Merbs, Charles F.
1982   "Kuru and Cannibalism." *American Anthropologist* 84:611–27.

Steegmann, A. T., Jr.
1975   "Human Adaptation to Cold." In *Physiological Anthropology.* A. Damon, ed. Pp. 130–60. New York: Oxford University Press.

Steward, Julian
1972   *The Theory of Culture Change: The Methodology of Multilinear Evolution.* Urbana: University of Illinois Press (first publ. 1955).

Stull, Donald D., and Schensul, Jean J., eds.
1987   *Collaborative Research and Social Change.* Boulder, Colo.: Westview Press.

Sturtevant, Edgar H.
1947   *An Introduction to Linguistic Science.* New Haven, Conn.: Yale University Press.

Talmon, Yohina
1964   "Mate Selection in Collective Settlements." *American Sociological Review* 29: 491–508.

Tannen, Deborah
1990   *You Just Don't Understand: Women and Men in Conversation.* New York: Morrow.

Tedlock, Barbara
1991   "From Participant Observation to the Observation of Participation: The Emergence of Narrative Ethnography." *Journal of Anthropological Research* 47(1):69–94.

Terrace, H. S.
1983 "Apes Who 'Talk': Language or Projection of Language by Their Teachers?" In *Language in Primates*. Judith de Luce and Hugh T. Wilder, eds. Pp. 19–42. New York: Springer-Verlag.
1979 *Nim*. New York: Knopf.

Tiger, Lionel
1978 "Omnigamy: The New Kinship System." *Psychology Today*, July.

Tocqueville, Alexis de
1956 *Democracy in America*, ed. by Richard D. Heffner. New York: Penguin.

Tomasic, Roman, and Feeley, Malcolm M.
1982 *Neighborhood Justice*. New York: Longman.

Tonkinson, Robert
1974 *The Jigalong Mob: Aboriginal Victors of the Desert Crusade*. Menlo Park, Calif.: Cummings.

Trice, Harrison M., and Beyer, Janice M.
1993 *The Cultures of Work Organizations*. Englewood Cliffs, N.J.: Prentice-Hall.

Turnbull, Colin
1972 *The Mountain People*. New York: Simon and Schuster.
1968 "The Importance of Flux in Two Hunting Societies." In *Man the Hunter*. Richard B. Lee and Irven DeVore, eds. Pp. 132–37. Chicago: Aldine.
1961 *The Forest People*. New York: Simon and Schuster.

Turner, Victor
1969 *The Ritual Process: Structure and Anti-Structure*. Ithaca, N.Y.: Cornell University Press.

Tylor, Edward
1920 *Primitive Culture*. 2 vols. New York: G. P. Putnam's Sons (first publ. 1873).

University of Chicago
1989 *Anthropologist's Work Revives Ancient Agriculture*. The Division of Social Sciences, No. 9 (Spring), pp. 1–4.

Valentine, Charles A., and Valentine, Betty Lou
1970 "Making the Scene, Digging the Action and Telling It Like It Is: Anthropologists at Work in a Dark Ghetto." In *Afro-American Anthropology*. Norman E. Whitten, Jr., and John F. Szwed, eds. Pp. 403–18. New York: Free Press.

van Gennep, Arnold
1961 *The Rites of Passage*. Chicago: University of Chicago Press.

van Willigen, John
1993 *Applied Anthropology: An Introduction* (Rev. Ed.). Westport, Conn.: Bergin and Garvey.

Vayda, Andrew P.
1976 *War in Ecological Perspective*. New York: Plenum.

Vincent, Joan
1974 "The Structuring of Ethnicity." *Human Organization* 33(4):375–79.

Volkman, Toby Alice
1984 "Great Performances: Toraja Cultural Identity in the 1970s." *American Ethnologist* 11(1):152–68.

Wagner, Roy
1975 *The Invention of Culture*. Englewood Cliffs, N.J.: Prentice-Hall.

Waite, Linda
1991 *New Families, No Families? The Transformation of the American Home*. Berkeley: University of California Press.

Wallace, Anthony
1970 *Death and Rebirth of the Seneca*. New York: Knopf.
1966 *Religion: An Anthropological View*. New York: Random House.

Wallerstein, I.
1974 *The Modern World System: Capitalist Agriculture and the Origins of the European World Economy in the Sixteenth Century*. New York: Academic Press.

Weatherford, J.
1981 *Tribes on the Hill*. New York: Rawson, Wade.

Weiner, Annette B.
1976 *Women of Value, Men of Renown: New Perspectives on Trobriand Exchange*. Austin: University of Texas Press.

White, Leslie A.
1949 "Energy and the Evolution of Culture." In *The Science of Culture*. Leslie A. White, ed.

Pp. 363–93. New York: Farrar, Straus and Cudahy.

Whitehead, Harriet, ed.
1981   *Sexual Meanings: The Cultural Construction of Gender and Sexuality*. New York: Cambridge University Press.

Whiting, Beatrice, ed.
1963   *Six Cultures: Studies of Child Rearing*. New York: Wiley.

Whiting, John, and Child, Irvin L.
1984   *Child Training and Personality: A Cross-Cultural Study*. Westport, Conn.: Greenwood (first publ. 1953).

Whiting, John, Kluckhohn, Richard, and Anthony, Albert
1967   "The Function of Male Initiation Ceremonies at Puberty." In *Personality and Social Life*. Robert Endelman, ed. Pp. 294–308. New York: Random House.

Whiting, John, and Whiting, Beatrice
1973   "Altruistic and Egoistic Behavior in Six Cultures." In *Cultural Illness and Health*. Laura Nader and Thomas W. Maretski, eds. Pp. 56–66. Washington, D.C.: American Anthropological Association.

Whorf, B. L.
1956   *Language, Thought and Reality*. Cambridge, Mass.: M.I.T. Press.

Wikan, Unni
1977   "Man Becomes Woman: Transsexualism in Oman as a Key to Gender Roles." *Man* (new series) 12:304–19.

Williams, Terry Moses
1989   *The Cocaine Kids: The Inside Story of a Teenage Drug Ring*. Reading, Mass.: Addison-Wesley.

Williams, Terry, Dunlap, Eloise, Johnson, Bruce D., and Hamid, Ansley
1992   "Personal Safety in Dangerous Places." *Journal of Contemporary Ethnography* 21(3):343–74.

Williams, Walter
1986   *The Spirit and the Flesh*. 2nd. ed. Boston: Beacon Press.

Wilson, Edward
1975   *Sociobiology: The New Synthesis*. Cambridge, Mass.: Harvard University Press.

Wissler, Clark
1926   *The Relation of Man to Nature in Aboriginal North America*. New York: Appleton.

Witkin, H. A.
1974   "Cognitive Styles across Cultures." In *Culture and Cognition: Readings in Cross-Cultural Psychology*. J. W. Berry and P. R. Dasen, eds. Pp. 99–118. London: Methuen.

Wolf, Arthur
1968   "Adopt a Daughter-in-Law, Marry a Sister: A Chinese Solution to the Incest Taboo." *American Anthropologist* 70:864–74.

Wolf, Eric R.
1982   *Europe and the People without History*. Berkeley: University of California Press.
1966   *Peasants*. Englewood Cliffs, N.J.: Prentice-Hall.

Woodburn, James
1968   "An Introduction to Hadza Ecology." In *Man the Hunter*. Richard B. Lee and Irven DeVore, eds. Pp. 49–55. Chicago: Aldine.

Worsley, Peter M.
1959   "Cargo Cults." *Scientific American* 200:117–28.

Zito, Laura
1982   "Settling Down: Bedouin in the Sinai." *Cultural Survival Quarterly* 6:22–24.

Index

in rituals, 355–356, 372, 428
See also Pastoralism; Primates
Animatism, 354–355, 378
Animism, 354, 378
Anthropology
    and advocacy, 446–449, 459
    and agricultural intervention,
        454–455
    and AIDS, 444–446
    applied, 8–9, 440–460
    archeology in, 6–7, 19
    "armchair," 23–24
    biological, 7–8, 19
    cognitive, 55
    and community-based action,
        445–446
    contemporary, 18
    contributions of, 9–17
    cultural, 6, 19
    defined, 4, 49
    development, 449–456
    ecological, 162–163
    economic, 191–195
    educative role of, 445
    ethnographic data in, 42–44
    and expert witnesses, 448–449
    feminist, 25, 61, 72, 74
    forensic, 8–9
    and history, 72, 73
    history of, 23–24, 73
    and human diversity, 4–5
    and intercultural communication,
        457–458
    interdisciplinary, 9
    interpretive, 36, 56, 61
    law, 319
    linguistics in, 6, 19, 111–112, 117,
        120–125, 449
    Marxist, 72, 74
    medical, 9, 443–446
    methodology of, 23–44
    paleontology in, 8
    problem testing in, 42–44
    and program evaluation, 446
    psychological, 9, 137
    public policy, 441–446, 458–459
    reflective, 37
    research techniques, 43–44
    specialization in, 5–9
    statistical approaches, 43
    theories, 51–55
    values in, 41
    See also Ethnography; Fieldwork
Anti-structure, 353–354
Anxiety, 350
Apache language, 126
Apache peoples, 121, 122–123

Apartheid, 297
Apollonian ethos, 59
Applebaum, H., 187
Applied anthropology, 440–460
Arab culture, 39–40, 83
Arapesh society, 4–5, 60, 92–93,
    228
Archeology, 6–7, 19, 163
Arctic/subarctic zones, 159, 163,
    166–169
Ardrey, Robert, 197
Arens, W., 397, 401
Ari'i peoples, 287
Armstrong, James, D., 19
Arnould, Eric J., 440, 456
Art
    anthropological perspectives on,
        383–387
    cultural context of, 385–390, 403
    dance, 394–395, 403
    defined, 383, 403
    folklore, 402–403
    functions of, 383–385, 402–403
    graphic/plastic, 387–391, 403
    Ice Age, 387, 388–389
    music, 391–394, 403
    and perceptual-cognitive style,
        87, 383
    and social organization, 387,
        390–391
    in society, 395–397
    and tourism, 425, 427
Artists, 395–397, 403, 404
Arunta peoples, 84
Ascribed statuses, 288, 301–303
Asoro society, 360
Assimilation, 420–421, 447
Association
    based on age, 273–274, 276–278,
        281
    based on kinship, 254–273
    based on religion, 376
    based on sex, 274–275, 279–280,
        281
    military, 325
    voluntary, 433–434
Astrology, 363
Australia, 84, 159–160, 165,
    232–233, 274, 362, 368–369
Authoritarian societies, 390–391
Authority, 289, 315
Autonomy, 422–423, 446, 447,
    449, 450
Avoidance, 317
Avunculocal residence, 249
Azande society, 362–363
Aztec society, 357, 360

Bacaner, Hadassah, 241
Badman hero, 403
Baffin Island, 87
Bahuchara Mata, 94–95
Bakairi Indians, 420–423, 436
Baker, Randall, 452
Balanced reciprocity, 210–211, 214
Bali, 398–400, 427
Balicki, Asen, 365
Baluchistan, 172–173, 186
Band societies, 319–321, 344
"Barbarism" stage, 51
Barrett, Richard A., 74
Barth, Frederik, 162, 303, 324
Bascom, William, 213
Basongye society, 391–392
Basseri society, 324, 335–336
Basso, Keith, 122–123
Batak peoples, 433
Bates, Marston, 101
Bear's Heart, 161
Bedouin, 39–40, 426
Beidelman, Thomas O., 357, 366
Beliefs, types of, 354–355
Bemba society, 146
Benedict, Ruth, 59, 60, 74, 137, 141,
    212, 355
Benet, Sula, 204
Berdache, 93, 97
Berreman, Gerald, 37, 301,
    302–303, 309
Berry, J. W., 84, 87
Bettelheim, Bruno, 145, 274
Beyer, Janice M., 458, 460
Bhopal disaster, 431
Bias, in ethnography, 24–25, 28, 36,
    37, 44
Bifurcation, 265, 267–268
Big-man, 324–325
Bilateral descent, 256, 263, 271, 281,
    319–320
Bilineal (double) descent, 262, 263
Bilocal residence, 249
Binary oppositions, 55
Biological anthropology, 7–8, 19
Biological determinism, 42
Biological diversity, 8, 10–11, 17, 19
Biology
    and aggression, 90
    and culture, 49–50, 100, 133–135
    and gender, 93, 135–136
    and incest taboo, 226
    and marriage, 223
    and sex roles, 200
    and spatial perception, 84
Bison, 161, 165
Black Elk, 79

Clark, Margaret, 203
Class distinctions, in language, 113. *See also* Social class
Class system, 290
Cleary, David, 187
Coca, 442
Cockfighting, 398–401
Cognition
  cultural patterning of, 83, 85–86, 88
  and education, 147, 148
Cognitive anthropology, 55
Cohen, Abner, 304
Cohen, Ronald, 106, 345
Cohen, Yehudi, 51, 163
Cole, Douglas, 219
Cole, Johnnetta B., 19
Cole, Michael, 83, 146, 148
Collaterality, 264
Collateral kin, 264
Collectives, 204, 244–246. *See also* Kibbutz
College, 143–144
Colombia, 442
Colonialism, 18, 19, 73, 316, 334, 375, 409, 414, 427
Color symbology, 385
Coming of Age in New Jersey (Moffatt), 143
Coming of Age in Samoa (Mead), 42
Communal cults, 365–369, 378
Communication
  defined, 105
  ethnography of, 117, 120–125
  human versus animal, 108, 128
  intercultural, 456–458
  joking as, 123
  and language, 108–111
  nonhuman primate, 106–107
  nonverbal, 108, 124–125
  and social status/class, 120
  written, 120
  See also Language
Communism, 338–341, 419, 424–425
Communitas, 353–354
Community-based action models, 445–446
Community development, 449–456
Comparative linguistics, 126–127, 128
Compensation payments, 329, 333
Competitiveness
  in cultures compared, 457
  in nonindustrial society, 206–208, 212–213
  in United States, 147, 151

Complementary opposition, 322–323
Composite/compound families, 243
Confession, 320, 365
Configurationalism, 59, 74
Conflict
  between age sets, 277–278
  in birth-ascription systems, 303
  class, 303
  culture, 148–149
  and development theory, 453, 456, 460
  and law, 318–319
  in nonviolent society, 90
  religious ritual and, 369
  theories about, 72–73, 74, 308–309, 342
Conflict resolution
  in band societies, 321
  in chiefdoms, 335–336
  intercultural communication in, 458
  in tribal societies, 324, 325–329, 333
Conflict theory, 72–73, 308–309, 342
Conformity
  and art, 396–397
  and child rearing, 87, 138–140, 150
  and law, 317–319, 337
  and political processes, 315–317
  and religion, 350, 363
Confucius, 339
Conklin, Harold C., 115, 159, 161
Connectedness, between cultures, 409
Consanguineal kinship, 243, 247–249, 264–265
Consumption of goods, 185, 191
  governmental control of, 337
  and modernization, 412, 429–430
  and time, 193
Contagious magic, 360
Controlled cross-cultural comparison, 43, 44
Conventionality, 108, 128
Coon, Carleton S., 209
Cooperation, 65–66, 457
Copper Eskimo, 165, 167–169, 186
Copra growing, 414–415
Cornplanter, Jesse, 279
Corporations, multinational, 427, 431–432
Cortez, Hernando, 357
Cosmology, 349

Council of the American Anthropological Association, 459
Counterculture, 353
Courts, 326–328, 337
Cousins, 230
Crack cocaine, 442
Crafts, labor division in, 201, 202. *See also* Art
Credit extension, 207, 208
Cronin, Constance, 306
Cross cousins, 230, 265
Cross-cultural comparison, 43, 44
Cross-cultural psychology, 83, 84
Cross-cultural studies
  of art, 390–391
  of marriage rights/exchange, 237–238
  of schoolchildren, 147–148
Crow culture, 93, 258, 272, 364
Cults
  communal, 365–369, 378
  ecclesiastical, 369–371, 378
  individualistic, 364, 378
  men's, 274–275, 279
  ritual, 274–275
  shamanistic, 364–365, 378
Cultural anthropology, 6, 19. *See also* Anthropology
Cultural configurationalism, 59, 74
Cultural continuity/discontinuity, 141–143, 144, 151
Cultural diffusion, 68–69, 72, 73
Cultural ecology, 51, 72, 84, 87
Cultural evolution, 51, 72
Cultural integration, 59–60, 72, 385, 401, 403
Cultural materialism, 54–55, 61, 72, 74, 357
Cultural patterning
  aggression, 89–92
  art and, 383
  behavior, 88–100
  cognition, 83, 85–86, 88
  and emotions, 88–89, 91–92
  gender, 92–97
  and language, 116–117
  perception, 83–85, 87
  reality, 79–83, 100
  selfishness, 89–92
  sexual practices, 96–100
  space, 81–83
  time, 81
Cultural relativity, 17, 19
Cultural specialization, 60–62
Cultural Survival, 446–448

and gender roles, 414–415
and human behavior, 191–195
and labor organization, 199–205
rank societies, 285
and residence rules, 249
stratified societies, 285
tourism, 425–427
Economic systems, 195–205
and exchange, 205–218
Rastafari, 65–66, 67
See also Exchange systems
Economizing, 191–192, 195
Ecosystem, 157
Edgerton, Robert B., 55, 141, 151
Education
and African-Americans, 124,
148–150, 449
in China, 339
culture conflict in, 148–149, 151
equity in, 449
initiation rites, 144
and Maasai society, 278
religion and, 350
socialization and, 146–150
Efficiency, in food-getting, 163, 164,
165, 171
Egalitarian societies, 165, 177, 285,
285–286, 306–307
art of, 390–391
band, 319
modernization of, 416, 420–423,
447
tribal, 321
Eggan, Fred, 261
Egoistic behavior, 89
Egypt, 69, 178–182, 183, 186, 226
Einstein, Albert, 63
Eisenhart, Margaret A., 151
Ekman, Paul, 89
Elderly, study of, 38–39
Elijah Muhammad, 377
Elkin, A. P., 369
El-Solh, Camillia Fawzi, 39, 45
Embedded Figures Test, 85
Ember, Carol R., 249
Ember, Melvin, 249
Emergence of Man, The, (Pfeiffer),
105
Emic perspective, 17, 19
Emotions
and art, 384, 394
cultural patterning of, 88–89,
91–92
expression of, 89, 138–139
Enculturation, 133, 150–151. *See
also* Culture; Socialization
Endogamy, 228–230, 250

Engels, Friedrich, 51
English language, 112, 113, 116, 117,
121, 124, 125, 264, 267–270,
449
Environment
adaptation to, 52–53, 157–162,
186, 358–359
and cultural diversity, 157
deforestation of, 451
effects of culture on, 162–163
effects of multinational
corporations on, 427, 431
effects of tourism on, 426
knowledge of, 161–162, 171
long-run variations in, 159–162
perception of, 79, 84–85
religious ritual and, 358–359
social, 162, 214
vocabulary and, 116
Environmental zones, 157–159
Errington, Frederick, 437
Escape, religion for, 350
Eskimo kinship terminology, 271
Eskimo language, 113
Ethics, 41–43, 44
Ethiopia, 65, 66, 272
Ethnic affiliation, and language,
121–124
Ethnicity, 303–306, 310, 427
Ethnocentrism, 9–10, 19
and art, 385
in cultural evolution theories, 51
in development programs, 449,
450, 451
about drug use, 442
in education, 120
about medicine, 443–444
in modernization, 411
and religion, 350
Ethnography
aim of, 36
bias in, 24–25, 28
changing directions in, 29, 36–37
of communication, 117, 120–125
defined, 23, 44
of ethnicity, 304
history/development of, 24–25,
36–37
of one's own society, 37–40
perspectives in, 25, 28
process, 446
versus quantitative design, 446,
456
of sexual behavior, 98
steps of, 30–35, 44
uses of, 42–44
See also Fieldwork

Ethnology, 23
Ethnomusicology, 394
Ethos, 59, 74
Etic perspective, 17, 19
European society, 73, 83, 98, 445
Evans-Pritchard, E. E., 323, 354,
362
Evolution
cultural, 51, 72
and language development, 105,
108
study of, 8
Evolutionary theory (classic), 51, 68,
72, 388
Exchange systems, 205–218, 219,
382
and caste, 297–298
governmental control of, 337
leveling mechanisms, 214–215
market exchange, 215–216,
412–414
reciprocity, 205, 209–211, 214
redistribution, 212–213, 214
Exogamy, 227–228, 230, 250, 258,
319
Exorcism, 15–16
Expert witnesses, 448–449
Exploitation, 411–412
Extended family, 224, 240–241,
243, 247–249, 250
Extensive cultivation (horticulture),
171, 174–177, 186
development program for, 451
efficiency of, 171
environmental zones for, 159
industrialization of, 420–423
labor division in, 200–201,
416–419
and land access, 196, 197–198
marriage in, 231, 232–233
music of, 394
versus peasant farmers, 184
productivity of, 171
seasonal variation and, 159
slash and burn, 174–176, 183,
333, 358, 420
social environment and, 162
social systems of, 177
tribal organization of, 321–325,
328–334
wealth/rank in, 206–208
work/free time of, 193

Facial expressions, 89, 100, 125
Factory work, 156
Fairy tales, 353
Fallers, Lloyd, 58

Familiarity-breeds-avoidance theory, 226

Family

as economic unit, 180, 215, 218, 242

extended, 224, 240–241, 243, 247–249, 250

functions of, 240

in India, 138–140, 228

marriage and, 223–225

nuclear, 240, 241–243, 245–246, 248–250, 269–271, 273

and poverty, 296

roles in, 241

Farb, Peter, 128, 448

Faris, James C., 378

Farmers, 141, 162, 178–182. *See also* Extensive cultivation; Intensive cultivation; Peasant society

Fatherhood, 255, 261

Feasting, 206–208, 212–213, 214, 215, 355–356, 358–359

Federal Bureau of Narcotics, 441–442

Feeley, Malcolm M., 328

Feinberg, Richard, 414

Feldman, Douglas, 460

Female infanticide, 231, 235, 330–331

Female initiation rites, 146

Feminist anthropology, 25, 61, 72, 74, 431

Ferguson, Brian R., 331, 332, 334

Fernea, Elizabeth, 251

Field dependent perceptual-cognitive style, 87

Field independent perceptual-cognitive style, 87

Fieldwork

analyzing data of, 35–36

choosing problem for, 30–31

collecting data in, 32–35

danger in, 41, 44

defined, 23

and development programs, 456

dilemmas in, 40–41, 43–44

ethics in, 41–42, 44

history/development of, 23–25, 29, 36–37, 44

in India, 30–35

in one's own culture, 37–40, 44

picking site for, 31–32

recording data in, 34–35

roles in, 33–34, 39–41, 44

steps of, 30–35, 44

See also Ethnography; Participant observation

Fijian society, 249, 336

Filmmaking, 382, 383

Finland, 415–416

Finnegan, Ruth, 349

Fischer, John, 387, 390–391

Fischer, Michael M. J., 17, 56

Fishing societies, 165, 176, 202, 286

Fiske, Shirley L., 460

Flannery, K., 163

Floods, 159

Flux, 321

Folklore, 402–403, 404

Folktales, 402, 404

Food-getting patterns, 163–186

environmental variation and, 159–162, 186

environmental zones and, 157–159

factors in, 51, 157

and family, 248

historical overview of, 163–164

labor specialization and, 165

land access and, 195–199

and occupational specialization, 165, 183

and polygyny, 233

and residence rules, 249

seasonal variation and, 159, 168, 172–173, 186

and sex roles, 202–203

social environment and, 162

See also Extensive cultivation; Hunters and gatherers; Intensive cultivation; Pastoralism

Food scarcity, 191, 320, 332, 357, 414, 421–422

Football, 397–398, 401

Foraging, 164, 165. *See also* Hunters and gatherers

Force, monopoly of, 337, 342

Ford, Clellan, 336

Forde, Daryll, 262

Foreign aid, 410

Forensic anthropology, 8–9

Formal economics, 191, 192, 218

Fouts, Roger, 106, 110

France, 81, 193

Frankel, Francine R., 417

Franquemont, Christine, 442

Fraternal polyandry, 234–235

Free association contract, 449

Freed, Ruth S., 151, 432–433

Freed, Stanley A., 151, 432–433

Freeman, Derek, 42–43

Free time, 193

Freilich, Morris, 75

French language, 120

French structuralism, 55

Freud, Sigmund, 137, 227, 338

Freudian psychoanalytical theory, 137, 338, 384–385

Fried, Morton, 342

Friedl, Ernestine, 200–201, 432

FUNAI (the National Brazilian Indian Foundation), 421–423

Functionalism, 50, 69, 73–74, 308–309

Functional specialization, 337

Fundamentalism, 370–371

Funerals, 367

Fur trade, 216–217, 334

Future, 81

Gambling, 398–401

Gamelan orchestra, 392, 427

Gardner, B. T., 106

Gardner, Peter, 200

Gardner, R. A., 106

Garn, S. M., 11

Gates, Hill, 156, 187

Gay, John, 148

Geertz, Clifford, 56, 183, 303, 398–400, 411

Gender

conversational patterns, 118–119

and cultural continuity/discontinuity, 144, 151

and cultural patterning, 92–97

cultural specialization and, 60

kin classification by, 264

language classification by, 113, 117

and networks, 436

role socialization, 135–136, 150

"third," 93, 94–97

See also Sex roles

Gender bias, 24–25

Genderlect, 118–119

Genealogy, 29

Generalized reciprocity, 205, 209–210

Generation

continuity of, 255–256

principle of, 263–264

Generosity, 192, 194, 208, 210, 211, 215

Genetics

and environment, 84

population, 8, 9, 226

and sex roles, 91

Geographic mobility, 243

German language, 113, 120

Gewertz, Deborah, 437

Gibbs, James L., Jr., 328

and kinship terminology, 265
segregation, 61
See also Gender
Sex roles
in American household, 242
association based on, 274–275,
279–280
and biology, 200
economic change and, 414–415
and kinship, 261
and labor division, 164, 165,
168–169, 175, 180, 199–203,
218, 223, 244–245
and sexual stratification, 306–308
socialization of, 135–136, 150
Sex trade, 426–427
Sexual behavior
and AIDS, 444, 445
and chastity, 236
in Cheyenne culture, 142
cultural patterning of, 96–100
and incest taboos, 225–227
of Maasai warriors, 278
and marriage, 223, 224, 235
and population control, 160
of Trobriand Islanders, 57, 97
in United States, 142
Sexual egalitarianism, 306–307,
310, 414
Sexual repression, 98, 142
Sexual stratification, 306–308, 310
Seychelles, 426
Shafer, Harvey, 241
Shaman, 320, 361, 364–365, 396
Shamanistic cults, 364–365, 378
Sheehan, Brian, 460
Shelter building, 52–53
Sicily, 306
Sierra Leone, 87, 280, 318
Silence (Cage), 392
Silent Language, The (Hall), 81
Sinai desert, 426
Singer, Merrill, 445, 446
Singer, Milton, 249
Sinha, Surajit, 348
Sioux Indians, 81
Siriono society, 320
Sisal growing, 413–414
Skinner, B. F., 338
Skinnerian psychology, 338
Skolt Lapp society, 415–416
Slash and burn cultivation (swidden),
174–176, 183, 333, 358, 420
Slave culture, 66, 287, 371, 372
Sluka, Jeffrey, 40–41
Smith, M. Estelli, 426

Social class
defined, 290, 310
endogamy and, 229–230
and exchange systems, 208
and industrialism, 185
and kinship, 291, 296
and life chances, 291, 296
prestige and, 290
psychological experience of,
292–295
and religion, 369–370
and school performance,
148–150, 151
and speech patterns, 120
in United States, 290–296
Social control
in band societies, 320
in chiefdoms, 335–336
informal/formal, 344
religion and, 350
in state societies, 337–342
in tribal societies, 325, 328–329,
333
Social environment, 162, 214
Social function, 50
Socialization
and biology, 133–135
continuity/discontinuity in,
141–143, 144, 151
and culture, 133–135
defined, 133
early, 136–143
folklore and, 402
and formal education, 146–150
gender-role, 135–136, 144–146,
150
informal versus formal, 147, 151
and kinship, 256
later life, 141–146, 151
and life cycle, 135
and personality, 136–143, 150
Social mobility
in caste system, 299–300
defined, 290
downward, 292–295, 310
and school performance, 149–150
Social protest, 402–403
Social status
and deep play, 399–400
as human value, 192, 194
and intercultural communication,
457
and lineage, 334
and marriage, 236
and ritual, 352–353, 365–367
and speech patterns, 120
and wealth, 206–208, 212–213

See also Prestige; Social class;
Social stratification
Social stratification, 185, 208, 310
and art, 390–391
birth-ascribed, 301–303
caste system, 296–300, 310
defined, 288
and development theory, 453
ethnicity and, 303–306
modernization and, 412
race and, 149–150, 300–303
and religion, 369–370, 377
by sex, 306–308
by social class, 290–296, 310
in state societies, 336–337, 342
theoretical perspectives on,
308–309, 310
See also Caste system; Social class
Societies, as subjects of
anthropology
complex, 44, 61, 137
contemporary hunting and
gathering, 164
nonindustrial, 192, 194–195
nonliterate, 69
one's own, 37–40
simple, 23, 137
types of, 285
See also Nonindustrial societies;
Western industrial culture
Sociobiology: The New Synthesis
(Wilson), 43
Sociolinguistics, 117, 120–121,
127–128, 449
Soga Society, 58
Song duels, 321
Sorcery, 361–362
Sororal polygyny, 235
Sororate, 230
South Africa, 143, 297
South America, 393
South/Southeast Asia culture area,
202, 392
Southworth, F. C., 109, 129
Soviet Union, 137, 203–204
Space, cultural patterning of,
81–83, 100
Spain, 217–218
Spanish language, 120, 126
Spatial ability, 84, 85, 87, 135–136
Speech behavior
functions of, 120
and gender, 118–119
versus language, 128
and social norms, 117, 120
and social status, 120
Spicer, Edward H., 441

West African societies (*continued*)
    peripheral markets in, 216
    polygyny in, 234
    slave culture from, 371
    in Sudan, 305
    women in, 201, 202, 306, 307,
        434
Western industrial culture
    anthropology and, 18
    art in, 386, 396–397, 403
    communication style of, 456–458
    conception of time in, 81
    education in, 147–150, 151
    egalitarian influence of, 415
    expansion of, 216–217, 308,
        331–332, 334, 374–375,
        409–436
    individualism in, 79, 140
    kindred groups in, 263
    perception of reality in, 79–80
    perspective of, 4–5
    religion in, 349, 350
    resistance to, 217–218, 376–377
    work/free time in, 193
West Indian peoples, 150
Weston, Kath, 251
White, Leslie, 51
Whitehead, Harriet, 93
Whitehead, Neil L., 334
"Whiteman" stories (Apache), 121,
    122–123
Whiting, Beatrice, 89
Whiting, John, 89, 141
Whiting, Robert, 404
Whorf, Benjamin, 116–117
Widows, 230, 233
Wikan, Unni, 94, 251
Wild boy of Aveyron, 78–79, 111
Williams, Terry, 41, 443

Williams, Walter, 94
Wilson, Edward, 43
Wilson, Monica, 281
Wiser, Charlotte V., 251, 311
Wiser, William, 311
Wissler, Clark, 69
Witchcraft, 194, 214, 215, 317,
    362–363, 378
Witchdoctors, 15–16
Witkin, H. A., 86
Wolf, Arthur, 226
Wolf, Eric R., 72, 73, 75, 186, 217
Women
    and anthropological study,
        24–25, 39, 232, 233
    associations of, 279–280,
        433–434
    and bridewealth, 238
    conversational patterns of,
        118–119
    Copper Eskimo, 168–169
    economic roles of, 136, 146,
        202–203, 307–308,
        414–415
    in families, 247
    in horticultural societies, 231,
        232–233
    in India, 59, 140, 239, 306,
        416–419, 433–434
    initiation rites for, 146
    in Israeli kibbutz, 244–245, 246
    and labor division, 199–205
    male conflict over, 356–357
    and matrilineal descent, 260–261
    in Nation of Islam, 377
    and patrilineal descent, 258
    in religion, 376
    and sexual stratification, 306–308
    and social networks, 436

    and technological modernization,
        416–419
    in United States, 242
    in West Africa, 201, 202, 306,
        307, 434
Woodburn, James, 165, 192
Work
    cultural attitudes about, 156
    as social participation, 199
    See also Labor
Worlds of a Maasai Warrior, The
    (Saitoti), 278
World systems theory, 72–73, 74,
    411–412, 436
Worsley, Peter M., 374–375, 412
Worth, Sol, 382, 383
Written communication, 109, 120
Wulff, Robert M., 460

Xhosa society, 143

Yako society, 262
Yanomamo society, 28–29, 201,
    211, 214, 330–332, 351
Yaqui Indians, 79–80
Yarahmadzai society, 172–173,
    186
Yoko, Madam, 280
Yoruba culture, 371
You Just Don't Understand
    (Tannen), 118–119
Youth culture, 61

Zaire, 162
Zito, Laura, 426
Zorn, Jean G., 238, 333
Zulu society, 369
Zuni culture, 59